ENVIRONMENTAL PRINCIPLE

Environmental Principles
From Political Slogans to Legal Rules

NICOLAS DE SADELEER

EU Marie Curie Chair holder at the University of Oslo
and
Professor of Environmental Law, Saint-Louis
University, Université Catholique de Louvain, and Oslo University
Senior Researcher at the Vrije Universiteit Brussel.

Translated by Susan Leubuscher

OXFORD
UNIVERSITY PRESS

OXFORD
UNIVERSITY PRESS

Great Clarendon Street, Oxford OX2 6DP

Oxford University Press is a department of the University of Oxford.
It furthers the University's objective of excellence in research, scholarship,
and education by publishing worldwide in

Oxford New York

Auckland Cape Town Dar es Salaam Hong Kong Karachi Kuala Lumpur
Madrid Melbourne Mexico City Nairobi New Delhi Shanghai Taipei Toronto

With offices in

Argentina Austria Brazil Chile Czech Republic France Greece
Guatemala Hungary Italy Japan South Korea Poland Portugal
Singapore Switzerland Thailand Turkey Ukraine Vietnam

Published in the United States by
Oxford University Press Inc., New York

© Nicolas de Sadeleer 2002

The moral rights of the author have been asserted

Crown copyright material is reproduced under Class Licence
Number C01P0000148 with the permission of HMSO
and the Queen's Printer for Scotland

Database right Oxford University Press (maker)

First published 2002

Published New in Paperback 2005

British Library Cataloguing in Publication Data

Data available

The Library of Congress has cataloged the hardcover edition as follows:

de Sadeleer, Nicolas
Environmental principles: from political slogans to
legal rules / Nicolas de Sadeleer
p.cm.
Includes bibliographical references and index.
1. Environmental law–History. 2. Environmental policy. I. Title.

K3585 .S23 2002   344'.046'09–dc21   2002029061

ISBN 0–19–925474–5 (hbk.)
ISBN 0–19–928092–4 (pbk.)

1 3 5 7 9 10 8 6 4 2

Typeset 9.5 on 12 pt Sabon
by Kolam Information Services Pvt. Ltd, Pondicherry, India
Printed in Great Britain on acid-free paper by
Biddles Ltd., King's Lynn

Preface to the Paperback Edition

Is international environmental law the carrier of a new normativity? This existential question emerges from the interstices of environmental law-making where new principles based on a new axiology for the national and international order emerge. These have matured entirely according to their own logic. Indeed, from their origins as vague political slogans, the principles have been incorporated in enforceable laws and instruments. Nicolas de Sadeleer's work, *Environmental Principles—From Political Slogans to Legal Rules*, reveals this phenomenological and consubstantial aspect of the evolution of environmental principles and unveils the intrinsic and extrinsic implications of such an evolution on the law.

Far from being similar to classical principles of law in general, they contribute to ensure the regulation, the assessment and the management of risk, a crucial function in modern society. Nicolas de Sadeleer underscores the autonomy of these new principles as well as, simultaneously, the central place occupied by environmental law in the international legal system, and at the domestic level, as a major influence on other areas of regulation, such as economic law.

Through the analytical description of three essential principles of international environmental law—the polluter-pays principle, the prevention principle and the precautionary principle—it is demonstrated how this new body of law varies both as to its functions and as to its material content. It varies in respect of its function in the sense that the functions of environmental principles shift between curative, preventive and anticipatory logic. The work excels in demonstrating that beyond their difference in nature, these principles lead to different degrees of protection whether for the environment or for human health. It varies in respect of its material aspect because of the interchangeability of these principles' status. Indeed, they appear in different legal guises, wearing alternatively or simultaneously, the form of rules, directing principles, standards or approaches.

Following this epistemic approach, the study concentrates on two essential points: on the one hand, the function of such principles in the assessment and the management of risk; on the other hand, the legal status of these principles, that is their proper place in the legal systems at different levels: in the spheres of international law, the European Union, and domestic legal orders. This original approach sets the work apart from more traditional analyses by inverting the usual tendency to start by evaluating the legal status of a rule and to scrutinise only then (and therefrom) the function such rules might play in practice. The author advances the idea of the emergence of an atypical process of norm formation, whereby the function of that rule will exert a significant influence over the legal status of that rule. In so doing, the book effectively reveals new grounds of legal force.

A strong emphasis is placed on various aspects of 'post-modern law'. This brings a fresh and original perspective to the study of international law, where influential doctrinal writings have remained relatively silent on the subject, while authors have been equally reluctant to bringing it to bear in the spheres of Community and domestic law. This makes this book one of the most comprehensive works written so far, when it comes to the usefulness of post-modern legal analysis and of its content, scope and limits, as illustrated here through the prism of the newly devised principles of environmental law. Through its rigorous description of what contemporary law is, Nicolas de Sadeleer demonstrates that a genuine transformation of the normative process has taken place and the changes of the international and domestic legal orders that have resulted from this transformation. The book is useful in helping legal scholars come to grips with this fact and stimulates the debate on new modes of legal regulation. The author's method effectively incorporates aspects and issues emanating from all spheres pertaining to the principles of environmental law, be they legal, political, scientific, technical, historical, economic or philosophical.

Another point to be highlighted is the legal treatment of scientific expertise. The book explores the stakes, the obstacles and the potential solutions that could reduce the tension in the often uneasy rapport between law and science. It thus breaks a path towards creative thinking in terms of setting up institutions and formulating national and international public policy, with appropriate pragmatism in putting forward new integrative elements of the decision-making process.

The book also stimulates its readers to think ahead about new issues and emerging challenges, notably in the relation between international environmental law and international economic law. Some fundamental questions are asked, with a view to providing appropriate solutions to crucial problems (regarding for instance biotechnology regulation, or the controversy surrounding the interpretation of the Agreement on the application of sanitary and phytosanitary measures (SPS agreement) or the Agreement on technical barriers to trade (TBT agreement)).

Lastly, this book constitutes a veritable fount of knowledge and facilitates access to both continental and Anglo-Saxon doctrine spanning the last 20 years. Its effort at achieving a synthesis of the various theories and opinions prevailing in the field of environmental law must be duly commended. Thus Nicolas de Sadeleer, who presently holds a prestigious European Union Marie Curie chair at the University of Oslo has written a very insightful and analytically powerful book that will have an abiding influence on the fields of theory of law, environmental law, as well of European and international law.

Laurence Boisson de Chazournes

Professor and Head of Department, Department of Public International Law and International Organization, Faculty of Law, University of Geneva

Contents

Acknowledgements

This book would not have seen the light of day without Mrs Susan Leubuscher, who did a remarkable job in translating my French into a coherent and enjoyable English text. It was her knowledge of international environmental politics and the philosophy of science, coupled with her dedication and constant support, which made it possible for me to draw on such extensive legal material from legal systems which are rather difficult to compare. I owe her an enormous and obvious debt.

This book has been long in the making. I became acquainted with environmental principles in 1992 while commenting for various European law journals on the famous *Walloon Waste* case, an unconventional judgement of the European Court of Justice providing new grounds for reflection on the ability of legal principles to redefine the scope of clear rules. In a 1995 book on EC law and waste disposal, *Le droit communautaire et les déchets* (Brussels: Bruylant-L.G.D.J., 1995) and in my 1998 dissertation on the application of environmental principles to positive law, *Les principes du pollueur-payeur, de prévention et de précaution* (Brussels: Bruylant-AUF, 1999) I drew attention to the specificity and legitimacy of a group of new directing principles that, while far from similar to traditional General Principles of International Law, are necessary to ensure the regulation and management of new environmental risks. Since then a good deal of water has flowed under the bridge. Discussions at WTO level, on the Codex alimentarius, in the EC institutions, in the USA, and in different European countries on the role of the highly controversial precautionary principle prompted me to continue my research on both the theoretical and practical aspects of this principle as well as other related principles. My participation at different seminars in Europe and in the US provided new grounds for my research in an ever developing field. As a guest lecturer in Paris, I also had the opportunity to discuss with French colleagues the implementation of the precautionary principle in France. Those discussions led to the publication of a number of new articles and a book (Fr. Ewald, Ch. Gollier, and N. de Sadeleer, *Le principe de précaution* (Paris: PUF, 2001)).

Based on these successive research projects, the present book provides a range of insightful, and sometimes provocative ideas on the future of environmental law, within the contexts of international law, EC law, and comparative law. The thoughts expressed here are the fruits of many and often passionate discussions with colleagues during these last ten years. I am in particular indebted to John. S. Applegate (Indiana University), Gerrit Betlem (Exeter University), Philippe Gérard (Saint-Louis University), Christian Hey (European Environmental Bureau), Franck Maes (Ghent University), Christine Noiville (Université

Paris 1), Joel Tickner (University of Massachusetts Lowell), Xavier Thunis (University of Namur), and Gehrard Roller (University of Bingen) who kindly gave helpful advice on different Chapters of the book.

Last but not least, I dedicate this book, written in the context of ever-increasing academic and scientific globalization, to my children Irmeline and Christopher and to my wife Åse.

Brussels, 22 December 2001

List of Abbreviations

AC	Appeal Cases Law Reports
ACCOBAMS	Agreement on the Conservation of Cetaceans of the Black Sea, Mediterranean Sea and Contiguous Atlantic Area
ACP	African, Carribean, and Pacific Group of States
AEWA	1995 Agreement on the Conservation of African-Eurasian Migratory Waterbirds
AIA	Advanced Informed Agreement
AJDA	Actualité juridique—Droit administratif (a French law review)
AJIL	American Journal of International Law
AJT	Algemene Juridische Tijdschrift (a Belgian law review)
ALARA	As low as is reasonably achievable
All ER	All England Law Reports (UK)
ALR	Australian Law Reports
Amén.-Env.	Aménagement-Environnement (a Belgian environmental law journal)
APA	Administrative Protection Act (US)
Arch Ph Dr.	Archives de philosophie du droit
ARIEL	Austrian Review of International and European Law
BAT	Best available technologies
BATNEEC	Best available technologies not entailing excessive costs
BGB	Bürgerliches Gesetzbuch (German Civil Code)
BGH	Bundesgerichtshof (German Federal Supreme Court)
Boston CILR	Boston College International Comparative Law Review
BSE	Bovine spongiform encephalopathy
BVerfG	Bundesverfassungsgericht (German Federal Constitutional Court)
BVerwG	Bundesverwaltungsgericht (German Federal Administrative Court)
BW	Burgelijk Wetboek (Civil Code-Netherlands, Belgium)
BYbIL	British Yearbook of International Law

CA	Cour d'arbitrage (Belgian Constitutional Court)
CAA	Cour administrative d'appel (French High Appellate Administrative Court)
Cah Dr Eur	Cahier de droit européen (a Belgian journal of European law)
Cass.b.	Cour de cassation (Belgium)
Cass.fr.	Cour de cassation (France)
CBA	Cost–benefit analysis
CBD	Convention on Biological Diversity
CC	Conseil constitutionnel (France)
CCAMLR	1980 Convention on the Conservation of Antarctic Marine Living Resources
C.civ.	Code civil (Civil Code-France, Belgium)
CEb.	Conseil d'Etat (High Administrative Court—Belgium)
CE fr.	Conseil d'Etat (High Administrative Court—France)
CEN	Comité Européen de Normalisation
CERCLA	Comprehensive Environmental Response, Compensation and Liability Act (US)
CFC	Chlorofluorocarbons
CFI	Court of First Instance of the European Communities
CITES	Convention on International Trade in Endangered Species
CMLR	Common Market Law Review
CMS	Convention on the Conservation of Migratory Species of Wild Animals
Colo J Int'l Env L & Pol'y	Colorado Journal of International Environmental Law and Policy
Colum J Transnat'l L	Columbia Journal of Transnational Law
Colum LR	Columbia Law Review
Conn Ins LJ	Connecticut Insurance Law Journal
Cornell ILJ	Cornell International Law Journal
CPB	Cartagena Protocol on Biosafety
DC	District Court (USA)
DS	Recueil Dalloz et Sirey (France)
DSBs	Dispute settlement bodies
Duke LJ	Duke Law Journal
EC	European Community
ECHR	European Convention on Human Rights
ECJ	Court of Justice of the European Community
ECommHR	European Commission of Human Rights

ECR	Reports of Cases before the Court of Justice of the European Communities and the Court of First Instance
ECSC	Treaty establishing the European Coal and Steel Community
ECtHR	European Court of Human Rights
EC Treaty	Treaty establishing the European Community
EEA	European Economic Area
EELR	European Environmental Law Review
EFLR	European Food Law Review
EFTA	European Free Trade Association
EIA	Environmental Impact Assessment
ELNI Newsl	Environmental Law Network International Newsletter
ELQ	Ecology Law Quarterly
Env and Planning LJ	Environmental and Planning Law Journal
Env L Rep	Environmental Law Reporter
Env P&L	Environment Policy and Law
EPA	Environmental Protection Agency (US)
ESA	Endangered Species Act (US)
EU	European Union
EuR	Europa Recht (a German journal of European law)
Eur J Int'l L	European Journal of International Law
EurLR	European Law Review
EuZW	Europäische Zeitschrift für Wirtschaftsrecht (a German law journal)
F.	Federal Reporter (US)
FAO	Food and Agriculture Organization
FFDCA	Federal Food and Drug Act (US)
GATT	General Agreement on Tariffs and Trade
Gaz. Pal.	Gazette du Palais (France)
Gen TG	Gesetz zur Regelung der Gentechnik (German Act on the Regulation of Genetic Engineering)
GESAMP	IMO/FAO/Unesco/WMO/WHO/IAEA/UN/ UNEP Joint Group of Experts on the Scientific Aspects of Marine Environmental Pollution
G Int'l Env LR	Georgetown International Environmental Law Review
GMO	Genetically modified organism
GYbIL	German Yearbook of International Law
Harv Env LR	Harvard Environmental Law Review
HL	House of Lords
HR	Hoge Raad (High Court, Netherlands)

HRC	Human Rights Commission
HRLJ	Human Rights Law Journal
Hum Ecol Risk Ass	Human and Ecological Risk Assessment
IAEA	International Atomic Energy Agency
ICJ	International Court of Justice
ICJ Rep	Reports of Judgments, Advisory Opinions, and Orders (International Court of Justice)
ICLQ	International and Comparative Law Quarterly
ILM	International Legal Materials
IMO	International Maritime Organization
Int'l Env LR	International Environmental Law Review
Int'l Env Rep	International Environment Reporter
Int'l J Estuarine & Coastal L	International Journal for Estuarine and Coastal Law
IOPC	International Oil Pollution Compensation Fund
IPPC	Integrated Pollution Prevention and Control
ISO	International Standard Organization
ITLOS	International Tribunal for the Law of the Sea
JD Int'l	Journal de Droit International
JEL	Journal of Environmental Law
J Int'l Econ L	Journal of International Economic Law
J Int'l Wildlife L & Pol'y	Journal of International Wildlife Law and Policy
J L & Econ	Journal of Law and Economics
JWT	Journal of World Trade
JT	Journal des Tribunaux (a Belgian law journal)
L & EA	Law and European Affairs
LGERA	Local Government and Environmental Reports of Australia
LMO	Living modified organism
LPA	Les Petites Affiches (a French law journal)
LQR	Law Quarterly Review
LRATP	Long-range transboundary air pollution
McGill LJ	McGill Law Journal
MEA	Multilateral Environmental Agreement
M en R	Tijdschrift voor Milieu en Recht (a Dutch law journal)
MFN	Most favoured nation rule
Mich J Int'l L	Michigan Journal of International Law
Mich LR	Michigan Law Review
MLR	Modern Law Review
MMPA	Marine Mammal Protection Act (US)
MPB	Marine Pollution Bulletin
MULR	Melbourne University Law Review
NAAQs	National ambient air quality standards (US)

NEPA	National Environmental Policy Act (US)
NILR	Netherlands International Law Review
NJ	Nederlandse Jurisprudentie (Dutch Law Reports)
NRC	US National Research Council
NRJ	National Resources Journal
NSWLEC	New South Wales Land and Environment Court
NVwZ	Neue Zeitschrift für Verwaltungsrecht (a German law journal)
NYU LR	New York University Law Review
OECD	Organization for Economic Co-operation and Development
OJ	Official Journal of the European Communities
OJLS	Oxford Journal of Legal Studies
OPRC	London International Convention on Oil Pollution Preparedness, Response, and Co-operation
OSCOM	Commission, 1972 Convention for the Prevention of Marine Pollution by Dumping from Ships and Aircrafts
OSHA	Occupational Safety and Health Act (US)
OSPAR	Convention for the Protection of the Marine Environment of the North-East Atlantic
OVG	Oberverwaltungsgericht (German Administrative Court of Appeal)
PARCOM	Commission, 1972 Convention for the Prevention of Marine Pollution from Land-Based Resources
PCBs	Polychlorinated biphenyls
PIC	Prior informed consent
POPs	Persistent organic pollutants
RCADI	Recueil de l'Académie de droit international
RDUE	Revue du droit de l'Union européenne
RECIEL	Review of European and International Environmental Law
REDE	Revue européenne de droit de l'environnement (a French journal of European environmental law)
R en K	Recht en Kritiek (a Dutch legal theory law journal)
Rev b dr intl	Revue belge de droit international
Rev Dr Amb	Revista de derecho ambiental
RFD Adm.	Revue française de droit administratif (a French administrative law journal)

RGDIP	Revue générale de droit international public
RIAA	Report of International Arbitral Awards
Riv Giur Amb	Rivista Giuridica dell'Ambiente (an Italian law journal)
RJE	Revue juridique de l'environnement (a French environmental law journal)
RMC	Revue du Marché Commun
RMUE	Revue du Marché Unique Européen
RSDIE	Revue Suisse de Droit International et de Droit Européen
RTD Civ.	Revue Trimestrielle de Droit Civil (a French civil law journal)
RTDE	Revue Trimestrielle de Droit Communautaire (a French journal of European law)
SAEDRC	South Australian Environment, Resources, and Development Court
SCt	US Supreme Court
SPS	Sanitary and Phytosanitary Agreement
TA	Tribunal administratif (Administrative Court, France)
TAC	Total allowable catches
TBP	Tijdschrift voor Bestuurwetenschappen en Publiekrecht (a Belgian law journal)
TBT	Technical Barriers to Trade
TBT antifoulant	Tributylin
Tex Intl LJ	Texas International Law Journal
TMA	Tijdschrift voor Milieu-Aansprakelijkheid/ Environmental Liability Law Review (a Dutch environmental civil liability law journal)
TMR	Tijdschrift voor Milieurecht (a Belgian environmental law journal)
TPR	Tijdschrift voor Privaatrecht (a Belgian civil law journal)
TREMs	Trade-related environmental measures
TSCA	Toxic Substances Control Act (US)
Tulane Env LJ	Tulane Environmental Law Journal
UmweltHG	Umwelthaftungsgesetz (German Liability Act)
UNCLOS	United Nations Convention on the Law of the Sea
UNECE	United Nations Economic Commission for Europe
UNFCCC	United Nations Framework Convention on Climate Change
UNGA	United Nations General Assembly

Univ Chicago LR	University of Chicago Law Review
UPR	Umwelt and Planungsrecht (a German law journal)
Va Envtl LJ	Virginia Environment Law Journal
Vand J Transnat'l L	Vanderbilt Journal of Transnational Law
Wash & Lee LR	Washington and Lee Law Review
WGBU	German Advisory Council on Global Change
WHO	World Health Organization
Willamette LR	Willamette Law Review
WTO	World Trade Organization
WTO DSB	World Trade Organization Dispute Settlement Body
WTO DSU	World Trade Organization Dispute Settlement Understanding
Yale LJ	Yale Law Journal
YbEEL	Yearbook of European Environmental Law
YbIEL	Yearbook of International Environmental Law
Z. Umweltrecht	Zeitschrift für Umweltrecht (a German law journal)

Tables of Cases

HUMAN RIGHTS JURISDICTIONS

EFTA COURT

NATIONAL COURTS

AUSTRALIA

BELGIUM

FRANCE

Tables of Legislation

I

Treaties and other International Instruments

II

European Community Legal Instruments

Soft-law documents

Environmental Action Programmes

Guidelines

Recommendations, Communications, Memoranda, and related documents

Regulations

Directives

Decisions

III

Domestic Statutes and Related Instruments

General Introduction

1. FUNDAMENTAL ISSUES

Principles are far more widely in evidence in environmental law than in any other field of law. International environmental law provides a particularly propitious breeding ground for principles, for while it is difficult to agree on fixed and precise rules at the international level, it is far easier to come to a public understanding about indefinite principles that can progressively be given more concrete form. The 1972 Stockholm Declaration on the Human Environment, the 1982 World Charter for Nature, and the 1992 Rio Declaration on Environment and Development—as well as Agenda 21, intended to clarify the scope of the 1992 UN Declaration—are replete with principles. These have been taken up, and often refined, by scores of international conventions adopted in their wake.

In fact, the EC Treaty even contains a Title that expressly sets out the principles meant to guide policy on the environment (Title XVI). Its Article 174(2) provides that European Community policy on the environment shall be based on 'the precautionary principle and on the principles that preventive action should be taken, that environmental damage should as a priority be rectified at source and that the polluter should pay'. Those principles have exercised considerable influence on the drafting of secondary EC legislation, as can be seen from their frequent inclusion in recitals; they have led to advances in national legislation owing to the interplay between EC and national legal orders. They have also had a decisive influence on some hard case rulings by the ECJ. These principles subsequently became influential beyond the spheres of international and EC law. German, French, Belgian, and Swedish legislators followed in the footsteps of the international institutions and set forth the principles in their domestic legal systems, in the process of attempting to codify environmental law.

Nonetheless, the fact that a number of principles of environmental law are put forward in the recitals and preambles of environmental conventions, EC directives and regulations, and national environmental codes, commented on in treatises and other specialist analyses, and set out in case-law does not mean that they have achieved their full legal effect. Their disparity leads to perplexity. Methodological problems are aggravated by the coexistence of an enormous number of entangled rules as well as by the fact that different legal systems have recognized almost identical principles in varying ways. Formulated at the international, national, and regional levels, principles are set out in extremely disparate legal instruments, ranging from 'soft law' to legally binding texts. Sometimes they are recognized by the law-maker, sometimes doctrine calls for them to be applied, sometimes the judge discovers them or simply creates them. They may assume an extremely general form (eg the principle of sustainable development) or a more technical form (as in the ALARA principle used in nuclear law). They are at times confined to a very specific area of environment law (eg the proximity and self-sufficiency principles used in waste legislation); at other times they are applied in a horizontal manner, cutting across all political sectors (as is the case for the polluter-pays, preventive, and precautionary principles). In addition, some principles have attracted the not fully reasoned approval of the legal community on the basis of the values, ideals, and presumptions they bring together rather than for their theoretical rigour. Last but not least, it is never simple to approach, comment on, and analyse principles: the concept of 'principle' changes from one legal culture to another and from one discipline to another. The task becomes even more daunting when it involves a wide range of legal regimes, each dealing with principles in its own way. Nor is the work made easier by the knowledge that principles constitute a special link between legal science and non-legal spheres such as ethics and policy creation.

Disparaged or praised, the principles of environmental law seem nevertheless to have a bright future. That said, does this success really represent a *significant advance* for environment law, or is it purely cosmetic, with no real legal effect?

The object of this book is to *determine the status* and *evaluate the contribution* made by the three foremost environmental principles—the polluter-pays, prevention, and precaution—to the construction of environmental law at the international, EC, and national levels. Given the numerous legal orders in question and the ambitious nature of our analysis, we must first discuss the two analytical threads that run through this research before embarking upon a general outline of the book.

2. ANALYTICAL BACKGROUND

The principles of the polluter pays, prevention, and precaution form the meeting ground of tremendous tensions: between supranational and national legal orders, between the global and the local, between law and science, and between modernity and post-modernity. We will have ample opportunity in the following Chapters to study the ecological, political, economic, and philosophical aspects of each of the three principles in the light of those tensions. First, however, we consider it useful to explain briefly the two analytical threads that will guide the discussions in this book.

2.1. The ascendancy of post-industrial risk

It will become clear in the course of this book that the concept of risk has become the activating concept of modern environmental law. In addition to natural risks, humanity is today exposed to a growing number of risks arising from modern technological development. While it is true that socio-economic development inevitably entails taking risks, it is also the case that the accumulation of these risks may threaten some areas of the environment, and even humankind itself.[1] The concept of risk has become a dominant organizing principle in late twentieth-century societies. Of course, different people tend to have very different concepts of what constitutes risk. In our analysis, risks are associated with the possibility that adverse effects may occur as a result of human activity. As we will see in Part I, however, the risks threatening our environment are not all of one type, but rather represent a succession of various categories of risk.

Most of the environmental risks produced by industrial society have been the subject of preventive regulatory measures. The most important criteria for assessing risks—probability of occurrence and damage—are therefore relatively well known. Science is able to determine thresholds intended to avoid detrimental effects. Listed installations, waste facilities, and water discharges are typical of this first generation of risks. Damage may also occur as the result of accident, but such damages are known to be reversible. In either case, the use of funds provided by taxes by virtue of the polluter-pays principle makes it possible to restore the environment to its state prior to damage (eg by reforestation, or decontamination of polluted soils). While the potential for damage is sometimes very high, the probability of occurrence in such cases remains low (eg nuclear facility accidents, bursting of dams).

However, more recently, issues such as the dissemination of genetically modified organisms (GMOs), ozone depletion, climate change, loss of biodiversity, and the discovery of latent health and environmental hazards such as endocrine disrupting substances and persistent organic pollutants (POPs) have come to symbolize the ascendancy of a new generation of risks. Those risks, particular to a post-industrial society, are characterized on one hand by the general inability of scientists to make reliable predictions about hazards due to uncertainties (identifiable, but not quantifiable) or insufficient knowledge and, on the other hand, by the impossibility of assessing the character of damage that might occur. Uncertainties can be related to the geographical scope of the potential for damage (eg chemical pollutants in the marine environment, spread of mad cow disease), to its temporal duration (eg persistence of chemicals or of radiation in the natural environment), to a delay in its manifestation (eg the impact of greenhouse gases on climate), or to its reversibility or irreversibility (eg ozone layer depletion, species damage due to cross-breeding between GM plants and

---

[1] WGBU, *World in Transition: Strategies for Managing Global Environmental Risks* (Berlin, Heidelberg, New York: Springer Verlag, 2000).

wild plants). In particular, this new generation of risks is characterized by the difficulty of identifying and quantifying causal links between a multitude of potential hazards (such as various types of emissions) and specific adverse effects (for example, sea-level rise, desertification). At this stage, science is largely dependent upon analogies or computer simulations to assess suspected risks. Furthermore, many of the adverse effects of these risks are global in nature (eg climate change). In contrast to natural, accidental risks and to those risks which industrial society can prevent by clear-cut preventive measures, this new generation of risks has given rise to a general attitude of disillusionment with scientific research and distrust of risk management and communication techniques. Researchers today therefore emphasize the central importance of intrinsically subjective value judgements in their assessments and the need to consider the benefits that might result from taking risks in order to create a dialogue with societal groups.

2.2. The pressure of post-modernity

Law has traditionally been represented as an autonomous system made up of general and abstract rules, which is both complete and coherent (modern law model). However, individualized, complex legal fields open to other societal spheres have recently emerged (post-modern law model), among them environment law. The complexity of environmental issues in both social terms (acceptance of risks by populations) and scientific terms (ascendancy of a new generation of ecological risks) confronts the law-maker with the following alternative: either to be prolix and regulate everything in a *pointilliste* manner, or to have recourse to more open concepts, particularly those principles for which no fixed definition can be found. It is this second choice—both original and baffling—which we have chosen to focus on in this book, in the form of the polluter-pays, preventive, and precautionary principles. These three principles contain within themselves all the ambiguities that characterize the shift from modernity to post-modernity.

3. GENERAL OUTLINE

3.1. The structure of the book

The aim of Part I below is to shed light on the origins, formulation, and application of the principles of the polluter pays, prevention, and precaution in international, EC, and various national legal orders. We devote particular attention to the difficulty of interpreting their definitions owing to their evolution within different legal systems. Throughout Part I, which comprises the empirical basis for our research, we consider a number of theoretical and practical questions raised by the relationships between these principles, which are at once harmonious and conflictual. We shall also determine whether it is already possible to draw precise legal consequences from the principles. This initial analysis serves as a basis for our first thesis, that a subtle shift has occurred in the battle against ecological risk: with the emergence of the principle of precaution, the battle against ecological risk has moved from its earlier position of *a posteriori* control (civil liability as a curative tool) to the level of *a priori* control (anticipatory measures). In particular, we shall show how this paradigmatic shift translates into a rather radical transformation of classical legal systems: a duty of care replaces scientific and technical certainties, non-fault liability is transformed into strict liability, environmental taxes aim to encourage certain types of behaviour rather than to achieve a redistributive objective, continuous monitoring replaces long-term authorizations, and end-of-pipe solutions give way to best available technology.

In considering this empirical evidence, Part II concentrates on *how these principles contribute to the balance and dynamics of environmental law* and their *legal character*. In particular, we concentrate on our second thesis: that principles constitute the interface in the *shift from modern to post-modern law*. Part II, examines the role and legal status of these principles in a horizontal manner. This theoretical analysis will apply to both international and European Community law, as well as to national legal systems. In its introductory section, we recall the substance of modern and post-modern law and the principles related to each; Chapter 5 explains more precisely how the three principles lend support to a number of ongoing legal developments, notably by enriching the instruments used by public authorities, such as the constitutional right to protection of the environment, codification, and the principle of proportionality. In Chapter 6 we present further evidence of the specificity of these three environmental law principles as they pass beyond the stage of simple guiding ideals to become true legal rules. Chapter 7 illustrates more particularly how environmental principles can reshape the 'trade-environment' debate at the international and EC levels.

3.2. Methodology

The complexity of the concepts we consider in this book required methodological choices to be made. These are briefly described below.

3.2.1. *The focus on three legal principles*

Instead of trying to demonstrate how the numerous principles found in environmental regulations have had a positive effect on the dynamic of environment law, we have concentrated our research on the specific contribution of three environmental law principles: those of the polluter pays, prevention, and precaution. We have chosen these three principles for a number of reasons. First, they are specifically devised to impose obligations on public authorities, by providing guidance on choices and methods concerning measures to limit environmental risk, with the aim of guaranteeing citizens the right to enjoy a healthy environment (Part II, Chapter 5). For that reason, they are sometimes characterized as *directing principles*, as opposed to *instrumental principles* which aim to grant procedural rights to those being administered. Secondly, as they are set out in substantive texts (international treaties, framework laws, etc.) they have become linked to *sources of binding law*. Thirdly, these three principles are also of particular interest in that they are explicitly or implicitly recognized in international and EC environment law, as well as in various national laws (France, Belgium, Germany, Switzerland, Sweden). Finally, an analysis of the three principles is justified by the fact that they are linked to models of thought which followed hard upon each other over an extremely short period of time and strongly influenced one another. The analysis of these three principles can be extrapolated to understand the legal status and function of other environmental principles not considered closely in this study.

3.2.2. Consideration of international, EC, and national legal systems

In the context of growing globalization, we have approached the issue of the legal status and function of these three environmental principles by jointly considering several legal systems that are not really comparable. We have tried to avoid confining ourselves to the logic of a single legal system for several reasons. First, there are a great number of studies on the role of the principles within international law and within national legal systems. Generally, however, such studies do not sufficiently consider the interactions between these various legal regimes and their underlying principles. Thanks to the theory of direct effect, EC law and the European Human Rights Convention have come to occupy a central role in legal reasoning in several European countries. As a result, it has become difficult to deal with environment law in Europe through a purely national approach, without taking into account the requirements of international and EC law; the latter, according to the doctrine of supremacy, comprises an integral part of Member State legal systems, which national courts are bound to apply. Conversely, we cannot consider EC law without understanding the principles at work in national law, even though the former constitutes an autonomous legal system. In addition, the European Court of Justice attaches particular importance to the European Convention on Human Rights as a main source of fundamental Community rights, owing to the fact that there is no written catalogue of rights in the EC Treaty. These elements may encourage lawyers from various European countries to rely more heavily on shared environmental principles. Secondly, we have tried to demonstrate that different legal spheres (international, EC, and national) engage in far greater interaction when they share a common set of principles. Our analysis therefore refers to case-law from WTO dispute settlement bodies, the International Court of Justice, the European Court of Human Rights, European Community courts, and civil, administrative, and constitutional courts of various States. Nor have we limited our analysis to a continental European perspective; we also consider the most interesting elements of US case-law related to standard-setting under conditions of uncertainty. In a world where ecological problems and our responses to them are undergoing 'globalization', leading to an increasing number of trade conflicts, jurists must bring to their analyses an understanding of developments in legal fields other than their own. Thus, rather than carry out an exercise in rigorous comparative analysis between national levels, we have chosen to focus—primarily but not exclusively—on international, EC, and selected, predominantly European, national systems, in order to provide a global understanding of environmental law today.

3.2.3. Environmental law and other legal branches

We have been led to consider legal fields other than environmental law in order to respond to the emergence of the concept of sustainable development and the integration principle. We must not forget that environment law did not take root in virgin soil. Its areas of concern are widely shared, including by health, food, energy, land use, and consumer law. Our analysis therefore accords wide scope to the concept of environmental protection, including aspects linked to natural resource management within a framework of sustainable development, as well as concepts linked to human protection (health, safety). We believe that contemporary political developments amply justify this approach. Indeed, given the growing importance of the precautionary principle, it is becoming increasingly difficult to separate problems of environment, food safety, and public health. Let us consider one example of this interaction: that of dioxins emitted by the incineration of household waste. This is a problem typical of waste disposal giving rise to atmospheric pollution; the environment thus becomes an issue early on. In addition, such dioxins are taken up by vegetation that is subsequently eaten by domestic animals, which are themselves a source of food. At that point, concern about environmental management becomes a food concern, which in turn becomes a health problem. This example demonstrates the extent to which traditional boundaries between the legal disciplines of consumer protection, health, and the environment are breaking down.

3.2.4. Public law and private law

Reflecting the fact that the dichotomy between public and private law in the field of environmental pollution is becoming increasingly outdated, our analysis does not limit itself to regulatory instruments but also devotes attention to the subject of civil liability.

3.2.5. Hard law, soft law, and case-law

We have sometimes emphasized instruments of soft law (eg the polluter-pays principle), at other times normative instruments (eg the preventive principle) and at yet other times case-law (eg the precautionary principle). There are a number of reasons for this. While it is difficult to understand the scope of the polluter-pays principle without considering the various recommendations that define its application, it is impossible to form a precise idea of the impact of the precautionary principle without also examining the relevant case-law. Of course, this study of how the three principles are used in different legal orders does not pretend to be exhaustive; our purpose is to provide the basis for analysing how they tackle ecological risk.

3.2.6. *The relative importance accorded each principle*

At first glance, the manner in which we approach these three principles may appear somewhat unbalanced, as we consider the polluter-pays principle largely within the context of the OECD and EC, the principle of prevention primarily in the framework of international law (duty of care obligations) and EC law (EIA, IPPC), and the precautionary principle much more broadly. Our reasons for this are as follows. These three principles did not arise simultaneously; nor did they appear with the same force in international law, EC law, and national legal regimes. Both OECD and EC institutions worked to disseminate the polluter-pays principle from the early 1970s, with the goal of economic integration. The precautionary principle, on the other hand, did not appear until the late 1980s, when it found its way into a few international conventions and subsequently crept into EC law and the law of several EU Member States. The principle of prevention, for its part, appears at the international, Community, and national levels in a far more straightforward manner. Nevertheless, we have tried in Part I to follow the same structural approach for each principle, considering its origin, definition, and legal applications.

3.2.7. *From positive law to legal theory: the need to blaze new trails*

While environment law has been in existence for almost three decades, most legal studies display only a modest interest in theoretical questions. Taken up with the task of commenting on a truly impressive number of texts, environmental law experts have had little time to reflect upon the fundamental nature of a subject that has not yet reached maturity. We have tried, albeit imperfectly, to fill that gap by straying from the beaten path. At the beginning of a new millennium, we attempt to offer a vision of environmental law that is at once comprehensive and critical. Faced with a multitude of texts, it is necessary to keep some distance by combining the critical consideration of the theoretician and the positivist view of the practitioner. In addition to considering the contribution made by three legal principles—the polluter-pays, prevention, and precaution—to the balance and dynamics of public policy, the first Part of this book develops a critical analysis of the epistemological bases of environment law, its relationship to science and technology, and its impact on the evolution of the concept of risk. This young legal discipline is both structurally complex and highly technical, in a state of rapid change yet applicable to a wide range of issues. On that basis, we seek in Part I to determine its essence using a multi-disciplinary approach in which elements of ecology, political science, legal theory, and positive law continuously interact.

The present work looks also to the future of both positive law and legal theory, in an attempt to contribute to the understanding of the processes of rule-making in use today and, more fundamentally, to analyse deep and often contradictory changes that will have a profound effect on the development of our entire legal system. For this reason, Part II puts to the test several speculative analyses formulated in the context of general legal theory and seeks to assess an entire series of legal instruments used by environmental jurists, such as teleological methods of interpretation, a welfare right such as the right to protection of the environment, the principle of proportionality, and the codification of environment law as a branch of law. These instruments challenge classical doctrinal thinking, in order to confront the problems being thrown up by a discipline that is nothing if not original.

PART I

THE POLLUTER-PAYS, PREVENTION, AND PRECAUTIONARY PRINCIPLES:

THREE APPROACHES TO ENVIRONMENTAL RISK

Part I   Introduction

The following Chapters examine the origins, formulations, and applications of the three environmental law principles with the greatest relevance for international, EC, and national legal regimes: the polluter-pays, prevention, and precautionary principles. We then consider how these three legal principles can alter the dynamics of public policy and decision-making. Part I aims to clarify when and how these principles co-exist: complementing, enriching, and in some cases contradicting each other. To that end, we first describe each principle individually, followed by a comprehensive analysis of the close links among them. We give particular consideration to the difficulty of interpreting these principles as they have evolved within very different legal regimes.

Our consideration of international law, in addition to assessing multilateral conventions, also examines recent legal developments in the context of the WTO and the European Human Rights Convention. In looking at the EC, we give careful consideration to the case-law of the European Court of Justice and the Court of First Instance, which are particularly relevant. In the context of national law, we consider examples taken primarily from French, British, German, Belgian, Dutch, Swiss, and Scandinavian legislation. Concomitantly, we evaluate a broad variety of legal instruments (civil liability regimes, environmental taxes, standards) used to implement these principles, and carefully assess the relevant case-law in order to gauge their practical legal impact.

We have not, however, limited our analysis to an exclusively European perspective. A growing number of trade conflicts between the United States and Europe (hormones, food safety, etc.) have the precautionary principle at their core. Thus we have also been at pains to demonstrate how United States law, without explicitly declaring the precautionary principle, as some European States and the EC have done, may implicitly have recourse to this type of norm. Just as United States legal experts could become better acquainted with certain specific aspects of European law—which, except in the United Kingdom, is strongly marked by the presence of principles—so European jurists could usefully examine the way in which the applicable US law takes scientific uncertainty into account.

As a first step, we must consider the polluter-pays, prevention, and precautionary principles as driving forces behind the processes shaping environment policy and confronting ecological risk. As every principle represents a first step in ordering ideas, it must be considered from an epistemological perspective before it can be systematically analysed. In fact, these principles represent differing (but in many ways complementary) models of thought, each with its own historical and sociological perspective and system of values. But before introducing those models we must first recall the profound changes in human thinking that have taken place during the twentieth century, when for the first time a temporal chasm opened between natural history and human history.

1. THE EPISTEMOLOGICAL BREAK

For over a century industrial societies have viewed nature both as a rich reserve of resources and as a dump for the refuse produced by resource exploitation. Natural resources appeared inexhaustible, following Lavoisier's law: 'Nothing is lost'. Nature seemed to be endowed with an almost limitless capacity to assimilate and purify the waste produced by human societies. As Anglo-Saxon decision-makers are fond of stating, 'The solution to pollution is dilution'. Natural phenomena, taking their course, would eliminate production and consumption residues. Nature thus provided for all of humanity's needs and mitigated the excesses committed in the name of development. Perpetually renewed, it could patiently bear the errors of human activity. Cleared forests grew again; polluting substances were borne away by wind and water. And if for some reason pollution could not be absorbed immediately, there was always the possibility of eventual regeneration. Failing that, clean-ups could be carried out in the future, using the increased wealth and improved technical means which would be an inevitable consequence of growth. Thanks to progress, environmental degradation seemed not merely a necessary but also a correctable evil.

Now that human time has caught up with natural time, however, this beatific vision is outdated. It took five million years for Homo sapiens to make his appearance, but only five thousand years for him to create civilization and only one century for him to metamorphize into Homo economicus. Scientific and technical progress have allowed man rapidly to dominate nature, a veritable Prometheus Unbound. That domination is reflected in an economic system based on headlong growth, accompanied by accelerated ecosystem degradation. But at the same time a series of environmental catastrophes has begun to make clear that nature cannot continue to endure unbridled development. Ecosystems retain their age-old rhythms, cycles, and periodicities; the lightning progress of the twentieth century has shaken these systems to their foundations. We are now bearing witness to a collision between a timeless and imperturbable, but increasingly threatened, natural order and a system of human activity which is undergoing dramatic changes. There is no question which system will be the final victor.

The public authorities have, after a fashion, tried to stem the threats posed by this precipitous rush to growth. Interventionist in several other areas, the State could not continue to ignore ecological imbalances that threaten not just the quality of life, but life itself. Environmental policy thus developed as a reaction to the excesses that accompany progress. But policy-makers intervened even before they saw catastrophe looming. Their intervention took place in stages, reflecting three successive models of thought.[1]

A *curative model* of nature characterized the early stages of environment policy: nature could no longer cure itself; it should be helped to repair the damage inflicted upon it. For reasons of equity and feasibility, the authorities sought to apportion the economic cost of such intervention by requiring polluters to pay the cost of pollution. It soon became apparent, however, that this model was practicable only if accompanied by a *preventive policy* intended to limit reparation to what could be compensated. This marks the second stage of State action for environmental protection, during which risks are still predictable. The emergence of increasingly unpredictable risks is at present causing the authorities to base their policy on a third, *anticipatory model*. Although still in its early stages, this model should make it possible to slow the pace at which we are approaching major, but still uncertain, risks.

2.   THE CURATIVE MODEL

The curative model counters the concept of nature as an inexhaustible resource reservoir. Its perspective is that natural resources are scarce and the wounds inflicted upon them will not heal without help. This model aims to eliminate the deleterious effects of over-exploitation, by decontaminating, re-introducing, cleaning up, restoring. If such actions are technically impossible, the destruction wrought in the name of progress must instead be compensated by providing or improving the protection accorded to as yet undamaged assets.

In this model, everything is seen as capable of being indemnified, replaced, repaid, compensated. Thus what has been polluted can be cleaned up; what has been destroyed can be restored; what cannot be safeguarded can be replaced, either by natural processes or through human action. Having proved unable to protect some resources, humans can always compensate for losses by protecting other resources.

Within this model, the intervention of State authorities is rather limited. The notion of environmental damages reparation is individualistic rather than collective. The principle of liability is central: the party responsible for damage must pay for its repair. Liability is clearly linked to the polluter-pays principle, since the person responsible for pollution is made to pay the cost of the resulting damage. By requiring the polluter to compensate the community for damage caused, the principle creates the economic conditions for reparation. It also

---

[1] For a discussion on this evolution, see N. de Sadeleer, 'Les enjeux de la temporalité dans le droit de l'environnement' in Fr. Ost, M. van de Kerchove, and Ph. Gérard (eds.), *L'accélération du temps juridique* (Brussels: Saint-Louis, 2000) 893–909; idem., 'Gli effetti del tempo, la posta in gioco e il dirrito ambientale' (2001) XVI:5 Riv Giur Amb 589–607.

allows the authorities to obtain the necessary financial resources in cases where they must substitute for defaulting polluters.

This model is inevitably open to criticism, which in effect says 'Pollute, then clean up'. It is merely an *a posteriori* response to a social problem. Considered in isolation, it rapidly reaches its limits: the logic of compensation comes up against the difficulty of assigning clean-up costs to liable parties. As soon as environmental effects become too diffuse or reparation proves too costly, public authorities find it difficult to identify responsible individuals or to require them to reimburse the costs they have incurred.

The legal institutions typical of this first model are also characterized by serious ambiguities. These are clearly brought out in the theory of good neighbourliness (*théorie des troubles de voisinage*), the precursor to environmental law. According to this theory, those responsible for damage are liable for reparation even though they have been granted the authorizations needed to carry out polluting activities. Compared to the measures typical of a preventive policy, this theory has the attraction of setting few constraints on production activities, since pollution is tolerated as long as it does not cause abnormal damage. In other words, the polluter only compensates victims after damage has occurred and been seen to be excessive. That being the case, in the absence of individual victims the environment becomes the victim.

3. THE PREVENTIVE MODEL

To be practicable, the curative model must be complemented by an administrative policy that sets standards aimed at preventing damage. Relying upon the adage 'prevention is better than cure' seems simply a return to good sense. The physical repair of environmental harm is an uncertain operation, given the technical and economic possibilities currently available. Often, moreover, repair proves to be more expensive than prevention. Good sense therefore dictates that problems be prevented from occurring in the first place and, once they have occurred, be prevented from spreading. The preventive model becomes essential in cases where damage could be irreversible.

In reality nature is not the perpetually renewed, inexhaustible fount of riches imagined by nineteenth-century liberalism—an irresistible force which always returns to its pristine state. Numerous actions give rise to consequences that cannot be remedied: a tropical forest that has been cleared is permanently destroyed; an endemic species that has become extinct cannot be replaced, because it is unique; the irradiation of the ground around Chernobyl will not dissipate for thousands of years . . . In each of these cases, the reversal of destruction is definitively excluded. If some form of compensation can generally be envisaged (for example, protecting one forest in the place of another which has been cleared) such remedies are always uncertain and makeshift, as well as expensive: the loss of any given ecosystem cannot be made good. Moreover, there is no guarantee that future generations will possess the means to efface the scars of the price paid for progress. 'Avoid the irreparable' must be the watchword.

Although it breaks down into a mosaic of general and special policies, the preventive model claims to be effective in minimizing risk while at the same time tolerating a certain degree of nuisance. Even though nature is vulnerable, it should be possible under the preventive model to exploit it without abusing it. This requires the prudent exploitation of natural resources in order to avoid the risk of unexpected damage that might be irreparable, owing either to its irreversible character or the limits inherent in compensation regimes. Within the preventive model, ecological damage should no longer be able to occur except accidentally—the dark side of scientific and technological progress. Being a rare occurrence, damage should be easy to remedy. Even if preventive measures do not totally avoid ecological damage, they at least have the merit of reducing risk to controllable levels.

In an effort to limit damage as far as possible, the preventive model must rely heavily on science and scientific expertise in order to establish some type of objective assessment of the risks being run. This schema is squarely grounded in the notion that science can determine with certainty and precision what level of damage will not compromise the restoration of ecosystems and their species. Under this 'assimilative' approach, the renewal of natural resources can be assured even while exploitation continues; loss would only occur once the self-cleaning capacity of ecosystems was exceeded. If one cannot eliminate all risks, they will at least have been reduced to the point where they may be dealt with collectively through indemnification funds.

Yet if prevention draws its force from scientific knowledge, it also comes up against the limits inherent therein. Where a risk is known preventive measures may be reasonably effective, since they address cause. However, we can only prevent what we understand; it is difficult to prevent a problem that is not understood, and even more difficult to prevent the unknown. And there, precisely, is the rub. The preventive model has a blind faith in science; for that reason it cannot prevent environmental degradation.

4. THE ANTICIPATORY MODEL

The emergence of a third model can be traced to the disenchantment with classical scientific culture, which, convinced of the linear nature of the universe, as predictable as the path of a cannon-ball, can find a remedy for any problem. Scientific predictability comes up against staggering limits in the field of environment.

The destructive effects of chemical substances, such as DDT and PCBs on wildlife or CFCs on the ozone layer, for example, could not be understood until these substances had been discovered. In many cases, moreover, scientists can only admit to ignorance. As the science of climatology advances, it becomes increasingly difficult to explain trends in global warming; as scientists discover new facts about how ecosystems operate, they find it increasingly difficult precisely to evaluate the scope and tempo of biodiversity loss. Contemporary science cannot deliver certainty; at the end of the day it throws up more questions than it solves. To some extent, the more science learns, the more it understands the limits to its knowledge.

Eventually, the only certainty is uncertainty. What was true in the past is not necessarily true any longer; what is accurate at the local level is not necessarily so at the global level; today's predictions will not necessarily come to pass. Metamorphosed into a 'factor for revealing uncertainty', science raises suspicions and doubts as often as it offers knowledge. In any case, our understanding of the environment is no longer able to keep pace with our ability to modify it, and this gap widens when it comes to controlling environmental impacts. The entire foundation of the 'assimilative' approach, which rests upon a blind confidence in science, is thus crumbling under the pressure of uncertainty.

This new model of conduct only came into effect once environmental damage had become planetary in scope. Lulled by promises of an increasingly certain world, Western civilization was brutally awakened at the beginning of the 1980s by the proof of unexpected vulnerability. Since then global threats have taken on a clearer, more precise form. Serious and irreversible damage that could have been avoided has occurred. Changes are unparalleled in their severity. The litany is alarming: climate change, destruction of the stratospheric ozone layer, sea level rise, poisoning of freshwater resources, ecosystem acidification, destruction of biological diversity, overexploitation of marine resources, increased technological risks, overpopulation, desertification...Scientific hypotheses until recently, these effects have in the space of a few years become the subject of global concern.

The fear we thought we could throw off by adopting a preventive approach combined with guarantee mechanisms has returned in a new guise. The threat is no longer local, but global; it is not individual, but collective and inescapable. Human history disrupted natural history; now the latter—rewritten by the hand of catastrophe—may in turn modify the course of human history. The certainty that we would witness the dawn of a radiant age where risks have been completely mastered has been succeeded by the spectre of a precarious future. Doubt clouds the positivist dream of a society governed by certainty of what is true and what false. The contemporary world is discovering the age of risk.

The mere possibility of rapid and possibly irreversible modifications to the physical environment justifies the demand that such risks be anticipated. This is the context in which a new anticipatory model based on the precautionary principle is emerging. In future, uncertainty should no longer delay the adoption of measures intended to anticipate environmental degradation. Precaution serves to prevent delay under the pretext that the true nature of risks is not known. Inversely, it serves to brake precipitate action, by urging delay in executing projects whose risks have not been sufficiently well identified. Precaution thus takes the form of an injunction against action when the nature of risk has not been clearly identified and of an obligation to refrain from action when such action might threaten the environment. This is a true Copernican revolution, whereby uncertainty becomes a central element of a decision-making process which formerly only recognized certainties.

By considering an uncertain future, the precautionary principle situates itself within a time dimension that has been conspicuously absent from earlier models. Yet this element is crucial; decisions taken today can no longer disregard ecological consequences, whose complexity is becoming increasingly clear as our knowledge advances. Environmental management decisions taken today will have effects beyond the boundaries of a political mandate, legislature, or human life. To regulate environmental effects in the present thus in fact amounts to regulating in haste. Recourse to the precautionary principle is therefore justified by consideration of the long term. From now on, time must be given time. This change in our perception of time will of course be reflected in a change of style: today's choices must also reflect a still uncertain future.

The three principles examined in the first Part of this book correspond to the three models described above. However, the chronological order in which we present them here does not necessarily tally with their historical evolution, which is not cut and dried. In fact, the process could more precisely be termed superposition rather than succession, to the extent that the appearance of a new model does not lead to the elimination of earlier models. We are therefore describing ideal types rather than clearly defined empirical structures. Nevertheless, these models have a heuristic value, allowing us to discern the evolution in thinking which has inspired the appearance of major environmental law principles.

1

The Polluter-pays Principle

1. INTRODUCTORY REMARKS

The use of environmental goods typically gives rise to what economists call externalities, which may be either positive or negative.

Farmers living near a well maintained forest benefit from reduced erosion and flooding and from wells that do not run dry. Yet the owner of the forest cannot charge for these benefits. The farmers are thus enjoying positive externalities.

On the other hand, negative externalities arise when the production or consumption of goods or services damages environmental goods without that damage being reflected in their price. For example, excessive use of fertilizers and pesticides, run-off of these into water, and over-abstraction of groundwater are not reflected in the price of agricultural produce. In this case, consumers benefit from market prices that do not reflect the true cost of their economic activity, becoming free riders at the expense of the environment.

The English economist Pigou argued that such external costs should be 'internalized': that is, integrated into the price of the goods or services in question, by charging those responsible for them. As long as these costs remain hidden, markets will react to distorted price signals and make inefficient economic choices.[1]

The polluter-pays principle is an economic rule of cost allocation whose source lies precisely in the theory of externalities. It requires the polluter to take responsibility for the external costs arising from his pollution. Internalization is complete when the polluter takes responsibility for all the costs arising from pollution; it is incomplete when part of the cost is shifted to the community as a whole. In all cases, the principle involves intervention by the public authorities. There are two ways to ensure that prices reflect the true cost of production and consumption: taxation that corresponds to the estimated economic value of the environmental damage, and regulatory standards to prohibit or limit the damage associated with an economic activity.

While the theory of externalities is a traditional subject of economics, the polluter-pays principle is rarely acknowledged or recognized outside of the OECD and EC texts which we consider below.

---

[1] A.C. Pigou, *The Economics of Welfare* (2nd edn., London: Macmillan, 1924). For an application of this thesis in the ecofiscal area, see A. Paulus, *The Feasibility of Ecological Taxation* (Antwerp-Apeldoorn: Maklu, 1997) 27.

On the other hand, the Coase theorem—which excludes polluter-pays elements—has been the subject of much recent debate. It states that under certain assumptions, such as low or zero transaction costs resulting from the availability of information to parties, it is as efficient to allow the victim of pollution a right to compensation as it is to recognize the polluter's right to pollute.[2]

Given that the polluter and the user compete for the same limited natural resources, there is no reason why the interest of one should outweigh that of the other. To the extent that each is ready to pay for use of a resource, they will naturally be inclined to conclude a transaction with a view to reducing pollution in order to reach optimal economic efficiency. For Coase, the question of externalities may thus be resolved through the attribution of ownership rights over natural resources.

If the polluter holds a right to pollute, it will be up to the victims to pay him to cease or reduce his activity. On the other hand, the polluter will have to compensate any party suffering from the pollution that has been assigned exploitation rights if he is to benefit from the resource in question. The attribution of ownership rights over a natural resource modifies the allocation of revenues without affecting the final result in terms of efficiency.

By rejecting intervention by public authorities in favour of free negotiation, the Coase theorem constitutes an apology for the liberal doctrine of *laissez-faire*. However, its practical significance is limited by a set of prerequisites: negotiation can only succeed if the rights of the parties are clearly defined, information is complete and reciprocal, and transaction costs remain negligible.[3] As Coase himself recognized, these conditions are rarely fulfilled.[4]

In any case, the theorem raises considerable difficulties of both a theoretical and a practical nature.[5] By focusing on the compensation due to victims, it eclipses the preventive dimension of Pigou's theory of externalities. It also neglects the important role played by the public authorities, who authorize access to natural resources. Finally, by failing to recognize that much environmental damage is independent of time, it ignores the needs of future generations.

With its origins in economic theory, the polluter-pays principle has progressively moved beyond the sphere of good intentions and scholarly commentary to become a frame of reference for law-makers. It is the essential conceptual basis for a range of legal instruments at the core of environmental legislation and has been used as an element of interpretation by the courts. We review its background below (Section 2) and detail various aspects of its content (Section 3) and analyse its effects on positive law, particularly from the perspective of taxation and civil liability (Section 4).

---

[2] R. Coase, 'The Problem of Social Cost' (1960) III J L & Econ 1–44.

[3] H.C. Bugge, 'The Principle of Polluter-Pays in Economics and Law' in E. Eide and R. Van den Bergh (eds.), *Law and Economics of the Environment* (Oslo: Juridisk Forlag, 1996) 63.

[4] R. Coase, *The Firm, the Market and the Law* (Chicago: Univ. of Chicago Press, 1988).

[5] M.S. Andersen, *Governance by Green Taxes: Making Pollution Prevention Pay* (Manchester: Manchester UP) 44–7.

2. THE ORIGIN OF THE PRINCIPLE

Following a brief summary of the form the principle takes in international law (Subsection 2.1) we consider in greater detail its progressive acceptance in the work of two economic organizations: the Organization for Economic Co-Operation and Development (OECD) and the European Community (EC) (Subsection 2.2). This section ends with a brief description of the principle's role in national legal regimes (Subsection 2.3).

2.1. International law

Besides having been adopted by the OECD and the EC, the polluter-pays principle has been expressly recognized in a number of multilateral conventions. Nevertheless, a distinction should be drawn between those conventions that proclaim the principle in their preambles (in this case, the role of the polluter-pays principle is merely to interpret the more precise norms contained in the convention) and those conventions that affirm the principle in an operative provision (in which case the principle is binding).

The principle is found in the preambles of the 1980 Athens Protocol for the Protection of the Mediterranean Sea against Pollution from Land-Based Sources and Activities (as amended in Syracuse on 7 March 1996),[6] the 1990 OPRC Convention,[7] the 1992 Helsinki Convention on the Transboundary Effects of Industrial Accidents,[8] the 1993 Lugano Convention on Civil Liability for Damage Resulting From Activities Dangerous to the Environment,[9] and the 2000 London Protocol on Preparedness, Response, and Co-Operation to Pollution Incidents by Hazardous and Noxious Substances.[10]

In its binding form, the principle is found in the operative provisions of the 1985 ASEAN Agreement on the Conservation of Nature and Natural Resources,[11] the 1991 Convention on the Protection of the Alps,[12] the 1992 Porto Agreement to establish the European Economic Area (EEA),[13] the 1992 OSPAR Convention,[14] the 1992 Helsinki Convention on the Protection and Use of

---

[6] Fifth Recital of the Athens Protocol as amended in Syracuse on 7 March 1996 (not yet in force).

[7] The Preamble of the OPRC Convention contains the following recital: 'taking account of the polluter-pays principle as a general principle of international environmental law'.

[8] The Preamble of the 1992 Helsinki Convention contains the following recital: 'Taking into account of the polluter-pays principle as a general principle of international environmental law'.

[9] The Preamble to the 1993 Lugano Convention (not yet in force) sets out 'the desirability of providing for strict liability in this field taking into account the "Polluter-Pays" Principle'.

[10] The Preamble sets out: 'Taking into account of the "polluter pays" principle as a general principle of international environmental law'.

[11] Article 10(d).

[12] Article 2(1): 'the Parties respect the polluter-pays principle'.

[13] Article 73.

[14] 'The Contracting Parties shall apply:... (b) the polluter-pays principle, by virtue of which the costs of pollution prevention, control and reduction measures shall be borne by the polluter' (Article 2.2(b)).

Transboundary Watercourses and International Lakes,[15] the 1992 Helsinki Convention on the Protection of the Marine Environment of the Baltic Sea Area,[16] the 1994 Agreements concerning the Protection of the Scheldt and Meuse Rivers,[17] the 1994 Convention on Co-Operation for the Protection and Sustainable Use of the Danube River,[18] the 1976 Barcelona Convention for the Protection of the Mediterranean Sea against Pollution (as amended in 1995),[19] the 1996 London Protocol to the Convention on the Prevention of Marine Pollution by Dumping of Wastes and Other Matter,[20] and the 1999 Bern Convention on the Protection of the Rhine.[21]

In addition, according to other treaties,[22] the polluter has primary responsibility for environmental harm and is directly accountable in national law. Liability conventions represent a sophisticated attempt to minimize resort to principles of State responsibility: applying the polluter-pays principle in private law, they must be seen as an alternative to State responsibility in international law.[23] However, the victim may not obtain compensation, or may not obtain it in full, if the liability of the operator cannot be established or has been limited. In order to give full effect to the polluter-pays principle with a view to enhancing the protection of victims, the source State should *de lege feranda* be held liable on a residual basis. The contribution to compensation of victims by States other than the source State or through the creation of an inter-State compensation arrangement must therefore be rejected, as such regimes find no support in the

---

[15] '... the Parties shall be guided by the following principles: ... (b) The polluter-pays principle, by virtue of which costs of pollution prevention, control and reduction measures shall be borne by the polluter' (Article 2.5(b)).

[16] 'In taking the measures referred to paragraphs 1 and 2 of the article, the Parties shall be guided by: ... the polluter-pays principle, by virtue of which costs of pollution prevention, control and reduction measures shall be borne by the polluter' (Article 2(5)).

[17] The principle is defined in the 1994 Agreements as that 'by virtue of which the costs of measures for the prevention, control and reduction of pollution are to be borne by the polluter' (Article 3(2)(d)).

[18] 'The polluter pays principle ... constitute[s] a basis for all measures aiming at the protection of the Danube River and of the waters within its catchment area' (Article 4(4)).

[19] 'The Contracting Parties shall apply the polluter pays principle by virtue of which the costs of pollution prevention, control and reduction measures are to be borne by the polluter with due regard to the public interest' (Article 4(3)(a)).

[20] The 1996 London Protocol (not yet in force) stipulates that: 'Taking into acccount the approach that the polluter should, in principle, bear the cost of pollution, each contracting Party shall endeavour to promote practices whereby those it has authorised to engage in dumping or incineration at sea bear the costs of meeting the prevention and control requirements for the authorised activities, having due regard to the public interest' (Article 3(2)).

[21] 'The Contracting Parties are guided by ... d) the polluter-pays principle' (Article 4).

[22] Eg Annex III, Art. 22 of the 1977 London Convention on Civil Liability for Oil Pollution Damage Resulting from Exploration for and Exploitation of Seabed Mineral Resources (not in force); Article 8 of the 1998 Wellington Convention on the Regulation of Antarctic Mineral Resource Activities (not in force).

[23] A. Boyle, 'Making the Polluter Pay? Alternatives to State Responsibility in the Allocation of Transboundary Environmental Cost' in Fr. Franzioni and T. Scovazzi (eds.), *International Responsibility for Environmental Harm* (London: Graham & Trotman/Martinus Nijhoff, 1991) 363.

polluter-pays principle. If the source State is held liable on a residual basis, it could always seek redress from the operator.[24]

At the 1992 Rio Conference, the principle was incorporated into Agenda 21[25] and the Rio Declaration on Environment and Development. The Declaration's Principle 16 states that:

National authorities should endeavour to promote the internalisation of environmental costs and the use of economic instruments, taking into account the approach that the polluter should, in principle, bear the cost of pollution, with due regard to the public interest and without distorting international trade and investment.

Yet this soft-law definition which is expressed 'in aspirational rather than obligatory terms'[26] is much less progressive than those previously set out by the OECD and the EC or contained in the 1992 Helsinki Convention on the Protection of the Marine Environment of the Baltic Sea or the 1992 OSPAR Convention. Devoid of any precise normative content ('should endeavour to promote', 'in principle'), Principle 16 is also dependent upon economic requirements for its application, since it may not 'distort international trade and investment' and is only applicable in a national context by reference to national authorities.

The fact that these treaty obligations and soft-law instruments which have expressly recognized the polluter-pays principle are relatively recent and generally limited to a purely regional application has led some authors to question whether, in the current state of international law, the polluter-pays principle may be considered to constitute a rule of customary international law.[27]

That said, the principle should nonetheless generate renewed interest as awareness of the close relation between development and environmental protection grows. In addition, the need for recourse to economic instruments is increasingly being felt, and these are largely justified by the polluter-pays principle. From a theoretical standpoint, generalization of the principle offers an ideal response to concerns that countries which apply lower protection standards will derive competitive advantage therefrom. If all countries were to ensure that environmental costs are fully reflected in industrial production costs, environmental cost differentials among nations would exclusively and legitimately reflect differences in local conditions.[28] Yet the implementation of the principle at a global level entails serious practical problems.

---

[24] R. Lefevere, *Transboundary Environmental Interference and the Origin of State Liability* (The Hague, London, Boston: Kluwer Law Int'l, 1996) 299–311, 322–3, 310.

[25] Paragraphs 30.3 and 2.14. of Agenda 21 endorse the polluter-pays principle at least implicitly by requiring that the price of goods and services should reflect environmental costs.

[26] A. Boyle and D. Freestone, *International Law and Sustainable Development* (Oxford: Oxford University Press, 1999) 4.

[27] A. Boyle, 'Making the Polluter Pay?', n. 23 above, 376; Ph. Sands, *Principles of International Environmental Law* (Manchester: Manchester UP, 1995) 213.

[28] D.C. Esty and D. Gerardin, 'Environmental Protection and International Competitiveness: A Conceptual Framework' (1998) 32 JWT 44–5. However, the Preambles of the 1990 OPRC

Finally, we would recall that GATT provisions are *a priori* neutral concerning adoption of the principle. In the *US Chemicals* case, the EC argued that a US tax on certain chemicals was not eligible for border tax adjustment because the taxation regime was contrary to the polluter-pays principle, as it was designed to finance environmental programmes which benefited only US producers. Since it was US production that was causing pollution in North America, the EC believed that the principle required the US to tax domestic products only. The Panel found that since the tax was directly imposed on products, it was eligible for border tax adjustment independent of its purpose. The Panel further noted that States were free to tax the sale of domestic products that are harmful to the environment and to exempt competing foreign products that would be less harmful. Thus, GATT rules on tax adjustment 'give the contracting party...the possibility to follow the polluter-pays principle, but they do not oblige it to do so'.[29]

2.2. Regional economic integration organizations

The fact that the presence of the polluter-pays principle in a series of international conventions is a relatively recent phenomenon should not disguise the importance of the work undertaken within the OECD and the EC over the past three decades, which has transformed a mere economic rule into a true legal principle, as it gradually shifts from soft law (OECD and EC recommendations) to hard law (treaties and EC secondary legislation).

2.2.1. The Organization for Economic Co-operation and Development

The polluter-pays principle was first adopted at international level in the 1972 OECD Council Recommendation on Guiding Principles concerning International Aspects of Environmental Policies.[30] The 1974 Council Recommendation on the Implementation of the polluter-pays principle, referred as a 'fundamental principle', is to be applied. The Council recommends Member countries 'not to assist the polluters in bearing the costs of pollution control

Convention, the 1992 Convention on the Transboundary Effects of Industrial Accidents, and the 2000 Protocol on Preparedness, Response, and Co-Operation to Pollution Incidents by Hazardous and Noxious Substances describe the polluter-pays principle as a 'general principle of international law'.

[29] GATT Dispute Settlement Panel, *US Chemicals Tax* case, 1987. Eg Ph. Sands, *Principles of International Environmental Law*, n. 27 above, 691–2; E.-H. Petersmann, *International and European Trade and Environmental Law after the Uruguay Round* (London: Kluwer Law Int'l, 1995) 86–9.

[30] 'The principle to be used for allocating costs of pollution prevention and control measures to encourage rational use of scarce environmental resources and to avoid distortions in international trade and investment is the so-called Polluter-Pays Principle. This principle means that the polluter should bear the expenses of carrying out the above mentioned measures decided by public authorities to ensure that the environment is in an acceptable state. In other words, the cost of these measures should be reflected in the cost of goods and services which cause pollution in production and/or consumption. Such measures should not be accompanied by subsidies that would create significant distortions in international trade and investment' (C (72) 128 (final), OECD, 1972).

whether by means of subsidies, tax or advantages'.[31] While it was meant to help do away with State aids by establishing a mechanism 'for allocating costs of pollution prevention and control measures to encourage rational use of scarce environmental resources', it was not intended to eliminate all forms of pollution. Indeed, according to both Recommendations, the polluter should only 'bear the expenses of carrying out the above mentioned measures decided by public authorities to ensure that the environment is in an acceptable state'.[32] The polluter-pays principle thus guaranteed only partial internalization of environmental costs; it was not intended to oblige polluters to assume the full consequences of their acts.

After a long period of calm—it was not until the end of the 1980s that the principle experienced a revival within the OECD—a new advance occurred when the OECD Council decided, in a 1989 Recommendation on the Application of the Polluter-Pays Principle to Accidental Pollution, that the principle would no longer be limited to chronic pollution.[33] Henceforth, the cost of measures to prevent and combat acts of accidental pollution should be charged to all potential agents, regardless of their actual contribution to the pollution. However, internalization of the cost of accidental pollution was still not complete; the polluter was only required to bear the cost of 'reasonable measures' taken by the authorities. This was nevertheless a significant advance in that it obliged potential polluters to cover the expense of remedying accidental pollution, which traditionally fell to public authorities.[34]

An additional step forward was taken in 1991, when the OECD Council admitted, in its Recommendation on the Uses of Economic Instruments in Environmental Policy, that 'a sustainable and economically efficient management of environmental resources' requires internalization of the costs of pollution prevention and control measures as well as damage costs.[35] Again, this represents an important step forward: the polluter must henceforth take responsibility not only for measures to prevent and control pollution (for example, treatment plant construction) as well as the associated administrative costs (such as monitoring) but also the cost of damage arising from the pollution (for instance, clean-up costs). Even if the principle's evolution is not yet complete, we can see it moving in the direction of full internalization of pollution costs.

2.2.2. *The European Community*

The polluter-pays principle has gradually commanded recognition as one of the pillars of the Community's environment policy; the EC has rapidly fallen

---

[31] C (74) 223 (final), OECD, 1974 .

[32] 1972 Recommendation, Annex A (a)(4); 1974 Recommendation, I(2).

[33] C (89) 88 (final), OECD, 1989.

[34] S. Gaines, 'The Polluter-Pays Principle: From Economic Equity to Environmental Ethos' (1991) 26 Texas Intl LJ 463.

[35] C (90) 177 (final), OECD, 1991.

into step with the Recommendations adopted by the OECD Council, clarifying the principle in a series of recommendations and resolutions and subsequently granting it legal effect. A brief review of that evolution is in order at this point.

The principle was originally set out in the First Environmental Action Programme (1973–76), according to which the polluter would normally be responsible for the costs occasioned by the prevention and control of nuisances. The procedures for applying the principle were specified in Recommendation 75/436/ Euratom, ECSC, EEC of 3 March 1975 regarding cost allocation and action by public authorities on environmental matters, which broadly takes up the rules elaborated by the OECD.

Twenty years later, this Recommendation remains indispensable for understanding the significance of the polluter-pays principle. It is particularly important in that the Recommendation is not devoid of legal effect even though it cannot confer rights on individuals upon which they may rely before their national courts. In effect, 'the national courts are bound to take recommendations into consideration in order to decide disputes submitted to them, in particular where they cast light on the interpretation of national measures adopted in order to implement them or where they are designed to supplement binding EC provisions'.[36] Therefore, Recommendation 75/436 can still have a decisive influence on the outcome of disputes brought to national courts.

According to Recommendation 75/436:

> natural or legal persons governed by public or private law who are responsible for pollution must pay the costs of such measures as are necessary to eliminate that pollution or to reduce it so as to comply with the standards or equivalent measures which enable quality objectives to be met or, where there are no such objectives, so as to comply with the standards or equivalent measures laid down by the public authorities.

The polluter is defined as whoever 'directly or indirectly damages the environment or who creates conditions leading to such damage'. The main instruments available to the public authorities for putting the polluter-pays principle into effect are *standards* and *charges*.

Typically, *standards* are policy measures of a preventive nature which have no direct link *a priori* with the theory of externalities that guides the principle under which the polluter pays. The Recommendation distinguishes between standards relating to environmental quality, procedure, and products. The first type of standards prescribes, through legally binding means, the levels of pollution and nuisance that may not be exceeded for a given medium. The second group refers to the operations and discharges of polluting installations. The last group sets out the ecological characteristics of products. These standards will be related to the principle of prevention in the following Chapter.

---

[36] Case C-322/88, *Grimaldi* [1989] ECR I-4407, para. 18.

By contrast, *charges* implement the theory of externalities to the extent that they include any type of financial instrument that requires the polluter to assume his share of the costs in controlling the pollution he has caused.[37]

Charges also have a preventive dimension, since they are primarily intended to 'encourage the polluter to take the necessary measures to reduce the pollution he is causing as cheaply as possible'. It is only as a secondary consideration that they may have a redistributive character, which consists in making the polluter bear 'his share of the costs of collective measures'.

Finally, we should note that the principle does not have absolute effect since it is subject to several exceptions analogous to those allowed within the OECD. Where the application of charges or overly stringent standards gives rise to serious economic disturbances, polluters may be granted limited aid by the public authorities, as well as transition periods to allow them to adapt their products or production processes.

Subsequent to the Recommendation of 3 March 1975, the polluter-pays principle recurred in all Environmental Action Programmes, with minor variations in meaning. According to the Fifth Environmental Action Programme, the adoption of economic incentives is necessary for effective implementation of the polluter-pays principle.[38] The initial desire to eliminate all public aids related to the environment by recourse to the principle was tempered by the 1994 and the 2001 EC Guidelines relating to State aids for the protection of the environment.[39]

The polluter-pays principle also appeared in secondary EC legislation throughout the 1970s and was expressly taken up in several waste management directives.[40] Since the adoption of the Waste Framework Directive in 1991, the principle has applied to this entire area of EC environment policy.[41] Article 10 of Directive 1999/31/EC on waste landfill has recently given concrete expression to the principle by requiring that the cost of waste disposal include all operation costs, including financial guarantees and restoration of the site once it ceases to

---

[37] It should be noted that this definition of charges has its basis in economic science; positive law assigns it a much more restricted scope. For instance, in EC law a *charge* is recompense for a service actually rendered to the importer or exporter of a product, which falls outside the scope of the prohibitions contained in Article 28 of the Treaty.

[38] COM (92) 23 final—Vol. II, 25, 68.

[39] Information from the EC Commission: EC Guidelines 94/C 72/03 on State Aid for Environmental Protection, replaced by EC Guidelines 2001/C 37/03 on State Aid for Protection of the Environment.

[40] Several waste management directives recall that the principle must be respected when setting out economic instruments (Directive 75/439/EEC on the disposal of waste oils, Directive 94/62/EC on packaging and packaging waste). In condemning a prohibition on the export of waste oils outside of France as incompatible with Article 30 of the Treaty (new Article 28), the ECJ rejected the economic argument invoked by the French authorities that an export ban was needed to avoid bankrupting recycling firms, since under the EC Waste Oils Directive Member States 'may, without placing restrictions on exports, grant to such undertakings "indemnities" financed in accordance with the principle of "polluter-pays"' (Case C-172/82, *Inter-Huiles* [1983] ECR 555, para. 18).

[41] According to Article 15 of Directive 75/442/EEC on waste, 'in accordance with the "polluter-pays" principle, the cost of disposing of waste must be borne by: the holder who has waste handled by a waste collector or by an undertaking and/or the previous holders or the producer of the product from which the waste came'.

be used for disposal. Such provisions oblige Member States to implement this environmental principle when carrying out pricing policy. Article 9 of Directive 2000/60/EC establishing a framework for Community action in the field of water policy has also given concrete expression to the principle, by requiring that 'Member States shall take account of the principle of recovery of the costs of water services, including environmental and resource costs'. In addition, Member States are required to ensure by 2010 that water pricing policies provide adequate incentives for the efficient use of water resources, thereby contributing to the environmental objectives of this Directive.

The principle was also invoked to justify a strict liability regime in the proposal for a Council Directive on civil liability caused by waste, in the 1993 EC Green Paper on remedying environmental damage and in the 2000 EC White Paper on Environmental Liability. EC directives dealing with atmospheric pollution, water protection, nature protection, and noise, however, do not expressly refer to the principle. Indeed, Council Directive 92/43/EEC on the conservation of natural habitats and of wild fauna and flora recognizes that 'the polluter-pays principle can have only limited application in the special case of nature conservation'.[42]

The polluter-pays principle finally received full recognition with the adoption of the Single European Act (SEA), thanks to the insertion of Article 130R(2) (new Article 174(2)), which states that 'action by the Community relating to the environment shall be based on the principle that the polluter should pay'. Like its fellow principles of prevention and precaution, the polluter-pays principle is meant to guide the definition and implementation of Community environment policy. The authors of the Treaty confirmed its essential role by recalling in Article 175 (former Article 130S(5)) that the principle continues to apply even when the Council uses its power to grant a temporary derogation to rules it has enacted, on behalf of Member States for whom Community measures would involve costs that are judged disproportionate. The 1992 Porto Agreement creating the European Economic Area (EEA) also states that 'action by the Contracting Parties relating to the environment shall be based on the principle that the polluter should pay'.

The culmination of this evolutionary process could in turn constitute a point of departure for new developments: not only will the polluter-pays principle henceforth play a role in all environment law, it will also have to be taken into account by the EC institutions: the Commission, the Council, the European Parliament, the Economic and Social Committee, and the Committee of the Regions.[43] They are legally obliged to consider the principle in the course of

---

[42] Eleventh recital of the Preamble.

[43] The European Commission has emphasized the need to apply the polluter-pays principle in transport policy in order to avoid distortion of competition: 'the fundamental principle of infrastructure charging is that the charge for using infrastructure must cover not only infrastructure costs, but also external costs, ie costs connected with accidents, air pollution, noise and congestion': see the White Paper on European Transport Policy for 2010 (COM(2001)370). Several provisions of EC Directives harmonising the rules of air, road, and railway transport implement—albeit imperfectly—the polluter-pays principle. In this regard, the Preamble of Directive 1999/62/EC on the

the normative process; in this way, all acts of secondary legislation will be subordinated to the principle.[44] In addition, the European Court of Justice (ECJ) must ensure respect for the principle in the cases it is called upon to settle.

This requirement does not, however, prevent the EC institutions from exercising a degree of discretion. The procedures for Community action relating to the environment set out in Article 174(3) could attenuate the principle's effectiveness;[45] nevertheless, the flexibility inherent in the principle does not authorize EC authorities systematically to exclude its use. The principle's place in the EC Treaty ensures that it may not simply be ignored on a regular basis, or even in a majority of cases.

That protection is reinforced by Article 230 of the EC Treaty, under which any natural or legal person may ask the ECJ to review the legality of acts of the institutions. If, for instance, the Commission were to authorize a national authority to grant State aids to a proven polluter for clean-up costs and those State aids provided the polluter with a competitive advantage over competitors from other Member States, a judicial review of the Commission's decision could take place, based on Article 87 of the Treaty and interpreted in the light of the requirements of the polluter-pays principle.[46]

Recently, the High Court of Justice of England and Wales referred to the ECJ for a preliminary ruling on the interpretation of Directive 91/676/EEC of 12 December 1991 concerning the protection of waters against pollution caused by nitrates from agricultural sources. Domestic farmers submitted that the Nitrates Directive infringes the polluter-pays principle laid down in Article 130R(2) (new Article 174) of the EC Treaty, on the ground that farmers were being singled out to bear the cost of reducing the concentration of nitrates in waters to below the threshold

---

charging of heavy goods vehicles for the use of certain infrastructure provides that 'the use of road-friendly and less polluting vehicles should be encouraged through differentiation of taxes or charges, provided that such differentiation does not interfere with the functioning of the internal market' (7th Recital). Directive 2001/14/EC on the allocation of railway infrastructure capacity and the levying of charges for the use of railway infrastructure and safety certification provides that 'the infrastructure charge may be modified to take account of the cost of the environmental effects caused by the operation of the train. Such a modification shall be differentiated according to the magnitude of the effect caused. Charging of environmental costs which results in an increase in the overall revenue accruing to the infrastructure manager shall however be allowed only if such charging is applied at a comparable level to competing modes of transport...' Last but not least, the Commission's Proposal for a Council directive on airport charges (COM(97)0154) defines the 'airport charges' as 'the sums collected at an airport for the benefit of the management body and paid by the airport's users ensuring the remuneration of facilities and services which, by their nature, can only be provided by the airport and which are related to...the environmental effects of handling aircraft and passengers...'.

[44] For the scope of the principle in EC law, see particularly L. Krämer, 'Polluter-Pays Principle in Community Law: The Interpretation of Article 130r of the EEC Treaty' in *Focus on European Law* (London: Graham & Trotman, 1997) 244. The following observations on the application of the principle are of course valid for the principles of prevention and precaution, which are recognized by the same provision of the Treaty. This holds true throughout the following discussion.

[45] For example, the Commission allows certain State aids in the field of environment although these are *prima facie* contrary to the principle; it does this by invoking the economic backwardness of the regions where enterprises receiving these aids are located.

[46] L. Krämer, 'The Polluter-Pays Principle in Community Law', n. 44 above, 252.

of 50 mg/l even though agriculture is acknowledged to be only one source of nitrates, while no financial demands were being made upon other sources.

Referring to the polluter-pays principle, the ECJ held that:

> the Directive does not mean that farmers must take on burdens for the elimination of pollution to which they have not contributed;...the Member States are to take account of the other sources of pollution when implementing the Directive and, having regard to the circumstances, are not to impose on farmers costs of eliminating pollution that are unnecessary. Viewed in that light, the polluter-pays principle reflects the principle of proportionality...[47]

According to this case-law, Member States cannot impose on farmers costs of eliminating pollution that are 'unnecessary': they must also take into account other sources of pollution.[48] Following that reasoning, the costs charged to some categories of economic agents arising from the designation of a protected zone should not be superior to the costs of the pollution generated by those agents.[49] This demonstrates clearly how a principle laid down in the EC Treaty may influence the interpretation of an act of secondary legislation and consequently determine national administrative practices.

2.3. National laws

The polluter-pays principle exercises a significant influence on the evolution of national law, given that many law-makers have expressly recognized it as a guiding norm of environment policy. This is particularly the case for Belgian[50] and French law,[51] which define the principle as that 'according to which the costs resulting from measures to prevent, reduce and control pollution should be borne by the polluter'. The principle was also specifically addressed in several Supreme Court of India Decisions in the course of 1996.[52]

Sometimes the principle takes a slightly different form. In German law, as well as in the German version of the EC Treaty, it is translated as the causality principle (*Verursacherprinzip*);[53] the *Verursacher* is the responsible party, and

---

[47] Case C-293/97, *Standley* [1999] ECR I-2603, paras. 51–2.   [48] Para 52.

[49] According to the Opinion of Advocate General Ph. Léger, the Directive had to be interpreted as requiring Member States to impose on farmers only the cost of pollution for which they were responsible, and he explicitly added 'to the exclusion of any other cost' (Opinion of 8 October 1998, Case C-293/97 (1999) ECR I-2603, para. 98).

[50] Article 1.2.1., §2 1995 Flemish Act containing general provisions concerning environmental policy: 'Environmental policy shall seek to achieve a high level of protection...It shall be based on, *inter alia*:—the polluter-pays principle'. Article 4 of the 1999 Federal Act concerning protection of the marine environment in marine areas under Belgian jurisdiction defines the principle as implying that 'the costs of preventing, reducing and controlling pollution, as well as the costs of reparation of damages, are to be borne by the polluter'.

[51] Article L 100–1 of the French Environmental Code.

[52] L. Kurukulasuriga, 'UNEP Regional Symposia on the Role of Judiciary in Promoting the Rule of Law in the Area of Sustainable Development' (1999) 10 YbIEL 761.

[53] This principle has been the subject of much doctrinal analysis. See M. Kloepfer, 'Die Prinzipien im einzelnen' in *Umweltrecht* (Munich, 1989) 83; B. Bender, R. Sparwasser, and R. Engel, 'Hauptprinzipien des Umweltrechts' (1995) 73: 3 *Umweltrecht* (Heidelberg: R. Müller) 27.

not necessarily the polluter as such.[54] In the Swiss legal system, the federal law on environmental protection envisages a causality principle by virtue of which 'the costs resulting from measures required under this law are to be borne by the person who has caused the damage'.[55] German doctrine considers that, in conformity with Article 20(a) of the Federal Constitution, the principle of collective burden sharing (*Gemeinlastprinzip*) deduced from the principle of the social State should give way to the polluter-pays principle (*Verursacherprinzip*) in the field of environment policy, whereby those responsible for pollution finance public policies in this area. Communities should not have to bear the responsibility for the costs of pollution, except in cases where the polluter-pays principle cannot be implemented owing to practical circumstances.[56]

The explanatory memoranda of numerous regulations relating to fiscal regimes, civil liability, waste management, competition among polluting enterprises, company subsidies, and economic instruments confirm the growing success of the polluter-pays principle at the national level.

3. Systematic analysis

The apparent simplicity of the polluter-pays principle masks a number of ambiguities and its outlines continue to be poorly defined at the legal level. In this section we synthesize the main analytical controversies concerning the principle. These are twofold: they concern, on one hand the function of the principle, and on the other hand identification of the polluter and what he must pay.[57]

3.1. The functions of the principle

The history of the polluter-pays principle reflects a gradual shift in meaning. At first, the Recommendations of the OECD and the EC referred to the principle as a means of preventing the distortion of competition (instrument of harmonization intended to ensure the smooth functioning of the common market); later it

---

[54] L. Krämer, *Focus on European Law*, n. 44 above, 1.

[55] Article 2 of the 1983 Federal Law on environmental protection.

[56] D. Murswiek, 'Der Bund und die Länder: Schutz der natürlichen Lebensgrundlagen' in M. Sachs (ed.) *Grundgesetz Kommentar* (Munich: Beck'sche Verlagsbuchhandlung, 1996) 661.

[57] Several analyses have been devoted to the legal effect of the polluter-pays principle. See M. Meli, 'Le origini del principio "chi inquina paga" e il uso accoglimento da parte della comunità europea' (1989) 2 Riv Giur Amb 217; U. Kettlewell, 'The Answer to Global Pollution? A Critical Examination of the Problems and Potential of the Polluter-Pays Principle' (1992) 3 Colo J Int'l Envtl L & Pol'y 431; L. Krämer, 'The Polluter-Pays Principle in Community Law', n. 44 above, 244; S. Gaines, 'The Polluter-Pays Principle', n. 34 above, 463; H. Smets, 'The Polluter-Pays Principle in the Early 1990s' in L. Campiglio *et al.* (eds.), *The Environment after Rio: International Law and Economics* (London: Graham & Trotman, 1994) 131; X. Thunis and N. de Sadeleer, 'Le principe du pollueur-payeur: idéal régulateur ou règle de droit positif?' (1995) Amén.-Env. 3; H.C. Bugge, 'The Principle of Polluter-Pays in Economics and Law', n. 3 above, 53; J.E. Hoitink, 'Het beginsel de vervuiler betaalt: "revival" van een milieubeginsel' in P. Gilhuis and A.H.J. Van den Biesen (eds.), *Beginselen in het milieurecht* (Alphen a/d Rijn: Kluwer, 2001) 41–54.

formed the basis both for internalizing chronic pollution (instrument of redistribution) and preventing it (instrument of prevention); finally, it served to guarantee the integrated reparation of damage (curative instrument). These various functions are at times complementary and at other times mutually exclusive.

3.1.1. *The function of economic integration*

Since the early 1970s the OECD and the EC have justified recourse to the polluter-pays principle to prohibit State aids from being used to finance anti-pollution investments. The 1972 OECD Recommendation on Guiding Principles Concerning International Economic Aspects of Environmental Policies stated that the principle was to be used 'to avoid distortions in international trade and investment'. In addition, the First (1973–76) and Second (1977–81) Community Environmental Action Programmes focused on trade harmonization, so that exceptions to the principle must 'cause no significant distortion to international trade and investment'. Allowing private enterprises to benefit from public assistance in financing such investments would obviously have run counter to the doctrine of free trade promoted by both economic organizations, since such aids distort competition between beneficiary firms and their competitors. Consequently, exceptions to this prohibition were authorized only in exceptional circumstances and on the condition that precise criteria were respected: aids could only be granted for a transitional period, to undertakings facing serious difficulties, and were not to give rise to serious distortions of commercial trade and international investment.[58] Responsible for approving State aids, the European Commission regularly applies the polluter-pays principle, refusing to allow State aids that violate Article 87 of the EC Treaty.[59]

Despite these conditions, this first function merely ensured a partial internalization of the costs arising from chronic and continuous pollution. In fact, only investments required by the public authorities fell under the terms of the principle, since there is as yet no question of forcing polluters to bear the full costs of their activities. We should recall that Pigou, in contrast, wanted to

---

[58] Three Commission Memoranda (1974, 1980, 1987) provided specific guidance on EC policy concerning State aids for pollution control. The intention of the first memorandum was to establish a framework for a transitional period, pending full implementation of the polluter-pays principle. It was subsequently stipulated in 1980 that a further transitional period was required. See Commission Memorandum C (80) 795, Community Approach to State Aids in Environmental Matters. Eg E. Grabitz and Ch. Zacker, 'Scope for Action by the EC Member States for the Improvement of Environmental Protection under EEC Law: the Example of Environmental Taxes and Subsidies' (1989) CMLR 423.

[59] The Commission considered incompatible with the polluter-pays principle the granting of aid to a paper firm that intended to rebuild its installations in an area that would give rise to fewer environmental problems, even though the grant met the principles of prevention and of reduction of pollution at source (Commission Decision 93/964/CE of 22 July 1993, OJ, L 273, 5 November 1993, 51). It also determined that, based on the polluter-pays principle, waste producers and holders are responsible for their disposal and recycling; if public authorities decide to take responsibility for disposing of the industrial ash emitted by a factory they are in effect granting the operation an aid, since such a decision serves to exempt the firm from having to pay to dispose of its residues (OJ, C-236 of 24 October 1997, 4).

encourage subsidies for positive externalities through revenues from a tax on negative externalities.[60] This aspect of the theory of externalities seems to have been forgotten by the two economic institutions that originally promoted the polluter-pays principle.

This neo-liberal philosophy continues to be put forward, although it has to some extent been called into question by the most recent Community framework on State aids for protection of the environment.[61] This has not, however, prevented the principle from progressively evolving within these two international organizations in the direction of a more complete internalization of pollution costs.

3.1.2. *The redistribution function*

While the first Community Environmental Action Programme emphasized the role of the polluter-pays principle in combating trade distortions associated with payments of subsidies, later programmes focused more closely on incentives for environmental improvements. The Third Community Environmental Action Programme, for instance, put greater emphasis on the principle as an environmental policy instrument, providing an 'incentive to reduce pollution . . . and to discover less polluting products or technologies'.

The main function of the polluter-pays principle is to internalize the social costs borne by the public authorities for pollution prevention and control. At this stage the principle serves as an economic rule according to which a portion of the profits accruing to polluters as the result of their activities must be returned to the public authorities responsible for inspecting, monitoring, and controlling the pollution these activities produce.

This function has attracted criticisms that are not entirely unfounded. It attaches a price to the right to pollute. Consequently, it is seen as accepting environmental degradation as inevitable provided that the agent pays: 'I pay, therefore I pollute'. For the polluting firm, however, a charge merely represents a supplementary tax. The result is to perpetuate pollution as long as its 'product'— the resultant charges—pays for the administrative authorities to carry out their regulatory tasks. Moreover, the purely distributive function may be subject to an even more fundamental criticism. To speak of a polluter is to evoke ecological damage, which in turn means that such damage has already taken place: that is, prevention is no longer of any use.

Of course, such criticisms must be nuanced. As we shall presently see, the polluter-pays principle can also contribute to reducing pollution (preventive function) and speeding up the process by which those responsible for pollution accept responsibility for ecological damage (curative function).

---

[60] A.C. Pigou, *A Study in Public Finance* (London: Macmillan, 1947) 101.

[61] Some authors consider that this remained the primary function of the polluter-pays principle until the 1992 Rio Conference. Eg P. Birnie and A. Boyle, *International Law and the Environment* (2nd edn., Oxford University Press, 2002) 92.

3.1.3. *The preventive function*

State financing of pollution control has no dissuasive value. On the contrary, it encourages polluters to pass their costs on to the community, with the aim of making the price of their goods and services more competitive. Recommendation 75/463 regarding cost allocation and action by public authorities on environmental matters was intended precisely to counter that tendency. The Recommendation stresses early on that the principle should demonstrate a preventive dimension. The adoption of pollution control measures, and particularly the charges associated with these, should according to the Recommendation 'encourage the polluter to take the necessary measures to reduce the pollution he is causing as cheaply as possible'.

This preventive function of the polluter-pays principle makes it possible to counter the criticisms levelled at it. Moreover, that function is justified on both the economic and legal levels. From the legal perspective, the polluter-pays principle should be consistent with the principle of prevention, which it complements; it would be absurd if principles intended to ensure a coherent environment policy could contradict one another. From the economic point of view, polluters are encouraged to reduce pollution as soon as the costs they must bear are seen to be greater than the benefits they anticipate from continuing nuisances.[62]

To the extent that charges increase in proportion to the seriousness of the pollution, it will be in the interest of operators to reduce their emissions. Moreover, charges are clearly superior to quality, process and product standards because those paying the charge may reduce their discharges to what they consider an optimal level; polluters therefore view economic standards as a flexible replacement for what they consider rigid binding rules.

Put at the service of prevention, the polluter-pays principle should no longer be interpreted as allowing a polluter who pays to continue polluting with impunity. The true aim of the principle would henceforth be to institute a policy of pollution abatement by encouraging polluters to reduce their emissions instead of being content to pay charges. In this way, the polluter-pays and preventive principles would constitute two complementary aspects of a single reality.

But we should not deceive ourselves: the distributive function for the most part remains more important than the preventive function. There are two explanations for this. First, hortatory mechanisms rest on the assumption that the polluter is behaving rationally, which is far from always being the case. Secondly, the dissuasive effect depends on the price charged the polluter—which is generally too low to encourage substantial reductions in pollution.

---

[62] The failure, in cases such as that of asbestos, to reflect the full market price of environmental and health costs gave these products an unjustifiable advantage in the market-place and delayed the adoption of preventive measures (warning signs that arose as early in 1898–1906 in the UK and France were not followed up with regulatory measures before the 1980s). Eg D. Gee and M. Greenber, 'Asbestos: From magic to malevolent mineral' in European Environmental Agency, *Late Lessons from Early Warnings: The Precautionary Principle 1896–2000* (Copenhagen: European Issues Report No. 22, 2001) 57.

3.1.4. The curative function

Whatever the importance or quality of preventive measures, the risk of environmental damage remains. Indeed, setting emission thresholds necessarily leads to degradation of water, soil, and air. It could undoubtedly be argued that most pollution effects, being relatively weak, do not compromise the regenerative capacity of ecosystems. However, this is a theoretical argument; from a scientific point of view, degradation relates more closely to introducing a polluting substance into the ecosystem than to crossing a threshold of irreversibility. The polluter-pays principle should therefore also give rise to liability for residual damage which occurs because of the inadequacy of discharge thresholds established by the public authorities.

Running like Ariane's thread throughout the corpus of environmental law, civil liability provides fertile ground for encouraging development of the curative dimension of the principle. By stressing the curative dimension, the polluter-pays principle could represent a further step forward; instead of simply obliging the polluter to pay for restoration carried out by the public authorities, it would also ensure that victims could obtain compensation from polluters, including for damage resulting from authorized activities. If civil liability guarantees a form of redistribution *ex post*, it differs from the classical distributive function in that it is more individual than collective in character. Nevertheless, to the extent that the obligation to repair damage is likely to modify individual and collective behaviour, civil liability also pursues a preventive objective which is not necessarily part of the distributive function.

In any case, there is an increasing tendency in international circles to ascribe a curative dimension to the polluter-pays principle. In a 1991 Recommendation on the Use of Economic Instruments in Environment Policy, the OECD Council admitted that a 'sustainable and economically efficient development of environmental resources' required internalizing the costs of preventing and controlling pollution as well as of the damage itself.[63]

The 1993 EC Green Paper on Remedying Environmental Damage and the 2000 White Paper on Environmental Liability considers that civil liability sets the polluter-pays principle in play by making it possible to force the polluter to bear the cost of damages. Similarly, the Preamble to the 1993 Lugano Convention on Civil Liability for Damage Resulting From Activities Dangerous to the Environment 'has regard to the desirability of providing for strict liability in this field, taking into account the "polluter-pays" principle'.

3.2. The ambivalence of the concepts of 'polluter' and 'payer'

The polluter-pays principle juxtaposes two terms whose meanings appear self-evident at first glance but become more elusive as one attempts to define them.

---

[63] C(90) 177 (final), OECD, 1991.

The act of definition is thus best approached from two different angles: first: who is the polluter, and secondly: how much must the polluter pay?

3.2.1. *Who is the polluter?*

Before determining what the polluter must pay, we should define who the polluter actually is: a thorny question that the work of the OECD has never tackled.

Discussions relating to the identification of the polluter for the most part hold to a precise notion of pollution; yet two contrasting concepts of pollution exist. According to the first, emission of a substance occurs when a threshold established to avoid the occurrence of ecological damage is exceeded (see Subsection 3.2.1.1 below). The second approach sees pollution as independent of this administrative technique and determined by the mere presence of damage (Subsection 3.2.1.2 below). The results of this conflict are not purely doctrinal. Were the theory that the mere existence of damage is sufficient to gain the upper hand, the person responsible for ecological damage would be obliged to bear all the consequences of his pollution, even if he had scrupulously respected the measures laid down by the public authorities. A further debate takes account of the difficulties that accompany the thesis linking pollution to the existence of damage (Subsection 3.2.1.3 below).

Finally, leaving aside the issue of what constitutes pollution, it remains to determine legally who will have to respect the obligations flowing from the polluter-pays principle. The scope of the discretion reserved to the law-maker to regulate this question forms the topic of a fourth discussion (Subsection 3.2.1.4 below).

3.2.1.1. The definition of pollution arising from unlawful acts

According to one theory, an emission does not necessarily constitute a pollution. In order to be considered pollution, the substance released to the environment must exceed discharge or quality standards set for the receiving environment by the public authorities.[64] The concept of pollution is thus dependent on exceeding a norm. As long as the thresholds fixed by the authorities are respected, the discharger is not subject to the polluter-pays principle. Following this reasoning, environmental effects authorized by the public authorities do not give rise to financial compensation.

At first sight Recommendation 75/436 appears to support this interpretation, since the second paragraph of its Annex states that the principle should make it possible to cover the costs of measures 'necessary to eliminate pollution or to reduce it so as to comply with the standards or equivalent measures . . . laid down by the public authorities'. This interpretation of what constitutes a polluter is based on the traditional view, according to which changes to the environment are only recognized as injurious when they exceed a certain threshold. Krämer

---

[64] L. Krämer, 'The Polluter-Pays Principle in Community Law' n. 44 above, 248.

supports this interpretation, arguing that the distinction between 'impairment' and 'pollution' is found in several places in the EC Treaty and secondary Community legislation.[65]

3.2.1.2. The definition of pollution based on emission impacts

According to the opposite thesis, the definition of pollution depends less on violation of a discharge threshold than on the impact of the substance in question on the environment or its victims. This interpretation is found in both binding and non-binding instruments of international and EC legal systems.

The 1975 Recommendation regarding cost allocation and action by public authorities on environmental matters already defined the polluter as being the person who 'directly or indirectly damages the environment or who creates conditions leading to such damage'. Despite its relatively vague character, this definition emphasizes that in order for there to be a polluter, there must be 'damage', in other words an injury to the environment. Similarly, a distinction may be drawn between contamination of the environment and pollution: contaminants are only regarded as pollutants when they cause damage.[66]

The definitions given to the term 'pollution' in international law tend to follow this reasoning. They generally comprise the following elements: the introduction by man, directly or indirectly, into a specific environment, of substances or energy giving rise or able to give rise to deleterious effects that could endanger human health, damage biological resources, or disturb the functioning of eco-systems, cause deterioration of material goods, or injure or damage amenities and other legitimate uses of the environment.[67] Convention definitions vary according to: the origin or source of the pollution being regulated (dumping or discharge, releases into the atmosphere, exploitation of the ocean bed, etc.); the polluting agent (petrol, waste, nuclear materials, chemicals, etc.); the environment affected by the pollution (atmosphere, international watercourse, marine environment, etc.); the nature and perception of nuisances; and the threshold of risk that is considered acceptable.

Under EC waste law, any disposal of waste that results in environmental harm must be regarded as environmental pollution. In the German version of Article 174(2) of the EC Treaty the concept of pollution does not even occur, as the

[65] Ibid., p. 248.

[66] Gesamp, *The Status of the Marine Environnement* (1990), UNEP Regional Seas Reports and Studies, no. 115.

[67] See, in this regard, the relatively similar formulations contained in the following Convention provisions: Article I(6) of the 1969 Brussels International Convention on Civil Liability for Oil Pollution Damage ; Article 2 of the 1976 Barcelona Convention for the Protection of the Mediterranean Sea Against Pollution; Article 1(6) of the 1977 London International Convention on Civil Liability for Oil Pollution Damage Resulting from Exploration for and Exploitation of Seabed Mineral Resources (not in force); Article 1(a) of the 1979 LRTAP Convention; Article 1(1)(4) of the 1982 UNCLOS; Article 21(1) of the 1997 New York Convention on the Law relating to the Uses of International Watercourses for Purposes other than Navigation (not in force); Article 1(d) of the 1992 OSPAR Convention; Article 2(2) of the Directive 96/61/EC on integrated pollution prevention and control [hereinafter the IPPC Directive].

principle applies only to 'acts which impair the environment' (*Verursacherprinzip*).[68]

While the first concept defines pollution solely by reference to passage beyond a threshold, without consideration of the damage produced, each of the definitions set out above defines pollution by reference to environmental effect, regardless of whether it is lawful or unlawful. In other words, pollution only exists as a function of an emission's impact on the environment; the effect is more important than the cause.

This definition of pollution should be welcomed for reasons of fairness, appropriateness, and legal coherence. First, it is justified from the perspective of fairness. To limit claims for financial compensation purely to cases of pollution caused by unlawful discharges, as proposed by those who defend the first definition, burdens the community with the cost of clean-up measures for damage caused by authorized discharges. This limitation on the internalization of pollution costs clearly runs counter to the evolution of the polluter-pays principle described above.

The second definition is also more acceptable for reasons of appropriateness. Limiting the application of the polluter-pays principle to unlawful impairment will not encourage polluters who are in compliance with emission standards to reduce the harmfulness or quantity of their polluting emissions even further. The principle of prevention will remain ill served as long as that of the polluter-pays does not cover every impairment of the environment.

Finally, at the level of civil liability, which is equally likely to be influenced by the polluter-pays principle, nothing prevents an act of wrongful pollution being evaluated from the perspective of the requirement for duty of care owed by the liable party, whether or not he respected the standards incumbent upon him. In fact, the granting of an administrative authorization does not automatically absolve its holder from liability.

3.2.1.3. The difficulties inherent in defining pollution through impact

Defining pollution as a function of the environmental impact of an emission does not, however, solve all the problems raised above. We may ask, for instance, whether the existence of damage is an essential condition for the polluter-pays principle to apply. During the 1970s conventions for protection of the marine environment defined marine pollution in a more restrictive manner, by considering that 'pollution' existed only when it had been demonstrated that the introduction into the sea of substances or energy had given rise to harmful effects.[69]

Since then the definition of pollution has evolved under the influence of the precautionary principle and now encompasses the risk of degradation. For example, under the IPPC Directive, pollution exists when the introduction of a

---

[68] L. Krämer, 'The Polluter-Pays Principle in Community Law', n. 44 above, 248–9.

[69] See the formulation set out in the 1974 Helsinki Convention on the Protection of the Marine Environment of the Baltic Sea (replaced); Article 1(1) of the 1974 Paris Convention for the Prevention of Marine Pollution from Land-Based Sources (replaced).

substance is 'likely to cause harm [...] or to entail deterioration'. Consequently, operators of hazardous activities might, on the basis of the polluter-pays principle, have to pay fees to guarantee the control and monitoring of tasks carried out by the authorities, even if they have not damaged the environment. Moreover, the OECD Recommendation of 5 July 1989 on the Application of the Polluter-Pays Principle to Accidental Pollution confirms the intention to apply the principle to accidental as well as chronic pollution and thereby to require potential polluters to contribute financially to preventive measures adopted by public authorities.

Even if the polluter-pays principle were to be applied as soon as the environment had suffered or was at risk of suffering degradation, it would still be necessary to determine what constitutes degradation. Can any disturbance of ecosystem functioning give rise to compensation? Does the polluter-pays principle include damage to future generations caused by the loss of potential scientific discoveries? There seems little doubt that a solution by which the agent of any disturbance would be considered a polluter could give rise to nonsensical situations.

Must we instead limit ecological damage to disturbances that are considered abnormal? This would imply using thresholds to define what categories of 'normal' damage do not give rise to compensation. However, the normal or abnormal character of damage is highly relative, as it tends to be a function of time, place, and the persons affected. A decibel level that would drive a musician mad would leave a deaf person unruffled; an oil slick that would devastate a fish farm presents less of a danger when it is spread over the high seas.

In addition, the very concept of abnormality is completely anti-ecological. Ecotoxicology shows us that notions of threshold are radically incorrect, being of almost no use when doses accumulate in living organisms. Moreover, the act of setting a threshold tends to reinforce the idea that some types of damage are acceptable and thus forces communities to accept a certain level of damage without being able to claim compensation. The polluter-pays principle of course provides no answers to the question of how to define damage; that must follow from a legislative choice.

3.2.1.4. Identifying the polluter

The 'polluter' should be the person who causes pollution. Now, even in the case of a specific installation, it is not always easy to identify who has actually caused pollution. The person in charge of the installation, the manufacturer of the defective plant, and the licence-holder or his representatives may all be liable for pollution. This question becomes even more complex in the case of diffuse pollution, where multiple causes produce single effects and single causes produce multiple effects. For reasons of economic efficiency and administrative simplicity, law need not necessarily adhere to reality, and it is sometimes preferable to apply this qualification to a single person rather than a number of people. For instance, Recommendation 75/436 regarding cost allocation and action by public authorities on environmental matters provides that the costs of pollution could be charged 'at the point at which the number of economic operators is least and control is easiest'. Consequently, the polluter may be the agent who plays a determining role in producing the pollution rather than the person actually causing the pollution (for example, the producer of pesticides rather than the farm worker).

We may ask ourselves, however, about the relevance of recourse to the concept of 'polluter' to ensure the implementation of a policy favouring sustainable development. Acts of pollution are not the only cause of today's ecological harm: the unbridled consumption of natural resources is also a problem, even if it is not a source of pollution properly speaking. The official positions of the OECD indicate a growing awareness of the need for prices to reflect the 'true' costs of natural resource use.[70]

According to the OECD, a 'user-pays' principle should complement the polluter-pays principle in order to guarantee more prudent resource management. By attributing a price to the consumption of natural resources, such a principle could contribute to sustainable development—a concept whose scope far exceeds that of mere pollution control. The main difference between these two principles is that the 'user-pays' principle would apply to resources and their users, while the polluter-pays principle applies entirely to discharges of pollutants, and consequently only to polluters. Other than that, these two principles arise from a single economic logic of internalizing external costs. By not making the slightest reference to the notion of pollution, the formulations of the polluter-pays principle in German law (*Verursacherprinzip*) and in Swiss law (*principe de causalité*) seem to correspond to this new principle.

3.2.2. How much must the polluter pay?

Once identified, the polluter will have to pay, but it still remains to agree on a price. At this point it is necessary to distinguish between the polluter-pays principle in the strict sense, which is limited to a partial internalization of costs, and the principle defined in a wider sense, which corresponds to a full internalization of externalities.[71]

The polluter-pays principle was originally defined strictly in order to exclude subsidies for pollution prevention and control measures financed by polluters.

---

[70] The user-pays principle is being seen in more and more OECD decisions. See the 1989 OECD Council Recommendation of 31 March 1989 Concerning the Management of Aquatic Resources: integration, demand management and protection of groundwaters (C(89) 12 (final)); the OECD Council Recommendation of 31 January 1991 Concerning the Use of Economic Instruments in Environmental Policy (C(90) 177 (final)); and the OECD Council Recommendation of 23 July 1992 on the Integrated Management of Coastal Zones (C(92) 114 (final)).

[71] Pezzey distinguishes between the 'Standard PPP' (the polluter pays only for measures intended to bring the pollution to an acceptable level) and the 'Extended PPP' (the polluter also pays to cover the social damages resulting from pollution at an acceptable level). Eg J. Pezzey, 'Market Mechanisms of Pollution Control: "Polluter-pays", Economic and Practical Aspects' in R. Kerri Turner (ed.), *Sustainable Environmental Management: Principles and Practice* (Boulder, 1988) 190.

Consequently polluters had no expenses other than those linked to financing prevention and control measures put in place by the authorities. This narrow perception of negative externalities, however, neglected the question of hidden debt: in other words, of environmental liability which must be borne by future generations when not immediately discharged by responsible parties.

On the other hand, in its widest sense the polluter-pays principle implies complete internalization. In addition to the cost of pollution prevention and control measures, it also covers ecological damage in its entirety.

This interpretation should be retained to the extent that it conforms to Principle 16 of the 1992 Rio Declaration, on one hand, according to which the polluter should 'bear the cost of pollution' rather than merely assume the cost of measures adopted by the public authorities, and on the other hand to the 1991 Recommendation of the OECD, wherein the OECD Council stated that: 'a sustainable and economically efficient management of environmental resources requires, *inter alia*, the internalisation of pollution prevention, control and damages costs'.[72]

In EC law this interpretation can be seen in Article 10 of Directive 1999/31/EC on the landfill of waste, which implies the complete internalization of all costs relating to management and control of a landfill in the price charged for the disposal of wastes. Nonetheless, internalization is not absolute in many international acts, where public authorities need only adopt such curative measures as are considered 'reasonable'.[73]

Full compensation for ecological damage raises the question of calculating its value, a calculation rendered even more delicate because attribution of a market value to a natural resource has a determining effect on the scope of liability. Of course the damage caused to nature could undoubtedly be valued in terms of forest surface destroyed or the number of animals or plants lost. However, even if such losses were quantifiable it would be difficult to evaluate them in monetary terms. What price can we attach to air, water, plants, and non-domestic animals? Some methods of calculation already make it possible to attach a monetary value to these, based on the efforts that would be needed to restore degraded environments to a pristine condition or to reintroduce animals and plants that have disappeared; but these remain approximative, since the development of species and natural spaces is impossible to master. The difficulty increases when the question of compensation is no longer limited to species or habitats but extends to interactions between biotic and abiotic elements.

---

[72] OECD Council Recommendation Concerning the Use of Economic Instruments in Environmental Policy, C(90) (117) final, OECD, 1991.

[73] See the 1969 Brussels International Convention on Civil Liability for Oil Pollution Damage; the OECD Recommendation of 5 July 1989 on the Application of the Polluter-Pays Principle to Accidental Pollution; the 1989 Geneva Convention on Civil Liability for Damage Caused During Carriage of Dangerous Goods by Road, Rail and Inland Navigation Vessels (not in force); and the not yet in force 1993 Lugano Convention on Civil Liability for Damage Resulting from Activities Dangerous to the Environment.

Clearly, this is where the shoe pinches. In the natural sciences, in effect, ecological damage is characterized by the disturbance of equilibria and ecological processes far more than by losses brought about by specific, and therefore quantifiable, elements.

Now, how is one to calculate these impairments? The destruction of a wild flower constitutes damage that can reasonably be quantified to the extent that its disappearance is not irreversible. As soon as the disappearance affects the entire species, however, the loss becomes inestimable because it relates to an irreversible phenomenon. Having disappeared, the species becomes irreplaceable. In such a case it is less a question of assessing the economic value of the species than of considering its intrinsic value. We must admit that it is impossible to evaluate the irreparable. Under those circumstances, is it reasonable to require a polluter to compensate the public authorities, given that the latter will no longer be able to repair the damage in question?

The polluter-pays principle thereby leads to another dead end. This merely confirms the relevance of the preventive and anticipatory approaches, which are the only approaches capable of averting the irreparable and consequently limiting the application of the polluter-pays principle to reversible damages.

4. APPLICATIONS OF THE PRINCIPLE

The polluter-pays principle has successively been invoked to address distortion of competition (objective of economic integration), as a preventive instrument to establish the internalization of chronic pollution (instrument of prevention *ex ante*), and finally to justify the adoption of fiscal measures or strict liability regimes (instrument of prevention *ex post*). We must now consider whether, as its protagonists claim, this principle is really capable of bringing about changes to two redistributive legal instruments: taxation and civil liability.

4.1. Environmental taxation

It is generally recognized that the polluter-pays principle implies setting up a system of charges by which polluters help finance public policy to protect the environment. According to the terms of the 1975 Council Recommendation regarding cost allocation and action by public authorities on environmental matters, this is in fact the most appropriate instrument for carrying out the principle.[74] This raises a number of questions, however, concerning how to identify who should pay charges (see Subsection 4.1.1 below), the tax base of charges (Subsection 4.1.2), and the allocation of charge revenues (Subsection 4.1.3).

---

[74] The Commission Communication of 26 March 1997 on taxes, fees and environmental charges in the Single Market considers that 'such levies could constitute an adequate means for implementing the polluter-pays principle, by including environmental costs in the price of goods and services' (COM(97) 9 final).

4.1.1. Who should pay pollution charges?

Identifying the person who must pay pollution charges has given rise to a great deal of controversy, since generally more than one identifiable individual contributes to pollution. May we charge each person who has contributed to the harm, no matter how small their share, on the grounds of equity? Or, for the sake of efficiency, is it preferable to charge the person who is best placed to pay? In Recommendation 75/436 the Commission gave as an example the case of motor vehicle emissions, which recurrently give rise to the question whether their costs should be charged to the vehicle manufacturer, the fuel producer, or the owner of the motor vehicle. Similarly, where noise from an airport disturbs those living in its vicinity, should one tax the operator of the airline, the operator of the airport, and the passengers, or only some of the above? If the latter, in what proportion?

Such an exercise would be little better than a lottery, for it is almost impossible to determine with any precision how each of these agents contributes to creating the nuisance. It is therefore necessary to ease the law-maker's task by permitting him to collect a charge at those points in the pollution chain which offer 'the best solution from the administrative and economic points of view and which make the most effective contribution towards improving the environment'.[75] 'Simplicity and clarity' of economic instruments have also been emphasized by the OECD in its 1991 Recommendation on the Uses of Economic Instruments: 'there should be a fine balance between undue complexity, which makes the economic instrument hard to apply, and excessive simplicity, which may mean that it is not very efficient'.[76]

Based on this position of principle, imprecise as it is, one can argue that the polluter should be identified by calling on the principles of prevention and of rectification of pollution at source. In conformity with those principles, it is preferable to charge the economic agent who is at the source of a nuisance. In effect, from the perspective of prevention there is no point in acting against a person who has no power over the nuisance. It is far more efficient to go as far upstream as possible, by identifying the economic agent without whose action the nuisance could not have occurred. As the first link in the chain of polluters, the producer of the polluting product is the individual who is best placed to bear the expense of pollution prevention and control. He will thereby make 'the most effective contribution towards improving the environment' when he is obliged to assume responsibility for prevention and elimination costs.

In this perspective, it is not the driver but the manufacturer of the motor vehicle who should pay a charge, to the extent that the latter is the only party able to control the technology that would make possible reductions of CO_2 and NO_x emissions to air.

---

[75] Recommendation 75/436/Euratom/ESCC/EEC, Annex, para 3; OECD, *The Polluter-pays Principle* (1992) 8.
[76] OECD, 1991, Annex III (14).

Of course, this option may appear iniquitous in that it will require someone who has not directly caused pollution to intervene financially, in the place of a multitude of other economic agents. We could also ask in what way the manufacturer of a motor vehicle or the manager of an airport are more responsible than a motorist, a driver, an airline, or its passengers. This point emphasizes the limits of a principle that does not definitively indicate who should be responsible for the cost of pollution when the responsible party is part of a collective phenomenon. The relevance of this criticism should not, however, prevent public authorities from making a single economic operator in the production chain bear the weight of taxation, given that we are discussing taxation and not civil liability, where every individual who is liable must bear the cost for the damage he has caused.

Is it necessary to attach great importance to this question, which may appear highly theoretical? In fact, if the economic operator pays, he is generally merely the first to pay; the consumer ultimately bears the additional cost arising from the charge to the producer. This assertion is accurate for monopolies insofar as a supplementary cost that reflects the charge will always be passed on to the consumer, who in a monopoly situation cannot turn to alternative producers for supplies. On the other hand, it is without foundation where companies are in competition, for the obligation to internalize pollution costs allows firms which pollute the least to gain market share. Required to pay a charge which increases as a function of the seriousness of the pollution caused, the most polluting producers in effect become less competitive. The play of competition thus makes it possible to avoid forcing consumers to bear over the long term the supplementary cost charged to the producer.

4.1.2. *Determining the basis of charges*

The basis of a charge will vary according to the redistributive or incentive function assigned to the polluter-pays principle. Recommendation 75/436 again serves to define the outlines of a solution.

4.1.2.1. Distributive function

In the case where the charge is fulfilling a redistributive function, the assessment should be proportional to the pollution caused, since the level of the charge should reflect the actual share in causing the pollution in question. In this perspective, Recommendation 75/436 foresees that 'the charges should be applied, according to the extent of pollution emitted, on the basis of an appropriate administrative procedure'.[77]

However, applying proportionality in a rigorous manner remains difficult. First, calculating the charge may prove a relatively complex operation owing to the multiple parameters which must be taken into account—among them: the nature of the nuisance, the hazards it presents, the means available to remedy its harmful effects, and the cost of meeting an environmental quality objective,

---

[77] Para. 4(b) of Recommendation 75/436/Euratom/ESCC/EEC.

including the administrative costs directly linked to carrying out anti-pollution measures. Aware of these difficulties, the authors of Recommendation 75/436 regarding cost allocation and action by public authorities on environmental matters admitted that 'insofar as the main function of charges is redistribution, they should at least be fixed [...] so that the aggregate amount of the charges is equal to the total cost to the Community of eliminating nuisances'.

Yet while the imperatives of tax law simplicity may lead to some attenuation of the proportionality requirement, it remains the case that a reasonable relation must exist between the charge and the importance of the nuisance. The charge must, in effect, correspond as closely as possible to the environmental risk created by commercialization.

Flat-rate tax regimes are therefore incompatible with the polluter-pays principle. A flat-rate tax charged to households for their production of domestic waste would also run counter to the polluter-pays principle, by making each taxpayer subject to an identical tax although waste generation may vary greatly from one household to another.[78]

4.1.2.2. Incentive function

The incentive character of taxation conforms to the polluter-pays principle insofar as the 1975 Community Recommendation strongly urges such an evolution. Environmental taxes are probably the most emblematic instruments of the simultaneous intervention of the polluter-pays and prevention principles: activities that are the most harmful to the environment pay the highest charges. In turn, the higher a charge, the more dissuasive its effect. Using such taxes, the legislator may be tempted to penalize undesirable behaviour through charges which are distinctly higher than the costs they are intended to cover. In that case the incentive function will overtake the requirement for proportionality. One should keep in mind, however, that the more effectively an eco-tax aims to prevent pollution, the less revenue it will bring in.[79]

As regards this second function, Article 15 of Directive 94/62/EEC concerning waste and waste packaging, which obliges Member States to respect the polluter-pays principle when adopting economic instruments intended to reduce their quantity of packaging waste, does not oppose the establishment of incentive-type tax regimes, the object of which would be to eliminate certain types of packaging from the market.

4.1.3. *Allocation of charge revenues*

Allocating the revenue from charges also gives rise to a number of questions. OECD and EC Recommendations do not indicate whether the sums collected should be set aside in a special fund for financing environmental policy or paid into the general State budget. The redistributive function generally assigned to

---

[78] See the debate in Belgium about the constitutionality of flat-rate tax regimes in the field of household waste management (CA no. 41/93, 3 June 1993).
[79] T. O'Riordan (ed.), *Ecotaxation* (London: Earthscan, 1997) 326.

charges argues in favour of the first option. Since a financial transfer from polluters to the public authorities is intended to spare the community from having to assume environmental liability, the proceeds of charges should primarily be allocated to the tasks of prevention, control, monitoring, and clean-up carried out by public authorities. In the case where charge revenue exceeds total expenditure, Recommendation 75/432 says that 'the surplus should preferably be used by each government for its national environmental policies'. Allocating charge revenues to a dedicated fund does not, however, conform to the principle of universality, according to which tax revenues should not be used for specific expenditure.

The question also arises whether the public authorities may assign part of the charges back to the polluters themselves. Recommendation 75/432 authorizes such mechanisms under certain conditions. Strictly applied, financial intervention by Member States in support of certain private investments should not be considered contrary to the polluter-pays principle. Methods for Member State financing have, moreover, been specified in several European Commission Communications.[80] In the 2001 EC Guidelines on State Aid for Environmental Protection, the European Commission asserts that 'firms had disposed of seven years for adapting gradually to the application of the pollution-pays principle'. Therefore, it is no longer necessary to grant environmental aid aimed at helping firms adapt to new environmental standards. Aid may only be granted where national standards are more stringent than those at the EC level.

4.1.4. Critical assessment

Their greater flexibility compared to preventive standards (environmental quality standards and product standards), their incentive character, and the financial resources they procure for the State all argue in favour of setting up charges based on the polluter-pays principle. As is evident from the explanatory memoranda of several environmental tax laws, the principle has succeeded in compelling recognition in this field, even if it does not resolve the questions of how to identify who should pay pollution charges, how to determine the basis for charges, and how to allocate charge revenues.

However, the difficulties inherent in interpreting the principle—particularly sensitive in relation to determining who should pay charges and the basis for determining them—should not lead to dismissing the principle, but rather to clarifying its meaning. In the past, recourse to other principles (eg prevention and rectification at source) has encouraged original approaches such as charging the producer rather than the consumer. Environmental taxation is in any case evolving in a more interventionist direction, with the aim of influencing the behaviour of economic agents by fiscal means. To the extent that the prospect of having to pay dissuades the polluter, the polluter-pays principle ties in with the

---

[80] See, most recently, Information from the EC Guidelines 94/C 72/03 on State Aid for Environmental Protection replaced by the EC Guidelines 2001/C 37/03 on State Aid for Protecting the Environment.

principle of prevention. Indeed, what objective does environmental taxation pursue if not to prevent the recurrence of a polluting activity through charges? Despite impressive progress, the rate of charges remains so low that these instruments rarely cover the combined costs of pollution control.[81]

4.2. Environmental liability

The OECD and EC intend the polluter-pays principle to assume a more curative dimension in future.[82] We may wonder, however, whether the principle is capable of helping victims to overcome the obstacle course that inevitably confronts attempts to obtain compensation for ecological damage without completely distorting civil liability. It is difficult to draw definitive conclusions about the influence of the principle on the evolution of civil liability. It is nonetheless possible to resort to the principle in order to evaluate the relevance of traditional positive law solutions requiring polluters to compensate the community for damage to the environment. We undertake that exercise in this section. Used as a critical filter for considering current positive law, the polluter-pays principle here serves to question solutions that have already been challenged by legal doctrine and to suggest improvements to civil liability law, where necessary.

4.2.1. The polluting event

4.2.1.1. Fault-based liability

In most European countries civil liability still rests largely on fault giving rise to damage.[83] Fault occurs when a statutory provision or regulation has not been

---

[81] In a comparative study on charges for wastewater discharges in France, Denmark, the Federal Republic of Germany, and the Netherlands, Skou Andersen concludes that these barely cover the costs of treatment plants, still less the full cost of ecological damage. According to Andersen, the pollution reduction achieved in these States is in part due to subsidies granted by the public authorities, which are explicitly forbidden by the original version of the polluter-pays principle. Eg *Governance by Green Taxes: Making Pollution Prevention Pay* (Manchester: Manchester UP, 1994) 204.

[82] The polluter-pays principle had already been mentioned in the first programme of action on the environment of 22 November 1973, in conjunction with civil liability. According to the EC White Paper on Environmental Liability (COM(2000) 66 final, 9 February 2000): 'Environmental liability is a way of implementing the main principles of environmental policy enshrined in the EC Treaty (Article 174(2)), above all the polluter-pays principle. If this principle is not applied to covering the costs of restoration of environmental damage, either the environment remains un-restored or the State, and ultimately the taxpayer, has to pay for it. Therefore, a first objective is making the polluter liable for the damage he has caused. If polluters need to pay for damage caused, they will cut back pollution up to the point where the marginal cost of abatement exceeds the compensation avoided. Thus, environmental liability results in prevention of damage and in internalisation of environmental costs. (Internalisation of environmental costs means that the costs of preventing and restoring environmental pollution will be paid directly by the parties responsible for the damage rather than being financed by society in general). Liability may also lead to the application of more precaution, resulting in avoidance of risk and damage, as well as it may encourage investment in R & D for improving knowledge and technologies' (para. 3.1). Unlike the harmonization of product liability, the harmonization of environmental civil liability at EC level will not be completed for many years to come.

[83] Most Continental civil liability regimes are fault-based. In France and in Belgium (C.civ., Article 1382) 'everyone is responsible for the damage caused not only by his own act but also by his negligence or carelessness'. Under the Dutch Civil Code (Article 6: 162 BW) the tortfeasor must

respected by the liable party, or when the latter has violated a general duty of care.

The need to demonstrate fault has always been considered a substantial obstacle by victims of ecological damage. The victim must prove fault; but what can he do when sophisticated techniques of which he is wholly ignorant are the origin of the injury he has suffered, other than turn to experts to establish the violation of specific standards? If he attempts to prove violation of a general norm of a duty of care, he is necessarily dependent upon the very wide discretion of the courts, which are entitled to define that norm. Moreover, the unforesee-ability of damage as well as exonerating justifications (Act of God, fortuitous event, *force majeure*, etc.) act as limitations which may exonerate the polluter from liability.

The picture is not necessarily as dismal as depicted above, however. The importance of fault should grow in step with the increase in regulations and standards of all types. The more numerous and complex regulations become, the more easily operators will incur liability. In addition, certain traditional provisions are being interpreted in innovative ways which could equally well apply to environmental liability. Moreover, the definition of negligence is being extended as civil liability is increasingly assigned a compensatory objective, and courts are tending to formulate that definition on the basis of damage caused.

4.2.1.2. Strict liability

Omitting the concept of fault reduces the time spent discussing the always delicate subject of whether fault has occurred. To ensure adequate compensation for losses, the core of civil liability (fault) will have to give way to its object (compensation for damage).[84] In other words, liability will have to break away from the requirement for fault in order to guarantee maximum compensation. Even if it sometimes results in unfairness to an innocent operator, the basis of the strict liability regime raises few difficulties. The operator responsible for a polluting activity should fully assume all the consequences of his operation, these being the counterpart of operating rights and the ensuing financial advantages.

Initiatives such as the 1993 Lugano Convention on Civil Liability for Damage Resulting from Activities Dangerous to the Environment,[85] the European

---

repair the damage another person suffers as a consequence of his act only if there is an unlawful act due to his fault. In Germany, under §823(1) BGB, liability arises when culpably unlawful behaviour has caused injury to a protected interest (*Rechtsgüter*). Italian Act no. 349 establishing the Ministry of Environment—the sole basis upon which a claim for purely environmental damage can be based—is based on fault and presupposes a violation of legal or administrative provisions. Like the fault-based regimes in Continental codes, those of the three Nordic countries which are members of the EC use fault-based liability regimes. Eg von Bar, *The Common European Law of Torts* (Oxford: Clarendon, 1998) para. 243.

[84] Explanatory report of the 1993 Lugano Convention on Civil Liability for Damage Resulting From Activities Dangerous to the Environment, not yet in force, recital no. 7.

[85] Sixth Recital of the 1993 Lugano Convention, not yet in force: 'Having regard to the desirability of providing for strict liability in this field taking into account the "Polluter-pays" Principle'.

Commission Green Paper on environmental liability,[86] Article 6:175 of the Dutch Civil Code,[87] and the chapter on liability for contaminated land of the Swedish Environment Code[88] clearly suggest that the polluter-pays principle calls for the establishment of a strict liability regime. More recently, in its White Paper on Environmental Liability, the European Commission stressed that liability independent of fault must be favoured for two reasons: first, it is very difficult for plaintiffs to establish fault in environmental liability cases; and secondly, it is the person who undertakes an inherently hazardous activity, rather than the victim or society in general, who should bear the risk of any damage that might ensue.[89]

This assumption is nevertheless questioned by one theoretical school, which argues that it is not possible to deduce from the polluter-pays principle that liability for damage exists even in the absence of fault.[90] The principle would thus not allow one to infer an obligation to establish a strict liability regime for environmental damage. Rather, the law-maker has a free hand to decide whether or not to base liability on fault.

This controversy expresses a political choice: it is up to the legislator to decide if operators must compensate all harmful consequences of their activities even if no fault attaches to them. Nonetheless, the polluter-pays principle could influence such a choice. In fact this is not a new trend in international law.[91] Recent

---

[86] Communication from the European Commission to the Council, the European Parliament and the Economic and Social Committee of 14 May 1993 (COM (93) 47 (final)), 25 and following, which states that a strict liability regime presents the advantage of favouring 'the implementation of the polluter-pays principle'.

[87] Article 6:175 BW imposes strict liability for damage caused by hazardous substances, justifying this option in the light of the polluter-pays principle. Eg E.A. Messer, *Risico-aansprakelijkheid voor milieu-verontreiniging in de BW* (Arnhem: Goude Quint, 1994) 120.

[88] Chapter X of the Environment Code, whose explanatory memorandum justifies strict liability in the light of the polluter-pays principle.

[89] COM(2000) 66 final, 9 February 2000.

[90] L. Krämer, n. 44 above, p. 257.

[91] The four nuclear Conventions (the 1960 Paris Convention on Third Party Liability in the Field of Nuclear Energy, the 1963 Brussels Agreement Supplementary to the Paris Convention of 1960 on Third Party Liability in the Field of Nuclear Energy, the 1963 Vienna Convention on Civil Liability for Nuclear Damage as amended by the 1997 Protocol, and the 1971 Brussels Convention Relating to Civil Liability in the Field of Maritime Carriage of Nuclear Material) create a common scheme based on the absolute liability of the operator of a nuclear installation.
The Conventions governing civil liability for oil pollution (the 1969 Brussels Convention on Civil Liability for Oil Pollution Damage (to be replaced by the 1992 Civil Liability Convention), the 1971 Brussels International Convention on the Establishment of an International Fund for Compensation for Oil Pollution Damage (to be replaced by the 1992 IOPC Protocol), and the 1977 London Convention on Civil Liability for Oil Pollution Damage Resulting from Exploration for and Exploitation of Seabed Mineral Resources (not in force) follow a similar pattern, but in a more liberal way, excusing the shipowner in certain cases.
The 1991 UN Treaty on Terminal Operator Liability in International Trade (not in force) imposes strict liability on the operator of the terminal. This is also the case for the 1996 International Convention on Liability and Compensation for Damage in Connection with the Carriage of Hazardous and Noxious Substances by Sea (not in force) and the 1989 Geneva Convention on Civil Liability for Damage Caused during Carriage of Dangerous Goods by Road, Rail and Inland Navigation Vessels, which impose strict liability on the carrier (not in force).

national environmental liability regimes tend to be based on the principle of strict liability, on the assumption that environmental purposes are more effectively achieved in that way.[92]

Insofar as the polluter may always avoid liability in the absence of fault, it is clear that a system of fault-based liability guarantees compensation for environmental damage less effectively than a strict liability regime. The polluter-pays principle is neutral as regards the elements of conscience or intention which should, if only tenuously, characterize a violation, for it is not up to the community to assume financial responsibility for environmental damage caused by individual economic operators, even if the latter are not guilty of any fault or have not been negligent. The cost of reparation of damage should thus be passed to those who caused the damage, insofar as possible; this is more likely under a strict liability regime.

4.2.2. Environmental damage

An environmental impact will only give rise to financial compensation to the extent that it generates damage. For there to be a polluter, there must therefore be damage. From Chernobyl to the destruction of a peat bog, from pollution of the seas by hydrocarbons to the poisoning of fish stocks through the discharge of municipal wastewater, a plethora of effects come under the rubric of ecological damage.

Infinitely variable by nature, this notion may cover both damage caused to *res propriae* (people or goods) and that caused to *res communes* (water, air, etc.) or to *res nullius* (wild flora and fauna). The first category of damage, where human beings or their goods are the victims, presents the least difficulty. Relating to elements that may be assessed monetarily, it allows compensation to be envisaged *a priori*.

By contrast, the category comprising 'pure ecological damage' or 'ecological damage *stricto sensu*' does not easily fit into the traditional legal system since the victim of pollution in this second category is the environment. Damage affecting the unowned environment does not have an individual and personal character and consequently does not generally give rise to compensation. This requirement

---

The first treaty to provide a general and comprehensive regulatory regime in the area of environmental law, the 1993 Lugano Convention on Civil Liability for Damage resulting from Activities Dangerous to the Environment, which is not yet in force, imposes strict liability on operators in respect of a dangerous activity.

More recently, the 2000 Basel Protocol on Liability and Compensation for Damage resulting from Transboundary Movements of Hazardous Wastes and their Disposal (not in force) makes the person who notifies the transfer strictly liable until the disposer has taken possession of the wastes.

[92] Strict liability is firmly established as the basis for all new national environmental legislation at European level. Germany: for civil liability the 1990 Environmental Liability Act (*UmweltHG*) and for public liability the 1998 Federal Soil Protection Act (*BSG*); Netherlands: Article 6:175 BW; Belgium: the 1995 Flemish Act on soil decontamination (*Bodemsaneringsdecreet*) and the 1999 Federal Act concerning protection of the marine environment in marine areas under Belgian jurisdiction; Denmark: the 1994 Environmental Damage Compensation Act; Finland: the 2000 Environmental Protection Act (86/2000); Sweden: chapter 32 of the 1998 Swedish Environmental Code.

prevents the reparation of damage caused to *res communes* or *res nullius*, which may appear unjustified in the light of the polluter-pays principle.[93] According to the principle, the responsible party should repair damage to both private goods and non-appropriable goods. This is the only reasonable solution, since the very object of the principle is to avoid forcing the community at large to bear the costs of damage to the unowned environment in the place of those truly responsible for such damage.

4.2.3. Causation

Victims are regularly confronted with pollution of a diffuse nature generated by multiple acts. Belgian and, to a lesser extent, French national courts tend to favour victims by applying the theory of *l'équivalence des conditions*, which puts all the acts that contribute to damage on an equal footing. In other words, each element which is considered a necessary condition of the damage is considered to have caused the damage. Where damage is caused by a plurality of conditions, the parties that caused the damage will be held jointly and severally liable. This theory enables the plaintiff to recover the whole of his damage from any tortfeasor, regardless of separate contributions to that damage.

The theory of *l'équivalence des conditions* nonetheless reaches its limits in dealing with the environment, for it does not make it possible to impute collective damage caused by the accumulation of many small acts of present or historic pollution to a large number of operators.[94] Each small polluting act is lawful; thus, escaping fault-based civil liability, such acts can only be controlled and limited through fiscal mechanisms of a preventive nature, which authorize recourse to the polluter-pays principle.

Criticism has recently been directed at joint and several liability on the ground of the polluter-pays principle; that is, by holding the most solvent party responsible for damages the system in effect encourages a 'deep pocket' approach. The European Commission seems to support this idea; in the 1993 Green Paper on environmental liability it observed that the system 'becomes unjust if the victim seeks redress from the party with the greatest financial resources rather than the party that has caused the greatest amount of damage'.[95] More recently, in the 2000 White Paper on Environmental Liability, the Commission stressed that 'circumstances might occur which would make it inequitable for the polluter to have to pay the full compensation for the damage caused by him. Some room might be granted to the court (or any other competent body, eg an arbiter) to decide—for instance in cases where the operator who caused the damage can prove that this damage was entirely and exclusively caused by emissions that

---

[93] A. Carette, *Herstel van en vergoeding voor aantasting aan niet-toegeèigende milieubestanddelen* (Antwerp-Groningen: Intersentia, 1997) 630.

[94] J. van Dunné, 'Legal Aspects of Non-Point Source Pollution of the River Meuse: a Comparative Analysis of Liability in Tort and Multiple Causation' in J. van Dunné (ed.), *Non-Point Source River Pollution: The Case of the River Meuse* (London: Kluwer Law Int'l, 1996) 46.

[95] *Green Paper*, 8.

were explicitly allowed by his permit—that part of the compensation should be borne by the permitting authority, instead of the polluter'.[96]

It is true that in a joint and several liability system the most solvent party will have to pay everything, although it may subsequently sue its fellow parties. Opposing this traditional regime, a system of mitigated joint and several liability would make each party liable for all damage unless it can prove it caused only part of the damage. As the party would then only be liable for that part, this system better protects the most solvent party, to the extent that it can prove responsibility for only a portion of the damage in question.

It would be paradoxical, however, to limit joint and several liability, which is quite favourable to victims, in the name of the polluter-pays principle at the same time as that principle is being used to ensure that polluters assume exclusive liability for damages.

Finally, in various national laws the costs to the public authorities of intervening to halt accidental pollution may not be recovered from third parties who contributed to the damage.[97] This represents a break in the causal link between the loss sustained by the authorities as the result of their intervention and the fault committed by polluters. This case-law is contradictory to the polluter-pays principle, particularly as the OECD Recommendation of 5 July 1989 on the Application of the Polluter-Pays Principle to Accidental Pollution envisages that clean-up costs for accidental pollution borne by the authorities should be charged to the polluter. In order both to escape the dangers of this case-law—which is at the very least unstable—and to conform better to the spirit of the polluter-pays principle, special laws should expressly require the polluter to reimburse clean-up costs taken on by the public authorities.[98]

4.2.4. *Canalization of liability*

4.2.4.1. Identifying the liable party

Even when the source of damage is identified, it is still necessary to determine the person liable for that damage. That task may prove highly complex, since the multiplication of potentially liable parties weakens joint and several liability. Such snags can be avoided only by canalizing liability. The canalization mechanism is linked to the establishment of strict liability regimes. Strict liability has both advantages and disadvantages: on one hand, it presents the advantage that the victim may act against a single person who is easily identifiable; on the other hand, it could be disadvantageous for the victim in cases where the designated operator is insolvent. It also provides certainty as to how liability will be assigned. Carrying out a preliminary designation of the operator also encourages

---

[96] *White Paper*, para. 4.3.

[97] In Dutch law, as regards pollution caused before 1975, see eg A. Kruisinga and J. Lefevere, 'De 30 september arresten: De historische vervuiler opnieuw buiten schot?' (1995) 2 TMR 99. In Belgian law, see Cass. 28 April 1978, (1979) RCJB 275; Cass. 28 June 1984.

[98] For instance, see in international law the 1969 Brussels Convention Relating to Intervention on the High Seas in Cases of Oil Pollution Damage.

the latter to improve safety measures or to choose more reliable operating systems. Canalization of liability therefore responds to the redistributive and preventive functions of the polluter-pays principle.

Determining that a single party is liable under strict liability is as difficult as determining who should pay a charge. Is it the person who possesses technical knowledge, or resources, or operational control of the activity at the time when damage occurs? The polluter-pays principle cannot answer that question.

Like Directive 85/374/EEC concerning liability for defective products, which considers the producer liable,[99] several international[100] and national[101] environmental liability regimes stress that the person who has the greatest degree of control over the source of the pollution should be liable. Those regimes usually tend to canalize liability towards the operator of the dangerous activity (the operator of the nuclear installation, the owner of the ship, etc.) since in principle he has both knowledge of and control over his installation.

4.2.4.2. Liability for diffuse pollution

Damage is often caused by one or several unidentified persons who are part of a larger group of economic operators whose identity is known. Such is the case, for example, when excessive levels of a dangerous substance are discharged into a river by a number of installations specifically authorized to discharge that substance into that body of water. In a fault-based regime only the firm carrying out unauthorized discharges would be held liable, since the other plants would have been operating within their authorized emission limits. Yet it is not certain that the victim will be able to identify which firm carried out the illegal discharge from among a group of installations situated upstream from his property. The

---

[99] Article 1 of Directive 85/374/EEC concerning liability for defective products traces liability for damage caused by a product back to its producer, as well as its importer and, under certain circumstances, their suppliers.

[100] According to Article II of the 1969 Brussels Convention on Civil Liability for Oil Pollution Damage, the liable party is the owner of the ship. According to Articles 6(1) and 7 of the 1993 Lugano Convention on Civil Liability for Damage Resulting from Activities Dangerous to the Environment (not in force), the liable party is the operator in respect of a dangerous activity. In the area of accidental pollution arising from dangerous installations the OECD designates the operator as the polluter. Under the 2000 Basel Protocol on Liability and Compensation for Damage resulting from Transboundary Movements of Hazardous Wastes and their Disposal (not in force) the person notifying the transfer and the disposer taking possession of the hazardous wastes is liable for damage. The EC White Paper on Environmental Liability proposes the establishment of a civil liability regime that would consist of one tier of liability only (the operator of the hazardous activity). The 1960 Paris Convention on Third Party Liability in the Field of Nuclear Energy and the Brussels Supplementary Convention provide for three tiers of liability: the operator of the nuclear plant tier, the installation state tier, and the international tier.

[101] For Belgium this is the owner of the polluted soil according to the 1995 Flemish Act on soil decontamination and the producer of the toxic waste according to the 1974 law on hazardous wastes. For the Netherlands it can be the person who uses the substance when the damage has occurred (6:175 BW), the landfill operator (6:176 BW), the water drill operator (6:177 BW), or the producer of the dangerous substance (6:185 BW). For Germany it can be the operator of certain classes of industrial plants and agricultural undertakings (*UmweltHG*) or the manufacturer of products manipulated by genetic engineering (*Gen TG*).

classical solution would then be to dismiss the case, sacrificing the interests of the victim on the altar of the principle of causation.

Based on this reasoning, the Paris Court of Appeal judged that when local residents complained about air traffic noise from an airport, they were criticizing isolated acts attributable to different airlines.[102] Since the damage was not indivisible in character, however, the victims were not able to prove which airline had been the cause of any given noise; therefore the companies could not be held liable. Such a solution is not compatible with the polluter-pays principle, in that it transfers negative externalities to the community.

An argument that is more favourable to the interest of the victims and could find support in the polluter-pays principle is set out in several legal systems. Some French courts, for instance, have extended joint and several liability to all potential agents of a hunting accident, to the benefit of the victim, even when the fatal shot has been fired by a single hunter who cannot be identified.[103] If it cannot be established which hunter actually shot a passer-by, all hunters are held liable. In a different case, faced with the impossibility of identifying the agricultural firm that had polluted fish farms through wastewater discharges, the German *Bundesgerichtshof* ruled that the two installations which had discharged a dangerous substance were both liable since no damage would have occurred had they not carried out those discharges.[104] In the latter case, in order for there to be a presumption of causation, the victim merely needs to prove that the substances that provoked the damage were discharged by an installation operated by the defendant; it is no longer necessary to demonstrate that a specific emission was the cause of the damage.

Taking these reflections a step further, the appearance of large-scale damage caused by substances that have been commercialized by several large firms (DES, thalidomide, PCP, asbestos, etc.) raises the question of collective liability of all those who might have been responsible for those damages. In contrast to the preceding examples, we are no longer dealing with a limited group of persons. Moreover, the potentially liable firms produce or place on the market substances that have been the subject of complaints over a period of time. Here as well, the polluter-pays principle could support the concept of collective fault based on the fact that each party produces the same risk. The cases that brought into question the damaging effects on foetuses of the drug DES when taken by pregnant women illustrates this argument. The victims sued a number of pharmaceutical companies in several US states; those firms marketed 90 per cent of all DES at the time of the events in question. Although the causal link between the product and the birth defect had been clearly demonstrated, the victims were nevertheless unable to prove exactly what make of medicine their

---

[102] Paris, 19 March 1979, (1979) DS 429.

[103] H. Aberkane, 'Du dommage causé par une personne indéterminée dans un groupe déterminé de personnes' (1958) RTD Civ 516.

[104] BGH, 22 November 1971, 52 BGHZ 257. On this point, see the commentary by P. Von Wilmowski and G. Roller, *Civil Liability for Waste* (Frankfurt: Peter Lang, 1992) 56.

mothers had taken during pregnancy. They were therefore unable to prove which firm was responsible for their illness, given that each of the defendants had placed the same substance on the market under different names. The plaintiffs were thus unable to establish the requisite causal connection owing to the existence of multiple tortfeasors.[105] The Supreme Court of California accepted in 1980 that each firm was liable for the damages caused to the victims according to its respective market share.[106]

Twelve years later a far more satisfactory solution was provided by the Dutch *Hoge Raad*, which judged that the eleven firms that had commercialized DES in the Netherlands were jointly and severally liable for damages to the victims.[107] Differently put, any one producer can be held liable for the full damage suffered by a large number of victims. As Jan van Dunné has noted, this decision has important implications for cases of diffuse pollution caused by a group of economic agents producing a homogeneous risk.[108] The market-share theory has been rejected by the *Hoge Raad*, which did not consider that the market share of each producer had to be established in the lawsuit. This case-law may be of some assistance to plaintiffs facing the probatory problem of identifying multiple tortfeasors of environmental damage.

According to van Dunné, this case-law has recently been extended to the area of ecological damage through the Dutch *Hoge Raad* transposing this solution to a case of water pollution. It judged that even if 'others than the designated parties had probably contributed to the pollution, it is established that the former are liable for an act which could have produced all the damage suffered by the victim'.[109]

Full internalization of pollution costs would appear to be the determining factor, since: 'the damage should not be borne entirely or partially by the victim, on the grounds that others could have caused part of the damage and that the victim has not been able to prove that all the damage he suffered stems from the act in question'.

This has interesting implications for the use of the polluter-pays principle in the field of civil liability, since the concept of the polluter—previously individual in character—here takes on a collective dimension.

The situation is easier when pollution has been caused by the accumulation of substances discharged by several installations, each of which holds a permit to discharge. In that case it is the accumulation that gives rise to damage rather than the substance *per se*. When the theory of *l'équivalence des conditions* applies, the victim has the right to engage the joint and several liability of each

---

[105] G. Betlem, *Civil Liability for Transfrontier Pollution* (London: Graham and Trotman/Martinus Nijhoff, 1993) 474.

[106] *Sindell v. Abbott Laboratories*, 26 Cal. 3d 588; 607 P.2d 924 (1980).

[107] HR, 9 October 1992; (1993) 1 TMA 15, comment by J. van Dunné.

[108] J. van Dunné, 'Legal Aspects of Non-point Source Pollution' n. 94 above, 46.

[109] HR, 17 January 1997, NJ 1997/230; (1997) 2 TMA 49, J. van Dunné. *Contra* E. Baun, 'Alternative causaliteit en milieuschade: Enkele opmerkingen naar aanleiding van het arrest Moerman-Baak' (1998) 2 TMA 30.

of the discharging installations. However, the operators must have acted unlawfully at the time of the release of the harmful substances without a strict liability regime.[110]

Accordingly, a number of authors have taken to emphasizing the need to elaborate a system of collective liability for such cumulative damages. Under such a system, all hazardous installations operating in the area affected by the pollution in question would be held jointly and severally liable for damages.[111]

4.2.5. Critical assessment

Use of the polluter-pays principle in the field of environmental taxation gives rise to a number of uncertainties and ambiguities. The question of how the principle should be applied becomes even more difficult when we attempt to describe exactly how it will affect civil liability. Will such liability derive from the concept of fault, or of risk? Must the 'polluter' always be a private person, or may it be the State as well? Is ecological damage included among those losses that can be compensated?

Purists will perhaps conclude that these difficulties doom the principle to failure. Yet despite its rather vague outlines and its inability to settle all the questions raised in connection with civil liability, the polluter-pays principle has the merit of clarifying criticisms that have been made of certain controversial doctrinal and legal solutions as well as strengthening arguments relevant for the purpose of environmental protection. We should not reject the polluter-pays principle in its entirety merely because it continues to present difficulties of interpretation and application. Such a general principle cannot, in fact, satisfactorily meet all objections and questions.

Although it is generally presented in the field of environmental protection as a law of 'failure', coming into play when it is too late, civil liability does to some extent contribute to preventing the repetition of injurious behaviour in future. This preventive orientation can only become significant, however, if compensation is set at a level that encourages the liable party to take adequate measures to avoid recurrence of the damage.

This analysis indicates that civil liability cannot on its own assume the compensatory and preventive function of the polluter-pays principle, for the victim always runs the risk that the agent may be unidentifiable or insolvent. Solutions must thus be sought outside of civil liability. Public authorities and hazardous installations have for many years been turning towards alternative mechanisms, such as collective compensation that guarantees automatic reparation.

---

[110] For a widely criticized judgment of the Dutch *Hoge Raad*, where a polluter escaped liability, see HR, 30 September 1994, NJ 1996/197.

[111] G. Teubner, 'The Invisible Cupola: from Causal to Collective Attribution in Ecological Liability', in G. Teubner and Farmer (eds.) *Environmental Law and Ecological Responsibility* (London: Kluwer Law Int'l, 1994) 17; G. Brüggermeier, 'The Control of Corporate Conduct and Reduction of Uncertainty by Tort Law' in R. Baldwin (ed.), *Law and Uncertainty: Risk and Legal Processes* (London: Kluwer Law Int'l, 1997) 71.

The notion of liability is totally absent from such compensation funds, which are based on solidarity rather than liability. These funds also have a subsidiary use in that they come into play when the person at the origin of the damage is unknown or insolvent. By assigning a charge to an industrial risk that has caused environmental damage, funds respond, at first glance, to the logic of the polluter-pays principle. On the other hand, by banalizing risks such compensation mechanisms are likely to distort preventive measures. Both negligence aspects and the objectionable nature of environmental damage, as well as respect for the standard of *bonus paterfamilias*, may be weakened by the interposition of funds that provide immediate indemnization. A charge paid into a fund does not produce a strong impression and thus has little effect in encouraging potential polluters to exercise care, as shown in the 1999 Erika oil-spill case. The semi-automatic payment of a fee takes the place of the right to pollute. According to Boyle, the limit of liability regimes in spreading the burden of serious accidents indicates how far removed from the polluter-pays principle the schemes found in conventions concerning civil liability for oil pollution and nuclear installations remain.[112] Thus it can be said that by putting a ceiling on the damages recoverable, none of these civil liability conventions fully implements this environmental principle.[113]

Funds also present other disadvantages. They are generally limited in the extent to which they cover third parties, thus preventing integral reparation of ecological damages. In addition, it weakens the polluter-pays principle when the parties asked to participate in a fund are those that present the greatest certainty of solvency rather than those really responsible for pollution.

5. Concluding observations

Given a name that is almost a slogan and the seeming clarity of its underlying logic, the polluter-pays principle easily wins approval. It has an important role to play in furthering environment law at the international, EC, and national levels. The principle answers to an economic logic, and its success in the field of environmental taxation is thus assured.

Nonetheless, a basic ambiguity remains inherent in the polluter-pays principle. On one hand, it appears essential for the implementation of a preventive environmental protection policy, by making it possible to obtain the funds needed to carry out that policy and, where necessary, modifying the behaviour of those being administered. It can even require polluters to compensate public authorities fully for damage they may have caused. On the other hand, the principle

---

[112] A. Boyle, 'Making the Polluter Pay? Alternatives to State Responsibility in the Allocation of Transboundary Environmental Cost' in Fr. Franzioni and T. Scovazzi (eds.), *International Responsibility for Environmental Harm* (London: Graham and Trotman/Martinus Nijhoff, 1991) 363; P. Birnie and A. Boyle, *International Law and the Environment* (2nd edn., Oxford University Press, 2002) 93.
[113] Ibid., 376.

contains neo-liberal overtones that appear to countenance the idea that the right to pollute can be purchased for the monetary equivalent of the environmental cost sustained.

In addition, the principle's outlines remain singularly difficult to trace at the legal level, despite the simplicity of its message. The more one attempts to refine its definition, the more elusive the principle becomes. The polluter cannot be pinpointed, because any act of pollution is the result of the act of production—the creator of added value—as well as of final consumption. The principle slips yet further from our grasp as pollution becomes increasingly diffuse and historic in nature, rather than clearly identifiable and contemporaneous with the damage produced.

Nevertheless, the principle's vagueness, which is considerable in relation to environmental taxation and even more so in relation to civil liability, should not lead us to condemn it. Rather, it is up to legal doctrine progressively to add the finishing touches that will clarify the definition and scope of the principle, as well as to re-evaluate traditional positive solutions in its light.

2

The Principle of Prevention

1. INTRODUCTORY REMARKS

The curative approach has been deeply engrained in environment law since its beginnings. The subsequent appearance of the principle of prevention modified the field radically, signalling a fundamental change of approach. Curative measures may remediate environmental damage, but they come too late to avert it. Preventive measures, on the other hand, do not depend on the appearance of ecological problems; they anticipate damage or, where it has already occurred, try to ensure it does not spread. In any case, common sense dictates timely prevention of environmental damage to the greatest extent possible, particularly when it is likely to be irreversible or too insidious or diffuse to be effectively dealt with through civil liability or when reparation would be extremely expensive. By requiring the adoption of measures intended to prevent such damage from arising, prevention forms a prudent complement to the polluter-pays principle, which does not necessarily compel polluters to reduce their pollution by requiring them to internalize their costs.

The outlines of the preventive principle are difficult to discern; it gives rise to so many questions that any attempt at interpretation calls for constant clarification. We may, for example, ask whether a preventive measure presupposes complete knowledge of the risk to be reduced, if all forms of injury must be foreseen, if intervention should take place at the level of the sources of damage or of their effects, and whether it is preferable to monitor the progress of damage or to prohibit damage the moment it becomes evident.

The following sections briefly review the evolution of the principle of prevention in international law, EC law, and several national legal systems (Section 2). We go on to consider the various aspects of the principle in some depth (Section 3). Finally, we examine the sometimes ambivalent nature of the instruments typical of the preventive principle, using three case studies (Section 4).

2. Origin of the principle

2.1. International law

2.1.1. The interaction between the preventive principle and the responsibility not to cause damage to the environment of other States or to areas beyond national jurisdiction

Several authors consider the *Trail Smelter* arbitration as the first manifestation of the principle of prevention.[1] In that case, the Dominion of Canada was judged liable for damage caused by pollutants discharged into the atmosphere by a foundry, on the ground that the Government should have ensured that the installation was being operated in conformity with the obligations incumbent upon all States under international law—that is, the duty at all times to protect other States against injurious acts caused by individuals from within its jurisdiction: 'Under the principle of international law [. . .] no state has the right to use or permit the use of territory in such a manner as to cause injury by fumes in or to the territory of another of the properties or persons therein, when the case is of serious consequence and the injury is established by clear and convincing evidence'.[2]

The arbitration ruling thereby recognized the existence of a rule of basic international law which obliges States to anticipate transboundary pollution. The principle of 'no appreciable harm' was reproduced *mutatis mutandis* in Principle 21 of the 1972 Stockholm Declaration on the Human Environment, a principle that most legal analysis considers a rule of customary international law:

States have, in accordance with the Charter of the United Nations and the principles of international law, the sovereign right to exploit their own resources pursuant to their own environmental policies, and the responsibility to ensure that activities within their jurisdiction or control do not cause damage to the environment of other States or of areas beyond the limits of national jurisdictions.[3]

While retaining the idea of prevention, the 1992 Rio Declaration on Environment and Development set the terms of this obligation in a more restrictive mould, in the form of Principle 2. According to this Principle, States henceforth have: 'the responsibility to ensure that activities within their jurisdiction or control do not cause damage to the environment of other States or of areas beyond the limits of national jurisdiction'.

---

[1] G. Handl, 'Environmental Security and Global Change: The Challenge to International Law' (1990) 1 YbIEL 1; J.G. Lammers, 'International and European Community Law: Aspects of Pollution of International Watercourses' in W. Lang, H. Neuhold, and K. Zemanek (eds.), *Environmental Protection and International Law* (London: Graham and Trotman/Martinus Nijhoff, 1991) 117; Ph. Sands, *Principles of International Environmental Law* (Manchester: Manchester UP, 1995) I 195.

[2] RIAA, vol. III 1907, at 1965.

[3] A. Kiss and D. Shelton, *International Environmental Law* (London: Graham & Trotman, 1991) 130; P. Taylor, *An Ecological Approach to International Law* (London: Routledge, 1998) 88.

Principle 21 of the 1972 Stockholm Declaration is fully incorporated into the 1979 LRATP Convention, the 1985 Vienna Convention for the Protection of the Ozone Layer, and the 1992 CBD—Article 3 lays down the text of the principle, unaltered—and 1992 Rio's Principle 2 is incorporated into the Preambles of the UNFCCC.[4]

Obligated by Stockholm's Principle 21 and Rio's Principle 2 'to ensure that activities within their jurisdiction or control do not cause damage to the environment of other States or of areas beyond the limits of national jurisdictions', States find themselves bound by a due diligence requirement to prevent transboundary pollution.[5] In other words, the State must have failed to show due diligence if it is to be held liable.[6] However, customary law does not specify what diligent conduct entails or what concrete measures States are required to take in order to fulfil their duties under Stockholm's Principle 21 and Rio's Principle 2.[7] The obligation to prevent transboundary harm is subject to a variety of interpretations as to what preventive actions may be required of a State, as well as what amount of damage is to be prevented.[8] We may thus legitimately ask: how specific is the obligation that States prevent pollution which would cause transboundary harm? Such specificity is essential if the principle of no appreciable harm is to fulfil a preventive function.

Clearly, not all instances of transboundary damage resulting from activities within a State's jurisdiction are unlawful. States are not required to guarantee that appreciable harm is prevented: they must merely exert due care or due diligence to prevent such harm.[9] Simply causing damage is thus not sufficient to render a State liable for damage caused by a source within its territory.

Most international treaties require States to comply with some sort of due diligence requirement (EIA, consultation, monitoring sources of potential

---

[4] Ph. Sands, 'International Law in the Field of Sustainable Development: Emerging Legal Principles' in W. Lang (ed.) *Sustainable Development in International Law* (London: Graham & Trotman, 1995) 63; J. Vessey, 'The Principle of Prevention in International Law' (1998) 3 ARIEL 181–207.

[5] The support given by States over the last 20 years to Principle 21 of the 1972 Stockholm Declaration on Human Environment and Principle 2 of the 1992 Rio Declaration on Environment and Development establishes a compelling basis for the view that it now reflects a general rule of customary international law. Eg K. Zemanek, 'State Responsibility and Liability' in *Environmental Protection and International Law*, n. 1 above, 192; Ph. Sands, 'International Law in the Field of Sustainable Development: Emerging Legal Principles' in W. Lang (ed.), *Sustainable Development in International Law* (London: Graham & Trotman, 1995) 62; D. Freestone, 'International Fisheries since Rio: The Continued Rise of the Precautionary Principle' in A. Boyle and D. Freestone (eds.), *International Law and Sustainable Development* (Oxford: OUP, 1999) 139.

[6] G. Handl, 'State Liability for Accidental Transnational Environmental Damage by Private Persons' (1980) AJIL 540.

[7] P. Birnie and A. Boyle, *International Law and the Environment*, (2nd edn., Oxford University Press, 2002) 113.

[8] A. Nollkaemper, *The Legal Regime of Transboundary Water Pollution: Between Discretion and Constraint* (London: Martinus Nijhoff/Graham & Trotman, 1993) 31.

[9] P.-M. Dupuy, 'Due Diligence in the International Law of Liability' in *Legal Aspects of Transfrontier Pollution* (OECD, Paris, 1977) 370; J.G. Lammers, *Pollution of International Watercourses* (The Hague: Martinus Nijhof, 1984) 348; A. Boyle, 'State Responsibility and International Liability for Injurious Consequences of Acts not Prohibited by International Law: A Necessary Distinction?' (1990) ICLQ 15.

transboundary harm, etc.). A State which complies with all such requirements may not be held liable, 'however devastating [the] harm may be'.[10]

However, Principles 21 and 2 differ from the principle of prevention in two ways. First, they are both grounded in respect for the principle of sovereignty, whereas the preventive principle seeks to minimize environmental damage as an objective in and of itself.[11] Secondly, the primary aim of Principles 21 and 2 is to prevent the abuse of rights over natural resource management. The preventive principle, in contrast, appears much wider in scope, in that pollution or environmental degradation must be anticipated, while States may not abuse their right of sovereignty.

As a result, the preventive principle is in fact an external element of the general obligation to 'due diligence' or 'due care' with respect to the environment and natural wealth and resources. Nonetheless, it is not without certain consequences for liability. By introducing an element of consistency for the general obligation of due diligence, the preventive principle should serve to strengthen the core of that obligation. Increased obligations of a preventive nature should in turn make it easier to engage State liability for unlawful acts. For instance, environmental impact assessment procedures may serve as a secondary standard for determining whether or not a State has complied with the due diligence requirement to prevent transboundary harm. A State that has failed to assess the impacts of its harmful activities on the territories of other States will find it difficult to argue that it has taken all possible measures to prevent damage.[12]

2.1.2. *The preventive principle in international treaties*

Prevention cannot be ensured merely by setting general rules whose credibility depends on the effective implementation of State liability. The basis for the preventive principle in international law must be sought in multilateral and bilateral conventions intended to ensure environmental protection rather than in international State liability. The proliferation of preventive mechanisms found in such conventions (environmental impact assessments, notification procedures, exchange of information on the impact of harmful activities, etc.) plays a crucial role in the implementation of the duty of diligence to prevent transboundary harm and therefore gives substance to the principle of prevention.

In addition, the preventive principle is implicitly or explicitly endorsed by an extensive body of international treaties and related instruments,[13] the subjects of which include:

---

[10] A. Boyle, 'Codification of International Environmental Law and the International Law Commission: Injurious Consequences Revisited' in A. Boyle and D. Freestone (eds.), *International Law and Sustainable Development*, n. 5 above, 76.

[11] Ph. Sands, *Principles of International Environmental Law*, n. 1 above, 194.

[12] P. Okowa, 'Procedural Obligations in International Environmental Agreements' (1996) LXVII BYbIL 275–336.

[13] Ph. Sands, n. 1 above, 195; M. Sunkin, D. Ong, and R. Wight, *Sourcebook on Environmental Law* (London, Sydney: Cavendish, 1998) 30.

- the marine environment[14]
- the management of high seas fisheries[15]
- the protection of rivers[16]
- atmospheric pollution[17]
- climate[18]
- the ozone layer[19]
- waste management[20]
- toxic substances[21]
- biodiversity[22]
- the Alps[23]

[14] The principle is reflected in the following provisions: Article 1 of the 1972 London Convention on the Prevention of Marine Pollution by Dumping of Wastes and Other Matter; Article 1 of the 1973 London International Convention for the Prevention of Pollution from Ships (not in force); Article 1 of the 1974 Paris Convention for the Prevention of Marine Pollution from Land-Based Sources (replaced by the 1992 OSPAR Convention); Articles 4 to 8 of the 1976 Barcelona Convention for the Protection of the Mediterranean Sea Against Pollution; Article 5(5) of the 1980 Athens Protocol for the Protection of the Mediterranean Sea against Pollution from Land-Based Sources and Activities (as amended in Syracuse on 7 March 1996, not yet in force); 1982 UNCLOS, Articles 192, 194(1)-(2), 195, 196, 204, 207, 208, 209, 210, 211, 212; Article 2 of the 1985 Montreal Guidelines on the Protection of the Environment Against Pollution from Land-based Sources; the Preamble to the 1990 OPRC Convention; Article 2(1)(a) of the 1992 OSPAR Convention; Article 3(1) of the 1992 Helsinki Convention on the Protection of the Marine Environment of the Baltic Sea Area; Articles 5(2)-10 of the 1992 Convention on the Protection of the Black Sea Against Pollution. See also Principle 7 of the 1972 Stockholm Declaration on the Human Environment.

[15] See Article 5 of the 1995 UN Agreement Governing the Application of the Articles of the United Nations Convention on the Law of the Sea of 10 December 1982 Concerning the Conservation and Management of Straddling Fish Stocks and Highly Migratory Stocks (hereinafter 1995 UN Fish Stocks Agreement). Eg F. Orrego Vicuna, *The Changing International Law of High Seas Fisheries* (Cambridge: CUP, 1999) 153–5.

[16] See, for example, Articles 2(1), 2(2), and 3 of the 1992 Helsinki Convention on the Protection and Use of Transboundary Watercourses and International Lakes; Article 3(2)(b) of the 1994 Scheldt-Meuse Agreements; Articles 2(2) and 5 of the 1994 Sofia Convention on Co-operation for the Protection and Sustainable Use of the Danube; Article 21 of the 1997 New York Convention on the Law Relating to the Uses of International Watercourses for Purposes other than Navigation (not in force); and Article 4 of the 1999 Bern Convention on the Protection of the Rhine.

[17] Article 2, 1979 LRATP Convention.

[18] See, for example, Article 3(3), 1992 UNFCCC.

[19] See Article 2 (2)(b) of the 1985 Vienna Convention for the Protection of the Ozone, as well as the 1987 Montreal Protocol on Substances that Deplete the Ozone Layer.

[20] See, among others, Article 4(2)(c) of the 1989 Basel Convention on the Control of Transboundary Movements of Hazardous Wastes and their Disposal; Article 6 of the 2000 Basel Protocol on Liability and Compensation for Damage Resulting from Transboundary Movements of Hazardous Wastes and their Disposal (not yet in force); Article 4(3)(e) of the 1991 Bamako Convention on the Ban of Import into Africa and the Control of Transboundary Movement and Management of Hazardous Wastes within Africa (not yet in force); Article 14 of the 1992 Rio Declaration on Environment and Development (prevention of relocation or transfer of harmful activities to other States).

[21] See, among others, Article 6 of the 1972 Stockholm Declaration on the Human Environment that set out the principle in sweeping terms: 'The discharge of toxic substances or of other substances and the release of heat, in such quantities or concentrations as to exceed the capacity of the environment to render them harmless, must be halted in order to ensure that serious or irreversible damage is not inflicted upon ecosystems'.

[22] See among others, Article 4 of the 1985 ASEAN Agreement on the Conservation for Nature and Natural Resources; the eighth recital of the Preamble and Article 14 of the 1992 CBD.

[23] Cf. Article 2 of the 1995 Salzburg Convention on the Protection of the Alps.

- the Antarctic[24]
- transboundary environmental risk assessment[25]
- notification and consultation.[26]

The stringency of preventive obligations will depend largely on the nature of the instrument (soft law or hard law) and the relevent provision (eg reference to the preventive principle in a preamble fulfils an interpretative function, while its enunciation in an operative provision is binding).[27] Nevertheless, the fact that general obligations of prevention are set out in so many conventions makes it possible to deduce a principle of customary international law. Indeed, the International Court of Justice (ICJ) has on several occasions in recent years recalled the obligation to respect and protect the natural environment:

The Court also recognizes that the environment is not an abstraction but represents a living space, the quality of life and the very health of human beings, including generations unborn. The existence of the general obligation of States to ensure that activities within their jurisdiction and control respect the environment of other States and areas beyond national control is now part of the corpus of international law relating to the environment.[28]

In the *Mox* case, ITLOS considered that the duty to co-operate in exchanging information concerning environmental risks is a 'fundamental principle in the prevention of pollution of the marine environment' under UNCLOS, Part XII and general international law.[29]

Sustainable development can draw support from a range of principles, among them the preventive principle.[30] The clearest recognition of the relationship between the preventive principle and the concept of sustainable development is found in the ICJ's ruling in the *Gabcíkovo-Nagymaros* case, relating to a project for a dam on the Danube:

---

[24] See, for example, Article 3(2) of the 1991 Madrid Protocol on Environmental Protection to the Antarctic Treaty.

[25] See Article 2(1) of the 1991 Espoo Convention on Environmental Impact Assessment in a Transboundary Context; Article 3(1) of the 1992 Helsinki Convention on the Transboundary Effects of Industrial Accidents.

[26] Those obligations are reflected in the following conventions: the 1974 Nordic Convention on the Protection of the Environment; Article 198 of the 1982 UNCLOS; 1986 IAEA Vienna Convention on Early Notification of a Nuclear Accident; 1986 Vienna Convention on Assistance in the Case of a Nuclear Accident or Radiological Emergency; the 1991 Espoo Convention on Environmental Impact Assessment in a Transboundary Context; Article 14(1)(d) of the 1992 CBD. See also Principle 19 of the 1992 Rio Declaration on Environment and Development.

[27] See the discussion in Chapter 3, Section 2 below.

[28] *Legality of the Threat or Use of Nuclear Weapons*, Advisory Opinion, ICJ Rep [1996] para. 29; Order of 22 September 1995, *New-Zealand v. France*, para. 64; *Gabcikovo-Nagymaros* (*Hungary v. Slovakia*), Judgment ICJ Rep [1997], para. 53.

[29] *The Mox Plant* case (*Ireland v. United Kingdom*) Order of 3 December 2001 on Provisional Measures (ITLOS, case no. 10), paras. 82–4 (hereinafter, Order no. 10).

[30] Ph. Sands, 'International law in the Field of Sustainable Development: Emerging Legal Principles' in P. Lang (ed.), *Sustainable Development and International Law* (London: Kluwer Law Int'l, 1995) 12.

The Court is mindful that, in the field of environmental protection, vigilance and prevention are required on account of the often irreversible character of damage to the environment and of the limitations inherent in the very mechanism of reparation of this kind of damage. [. . .] Owing to new scientific insights and to a growing awareness of the risks for mankind—for present and future generations—of pursuit of such interventions at an unconsidered and unabated pace, new norms and standards have been developed, set forth in a great number of instruments during the last two decades. Such norms have to be taken into consideration, and such new standards given proper weight, not only when States contemplate new activities but also when continuing with activities begun in the past. This need to reconcile economic development with protection of the environment is aptly expressed in the concept of sustainable development.[31]

The emphasis placed by this judgment on the prevention of environmental harm clearly indicates general acceptance of a principle of customary law. However, in referring to sustainable development as a concept, the Court left unanswered the question whether this was an embryonic principle or at best a political objective.[32] Although Judge Weeramantry in his separate opinion to this judgment argued that the principle of sustainable development has become part of modern international law and practice, the Court characterized the 'concept of sustainable development' as expressing the need to reconcile economic development with the protection of the environment.[33]

The practice of including general obligations of prevention in international treaties has profound implications for States; it suggests that the lawfulness of transboundary pollution is determined by treaty obligations rather than by any obligations under general international law.[34] However, as is the case under the rules of liability for transboundary pollution, prevention of all transboundary pollution is not absolute in international treaty law. Harm is an inherent aspect of interaction among States. Therefore, a number of international instruments specify that their provisions apply only when harm is 'significant', 'substantial', or 'appreciable'.[35] Nevertheless, the 'significant' threshold—which is less stringent than the 'serious' threshold established by the *Trail Smelter* case but

---

[31] *Gabcíkovo-Nagymaros*, para. 140.

[32] A. Khavari and D. Rothwell, 'The ICJ and the Danube Dam Case: A Missed Opportunity for International Environmental Law?' (1999) 507 MULR 15.

[33] Judge Weeramantry considered in his dissenting opinion that sustainable development was 'more than a mere concept; [it is]...a principle with normative value'. However, according to V. Lowe, sustainable development is 'a meta-principle, acting upon other legal rules and principles—a legal concept exercising a kind of interstitial normativity, pushing and pulling the boundaries of true primary norms when they threaten to overlap or conflict with each other'. Eg 'Sustainable Development and Unsustainable Development' in A. Boyle and D. Freestone (eds.), *International Law and Sustainable Development*, no. 5 above, 19–37. See also Fr. Maes, 'Environmental Law Principles' in M. Sheridan and L. Lavrysen (eds.), *Environmental Law Principles in Practice* (Brussels: Bruylant, 2002) 72–3.

[34] A. Nollkaemper, *The Legal Regime of Transboundary Water Pollution*, n. 8 above, 32.

[35] See, for instance, Article 1(2) of the 1985 Vienna Convention for the Protection of the Ozone Layer; Article 1(2) of the 1992 Helsinki Convention on the Protection and Use of Transboundary Watercourses and International Lakes. According to the EC White Paper on Environmental Liability, the proposed liability regime should apply only to significant damage to biodiversity.

nonetheless more than 'minor'—has become the central qualification for transboundary environmental harm. The 1991 Espoo Convention, for instance,
obliges States to prevent 'significant transboundary environmental effects',[36]
and the 1992 Helsinki Convention on the Protection of Transboundary Watercourses obliges States to prevent 'significant adverse effects on the environment
within the jurisdiction of another party'.[37] This approach is also followed in
EC law by the Directive 96/61/EC concerning integrated pollution prevention
and control.[38] Other international instruments, such as the 1992 OSPAR
Convention, simply oblige States to prevent pollution.

The main function of such a threshold is that of limiting the scope of general
rules on prevention to 'significant' harm, thereby avoiding a total ban on
activities that cause only minor interferences.[39] Therefore, the use of such
language in a number of international instruments indicates acceptance of a
certain level of environmental harm (threshold of tolerance). That threshold
may at first glance appear vague and subjective, but it could easily be established
in a more objective fashion, thus limiting the discretion of States.[40]

2.2. European Community law

Originally oriented primarily towards industrial pollution, Community environmental policy has progressively evolved towards a global and preventive
approach. Even before being formally integrated into the EC Treaty, the preventive principle played a key role in determining Community environment policy.
The EC's first Action Programme laid down the basis for what has become the
prevention principle, stating that 'the best environmental policy consists in
preventing the creation of pollution and nuisances at source, rather than subsequently trying to counteract their effects'. The Second and Third Environmental
Action Programmes, which exerted an important influence on a significant
proportion of Community legislation in the 1980s, strongly focused on the
prevention principle.

Since the amendment of the Treaty of Rome by the Single European Act, the
preventive principle has been recognized by Article 174(2), together with
the principle that environmental damage should as a priority be rectified at
source and the polluter-pays principle. It also strengthens one of the objectives
assigned to Community environment policy by Article 174(1): namely, 'to ensure
a prudent and rational utilisation of natural resources'.

In addition, as will be seen subsequently, secondary Community legislation
has contributed substantially to the development of legal instruments of a

---

[36] Article 2(1).   [37] Article 2(1).

[38] According to Article 3(h) of the IPPC Directive, installations have to be operated in such a way
that 'no significant pollution is caused'.

[39] K. Sacharien, 'The Definition of Thresholds of Tolerance for Transboundary Environmental
Injury under International Law: Development and Present Status' (1990) XXXVII NILR 193.

[40] A. Nollkaemper, *The Legal Regime of Transboundary Water Pollution*, n. 8 above, 37.

preventive nature, notably procedures for authorizing and evaluating effects, setting thresholds for harmful effects, and recourse to best available technology.

In the context of EC waste policy, prevention has been transformed into a serious policy objective. Since wastes pose a threat to human health and the environment, their production and harmfulness should be avoided, or at least reduced. According to Directive 75/442/EEC on waste, 'Member States shall take appropriate measures to encourage firstly the prevention or reduction of waste production and its harmfulness...' and secondly 'the recovery... or the use of waste as a source of energy'.[41] Directive 94/62/EEC on packaging and packaging waste makes it quite clear that the best means of preventing the creation of packaging waste is to reduce the overall volume of packaging.

The presence of the preventive principle in the EC Treaty allows Community courts to interpret the provisions of the Waste Framework Directive to favour protection of the environment. Thus, the Court of Justice has ruled that:

Article 4 of Directive 75/442, adopted on the basis of Article 130S of the EC Treaty (now Article 175), aims to put into practice the principles of precaution and preventive action found in Article 130R, paragraph 2, second sentence, of the Treaty. These principles oblige the Community and the Member States to anticipate, reduce and, as far as possible, to cut off at their origin sources of pollution or nuisances through the adoption of measures intended to eliminate known risks... To the extent that wastes, even those in temporary storage, may give rise to serious damage to the environment, there is reason to consider that the provisions of Article 4 of Directive 75/442, which aims to implement the precautionary principle, are equally applicable to operations involving temporary storage.[42]

Closely related to the preventive principle, the principle of rectification of environmental damage at source as a priority plays an important role in the control of transboundary movements of wastes intended for disposal, according to the case-law of the European Court of Justice. The Court held that the principle means that any region, municipality, or other local authority is entitled to adopt measures to limit the transport of wastes and to ensure that their disposal takes place as close as possible to their place of production.[43]

In the field of permits, the IPPC Directive serves as an important instrument for implementing the principle. Article 1 of the Directive lays down the measures designed to prevent or, where that is not practicable, to reduce emissions to air,

---

[41] Article 3(1) of Directive 75/442/CEE on waste, as amended by Directive 91/156/CE.

[42] Cases C-175/98 and C-177/98, *Francesca Bizzaro et Paolo Lirussi* [1999] ECR I-6881, paras. 51–3. The English version of this judgment is not yet available. The original reads: '*L'article 4 de la directive 75/442, adoptée sur le fondement de l'article 130 S du traité CE (devenu, après modification, article 175 CE), vise à mettre en oeuvre les principes de précaution et d'action préventive qui figurent à l'article 130 R, paragraphe 2, deuxième phrase, du traité. En vertu de ces principes, il incombe à la Communauté et aux États membres de prévenir, de réduire et, dans la mesure du possible, de supprimer, dès l'origine, les sources de pollutions ou de nuisances par l'adoption de mesures de nature à éradiquer les risques connus. [ ]Dans la mesure où les déchets, même stockés temporairement, peuvent causer des dommages importants à l'environnement, il y a lieu de considérer que les dispositions de l'article 4 de la directive 75/442, qui visent à mettre en oeuvre le principe de précaution, sont également applicables à l'opération de stockage temporaire.*'

[43] Case C-2/90, *Commission v. Belgium* [1992] ECR I-1, para. 34.

water, and land from installations. As regards prevention, Article 3 stipulates that the operator of an installation is to take all appropriate preventive measures against pollution and 'the necessary measures to prevent accidents'. However, there is no general requirement that the operator prevent pollution; rather, his obligations are determined by permit conditions.[44] Another good example of the implementation of the principle of prevention in EC secondary legislation is found in Directive 96/82/EC on the control of major accident hazards involving dangerous substances, which aims to prevent such accidents. Article 5(1) of the Directive requires that 'Member States shall ensure that the operator is obliged to take all measures necessary to prevent major accidents and to limit their consequences for man and the environment'.

If national policies do not observe the preventive principle, this makes it more difficult for the Community to achieve its environmental policy in accordance with Articles 10 and 174(2) of the Treaty. In order to respect those two Treaty provisions, national authorities must take account of the principle of prevention in the administration of any licensing regime emanating from EC legislation. If it could be shown that a national authority had not applied the principle at all, had applied it improperly, or had failed to consider relevant evidence, the national permit would be in breach of EC law and would therefore be defective. According to some authors, individuals may rely on such a Community obligation to review administrative decisions.[45]

2.3. National laws

Recognized in the field of international law, the principle of prevention has exercised a decisive influence on the evolution of national environment legislation in Europe and in the USA. National regimes are fundamentally preventive in nature, since they prompt the public authorities to take measures to protect the environment even when environmental damage has not yet occurred.[46] The preventive principle may be recognized in either of two ways: first, it may be drawn from a number of important preambular provisions of sectoral laws governing air, water, soil, nature, wastes, and dangerous substances. Secondly, as will be seen from the following examples, it is expressly set forth in various framework laws on environmental protection.

In Swiss legislation, the Federal Act of 7 October 1983 on the protection of the environment requires that 'infringements that could give rise to harm shall be reduced as early as possible as a preventive measure', and that 'atmospheric pollution, noise, vibrations and rays be limited by measures taken at source'. It states that: 'Independently of existing nuisances, prevention makes it important

---

[44] L. Krämer, *Focus on European Environmental Law* (2nd edn., London: Sweet & Maxwell, 1997) 231.

[45] A. Doyle and T. Carney, 'Precaution and Prevention: Giving Effect to Article 130r Without Direct Effect' (1999) EELR 47.

[46] L. Krämer, *EEC Treaty and Environmental Protection* (London: Graham & Trotman, 1990) 61.

to limit emissions to the extent that is technically and operationally possible and economically acceptable'.[47]

In Danish law, the Environmental Protection Act No. 358 of 6 June 1991 sets out, on one hand, that: 'In the administration of this Act weight shall be given to the results achievable by using the least polluting technology, including least polluting raw materials, processes and plants and the best practicable pollution control measures. In this evaluation special consideration shall be given to preventive measures in the form of cleaner technology'[48] and, on the other hand, that: 'Any party proposing to commence activities likely to cause pollution shall choose such a site for the activities that the risk of pollution is minimised [and] shall take measures to prevent and combat pollution'.

Article 1(1)(a) of the Dutch Environmental Management Act of 1 March 1993 (*Wet milieubeheer*) requires that:

All persons give sufficient consideration to the environment;
The consideration set out in paragraph 1 presumes in all cases that any person who knows or has reason to assume that damage to the environment may be caused by his activities or his omissions is required to abandon those activities, to the extent that this may reasonably be expected of him, and must take all measures that may reasonably be required of him in order to prevent such harmful consequences and, if this proves not to be possible, to limit or attenuate them.

Section 9(1) of the chapter concerning the objectives of the 1998 Swedish Environmental Code (*Miljöbalk*) stipulates that: 'If an activity or measure is likely to cause significant damage or detriment to human health or the environment, even where protective measures and other precautions are taken as required by this Code, the activity or the measure may only be undertaken in special circumstances.'

In Belgian legislation, the Federal Act of 20 February 1999 requires that when carrying out activities in marine areas, users of those areas as well as the public authorities must take into consideration the preventive principle, which implies that 'it is necessary to act in such a way as to prevent damage rather than to have to repair such damage after the fact'. This principle also guides regional policies; it is set out in the Flemish Region's Decree on Environmental Policy of 5 April 1995 and appears among the objectives of several sectoral laws.[49]

In French law, the principle of preventive action is proclaimed in the Environmental Code, although it is not defined. It is accompanied by the principle of rectification at source of environmental effects, as a priority.[50]

It also seems that the use of the preventive principle may be deduced from constitutional law relating to environmental protection. In several decisions, the Greek High Administrative Court has ruled that Article 24 of the Constitution

---

[47] Article 11, first and second indents of the Federal Act of 7 October 1983 on protection of the environment.
[48] Article 3(1) of Environmental Protection Act No. 358 of 6 June 1991.
[49] Article 1.2.1, §2, 1995 Act of the Flemish Region on Environmental Policy.
[50] Article L 100–1, Environmental Code.

contains a basic principle of preventing damage to the natural environment; the consequent limitations require public authorities to carry out a policy of sustainable development.[51]

Finally, in US law, the 1990 Pollution Prevention Act (PPA) declares: 'It is the policy of the United States that pollution should be prevented at source.'[52] The PPA requires EPA to consider source reduction in all of its decision-making processes and to co-ordinate source reduction activities throughout the federal government. Nevertheless, the Act focuses on voluntary (voluntary pollution prevention activities by industry) rather than mandatory compliance.

3. Systematic analysis

Given the abundance of essentially preventive norms (Subsection 3.1. below) it is possible to describe the outlines of the principle of prevention and to specify its contents. Having determined the scope of the preventive principle in relation to other principles of environmental law (Subsection 3.2.) and systematized its various aspects (Subsection 3.3.) we go on to consider the role of proportionality in determining the degree of prevention sought (Subsection 3.4.).

3.1. The multiple aspects of the principle

Preventive measures aim to avoid environmental harm and reduce or eliminate the risk of harm.[53] Yet despite that clear objective, the principle of prevention is quite complex, owing to the number and diversity of the legal instruments in which it occurs. It may be expressly recognized in framework laws or deduced from normative texts of both constitutional and legislative origin.

In practice, the main use of the principle is in issuing authorizations that set out the conditions for administrative controls, and in some cases criminal penalties. These authorizations use technical specifications to determine means of operation, quantities and concentrations of pollutants that may be discharged, and what type of security measures must be put in place by the permit holder during the duration of the permit. Increasingly, permits are based on concepts such as 'best available techniques', 'best environmental practice', 'clean production methods', or 'best available technology not entailing excessive cost'.

Prevention may be linked to both pollution sources and points of impact. As regards sources, public authorities may adopt product norms, regulate manufacturing processes in order to make them less damaging, or assess the

---

[51] G. Sioutis, 'La notion de développement durable dans la jurisprudence du Conseil d'Etat hellénique', (1998) 1 REDE 56.

[52] 42 USC paras. 13102 (1999). See J.S. Applegate, J. Laitos, and C. Campbell, *The Regulation of Toxic Substances and Hazardous Wastes* (New York: Foundation Press, 2000) 1165–76.

[53] For examples of preventive measures, see D. Shelton and C. Kiss, *Manual of European Environmental Law* (2nd. edn., Cambridge: CUP, 1997) 114.

environmental impacts of projects before authorizing them. As regards impacts, they may establish quality standards for receiving environments; these fix maximum amounts of polluting substances for the environment that is to be protected or, in some cases, extend special protection status to threatened areas. The creation of special areas allows environmental aggression to be controlled according to the sensitivity of receiving environments.

Action programmes seem to be a response to efforts to carry out comprehensive and anticipatory planning and play an important role in organizing the progressive achievement of protective objectives.

Finally, we should note that prevention is extending its reign to instruments which *a priori* have no direct relation to environmental protection. This is particularly the case as regards civil liability, environmental taxation, and criminal law; under the influence of the preventive principle, provisions are increasingly being formulated in all these areas in a manner that accentuates their preventive effect.

Despite its essentially curative function, civil liability also includes a preventive function, since it always involves loss or impoverishment for the party found to be liable. The extent of the reparation required thus serves the purpose of prevention to the extent that potentially liable parties will adapt their behaviour with a view to the likelihood of liability. The elimination of fault in determining responsibility for damage which is inherent in strict liability regimes has also helped to reinforce the preventive dimension of civil liability. In such regimes the preventive function has overtaken the curative function that civil liability is intended to fulfil. The party responsible for environmental damage, no longer able to plead the absence of fault, henceforth has an interest in exercising extreme care. It will verify the qualifications of the operators with whom it deals, carry out audits of the lands it buys, and equip its installations with the best available technologies.

Prevention may also be carried out via a fiscal approach through the use of 'economic instruments', which are being held up as alternatives to binding administrative measures: in other words, 'command and control' instruments. If the object of taxes on nuisances is to provide the public authorities with sufficient financial means to repair the damage caused by authorized pollution, a sizeable increase in levels of taxation should encourage polluters to curb their releases. Eco-taxes symbolize this shift from redistributive taxation to a strongly dissuasive approach.

In the area of criminal law, we must recognize that dissuasive sanctions and penalties specifically adapted to environmental delinquency help prevent environmental violations from being committed. Reparatory sanctions occupy a central position in penal policy concerning the environment, for they form the junction between a retributional concept of punishment largely oriented towards the past and a more future-oriented preventive approach. In addition, the right of a court to order that polluted areas be returned to good condition not only prevents perpetuation of a violation but also serves to dissuade behaviour that seeks to continue and profit from unlawful activities. But attempts to reinforce the dissuasive effect of sanctions will primarily result in a widening of the range of sanctions, since an overly narrow definition of these—as a function of the seriousness of the violation—could compromise the effectiveness of dissuasion.

3.2. Interactions between the preventive principle and other principles of environmental law

Our analysis has indicated that the preventive principle is too broad to provide clear guidelines for State authorities as to precisely how they should prevent transboundary harm. Other principles emerging at the level of international customary law and recognized by the EC legal order (the polluter-pays principle, the precautionary principle, and the principle of rectifying pollution at source) can reinforce the principle of prevention by providing indications as to the actions to be taken by public authorities.[54] We consider in this section how the preventive principle differs from both the polluter-pays principle, which focuses on the repair of existing damage, and the precautionary principle, which serves to counter risks that are still uncertain. Prevention may, but will not necessarily, combine with the principle of rectifying pollution at source when it is applied before damage has occurred.

3.2.1. *Relationship with the polluter-pays principle*

A distinction should be drawn between the obligation to reduce and control existing pollution and the obligation to prevent new cases of pollution. When damage has already occurred prevention is no longer relevant: the damage must be either halted or repaired. In the latter case, reparation presupposes causation of damage, or at least an injury which will become evident in the future. The polluter-pays principle should free sufficient financial resources to avoid the cost of repair falling to the community and, in certain cases, to prevent future repetition of the damage.

Preventive measures, on the other hand, seek to avoid the problem of reparation arising in the first place. That is, prevention only applies when damage has not yet occurred or when its spread and/or recurrence can be averted. For example, an injunction to cease an unlawful act is a preventive measure: while not affecting the damage that has already occurred, it prevents its recurrence in the future.

3.2.2. *Relationship with the precautionary principle*

The distinction between the preventive principle and the precautionary principle rests on a difference of degree in the understanding of risk. Prevention is based on certainties: it rests on cumulative experience concerning the degree of risk posed by an activity (Russian roulette, for example, involves a predictable

---

[54] L. Soljan, 'The General Obligation to Prevent Transboundary Harm and its Relation to Four Key Environmental Principles' (1998) 3 ARIEL 209–32.

one-in-six chance of death). Therefore, prevention presupposes science, technical control, and the notion of an objective assessment of risks in order to reduce the probability of their occurrence. Preventive measures are thus intended to avert risks for which the cause-and-effect relationship is already known (for example, chronic pollution, repetitive risks). In such situations, the goal is to prevent the recurrence of a risk that has already taken place—a risk to which a probability can be attached, so that it may be characterized as 'certain'.[55]

Precaution, in contrast, comes into play when the probability of a suspected risk cannot be irrefutably demonstrated. The distinction between the two principles is thus the degree of uncertainty surrounding the probability of risk. The lower the margin of uncertainty, the greater the justification for intervention as a means of prevention, rather than in the name of precaution. By contrast, precaution is to be used when scientific research has not yet reached a stage that allows the veil of uncertainty to be lifted.

3.2.3. *Relationship with the principle of rectification at source*

The principle of prevention also tends to merge with the principle of rectification at source, which has been recognized in the 1992 Helsinki Convention on the Protection of Transboundary Watercourses,[56] the 1994 Scheldt-Meuse Agreements,[57] the 1992 Porto Agreement on the EEA,[58] and Article 174(2) of the EC Treaty, which states that 'environmental damage should as a priority be rectified at source'. This principle marks a significant departure from an 'end-of-pipe' policy. For instance, it implies a preference for emission standards rather than environmental quality standards.

The scope of the preventive principle is wider than that of the principle that environmental damage should as a priority be rectified at source. The principle of prevention posits the anticipation of potential damage without necessarily tackling the source of the pollution. Thus, respect for environmental quality standards could well suffice to prevent pollution. On the other hand, the principle of rectification at source of environmental damage as a priority aims to correct the nature of the activity producing environmental damage. At this level quality objectives no longer suffice; rather, it is appropriate to tackle the source of pollution by requiring polluters to make use of best available technologies. The principle of rectification thereby refines the scope of the preventive principle by demanding stronger intervention on the part of the public authorities in the fight against environmental degradation.

3.3. The dimensions of the preventive principle

The preventive principle translates into a number of disparate instruments. Their scope may be widespread or local, global or narrow; their duration may be brief

---

[55] See the discussion in Subsection 3.2.1.2., Chapter 3 below.   [56] Article 3(1)(d).
[57] Article 3(2)(d).   [58] Article 73(2).

or lasting; their intensity varies from one extreme to another. Below, we seek to establish a hierarchy among the different types of preventive measures with regard to their temporal, spatial, material, and sectoral dimensions.

3.3.1. *The temporal and spatial dimension of preventive measures*

The complexity of pollution arises from the fact that it evolves in time and in space, simultaneously but in a differentiated fashion. While preventive measures may be taken at any stage in its progression, it is nevertheless possible to arrange such measures in a hierarchy based on the time and distance that separate the ecological damage from its source.

Lead, a metal whose polluting effects at almost all stages of pollution have been regulated by EC secondary legislation, provides a marvelous illustration of the range of preventive measures that may be used by public authorities.[59] Lead constitutes a particularly diffuse threat to human health as it is able to contaminate a variety of environmental systems. Found in soils in its natural state, it may enter surface waters and thence find its way into water used for food processing. Lead pipes also pose a threat to human health by contaminating the drinking water that passes through them. Lead pollutes the aquatic environment when it is discharged into water by various industries. As a constituent of paint or petrol, lead enters the atmosphere by mixing with other gaseous emissions.

In brief, lead may pollute air, water, and soil and, in contaminating each of these mediums, may poison humans. The widespread presence of this toxic metal in the environment poses a significant health risk.[60] Yet at each stage of lead's journey, its harmful effects may be forestalled by the implementation of an appropriate legal instrument. As will be seen below, the prevention of pollution caused by lead becomes increasingly efficient the closer one gets to its source.

The potential victim of lead pollution may be directly protected by the adoption of exposure standards. For example, Directive 98/83/EEC on the quality of water intended for human consumption sets maximum concentrations for lead in abstraction waters in order to protect consumer health,[61] and Directive 76/160/EEC concerning the quality of bathing waters fixes maximum concentrations of lead allowed in such waters in order to protect the health of bathers. Similarly, Directive 1999/30/EC relating to limit values for sulphur dioxide, nitrogen dioxide, and oxides of nitrogen, particulate matter, and lead in ambient air sets limits for lead in the atmosphere.

The protection of health is also indirectly ensured by Directives that aim to guarantee food quality by setting exposure standards. Directive 74/63/EEC, for example, limits the quantities of lead in food intended for domestic animals, not merely in order to secure the protection of the animals themselves, but also indirectly to protect humans. Similar thinking lies behind Directive 78/659/EEC

---

[59] This example is taken from the work of N. Haigh, *EEC Environmental Policy and Britain* (2nd edn., London: Longman, 1990) 15.

[60] *Lead Industry Ass'n v. EPA*, 647 F.2d 1130, 1148–49 (DC Cir. 1979).

[61] Case C-42/89, *Commission v. Belgium* [1990] ECR I-2821.

on the quality of fresh waters needing protection or improvement in order to support fish life; the object of the Directive, as confirmed by the ECJ, is to protect the health of consumers.[62]

The above preventive measures focus more closely on symptoms of contamination than on eliminating their cause. Preventive action may move upstream, however, if public authorities decide to act against pollution directly rather than to protect potential victims or environmental components. This is the case for so-called emission standards, which aim to limit releases of lead from anthropogenic sources. Thus, for instance, Directive 76/464/EEC on pollution caused by certain dangerous substances discharged into the aquatic environment of the Community and Directive 80/68/EEC on the protection of groundwater against pollution caused by certain dangerous substances require Member States to set concentration thresholds for discharges of lead-containing waste waters.

At this stage, prevention equates to an 'end-of-pipe' policy, since emission limits do not alter the source of pollution but merely limit it. It is possible, however, for public authorities to intervene at an earlier stage by directly regulating the production processes that give rise to pollution. The IPPC Directive requires industrial operators to adapt their production processes to take into account the development of best available technologies. The advantages of this option are clear: while discharge standards may rapidly become obsolete in the wake of technical and scientific progress, the obligation to use best available technologies requires a continuous effort by industrial operators to reduce the environmental impact of their methods of production.

Even further upstream, the authorities may regulate the products used in polluting installations. Directive 98/70/EC relating to the quality of petrol and diesel fuels and amending Council Directive 93/12/EEC, for instance, obliged Member States to prohibit the marketing of leaded petrol within their territory by 1 January 2000. Product standards also include ceilings for lead in packaging under the provisions of Directive 94/62 on packaging and packaging waste.

3.3.2. *The material dimension of preventive measures*

The preventive principle varies as a function of the degree of constraint set by implementing standards. Prevention may be absolute in character, if damage is prevented from occurring by the adoption of prohibitory measures (embargo, prohibition on commercialization of a product or operation). By going so far as to halt activities suspected of causing environmental damage, this option clearly meets problems head on, even if it does not necessarily appeal to public authorities, which generally prefer to reconcile differing societal aims.

Contrasting with this first approach is that of information. In EC law information requirements relating to the ecological quality of products[63] and

---

[62] Case C-298/95, *Commission v. Germany* [1996] ECR I-6747.
[63] Regulation (EC) No. 1980/2000 of 17 July 2000 on a revised Community eco-label award scheme.

services[64] serve to inform both industry operators and the public about how these should be produced and used. A number of international conventions set out information and notification requirements for neighbouring States for certain types of activities.[65] This is also the case for the obligation to set thresholds for alerting populations to the dangers they face.[66] By taking an informative rather than interventionist dimension, this approach should allow public authorities to adopt appropriate measures in a timely fashion. It is no longer a question of following the evolution of a situation that could lead to problems, any more than of immediately acting to prohibit it.

Finally, the constraint posed by preventive measures may range between an absolute requirement and notification obligations. This is the case for all permitting mechanisms which authorize a certain degree of disturbance, nuisance, pollution, and hazard but do not question the existence of the regulated activity. This intermediate form of prevention is at present found at the heart of most environmental law institutions. This approach, based on the principle that 'the solution to pollution is dilution', paints a deliberately reassuring picture of the phenomena that underlie pollution.[67] It assumes that as long as polluting emissions do not exceed a certain critical threshold, receiving environments may absorb and disperse them. Ecological deterioration only takes place when the self-cleansing capacity of environments is saturated as the result of too high concentrations or too rapid accumulations of polluting substances. It is therefore not absolutely necessary to reduce discharges of polluting substances to zero level, since legal instruments may easily provide an appropriate response to any type of pollution by setting the exact level of a pollutant that an ecosystem can assimilate.[68]

This form of prevention is favoured by public authorities since it makes it possible to reconcile the factors of production that generate economic wealth and social well-being with the need to guarantee an environment of high quality. The private sector prefers this approach to a more aggressive mode of prevention because it distances itself from prohibitions, in the name of scientific and tech-

[64] The objective of the Regulation (EC) No. 761/2001 of 19 March 2001 allowing voluntary participation by organizations in a Community eco-management and audit scheme (EMAS) is to promote continual improvements in the environmental performance of organizations by 'the provision of information on environmental performance and an open dialogue with the public and other interested parties' (Article 1(2)(c)).

[65] See, among others, 1974 Nordic Convention on the Protection of the Environment; 1986 IAEA Vienna Convention on Early Notification of a Nuclear Accident; 1986 Vienna Convention on Assistance in the Case of a Nuclear Accident or Radiological Emergency; 1992 Helsinki Convention on the Transboundary Effects of Industrial Accidents; Principles 18 and 19 of the 1992 Rio Declaration on Environment and Development. Ireland and the United Kingdom have been required by ITLOS to co-operate in exchanging information concerning risks or effects of the operation of the MOX plant in Sellafield (Order no. 10, paras. 82–4).

[66] See Directive 92/72/EC on air pollution by ozone.

[67] M.W. Holdgate, *A Perspective of Environmental Pollution* (Cambridge: CUP, 1979).

[68] In the chemical sector, few preventive legislation appear to aim for a zero threshold of risk. For instance, a *de minimus* risk approach transpires from Council Directive 91/414/EEC which provides that a pesticide may only be authorized if it has no *unacceptable* effects on the environment or human health; this implicitly confirms the acceptance of a residual risk.

nical management of problems: polluting activities remain authorized, even if their discharges are regulated.

This intermediate approach is less radical—and probably less effective—than the absolutist approach, which is criticized by industry and public authorities as too extreme. Yet it supplants prevention by notification, which for its part is considered too timid. Based on forestalling and notifying the occurrence of ecological damage, this middle path requires energetic intervention by the public authorities to control, regulate, intervene in, and limit pollution at an acceptable level. On the other hand, it also demonstrates an almost blind confidence in science and technology, with the risk that new types of ecological damage will not be anticipated and understood.

3.3.3. *The sectoral dimension of preventive measures*

Prevention perceptibly wavers between localized or sectoral intervention and a global approach based on ecosystems. In fact, preventive measures can both halt the highly specific impacts of an activity (for instance, a sectoral authorization concerning waste, air, or water) and apprehend all the impacts of an activity on the environment (for example, assessment of all direct and indirect impacts of a project, or an integrated permit).

Environment law has developed piecemeal, as a function of successive perceived needs. From its beginnings it has taken shape around sectoral policies, whose fragmented nature can mask transfers of pollution from a regulated sector to other sectors. For example, a prohibition on the production of waste may easily translate into an increase in energy production, contributing to atmospheric pollution. There is thus no point in dealing with nuisances in an isolated manner, since only a comprehensive perspective is capable of grasping the full complexity of ecological reality.

Since the late 1980s the scope of the preventive dimension has been the subject of a major policy debate at European level. New legal regimes, following the example of the IPPC Directive and control, are today tending towards greater integration, in particular by establishing single permitting systems that aim to cover all the nuisances generated by a single industrial installation. A more holistic understanding is also reflected in the 'cradle-to-grave' approach set out in Regulation No. 1980/2000 of 17 July 2000 on a revised Community eco-label award scheme. However, the widening of the preventive dimension of such instruments should not disguise the fact that they are proving less effective than more precise instruments. Thus, the provisions of the IPPC Directive allow Member States very wide discretion, while Regulation No. 1980/2000 is a voluntary instrument.

3.4. Application threshold for the principle of prevention

Everyone agrees that it is better to prevent ecological damage than to repair it. It is thus undoubtedly preferable to favour those instruments that most efficiently prevent damage, particularly when these are intended to bring into play a constitutional right relating to the environment. Is it, however, necessary to prevent damage at any price? This seems unlikely, since the content of any preventive measure remains largely determined by a more general principle of proportionality according to which the probability of damage must be balanced against its extent, and restrictions set on other interests must be justified by the need to adopt the measure in question.

Below, we consider the concrete consequences of the preventive principle on the scope of preventive measures. Before adopting such a measure, public authorities first verify the probability of damage and then weigh ecological benefits in the absence of such measures against the potential socio-economic consequences if preventive measures are taken.

3.4.1. *The relationship between the probability and the extent of damage*

The preventive principle, as noted earlier, rests on a certain mastery of environmental risks. In some cases the negative impact of pollution is recognized; in other cases pollution is suspected of affecting ecosystems at a certain moment.[69]

When pollution is likely to have a transboundary impact, the degree of risk posed by a polluting activity is an essential element of the obligation to prevent environmental harm. Where the probability of a risk occurring is seen to be extremely low, the authorities generally find themselves caught between intervention and non-intervention.

A due care or due diligence obligation implies that States must prevent activities which involve a 'significant risk' of causing environmental harm.[70] Significance depends on the probabilility that a risk will materialize, but also on the magnitude of harm which might be caused. When damage is not expected to be serious, due diligence will only be required if such damage is highly likely to occur; the higher the risk, the greater the diligence required from the polluter. A risk with a low degree of probability may still be regarded as significant if it is likely to cause enormous harm. Despite the likelihood of a nuclear accident being one in a million, for example, such an accident is as likely to occur tomorrow as in 100 years, with catastrophic results. Thus, the occurrence of that risk must be averted even if it is minimal. In other words, where there is a high degree of uncertainty concerning the occurrence of extreme adverse effects, risk reduction is unconditional; even a ban or moratorium can be appropriate.

Similarly, German doctrine recognizes limits to the application of the principle of protection against danger (*Schutzprinzip*)—the equivalent of the preventive principle—by recourse to probability theory (*die Je-Desto Formel*).[71] A major

---

[69] For instance, Article 2(2)(a) of the 1992 Helsinki Convention on the Protection of Transboundary Watercourses obliges parties 'to take all appropriate measures to prevent pollution of waters causing or likely to cause transboundary impact'.

[70] J.G. Lammers, 'International and European Community Law: Aspects of Pollution of International Watercourses', n. 1 above, 119.

[71] For a critical analysis of this theory, see G. Roller, *Genehmigungsaufhebung und Entschädigung im Atomrecht* (Baden-Baden: Nomos, 1994), p. 62.

accident of low probability must be avoided owing to its disastrous implications. By contrast, a very high risk of relatively negligible damage need not be countered in the name of prevention.

3.4.2. Cost–benefit analysis

There is little doubt that most of the obligations of prevention, in both international and national law, leave a margin for socio-economic analysis. UNCLOS provides that States shall take all necessary measures to prevent pollution of the marine environment, using the best practical means 'at their disposal and in accordance with their capabilities'. According to the 1994 Charleville-Mézières Agreements on the protection of the Scheldt and the Meuse, the principle of rectification of pollution at source as a priority should only be used to guide contracting Parties to the extent that its implementation is carried out 'under economically acceptable conditions'. Similarly, the words 'when that is not practicable' inserted in Article 1 of the IPPC Directive allow operators to include considerations of an economic nature when they reduce their pollution.[72] Integrated pest control is meant to take into account the economic costs of risk reduction measures, and the use of chemical plant protection must be restricted to the strict minimum necessary to maintain the pest population 'at levels below those causing economically unacceptable damage or loss'.[73] Similarly, the current chemical substances Regulation calls for the balancing of 'advantages and drawbacks' before control measures can be recommended by a national *rapporteur*.[74]

The same trend can be observed in national environmental framework laws. The Swiss Federal Law of 7 October 1983 on protection of the environment envisages preventive emission limits 'in keeping with the current state of technology and conditions of use and to the extent that this is economically acceptable'. The French Environmental Code foresees recourse to best available techniques in order to carry out the principles of preventive action and of rectification at source as a priority, on the condition of an 'economically acceptable cost'. According to the 1998 Swedish Environmental Code, 'particular importance shall be attached in this connection to the benefits of protective measures [...] in relation to their cost. The cost–benefit relationship shall also be taken into account in assessments relating to total defence activities or where a total defence measure is necessary.'[75]

According to those international and national provisions, before adopting a preventive measure public authorities should evaluate whether the cost of their action will or will not exceed the cost of the damages that might be avoided.

---

[72] L. Krämer, *Focus on European Environmental Law*, n. 44 above, 230.

[73] Article 2(13) of Directive 91/414/CEE concerning the placing of plant protection products on the market.

[74] Council Regulation (EEC) No. 793/93 on the evaluation and control of the risks of existing substances.

[75] Section 7, Chapter 2 of the 1998 Swedish Environmental Code.

Thus, hypothetically, a cost–benefit analysis should be carried out if an industrial discharge is harming the environment and could only be prevented by closing down the polluting plant, at a high socio-economic cost. If calculations were to indicate that the costs of terminating the activity would be disproportionate, the operation should not be shut down. In the case of transboundary pollution, activities should not be considered as unlawful *a priori*. Rather, States must negotiate on the modalities of reducing pollution.[76]

There is a serious danger that this balancing exercise will rely entirely on classical economic analysis, which does not accord equal value to threatened environmental elements. Yet public authorities find it more difficult to justify the adoption of preventive measures in cases where the cost allocated to environmental elements is modest—or even nil—than where it is high. In this equation, the cost of the redistribution of resources to the detriment of other needs—an inevitable result of adopting a preventive measure (for example, the economic and social costs implicit in closing down a polluting activity)—can easily surpass the benefits obtained through use of the preventive measure (for instance, the advantages gained by halting a polluting activity). The difficulty lies in the fact that the cost of socio-economic injury is quantifiable, which is not necessarily the case for the cost of ecological damages—particularly those caused to *res communes*.

For environmental protection to be raised to the level of a fundamental value in most of the legal systems we are examining would require that ecological damage take its rightful place in the cost–benefit analysis procedure. Such integration would serve to temper the rigour of classical economic analysis by permitting consideration of non-quantifiable data.

4. Applications of the principle

Owing to its wide-ranging definition, prevention covers a plethora of legal instruments, ranging from monitoring mechanisms to legal prohibitions. Three instruments representative of the principle of prevention are evaluated below. These are the technique of thresholds (Subsection 4.1), best available technology (Subsection 4.2), and impact assessment (Subsection 4.3).

4.1. Setting thresholds

It is clearly impossible for the public authorities to anticipate all forms of environmental degradation. Nor is it possible to prohibit all noise, pollution, nuisances, and damage to the natural environment; if it were, life in society as we know it would become impossible. The only viable solution is thus to authorize activities that are injurious to the environment within binding thresholds,

---

[76] A. Nollkaemper, *The Legal Regime of Transboundary Water Pollution*, n. 8 above, 46.

beyond which environmental deterioration is judged to be unacceptable. This technique requires the public authorities to determine the level at which the natural absorption capacities of receiving environments are able to function.

Thus, discharge standards for pollutants to air, water, and soil, quality objectives for each of these environmental compartments and product norms must respect thresholds. Expressed in an extremely diverse manner—by percentages of materials, concentrations of substances, decibels, etc.—thresholds have permeated all areas of environment policy. Respect for these thresholds is best guaranteed when their breach is automatically considered an infringement leading to criminal or administrative sanctions (eg withdrawal of a permit).

From the perspective of achieving the internal market of the European Community, harmonization of standards at EC level implies adoption of directives or regulations setting uniform thresholds, based on Article 95.[77] The choice of this legal basis avoids distortions of competition arising from national decisions taken on a case-by-case basis; these give rise to security for economic operators to the extent that Member States may in principle no longer derogate from the rule of Community harmonization.

Despite its obvious merits, the threshold technique may be criticized on two counts. First, it reinforces the power of experts, thereby camouflaging the resurgence of technocratic decision-making. Secondly, by conciliating the needs of economic development with requirements for environmental protection, it runs counter to a fundamentally protective orientation based on the principle of non-degradation, which calls for general and absolute prohibitions on activities that damage the environment. By legalizing a certain level of nuisance, thresholds stand in the way of integrated protection of the environment.

The usual response to such criticism is that tolerance of pollution under the threshold technique is scientifically justified. According to an 'assimilative' approach, it should be possible to determine the precise quantity of pollutants that ecosystems can absorb without damage.[78] This thesis, however, may be disputed on three levels.

First, there is no definition of what constitutes an undesirable effect or unacceptable impact on an ecosystem or of how it will be measured.[79] Secondly, in order to be effective, emission levels must coincide with receiving thresholds, known as ecological quality standards. Only the latter unequivocally correspond to an optimal policy of prevention, since they are calculated with a view to guaranteeing the quality of receiving environments. In practice, however, emission limit values seem to be established on the basis of the economic or technical

---

[77] See particularly Case C-300/89, *Commission v. Council* [1991] ECR I-2867.

[78] The assimilative capacity is 'a property of the environment, defined as its ability to accommodate a particular activity, or rate of activity, without unacceptable impact'. Eg V. Pravdic, 'Environmental Capacity: Is a New Scientific Concept Acceptable as a Strategy to Combat Marine Pollution?' (1985) 16 MPB 295.

[79] J.S. Gray, 'Integrating Precautionary Scientific Methods into Decision-Making' in D. Freestone and E. Hey (eds.), *The Precautionary Principle and International Law* (London: Kluwer Law Int'l, 1995) 133.

capacities of the polluter rather than with regard to the absorption capacities of the receiving environment. They are more often linked to quality objectives by coincidence than on the basis of a planned policy, given the extent to which considerations having nothing to do with environmental protection play a role in their determination. In addition, the scientific certainty upon which emission limits are based has increasingly become a subject for caution, since it consistently ignores the cumulative effects of pollution. Attempts to establish safe levels for the marine ecosystem, for example, are severely flawed.[80] Indeed, such difficulties were at the origin of the emergence of the precautionary principle in international law.

Although constituting the vanguard for the preventive principle, the technique of thresholds thus remains open to criticism on several fronts, owing to its tolerance of a certain degree of damage.

4.2. Use of best available technologies

Some authors consider that the use of best available technologies naturally follows from the precautionary principle[81]—an analysis that appears overly categoric. We believe their use is linked to the principle of prevention, since recourse to best available technologies is required of operators when the impacts of their pollution are known. By contrast, when recourse to best available technology is required in a context of uncertainty, that obligation is rather in response to the precautionary principle. In either case the requirement to turn to best available technology, which is found in both international and EC law, is generally related to the preventive principle.

In many international treaty regimes the obligation to prevent harmful releases to the environment is directly related to the obligation to apply 'best available technologies' (BAT). Thus, the 1992 Helsinki Convention on the Protection and Use of Transboundary Watercourses and International Lakes states that 'to meet the aims of prevention' Parties must act in such a way that 'limits for waste-water discharges stated in permits are based on the best available technology for discharges of hazardous substances'.[82] These are defined as 'the latest stage of development of processes, facilities or methods of operation which indicate the practical suitability of "particular measures" for limiting discharges, emissions and waste.'[83]

The 1994 Agreements concerning the Protection of the Scheldt and Meuse Rivers define the principle of prevention as being 'the principle by virtue of

[80] M. MacGarvin, 'Precaution, Science and the Sin of Hubris' in T. O'Riordan and J. Cameron (eds.), *Interpreting the Precautionary Principle* (London: Cameron & May, 1994) 88.

[81] E. Rehbinder, 'The Precautionary Principle in an International Perspective' in *Miljørettens grundsporgsmaal* (Copenhagen, 1994) 94; J. Cameron, W. Wade-Gerey, and J. Abouchar, 'Precautionary Principle and Future Generations' in E. Agius and S. Busuttil (eds.), *Future Generations and International Law* (London: Earthscan, 1998) 109.

[82] Article 3(c).

[83] See Annex I (1).

which, in particular, clean technologies are implemented under economically acceptable conditions'. Under the 1992 OSPAR Convention, States are obliged to require the use of the 'best available techniques, including, where appropriate, clean technology'.[84] The 1992 Baltic Convention includes a requirement to use the 'Best Available Technologies'.[85] while the 1998 Århus Protocol on POPs to the LRTAP Convention insists on the use of 'best available techniques'.[86]

Similarly, the obligation to use best available technologies is found in EC law, and more particularly in the IPPC Directive. According to this Directive, installations shall operate under a regime of 'best available techniques',[87] which are defined as follows: 'the most effective and advanced stage in the development of activities and their methods of operation which indicate the practical suitability of particular techniques for providing in principle the basis for emission limit values designed to prevent and, where that is not practicable, generally to reduce emissions and the impact on the environment as a whole'.

From the perspective of prevention, such obligations should in any case be welcomed. They shift the focus from 'end-of-pipe' solutions to the regulation of industrial processes with a view to preventing harmful discharges in the first place. Is the best means for averting the risk of pollution not precisely that of requiring firms to make use of the most effective technologies available?

That said, use of best available technologies is not an absolute. As soon as the cost of new technologies is considered too onerous, firms renege on approvals of new investment, arguing that what is being asked of them is disproportionate in relation to the environmental improvements anticipated. In order to avoid driving companies into bankruptcy or weakening their competitive position, legislation balances the requirement to use best available technologies against an economic factor: the purchase of such technologies should not entail excessive costs for the operator. Their use should not only be technically feasible, it must also be economically acceptable.

According to most definitions in international and EC law, the obligation to apply BAT involves a balance between costs and the nature of the harm being caused to the environment. The 1979 LRATP Convention obliges Parties to use the best available technology that is 'economically feasible'.[88] The 1992 Helsinki Convention on the Protection of Transboundary Watercourses indicates among the factors which should be considered in the determination of clean technology 'the economic feasibility of such technology'. In the Scheldt-Meuse Agreements, the use of 'Best Available Technologies' is linked to an 'economically acceptable cost'.[89]

Similarly, a close reading of the definitions of the IPPC Directive makes clear that 'best available techniques must have been developed on a scale which allows

---

[84] Article 2(3)(b) and Annex I.   [85] Article 3(1) and Annex II.
[86] See practice-oriented guidance document on available methods to determine the techniques to reduce POPs emissions.
[87] Articles 3, 8, and 10.   [88] Article 7(a).   [89] Annex I (1)(c).

implementation under economically and technically viable conditions'.[90] This combination of technical performance and economic capacity is translated by an obligation to use 'best available technologies not entailing excessive costs' (BATNEEC).

In each case costs must be balanced against the nature and volume of the discharges in question.[91] The preventive principle thereby risks becoming considerably weakened by recourse to cost—benefit analysis. First, the inevitable consequence of this balancing will be to redefine appropriate technologies as a function of the financial capacity of individual operators. Highly polluting operations could easily evade this obligation by claiming insufficient financial resources, while less polluting but more affluent firms would comply with their obligations. The differential treatment that would result, particularly in setting operating conditions, could cause discrimination among firms.

In addition, administrations might be tempted to verify whether the use of best available technologies is actually necessary to respect the environmental quality standards they have set by employing the proportionality principle. If an administration considers the requirement to acquire new technologies disproportionate—that is, the environmental improvement is relatively small in relation to the socio-economic sacrifices required—it may well decide to abandon the requirement. Yet such an analysis must take into account all the risks inherent in the activity in question. It is of course at this point that proportionality becomes problematic, because it generally disregards such considerations. Seen in this perspective, the requirement to use best available technologies is not necessarily strongly preventive in character.

4.3. Environmental impact assessment

The favoured terrain for the preventive principle is undoubtedly the environmental impact assessment (EIA) applied to certain projects or activities. According to Principle 17 of the Rio Declaration: 'environmental impact assessment, as a national instrument, shall be undertaken for proposed activities that are likely to have a significant adverse impact on the environment'. At first glance, such a procedural requirement seems likely to require States to show due diligence. Nevertheless, closer examination of the relevant international and EC obligations indicates that the EIA procedures are still at an embryonic stage.

A large number of international conventions require EIAs in a transboundary context.[92] With the exception of the 1992 ECE Espoo Convention on

[90] Article 2(11).

[91] A. Nollkaemper, *The Legal Regime of Transboundary Water Pollution*, n. 8 above, 132.

[92] See also, among others, Article 6 of the 1974 Nordic Environmental Protection Convention; UNCLOS, Article 206 requires States to assess the potential effects of planned activities which might cause substantial pollution or significant and harmful changes to the marine environment; the 1991 Madrid Protocol on Environmental Protection to the 1959 Antarctic Treaty requires prior assessment of environmental impacts for all activities undertaken in Antarctica; Article 14(1) of the 1992 CBD requires the contracting parties to 'introduce appropriate procedures requiring environmental impact

Environmental Impact Assessment in a Transboundary Context, however, none of those conventions define the minimum content for a proper EIA. Thus, uncertainty persists as to the essential components of this procedural obligation (independence of the author of the EIA, quantity and quality of the information, public participation, etc.).[93]

In EC law, Directive 85/337/EEC on the assessment of the effects of certain public and private projects on the environment is often held up as one of the most striking examples of the principle of prevention. Directive 85/337/EEC is grounded in a resolutely preventive approach, as is evident from its Preamble, which states that 'the best environmental policy consists in preventing the creation of pollution or nuisances at source, rather than subsequently trying to counteract their effects'.[94] This formulation leaves no doubt as to the clear preference given to considering environmental impacts as far upstream as possible.

However orderly it may appear, this procedure gives rise to innovations that force truly revolutionary changes upon traditional administrative processes. The underlying philosophy of the Directive is that when authorities are fully aware of all the environmental consequences of a given project, they will be in a better position to consider whether the project should be approved at all, and if so what could be done to minimize its negative consequences.[95]

All the 'environmental impacts' of a given project—that is, all its direct as well as indirect effects, both short-term and long-term, temporary and permanent, accidental or intended—on the various elements of the environment must be evaluated from a trans-sectoral perspective, in a holistic and systematic manner. This procedure gives rise to a dynamic which informs administrators, project initiators, and third parties and provides them with an opportunity to require fuller integration of environmental concerns into the decision-making process.

assessment of its proposed projects that are likely to have significant adverse effects on biological diversity'. See also the 1976 Barcelona Convention for the Protection of the Mediterranean Sea against Pollution (as amended in 1995), Article 4(3)(c); 1992 UNFCCC, Article 4(1)(f); 1995 Barcelona Protocol concerning Specially Protected Areas and Biological Diversity in the Mediterranean, Article 17; AEWA Actions Plan, Article 4(3)(a). In the case of *Hatton and Others v. the United Kingdom*, the ECHR considered that States are required 'to minimise, as far as possible, the interference with (fundamental) rights, by trying to find alternative solutions and by generally seeking to achieve their aims in the least onerous way as regards human rights. In order to do that, a proper and complete investigation and study with the aim of finding the best possible solution which will, in reality, strike the right balance should precede the relevant project.' *Hatton and Others v. the United Kingdom* Case, 2 October 2001, not yet reported, para. 97. This case-law strongly supports the use of EIAs. Last but not least, Birnie and Boyle consider that EIAs are so well established in national law that they might be regarded as 'a general principle of law or even a requirement of customary law for States to conduct an EIA in accordance with Principle 17 of the 1992 Rio Declaration': Birnie and Boyle, see n. 7 above, 131.

[93] P. Okowa, 'Procedural Obligations in International Environment Agreements' (1996) Lxvii, BYbIL, 275–336.

[94] First recital of Directive 85/337/EEC on the assessment of the effects of certain public and private projects on the environment [hereinafter Directive 85/337/EEC on EIA].

[95] L. Krämer, *Focus on European Environmental Law*, n. 44 above, 132.

Unfortunately, despite its innovative aspects, Directive 85/337/EEC contains several gaps that weaken its preventive effect. One weak point is the inappropriateness of the time requirement for impact assessment. The Directive lays down an obligation to assess a project prior to granting it authorization, but practice clearly demonstrates that project conception is at this stage so advanced so that it is difficult to modify it in any substantial way.

The current EIA regime is carried out much too late to allow the course of the project to be appreciably altered. There is little sense in requiring an impact assessment for the operation of a nuclear reactor, for example, if there is no EIA requirement for the national energy programme used to justify the need for a reactor. Within a strongly preventive perspective of the latter type, an evaluation would be effected as far upstream as possible and would require that project plans and programmes be submitted for a preliminary assessment even before the project itself becomes subject to assessment.[96] The new Directive 2001/42/EC on environmental assessment of certain plans and programmes fills this gap by requiring Member States to ensure that environmental consequences of certain plans and programmes are identified and assessed during their preparation and before their adoption.

A further difficulty, and not the least of them, has to do with the relatively narrow field of application *ratione materiae* of Directive 85/337/EEC, in that only those projects that have a significant impact on the environment must be subjected to the assessment procedure. The Directive adopts a dichotomous approach based on the nature of a given project. Annex I projects must be subjected to an impact assessment since they are assumed to have a significant impact. Member States enjoy no discretion for such projects. These are few in number, however: only projects with a very significant impact (nuclear installations, motorways, etc.) must undergo an impact assessment.

By contrast, Annex II projects *may* be subjected to an EIA procedure. The Directive recognizes that these projects do not always have significant effects but acknowledges that in particular cases this may nonetheless be the case. Although Annex II projects are significantly greater in number than those set out in Annex I, Member States are accorded some discretion as to how to treat them. An assessment procedure is required only when a project is likely to have important impacts on the environment, notably as the result of its nature, size, or location.[97] This should imply a case-by-case examination to determine at what point

---

[96] For submission of a plan for an EIA, see Case C-81/96, *Gedeputeerde Staten van Noord-Holland* [1998] ECR I-3923, para. 20.

[97] However, the ECJ ruled that a Member State may not exclude Annex II projects from any form of assessment (Case C-133/94, *Commission v. Belgium* [1966] ECR I-2323, para 42). The possibility to lay down specifications is secondary to 'a comprehensive evaluation of the characteristics of projects likely to have important impacts on the environment' (Case C-72/95, *Aannemersbedrijf PK Kraaijeveld* [1996] ECR I-5403, para. 52). Recently the ECJ ruled that by setting thresholds for classes of projects to be covered by Annex II without at the same time ensuring that this technique would not circumvent the objective of the legislation, Ireland had exceeded the limits of its discretion under Articles 2(1) and 4(2) of the Directive (Case C-392/98, *Commission v. Ireland* [1999] ECR I-5901, para. 82).

the impact is important. Yet the latest revision of the Directive authorizes Member States to use nationally determined thresholds or criteria as a guideline, thereby enabling them to avoid case-by-case consideration.[98] This significantly increases Member States' power of discretion. By setting low thresholds, they may permit a sizable number of projects to avoid the requirements of the impact assessment procedure.

Last but not least, we should recall that if the EIA procedure is a *sine qua non* for granting an administrative authorization, it is nonetheless a procedural requirement. In the current state of EC law, submission of a project to an EIA is a purely formal guarantee, which does not in itself entail any strengthening of ecological controls.[99]

Thus, while the EIA procedure has the merit of informing various interested parties about the damaging effects certain types of activities have on the environment and requiring authorities to provide a statement of reasons for their authorization decisions, it at no time imposes an obligation to reject or modify a project on the ground of damaging environmental impacts. The adoption of preventive measures based on assessment results thus continues to depend on the goodwill of the public authorities. The Directive's critics therefore consider it an alibi, a *trompe-l'œil*, a smokescreen which, owing to its purely informative nature, in the end provides no more than illusory guarantees of protection.

5. CONCLUDING OBSERVATIONS

At times prevention is elevated to the level of a general principle; at other times it is formulated in very general declaratory rules; sometimes it may be deduced from the objectives of normative instruments of a more technical nature. Its omnipresence affirms that it acts as a beacon for environmental law at both the international level and in national legal orders: a sort of golden rule.

But anyone trying to abstract the quintessential nature of such a principle is likely rapidly to become lost in the maze of legal mechanisms to which prevention gives rise. The level of generality of the principle is such that its efficiency may be questioned; the obligations that follow from it appear as vague as their legal content is ephemeral.

A legal principle can only be effective if everyone agrees upon its effect, even in an imprecise manner. In this regard the systematic examination carried out above makes it possible to identify various forms of prevention and to specify which are the most effective in achieving the protection sought. Critical analysis of the various legal instruments stemming from the preventive principle also makes it possible to determine their strong points, which include the procedures

---

[98] Article 4(2) of Directive 85/337/EEC, as amended by Directive 97/11/EC.
[99] Advocate General M.B. Elmer's opinion in Case C-431/92, *Commission v. Germany* [1995] ECR I-2189.

for fixing nuisance thresholds, best available technologies, and environmental impact assessment procedures. We may nevertheless ask if these instruments, in their current state of development, constitute a sufficiently strong rampart against increasing incursions by environmental degradation.

Examined more closely, most of these instruments may be seen to be highly ambiguous. Quality standards intended to limit pollution on the basis of the self-cleansing capacity of ecosystems in reality mask an approach that seeks to conciliate economic needs and protection of the environment and in no way questions an unshakeable faith in technology. While impact assessment procedures have the merit of providing information to the various actors concerned, they present no obstacle to the adoption of decisions that will lead to serious environmental damage. Examples of this are not lacking. In fact, do all these procedures in one way or another not legitimize a certain level of environmental degradation? But these ambiguities arise less from the principle upon which these instruments are based than from the interaction between a litany of limitations and an ideal of proportionality.

In order for the preventive principle to be able truly to serve environmental protection law, it appears indispensable to define its scope more precisely. Several principles that have appeared in its wake could contribute to that result. Among these, the precautionary principle (examined in greater detail below) should make it possible to consolidate the preventive approach by forcing the public authorities to act even when they do not have conclusive proof to provide grounds for their action. As for the principle of rectification of environmental effects at source as a priority, it should be combined with the preventive principle in order to require public authorities to act as far upstream as possible in tackling the causes of environmental damage. The polluter-pays principle should also be called upon to evolve within the intellectual framework of prevention. In addition, recourse to the principle of integration would enlarge the scope of prevention by requiring those responsible for other public policies to attenuate their impacts on the environment. Were such adjustments to be made, the preventive function of environmental law would be able to flower fully.

3

The Precautionary Principle

1. Introductory Remarks

Policy measures intended to counter environmental damage have undergone a succession of radical modifications over time. A first phase took the form of remedial action, which translates into late intervention by the public authorities. At this stage damage has already occurred; the only possible course of action is remedy.

This approach evolved to include a preventive dimension, by which public authorities intervene prior to the occurrence of damage that is likely to take place if nothing is done to prevent it. This second stage is marked by an understanding that threats to the environment are tangible and that situations may rapidly become critical; for that reason, timely prevention of damaging consequences should be undertaken.

Finally, the third variation is marked by anticipation. It differs from the other two in that the authorities are prepared for potential, uncertain, or hypothetical threats: indeed, for all cases where no definitive proof exists that a threat will materialize. The most recent phase in the evolutionary process, precaution is the end point of a range of public measures meant to counter ecological damage. Not only has damage not yet occurred, but there is no irrefutable proof that it will occur.

This progression is evidence of a genuine paradigm shift. While prevention is based on the concept of certain risk, the new paradigm is distinguished by the intrusion of uncertainty. Precaution does not posit a perfect understanding of any given risk: it is sufficient that a risk be suspected, conjectured, or feared. The rational view, 'ascertain the facts, then act', must be reversed, to become 'act first, then ascertain the facts'.

Envisaging anticipatory preventive action in response to uncertainty, precaution represents an important milestone in risk reduction. The question is no longer merely how to prevent assessable, calculable, and certain risks, but rather how to anticipate risks suggested by possibility, contingency, plausibility, probability. Decision-making processes must henceforth take all risks into account, whatever their degree of certainty. By leaving behind the realm of rational certainty, precaution necessarily gives rise to controversy and its practical application to conflict.

The precautionary principle is invoked increasingly often: in relation to WTO negotiations, mad cow disease, the spread of genetically modified organisms, urban smog, the Belgian dioxin scandal, the French HIV blood-contamination scandal, health claims linked to phthalates in PVC toys, and endocrine disruptors, among other issues. Reflecting the adage 'better safe than sorry', the principle calls for risk to be anticipated. It has also assumed a legal role; legislators cite it, some courts draw inspiration from it, and important scholarly analyses have been devoted to it. Its value amply justifies in-depth consideration.

Yet despite the success of the precautionary principle in the fields of national, EC, and international law, its outlines are far from clear. Accorded diverse definitions in these legal orders and case-law applications, the principle can in fact be understood in a variety of ways.

A retrospective of positive law is necessary at this point. Section 2 below reviews the definitions given to the principle in various legal systems, as well as representative court decisions, in order to set out the problematic elements inherent in this norm. Variations in terminology have emerged, reflecting the considerable controversy surrounding the principle. International law is rather confusing in this respect.[1] To avoid the more extreme versions of the precautionary principle, which press for absolute environmental protection, some—including US policy-makers—prefer to use the term precautionary *approach* rather than precautionary *principle*; the latter term is preferred by the European Community institutions. For our part, we consider this an irrelevant debate, a semantic squabble between decision-makers. From a legal point of view the question is whether precaution will become a principle of customary law in international law, on one hand, and a general principle at the national level on the other hand. Based on a substantive analysis of the mechanisms that have developed around the concept of precaution, our response to both aspects of this question would be affirmative. We will therefore use the terms precautionary principle and precautionary approach interchangeably.[2]

On the basis of these empirical materials, we consider the various thresholds for application of the precautionary principle: the concepts of risk, damage, and

---

[1] For instance, in the 1992 Rio Declaration on Environment and Development, the 1996 Protocol to the London Dumping Convention, and the 2001 Stockholm POPs the principle is called an 'approach', while the 'approach' became a principle in the 1992 OSPAR Convention, the 1992 Helsinki Convention on the Protection of the Marine Environment of the Baltic Sea Area, and the Barcelona Convention to Protect the Mediterranean. In the field of waste management, the 1991 Bamako Convention, not yet in force, uses both the terms 'precautionary approach' and 'precautionary principle' in the same provision (Art. 4.3(f)). Lastly, the CPB refers to the 'precautionary approach' in its Preamble, but uses terminology which clearly reflects the same basic rationale for application of the precautionary principle in Articles 10 and 11.

[2] Other authors use both terms interchangeably. Eg E. Hey, 'The Precautionary Concept in Environmental Policy and Law: Institutionalizing Caution' (1992) 4 G Int'l Env L Rev 303; D. Freestone, 'The Road from Rio: International Environmental Law after the Earth's Summit' (1994) 6 JEL 210–13. Those authors suggest that the 'precautionary approach' can only be defined by reference to the principle. See also P. Birnie and A. Boyle, *International Law and the Environment* (2nd edn., Oxford University Press, 2002) 116.

proportionality (Section 3 below). This third section sets out the difficulties that characterize the principle and recommends ways in which these weaknesses might be remedied.

More forward-looking in character, Sections 4 and 5 below—based on the empirical materials of Section 2—assess how the principle might provide fresh impetus to the evolution of environmental law by introducing uncertainty to an unparalleled extent in both rulings and sanctions. For the sake of greater clarity, we have distinguished between the role scientists should play in the decision-making process (Section 4) and the effects of the principle on positive law (Section 5), despite numerous points of overlap. Section 4, based on a multidisciplinary approach, demonstrates that opposing science to precaution is unproductive and proposes practical solutions in the field of risk assessment and risk management. Section 5, which takes a more classical legal approach, demonstrates how the principle could influence the elaboration of standards and civil liability.

Economic factors do not play the same central role in discussions about the precautionary principle as they do in debates about the polluter-pays principle. While the latter is derived from economic theory, the precautionary principle is a decision-making principle related to the principle of prevention, in which economic elements are not of prime importance. [3]

2. THE ORIGIN OF THE PRINCIPLE

Arising in the mid-1980s from the German *Vorsorgeprinzip*, the precautionary principle was widely invoked throughout the 1990s within international legal circles and legitimated in any number of international treaties. It has come to occupy an uncontested position in international (Subsection 2.1 below) and EC law (Subsection 2.2) as well as in certain national legal regimes (Subsection 2.3) to the point where it overshadows a number of other principles.

In this section, we try to demonstrate how the precautionary principle is capable of slowly but inexorably permeating the numerous crevices of positive law, whether through the declaration of public policy objectives (soft law, preambles to international conventions), regulatory acceptance (hard law), or new methods of judicial interpretation (case-law). We also examine to what extent the boundaries between international law and national legal regimes are porous; in any event, developments in international environment law cannot be understood without being related to national laws and *vice versa*.

The diversity of applications described above in any case indicates the potential of a principle which, born of environmental law, is being called upon to govern wide sections of positive law in the longer term (see examples given below in the field of food safety and health).

---

[3] We thus approach the economic implications of the precautionary principle in a more diffuse manner, both in various parts of this Chapter (Subsections 3.2.3.2. and 4.3.3.4) and in Chapter 5.

2.1. International law

2.1.1. Hard law and soft law

The decisions adopted by States within the North Sea Ministerial Conferences mark the first use of the precautionary principle in international law. Explicit reference is made to it in the 1984 Bremen Ministerial Declaration of the International Conference on the Protection of the North Sea,[4] the 1987 London Ministerial Declaration of the Second International Conference on the Protection of the North Sea,[5] the 1990 Hague Declaration of the Third Conference on the Protection of the North Sea,[6] and the 1995 Esbjerg Declaration of the Fourth Conference on the Protection of the North Sea.[7]

The precautionary principle has steadily expanded its dominion in the field of marine pollution, where an abundance of ecological data on pollution yielded little understanding but much concern. During the 1980s it was invoked in decisions adopted by both the Paris and Oslo Commissions.[8] Since the beginning of the 1990s the principle has been set out in the 1990 OPRC Convention,[9] the

---

[4] 'A.7. Conscious that damage to the marine environment can be irreversible or remediable only at considerable expense and over long periods and that, therefore, coastal states and the EEC must not wait for proof of harmful effects before taking action . . .'

[5] 'VII . . . In order to protect the North Sea from possibly damaging effects of the most dangerous substances, a precautionary approach is necessary which may require action to control inputs of such substances even before a causal link has been established by absolutely clear scientific evidence.'

Putting this principle into effect in relation to inputs of 'dangerous substances' via rivers and estuaries as well as in relation to dumping and incineration at sea, the participants then agreed to:

'XVI.1. accept the principle of safeguarding the marine ecosystem of the North Sea by reducing polluting emissions of substances that are persistent, toxic and liable to bioaccumulate at source by the use of the best available technology and other appropriate measures. This applies especially when there is reason to assume that certain damage or harmful effects on the living resources of the sea are likely to be caused by such substances, even where there is no scientific evidence to prove a causal link between emissions and effects ("*the principle of precautionary action*").'

[6] The Parties adopted the following premises as a basis for their future work:

'They will continue to apply the precautionary principle, that is to take action to avoid potentially damaging impacts of substances that are persistent, toxic and liable to bioaccumulate even where there is no scientific evidence to prove a causal link between emissions and effects.'

[7] The Esbjerg Declaration of the Fourth Conference on the Protection of the North Sea attaches particular importance to the principle, as regards the management of marine resources (point 16), the prevention of pollution by hazardous substances (point 17), and prevention of pollution by ships (point 42, iii). In any case, the principle is meant to lead to the halting of pollution of the North Sea by dangerous substances within 25 years.

[8] The Paris Commission, created in the context of the 1974 Convention for the Prevention of Marine Pollution from Land-Based Sources, adopted a Recommendation on 22 June 1989 that incorporated almost verbatim the definition of the precautionary principle contained in the 1987 London Declaration on the Protection of the North Sea. The Oslo Commission, established by the 1972 Convention for the Prevention of Marine Pollution by Dumping from Ships and Aircraft, on 14 June 1989 adopted Decision 89/1 on the Reduction and Cessation of Dumping Industrial Wastes at Sea, in response to the risks inherent in this method of eliminating industrial wastes.

[9] The Preamble notes the 'importance of precautionary measures and prevention in avoiding oil pollution in the first instance' and taking 'account of the polluter-pays principle as a general principle of international environmental law'.

1992 OSPAR Convention,[10] the 1992 Helsinki Conventions on the Protection and Use of Transboundary Watercourses and International Lakes,[11] the 1992 Helsinki Convention on the Protection of the Marine Environment of the Baltic Sea Area,[12] the 1994 Charleville-Mézières Agreement concerning the Protection of the Scheldt and Meuse Rivers,[13] the 1994 Sofia Convention on Cooperation for the Protection and Sustainable Use of the Danube,[14] the 1976 Barcelona Convention for the Protection of the Mediterranean Sea against Pollution (as amended in 1995);[15] the 1980 Athens Protocol for the Protection of the Mediterranean Sea against Pollution from Land-Based Sources and Activities (as amended in 1996),[16] and the 1999 Bern Convention on the Protection of the Rhine.[17] Since the mid-1990s the principle has been applied to new areas and activities such as coastal management[18] and the international fisheries sector.[19] For the first time, an international fisheries convention, the 1995 UN Agreement

[10] The Paris Convention defines the precautionary principle as that 'by virtue of which preventive measures are to be taken when there are reasonable grounds for concern that substances or energy introduced, directly or indirectly, into the marine environment may bring about hazards to human health, harm living resources and marine ecosystems, damage amenities or interfere with other legitimate uses of the sea, even when there is no conclusive evidence of a causal relationship between the inputs and the effects' (Article 2(2)(a)).

[11] 'The Parties shall be guided by... (a) The precautionary principle, by virtue of which action to avoid the potential transboundary impact of the release of hazardous substances shall not be postponed on the ground that scientific research has not fully proved a causal link between those substances, on the one hand, and the potential transboundary impact, on the other hand' (Article 2(5)).

[12] The contracting Parties of the Helsinki Convention undertake to apply the precautionary principle, which consists in 'taking preventive measures when there is reason to assume that substances or energy introduced, directly or indirectly, into the marine environment may cause harm to human health, harm living resources and marine ecosystems, damage amenities or interfere with other legitimate uses of the sea, even when there is no conclusive evidence of a causal relationship between inputs and their alleged effects' (Article 3(2)).

[13] The Charleville-Mézières Agreement defines the principle as that 'by virtue of which the implementation of measures intended to avoid potential significant transboundary impacts from the discharge of dangerous substances is not postponed on the grounds that scientific research has not fully established a causal link between the discharge of those substances on the one hand and a potentially significant transboundary impact' (Articles 2(a) and 3(2)(a)).

[14] '...the precautionary principle constitute[s] a basis for all measures aiming at the protection of the Danube River and of the waters within its catchment area' (Article 2(4)).

[15] The Contracting Parties shall apply, in accordance with their capabilities, the precautionary principle, by virtue of which where there are threats of serious or irreversible damage, lack of full scientific certainty shall not be used as a reason for postponing cost-effective measures to prevent environmental degradation' (Article 4(3)(a)).

[16] Fifth Recital of the Athens Protocol as amended in Syracuse on 7 March 1996 (not yet in force).

[17] Article 4.

[18] Paragraph 17.21 of Agenda 21 adopted at the 1992 Rio Conference on the Environment and Development calls for 'new approaches to the marine and coastal area management and development, at the national, regional and global levels, approaches that are integrated in context and are precautionary and anticipatory in ambit...'

[19] F. Orrego-Vicuna, *The Changing International Law of High Seas Fisheries* (Cambridge University Press, 1999) 157–64; D. Freestone, 'International Fisheries since Rio: The Continued Rise of the Precautionary Principle' in A. Boyle and D. Freestone (eds.), *International Law and Sustainable Development*, (Oxford University Press, 1999) 135–64; S. Kaye, *International Fisheries Management* (London: Kluwer Law Int'l, 2001) 163–265; P. Birnie and A. Boyle, n. 2 above, 675–6.

on Straddling Fish Stocks and Highly Migratory Fish Stocks, elaborated a precautionary approach to be applied to conservation, management, and exploitation measures.[20] That Agreement signals a significant shift in the burden of proof, by creating a presumption in favour of conservation.[21] It also represents 'a major change in the traditional approach of fisheries management, which has tended to react to management problems only after they arrive at crisis levels'.[22]

The uncertainty surrounding the causes and effects of atmospheric pollution has also served to favour the use of the precautionary principle: putting off measures to limit emissions of greenhouse gases or ozone-depleting substances risked allowing serious and irreversible accumulation of these gases in the atmosphere. Paradoxically, the 1985 Vienna Convention for the Protection of the Ozone Layer was adopted just as the scientific controversy over the effects of global ozone layer depletion had reached its height.[23] The Convention did not fix a reduction quota for emissions of chlorine into the atmosphere, but it did set in motion a regulatory process which rapidly resulted in the 1987 adoption of the Montreal Protocol on Substances that Deplete the Ozone Layer, subsequently amended several times in order to achieve the phase-out of all CFCs by 1995.[24] Since then the principle has been endorsed by other instruments concerning air pollution.[25]

The precautionary principle rapidly moved beyond the fields of marine and atmospheric pollution to other areas of international environmental law. It was successively established as a general principle of environmental policy in various soft law documents: on 16 May 1990 by the United Nations Economic

[20] Article 6(2) embodies this approach: 'States shall be more cautious when information is uncertain, unreliable or inadequate. The absence of adequate scientific information shall not be used as a reason for postponing or failing to take conservation and management measures'. Eg D. Nelson, 'The Development of the Legal Regime of High Seas Fisheries' in A. Boyle and D. Freestone (eds.), *International Law and Sustainable Development* (Oxford University Press, 1999) 128. See also J. Cooke and M. Earle, 'Towards a Precautionary Approach to Fisheries Management' (1993) 3 RECIEL 252–9 ; S.M. Garcia, 'The Precautionary Principle: Its Implications in Capture Fisheries Management' (1994) Ocean and Coastal Management 99–125 ; G.J. Hewison, 'The Precautionary Approach to Fisheries Management: An Environmental Perspective' (1996) 3 Int'l J Marine & Coastal L 301–32.

[21] D. Freestone, 'International Fisheries since Rio . . . ', n. 19 above, 158.

[22] D. Freestone, 'Caution or Precaution: "A Rose By Any Other Name . . . "?' (1999) 10 YbIEL 30.

[23] The sixth Recital of the 1985 Vienna Convention presented the Parties as 'Mindful . . . of the precautionary measures for the protection of the ozone layer which have already been taken at the national and international levels'.

[24] Noting that adverse effects resulted from or were likely to result from human activities which 'modify or are likely to modify the ozone layer', the Parties to the 1987 Montreal Protocol declared themselves 'Determined to protect the ozone layer by taking precautionary measures to control equitably total global emissions of substances that deplete it, with the ultimate objective of their elimination on the basis of developments in scientific knowledge, taking into account technical and economic considerations' (Montreal Protocol, second and sixth Recitals).

[25] The Preambles of the 1998 LRTAP Protocols on POPs and on Heavy Metals state that the Parties are 'resolved to take measures to anticipate, prevent or minimize emissions of persistent organic pollutants, taking into account the application of the precautionary approach, as set forth in principle 15 of the 1992 Rio Declaration on Environment and Development'.

Commission for Europe (UNECE) in Bergen,[26] on 25 May 1989 by the Governing Council of the United Nations Environment Programme (UNEP),[27] in July 1990 by the Council of Ministers of the Organization of African Unity (OAU) meeting in Addis Ababa,[28] in October 1990 by the Ministerial Conference on the Environment of the UN Economic and Social Commission for Asia and the Pacific (ESCAP),[29] and finally in January 1991 by the Environment Ministers of the Organization for Economic Co-Operation and Development (OECD).[30]

It was eventually accorded universal recognition at the UN Conference on Environment and Development[31] in Rio de Janeiro, which resulted in a Declaration and two framework Conventions. Principle 15 of the non-binding 1992 Declaration on Environment and Development declares: 'In order to protect the environment, the precautionary approach shall be widely applied by States according to their capabilities. Where there are threats of serious or irreversible damage, lack of full scientific certainty shall not be used as a reason for postponing cost-effective measures to prevent environmental degradation'.

Similarly, the 1992 Framework Convention on Climate Change (UNFCCC) obliges Parties:

to take precautionary measures to anticipate, prevent or minimise the causes of climate change and mitigate its adverse effects. Where there are threats of serious or irreversible damage, lack of full scientific certainty should not be used as a reason for postponing such measures, taking into account that policies and measures to deal with climate change should be cost-effective so as to ensure global benefits at the lowest possible cost.[32]

The Preamble of the 1992 Convention on Biological Diversity (CBD) also provides that: 'where there is a threat of significant reduction or loss of biological diversity, lack of full scientific certainty should not be used as a reason for postponing measures to avoid or minimize such a threat'.[33]

Although subject to varying interpretations and accorded over twelve different definitions in international treaties and declarations, the precautionary principle is fast becoming a fundamental principle of international environmental law.

---

[26] Bergen Ministerial Declaration on Sustainable Development in the ECE Region, para. 7: 'Where there are threats of serious or irreversible damage, lack of full scientific certainty should not be used as a reason for postponing measures to prevent environmental degradation'.

[27] UNEP Governing Council Decision 15/27 (1989) on the Precautionary Approach to Marine Pollution.

[28] See also the 1991 Bamako Convention on the Prohibition of International Trade in Waste with Africa, not yet in force, which defines the precautionary approach as entailing, *inter alia*, 'preventing the release into the environment of substances which may cause harm to humans or the environment without waiting for scientific proof regarding such harm' (Article 4(3)(f)).

[29] 1990 Bangkok Declaration on Environmentally Sound and Sustainable Development in Asia and the Pacific: '. . . in order to achieve sustainable development, policies must be based on the precautionary principle'.

[30] In their Declaration, the Ministers stated that: 'The absence of full scientific certainty is not an excuse for postponing measures aimed at preventing environmental degradation'.

[31] The principle is also recognized in the non-binding *Agenda 21* of 16 June 1992, UN Doc.A/Conf. 151/26, Vol. III (1992).

[32] Article 3(3).

[33] Ninth Recital.

Since the 1992 Rio Conference, it has been taken up in the majority of bilateral and multilateral international treaties relating to environmental protection.[34] The principle was, for instance, explicitly endorsed in 1994 by CITES[35] and in several of the Agreements on the conservation of migratory species, established under the CMS.[36]

However, the principle has also become a major point of controversy in the strained relationship between trade and environment, with the EC pleading for its expansion while the US calls for trade measures to be based on 'sound science'.[37] On one hand, it is not mentioned explicitly in any of the constitutive agreements of the WTO, although recourse to the principle has been somewhat unsatisfactorily addressed on a case-by-case basis by various WTO dispute settlement panels;[38] on the other hand, the EC did not manage to obtain the inclusion of the principle in any of the WTO agreements during the 1999 Seattle Ministerial conference and the 2001 Doha Ministerial conference of the WTO.

Finally, the year 2000 saw the adoption of two new multilateral agreements where the precautionary principle dominated the negotiations and often led to conflicts between the supporters of the softer 'precautionary approach' and the supporters of a more legalistic 'precautionary principle'. The principle was at the core of the Cartagena Protocol on Biosafety (CPB) adopted under the auspices of the Convention on Biological Diversity (CBD). As the first binding international agreement dealing with modern biotechnology, the CPB articulates what may be the most advanced expression of the precautionary principle in any international agreement.[39] The CPB specifically focuses on the transboundary movement of GMOs, called 'living modified organisms' (LMOs). The Parties to the Protocol reaffirmed the precautionary approach contained in Principle 15 of the Rio Declaration on Environment and Development in several operative provisions of the Protocol.[40] In addition to referring to the precautionary principle, the CPB

[34] For recent developments concerning the precautionary principle in international law, see D. Freestone and E. Hey, 'Origins and Development of the Precautionary Principle', in D. Freestone and E. Hey (eds.), *The Precautionary Principle and International Law* (London, Boston, The Hague: Kluwer Law Int'l, 1995) 3; P. Birnie, 'The Status of Environmental "Soft Law": Trends and Examples with Special Focus on IMO Norms, in Competing Norms', in *The Law of Marine Environmental Protection* (London: Kluwer, 1997), 51.

[35] CITES Resolution of the Ninth Conference of the Parties, known as Conf. 9.24. Eg B. Dickson, 'The Precautionary Principle in CITES: A Critical Assessment' (1999) 39 NRJ 211.

[36] Article 2(2) AEWA; Article 2(4) ACCOBAMS; Article 2(3) of the 2001 Canberra Agreement on the Conservation of Albatrosses and Petrels.

[37] Ph. Sand, *Transnational Environmental Law* (London: Kluwer Law Int'l, 1999) 134.

[38] Although not mentioning the principle, the Sanitary and Phytosanitary Measures (SPS) Agreement does decidedly support the application of crucial aspects of the principle. See the discussion in Subsection 2.1.2.3. below.

[39] P.-T. Stoll, 'Controlling the Risks of GMOs: The Cartagena Protocol on Biosafety and the SPS Agreement' (1999) 10 YbIEL 98; S. Shaw and R. Schwartz, 'The CBP and the WTO: Reflections on the Precautionary Principle' (2000) 10:4 RSDIE 536–42; Cameron Hutchison, 'International Environmental Law Attempts to be "Mutually Supportive" with International Trade Law: A Compatibility Analysis of the CPB with the SPS Agreement' (2001) 4:1 J Int'l Wildlife L & Pol'y 1–34.

[40] 'In accordance with the precautionary approach contained in Principle 15 of the Rio Declaration on Environment and Development, the objective of this Protocol is to contribute to ensuring an

expressly authorizes Parties to refuse the import of LMOs on a precautionary basis.[41] Furthermore, Annex III (4) reflects the principle at the level of risk assessment, as it states that 'lack of scientific knowledge shall not necessarily be interpreted as indicating a particular level, an absence of, or an acceptable risk'.

The precautionary principle is not formulated as an obligation in the CPB, but merely as the right to take a precautionary measure. Furthermore, that right is limited by the obligation of the Party of import to review a decision in the light of new scientific evidence upon request by an exporting country.[42] Nevertheless, the insertion of precautionary provisions in the CPB is significant for potential trade conflicts concerning LMOs. The recognition of the precautionary principle should enrich the SPS Agreement in the context of LMOs by filling the gap in current SPS risk assessment procedures. WTO DSBs might therefore have to take those provisions into account when interpreting ambiguous provisions of the SPS Agreement, such as Article 5(7). This cross-fertilization between the Protocol and CBD and WTO instruments will give substance to the CPB's preambular recognition that trade and environment agreements should be mutually supportive.

The precautionary principle has also recently been at the core of negotiations on two major international conventions on chemical pollutants. Recognizing the risk posed by persistent organic pollutants to human health and the environment, the 2001 Stockholm Convention on Persistent Organic Pollutants (POPs) lays down the precautionary approach as its main objective.[43] Precaution also underpins the listing procedure for new POPs.[44] In addition, the 2001 London IMO Convention on the Control of Harmful Anti-Fouling Systems on Ships, which prohibits the use of harmful organotins in anti-fouling paints used on ships, establishes a precautionary mechanism to prevent the potential future use of other harmful substances in anti-fouling systems.[45]

---

adequate level of protection in the field of the safe transfer, handling and use of living modified organisms resulting from modern biotechnology that may have adverse effects on the conservation and sustainable use of biological diversity, taking also into account risks to human health, and specifically focusing on transboundary movements' (Article 1).

[41] 'Lack of scientific certainty due to insufficient relevant scientific information and knowledge regarding the extent of the potential adverse effects of a living modified organism on the conservation and sustainable use of biological diversity in the Party of import, taking also into account risks to human health, shall not prevent that Party from taking a decision...in order to avoid or minimize such potential adverse effects' (Articles 10(6) and 11(8)).

[42] B. Eggers and R. Mackenzie, 'The Cartagena Protocol on Biosafety' (2000) 3 JIEL 525–43.

[43] Article 4.

[44] Each Party can propose that the Secretariat list a chemical in Annexes A, B and/or C. The POPs Review Committee can decide that the chemical is likely as a result of its long-range environmental transport to lead to significant adverse human health and environmental effects, such that global action is warranted. However, the lack of full scientific certainty shall not prevent the proposal from proceeding (Article 8(7)(a)). 'Taking due account of the recommendations of the Committee, including any scientific uncertainty', the Conference of the Parties is to decide, 'in a precautionary manner', whether to list the chemical in the Annexes of the Convention (Article 8 (7)(e)).

[45] Article 6(3) and (5); Preamble, fifth recital.

The analysis of these historical developments is important from the perspective of creating a new principle of customary law. Owing to its near universality and to the development of certain State practices that recognize its validity, the precautionary principle should be considered a rule of customary law, although this position does not yet enjoy unanimous support.[46] We consider this question in greater depth in Chapter 6 below.

Equally important, the use of the precautionary principle must be complemented by a principle of substitution which requires State authorities to eliminate or reduce risks by replacing one dangerous activity with another, less dangerous, activity. This principle is being increasingly widely recognized in international law, and can be seen in provisions of the POPs and Anti-Fouling Conventions discussed above.[47] Part II below examines how these different principles support and strengthen one another.

2.1.2. *Case-law*

International courts have until recently remained reluctant to accept the precautionary principle, despite its wide recognition in international treaties. Several decisions indicate the absence of a common approach to risk assessment under conditions of uncertainty and to the possibility of invoking this environmental principle. While the International Court of Justice (ICJ) and the European Court of Human Rights (ECtHR) are not favourable either to addressing the principle directly or to adopting a precautionary approach, some elements of the principle can already be found in the case-law of the WTO Dispute Settlement Bodies (DSBs) concerning the SPS Agreement and the International Tribunal for the Law of the Sea (ITLOS).

2.1.2.1. International Court of Justice

In the *Gabcikovo-Nagymaros* case before the ICJ, Hungary invoked the precautionary principle to justify unilateral suspension of works on its section of a dam on the Danube, on the ground that the project was likely to cause significant or irreversible damage to its environment. To justify its suspension of the treaty obligations it had jointly engaged with the former Czechoslovakia, Hungary had to fulfil the requirements of a state of necessity: on one hand, the state of necessity had to be occasioned by an 'essential interest' of the State; on the other hand, the interest had to have been threatened by a 'grave and imminent

---

[46] See the discussion in Chapter 6, Subsection 3.2.3. below.

[47] The substitution principle can also be found in OSPAR Decision 90/2 on a harmonized mandatory control system for the use and reduction of the discharge of offshore chemicals, the 1991 Agreement on the Conservation of Bats in Europe (Article 3(8)), the 1991 Geneva Protocol on Volatile Organic Compounds (VOCs) to the LRATP Convention (Article 2(5)), the 1998 Århus Protocol on Heavy Metals to the LRTAP Convention (Article 3(4)), the 2001 Stockholm POPs Convention (Article 5) and the 2001 London IMO Convention on the Control of Harmful Anti-fouling Systems on Ships (Article 6(4)(a)(v)).

peril'.[48] A State invoking a 'grave and imminent peril' does not have to show current material damage.

While recognizing the seriousness of the environmental concerns put forward by Hungary to justify its refusal to observe the treaty it had concluded with the former Czechoslovakia to construct a system of locks on the Danube,[49] the ICJ refused to accept the existence of a 'grave and imminent peril' because of the uncertain nature of the dangers invoked by the Hungarian authorities.

The Court noted that verification of the 'grave and imminent nature' of the peril invoked by Hungary was a complex process:

serious though these uncertainties might have been they could not, alone, establish the objective existence of a 'peril' in the sense of a component element of a state of necessity. The word 'peril' certainly evokes the idea of 'risk'; that is precisely what distinguishes 'peril' from material damage. But a state of necessity could not exist without a 'peril' duly established at the relevant point in time; the mere apprehension of a possible 'peril' could not suffice in that respect. It could moreover hardly be otherwise, when the 'peril' constituting the state of necessity has at the same time to be 'grave' and 'imminent'. 'Imminence' is synonymous with 'immediacy' or 'proximity' and goes far beyond the concept of 'possibility'. As the International Law Commission emphasized in its commentary, the 'extremely grave and imminent' peril must 'have been a threat to the interest at the actual time'.... That does not exclude, in the view of the Court, that a 'peril' appearing in the long term might be held to be 'imminent' as soon as it is established, at the relevant point in time, that the realization of that peril, however far off it might be, is not thereby any less certain and inevitable.[50]

Hungary was found not to have met this test. As to a specific part of the project where the peril had not yet materialized, the Court concluded that:

the peril claimed by Hungary was to be considered in the long term, and, more importantly, remained uncertain. As Hungary itself acknowledges, the damage that it apprehended had primarily to be the result of some relatively slow natural processes, the effects of which could not easily be assessed...However 'grave' it might have been, it would accordingly have been difficult, in the light of what is said above, to see the alleged peril as sufficiently certain and therefore 'imminent' in 1989.[51]

Consequently, a state of necessity can only be invoked under international law of State responsibility if there is a sufficient degree of certainty and inevitability that a peril will materialize. In a separate opinion, however, Judge Weeramantry saw

---

[48] *Gabcikovo-Nagymaros* (Hungary v. Slovakia), Judgment ICJ Rep [1997] 7, para. 52. Eg A. A-Khavari and D. Rothwell, 'The ICJ and the Danube Dam Case: A Missed Opportunity for International Environmental Law?' (1993) MULR 507; R. Higgins, 'Natural Resources in the Case Law of the International Court' in A. Boyle and D. Freestone (eds.), *International Law and Sustainable Development*, n. 19 above, 103–11.

[49] Judgment, para. 53.

[50] Ibid., para. 54.

[51] Ibid., para. 56.

the precautionary principle as a constituent of the wider legal principle of sustainable development.

2.1.2.2. European Court of Human Rights

Requiring that petitioners demonstrate a significant degree of probability that the rights recognized in the Convention will be violated, the case-law of the organs of the European Convention on Human Rights (ECHR) indicates that these bodies are not keen to take the precautionary principle into account.

In the case of French nuclear testing in French Polynesia, the European Commission of Human Rights granted that the risk of a future violation could, in exceptional circumstances, qualify the applicant as a victim. In that case, however, the victim would have to produce 'reasonable and convincing indications of the probability of the occurrence of a violation that personally concerned him; mere suspicions or conjectures are in this respect insufficient'.[52] Although the applicants had produced several scientific reports to support their fear of a violation of Articles 2(3) and 8 of the ECHR and of Article 1 of Protocol No. 1, the Commission considered that it could not take a position, especially as there was disagreement between the parties and the experts. The Commission added that:

> Merely to invoke the risks inherent in the use of nuclear energy, for both civil and military uses, is not sufficient grounds to claim to be a victim of a violation of the Convention, since many activities give rise to risks. A claim must demonstrate in a defensible and detailed manner that owing to failure by the authorities to take sufficient precautions, the probability that damage will occur is high enough that it constitutes a violation, provided that the repercussions of the act in question are not too remote.

In the case of *LCB v. The United Kingdom*, the ECtHR stated that in going ahead with nuclear tests the United Kingdom had not violated Article 2 of the ECHR since the applicant, who was suffering from leukaemia, had not demonstrated a causal link between the exposure of her father to radiation and her subsequent illness. The British authorities could only have been required to inform a serviceman about the risks of nuclear radiation if 'it had appeared likely at that time that any such exposure . . . to radiation might have endangered a real risk' to the health of the father of the applicant. In other words, it was not reasonable to expect the national authorities to provide health advice during the testing period unless, at that time, it had appeared likely that radiation could entail real risks.[53] In its decision in *McGinley and Egan v. United Kingdom*, the ECtHR judged that the British authorities had fulfilled their positive obligation according to Article 8 of the ECHR to inform the persons engaged in hazardous activities about radiation risks.[54] Even when involved in activities that could give rise to long-term health effects, the applicants must demonstrate that, at the time of the

---

[52] Report of 4 December 1995, re. No. 28204–95.
[53] *LCB v. United Kingdom* Case, 9 June 1998, Reports 1998–III, para. 38.
[54] *McGinley and Egan v. United Kingdom* Case, 9 June 1998, Reports 1998–III, para. 98.

occurrence in question, the national authorities withheld relevant documents concerning the risks of ionising radiation. In the absence of such proof, they may not claim a violation of their right to respect for their private lives based on a past failure to provide them with access to relevant information.

The ECtHR ruled in the case *Balmer-Schafroth v. Switzerland* that the connection between the decision by the Swiss Federal Council to continue operating an outdated nuclear power plant and the right to protection of physical integrity invoked by the petitioners was 'too tenuous and remote' for the latter to invoke the right to a fair hearing by a tribunal within the meaning of Article 6(1) of the ECHR.[55] Even if the victims had successfully challenged the technical defects of the plant, they had not convincingly demonstrated a causal relationship between the alleged risk and their right to protection of their physical integrity. They had not established:

a direct link between the operating conditions of the plant which were contested by them and their right to protection of their physical integrity, as they failed to show that the operation of M. power station exposed them personally to a danger that was not only serious but also specific and, above all, imminent. In the absence of such a finding, the effects on the population of the measures which the Federal Council could have ordered to be taken in the instant case remained hypothetical.

This case-law, which represents a missed opportunity from the perspective of the precautionary principle, was confirmed in *Athanassoglou v. Switzerland*.[56] As in the *Balmer-Schafroth* case, the ECtHR had to decide whether the link between an administrative decision to operate a nuclear plant and the applicants' rights to adequate protection of their life, physical integrity, and property was sufficiently close to bring Article 6(1) of the ECHR into play and was not too tenuous or remote. The Court did not perceive any material difference between this second case and that of *Balmer-Schafroth*. The applicants considered that only a court could possess the independence to assess if the authorities had taken proper account of a 'high residual risk of unforeseen scenarios and of an unforeseen sequence of events leading to serious damage'. The Court judged, however, that how best to regulate the use of nuclear power was a policy decision for each Contracting State to take according to its democratic processes and that Article 6(1) cannot be read as dictating any one scheme rather than another.[57]

2.1.2.3. WTO Dispute Settlement Bodies

WTO dispute settlement bodies (DSBs) have already tackled the precautionary principle in a number of cases concerning health measures. These cases are of

---

[55] *Balmer-Schafroth and Others v. Switzerland* Case, 26 August 1997, Reports 1997–IV. In a dissenting opinion, Judge Pettiti expressed the view that such reasoning 'appeared to have ignored the whole trend of international institutions and public international law towards protecting persons and heritage', particularly as seen in 'the development of the precautionary principle and the principle of conservation of the common heritage'.

[56] Case, 6 April 2000, not yet reported.

[57] Para. 54.

interest to environmental lawyers because the public health issues that they raise concerning the nature of risk assessment may be similar to issues that arise in environmental cases.

In two decisions of 18 August 1997 a WTO Panel determined that identification of the risk posed by hormones in meat was a condition *sine qua non* for the risk assessment required by Article 5 of the Agreement on the Application of Sanitary and Phytosanitary Measures (SPS Agreement). Failing such an identification, the European Community was not justified in having recourse to the precautionary principle to justify its ban on hormones in beef, which was being challenged.[58] According to the Panel, the precautionary principle is applicable only in the case of provisional measures under Article 5(7) of the Agreement. The Panel could not have been clearer: any measure that restricts trade must be based on fully assessed risks and not on the uncertainties inherent in scientific research.[59]

The Appellate Body in this case, for its part, accorded a broader role to the precautionary principle but left open the way in which it should be applied.[60] While the Appellate Body stated that it was 'unnecessary, and probably imprudent' for it to take a position on the legal status of the precautionary principle,[61] it nevertheless confirmed that the precautionary principle 'finds reflection in Article 5(7) of the Agreement', where it is not expressly recognized.[62] Furthermore, it noted that the principle is reflected in the sixth paragraph of the SPS Agreement's Preamble and in Article 3(3), both of which recognize the right of Members individually to determine the appropriate level of sanitary protection even if this is different from the level of protection which would be achieved by

---

[58] *EC Measures Concerning Meat and Meat Products (Hormones)*, Complaint by the United States, OMC WT/DS 26/R/USA of 18 August 1997; *EC Measures Concerning Meat and Meat Products (Hormones)*, Complaint by Canada, OMC WT/DS 48/R/Can of 18 August 1997. For a critical examination of these decisions, see S. Deimann, 'WTO Panel on EC Measures concerning Meat and Meat Products' (1997) 2 Elni Newsl. 1.

[59] Ibid., sub. VIII D5 (b)(iii).

[60] Appellate Body Report in *EC Measures Affecting Meat and Meat Products (Hormones)* ('EC Hormones') (WT/DS26&48/AB/R), adopted 13 February 1998 [hereinafter Appellate Body, *EC Hormones*]. Eg Th. Douma, 'The Beef Hormones Dispute and the Use of National Standards under WTO Law' (1999) EELR 137; B. Eggers, 'Die Entscheidung des WTO Appellate Body im Hormonfall: Doch ein Recht auf Vorsorge?' (1998) 5–6 EuZW 147; D. Hurst, 'Hormones: European Communities-Measures Affecting Meat and Meat Products' (1988) 9 Eur J Int'l L 182; K. Van der Borght, 'Risico-evaluatie, Groeihormonen en de WTO' (1998) 4 TMR 239; L. Hughes, 'Limiting the Jurisdiction of Dispute Settlement Panels: The WTO Appellate Body Beef Hormone Decision' (1998) Int'l Envt L Rev 915; G. Goh and A. Ziegler, 'A Real World where People Live and Work and Die: Australian SPS Measures after the WTO Appellate Body's Decision in the Hormones Case' (1998) 32:5 JWT 271; V.R. Walker, 'Keeping the WTO from Becoming the "World Trans-Science Organisation": Scientific Uncertainty, Science Policy, and Factfindings in the Growth Hormones Dispute' (1998) Cornell ILJ 251; J. Pauwelyn, 'The WTO Agreement on SPS Measures as applied in the First Three SPS Disputes' (1999) J Int'l EL 641; R.D. Thomas, 'Where's the Beef? Mad Cows and the Plight of the SPS Agreement' (1999) 32 Vand J Transnat'l L 487; C. Noiville, 'Principe de précaution et Organisation mondiale du Commerce: Le cas du commerce alimentaire' (2000) 2 J D Int'l 263.

[61] Concerning the customary value of the principle, see the discussion in Chapter 6, Subsection 3.2.3. below.

[62] Para. 124.

measures based on 'international standards, guidelines or recommendations'. However, the precautionary principle does not by itself, and without a clear textual provision to that effect, relieve a Panel of the duty to apply the normal principles of treaty interpretation. The Appellate Body consequently held that the EC ban on hormone-treated beef was incompatible with the SPS Agreement: a principle such as precaution may not override the provisions of Article 5(1) and (2) of the SPS Agreement.[63]

Nonetheless, the Appellate Body in that case endorsed a precautionary approach. It drew a clear distinction between risk assessment, which must be based on a scientific approach, and the political decision (risk management) that determines the level of protection, which may be 'zero risk'. The results of the risk assessment must sufficiently warrant—that is to say, reasonably support—the SPS measure at stake. Moreover, it agreed with the EC that risk assessment cannot be restricted to laboratory testing but must also address potentially adverse effects to human health in the real world. What matters is not only risk ascertainable by standard laboratory methods but tangible risk in the 'real world' and its 'actual potential for adverse effects on human health in the real world where people live and work and die'.[64] Furthermore, divergent scientific opinions coming from qualified and respected sources can be taken into account by Governments acting responsibly and in good faith. It also rejected the inclusion of the word 'probability' in the panel's interpretation of the definition of risk assessment, considering that it introduced a quantitative dimension of the notion of risk and therefore implied a 'higher degree or a threshold of potentiality or possibility', whereas the word 'potential' in paragraph 4 of Annex A of the Agreement only relates to the possibility of an event occurring.[65]

The second dispute in which the precautionary principle was invoked, *Australia Salmon*, arose from a decision by Australia to ban salmon coming from Canada. The Australian measure was based on a risk assessment that, according to the Panel, 'addressed and to some extent evaluated a series of risk reduction factors, in particular, on a disease-by-disease basis'. Referring to its *EC Hormones* Report, the Appellate Body stated in its 20 October 1998 report that in this kind of case a risk assessment must evaluate, among other things, the likelihood of adverse health effects: 'the "risk" evaluated in a risk assessment must be an "ascertainable risk"'; theoretical uncertainty is not the kind of risk which, under Article 5(1) of the SPS Agreement, is to be assessed. This does not mean, however,

---

[63] According to Article 5(1), 'Members shall ensure that their sanitary or phytosanitary measures are based on an assessment, as appropriate to the circumstances, of the risks to human, animal or plant life or health, taking into account risk assessment techniques developed by the relevant international organizations'. Article 5(2) states: 'In the assessment of risks, Members shall take into account available scientific evidence; relevant processes and production methods; relevant inspection, sampling and testing methods; prevalence of specific diseases or pests; existence of pest- or disease-free areas; relevant ecological and environmental conditions; and quarantine or other treatment'.

[64] Para. 187.

[65] Paras. 183–4.

that a Member cannot determine its own appropriate level of protection to be 'zero risk'. However, in the *Australia Salmon* case, the Appellate Body concluded that the import prohibition on fresh, chilled, or frozen salmon was not based on a risk assessment as required by Article 5(1) of the SPS Agreement and that Australia had therefore acted at variance with this provision.[66]

Finally, in a report of 22 February 1999, *Japan Varietals*, the Appellate Body again based a decision on the *EC Hormones* case to reject direct application of the precautionary principle and rule against a Japanese import prohibition that was not based on a risk assessment.[67]

Although the SPS Agreement provides little guidance as to the characteristics of risk assessment, the above case-law provides important lessons which could be transposed to other types of risk assessment procedures, particularly in the field of environmental protection. Those principles will help us at a later stage to elaborate recommendations for reconceptualizing risk assessement procedures.[68] The following conclusions can be drawn from the *EC Hormones*, *Australia Salmon*, and *Japan Varietals* cases.

—Risk assessment can be conducted either quantitatively or qualitatively.[69] When a Panel is charged with determining whether sufficient scientific evidence exists to warrant a WTO member maintaining a particular measure, it 'may of course, and should, bear in mind that responsible, representative governments act from perspectives of prudence and precaution where the risk of irreversible, eg life-terminating, damage to human health is concerned.'[70]

—Risk assessment can set out both the prevailing view representing the mainstream of scientific opinion and the opinions of scientists taking a divergent view.[71]

—There is no requirement for a proper risk assessment to establish a 'minimum magnitude' or threshold level of degree of risk.[72] An SPS member's acceptable level of risk could even be set at 'zero risk'; therefore a risk assessment indicating a slight degree of risk can serve as a valid basis for State action.

—That said, the risk must be 'ascertainable' and not 'theoretical', since science can never provide absolute certainty that a given substance will never give

---

[66] Appellate Body Report in *Australia-Measures Affecting the Importation of Salmon*, WT/DS18/AB/R, adopted 6 November 1998 (hereinafter Appellate Body, *Australia Salmon*).

[67] Appellate Body Report in *Japan Varietals, Japan Measures Affecting Agricultural Products*, WT/DS76/AB/R, adopted 19 March 1999 (hereinafter Appellate Body, *Japan Varietals*).

[68] See the discussion in Section 4 below.

[69] Appellate Body, *EC Hormones*, paras. 184–6; *Australia Salmon*, para. 124.

[70] Appellate Body, *EC Hormones*, para. 194.

[71] Ibid., para. 194.

[72] While the Panel required a risk assessment to establish a minimum magnitude of risk, the Appellate Body noted that imposition of such a quantitative requirement finds no basis in the SPS Agreement (Appellate Body, *EC Hormones*, para. 186). This was confirmed in a recent report of the panel (*European Communities—Measures Affecting the Prohibition of Asbestos and Asbestos Products* (WT/DS 135), para. 8.171) and the Appellate Body in the Asbestos case (*European Communities—Measures Affecting the Prohibition of Asbestos and Asbestos Products*, WTO Doc. WT/DS135/AB/R (12 March 2001), para. 167) (hereinafter Appellate Body, *EC Asbestos*).

rise to adverse health effects.[73] However, the risk need not be 'ascertainable' in a scientific laboratory operating under strictly controlled conditions; actual potential for adverse effects on human health in the real world where people 'live, work and die' must also be taken into account.[74]

—Risk assessment criteria are ambiguous: on one hand, the object and purpose of the SPS Agreement justify the examination and evaluation of all such risks for human health whatever their precise and immediate origin; on the other hand, any risk assessment must be sufficiently specific (risk assessment must be conducted for each substance).[75]

—The obligation that an SPS measure may not be maintained without sufficient scientific evidence requires that there be a 'rational or objective relationship between the SPS measure and the scientific evidence'.[76] Whether such a rational relationship exists between an SPS measure and scientific evidence is to be determined on a 'case-by-case basis' and will depend upon the particular circumstances of a case, including the characteristics of the measure at issue and the quality and quantity of the scientific evidence.[77] Although it is not entirely clear, the Appellate Body's analysis suggests that this 'rational relationship' standard is quite easily satisfied.[78]

Once a proper risk assessment has been conducted and in cases where an 'ascertainable risk' is detected, WTO Members have the right to establish their own appropriate level of sanitary protection, which may be higher (ie more cautious) than that implied in existing international standards, guidelines, and recommendations.[79] Members are not required to carry out a cost–benefit analysis. Therefore, the WTO Member concerned must make a 'societal value judgement' as to whether or not it can accept a given risk. This requires a qualitative decision involving social and political consideration.

In cases where it is not possible to conduct a proper risk assessment, Article 5(7) of the SPS Agreement allows Members to adopt and maintain a provisional SPS measure. According to the Panel and the Appellate Body, this provision incorporates the precautionary principle. However, it must be stressed that it does so only to a limited extent,[80] as this safety clause is submitted to four requirements, which are cumulative:

---

[73] Appellate Body, *EC Hormones*, para. 186. In the *Australia Salmon* case the Appellate Body stated that it will not be sufficient for governments to impose regulations simply on the basis of the 'theoretical' risk that underlies all scientific uncertainty (para. 129).

[74] Appellate Body, *EC Hormones*, para. 187.

[75] Ibid., para. 206.

[76] Ibid., paras. 186, 189, 193, 197, 253.

[77] Appellate Body, *EC Hormones*, para. 195; *Japan Varietals*, para. 84.

[78] D. Hurst, n. 60 above, 182.

[79] Appellate Body, *EC Hormones*, para. 124.

[80] Th. Douma, 'The Beef Hormones Dispute', n. 60 above, 140; C. Noiville and P.-H. Gouyon, 'Principe de précaution et organismes génétiquement modifiés' in P. Kourilsky and G. Viney, *Le principe de précaution* (Paris: La Documentation Française-O. Jacob 2000) 306.

(1) the 'relevant scientific information' must be insufficient;

(2) the measure should be adopted 'on the basis of available pertinent information';

(3) the Member must seek to obtain the 'additional information necessary for a more objective assessment of risk', which must be sought in order to allow the Member to conduct 'a more objective assessment of risk';[81]

(4) the Member is obliged to 'review the . . . measure accordingly within a reasonable period of time'. The requirement of a 'reasonable period of time' must be established on a case-by-case basis and depends on the specific circumstances of each case, including the difficulty of obtaining the additional information needed for review and the characteristics of the SPS measure.[82]

Whenever one of these four requirements is not met, the measure at issue is inconsistent with Article 5(7).[83]

2.1.2.4. International Tribunal for the Law of the Sea

The ITLOS order of 27 August 1999 in the *Southern Bluefin Tuna* cases seems to view the precautionary principle in a much more favourable light than decisions by other international courts. In those cases, there was disagreement between Australia and New Zealand on one hand and Japan on the other concerning an experimental fishing programme for southern bluefin tuna being carried out by the Japanese authorities.[84] The complainants alleged that Japan, by unilaterally undertaking experimental fishing, had failed to comply with its obligation to co-operate in conserving southern bluefin tuna stock. The provisional measures requested by New Zealand were, *inter alia*, that the parties' fishing practices be consistent with the precautionary principle pending a final settlement of the dispute.

Although ITLOS could not conclusively assess the scientific evidence presented by the parties, since there was scientific uncertainty regarding the conservation measures to be taken,[85] it found that action should be taken as a matter of urgency to avert further deterioration of southern bluefin tuna stock. Even

---

[81] Appellate Body, *Japan Varietals*, para. 92.

[82] Ibid., para. 93. The CPB does not impose a comparable follow-up obligation for precautionary measures taken under its Articles 10(6) or 11(8). Article 7(2) of EC Regulation No. 178/2002 laying down the general principles and requirements of food law, establishing the European Food Safety Authority, and laying down procedures in matters of food safety (hereinafter EC Regulation No. 178/ 2002 laying down the general principles and requirements of food law) requires that the precautionary measures 'shall be reviewed within a reasonable period of time, depending on the nature of the risk to life or health identified and the type of scientific information needed to clarify the scientific uncertainty and to conduct a more comprehensive risk assessment'.

[83] Ibid., para. 89.

[84] *Southern Bluefin Tuna Cases* (Australia v. Japan; New Zealand v. Japan), Provisional measures, Order of 27 August 1999 (ITLOS, cases nos. 3 and 4) (hereinafter, Order nos. 3 and 4). Eg H.S. Schiffman, 'The Southern Bluefin Tuna Case: ITLOS Hears Its First Fishery Dispute' (1999) 3 J Int'l Wildlife L & Pol'y 318; B. Kwiatkowska (2000) 24 AJIL 150; K. Leggett, 'The Southern Bluefin Tuna Cases: ITLOS Order on Provisional Measures' (2000) 9 RECIEL 75.

[85] Order, paras. 73 and 74.

though the precautionary principle is not invoked as such,[86] ITLOS does acknowledge it:[87]

Considering that the conservation of living resources of the sea is an element in the protection and preservation of the environment,

[...]

Considering that, in the view of the Tribunal, the parties should in the circumstances act with prudence and caution to ensure that effective conservation measures are taken to prevent serious harm to the stock of southern bluefin tuna.[88]

As a result, ITLOS prescribed a limitation to experimental fishing in order to prevent further damage to tuna stock. While it is true that ITLOS urged caution rather than precaution, the fact remains that it prescribes *de facto* precautionary measures.[89] The Tribunal's recommendation indicated an awareness of the environmental rights and duties of States in modern international law, based on the standard of preventing 'serious harm to the marine environment' set forth in Article 290(1) UNCLOS. This standard broadens the grounds on which provisional measures may be ordered so as to prevent serious harm to the marine environment. In this case, both parties were required to refrain from conducting experimental programmes that involved catching bluefin tuna.

In the *Mox* case Ireland requested provisional measures to suspend immediately the authorization of the Mox plant at the Sellafield nuclear power station in Cumbria. Ireland argued, among other things, that the United Kingdom had breached its obligations under various Articles of UNCLOS, including failing to take the necessary measures to prevent, reduce, and control pollution of the marine environment of the Irish Sea from intended or unintentional releases of radioactive materials and wastes from the plant. According to Ireland, the precautionary principle required the UK to demonstrate that no harm would arise from discharges of these Mox operations.

ITLOS did not find that the urgency of the situation required prescribing the provisional measures requested by Ireland. Nevertheless, the Tribunal considered that 'prudence and caution require that Ireland and the United Kingdom cooperate in exchanging information concerning risks or effects of the operation of the Mox plant and in devising ways to deal with them, as appropriate'.[90]

---

[86] Judge Laing observed that the Tribunal adopted 'the precautionary approach rather than the precautionary principle'; he concluded that 'adopting an approach, rather than a principle, appropriately imports a certain degree of flexibility and tends, though not dispositively, to underscore reticence about making premature pronouncements about desirable normative structures' (Separate opinion of Judge Laing at paras. 13 and 19).

[87] A. Fabra, 'The LOSC and the Implementation of the Precautionary Principle' (1999) 10 YbIEL 17.

[88] Order, paras. 70, 77.

[89] D. Freestone, 'Caution or Precaution?', n. 22 above, 29.

[90] Order no. 10, para. 84. As Judge Wolfrum stated in his separate Opinion, 'Ireland could not, for several reasons, rely on the precautionary principle or approach in this case even if it were to be accepted that it is part of international customary international law'. If ITLOS had followed Ireland's argument it would have had to decide on the merits, thus going beyond the scope of provisional measures.

2.2. European Community law

2.2.1. Primary law

The precautionary principle was not among the first group of principles incorporated in the Treaty of Rome through its amendment by the Single European Act (SEA). It had to await the adoption of the Maastricht Treaty to take its place—without definition—beside the principles of prevention, rectification at source, and the polluter pays.[91] Since then, however, the precautionary principle has also found its way into the Preamble of the Agreement on the European Economic Area (EEA).

Since Article 6 of the EC Treaty requires that environmental protection requirements be integrated into the definition and implementation of all EC policies and activities, and since according to Article 174(2) EC environment policy must be based on the precautionary principle, it follows that this principle should be reflected in all EC policies.[92]

2.2.2. Soft law

The precautionary principle has not been defined in the EC Treaty. To fill this gap the European Commission produced a Communication in February 2000 that seeks to inform all interested parties—in particular the European Parliament, the Council, and the Member States—of the manner in which the Commission applies or intends to apply the principle when faced with taking decisions relating to the containment of risk.[93]

The Communication describes precaution as a risk management tool which is part of a risk analysis framework rather than an overall guide to implementation. According to this argument, precautionary action should only be taken after experts prepare an 'objective' quantitative risk assessment.[94] Precaution is seen as a temporary measure pending further scientific information. The importance of assessing alternatives to potentially harmful activities is completely

---

[91] In the absence of EC legislation that sets forth the precautionary principle either explicitly or implicitly, courts may not invoke this or other principles set out in Article 130R of the EC Treaty, since these are addressed solely to Community institutions (Queen's Bench Division, 3 October 1994, *R v. Secretary of State for Trade and Industry, ex parte Duddridge and Others* (1995) 2 JEL 237, comment by D. Hugues).

[92] N. de Sadeleer, 'Le statut du principe de précaution en droit communautaire' (2001) 1 Cah Dr Eur 79–120. For instance, it remains to be seen if the obligation for the EC institutions to ensure high health and consumer protection levels according to Articles 152 and 153 of the EC Treaty includes the adoption of precautionary measures.

[93] Communication from the Commission on the Precautionary Principle (COM(2000) 1), para. 2. The Communication was intended to build a consensus among the various Commission Directorates General, paving the way for a common position among EC institutions and a common understanding among the Member States.

[94] According to the Commission, 'The implementation of an approach based on the precautionary principle should start with a scientific evaluation, as complete as possible, and where possible, identifying at each stage the degree of scientific uncertainty' (para. 4). Furthermore, 'Decision-makers have to obtain, through a structured approach, a scientific evaluation, as complete as possible, of the risk to the environment, or health, in order to select the most appropriate course of action' (para. 6.1.).

missing from the Communication. On a more positive note, however, the Communication emphasizes the need to incorporate qualitative as well as quantitative scientific evidence, acknowledges that protection of health and the environment should be put before economic concerns, and encourages a decision-making procedure that is transparent and involves all interested parties as early as possible and to the extent reasonably possible. According to the Commission's Communication, determination of what constitutes an 'acceptable' level of risk for society is an eminently *political* responsibility. The Commission consequently claims that it has the right to fix levels of protection—particularly of the environment, and of human, animal, and plant health—although it acknowledges that the precautionary principle must be submitted to the principles of proportionality and non-discrimination, to cost–benefit analysis and to review. Thus, the thresholds determined in the Communication do not constrain the EC institutions to act in a strictly determined manner.[95]

The European Council adopted a resolution endorsing 'the broad lines' of the Commission's Communication at Nice in December 2000. This considers that 'use should be made of the principle where the possibility of harmful effects on health or the environment has been identified and preliminary scientific evaluation, based on the available data, proves inconclusive for assessing the level of risk'. The Council took the matter one step further, stating that the principle should apply to Member State policies as well as EC institutions. The Communication also asked the European Commission to incorporate the principle when drawing up legislative proposals and in all its actions.

2.2.3. Secondary law

The hopes placed in the precautionary principle are just beginning to find concrete expression, although this development appears more advanced in the field of public health than in that of environment.[96] Its main appearance in

---

[95] Referring to the Fifth Action Programme, the ECJ judged that the Programme was 'designed to provide a framework for defining and implementing Community environment policy, but does not lay down legal rules of a mandatory nature (Case C-142/94P, *Rovigo* [1996] ECR I-6669, para. 32).

[96] This is particularly the case for food safety. Eg S. Schlacke, 'Foodstuffs Law and the Precautionary Principle: Normative Bases, Secondary Law and Institutional Tendencies' in C. Joerges, K.-H. Ladeur and E. Vos (eds.), *Integrating Expertise into Regulatory Decision-Making* (Baden-Baden: Nomos, 1997) 169; R. Streinz, 'The Precautionary Principle in Food Law' (1998) 8 : 4 EFLR 413–32; L. Gonzalez Vaqué, L. Ehring, and C. Jacquet, 'Le principe de précaution dans la législation communautaire et nationale relative à la protection de la santé' (1999) 1 RMUE 79–128. EC Regulation No. 178/2002 laying down the general principles and requirements of food law reflects the Communication on the Precautionary Principle in relation to its application in food law. According to this Regulation, the precautionary principle is relevant in those specific circumstances where risk managers have identified reasonable grounds for concern that an unacceptable level of risk to health exists but the supporting information and data may not be sufficiently complete to enable a comprehensive risk assessment to be made. When faced with these specific circumstances, decision makers or risk managers may take measures to protect health based on the precautionary principle while seeking more complete scientific and other data in order to ensure the high level of health protection provided for by the Community. This Regulation is in step with the growing international acceptance of the principle as it applies in the field of food safety.

the field of environment is in regulations concerning dangerous substances and genetically modified organisms (GMOs) as they relate to people and the environment.

2.2.3.1. Biotechnology

The extent to which GMOs pose a risk of adverse effects on the environment or human health is controversial and remains uncertain. The ultimate avatar of the Promethean myth, biotechnology has been the favoured field for implementation of the precautionary principle in EC law. Its enormous possibilities, lightning progress, and seemingly limitless applications have led EC law-makers to adopt two directives intended to cope with its potential dangers.

While Directive 90/219/EEC on the contained use of genetically modified micro-organisms shares a certain number of mechanisms with the Seveso Directive,[97] one fundamental difference remains. Directive 90/219/EEC introduces a new stage in risk prevention by requiring users of modified micro-organisms to assess the risks their activities pose to human health and the environment even when these are still in doubt.[98] As amended by Directive 98/81/EEC, its Article 4 leads to the adoption of a precautionary approach by providing that: 'where there is doubt as to which class is appropriate for the proposed controlled use, the more stringent protective measures shall be applied, unless sufficient evidence, in agreement with the competent authority, justifies the application of less stringent measures'.

This provision reflects the precautionary principle, as it provides for containment and other protective measures appropriate to a higher classification 'until such time as less stringent measures have been justified by appropriate data'.[99]

The deliberate release of GMOs has been regulated by Directive 90/220/EEC on the deliberate release into the environment of genetically modifed organisms, which was designed to control both experimental and market releases of GMOs. In the early 1990s this Directive represented a conceptual revolution by having a law anticipate a risk that was poorly understood. This constituted a genuine paradigm shift, from both the scientific and legal points of view.[100] Directive 90/220/EEC was based on the idea that Member States could easily reach agreement on each application for placing new GMOs on the market. However, such agreement has proved difficult to achieve in practice; the procedure appears unsuited for its intended purpose. An earlier procedure had been criticized for not taking the precautionary principle into account, as it allowed a single

---

[97] In the framework of the latter Directive technological risks are sufficiently well known to allow the adequate preparation of safeguard measures, so that a system of preliminary authorisation and the elaboration of emergency and public information plans are sufficient to allow the authorities to ensure an acceptable level of safety.

[98] Article 1 and Recitals four, six and especially seven of Directive 90/219/EEC: 'Whereas the precise nature and scale of risks associated with genetically modified micro-organisms are not yet fully known and the risk involved must be assessed case by case . . .'.

[99] Third Recital, amended Directive.

[100] C. Noiville, *Ressources génétiques et droit* (Paris: Pédone, 1997) 206 *et seq.*

Member State to block Council refusal to approve the marketing of a GMO. The case of genetically modifed maize clearly demonstrated these dysfunctions.[101] As a result, Member States decided to impose a moratorium on the placing on the market of all new GMOs, based on the precautionary principle.

As the result of this moratorium, Directive 90/220/EEC was replaced by Directive 2001/18/EC in 2001; the latter seems to better implement the precautionary principle, which is explicitly set out in several provisions.[102] In accordance with the precautionary principle, the objective of this Directive is 'to protect human health and the environment'; national authorities can only permit GMOs if it is ensured that 'all appropriate measures are taken to avoid adverse effects on human health and the environment which might arise from the deliberate release or the placing on the market of GMOs'.[103] According to its Article 4, 'Member States, in accordance with the precautionary principle, shall ensure that all appropriate measures are taken to avoid adverse effects on human health and the environment which might arise from the deliberate release or the placing on the market of GMOs'.

In addition, a number of provisions of the new Directive implicitly implement the precautionary principle. Applicants must carry out an environmental risk assessment of the GMO being proposed for authorization. Whereas the former

---

[101] The consent procedure in the 90/220/EEC Directive involves both national and EC authorities. The national authorities are responsible for submitting applications to a risk assessment. If a national competent authority takes a decision in favour of the application, it must then send the dossier to the European Commission, which must in turn forward it to other national authorities. If objections are put forward (which has until now been the case) a Regulatory Committee must take a decision on the requested authorization. If no decision is taken by the Regulatory Committee, the question of whether to authorize the GMO passes to the Council of Ministers. Under the former comitology procedure, Ministers could only refuse approval by unanimity, ie all 15 Member States must vote against. In other words, a single Member State could stop the others from refusing approval of a GMO. If no decision was taken by the Council of Ministers, the final decision reverted back to the European Commission, which has consistently been in favour of authorizing deliberate releases of GMOs. The Commission had in some cases decided that a particular GMO had to be placed on the market or released into the environment even though not all the Member States agreed. The most notable example was the case of Novartis Bt 176 maize, which is genetically modified to be both herbicide-tolerant and insect-resistant and carries a 'marker' gene conferring resistance to a widely used antibiotic, Ampicillin. The Commission authorized the placing on the market of this Bt maize despite opposition from 13 Member States. This led Austria and Luxembourg to ban this type of genetically modified maize. The French Council of State also suspended authorization of this maize (see the discussion in Subsection 2.3.2. below). See also EC Decision 1999/468/EC, which amends the decision-making procedure at the level of the Council of Ministers (qualified majority instead of unanimity). Eg W.T. Douma and M. Matthee, 'Towards new EC rules on the Release of GMOs' (1999) 8 RECIEL 152; B. Sheridan, *EU Biotechnology Law and Practice* (Benbridge: Palladion Law Press, 2001) 29–96.

[102] Directive 2001/18/EC on the deliberate release into the environment of genetically modified organisms and repealing Council Directive 90/220/EEC (hereinafter Directive 2001/18/EC on the deliberate release of GMOs). Eg N. de Sadeleer and C. Noiville, 'La Directive Communautaire 2001/18/EC sur la dissémination volontaire d'organismes génétiquement modifiés dans l'environnement: Un examen critique' 58 (2002) JDTE 81.

[103] Articles 1 and 4. These explicit references to the principle in Directive 2001/18/EC are of the utmost importance, as Member States are obliged to abide by the principle when carrying out risk assessments. The precautionary principle will thus apply the actions of both the EC institutions and the Member States. See the discussion later in this Chapter.

Directive 90/220/EEC provided no indication of what types of risks must be subjected to such an assessment, the new definition of 'environmental risk assessment' represents an improvement on the earlier text, in that it incorporates the thrust of the precautionary principle by specifying that 'direct or indirect, immediate or delayed risks' shall be evaluated by the national competent authority.[104] When performing the risk assessment, assessors may not 'discount any potential adverse effect on the basis that it is unlikely to occur'.[105] The authorization system of Directive 2001/18/EC also seeks to guarantee safety by requiring a case-by-case evaluation of potential risks.[106] Product approvals for GMOs will expire within ten years and can only be renewed if monitoring carried out during this period shows no negative results. The notifier would then need to apply for a renewal of the consent.[107] The new Directive also requires that traceability be ensured through labelling.[108]

Nevertheless, owing to its legal basis (Article 95 of the EC Treaty) Directive 2001/18/EC deals not only with the protection of the environment and human health, but also with the functioning of the internal market. The Directive provides that once the introduction of a product has been permitted in one Member State, other Member States may no longer prohibit, restrict, or impede its placing on the market in their territory.[109] A Member State may temporarily prohibit or restrict the use and/or sale of that product on its territory only in the case of 'new or additional information [being] made available since the date of the consent' that would lead it to consider that the authorized product constitutes a risk to human health or the environment.[110] Thus, exclusionary measures may only be taken to protect the environment or human health and must be of a provisional nature.

2.2.3.2. Dangerous substances

Set up in the early days of the environmental debate, EC chemicals policy consists of a complex regulatory system made up of an intricate network of directives and regulations. These instruments were primarily motivated by a desire to complete the internal market and have only recently begun to consider

---

[104] Article 2(8) and Annex II.   [105] Annex II, C(2)(1).   [106] Article 4(3).

[107] Article 17. Without this requirement, GM products could continue to be sold while discussions take place about whether there really is evidence of harm. This limitation of the authorization is a clear expression of the precautionary principle, as the authorization is not unconditional.

[108] Articles 4(6), 21, and 26.

[109] Article 22.

[110] Article 23. The ECJ ruled in the case *Greenpeace France* that if new evidence appears of an environmental or health risk which was unknown at an earlier stage of the risk assessment procedure, the Member State can, according to the safeguard clause, refuse to give its 'consent in writing' at the second stage of the procedure. According to Advocate General Mischo, the possibility of acting on the safeguard clause at any time 'should, it seems to us, reassure the most demanding [critic] that the precautionary principle is being scrupulously respected' (Opinion of the 25th November 1999, paras. 86–87). However, the Advocate General stated that such a ban would be exceptional (para. 89). See our analysis in Subsection 2.2.4.3. below of Case C-6/99, *Greenpeace France* [2000] ECR I-1676, para. 47.

environmental concerns. Owing to a huge backlog of data sets, this system has been unable to cope with the increasing problems caused by hazardous chemicals.

Without going into the details of risk assessment methodology, we discuss briefly how the regulatory approach to new and existing substances and directives covering certain categories of chemicals such as pesticides and biocides are coping with scientific uncertainty. This analysis will serve as an empirical basis for further discussion on how risk assessment and risk management procedures could be conceptualized in a different manner.

The sixth amendment to Council Directive 67/548/EEC on the classification, packaging, and labelling of dangerous substances, which established an EC-wide notification procedure for newly marketed substances (ie substances placed on the market before 1981) was intended to increase knowledge of the effects of substances and thereby facilitate subsequent decision-making. Since 1982 producers and importers of new substances have been obliged to notify the competent national authority about and provide full information on any substance that is to be placed on the market. The notifier may furnish the competent authority with a preliminary risk assessment. Existing substances are exempt from notification.[111] On the basis of the data provided by the manufacturer or the importer, the competent authority assesses the 'real and potential' risks to man and the environment posed by the notified substance according to the provisions of Commission Directive 93/67/EEC.[112] After the European Commission has provided this information to all other Member States, the Community decides by way of a committee procedure whether and how to classify the new chemical substance. From a precautionary point of view, the procedure is marred by a number of inadequacies. First, the notifier supplies 'information necessary for evaluating the foreseeable risks' to the competent authority. The emphasis is clearly on the collection of scientific data and test results, while contextual issues pertaining to risk (such as familiarity, immediacy, latency, scope, or novelty) are not included in the notification.[113] In addition, because the procedure applies only to new substances, which represent a very small percentage of substances on the market, most chemicals have never been assessed in terms of their harmful effects on health and the environment.[114]

---

[111] Chemicals existing before 1981 must be classified and labelled by manufacturers and producers under their own responsibility, until such time as they are classified by the competent authorities under the EC procedure.

[112] Commission Directive 93/67/EEC on the assessment of risks of dangerous substances to man and the environment stresses that the competent authority shall take into account 'reasonably foreseeable' exposure of man and the environment to that substance (Article 3(3)). Risk assessment principles do not appear overly rigid, as they grant Member States a reasonably broad degree of discretion, in some cases leaving open the possibility of choosing between a qualitative or quantitative approach.

[113] V. Heyvaert, *Coping with Uncertainty: The Regulation of Chemicals in the EU* (Florence: Institute of European Affairs) 74.

[114] Public authorities know surprisingly little about the risks presented by the most problematic chemicals. Of the more than 100,000 chemical substances in circulation, the classification of only 4,500 existing and new substances has been agreed upon. For many of the rest, public authorities must

In order to fill the information gap relating to chemicals placed on the market before 1981, Council Regulation (EEC) 793/93 envisages a system of evaluation and control of the risks posed by existing substances. Any Community importer or producer of an existing substance in quantities exceeding 1,000 t/year must submit data on the ecotoxicity and environmental fate and pathways of that chemical to the Commission. Member States are given responsibility for assessing the risks of specific substances on a list of priority substances requiring immediate attention because of their potential effects on man or the environment.[115] To this end, a *rapporteur* is appointed to conduct a risk assessment.[116] The risk assessment rules allow the *rapporteur* a wide margin of discretion, as he may choose between a quantitative or qualitative approach. Where appropriate, the *rapporteur* is to propose a strategy for limiting these risks. Such proposals could ultimately lead to measures being taken under Directive 76/769/EEC on restrictions on the marketing and use of certain dangerous substances and preparations.

However, the implementation of risk assessment principles is so laborious that it paralyses regulatory action.[117] First, an assessment of the advantages and drawbacks of the substance and of the availability of replacement substances is

rely on a provisional classification established by industry. An EC report from 1999 shows that only 14% of the approximately 2,500 high-production-volume chemicals registered in the EC's IUCLID database are accompanied by data complying with the basic requirements of Council Directive 67/548/EEC, 65% have some data, and 21% have no data whatsoever. It can be assumed that the data shortage is even more pronounced for lower-volume substances. For further analysis see eg G. Winter (ed.), *Risk Assessment and Risk Management of Toxic Chemicals in the EC* (Baden-Baden: Nomos, 2000) 261; F. Bro-Rasmussen, 'The Precautionary Principle and Science-Based Limits in Regulatory Toxicology' in D.M. Pugh and J.V. Tarazona (eds.), *Regulation for Chemical Safety in Europe: Analysis, Comment and Criticism* (Dordrecht: Kluwer, 1998) 97–110.

[115] A first priority list containing 42 substances (or substance groups) was published in the Annex to Commission Regulation (EC) No. 1179/94. A second and third list followed in 1995 and 1997 respectively. One factor for listing a substance is 'the lack of data on the effects of the substance on the environment' (Article 8, Regulation (EC) No. 1179/94). However, these lists cover less than 0.1% of existing chemicals.

[116] Risk to man and the environment is assessed on the basis of the principles laid down in Commission Regulation (EC) No. 1488/94 of 28 June 1994. This Regulation contains a detailed list of evaluation steps in its Annexes. A 1994 Technical Guidance Document lays down the methodology. In their technical aspects, these provisions are quite similar to those applying to the assessment of new substances according to Directive 93/67/EEC.

[117] By 1999 only 19 of the prioritized existing substances had been assessed for risk. The majority of assessments have taken between 2.5 and 4.5 years to carry out (eg M. Postle, 'Cost—Benefit Analysis and the Development of Risk Reduction Strategies' in G. Winter (ed.), *Risk Assessment and Risk Management of Toxic Chemicals*, n. 114 above, 126). Risk reduction measures were recommended by the Commission for 14 of the assessed substances, but not a single one of these recommendations has been taken up by the EC institutions as a basis for regulatory restrictions under Directive 76/769/EEC. If this slow pace continues, the assessment of 4,000 highly problematic chemicals will not be completed before the year 3000. The obligation to conduct a risk assessment thus prevents restrictions rapidly being set for the use of substances based on their hazardous properties only. In June 1999 the Council stated that 'as risk assessments have only been drafted for a very small number of existing substances pursuant to EC legislation on existing substances, but none have been adopted, maintaining the current approach is unlikely to tackle the problem of existing substances with a view to achieving an appropriate limitation of all significant risks posed by these substances to man and the environment'. The Council therefore called upon the Commission to base its reform proposals on the precautionary principle.

a prerequisite to establishing a risk reduction strategy.[118] Secondly, despite the results of the few risk assessments performed, the Council has not been willing to place restrictions on the marketing and use of certain dangerous substances and preparations according to Council Directive 76/769/EEC.[119] A number of environmental groups have called for risk assessment to be abandoned in the name of the precautionary principle,[120] thus accelerating the decision-making process as it relates to risk. A Commission White Paper published on 13 February 2001 now serves as the basis for a new policy in this field.

Establishing an approved list of substances at EC level, coupled with the authorization of products by national authorities and mutual recognition of authorizations, Directive 91/414/EEC concerning plant protection products contains some elements of the precautionary principle. In interpreting evaluation results of requests for authorization of plant protection products, Member States shall 'take into consideration possible elements of uncertainty in the information obtained during the evaluation, in order to ensure that the chances of failing to detect adverse effects or of underestimating their importance are reduced to a minimum'.[121] However, as is the case for Regulation (EEC) 793/93, no risk reduction measures have been taken for the 91 active priority substances listed in Annex I of this Directive, which can therefore still be used within the EC.

Nonetheless, the EC has embraced an important element of the precautionary principle through recognition of the substitution principle, according to which the mere existence of an alternative substance that appears to be less dangerous than the substance in question is sufficient basis for a prohibition. The substitution principle can be found in both Directive 89/391/EEC on the introduction of measures to encourage improvements in the health and safety of workers at work and Directive 90/394/EEC on the protection of workers from the risks related to exposure to carcinogens at work, which require employers to eliminate or reduce risks by replacing one dangerous substance with a less dangerous substance. For its part, Directive 98/8/EC concerning the placing of biocides on the market provides that the inclusion of an active substance in Annex I may be refused or withdrawn 'if another Annex I active substance exists for the same type of product which, taking account of the state of scientific or technical knowledge, presents significantly less risk for health or for the environment'.[122]

---

[118] Article 10(3), Council Regulation (EEC) No. 793/93. Advantages could include benefits to users, producers, processors, and society in general; drawbacks might include risks to human health and the environment as identified in risk assessments. Such an obligation appears, however, to be a time-consuming exercise.

[119] At present there are restrictive measures for 41 substances or groups of substances, covering about 900 substances in total. These restrictions vary from an almost total prohibition to a prohibition limited to specific applications.

[120] V. Heyvaert, 'Reconceptualizing Risk Assessment' (1999) 8 RECIEL 139.

[121] Annex VI (A)(4) of Directive 91/414/EEC concerning the placing of plant protection products on the market.

[122] Article 10(5). It remains to be seen, however, how this significant but controversial requirement will be used in practice in the authorization procedure. Eg E. Vogelzang-Stoute, 'EC Legislation on the Marketing and Use of Pesticides' (1999) 8 RECIEL 147. The substitution principle can also be found in EC law, in Article 4(2)(a)(iii) of Directive 2000/53/EC on end-of-life vehicles.

The substitution principle can play an important role in assessing the proportionality of measures that distort the free movement of goods. For instance, the ECJ ruled in *Kemikalieinspektionen* that a Swedish ban on the toxic substance trichloroethylene, a measure having an effect equivalent to a quantitative restriction within the meaning of Article 28 of the EC Treaty, was compatible with the Treaty in that it was necessary for the effective protection of the health and life of humans. In particular, the Court stressed that the system of individual exemptions to the Swedish ban appeared to be appropriate and proportionate in that 'exemptions are granted on condition that no safer replacement product is available and provided that the applicant continues to seek alternative solutions which are less harmful to public health and the environment'.[123] The Court stressed that those requirements were compatible with the 'substitution principle', which emerges *inter alia* from Directives 89/391/EEC and 90/394/EEC.

To conclude, the failure of EC chemicals policy to reduce health and environmental risks is related to a general preference for a certainty-seeking regulatory style in which formal, science-based, and standardized risk assessment has been singled out as the predominant tool for decision making relating to chemicals. While risk assessments draw extensively on science, data is often incomplete and results may be unclear or contradictory. As it is difficult to establish causal links between exposure to chemicals and health or environmental effects, there is generally a significant degree of uncertainty in estimates of the probability and magnitude of effects associated with a chemical agent. As the result of limited knowledge, it is difficult to provide conclusive evidence of a threat to human health and the environment. Despite the fact that the precautionary principle enables the adoption of risk reduction measures even where there is a suspicion of risk, assessment procedures still call for absolute certainty. In addition, these procedures are cumbersome, time-consuming, and expensive, as they require analysis of an enormous quantity and variety of data. In consequence, the risk reduction measures achieved by the EC chemicals policy appear relatively modest in the context of the human and financial resources required by the assessment procedures.

This led the Council to call for a substantial revision of the current policy in 1999. Needless to say, the precautionary principle will be at the core of the debates that accompany that reform. To allow more efficient risk reduction measures it will be necessary to improve various EC procedures in the light of the precautionary principle.[124] Where experts are not able fully to perform all the stages of the assessment procedure because available data is incomplete,

---

[123] Case C-473/98, *Kemikalieinspektionen and Toolex Alpha AB* [2000] ECR I-5702, para. 47; comment by O. Segnana (2001) 2 Amén.-Env. 110–19; comment by V. Heyvaert (2001) 2 TMR 149–53.

[124] On 13 February 2001 the European Commission adopted a White Paper setting out the strategy for a future Community Policy for Chemicals (COM(2001) 88 final). The main objective of the new Chemical Strategy is to ensure a high level of protection for human health and the environment in the light of the precautionary principle, while ensuring the efficient functioning of the internal market and stimulating innovation and competitiveness in the chemical industry.

inaccurate, or inconclusive, preliminary assessment should be sufficient to allow public authorities to take risk management decisions.[125]

2.2.4. *Case law*

In addition to the incorporation of the precautionary principle into the Chapter of the EC Treaty relating to protection of the environment, the ECJ has not hesitated to consider the context of scientific uncertainty in various cases concerning health policy and biodiversity. Since the EFTA Agreement provisions regarding the free movement of goods are almost identical to those of the EC Treaty, we consider EFTA case-law together with ECJ case-law.

2.2.4.1. Case law concerning health policy

While the precautionary principle entered into EC law via recognition in the Treaty Chapter relating to environmental protection, it seems rapidly to have found a niche in the field of health protection, where it has been expressly put forward by the European Court of Justice (ECJ) and the Court of First Instance (CFI). The importance of this case-law, particularly from the perspective of the weighing of interests, amply justifies extensive analysis.

Ironically, the precautionary principle was implicitly put forward by the ECJ in litigation concerning the prohibition of hormones—an issue over which the European Commission was to lose its case a few years later before the WTO Appellate Body.[126] In the *Fedesa* case the ECJ rejected a complaint based on the existence of scientific proofs demonstrating the innocuousness of five hormones, on the ground that the Council had acted within the limits of its discretion in choosing to retain a ban on the hormones in question, thus responding to the concern expressed by the European Parliament and the Social and Economic Committee, as well as by several consumer organizations.[127] Setting out the grounds for this judgment, the Court noted that the Directive did not:

frustrate the legitimate expectations of traders affected by the prohibition of the use of the hormones in question. It is true that the Council Directive ... refers to the fact that the harmless or harmful effects of the substances in question have yet to be examined in detail, and requires the Commission to take account of scientific developments. However, that Directive does not pre-empt the conclusions which may be drawn therefrom by the Council in exercise of its discretion. Moreover, in view of the divergent appraisals which had been made, traders were not entitled to expect that a prohibition on administering the substances in question to animals could be based on scientific data alone.

The EC courts also adopted a precautionary approach in determining that the Commission had not committed a manifest error of appraisal by instituting a ban on the export of beef, since no delay was permissible when the most probable

---

[125] D. Santillo, P. Johnston, A. Singhofen, and M. Krautter, 'Hazard Based Risk Assessment and Management' in G. Winter (ed.), *Risk Assessment and Risk Management of Toxic Chemicals*, n. 114 above, 98.

[126] See the discussion in Subsection 2.1.2.3. above.

[127] Case C-331/88, *Fedesa* [1990] ECR I-4023, para. 9.

explanation of Creuzfeldt-Jakob's disease was exposure to bovine spongiform encephalopathy (BSE).[128] The ECJ ruled that: 'At the time when the contested decision was adopted, there was great uncertainty as to the risks posed by live animals, bovine meat and derived products. Where there is uncertainty as to the existence or extent of risks to human health, the institutions may take protective measures without having to await the reality and seriousness of those risks become fully apparent.'[129]

According to the ECJ, this approach is supported by Article 174 of the Treaty, which embodies the precautionary principle.

Recourse to the precautionary principle was subsequently confirmed by the *Bergaderm* decision, in which the CFI rejected the action introduced by a pharmaceutical company contesting a Commission decision to prohibit the use of psoralenes in sun creams. The CFI decided, with reference to para. 63 of the *National Farmers' Union* decision, that in the presence of uncertainties concerning the existence or scope of a risk to human health, the EC institutions may adopt measures of protection without waiting for the existence and seriousness of these risks to be fully proved.[130]

In an order of 30 June 1999 the President of the CFI dismissed an application for interim measures against an EC Regulation prohibiting the use of antibiotic additives in livestock feed which was being justified by the risk that BSE might be transmitted from animals to humans.[131] The applicant claimed that the precautionary principle had been improperly applied by the EC legislator, since an objective risk assessment had not been carried out; he argued that differences existed between his case and that which gave rise to the order of 12 July 1996 in the case *United Kingdom v. Commission*, based on the fact that the terminal nature of Creuzfeldt-Jakob's disease and the grave risk it posed to human health was not an element in the present case. This argument was rejected by the President, according to whom: 'without prejudging the examination by the Court of the assessment of the extent of the risk, which must be established by the institutions concerned when adopting a precautionary measure, the mere existence of the risk so identified is enough in itself to justify taking into account, in the balancing of interests, the protection of human health'.[132]

---

[128] Case C-180/96 P, *United Kingdom v. Commission* [1996] ECR I-3903, para. 93; Case T-76/96 R, *National Farmers' Union (NFU)* [1996] ECR II-815, para. 88. For a comparison with the WTO Hormones case, eg N. McNelis, 'The role of the Judge in the EU and WTO: Lessons from the BSE and Hormones Cases' (2001) J Int'l Eco L 189–208.

[129] *NFU*, para. 63.

[130] Case T-199/96, *Bergaderm* [1998] ECR II-2805. In the appeal against the judgment of the Court of First Instance, the ECJ stressed that the reference to the precautionary principle in para. 66 of the judgment of the Court of First Instance was a 'statement of reasons added for completeness', since the CFI had already concluded its reasoning in para. 65 by stating that the Commission could not be criticized for placing the matter before the Scientific Committee or for complying with that body's opinion, which was drawn up on the basis of a large number of meetings, visits, and specialist reports (Case C-352/98 P, *Bergaderm* [2000] ECR I-5291, para. 53).

[131] Case T-79/99P, *Alpharma* [1999] ECR II-2027.

[132] Para. 66.

Consequently, this case law implies that EC institutions may adopt measures on a precautionary basis in the absence of serious factors such as the grave risk posed to human health by BSE.

The precautionary principle was invoked by the French authorities in 1999 as a basis for banning the import of British beef, on the ground of unknown effects on human health due to possible BSE transmission.[133] The French Government argued that the European Commission had not taken into account the minority opinions within the *ad hoc* Scientific Committee, thereby infringing the precautionary principle. Since bans within the EC contravene the free movement of goods, as embodied in Article 28 of the EC Treaty, the European Commission took France to the ECJ. The Commission contended that the French authorities could not, by relying on the scientific opinion of its own national scientific body,[134] substitute its own assessment of risks for that carried out by the Commission in accordance with secondary EC law. The Commission also maintained that the precautionary principle, 'which guides its actions', does not require that it act on any and every scientific opinion resulting from committee deliberations. According to the ECJ, once general rules for a beef tracing and labelling system came into force at the EC level, France could no longer rely on Article 30 of the EC Treaty to support its refusal to import British beef subject to the Date-Based Export Scheme (DBES). However, until 30 December 1999 France was entitled to rely on Article 30 of the EC Treaty to ban British beef imports in order to protect public health, on the ground that existing EC rules on traceability did not constitute exhaustive and coherent harmonization in the field of food safety. [135]

Within the context of the European Free Trade Association (EFTA) the precautionary principle was recently endorsed by the EFTA Court in the case *EFTA Surveillance Authority v. Norway*. In that case the Norwegian Food Control Authority refused the application of a Danish company for authorization to sell 'fortified' cornflakes in Norway, on the ground that the addition of nutrients—which might entail allergy risks for some consumers—is only justified if there is an unmet nutritional need among the Norwegian population at large. The EFTA Court held that: 'a Contracting Party may invoke the precautionary principle, according to which it is sufficient to show that there is relevant scientific uncertainty with regard to the risk in question. That measure of discretion must, however, be exercised subject to judicial review'.

---

[133] The French experts claimed that the risk of cattle being infected with BSE could come from a third route, and not only from the two routes already known about, namely feed and maternal transmission. Given the incubation period for the disease, there were no scientific data enabling the validity of the eligibility criteria for animals under the DBES to be established. Only diagnostic tools helped to control the risk.

[134] In addition to its ban, France had brought an action before the Court for annulment of the decision by which the Commission was alleged to have refused to amend its decision allowing the exports of British beef. Ruling on an objection of inadmissibility raised by the Commission, the ECJ declared that action manifestly inadmissible by order of 21 June 2000 in Case C-514/99, *France v. Commission* [2000] ECR I-4705.

[135] Case C-1/00, *EC Commission v. France* [2001] ECR I-9989.

According to the Court, a proper application of the precautionary principle presupposes, first, an identification of potentially negative health consequences arising from an additive, and secondly, a comprehensive evaluation of the risk to health based on the most recent scientific information.[136] When the insufficient, inconclusive, or imprecise nature of the conclusions to be drawn from those considerations makes it impossible to determine risk or hazard with any certainty, but the likelihood of considerable harm persists, the precautionary principle would justify taking restrictive measures.[137] However, precautionary measures must be submitted to the following criteria: 'Such restrictive measures must be non-discriminatory and objective, and must be applied within the framework of a policy based on the best available scientific knowledge at any given time. The precautionary principle can never justify the adoption of arbitrary decisions, and the pursuit of the objective of "zero risk" only in the most exceptional circumstances.' [138]

In this case, the Court found no indication that the precautionary principle had been inappropriately used as a disguised form of protectionism, although they deemed that the Norwegian authorities had in fact dealt with the application in an inappropriate manner.

2.2.4.2. Case law concerning biodiversity

The precautionary principle also appears in more traditional environmental case-law, although it is not necessarily explicitly expressed as such. In a judgment concerning wild birds, *L'Association pour la Protection des Animaux Sauvages et Préfet de Maine-et-Loire et Préfet de La Loire-Atlantique*, the Court favoured determining the end of the hunting season in a manner that guaranteed the optimal level of protection for avifauna. It judged that in the absence of 'scientific and technical data relevant to each individual case'—that is, in cases of uncertainty—Member States should adopt a single date for ending the season, equivalent to 'that fixed for the species which is the earliest to migrate',[139] and not 'the maximum period of migratory activity' which had been set by the French *Conseil d'Etat*.[140] That is, as long as a degree of uncertainty remains concerning the timing of pre-mating migrations of migratory birds, the strictest method of determining the close of hunting should override methods attempting to accommodate hunting interests on the basis of scientific approximation. However, Directive 79/409/EEC on the conservation of wild birds does empower Member States to stagger the closing dates for hunting if they can prove, on the basis of scientific and technical data, that such action will not hinder the complete protection of the species of bird that might be affected by the measure.[141] In this way, the concern to give full useful effect to Community legislation is joined with concerns reflecting precaution.

---

136 Case E-3/00, *EFTA Surveillance Authority v. Norway*, paras. 16 and 21.
137 Ibid., para. 22.   138 Para. 23.   139 Case C-435/92, [1994] ECR I-67, para. 21.
140 C.E. fr., 25 May 1990 (1990), 10 AJDA 730, comment by P. Le Mire.
141 Paras. 21–22.

By ruling against the Kingdom of Spain in its judgment in *Marismas de Santoña* for not having protected a wetland area of importance for certain migratory species of birds, in conformity with Directive 79/409/EEC, the ECJ adopted a precautionary approach. As no reduction in the number of protected birds had been observed, the Spanish authorities disputed that the destruction of this valuable ornithological site violated the requirements of the Directive. Their argument was rejected, however, on the ground that the obligation to preserve the natural habitats in question applied whether or not the population of protected birds was disappearing from these areas.[142] In so ruling, the ECJ had considered the context of uncertainty resulting from the fact that destruction of a natural habitat does not necessarily translate into an immediate decline in its animal populations: 'The obligations on Member States...exist before any reduction is observed in the number of birds or any risk of a protected species becoming extinct has materialised'.

The judgment in *Armand Mondiet* of 24 November 1993 provides a further illustration of the role that the precautionary principle can play in decisions taken in a context of scientific uncertainty. In this case a ship owner challenged EC Regulation 345/92 forbidding tangle nets of over 2.5 kilometres, on the grounds that no scientific data justified this measure and that it did not conform with the only information available, although the Regulation provided that conservation measures should be drawn up 'in view of the information that was available'. Advocate General Gulmann concurred with the Commission's argument that 'it is sometimes necessary to adopt measures as a precaution'. In order to conserve tuna stocks, for which insufficient scientific data existed, total allowable catch (TAC) had been based on that principle.[143] The ECJ followed the opinion of Advocate General Gulmann by ruling that in the exercise of its powers, the Council of Ministers could not be forced to follow particular scientific opinions.[144] That is, the fact that the benefit to be derived from a ban on tangle nets is uncertain does not alter the requirements of EC legislation.

In *Bluhme*, the ECJ ruled that a Danish wildlife measure prohibiting the import of any species of bee other than the endemic subspecies *Apis mellifera mellifera* into a Baltic island was justified under Article 30 of the EC Treaty, notwithstanding the lack of conclusive evidence establishing both the nature of the sub-species and its risk of extinction.[145]

2.2.4.3. Case-law concerning GMOs

In a case concerning marketing approval for genetically modified maize,[146] the French *Conseil d'Etat* asked the ECJ for a preliminary ruling on whether, among other things, the national competent authority, following a favourable decision

---

[142] Case C-355/90, *Commission v. Spain* (1993) ECR I-6159, para. 28.
[143] Opinion of Advocate General M. Gulmann, ECR I-6159, para. 28.
[144] Case C-405/92, *Armand Mondiet* [1993] ECR I-6176, paras. 31 to 36.
[145] Case C-67/97, *Bluhme* ('*Danish Bees*') [1998] ECR I-8053.
[146] See the discussion in Subsection 2.3.2. below.

by the Commission, 'is obliged to give consent in writing allowing the product to be placed on the market' or whether that authority 'retains a discretion not to give such consent'.

According to the Court's decision, the precautionary principle does not alter the wording of Article 13 of Directive 90/220/EEC, according to which national authorities are under an obligation to give their consent.[147] One of the arguments made by the ECJ is that the precautionary principle is already reflected in the Directive, in both the notifier's obligation to inform the competent authorities immediately of new information regarding the risks of the product to human health or the environment and the subsequent duty of these authorities to inform the Commission and the other Member States about such information, and in the right of a Member State to provisionally restrict or prohibit the use and/or sale on its territory of a GMO under the conditions set out in Article 16.[148] However, 'the system of protection put in place by Directive 90/220/EEC, in particular by Articles 4, 12(4) and 16, necessarily implies that the Member State concerned cannot be obliged to give its consent if in the meantime it has new information which leads it to consider that the product for which notification has been received may constitute a risk to human health and the environment'.[149]

In English, the mood, verb tense, and construction of this phrase all constituted an *a priori* invitation to the court to recognize that the French State is bound (*compétence liée*) by the decision of the European Commission to allow commercialization of modified maize.[150] Nevertheless, the precautionary principle allowed the ECJ to reach a far more nuanced solution, by recognizing the right of a Member State to oppose commercialization of GMOs on grounds of the appearance of new risks. In this decision the precautionary principle took the form of an interpretative principle of law, which served to correct the effect of a provision whose meaning could nevertheless be directly established. In other words, the principle of precaution appears capable of modifying the meaning even of a relatively clear text.

2.3. National laws

As the precautionary principle has met with unparalleled success in the international legal order, national legislators in EC Member States have followed suit by increasingly setting it out in the recitals of environmental codes of law or in framework laws (Germany, France, Belgium, Sweden). In German law, for example, the principle has for some time now implicitly followed from sectoral laws relating to listed installations, biotechnology, nuclear energy, and water management, while it has been set out explicitly in the French and several

---

[147] Case C-6/99, *Greenpeace France et Ministère des Affaires Etrangères* [2000] ECR I-1676.
[148] Ibid., para. 44.
[149] Ibid., para. 45.
[150] Ibid., paras. 28–30.

Belgian framework laws. It remains questionable, however, whether the understanding of this principle is the same in the various legal orders that we describe below, as they are characterized by rather distinct legal traditions.

It will undoubtedly be some time before the principle becomes more substantially entrenched in national environment laws. Since the objective of the principle is to govern decision making under conditions of uncertainty in a global manner, it still needs to advance—perhaps in a more striking fashion—in other fields of law closely connected to environment law, such as health law and safety regulations.

Nonetheless, it soon becomes apparent that substantive indications of the principle are more clearly in evidence in national legal regimes than one might think. By according increasing importance to uncertainty, several legislative systems have already brought the principle into play without expressly referring to it. Doctrine acknowledges, at any rate, that national biotechnology laws represent one of its most important advances.

It is above all at the level of litigation, however, that the principle comes into play, since courts have for years been enacting precaution without being aware of it. As demonstrated by the following case-law, a number of national courts in EC countries, as well as the United States and Australia, have already made a breakthrough by integrating uncertainty into their reasoning. We first consider continental European systems (Germany, France, Belgium, and Sweden) and then look at countries sharing an Anglo-Saxon legal tradition (the UK, Australia, and the US). Our focus will be on those court decisions that are most significant in furthering the implementation of precaution.

2.3.1. Federal Republic of Germany

In Germany the concepts of precaution and prevention tend to be merged into the term *Vorsorge*. Nonetheless, German legal literature distinguishes between prevention (*Prävention*), which refers to foreseeing known dangers (*Gefahr*), and precaution (*Vorsorge*), which does not require certainty of the occurrence of the risk to be averted (*Risiko*).[151] As we shall see, this distinction has been confirmed by case-law.

---

[151] For a fuller discussion of the role of the principle in the evolution of environmental law in Germany, see: M. Bothe and H. Scharp, 'La juridiction administrative allemande empêche-t-elle le développement de l'utilisation pacifique de l'énergie nucléaire?' (1986) 4 RJE 420; E. Rehbinder, 'Vorsorgeprinzip im Umweltrecht und Präventive Umweltpolitik' in U.E. Simonis (ed.), *Präventive Umweltpolitiek* (1988) 129–41; M. Kloepfer, 'Die Principien im einzelnen' in *Umweltrecht* (München, 1989) 74; E. Rehbinder, 'Prinzipien des Umweltrechts in der Rechtsprechung des Bundesverwaltungsgerichts: Das Vorsorgeprinzip als Beispiel' in *Bürger-Richter-Staat, Festschrift für Horst Sendler* (Münich: Hg. Franssen/Redeker/ Schlichter/Wilke, 1991) 269; A. Reich, *Gefahr-Risiko-Restrisiko* (Düsseldorf:Werner-Verlag, 1989); G. Roller, *Genehmigungsaufebung und Entschädigung im Atomrecht* (Baden-Baden: Nomos, 1994); S. Boehmer-Christiansen, 'The Precautionary Principle in Germany' in T. O'Riordan and J. Cameron (eds.), *Interpreting the Precautionary Principle* (London: Cameron & May, 1994) 31; K.-H. Ladeur, 'Zur Prozeduralisierung des Vorsorgebegriffs durch Risikovergleich und Prioritätensetzung' in *Jahrbuch des Umwet und Technikrechts* (Heidelberg: TechnikelB, 1994) 297; B. Bender *et al.*, 'Hauptprinzipen des Umweltrechts' in *Umweltrecht*

For the administrative agencies concerned with listed installations, nuclear plants, and biotechnology, German case-law has succeeded in fashioning a true legal principle of precaution on the basis of texts which had not been intended in that way. Section 5, no. 2 of the Federal Emissions Control Act (*Bundesimmissionsschutzgesetz*), for instance, specifies that: 'Installations subject to authorization are to be constructed and operated in such a manner that precaution is taken against damaging environmental effects...'

In a perspective of precaution, the German Federal Administrative Court (*Bundesverwaltungsgericht*) accepts the use of administrative measures which limit freedom of action and which are taken without clear proof of a causal link between the activity being regulated and environmental damage. This case-law is particularly interesting in that it draws a fine distinction between dangers, risks, and residual risks, considered later in this section.

In a judgment of 17 February 1978 concerning the operation of a coal-fired power plant,[152] the German Federal Administrative Court ruled that: 'according to §5 of the Federal Emissions Control Act, installations must be established and operated in such a way that harmful effects on the environment and other dangers, disadvantages and considerable nuisances are avoided and that the necessary precautions are taken against pollution, particularly by limiting emissions on the basis of best available techniques'.

The same court, in a judgment of 14 February 1984,[153] specified the conditions under which it was possible to appeal to the principle: 'Precaution... is indicated when there are sufficient grounds to believe that there is the danger that emissions might lead to environmental damage—even if a causal link has not been proved for the case under consideration'.

The precautionary principle also made remarkable progress in the area of nuclear law, owing to the legal interpretation of §7 of Germany's Atomic Energy Act (*Atomgesetz*), which provides that authorization may only be granted if 'precautions demanded by the current level of scientific and technical knowledge are taken against possible damage caused by the establishment or operation of the installation'.

The Federal Constitutional Court (*Bundesverfassungsgericht*) ruled, in a judgment of 8 August 1978 relating to the operation of the Kalkar nuclear reactor,

(3 Aufg., Heidelberg: R. Müller, 1995) 24; D. Murswiek, 'Der Bund und die Länder Schutz der natürlichen Lebensgrundlagen' in M. Sachs (ed.), *Grundgesetz: Kommentar* (Munich: Beck'sche Verlagsbuchhandlung, 1996) 653; Th. Lundmark, 'Principles and Instruments of German Environmental Law' (1997) 4 J Env L & Practice 43; K. von Moltke, 'The *Vorsorgeprinzip* in West German environmental policy' in *Royal Commission on Environmental Pollution*, 12th report: Best practicable environmental option, Cmnd 310, (London: HMSO, 1988); H. Von Lenser, 'Vorsorgeprinzip' in *Handwortbuch des Umweltrecht*, Bd. II, (Berlin, 1988) 1086; P. Sand, *Transnational Environmental Law* (London: Kluwer Law Int'l, 1999) 136–7; N. de Sadeleer, 'The Enforcement of the Precautionary Principle by German, French and Belgian Courts' (2000) 9 : 2 RECIEL 144–51; G. Roller, 'Environmental Law Principles in the Jurisprudence of German Administrative Courts' in M. Sheridan and L. Lavrysen (eds.), *Environmental Law Principles in Practice* (Brussels: Bruylant) 157–71.

[152] BVerwG, 17 February 1978, Bd. 55 (1978) 250.
[153] (1985) 69 BVerwG, 17 February 1984, 43.

that §7 of the Atomic Energy Act was consistent with the Constitution and aimed to ensure the optimal defence against dangers and the greatest precaution against risks, based on the protection afforded by fundamental constitutional rights, including the right to health protection.[154] The Constitutional Court also ruled, in the same case, that indeterminate concepts such as 'precaution' and 'the current level of scientific and technical knowledge' should be made more precise by administrative authorities rather than by courts and that it was therefore legitimate to confer upon the executive the task of implementing the principles laid down by the law:

Evaluation of the probability of future damage due to the construction and operation of a nuclear installation must take account of similar situations in the past. In the absence of specific past situations, the evaluation must be based on simulations. To the extent that in this field only approximations, rather than certainties, exist, any new event as well as any new development in knowledge should be taken into account as it arises. Thus, to require legislation definitively to exclude any impairment (*Gefährdung*) of a fundamental right would make it impossible for the administrative authorities to grant an authorization. It is therefore proper to undertake a reasonable assessment of the risks. As concerns injurious effects on life, health and goods, the federal legislator has established an assessment scale based on optimal prevention of potential dangers and risks as set out in §§1 and 7 of the Atomic Energy Act: authorizations may not be granted unless, based on the current level of scientific and technical knowledge, the occurrence of damage may be practically excluded.

The contribution of the judgment is fundamental on this latter point. Precautionary measures must be adopted with reference to the latest scientific knowledge. If they cannot be carried out because of technical difficulties, operational authorization must simply be refused, based on the fact that, as the Court stressed, 'precaution is not limited by what is technically achievable'. This said, the Constitutional Court held that it was not the function of courts to substitute their judgment for that of political bodies, particularly in the absence of legal criteria. Moreover, if the legislator had to exclude all danger in order to secure fundamental rights, he would disregard the potential of human intelligence and would forbid practically any State authorization of technical operations.

Risks should therefore be submitted to criteria of practical reason (*Abschätzungen anhand praktischer Vernunft*): that is, a reasonable assessment. Beyond the threshold of practical reason, uncertainties are inevitable; these are the residual risks (*Restrisiko*) that every citizen must tolerate as a socially fair distribution of burdens (*sozialadäquate Lasten*). The basic argument is thus: if a residual risk must be tolerated by everyone, no one has a subjective right to contest exposure to such risk.

Despite the Constitutional Court's judgment, the majority of German legal opinion in the early 1980s continued to consider that §7 of the Atomic Energy Act only covered protection from or prevention of hazards (*Gefahrenabwehr*): that is, the adoption of policy measures needed to avert known dangers. This

---

[154] BVerfGE 49, 89 (143) and 53, 30 (58/58).

provision could not cover the anticipation of risks (*Risikovorsorge*) or the prevention of minimal residual risks (*Restrisiko*).[155]

In a judgment related to the operation of the nuclear power station in Wyhl, the Federal Administrative Tribunal rejected this overly narrow interpretation. In this case, the complaint concerned the legality of the operating authorization for the power station, in that it did not envisage protection in the case of reactor accident. Failure to set conditions that would trigger a strong protection mechanism to protect the population against the risk of nuclear radiation led the Administrative Tribunal of Freiburg to rescind the contentious authorization in March 1978. The administrative authority that had granted the authorization had relied on the opinion of a number of experts who considered that protection against a nuclear reactor accident was not required as a necessary precaution, based on the current level of science and technology (*Stand von Wissenschaft und Technik*) as set out in §7 of the Atomic Energy Act.

This first decision was nevertheless reversed on 30 March 1982 by the Mannheim Administrative Appeals Court, which judged that 'one aspect of the natural sciences is to choose which facts should be taken into account when investigating risks' and that the analyses which had been ordered by the public authorities prior to authorizing the nuclear power station respected the requirements set out in §7 of the Atomic Energy Act.

On 19 December 1985 the Federal Administrative Court in Berlin (*Bundesverwaltungsgericht*), ruling in a second-stage appeal, granted the administrative authority a relatively significant discretion in assessing risks that did not fall under judicial control.[156] This ruling produced particularly interesting clarifications regarding the obligation for precaution set out in §7 of the Atomic Energy Act, which had a considerable impact on the evolution of German administrative case-law:

§7, indent 2, no. 3 should be interpreted not in terms of the predetermined notion of 'danger' of classical administrative law, but with regard to the specific protection which appears in §1, no. 2 of the Atomic Energy Law. Consequently, precaution in the sense of the standard in question does not mean that measures of protection may only be taken if 'certain situations or facts can, by the law of causation, give rise to other, prejudicial, situations or facts' (definition given by the Superior Administrative Court of Prussia, judgment of 15 October 1894). On the contrary, it is necessary to take account of the possibilities for damages that do not yet represent 'dangers' in this sense, since science in its present state is not capable of predicting with certainty the consequences of certain acts and can therefore not say whether or not these effects represent a danger...

It is necessary to take into consideration suspicion of danger or of 'reasons for concern' (*Besorgnispotential*). Precaution also means that in assessing the probability of damage, reference to practical technical knowledge is not sufficient; security measures should also

---

[155] E. Rehbinder, 'Prinzipien des Umweltrechts in der Rechtsprechung des Bundesverwaltungsgerichts: Das Vorsorgeprinzip als Beispiel' in *Bürger-Richter-Staat, Festschrift für Horst Sendler* (Munich: Hg. Frannsen/Redeker/Schlichter/Wilke, 1991) 272; G. Roller, *Atomrecht*, n. 151 above, 54.

[156] (1986) NVwZ 208.

be considered according to 'purely theoretical' thinking and calculations, so as adequately to exclude risks arising from uncertainties and lacunae in scientific understanding... In order to take the precautions required according to §7, indent 2, no. 3 of the Atomic Energy Act, dangers and risks must be practically excluded. The evaluation needed for this task should refer to 'the current level of science and technology'. Uncertainties relating to research and risk assessment must be considered according to the reasons for concern associated with them under sufficiently conservative hypotheses. In this process, the administrative authority charged with granting the authorization should not just rely on dominant theory but should take account of all tenable scientific knowledge.

Following from these considerations, the Federal Administrative Court defined the notion of residual risk in the strictest possible manner. It imposed an obligation to act, because 'dangers and risks must be practically excluded'. Since science is no longer omniscient, precaution must apply to 'possibilities for damage which do not yet represent a danger'. By attaching greater importance to probabilities than to certainties, the Court correctly distinguished risks whose causation is uncertain from the classical concept of danger. By not allowing the public authorities to take refuge behind a 'dominant theory', since 'science in its present state is not capable of predicting with certainty the consequences of certain acts and can therefore not say whether or not these effects represent a danger', the Court also recognized the plurality of truth.

The German Federal Administrative Court thus applied a greatly widened concept of precaution, which goes much further than that originally envisaged by the drafters of national legislation and allowed at the time by most legal analysis.[157] This case-law demonstrated that courts are likely to draw from such a principle those elements that permit them to ensure firm control of administrative decisions without, however, taking the opportunity to weaken the separation of powers. While legal control is thereby increased, it nonetheless remains marginal in verifying respect for the current state of science and technology. Based on the case-law related to the Kalkar fast breeder reactor, the Federal Administrative Court expressed the opinion that it was not up to administrative tribunals to substitute their assessment of scientific controversies for the evaluation carried out by administrative authorities. The Court rejected the appeal on the ground that the competent authority had studied differing scientific opinions in the case of the Whyl power plant.

More recently, litigation concerning the implementation of the precautionary principle in German environmental law has also taken place in the field of biotechnology, based on the provisions of the Act of 16 December 1993 (*Gentechnikgesetz*) that state:

§ 6, no. 2. In conformity with the current level of science and technology, the operator must take all measures to protect the rights set out in §1, no. 1 and to anticipate the creation of dangers...

---

[157] E. Rehbinder, 'Vorsorgeprinzip im Umweltrecht und Präventive Umweltpolitik', n. 151 above, 269; G. Roller, *Atomrecht*, n. 151 above, 54 *et seq.*

§13. Authorization for the operation and establishment of a biotechnology installation . . . may not be granted until:

(4). It is guaranteed that the measures required have been taken at all necessary levels of protection, in conformity with the current level of science and technology, and this without it being necessary to wait for damaging effects by emissions on the rights protected under §1, no. 1.

In a judgment of 27 January 1995 the Administrative Appeals Court of Hamburg specified the scope of the precautionary principle set out in §6, no. 2 of the Biotechnology Act, which requires an operator to take steps to protect against and prevent the occurrence of potential dangers. After recalling that the concept of the current level of science and technology could be submitted to review by the court, the Court stressed that this concept comprises both the prevention of danger (*Gefahrenabwehr*) and precaution against risks (*Risikovorsorge*).[158] The Court then recalled the case-law of the Federal Administrative Court in the *Whyl* case, which conferred a power of assessment upon the administrative authorities. It inferred from this that its judicial review should be limited to verifying that the contentious assessment was based on sufficient information and non-arbitrary assumptions.

This case-law, which assigns a significant degree of discretion to the administrative authorities in cases of scientific uncertainty, was confirmed by the German Federal Administrative Court. On 15 April 1999 the Federal Court ruled that the competent authorities charged with issuing operating permits for genetics laboratories under the *Gentechnikgesetz* enjoyed the same freedom to evaluate evidence as that accorded to the administrative authorities under the *Atomgesetz*.

In keeping with the Federal Administrative Court's reasoning in the *Whyl* case, administrative courts will exercise their jurisdiction to control the procedural aspects of risk assessment. They may henceforth go beyond the earlier limits of merely formal control (for example, verifying if all relevant scientific literature has been cited, although without being allowed to determine how scientific facts have been integrated into an administrative decision).[159] In addition, while they can verify whether competent authorities have taken all relevant aspects of an issue (such as non-mainstream scientific studies) into account and have accordingly come to a reasonable conclusion, they cannot decide what measures are necessary to comply with the precautionary principle.

2.3.2. *France*

The *Conseil d'Etat*, the highest French administrative court, took a precautionary position for the first time in a case having nothing to do with the environment, but concerning AIDS-contaminated blood. One of the recitals of its

---

[158] OVG Hamburg, 27 January 1995 (1995) 2 Zeitschrift für Umweltrecht 93.
[159] BVerfG, 15.4.1999, 7B278.98, (1999) DVBL 1138. Eg G. Roller, 'Environmental Law Principles . . .', n. 151 above, 157.

judgments of 9 April 1993 reproves the French Government for not having acted in the presence of 'a serious risk' when there was no need to 'wait for certainty' on the issue. The argumentation of *Commissaire du Gouvernement* Legal was even more explicit. He concluded that: 'In a situation of risk, a hypothesis that has not been invalidated should provisionally be considered valid, even if it has not been formally demonstrated'.[160]

The *Conseil d'Etat* adopted an identical argument in the *Rossi* judgment, where it questioned the legality of a prefectoral decision which found water abstraction works to be in the public interest and established a narrow safety perimeter around the abstraction site. The *Conseil* adjudged that the administration could not base its decision on scientifically proven data alone: 'the fact that a fluorescine infiltration test may not have confirmed such risks and that the hydrogeological report... may not have considered the narrow safety perimeter insufficient do not in themselves demonstrate that there is no need to enlarge the said safety perimeter in order to guarantee the quality of the waters in question'.[161]

This judgment can be seen as implementing the precautionary principle, since the *Conseil d'Etat* in effect reproaches the administration for not having demonstrated that there was no need to enlarge the safety perimeter when the risk of infiltration had not been established with certainty. The judgment thus marks a profound change in perspective concerning the legality of administrative action on the environment. In case of doubt, an administration must be able to prove that it is not necessary to go beyond what has been laid down or fall short of what has been authorized.

The *Conseil d'Etat* also took a precautionary stance in the case of *Commune De Quévillon*, where it ruled that modification of a planning instrument (*Plan d'occupation des sols*) in order to set apart agricultural land for the deposition of dredging spoil violated its terms, even though the land was eventually to be restored to its original use.[162] The infringement could be gathered 'from the risk of harmful effects linked, in particular, to the final restoration to agricultural use of lands used for dredging spoil, whose toxicological effects are not guaranteed to be harmless'. It thus fell to the author of the planning instrument to demonstrate that the stored spoil would not give rise to toxicological effects.

The precautionary principle has recently been discovered by French environmental lawyers.[163] Introduced by the Law of 2 February 1995 reinforcing

---

[160] C.E. fr., 9 April 1993, M et Mme B.

[161] C.E. fr., 4 January 1995, Ministre de l'Intérieur c/ M Rossi. The Administrative Court of Versailles adopted a similar position in a separate borehole case (TA Versailles of 8 October 1996). It held that insofar as the impact assessment was at variance with the opinions submitted by specialized services, 'the prefect should have had more thorough studies carried out to complete the dossier, particularly concerning the foreseeable future effect of borehole exploitation on underlying waters'. That is, uncertainty is no excuse for incomplete investigations.

[162] C.E. fr., 30 April 1997, Commune de Quévillon.

[163] Ch. Cans, 'Grande et petite histoire des principes généraux du droit de l'environnement dans la loi du 2 février 1995' (1995) 2 RJE 195); Y. Jegouzo, 'Les principes généraux du droit de

environmental protection, which initiated the codification of environmental law, and taken up at the end of the year 2000 in the French Environmental Code, the precautionary principle is defined by the French legislator as: 'the principle according to which the absence of certainty, taking account of current scientific and technical knowledge, ought not to delay the adoption of effective and proportionate measures aimed at preventing a risk of serious and irreversible damage to the environment, at an economically acceptable cost'.

Moreover, the precautionary principle is specified as the principle that should take precedence in environmental protection policies.

Administrative case-law did not really reflect this new legal principle, however, until its application in the case of transgenic maize, where application had been made to the *Conseil d'Etat*, among others by Greenpeace France, to suspend the execution of an Agriculture Ministry order which would have registered three varieties of genetically modified maize in the catalogue of species and varieties of plants grown in France. In his conclusions of 25 September 1998, *Commissaire du Gouvernement* J-H Stahl cast doubt on whether the precautionary principle could be said to have direct effect: the principle could not be appealed to directly owing to the provision in the Barnier Law of 2 February 1995 which states that the principles set out in the Law 'inspire' environmental policies 'in those laws which define its range':

Moreover, we do not consider it possible that the other principles established by this article—the principle of preventive action and of prevention at source, the polluter pays principle, the principle of participation—can be directly applied in the absence of legislative provisions which give them concrete form. We are dealing here with a political principle intended to guide legislative and regulatory action in the field of environment . . .

Further, the *Commissaire du Gouvernement* proposed to combine the precautionary principle with other applicable legislative provisions:

The combination of legislative provisions should thus rather lead to application of the Law of 13 July 1992 (by which the legislator authorized, organized and set conditions for the dissemination of genetically modified organisms) in the light of the precautionary principle of Article L200–1 of the Rural Code. In carrying out the procedure of the 1992 Law, the conduct of the administration should be marked by a high degree of precaution. And the judge considering its legality may assess this conduct. Under the control of the judge, the administrative authority must thus carefully study the risks—at least those that can be identified; take into consideration all opinions that appear useful—perhaps beyond what is required by law . . .

In its ruling of 25 September 1998, which gave rise to some comment since it expressly invoked the precautionary principle for the first time, the *Conseil d'État* departed from the conclusions of its *Commissaire du Gouvernement*;

l'environnement' (1996) 12: 2 RFD Adm. 209 ; P. Kourilsky and G. Viney, *Le Principe de Précaution* (Paris: La Documentation Française—O. Jacob, 2000). For a critical analysis of French doctrinal positions, see N. de Sadeleer, 'Les avatars du principe de précaution en droit public. Effet de mode ou révolution silencieuse?' (2001) 17: 2 RFD Adm. 547–62.

the ruling stated that the grounds put forward by the plaintiffs, who claimed the procedure leading to the decision was irregular owing to insufficient information on the one hand and to a violation of the precautionary principle on the other hand, appeared sufficiently serious to suspend the contested decision.[164] Thus, violation of the precautionary principle must be considered an infringement of a legal obligation; the fact that specific laws do not give concrete form to the principle does not prevent a court from applying it directly.

In a preliminary ruling of 20 March 2000 the ECJ declared that the French State was bound by the preliminary decision taken by the European Commission to consent to the commercialization of genetically modified organisms unless new scientific evidence of risk had become available.[165] Required to conform to the ECJ's interpretation in its decision of 21 March 2000, the French *Conseil d'Etat* stated in a ruling of 22 November 2000 that, given the absence of new elements relating to potential environmental risks arising from Bt maize, the French Government was required to consent to Novartis' application. The procedural complaints put forward by the plaintiff regarding the French proced-ure preceding transmission of the application to the European Commission had no effect on the legality of the decision being challenged.[166]

In another decision, the *Conseil d'Etat* considered the legality of a decree extending the prohibition of the marketing of products of bovine origin that might present a risk of BSE transmission to ovine and caprine products.[167] On the basis of the precautionary principle, which would urge that the Government take particular account of 'the care required for the protection of public health', the *Commissaire du Gouvernement* decided that it would be difficult for the French Government to have committed a manifest error of appraisal. The *Con-seil d'Etat* rejected a request for nullification by the sheep breeders' union, indicating that even if the risk of transmission had not yet been established, decisions on the point could not be made with any certainty. From which it concluded that: 'With regard to the precautionary measures that are indispens-able when dealing with public health . . . the Prime Minister has not committed an error of appraisal'.

Recalling the principle of the autonomy of political decision-making with respect to scientific evaluation in the *Rustica Prograin génétique* and *Bayer* cases, the *Conseil d'Etat* accepted the validity of the withdrawal from the market of a pesticide because of its possible deleterious effect on bees even though the competent minister had not concurred with the opinion of an *ad hoc* committee that had recommended a less severe measure.[168] From the perspective of classical case-law, the administrative decision to prohibit the insecticide could have been

---

[164] C.E. fr., 19 February 1998, Association Greenpeace France.
[165] Case C-6/99, *Greenpeace France*. See the discussion in Subsection 2.2.4.3. above.
[166] CE fr., 22 November 2000, Association Greenpeace France et autres.
[167] C.E. fr., 24 February 1999, Société Pro-Nat, req. no. 192465.
[168] CE fr., 29 December 1999, Société Rustica-Prograin génétique SA et autres, no. 206687, 207303.

deemed illegal because the dossier contained so few conclusive elements. Nevertheless, the precautionary principle allowed the *Conseil d'Etat* to rule that the administrative decision was not vitiated by a manifest error of appraisal.

Finally, the precautionary principle appears recently to have made important advances at the level of lower administrative courts, which no longer hesitate to nullify administrative decisions on the ground that they have not respected the principle.[169]

2.3.3. Belgium

Although relatively rare, rulings underpinned by a precautionary stance are not exceptional in litigation under Belgian law.[170] Use of the precautionary principle is implicit in two decisions of the Belgian constitutional *Cour d'arbitrage*. In the first the Court accepted as admissible an environmental tax which set a higher tax for PVC packaging than for packaging made of other materials, despite the absence of unanimity among experts on the justification for such a measure: 'Despite the absence of unanimous scientific agreement that PVC causes a particular threat to the environment, it was reasonable for the legislator on the basis of available data to deem that PVC containers would lead to more environmental problems than other containers'.[171]

The Court applied similar reasoning with respect to a Flemish regional law that 'was progressively dismantling gravel quarrying in Limbourg province with a view to halting environmental damage'.[172] The judgment explicitly stressed that a regulatory measure may always be reversed, while the continuation of quarrying could have irreversible consequences for the ecosystem under threat:

the legislator must weigh the environmental benefits and threats posed by quarry works and thus has sole responsibility for determining whether or not the environmental impact of these works should be considered negative on the whole and, if necessary, to decide if they should be halted as soon as possible... All the more so since, if the environmental discussion later results in a reappraisal of current conclusions, the legislator can always reconsider this measure rather than allowing quarry works to continue with the risk of irreversible damage occurring.

---

[169] Thus, on 19 April 2000 the Lille Administrative Court annulled alterations to Lille's main road on the ground that proposed changes for bypassing the urban centre through use of a motorway did not sufficiently consider all the potential pollution impacts on groundwater and therefore did not satisfy the precautionary principle (T.A. Lille, 19 April 2000, Fed. Nord-Nature, no. 98–552). In a decision of 20 April 2000 the Toulouse Administrative Court revoked a prefectoral decision to increase the flow of a watercourse in order to make possible a kayak race, on the ground that the decision was likely to cause serious and irreversible damage to certain protected wild species and thus did not satisfy the requirements of the precautionary principle (T.A. Toulouse, 20 April 2000, Fédération du Tarn pour la pêche et le milieu aquatique, no. 97/2846).

[170] L. Lavrysen, 'The precautionary principle in Belgian jurisprudence: Unknown, unloved?' (1998) EELR 75–82; N. de Sadeleer, 'The Enforcement of the Precautionary Principle by German, French and Belgian Courts' (2000) 9 : 2 RECIEL 144–51; I. Larmuseau, 'The precautionary principle in Belgian jurisprudence: So many men, so many minds?' in M. Sheridan and L. Lavrysen (eds.), *Environmental Law Principles*, n. 151 above, 173–92

[171] C.A., no. 7/95 of 2 February 1995.

[172] C.A., no. 35/95 of 25 April 1995.

Thus applied, the precautionary principle has served to guide the reasoning of the Belgian Constitutional Court towards recognition of certain legal measures taken to deal with injurious activities even when scientific proof about the effects of those activities on the aquatic environment was not conclusive. These two decisions are the more remarkable in that they were handed down at a time when the precautionary principle was not recognized in Belgian law.

Some judgments of the Belgian *Conseil d'Etat* similarly draw inspiration from the precautionary principle. Demonstrating a risk of serious damage which cannot easily be remedied, as required by the preliminary ruling, also appears to open the way to the principle. In particular, the *Conseil d'Etat* was of the opinion that this condition should be considered as established in cases where an environmental impact assessment had not been carried out.[173] This is also the case where industrial expansion of a site heightens the risk of malfunctions which have in the past endangered local residents although the objective increase in risk does not appear to warrant the adoption of supplementary safeguard measures as part of a modified licence.[174] Since the *Venter* decision, consideration of the precautionary principle appears to be required by constitutional law when dealing with protection of health and a healthy environment. Although the complainant could not present supporting evidence for his claim that electric cables passing above his home or mobile telephone stations posed a risk to neighbourhood health, the *Conseil d'État* decided there were sufficient grounds for reasonable suspicion of a health risk, even if existing standards were being respected.[175] Since it was not its role to settle this scientific controversy, the Administrative High Court decided that while a risk to health could not be proved, neither could it be excluded. To the extent that the risk threatened basic constitutional rights to health and environmental protection, the injury could be considered sufficiently serious to warrant suspending the contentious administrative act.

The use of the precautionary principle in environment policy in Belgian law was first recognized in a decree of the Flemish Region of 5 April 1995, which states that: 'Environmental policy shall seek to achieve a high level of protection ... It shall be based on, *inter alia*: the precautionary principle'.[176]

The legal implications of this principle remain controversial. On one hand, in its suspension judgment of 25 January 1999 concerning a licence for the construction of a new incineration plant close to Brussels, the *Conseil d'Etat* dismissed as not serious the violation of the precautionary principle found in the Flemish Decree:

That a first reading of the provisions that we invoked prompts the conclusion that these provisions do not contain any enforceable rules, merely general principles in the area of

---

[173] C.E. b., no. 45.755, 26 January 1994, Maniquet et Lecomte (1994) 4 Amén.-Env. 65.
[174] C.E. b., no. 56.416, 22 November 1995, a.s.b.l. Environnement Assistance (1996) 2 Amén.-Env. 80.
[175] C.E. b., no. 82.130, 20 August 1999, *Venter*; no. 85.836; no. 85.835, 6 March 2000, *Daeten*.
[176] Article 1.2.1, §2.

general environmental policy, principles that do not need to be worked out further and translated into enforceable regulations; that consequently, leaving aside the question whether or not these principles have been ignored, in the current state of the proceedings there is nothing to indicate that a possible violation of the principles should, or even could, lead to the annulment of the disputed licence'.[177]

On the other hand, the President of the Court of First Instance of Antwerp held, in a case concerning an incineration plant close to Antwerp, that the prevention and precautionary principles had been ignored by the granting of a new operating licence to a plant that has been closed in the past because its operations were suspected of causing birth defects. The President of the Court considered that there could not be absolute certainty that the incineration plant would not pose any further risk to the surrounding population. Ordering that the plant be closed, he concluded his judgment of 2 February 1999: 'whereas with regard to public health no compromises should be made, precisely because it is the future of residents and their quality of life that are at stake'[178]. However, on 11 October 1999 the Antwerp Court of Appeal decided to reverse the First Instance decision:

whereas ... principles are only to be taken into account in so far as they can be transposed to provisions of laws, decrees, ordinances, regulations or decisions concerning environmental protection, against which an evident violation or the serious risk of a violation is presented; ...

whereas the government has given shape to the precautionary principle by imposing on ISVAG the emission standards stated in the environmental licence; whereas these permits, as regular unilateral administrative legal acts of the competent administrative authority, should be deemed to be in accordance with the law and are therefore applicable in this respect; ...

the dioxin emission standard of 0.1 ngTEQ/Nm^3 ... is perfectly acceptable and that it meets the legal emission limits and the objectives of the precautionary principle; ...

Finally, recognition of the principle was reiterated in Article 4 of the federal law of 30 January 1999 aimed at protecting the marine environment in the maritime areas under Belgian jurisdiction, which set out that: ' ... when carrying out activities in maritime areas, operators must take into consideration the precautionary principle ... which means that preventive measures must be taken when there are reasonable grounds for concern about pollution of marine areas, even if conclusive proof of a causal link between the introduction of substances ... and deleterious effects does not exist'.

Moreover, the Federal law stipulates that 'the users of the marine environment and the government shall take into consideration ... the precautionary principle ... when carrying out their activities in the marine environment'; the principle is thus directly binding on all users of the marine environment, both public and private.

[177] C.E. b., no. 78340 and 78341, 25 January 1999, *Vlabraver.*
[178] Antwerp Trib., 2 February 1999.

2.3.4. *Sweden*

Sweden has often been in the forefront in implementing the precautionary principle. The written history of the precautionary principle in Swedish legislation can be traced back to the 1973 Act on Products Hazardous to Man or the Environment.[179] Implementing the 1973 Act, the Swedish authorities considered that they did not need to wait until harm had been done before restricting chemical products. Restrictions could also occur in cases where less hazardous alternatives existed. For instance, several pesticides (aldrin, dieldrin, endrin, etc.) were banned in the 1970s and early 1980s because less hazardous alternatives were available. Furthermore, to avoid restrictions on a product, its producer must show, beyond reasonable doubt and on the basis of scientific knowledge, that suspicion of harm is unfounded.

More recently, Sweden has put precaution into a central position in its 1998 environmental Code, whose §3 states that:

(1) Persons who pursue an activity or take a measure, or intend to do so, shall implement protective measures, comply with restrictions, and take any other precautions that are necessary in order to prevent or hinder damage or detriment to human health or the environment as a result of the activity or measure. For the same reason, the best available technology shall be used in connection with professional activities.

(2) Such precautions shall be taken as soon as there is cause to assume that an activity or measure may cause damage or detriment to human health or the environment.

Preparatory work being carried out envisages that this provision would apply the precautionary principle in Swedish national law in the form in which it has been developed at international level.[180]

In addition, the precautionary principle combines with the substitution principle, set out in §6 of the Code, which lays down that: 'Persons who pursue an activity or take a measure, or intend to do so, shall avoid using or selling chemical products or biotechnical organisms that may involve risks to human health or the environment if products or organisms that are less dangerous can be used instead. The same requirement shall apply to goods that contain or are treated with a chemical product or a biotechnical organism'.

To achieve the environmental quality objective of a non-toxic environment according to the Bill 'Swedish Environmental Quality Objectives', the Government proposed in April 1998 among other objectives that 'the environment must be free from man-made substances and metals that represent a threat to health or biological diversity'. It later issued new guidelines on chemicals policy, including implicit implementation of the precautionary principle: 'Man-made organic

---

[179] B. Wahlström, 'The Precautionary Approach to Chemicals Management: A Swedish Perspective' in C. Raffensperger and J. Tickner (eds.), *Protecting Public Health and the Environment: Implementing the Precautionary Principle* (Washington: Island Press, 1999) 51; E. Sandberg, 'The Precautionary Principle in Swedish Chemicals Policy' in E. Freytag, T. Jackl, G. Loibl, and M. Wittman (eds.), *The Role of Precaution in Chemicals Policy* (Vienna: Diplomatische Akademie, 2002) 63–8.

[180] Regjeringen Proposition 1997/98: 45, Miljöbalk, *Riksdagen* (1997/98), 1 saml., no. 45, Del. 1, 208.

substances that are persistent and bioaccumulative occur in production processes only if the producer can show that health and the environment will not be harmed. Permits and terms of the Environmental Code are devised in such a way as to guarantee this guideline.'

To that end, the Swedish Chemicals Policy Committee set the target that products should not contain persistent and bioaccumulative substances by the year 2007.

2.3.5. United Kingdom

Establishing principles is standard practice in the legislation of the founding States of the European Community. The Anglo-Saxon legal system, on the other hand, has always resisted the intrusion of legal principles. Legislative drafters, particularly in the English tradition, have habitually sought to avoid broad statements of principle, and it is noticeable that courts still have some difficulties in applying principles, particularly to over-ride clear rules.[181] For this reason the precautionary principle is not found in any British statutory law. However, the use of precautionary action was foreseen by the British Government in 1990, in the White Paper *This Common Inheritance*:

> ... Where there are significant risks of damage to the environment, the government will be prepared to take precautionary action to limit the use of potentially dangerous materials or the spread of potentially dangerous pollutants, even where scientific knowledge is not conclusive, if the balance of likely costs and benefits justifies it. The precautionary principle applies particularly where there are good grounds for judging either that action taken promptly at comparatively low cost may avoid more costly damage later, or that irreversible effects may follow if action is delayed.[182]

In stressing the need to consider the costs and benefits of taking action, this is a rather weak version of the principle. A more recent government policy, the 1999 strategy on sustainable development, which states that 'precautionary action requires assessment of the costs and benefits of action, and transparency in decision-making', is equally weak.[183]

While the courts of the founding States of the EC do not hesitate to develop teleological methods of interpretation based on broad provisions, English courts are uncomfortable when confronted with such norms. Applicants who have referred to the precautionary principle as set out in Article 174(2) of the EC Treaty before British courts have consequently tended to be unsuccessful.

In fact there has thus far been only one significant UK case where the principle has been considered non-justiciable. In the *Duddridge* case, where the laying of a high-tension electric cable in front of a school was challenged as posing a possible

---

[181] D. Freestone and E. Hey, 'Implementing the Precautionary Principle: Challenges and Opportunities' in D. Freestone and E. Hey (eds.), *The Precautionary Principle and International Law* (London, Boston, The Hague: Kluwer Law International, 1995) 255.

[182] Dept. of the Environment, *This Common Inheritance: Britain's Environmental Strategy*, UK White Paper on Environmental Policy (London: HMSO, 1990) 7.

[183] C. Hilson, *Regulating Pollution: A UK and EC Perspective* (Oxford: Hart, 2000) 89.

risk of leukaemia to students, the applicants argued that the Secretary of State for Trade and Industry was legally obliged under Article 174 (former 130R) of the EC Treaty to review the project in the light of the precautionary principle. The UK court rejected this argument, based on the *Peralta* judgment of the European Court of Justice,[184] which it took to say that Article 174(2) does not impose an obligation on national administrative authorities.[185] We believe the decision would have been different had the applicants challenged the Secretary of State's decision on the basis of an EC Directive that applied the precautionary principle. The court's interpretation would then have had to consider the national legal measures transposing the relevant EC law. This was not the case in *Duddridge*.

However, like other EC Member State jurisdictions discussed above, UK courts are not reluctant to take into account questions concerning unsubstantiated risk. Courts have had little problem in accepting a broad definition of risk, allowing decision-makers to act without full proof of harm.[186]

2.3.6. United States of America

While the precautionary debate has often been characterized as a clash, with the EC promoting the principle and the US opposing it, historical studies suggest otherwise. In fact US authorities have implemented precautionary approaches *avant la lettre*.[187] As we will see below, a careful examination of US case-law confirms this conclusion.

Legal drafters in the United States have habitually sought to avoid broad statements of principle. The precautionary principle is therefore not found as such in US environmental protection or health and safety legislation, even though the general notion of precaution underlies much of the early environmental legislation in the United States.[188] However, recent US environment law has increasingly stressed cost–benefit analysis and risk assessment, both of which contradict the precautionary principle since they assume that the

---

[184] ECJ, 14 July 1994, *Peralta*, as above.

[185] *R v. Secretary of State for Trade and Industry, ex parte Duddridge and Others* [1995] Env. LR 151 and [1995] 2: 7 JEL 237, comment by D. Hugues; J. Holder, 'Safe science? The Precautionary Principle in UK Environmental Law' in J. Holder (ed.), *The Impact of EC Environmental Law in the UK* (Chichester: Wiley, 1997) 123.

[186] The Court of Appeal held that it was correct to interpret 'risk' under 3(1) of the Health and Safety at Work Act 1974 not as simply referring to proven risks but also to possibilities of danger and that such an interpretation was consistent with the public health and safety aims of that legislation (*R v. Board of Trustees of the Science Museum* (1993) ICR 876). Likewise, the public perception of an unsubstantiated risk was held to be a relevant consideration for a planning inspector to take into account in refusing planning permission (*Newport BC v. Secretary of State for Wales and Browning Environmental Services Ltd* [1998] Env L R 174). Eg E. Fisher, 'Drowning by Numbers: Standard Setting in Risk Regulation and the Pursuit of Accountable Public Administration' (2000) 20: 1 OJLS 114; id., 'Is the Precautionary Principle Justiciable?' (2001) 13:3 JEL 324.

[187] See the different case studies in European Environmental Agency, *Late Lessons from Early Warnings: The Precautionary Principle 1896–2000* (Copenhagen: European Issues Report No. 22, 2001).

[188] Although US authorities oppose the use of the principle in international forums, elements of the precautionary principle are firmly entrenched in early US domestic environment law. Eg J.S. Applegate, 'The Precautionary Preference: An American Perspective on the Precautionary Principle' (2000) 3: 6 Hum Ecol Risk Ass 413.

decision-maker is acting in full knowledge of the facts in any given situation. We will consider some of the most relevant cases relating to precaution, in order to demonstrate both the successes and setbacks encountered by the precautionary approach in US case-law.

2.3.6.1. Acting on the frontiers of scientific knowledge

While European regulatory bodies are prone to take decisions in areas characterized by scientific uncertainties—such as chemicals policy—in a flexible and informal manner, the US approach is far more rigid and rule-oriented. US regulatory authorities tend to be much more demanding than their European counterparts with respect to the quantity of scientific data on which regulatory decisions should be based, although quality criteria vary enormously from one area to another.[189]

Several factors might explain the US insistence on extensive documentation. Under the provisions of the Federal Administrative Procedure Act (APA) scientific decision-making should involve the public: various stakeholders such as states, local authorities, and interest groups are entitled to comment on regulatory initiatives according to a 'notice and comment' procedure. This procedure is intended to be quite simple; any complexity resides in the various mechanisms for obtaining input, and primarily the requirement to create a detailed record to support eventual judicial review. Having to justify their decisions in the face of possible litigation, US regulatory agencies depend heavily on scientific data. Furthermore, the US Supreme Court has placed progressively higher burdens on agencies to rely on scientific evidence: an obligation that reduces their margin of discretion in the exercise of their regulatory duties. US courts are also known to be less reluctant than their European counterparts to amend standards. In contrast, European public authorities can count on deference from national and EC courts, which exercise only a marginal form of review. Pressure from judicial review and the influence of interest groups only partly explain the reliance of US agencies on risk assessment; the fact that this method provides an aura of

---

—The Clean Water Act (CWA) establishes strict goals in order to 'restore and maintain the chemical, physical, and biological integrity of the Nation's waters'. In enacting this statute Congress rejected the assimilative capacity approach, for essentially precautionary reasons. In Congress' view, the assimilative capacity approach 'assumes more knowledge about our complex ecosystem than we actually have'.

—The Clean Air Act (CAA) contains unequivocal obligations to prevent an activity once a health or environmental risk is established. Under §109(b), the EPA is to set national ambient air quality standards allowing for an adequate margin of safety. The EPA is neither required nor allowed to consider costs and technology. See *Lead Industry Ass'n v. EPA*, 647 F.2d 1130, 1148–1149 (D.C. Cir. 1980); *American Petroleum Institute v. Costle*, 665 F.2d 1176, 1185 (D.C. Cir. 1981).

—The Occupational Safety and Health Act (OSHA) was designed to 'assure so far as possible every working man and woman in the Nation safe and healthful working conditions'.

[189] V. Heyvaert, 'The changing role of science in environmental regulatory decision-making in the European Union' (1999) 3: 4 L&EA 427.

objectivity and precision in dealing with environmental hazards might also explain its success.

Does this mean that a precautionary approach has no role to play in the US decision-making process? This is far from certain. In fact the US Supreme Court as well as Federal courts were forerunners in applying a precautionary approach during the 1970s and 1980s in several cases challenging the validity of federal laws adopted under conditions of uncertainty.[190]

(a) Clean Air Act (CAA) and Clean Water Act (CWA)
Early court decisions gave substantial deference to the Environmental Protection Agency (EPA) to take action to prevent harm even before evidence of cause and effect had been assembled. In other words, they held that certain environmental or health risks justify the abatement of hazards despite the absence of evidence of actual harm.

In a case concerning unknown health effects of discharges of taconite tailings (*Reserve Mining Co. v. US EPA*), the Eighth Circuit Court reversed its earlier decision[191] and endorsed precautionary measures. It found that the 'public's exposure to asbestos fibres in air and water creates some health risk' that justified the 'abatement of the health hazard on reasonable terms as a precautionary and preventive measure to protect public health'.[192] The Court was satisfied that 'under an acceptable but improved medical theory [asbestos fibres] may be considered as carcinogenic' and a reasonable medical concern as regards public health had therefore been established[193] and ruled: 'In the context of [the CWA], we believe that Congress used the term "endangering" in a precautionary or preventive sense, and, therefore, evidence of potential harm as well as actual harm comes within the purview of that term'.

In a similar case the Minnesota Supreme Court held that, even though there was no evidence of the level at which asbestos posed a risk in drinking water,

---

[190] M. Belsky, 'Environmental policy law in the 1970s: Shifting back the burden of proof' (1988) 12: 1 ELQ 5; D. Bodansky, 'The Precautionary Principle in US Environmental Law' in T. O'Riordan and J. Cameron (eds.), *Interpreting the Precautionary Principle*, n. 151 above, 203; D. Shelton, 'The Impact of Scientific Uncertainty on Environmental Law and Policy in the USA' in D. Freestone and E. Hey (eds.), *The Precautionary Principle and International Law*, n. 181 above, 209; G.D. Fulem, 'The Precautionary Principle: Environmental Protection in the Face of Scientific Uncertainty' (1995) Willamette L Rev 495; M. Shapiro, 'The Frontiers of Science Doctrine: American Experiences with the Judicial Control of Science-Based Decision-Making' in C. Joerges, K.-H. Ladeur, and E. Vos (eds.), *Integrating Expertise into Regulatory Decision-Making* (Baden-Baden: Nomos, 1997) 325 ; J. Tickner and C. Raffensperger, 'The American View on the Precautionary Principle' in T. O'Riordan, J. Cameron, and A. Jordan (eds.), *Reinterpreting the Precautionary Principle* (Cameron and May, London, 2001) 183–214.

[191] The Court first held that such discharges 'may or may not result in detrimental health effects, but for the present that is unknown'. As the plaintiffs had failed to prove a demonstrable health hazard, discharges could continue and populations continue to be exposed. *Reserve Mining Company v. United States*, 498 F.2d 1073, 1083–1084 (8th Cir. 1974).

[192] *Reserve Mining Co. v. EPA*, 514 F. 2d at 520 (8th Cir. 1975).

[193] Ibid., at 529.

the regulatory agency was free to apply a worst-case standard until better evidence became available.[194]

Similarly, US federal courts have considered that a precautionary approach follows from the CAA. In a case concerning regulation of gasoline additives under the CAA (*Ethyl Corp. v. EPA*)[195] the Court of Appeals for the District of Columbia Circuit ruled that the EPA could order reductions of lead levels in petrol, despite the fact that the risk assessment only established a 'significant risk of harm'[196] and that the evidence was 'difficult to come by, uncertain or conflicting',[197] given that: '...more commonly, "reasonable medical concerns" and theory long precede certainty. Yet the statutes—and common sense—demand regulatory action to prevent harm, even if the regulator is less than certain that the harm is otherwise inevitable [...] awaiting certainty will often allow for only reactive, not preventive regulation'.

The Court went on to find that the CAA follows a precautionary approach:

Case law and dictionary definition agree that endanger means something less than actual harm...Where a statute is precautionary in nature, the evidence difficult to come by, uncertain, or conflicting because it is on the frontiers of scientific knowledge, the regulations designed to protect the public health, and the decision that of an expert administrator, we will not demand rigorous step-by-step proof of cause and effect. Such proof may be impossible to obtain if the precautionary purpose of the statute is to be served. Of course, we are not suggesting that the Administrator has the power to act on hunches or wild guesses...However, we do hold that in such cases the Administrator may assess risks. He must take account of available facts, of course, but his inquiry does not end there. The Administrator may apply his expertise to draw conclusions from suspected, but not completely substantiated, relationships between facts, from trends among facts, from theoretical projections from imperfect data, from probative preliminary data not yet certifiable as 'fact,' and the like. We believe that a conclusion so drawn...may, if rational, form the basis for health-related regulations under the 'will endanger' language of Section 211.

Based on similar reasoning, the same Court judged that it would have been contrary to the intent of the CAA to forbid the EPA to adopt national ambient air quality standards (NAAQs) 'until it can conclusively demonstrate' adverse health effects (*Lead Indus. Ass'n Inc. v. EPA*).[198] Another court similarly found that the 'margin of safety' test was 'intended to provide protection against hazards which research has not yet identified'.[199] The court in this case allowed the EPA to establish very stringent emission standards for substances whose dangers were not well established, based on extrapolations from data about more familiar substances:

---

[194] *Reserve Mining Co. v. Minnesota Pollution Control Agency*, 267 N.W.2d 720 (Minn. 1978).
[195] *Ethyl Corp. v. EPA*, 541 F.2d1, 24–25 (D.C. Cir. 1976).
[196] Ibid., at p. 12ff. Followed in *Industrial Union Dep't. v. American Petr. Inst.*, 448 U.S. 607, 714.
[197] Ibid., at 25, 28.
[198] *Lead Indus. Ass'n Inc. v. US EPA*, 647 F.2d 1130 (D.C. Cir. 1979).
[199] *EDF v. EPA*, 598 F.2d at 81.

The public and the environment were not to be exposed to anything resembling the maximum risk. Not only was EPA to provide a 'margin of safety', but the margin was to be greater than 'normal' or 'adequate': the margin was to be 'ample'. 'Ample' is defined as 'abundant; plentiful; more than adequate'. Clearly Congress intended that in dealing with toxic pollutants that pose a threat to human health, margins of safety should be generous to ensure protection of human health and aquatic ecosystems to the greatest extent possible.[200]

That does not, however, require setting limits that would assure a 'risk-free' environment. Rather, the Agency must decide 'what risks are acceptable in the world in which we live' and set limits accordingly. [201]

In 1999 the Court of Appeals for the District of Columbia remanded the EPA's 1997 decision to tighten health-based air quality standards for ozone and particulate matter, ordering the Agency to provide an 'intelligible principle' explaining how it selected such standards (*American Trucking Associations Inc. v. EPA*). The District Court stated that the EPA may not ignore the possible health benefits of a pollutant such as tropospheric ozone; in formulating air quality standards, the Agency must consider identifiable effects and then assess the ozone's net adverse health effect by whatever criteria it adopts (*American Trucking Associations Inc. v. EPA*).[202] The Supreme Court reversed the Court of Appeals decision in 2001, holding that the CAA does not delegate legislative power to the EPA in contravention of the Constitution.[203]

(b) Occupational Safety and Health Administration (OSHA)
The early CAA cases were supplemented by several occupational health cases where the Federal courts noted the ability of the OSHA to act when information was 'on the frontiers of scientific knowledge' and the right of the agency to issue regulations that are 'technology forcing' in nature, even if some companies might be put out of business by such regulations.[204] For example, in a case regarding OSHA regulation of asbestos exposures, the District of Columbia Circuit Court noted that: 'some of the questions involved in the promulgation of these standards are on the frontiers of scientific knowledge, and consequently as to them insufficient data is presently available to make a fully informed factual determination. Decision making must in that circumstance depend to a greater extent upon policy judgements and less upon purely factual analysis.'[205]

In the 1980 *Benzene* decision,[206] however, the Supreme Court ordered the OSHA to demonstrate, on the basis of substantial evidence, that a hazard

---

[200] Ibid., at 83.

[201] See *NRDC, Inc. v. EPA*, 824 F.2d 1146, 1164–65 (D.C. Cir. 1987).

[202] 175 F.3d 1027, 48 ERC 1417 (D.C. Cir., 1999) 94. Eg J. Brax, 'American Trucking Ass'ns, Inc. v. EPA' (2000) 27 ELQ 549.

[203] *Whitman v. American Trucking Associations*, 531 U.S. 457 (2001).

[204] E. Fisher, 'The Risks of Quantifying Justice: The Use of the Substantial Evidence Test in Judicial Review of OSHA Rule-Making' in R. Baldwin (ed.), *Law and Uncertainty: Risks and Legal Processes* (London: Kluwer Law Int'l, 1997) 293–311.

[205] *AFL-CIO v. Hodgson*, 99 F.2d 467, 1974.

[206] *Industrial Union Dep't. AFL-CIO v. American Petroleum Inst.*, 448 U.S. 607, 656 (1980).

represented a significant risk before establishing an occupational health stand-ard.[207] Where scientific knowledge is imperfect and the precise quantification of risks is therefore impossible, the burden of proving the significance of the risk is thus on the Agency and not on the industry. The Supreme Court acknowledged, however, that imposing the burden of demonstrating a significant risk of harm on the Agency would not strip it of its ability to regulate carcinogens, nor would it require the Agency to wait for deaths to occur before taking any action. The requirement that a 'significant' risk be identified is therefore not a mathematical straitjacket. Although the Agency's findings must be supported by substantial evidence, it is not required to support its finding that a significant risk exists with anything approaching scientific certainty, as it has 'some leeway where its findings must be made on the frontiers of scientific knowledge'. So long as those findings are supported by a body of reputable scientific thought, the Agency is free in its risk assessment of hazardous substances 'to use conservative assumptions in interpreting the data with respect to carcinogens, risking error on the side of overprotection rather than underprotection'.

The *Benzene* case-law was taken up by other courts and has had a chilling effect on environmental and occupational health regulation in the US, hindering the OSHA as well as other agencies from issuing further health protection measures.[208] Agencies felt obliged to devote significant financial and human resources to developing voluminous scientific dossiers based on quantified risk assessment to support their standards. Criticisms of judicial review of agency actions have increased in recent years, with time-and-resource intensive assess-ments characterized as 'ossification' of a previously flexible regulatory pro-cess,[209] forcing regulatory agencies to emphasize narrow issues that may not have particular policy importance.[210]

Additional court decisions, such as those made by the Fifth Circuit court on formaldehyde in consumer products and the EPA's regulation of asbestos under the Toxic Substances Control Act (after ten years of studying the problem) have heightened the reluctance of administrative agencies to take precautionary action to protect public health without quantitative estimates of risk. A 'sub-stantial evidence' standard of review has been applied in a case involving the

[207] The Court noted that 'Congress was concerned, not with absolute safety, but with the elimin-ation of significant harm . . . As we read the statute, the burden was on the Agency to show, on the basis of substantial evidence, that it is at least more likely than not that a long-term exposure to 10ppm of benzene represents a significant risk of material health impairment.'

[208] Agencies now interpret this decision to mean that they must have quantitative estimates of risk before regulating. Eg C.F. Cranor, 'Asymmetric information, Precautionary Principle and burdens of proof' in C. Raffensperger and J. Tickner (eds.), *Protection of Public Health & the Environment. Implementing the Precautionary Principle* (Washington: Island Press, 1999) 91.

[209] T. McGarity, 'Some Thoughts on "Deossifying" the Rulemaking Process' (1992) 41 Duke LJ 1; J.S. Applegate, 'The Precautionary Preference: An American perspective on the precautionary Principle' (2000) 3 Hum Ecol Risk Ass, 431.

[210] R. O'Leary, 'The Impact of Federal Court Decisions on the Policies and Administrations of the U.S. Environmental Protection Agency' (1989) 41 Administrative Law Review 549; S. Rose-Ackerman, *Controlling Environmental Policy* (New Haven: Yale UP, 1994) 134.

OSHA's Air Contaminants Standard. The eleventh court of appeals nullified the OSHA regulation establishing baseline standards for 428 chemical substances because the Federal Administration failed to establish a significant risk for each substance and failed to establish economic and technical feasibility on a substance-by-substance basis.[211] The court's rejection of generic rule making forced the OSHA to develop an elaborate record for each chemical. Noting that an EPA ban on asbestos failed to examine the effect of non-asbestos brakes on automotive safety in light of credible evidence that non-asbestos brakes could significantly increase the number of highway fatalities, a Federal court decided to suspend the EPA standard.[212]

2.3.6.2. Balancing risks and benefits

Critics of a precautionary approach emphasize the financial burden that accompanies overprotection in the face of uncertainty. Nevertheless, when regulatory agencies have to balance the protection of human health against economic interests, US courts and Congress clearly favour human health. Consequently, early US case-law supported standards that had important economic consequences.

(a) Endangered Species Act (ESA)

In a now celebrated judgment, *Tennessee Valley Authority v. Hill*, the Supreme Court had to rule on the prohibition by a Federal judge of continued construction of a dam which would have resulted in the extinction of an endemic fish, the Snail Darter, whose habitat was protected under the ESA.[213] The Court considered that, if there was any question about the survival of the endangered species, actions threatening its conservation should be prohibited because:

The value of this genetic heritage is, quite literally, incalculable . . . From the most narrow possible point of view, it is in the best interests of mankind to minimize the losses of genetic variations. The reason is simple: they are potential resources. They are keys to puzzles which we cannot solve, and may provide answers to questions which we have not yet learned to ask . . . The institutionalization of caution lies at the heart of the Act.

This example demonstrates that, in passing the ESA, Congress was concerned about the as yet unknown uses of endangered species[214] and the unforeseeable role such creatures might play in the planet's chain of life. Thus interpreted, the ESA seems to represent an absolutely precautionary approach: a finding of endangerment results automatically in order fully to protect the natural habitat of the species. Neither the value of the species nor the economic costs of preservation may be considered.[215]

---

[211] *AFL-CIO v. OSHA* 965F.2d. 962 (11th Cir. 1992).
[212] *Corrosion Proof Fittings v. EPA*, 947 F.2d 1201, 1224–1225 (5th Cir. 1991).
[213] *Tennessee Valley Authority v. Hill et al.*, 437 U.S. 153, 180 (1978).
[214] Ibid., 437 U.S. 153, 179.
[215] J.S. Applegate, n. 209 above, 433.

(b) Clean Air Act (CAA)

In implementing the CAA, the EPA must set NAAQs that allow for an adequate margin of safety, and it is not allowed to consider costs and technological feasibility. The CAA does not prevent the EPA from adopting measures which are not based on certainty; it does, however, forbid the Agency from limiting the scope of protection justified by a situation of uncertainty in the name of economic considerations. The Federal Court of Appeal for the District of Columbia reads the CAA as barring the EPA from considering any factor—eg the costs of implementing standards—other than 'health effects relating to pollutants in the air'.[216] In 2001 the Supreme Court affirmed the case-law of the Court of Appeals on this point: 'CAA unambiguously bars cost considerations from the NAAQs-setting process'.[217]

(c) Federal Food, Drug, and Cosmetic Act (FFDCA)

The Delaney Clause in Section 409 FFDCA which applies 'zero risk' to food additives that are or contain carcinogens is a prominent example of a precautionary approach in the US.[218] The EPA has interpreted that clause to mean that some residues of carcinogenic pesticides may be present in processed foods as long as they pose a 'negligible risk', meaning that consumption of the maximum concentration of the substance over a lifetime would be expected to cause no more than one death from cancer in an exposed population of one million. The District Court of Columbia[219] as well as the Ninth Circuit Court[220] have strictly interpreted that clause, stressing that it must be understood literally, without regard to any concept of sensible policy-making.

2.3.6.3. Reversal of the burden of proof in litigation

State constitutional rights to a clean and healthful environment could provide fertile ground for the development of the precautionary principle in the US. A good example of this trend can be found in a 1999 decision by the Supreme Court of Montana.[221] Plaintiffs alleged that, by amending a mineral exploration licence, the Montana Department of Environmental Quality violated the right to a clean and healthy environment and the clear non-degradation policy estab-

---

[216] *NRDC*, 902 F.2d at 973; *Lead Industries*, 647 F.2d at 1148; *American Lung Ass'n v. EPA*, 328 U.S. App. D.C. 232, 134 F.3d 388, 389 (D.C. Cir. 1998); *American Petroleum Inst.*, 665 F.2d at 1185; *American Trucking Associations, Inc. v. EPA*, 175 F.3d 1027, 48 ERC 1417 (D.C. Cir., 1999) 94; *Whitman v. American Trucking Associations*, 531 U.S. 457 (2001).

[217] *Whitman v. American Trucking Associations*, 531 U.S. 457 (2001).

[218] In 1985 Congress enacted Section 409(c)(3)(A), commonly known as the 'Delaney Clause', which established an absolute standard of safety for carcinogenic food additives: 'No additive shall be deemed to be safe if it is found to induce cancer when ingested by man or laboratory animals, or if it is found, after tests which are appropriate for the evaluation of the safety of food additives, to induce cancer in man or animal'.

[219] *Public Citizen v. FDA*, 831 Fed 1108 (D.C. Cir 1987).

[220] *Les v. Reilly*, 968 F. 2d 985 (9th Cir. 1992).

[221] *Montana Environmental Information Center v. Department of Environmental Quality*, MT 248.

lished by Montana's Constitution.[222] The District Court refused to apply strict scrutiny because the plaintiffs were not able to demonstrate that discharges from the mine exceeded water quality standards and that there was a risk to human or environmental health; according to the District Court, an actual threat to human health or the health of the environment had to be demonstrated. The Supreme Court of the State of Montana reversed this judgment, ruling that the plaintiffs only needed to show degradation to the environment in order to demonstrate that their right to a clean and healthful environment as guaranteed by the Constitution had been abridged:

Our constitution does not require that dead fish float on the surface of our state's rivers and streams before its farsighted environmental protections can be invoked.(....) We conclude, therefore, that the District Court erred when it held that Montana's constitutional right to a clean and healthy environment was not implicated, absent a demonstration that public health is threatened or that current water quality standards are affected to such an extent that a significant impact has been had on either the Landers Fork or Blackfoot River.

2.3.6.4. Development risks

Liability for so-called development risks would also be desirable. On one hand, it is impossible to react to unknown risks with preventive measures and an adjustment of the level of activity. On the other hand, the manufacturer or operator of a plant is in the best position to carry out research on the impacts of his operation's products and emissions. Thus far, however, it is only in asbestos cases that some US jurisdictions have taken steps in the direction of strict liability for development risks and thus precluded the defence of unfeasibility.[223]

2.3.7. *Australia*

In Australia[224] the precautionary principle emerged in February 1992 through the Intergovernmental Agreement on the Environment, where the Commonwealth, States, Territories, and Local Governments agreed to follow the precautionary principle as part of a commitment to ecologically sustainable development.[225] The Agreement is not binding on parties, however. Subsequently, specific

---

[222] Article II, Section 3 and Article IX, Section 1 of Montana's Constitution.

[223] *Beshada v. Johns-Manville Prods. Corp.*, 90 NJ 191, 447 A 2d 539 (1982). Contrary to Beshada: *Anderson v. Owens-Corning Fiberglass Corp.*, 53 Cal. 3d 987, 810 P 2d 549 (1991).

[224] C. Barton, 'The Status of the Precautionary Principle in Australia: Its Emergence in Legislation and as a Common Law Doctrine' (1998) 2: 22 HELR 509; W. Gullett, 'Environmental Protection and the Precautionary Principle: A Response to Scientific Uncertainty in Environmental Management' (1997) Envtl and Planning LJ 61; P. Stein, 'Turning Soft Law into Hard: An Australian Experience with ESD Principles in Practice' (1997) 3: 2 Judicial Review 91; E. Fisher and R. Harding, 'The Precautionary Principle in Australia: From Aspiration to Practice?' in T. O'Riordan, J. Cameron, and A. Jordan (eds.), *Reinterpreting the Precautionary Principle*, n. 190 above, 215–33.

[225] The parties agreed that: 'Where there are threats of serious or irreversible environmental damage, lack of full scientific certainty should not be used as a reason for postponing measures to prevent environmental degradation. In the application of the precautionary principle, public and

reference has been made to the precautionary principle in more than twenty statutes and policy documents. [226]

In addition, Australian courts have been at the forefront in implementing the principle; Australian case-law thus contains a wealth of information on its contents and legal application. The first and most significant judicial consideration of the precautionary principle was carried out in 1993 by Stein J of the New South Wales Land and Environment Court in *Leatch v. National Parks and Wildlife Service*.[227] In order to verify the grounds for administrative decisions, the Land and Environment Court of the Australian State of New South Wales has several times had recourse to the precautionary principle, based on a provision of the legislation relating to national parks and wildlife. On that basis, the Court rescinded an administrative authorisation to eliminate a rare species of toad from a natural site that was to be crossed by a high-speed trunk road. It considered that the administration which had granted the disputed authorization had not taken due account of the risk that the species would disappear, and that no lower-risk alternative had been seriously evaluated:

...the precautionary principle is a statement of commonsense and has already been applied by decision-makers in appropriate circumstances prior to the principle being spelt out. It is directed towards the prevention of serious or irreversible harm to the environment in situations of scientific uncertainty. Its premise is that where uncertainty or ignorance exists concerning the nature or scope of environmental harm (whether this follows from policies, decisions or activities), decision-makers should be cautious. Given that the Giant Burrowing Frog has only recently been added to the schedule of endangered species by the scientific committee as vulnerable and rare... caution should be the keystone to the Court's approach. Application of the precautionary principle appears to be

private decisions should be guided by: (i) careful evaluation to avoid, wherever practicable, serious or irreversible damage to the environment; and (ii) an assessment of risk-weighted consequences of various options.'

[226] Of the Commonwealth's legislation, the Environment Protection and Biodiversity Conservation Act 1999 provides the most detailed legislative exercise in its reference to the precautionary principle. Section 391 requires that the Minister take account of the precautionary principle in making decisions or granting permits. The New South Wales Parliament has been particularly active in promoting the principle. The Protection of the Environment Administration Act 1991 adopted the precautionary principle as an objective. The principle is worded in a traditional manner: 'If there are threats of serious or irreversible environmental damage, lack of full scientific certainty should not be used as a reason for postponing measures to prevent environmental degradation'. Section 30(1)(c) of the Fisheries Management Act 1994 provides that in determining TAC, the Total Allowable Catch Setting and Review Committee is to have regard to the precautionary principle, namely, that if there are threats of serious or irreversible damage to fish stocks, lack of full scientific certainty should not be used as a reason for postponing measures to prevent that damage. The Parliament of South Australia has also adopted a precautionary approach, in the Environment Protection Act 1993. The 'objectives' section of the Act provides a commitment 'to apply a precautionary approach to the assessment of risk of environmental harm and ensure that all aspects of environmental quality affected by pollution and waste (including ecosystem sustainability and valued environmental attributes) are considered in decisions relating to the environment...'

[227] [1993] 81 LGERA 270. On the other hand, the same Court refused to rescind an administrative decision authorizing logging in a wooded massif, on the ground that the environmental impact assessment had sufficiently considered the risks to various species of protected animals inherent in the planned exploitation: *Northcompass Inc. v. Hornsby Shire Council* [1996] NSWLEC 213.

most apt in a situation of a scarcity of scientific knowledge of species population, habitat and impacts. Indeed, one permissible approach is to conclude that the state of knowledge is such that one should not grant a licence to 'take or kill' the species until much more is known.

However, in most other cases the principle has not been a particularly sharp 'sword' for litigants.[228] Generally, Australian courts—like their European counterparts—tend to be deferential to the authorities, considering that the principle has already been integrated into administrative decisions. In cases such as the licensing of a combustion plant that would contribute to the greenhouse effect,[229] of an aluminium dross plant,[230] of the construction of a tourist resort close to a World Cultural and Natural Heritage site,[231] and of exposure to radiation,[232] the courts considered that elements of the inquiry carried out by the public authorities were in conformity with the precautionary principle.

In a recent case concerning the ecological sustainability of tuna feedlots in Australian waters, the South Australia Environment Resources and Development Court held that the onus was on the developer to show that the feedlots were sustainable, rather than the burden being on conservationists to demonstrate that they were not. [233]

On the whole, these various decisions demonstrate that the precautionary principle has been afforded a degree of legal recognition by Australian courts.

3. Systematization of the principle

Analysis of the precautionary principle requires clarification of the concept of risk, and particularly ecological risk. In carrying out this examination, we identify the essential elements of the three threshold levels to which precautionary

---

[228] The principle could be used, however, to grant shorter licence periods for logging which will allow public authority to obtain additional informations (eg *Nicholls v. National Parks and Wildlife Service and Others* [1994] 84 LGERA 397).

[229] In dismissing an appeal against the grant of a development application for the establishment and operation of a coal-fired power station, the court stated: 'The application of the precautionary principle dictates that a cautious approach should be adopted in evaluating the various relevant factors in determining whether or not to grant consent; it does not require that the greenhouse issue should outweigh all other issues.' See *Greenpeace Australia LTD v. Redbank Power Company and Singleton Council* [1994] 86 LGERA 143.

[230] *Alumino (Aust) Pty. Ltd. v. Minister Administering the Environmental Planning and Assessment Act 1979* [1996] NSWLEC 102. The court stated: 'It is obvious that where development involves the handling and processing of materials which have the potential to cause significant harm to the health of human beings and vegetation, extreme caution must be used in determining whether development consent will be forthcoming'.

[231] *Friends of Hinchinbrook Society Inc. v. Minister for Environment* [1997] 142 ALR 622 and [1997] 87 LGERA 10.

[232] *Optus v. Corporation of the City of Kensington and Norwood* [1998] SAERDC 480.

[233] *Conservation Council of SA Inc. v. Development Assessment Commission and Tuna Boat Owners' Association of Australia* [1999] SAERDC 86. Eg M. Parnell, 'Southern Bluefin Tuna Feedlotting ESD, the Precautionary Principle and Burden of Proof' (1999) 2 J Int'l Wildlife L & Pol'y 334.

measures appear to be subject: risk (Subsection 3.1 below), damage (Subsection 3.2), and proportion (Subsection 3.3).

3.1. The centrality of post-industrial risk

3.1.1. *The ambiguity of the concept of risk*

The precautionary principle is so intimately linked to risk that we must examine the scope of the concept before systematically considering the subject as a whole. The success of the concept of risk in legal systems should not obscure the fact that its multiple meanings continue to give rise to difficulties. In current usage, risk is generally understood as a synonym for danger, peril, an unfortunate event. Risk is inherently uncertain. It is by nature erratic, unforeseen, unexpected. Where the slightest doubt exists as to whether an event will occur, risk is present. Insurance policies, whose purpose is to cover risk, exclude intentional misconduct by the policy holder.[234] Insurance only covers the *probability* of loss of a good: that is, uncertainty. However, the concept is ambiguous in that it covers both loss and the event causing the loss. It is thus necessary to distinguish clearly between risk in its wider sense and in its strict sense.

Sensu lato, risk is a two-sided concept: on one hand, chance, accident, the possible occurrence of an event; on the other hand, the resultant loss or damage. It embraces both probability of occurrence and damage. This twofold approach is made necessary by the fact that risk has no meaning in and of itself. The concept is usually associated with adverse effects that occur as the result of human activity (eg cancer caused by smoking or drinking, AIDs due to unsafe sex, driving accidents) or natural phenomena (eg floods, earthquakes). The notion of risk thus only becomes fully effective when it affects values or interests. Environmental risk, for instance, did not exist so long as nature could be casually destroyed; the concept only took shape once such destruction came to be seen as affecting collective interests.

Sensu stricto, risk refers to the possibility of an unfortunate event occurring. The ensuing damage is consequential. The need clearly to distinguish between risk and damage has led us to adopt this second meaning of the term. With only a few exceptions, 'risk' is used here *sensu stricto* to designate the probability of an event or process with injurious consequences.

3.1.2. *The character of post-industrial risk*

The appearance of the precautionary principle is linked to the emergence of a new type of risk, which we qualify as post-industrial risk. In this section we examine what distinguishes this from other forms of risk in an historical perspective.

---

[234] The principle that insurance cannot be provided for intentional fault does not, however, exclude that simple fault or negligence may be insured against.

The concept of risk has recently undergone lightning progress. Put forward by French legal authors such as Salleilles and Josserand at the end of the nineteenth century, the theory of risk seemed to provide a new basis for civil liability, which would progressively allow worker—and subsequently consumer—related damages to be compensated without the fault of the installation owner/operator or producer having to be proved.

Risk theory rapidly shaped the welfare state, a model which thoroughly permeated the majority of political systems in the course of the twentieth century. In that context, social risk (illness, old age, unemployment) gave rise to a 'right' to compensation within the framework of mechanisms that ally solidarity with insurance. Whether through private or public compensation mechanisms (unemployment insurance, workplace accident funds, etc.) insurance guaranteed optimal indemnification for victims. In order to be covered by the welfare state, or if necessary by private insurers, risks had to be regular, foreseeable, and calculable.[235] This model of 'insurability' is thus based entirely on knowledge.

Particular to industrialized society, the concept of 'environmental risk' first appeared in the mid-1960s, with the sudden awareness of environmental degradation. Environmental risks rapidly became a major concern, in that they affected all socio-economic sectors: industry (risk of accidental release of pollutants, hazardous wastes, etc.), energy (risk of air pollution resulting from the combustion of fossil fuels, nuclear wastes), transport (potential impacts of photochemical oxydants, introduction of non-indigenous species), exploitation of natural resources (precipitous depletion of fish stocks, loss of biodiversity), intensive farming (eutrophication of surface and ground waters, acidification or salinization of soils).[236] At that stage it was believed that potential adverse impacts could be reduced to tolerable levels thanks to science, which made it possible to assess the probability of adverse effects and the extent of the ensuing damage. A preventive approach (land use planning, emission controls, quality standards, BAT, IPPC, emergency planning) was expected to prevent further degradation.[237]

The end of the twentieth century has taken us fully into a 'risk civilization' or 'risk society'.[238] Scientific development gives rise to so many new risks that it has

[235] Fr. Ewald, *L'Etat Providence* (Paris: Grasset, 1980).

[236] D. Stanners and P. Bourdeau (eds.), *Europe's Environment: The Dobris Assessment* (Copenhagen: European Environmental Agency, 1995).

[237] While it is rarely defined in normative texts, risk has now become a familiar word in environmental law. The legal regimes that apply to nuclear risks, risk of major accidents involving dangerous substances, or natural risks are legion, and many general legal texts take this branch of law as an example when considering the question of risk. See, in this connection, the definition of risk set out in Article 3(7) of Directive 96/82/EC on the control of major accident hazards involving dangerous substances: 'the likelihood of a specific effect occurring within a specified period or in specified circumstances'.

[238] P. Lagadec, *La civilisation du risque* (Paris: Seuil, 1981); A. Giddens, *Modernity and Self-Identity: Self and Society in the Late Modern Age* (London: Polity, 1990); N. Luhmann, *Risk: A Sociological Theory* (Berlin: de Gruyter, 1991).

become difficult to know which are real and which hypothetical. In this context the abstract concept of risk has become a dominant ordering principle, helping to structure and condition social and institutional relations and, to some extent, replacing monetary wealth and cultural privilege as the focus of distributional tensions and political conflict.[239] In his book *Risikogesellschaft*, the German sociologist Ulrich Beck characterizes risk as the central concept of the century.[240] Although contemporary societies are undoubtedly less exposed to danger than earlier societies, they nevertheless have a much keener perception of risk. According to Beck, the notion of risk encapsulates the readiness of the modern spirit to confront the multiple hazards of a rapidly changing socio-economic culture, just as earlier societies braved the perils of the sea. Risk is inherent in all aspects of our civilization. Life is replete with risks, including sickness, unemployment, scholastic failure, criminality, etc. Consequently risk is becoming a tool for objectifying social problems.

The globalization of the economy and the rise of new technologies characteristic of post-industrialized society have caused a new generation of risks to emerge (CFCs, POPs, GMOs, BSE, greenhouse gases, hormone-disrupting chemicals, electromagnetic fields, etc.). Presenting unique challenges to the ability of science to anticipate and prevent harm, these 'post-industrial risks' are fundamentally different from earlier types of risks for three reasons. First, while the risks assumed by the Welfare State primarily concerned either individuals (consumers, workers) or specific groups (neighbourhood, local communities), post-industrial risks have much wider and diffuse impacts. In fact, it is more a question of accumulation of ecological impacts (eg the tremendous increase of transportation by road and by air) due to mass production, globalization, and free trade than of radical technological change (eg genetic engineering which is revolutionary in comparison with traditional industrial processes). Therefore, the impacts of post-industrial risks are more global (ozone depletion, climate change) than local (pollution of the Great Lakes or the North Sea). Secondly, post-industrial risks may give rise to damage outside the realm of commerce (eg to human health) and thus be impossible to evaluate. Finally, and this is undoubtedly the crucial difference, post-industrial risk is permeated with uncertainty.

Scientific knowledge is relativistic, and uncertainty weighs heaviest on those factors determining causation for post-industrial risk. In cases where causation cannot be fully established, it is replaced by a relationship of possibility, eventuality, or plausibility between a cause and its effect. For example, the exact nature of various greenhouse gases and the extent to which each contributes to climate change is not clear. Despite the efforts of the scientific community there is still no hope of fully understanding the complexities of the interactions of the

---

[239] A. Stirling, *On Precautionary and Science Based Approaches to Risk Assessment and Environmental Appraisal: Field Study* (Sevilla: Institute for Prospective Technological Studies, 2001) 3.

[240] U. Beck, *Risiko Gesellschaft: Auf dem Weg in eine andere Moderne* (Frankfurt: Suhrkamp, 1986); Eng. translation: *Risk Society: Towards a New Modernity* (London: Sage, 1992).

atmosphere, the oceans, and greenhouse gases. This type of complexity is the rule, rather than the exception, in ecosystems. In approaching such questions, scientists therefore put forward hypotheses rather than assertions. The uncertainty that attaches to causation of post-industrial risks affects the calculation of their probability as well as the nature and scope of the damages they may entail.

To begin with, insufficient experience makes it impossible to determine the regularity and probability of such risks.[241] It is also difficult to determine the damages post-industrial risks may provoke, in terms of localization (eg the impacts of acid rain or radioactivity vary with thermal currents), time of latency between the first exposure and the actual impact of damage (eg mutations due to thalidomide), frequency (repetitive or single), duration (persistent, reversible, slowly reversible, irreversible, multigenerational), extent (cumulative or synergistic, serious or insignificant), nature (human health, biodiversity) and scale (global, regional).[242] Uncertainty may touch all these factors (eg in the case of climate change). In other situations, it may be restricted to specific aspects of the problem (eg aquifer pollution by pesticide dispersion).

Finally, surprises are inevitable as scientists regularly confront the greatest uncertainty: ignorance.[243] The consequences of ignorance can be dramatic, as shown by the late discovery of the impacts of asbestos mesothelioma cancer (unknown prior to 1974), of CFCs (unknown prior to 1977), and of TBT antifoulants (grossly underestimated until the middle of the 1980s).

Given the above, is it possible to insure against post-industrial risks, since insurance is neither a lottery nor a wager? For a risk to be insurable, it must be as objective as possible. Yet the dearth of statistical data concerning the frequency and average cost of ecological risks, as well as the difficulty in identifying and controlling the risk to be indemnified, encourages prudence among insurers. This is hardly surprising, now that atmosphere-related risks have turned the insurance world on its head (for example, possible future compensation for victims of cancers that might result from the depletion of the ozone layer).

Each new concept of risk (social risk, environmental risk characteristic of industrial societies) has disturbed existing legal regimes, in some cases 'subverting' and in all cases at least destabilizing the established order; we can expect that the concept of 'post-industrial risk' will also give rise to major legal transformations.

---

[241] Before one of the nuclear reactors at Chernobyl exploded in 1987 no expert could have stated with certainty the probability of an explosion, for the simple reason that verification would not have been possible. Simulations had not predicted its occurrence.

[242] WGBU, *World in Transition: Strategies for Managing Global Environmental Risks* (Berlin, Heidelberg, New York: Springer Verlag, 2000); A. Klinke and O. Renn, 'Precautionary Principle and Discursive Strategies: Classifying and Managing Risks' (2001) 4:2 Journal of Risk Research 159–73.

[243] The concept of ignorance is no less scientific than is the probabilistic notion of risk. This concept can be defined as 'a state under which there exist neither grounds for the asignment of probabilities, nor even a basis for the definition of a comprehensive set of outcomes'. A. Stirling, n. 239 above, 17; European Environmental Agency, *Late Lessons from Early Warnings: The precautionary principle 1896–2000* (Copenhagen: Environmental Issues Report No. 22, 2001) 169–70.

3.1.3. The dilemma of post-industrial risk

In the 1980s, on the basis of almost identical scientific hypotheses about ozone layer depletion, public authorities in the UK and the US set in motion diametrically opposed policies concerning possible limitations on the production of chlorofluorocarbons (CFCs). The Americans adopted a precautionary strategy, limiting CFCs in response to the threat they posed to stratospheric ozone. The representatives of Her Majesty's Government, on the other hand, delayed the adoption of regulations until the hypothesis had been validated. This example illustrates the dilemma confronting public authorities when action is required to protect against an ecological risk.[244] Should they act under conditions of uncertainty to parry a threat that is merely suspected? Or should they first reduce the margin of uncertainty, even if it means delaying action?

Uncertainty affects both the likelihood of an event and when—and to what extent—it will produce damage. In response, public authorities will opt for either a delayed or an immediate preventive strategy.

The former strategy aims to delay action until the authorities have determined the exact nature of the risk. This strategy gives priority to research, even if it means delaying decisions until investigations have been completed. The accumulation of scientific knowledge resulting from this delay offers decision-makers some hope of reaching a suitable and carefully planned decision. By avoiding hasty and precipitate measures, this stance appears to favour a more efficient allocation of economic resources; however, the uncertainties inherent in scientific investigation could delay the adoption of essential measures in the absence of incontrovertible proof. Over the long term, this strategy could therefore prove to be as expensive as, or even more expensive than, an immediate strategy.

The latter approach does not condone any hesitation by public authorities. Although they may be torn between waiting and acting, the authorities may not vacillate even if conclusive evidence to support their suspicions is not available. Serious risks must immediately be prevented. Although it may allow the authorities to avert potentially expensive damages at low cost, this tactic presents certain drawbacks. Thus, if an anticipatory measure turns out not to have been necessary because the perception of risk was exaggerated, its proponents will be reproached for having acted irresponsibly, sacrificing innovation for the sake of security. This strategy can prove onerous in cases where preventive measures cost more than damages.[245]

Taken to the extreme, neither strategy is defensible: the one would forbid action in the present for fear of uncertain eventual effects, while the other would allow pressure for short-term gain to appropriate the future. The strategy of

---

[244] S. Rowland, 'EU Policy for Ozone Layer Protection' in Golub (ed.), *Global Competition and EU Environmental Law* (London: Routledge, 1998) 39.

[245] D. Pearce, 'The Precautionary Principle and Economic Analysis' in T. O'Riordan and J. Cameron (eds.), *Interpreting the Precautionary Principle*, n. 151 above, 145.

delayed preventive action can paralyse technological development; its rival may allow irreversible ecological damage to occur.

This paradox illustrates the dilemma confronting public authorities when they need to act in a context of incomplete knowledge. Should they await the results of full scientific investigations before acting, thereby risking irreversible damage in the future? Or should they act in an anticipatory fashion, even if the real nature of the threat remains less than certain?

Whether a risk is merely suspected or has been clearly demonstrated, the authorities will not intervene until they have taken the measure of the interests at stake. At this point choice of action is still largely determined by the import-ance accorded to environmental as opposed to competing socio-economic inter-ests. Authorities with a high level of environmental awareness will do everything in their power to avoid a disaster, even if it means wasting money, since they value the environment beyond price. On the other hand, authorities which consider problems from a purely economic perspective will refuse to sacrifice progress for the sake of hypothetical stakes and will refrain from intervening until it has been clearly demonstrated that a catastrophe is taking place.

In this way, the notion of objective evaluation of ecological risk depends by turn upon what information is available and what values the public authorities are upholding. Intervention receives further justification when uncertainty de-creases and it has been admitted that a risk may affect a recognized value. Inversely, inaction tends to triumph when uncertainty remains strong and the consequences of triggering the risk in question are not considered injurious.

3.2. Risk thresholds

Although various legal definitions of the precautionary principle share common elements, the thresholds intended to limit their scope are strongly nuanced. These restrict the application of the principle by defining the risk to be averted (with proof based on 'technical knowledge' required in some instances) or specifying the damage likely to occur (which, according to some definitions, should be 'serious or irreversible'); moreover, these two thresholds may apply cumulatively. Once these thresholds have been crossed, a precautionary measure may be taken to avert the anticipated risk, but it should be proportionate. This last condition also gives rise to divergent interpretations (some definitions require that risk reduction measures not 'entail excessive costs').

This is not the place to examine the varying thresholds set out by different definitions, as this would entail retracing the principle's history. Instead, we attempt to elaborate a systematic theory of the application thresholds governing the use of the precautionary principle.

These thresholds are critical because of the context of uncertainty which justifies the use of precaution. We will examine the difficulties of interpretation raised by *stricto sensu* risk, damage, and proportionality and link these to the concept of post-industrial risk. Each section below presents a brief summary of the question before setting out solutions which should be encouraged in view of the objectives of the precautionary principle. International and national definitions of the principle provide the empirical basis for these reflections.[246]

3.2.1. *The effect of uncertainty on establishing* stricto sensu *risk*

3.2.1.1. Introductory note

Lawyers do not baulk at considering risk, even if their concept of science is still grounded much more firmly in certainties than in probabilities. As evidenced by the evolution of liability and insurance law, the legal system no longer ignores the concept of risk. Nonetheless, the risks that set the precautionary principle in motion give rise to certain problems.

When an event characteristic of *stricto sensu* risk tends to recur, risk can be calculated on the basis of probability. It is possible, for instance, to calculate a driver's risk of accident by reference to elevated alcohol levels, exceeding the speed limit, or failing to exercise particular care in bad weather. However, when an event is merely anticipated and normal experience provides no basis for forecasting its likelihood, risk cannot be ascertained by calculating probability. Therefore, standard prerequisites for calculating probabilities cannot be satisfied for this class of risks, since any given problem is bound to remain controversial until the relevent scientific knowledge has stabilized. The question then arises: in which category of foreseeability should we range risks anticipated on the basis of the precautionary principle? Should the principle apply to any suspected risk, or only to known risks?

3.2.1.2. Recommended solutions

• A hierarchy of risks corresponding to degree of knowledge

Risk can be categorized as a function of knowledge, using the German theory[247] that distinguishes three types of risk.[248] The highest category is that of 'dangers' (*Gefahren*), unacceptable risks to which the principle of prevention (*Schutzprinzip*) corresponds. Dangers must be prohibited. 'Residual risks' (*Restrisiko*) form the lowest category. Purely hypothetical, such risks must be tolerated by society and therefore escape regulatory measures. As a result neither the principle of prevention nor the precautionary principle (*Vorsorgeanlaß*) applies to them. Only the final category, that of 'risks' (*Risiko*), which are located between unacceptable risks and residual risks, falls within the scope of the precautionary

---

[246] See Appendix I, Table of Materials, at the end of the book for a better understanding of the nuances inherent in the various definitions of the precautionary principle.

[247] This is only one of a number of approaches used to determine the concept of risk; see the synthesis of various possible classifications by R. Baldwin, 'Introduction—Risk: The Legal Contribution' in R. Baldwin (ed.), *Law and Uncertainty: Risks and Legal Processes* (London: Kluwer Law Int'l, 1997) 2.

[248] As regards this distinction, see among others A. Reich, *Gefahr-Risiko-Restrisiko* (Düsseldorf: Werner, 1989).

principle.[249] In order to minimize such risks in situations of recognized uncertainty (*Minimierungsgebot*) the authorities are obliged to act under the precautionary principle.[250]

By slightly modifying this hierarchy of risks, we may distinguish:

—*residual risks*, which do not require regulatory measures;
—*certain risks*, which fall within the scope of the principle of prevention; and
—*uncertain risks*, which come under the precautionary principle.

(1) Residual risks

If the precautionary principle imposes upon the decision-maker a mode of thinking that seeks to limit risks, must it therefore necessarily reduce him to inaction as soon as a risk is suspected? Does it apply in the same way to purely speculative risks? Must all Cassandras be taken seriously?

Such strictness would be an exaggeration. Most authors reckon that it would be excessive to try to avert all risks.[251] In any case, many of the consequences of our activities are unforeseeable because they arise in a context that is itself unpredictable. Risks are everywhere. We accept some of them while rejecting others. Driving a car, travelling by aeroplane, using electricity, having sexual relations: all of these involve some risk or another. To avert all risks we would have to forbid gas cookers because electric cookers are less likely to give rise to accidents: clearly an absurd suggestion. Hanging a Damoclean sword over any technical activity suspected of entailing environmental risk would put an end to innovation, discourage the spirit of enterprise, and compromise technological progress.

For instance, in the 1980 *Benzene* decision[252] the US Supreme Court stated that:

Some risks are plainly acceptable and others are plainly unacceptable. If, for example, the odds are one in a billion that a person will die from cancer by taking a drink of chlorinated water, the risk clearly could not be considered significant. On the other hand, if the odds are one in a thousand that regular inhalation of gasoline vapors that are 2% benzene will be fatal, a reasonable person might well consider the risk significant and take appropriate steps to decrease or eliminate it.

Similarly, the German Constitutional Court has stated that the right to life and physical integrity embodied in Article 2 of the German Constitution does not require the authorities, or Parliament, to prohibit a technology in the name of a

---

[249] E. Rehbinder, 'The Precautionary Principle in an International Perspective' in *Miljørettens grundsporgsmaal* (Copenhagen, 1994) 95; idem., 'Precaution and Sustainability: Two Sides of the Same Coin?' in *A Law for the Environment* (Gland: IUCN, 1994) 93.

[250] M. Kloepfer, *Umweltrecht* (München: Verlag C.H. Beck, 1989) 167.

[251] Some characterize such an approach as 'absolutist': eg A. Nollkaemper, 'What You Risk Reveals What You Value and Other Dilemmas Encountered in the Legal Assaults on Risks' in D. Freestone and E. Hey (eds.), *The Precautionary Principle*, n. 181 above, 73.

[252] *Industrial Union Dep't. AFL-CIO v. American Petroleum Inst.*, 448 U.S. 607, 656 (1980).

'zero risk' precautionary standard.[253] More recently the EFTA Court held that 'a purely hypothetical or academic consideration will not suffice to base a precautionary measure in order to protect the health and life of humans'.[254]

Adherence to the adage 'when in doubt, do nothing' should not overshadow the complementary wisdom that 'there's such a thing as being too careful'. To avoid having the best become the enemy of the good, the principle's field of application must exclude those risks characterized as residual, that is, hypothetical risks resting on purely speculative considerations without any scientific foundation.[255] Speculation, conjecture, intuition, warnings, denunciations, or implications should not suffice in and of themselves to justify an attitude of precaution.

(2) Certain risks

Risks for which causation between an event and damage is demonstrated by irrefutable scientific proof do not in any case come under the precautionary principle. Such risks can be qualified as *certain*, since it is possible to establish the causal link between the initial event and its adverse effects, to calculate the probability of their occurrence, and on that basis to insure against them. This characterization may be surprising, since risk is by nature a question of chance and its occurrence is always uncertain. Yet what is 'certain' here is precisely the link of cause and effect between an event that might occur and the damage anticipated as a result. Only the length of time that will elapse before the risk occurs is unpredictable.

For example, since we know that global warming due to increased greenhouse gas emissions will cause sea levels to rise, this is a certain risk to the extent that we know it will happen, if not the exact rate at which it will happen. In the same way, the risk of flooding caused by intensified use of agricultural land or of eutrophication caused by discharges of urban wastewater or slurry are certain risks, since we can establish causation between these human activities and the resultant ecological phenomena. That knowledge justifies adopting preventive measures. In the context of the German theory referred to above, these risks are *unacceptable*, because they are known.

Originally, the German precautionary principle primarily concerned certain risk. Two conditions had to be met for it to be invoked: first, the risk had to be imminent rather than latent; secondly, environmental degradation had to have already occurred.[256] The principle was thus limited to anticipating the extension of an environmental disaster and, in this interpretation, was situated midway between the principle of prevention and the more modern interpretation of the precautionary principle. It differed from the principle of prevention in that it was

---

[253] BVerfG, Beschl. v. 20.12.1979, 1 BvR 385/77 (*Nuclear Power Plant Mülheim-Kärlich*), vol. 53, 30.

[254] *EFTA Surveillance Authority v. Norway*, para. 20.

[255] E. Rehbinder, 'Precaution and Sustainability...', n. 249 above, 98–9.

[256] E. Rehbinder, 'The Precautionary Principle...', n. 249 above, 95.

no longer necessary to demonstrate a causal link between the activity giving rise to damage and the good that had suffered damage, but it was still far removed from today's precautionary principle since it required imminence and pre-existing environmental degradation. This concept was strongly criticized by Rehbinder for not distinguishing between a situation of known degradation and one where there is a risk to the environment.[257]

(3) Uncertain risk

If 'certain' and 'residual' risks elude the precautionary principle for the reasons set out above, the principle should nevertheless apply to risks situated between these two extremes. The occurrence of such risks remains controversial at the scientific level, but it is not unreasonable to anticipate their occurrence on the basis of certain data, even if those data have not yet been fully validated. In other words, strong presumption should be sufficient basis for an appeal to precaution, whereas simple intuition excludes its use. The application of the principle should depend on minimal evidence of the probability of a risk; failing this, scientific uncertainty—which serves to advance knowledge—would be transformed into a sterile debate and would eventually serve to discredit research. The precautionary measure must therefore be linked to a minimum of knowledge: that is to say, to scientific grounds with a demonstrated degree of consistency.

The wording of several definitions confirms this desire to maintain the principle within the limits of the reasonable. For example, the 1992 OSPAR Convention calls for 'reasonable grounds for concern', while the preparatory text for the French Environmental Code stresses that a precautionary measure may only be taken 'when there are serious grounds for concern about the state of the environment'. Article 5(7) of the SPS Agreement, which addresses the question of precaution for food safety issues, requires that the sanitary or phytosanitary measure may only be taken 'on the basis of available pertinent information' as opposed to general concerns. However, certain definitions of the precautionary principle go so far as to exclude the scientific demonstration of causation, for example, the formulation of the Declarations of the Parties at the Second Conference on the North Sea and of the Nordic Council at the International Conference on Pollution of the Seas in October 1989.

On the other hand, precaution demands by definition that knowledge of the more or less predictable nature of a danger need not be entirely validated. Indeed, consideration of numerous definitions makes clear that the principle is to apply even if certainty about the occurrence of an event is not 'absolute' or 'total',[258] in the 'absence of adequate scientific information',[259] in the case of

---

[257] Ibid., 95.

[258] See, among others, the formulations set out in the Ministerial Declaration of the Second International Conference on the Protection of the North Sea, the ninth recital of the Convention on Biological Diversity, Article 3(3) of the 1992 UNFCCC, and Principle 15 of the 1992 Rio Declaration on Environment and Development.

[259] 1995 UN Fish Stocks Agreement, Article 6(2).

'insufficient relevant scientific information and knowledge',[260] 'if there is no conclusive proof of a causal link between causes and effects',[261] or if 'scientific research has not fully demonstrated the existence of a causal link'.[262]

The precautionary principle may henceforth be applied if there are 'reasonable grounds' for concern even when irrefutable proof is lacking. That is to say, the threshold should be set neither too high nor too low. If it is too high, the principle would be devoid of substance; if too low, the principle would become inoperable. A middle course should thus require public authorities to demonstrate that a risk is considered scientifically likely ('reasonable scientific plausibility').[263] That condition would be fulfilled when empirical scientific data (as opposed to simple hypothesis, speculation, or intuition) make it reasonable to envisage a scenario, even if it does not enjoy unanimous scientific support.

When is there 'reasonable scientific plausibility'? When risk begins to represent a minimum degree of certainty, supported by repeated experience. But a purely theoretical risk may also satisfy this condition, as soon as it becomes scientifically credible: that is, it arises from a hypothesis formulated with methodological rigour and wins the support of part of the scientific community, albeit a minority.[264]

The principle may consequently apply to all post-industrial risks for which a cause-and-effect relationship is not clearly established but where there is a 'reasonable scientific plausibility' that this relationship exists. This would be particularly appropriate for delayed pollution, which does not become apparent for some time and for which full scientific proof is difficult to assemble. In the case of delayed pollution, analytical results do not provide a sufficient basis for evaluating the efficacy of actions already taken or measuring the extent of damages avoided. Since feedback from experience is too slow, the expert must extrapolate what is known beyond normally permitted limits and assign a greater or lesser degree of probability to possible future developments.[265] In this way he will find himself led by circumstances to predict the unpredictable. As a result, a new understanding of duration in causality is urgently needed. The precautionary principle invites the decision-maker to take account of considerably extended

[260] 2000 CPB, Articles 10(6) and 11(8).

[261] Eg the definition of the precautionary principle in the 1992 OSPAR Convention.

[262] Eg the definitions of the precautionary principle in the 1994 Scheldt-Meuse Agreements and in the 1992 ECE Helsinki Convention on the Protection and Use of Transboundary Watercourses and International Lakes.

[263] J. Hickey and V.R. Walker, 'Refining the Precautionary Principle in International Environmental Law' (1995) Va Envtl L J 447; V.R. Walker, 'Keeping the WTO from Becoming the World Trans-Science Organisation' (1998) Cornell ILJ 251, 262 and 279–85; D. Wirth, 'The Role of Science in the Uruguay Round and NAFTA Trade Disciplines' (1994) Cornell ILJ 855–6; N. de Sadeleer, 'The Effect of Uncertainty on the Threshold Levels to which the Precautionary Principle Appears to be Subject' in M. Sheridan and L. Lavrysen (eds.), *Environmental Law Principles*, n. 151 above, 31.

[264] Ph. Kourilsky and G. Viney, n. 163 above, 145; C. Noiville, 'Principe de précaution et gestion des risques en droit de l'environnement et en droit de la santé' (2000) 239 LPA 41.

[265] OECD Environment Committee, Group of Economic Experts, ENV/EC/ECO (92) 12, 3–4.

timescales, as uncertainty largely resides in the period between a cause and the subsequent manifestation of a harmful effect.[266] Therefore it should be possible to counter delayed pollution in the name of the precautionary principle, without having to use weak evidence to try to demonstrate the likelihood of ecological damage.

The principle also applies to biotechnologies, even if the damage these techniques may cause is very poorly understood. The risk posed by certain GMOs is beginning to constitute a minimum supported by repeated experience: for example, some indications have arisen that transgenic Bt maize may kill certain types of butterflies. This risk, while not yet proved, is nonetheless plausible.

Decision-makers should also be aware that in some cases the very possibility of an adverse impact may be unknown. Even more than uncertainty, ignorance underscores the need to accept the limits of scientific assessment. Therefore regulatory appraisal in complex situations should tackle not only uncertainty but also ignorance.[267]

The degree of uncertainty peculiar to post-industrial risk marks a break with the character of certain risk and residual risk. It is thus possible to conclude that if the precautionary principle *a priori* excludes purely residual risk and does not concern certain risk, it nonetheless requires a highly sophisticated understanding of the probability of the risks situated between these two extremes. In this way it strongly resembles the strategy of delayed preventive action, although the two should not be confused.[268] We will see below that the need to avert uncertain risk is even more essential when damage may prove to be significant or irreversible.

3.2.2. The effect of uncertainty on damage

3.2.2.1. Introductory note

Having weighed the probability of a suspected risk, the decision-maker will naturally wonder how to protect against it. Should he reduce, if not eliminate, the risk in question, whatever the importance or severity of the damages it may entail? Or should he intervene only if the stakes are high enough?

His attitude is likely to vary depending on the probability that a risk will materialize and, above all, the importance of the anticipated damage. He will have to avert risks that are likely to give rise to serious damage, even if they are of low probability. On the other hand, he could not reasonably be expected to act to avert a weak risk or a high risk of negligible damage. Thus, the scope of possible damage gives meaning to *sensu lato* risk.

The disappearance of natural habitats and their species as a result of human land-use patterns, global warming resulting from emissions of greenhouse

---

[266] Fr. Ewald, 'The Return of the Crafty Genius: An Outline of a Philosophy of Precaution' (1999/2000) 6: 1 Conn Ins LJ 12.

[267] See the discussion in Subsection 3.1.2. above.

[268] See the discussion in Subsection 3.1.3. above.

gases into the atmosphere, and diseases and fatalities due to atmospheric pollution and contaminated water are all damages whose precise form is not easily defined. Climate change is one of the clearest illustrations of this. The scientific community is now convinced, for example, that sea levels will continue to rise if nothing is done to reduce emissions of greenhouse gases into the atmosphere. Yet despite this consensus scientists have not yet reached full agreement on the scope or rapidity of the phenomenon. Most recent estimates indicate that sea-level rise due to a few degrees' increase of the average temperature at the Earth's surface during the coming decades could vary between ten centimetres and one metre. It is still impossible accurately to determine the extent of the ensuing disturbances (melting of the ice sheet, dwindling of estuarine environments, flooding of coastal plains, droughts, etc.). Will these phenomena occur suddenly or progressively? In thirty years or a century from now? Will their impact be global or regional? To date, no precise answers to these questions have been found.

Our only certainty at present is precisely the *uncertainty* surrounding these phenomena, which could evolve in a completely unforeseen manner. Oceans and forests can undoubtedly reabsorb some portion of CO_2 emissions; however, natural catastrophes such as the fires which ravaged South-East Asia and Latin America during 1997–98 will become more frequent, in turn giving rise to further emissions. If warming accelerates evaporation, resulting in the formation of clouds, the latter could in turn strongly amplify the warming phenomenon (by trapping infra-red radiation) rather than serving to stabilize it (by reflecting solar rays).

Even greater uncertainties affect the regional impact of climate change. Some regions of the world will experience unusually heavy rainfall; others will be affected by drought.[269] Will lemon trees eventually flourish on the banks of Scandinavian fjords or almond trees in northern Europe? Unable to respond to such questions with any precision, experts can only provide forecasts heavily encumbered with uncertainty. Alterations in animal and insect migration and breeding patterns have already been observed in northern Europe, affecting the predictability of traditional ecosystem behaviour and agricultural patterns. Such changes will be exacerbated by the continuing severity of extreme weather events such as droughts, floods, and heat waves which characterize the phenomenon of climate change.

3.2.2.2. Possible solutions

• Determination of a threshold

Although inter-ministerial declarations relating to the protection of the North Sea note the existence of potential damage without specifying its precise nature, most authors believe that a threshold must be set in order to avoid the

---

[269] T. Downing, A. Olsthoorn, and R.S. Tol, *Climate, Change and Risk* (London: Routledge, 1999).

precautionary principle being watered down through over-use. They consider that it should only apply to risks entailing non-negligible damage.[270] Several definitions lend support to this theoretical interpretation. Thus, the 1992 UNFCCC, the 1976 Barcelona Convention for the Protection of the Mediterranean Sea against Pollution (as amended in 1995), and the 1990 Bergen and 1992 Rio Declarations only recognize recourse to the principle in order to avert 'threats of serious *or* irreversible damage', while the French Environmental Code authorizes the principle (and this is an important nuance) only to 'avert a threat of serious *and* irreversible damage' [emphases added].

For other issues damage is specified in slightly less abstract terms. In the 1992 CBD, the principle should counter a 'threat of significant reduction or loss of biological diversity'. The 1992 OSPAR Convention turns to the principle when pollution 'may bring about hazards to human health, harm living resources and marine ecosystems', while the 1994 Scheldt-Meuse Agreements require that dangerous substances have 'a significant transfrontier impact' in order for the principle to come into play. In the 2000 Cartagena Biosafety Protocol (CPB) precautionary measures are limited to cases where scientific uncertainty relates to a lack of evidence regarding the 'extent' of the potential adverse effects.[271]

Such requirements can also be found in national case-law. In the *Benzene* case, the US Supreme Court required the OSHA to carry out a threshold determination of 'significant risk' of cancer before the Agency could promulgate standards for air-borne benzene intended to counter that risk: ' "Safe" is not the equivalent of "risk-free". There are many activities that we engage in every day—such as driving a car or even breathing city air—that entail some risk of accident or material health impairment; nevertheless, few people would consider these activities "unsafe". Similarly, a workplace can hardly be considered "unsafe" unless it threatens the workers with a *significant* risk of harm' [emphasis added].[272]

The decision-maker is thus obliged to restrict the application of the precautionary principle to certain categories of damage; however, agreement has not yet been reached on how to define those categories.

Most definitions require the presence of at least serious—or significant—damage. These are highly subjective concepts, which are perceived quite differently depending on location, period in time, and persons affected. The fundamental importance of climatic conditions to maintaining life on earth leads people to take the prospect of global warming seriously. The wide range of disturbances which will result from this process obliges States to demonstrate

---

[270] A. Nollkaemper, 'What You Risk Reveals What You Value . . .', n. 251 above, 83; J. Cameron and J. Abouchar, 'The Precautionary Principle: A fundamental principle of law and policy for the protection of the global environment' (1991) Boston CILR 1–27, 100; N. de Sadeleer, 'The Effect of Uncertainty . . .', n. 263 above, 32–6.

[271] The term 'extent' embodies a notion of quantity that is not appropriate for the type of risk in question. Eg P.-T. Stoll, 'Controlling the Risks of GMOs: The Cartagena Protocol on Biosafety and the SPS Agreement' (1999) 10 YbIEL 82–119, 98.

[272] *Industrial Union Dep't. AFL-CIO v. American Petroleum Inst.*, 448 U.S. 607, 656 (1980).

their duty of care. No one doubts that the issue is one where humankind confronts a threat of serious damage. But what about other types of risks that might arise? In the eyes of the layman, the loss of an endemic species of flower from a tropical forest may appear insignificant. After all, such forests contain thousands of other, similar species. However, if the species that is threatened with extinction conceals as yet undiscovered medicinal potential, firms that might engage in its commercialization and the sick whom it might cure will sustain a real loss.

Gauging the serious or significant character of the consequences of a risk is even more difficult when interaction with other risks is likely. As long as it remains isolated, a blow to the environment will not necessarily give rise to serious damage. However, it need only be repeated or interact with other assaults on the environment suddenly to take on unexpected dimensions. Economists call this phenomenon the 'tyranny of small decisions' because of the perverse effects that may result from a large number of micro-decisions that individually have no importance for environmental protection but which, taken together, give rise to considerable damage.[273] Should such risks be disregarded? Or should they be countered with a view to their cumulative effects? *A priori*, the latter. In the framework of the North Sea Conference, at any rate, the precautionary principle is formulated to ensure that low-level threats whose accumulation could pose a serious danger are taken into account. The ECJ, for its part, has adopted a very broad definition of the types of damage to human health that the principle should address.[274]

The degree of severity needed to trigger the implementation of the precautionary principle could certainly be made more objective by the use of economic criteria. For instance, the principle might apply only when the cost of repairing damage exceeds a specified sum of money. However, this would be to forget that the principle fits into a logic of decision-making rather than one of indemnization. In contrast to the polluter-pays principle, it seeks to prevent, delay, regulate, or even forbid an activity rather than to indemnify its victims. Precaution is above all conceived as a means of avoiding damage that might give rise to extremely high levels of compensation. The principle therefore does not really fit into the concept of risk coverage that characterizes the welfare state, where everything is considered ultimately reparable. Rather, it reminds us that we cannot always attribute an economic value to things; some damages are irreparable, beyond the power of money to fix. In such cases precaution provides a boldly innovative approach which recognizes the importance of the individual elements that make up the environment. Determining the seriousness of

---

[273] J. Van Dunné (ed.), *Non-Point Source River Pollution: The Case of the River Meuse* (London: Kluwer Law Int'l, 1996).

[274] 'Where there is uncertainty as to the existence or extent of risks to human health, the institutions may take protective measures without having to wait until the reality and seriousness of those risks become fully apparent': Case C-157/96, *NFU*, para. 63. See the discussion in Subsection 2.2.4.1. above.

environmental damage on the basis of purely monetary criteria makes no sense in this framework.

• Serious or irreversible damage

The risk of irreversible damage might appear easier to determine than the risk of serious damage, since irreversibility may be scientifically, objectively determined. An irreversible situation is irrevocable: it is impossible to return to the point of departure. Neither corpses nor extinct species can be brought back to life.

But does all irreversible damage necessarily fall within the scope of the precautionary principle? Is not any serious bodily injury, not to speak of death, a form of irreversible damage for its victim, which no amount of money can truly compensate?[275] If we follow that logic the majority of damage could be considered irreversible, and the principle would thus have to apply to a multitude of risks, undoubtedly reducing its effectiveness. For that reason the criterion of irreversibility does not necessarily constitute a satisfactory approach to the question. We should also note that in its 1999 Order, ITLOS required a risk of 'serious harm', not of irreversible damage, to southern bluefin tuna stocks in order to take provisional measures to avert their further deterioration.[276]

• Serious and irreversible damage

The French definition of the precautionary principle combines criteria of seriousness and irreversibility.[277] This may at first glance appear obvious, since irreversible damage is by definition serious. We should ask ourselves, however, if it is correct to equate the concepts of seriousness and irreversibility: while irreversible damage is always serious, the opposite is not necessarily the case.[278] For example, experience has taught us that the often spectacular marine pollution caused by oil spills is largely reversible. Yet marine spills certainly fall within the scope of the precautionary principle owing to their seriousness.

• Collective damage

Given the difficulty of interpreting the terms 'significant', 'serious or irreversible', and 'serious and irreversible', the precautionary principle should probably apply only to collective damage which is catastrophic in nature. The effect of this, however, would be to exclude individual damage. Moreover, no criterion for collective damage appears in either the explanatory memoranda or commentaries of the various national and international instruments establishing the precautionary principle.

Injury to a worker resulting from a technological risk may well be serious and irreversible. In such a case, would the operator not be blamed for failing to take proper precautions? Following this logic, we may seek the equivalent to this criterion for cases of damage to the *res communes*. The fact that the environment

---

[275] Fr. Ewald, n. 266 above, 62.   [276] Order, paras. 77 and 80.
[277] See also the Second World Climate Conference Ministerial Declaration, 7 November 1990.
[278] Fr. Ewald, n. 266 above, 62.

is considered *res communes* tends to transform any type of ecological damage into collective damage. If a species of butterfly vanishes, strollers will be deprived of the pleasure of seeing it flit from flower to flower, photographers will no longer be able to capture its essence on film, entomologists will lose their subject of study, and so on. The damage in this case affects the collectivity, even if it concerns a very small element of the natural environment.

As a result, recourse to a criterion of collective damage is on one hand overly restrictive, since it excludes damages caused to individuals by technological risks; on the other hand it is superfluous in cases of damage to the *res communes*.

• Damage under conditions of uncertainty

We must ask ourselves whether the desire to determine damage on the basis of these criteria leads to a paradox since its occurrence remains subject to scientific uncertainty. How can one anticipate the seriousness, irreversibility, or collective character of damage that may never arise? The scope of the damage feared is in effect no more assessable than *sensu stricto* risk. Given the complexity of ecological processes and their reactions to possible assault, determining what damage may be anticipated is always a gamble.

The threshold models described above assume that the environment or the human body can assimilate a certain level of contaminants without being harmed. This assumption might, however, be incorrect in many cases. For example, for hazards such as harm to the reproductive systems of animals or human beings due to endocrine disruptors, thresholds may simply not exist.

A time element also comes into play. Ecological damage may show up belatedly, since chemical and biological effects do not necessarily become evident immediately; but when they do appear they tend to require major elimination efforts or be irreversible. Low levels of chemical contaminants exert impacts that are difficult to detect in short-term laboratory tests but show up later, often in the next generation. The principal tenet of toxicology—the 'poison is in the dose'- should be supplemented by the observation that 'duration reveals the poison'.[279]

We can of course learn from past experience when facing similar situations. However, that would be to overlook the fact that the precautionary principle applies precisely to hypotheses where clear experience is lacking. Any attempt to establish a hierarchy for damages that are serious or insignificant, irreversible or reversible, collective or individual would come up against the uncertainty inherent in the anticipated risk.

The precautionary principle is therefore not a comprehensive means by which to evaluate the scope of damage. In the long run, the political process rather than legal inference will have to determine which goods are most precious to us and then erect a firewall of precaution to protect them from external threats. For that

---

[279] P.L. de Fur, 'The Precautionary Principle: Application to Policies Regarding Endocrine Disrupting Chemicals' in C. Raffensperger and J. Tickner (eds.), *Protecting Public Health and the Environment*, n. 179 above, 342.

reason perhaps, in contrast to the Rio Declaration which submitted the precautionary principle to 'serious or irreversible damage', the 1992 OSPAR Convention, the 1992 Helsinki Convention on the Protection of the Marine
Environment of the Baltic Sea Area, and the 2000 CPB do not apply any
threshold requirements to threats of serious or irreversible damage: it is sufficient
that a substance may give rise to a hazard to human health or harm living
resources or marine ecosystems in order for the principle to be implemented.

3.2.3. *The effect of uncertainty on the proportionality of precautionary measures*

3.2.3.1. Introductory note

Even if we agree to recognize that suspected risk is real and may entail considerable damage, the decision-maker must still be convinced that the game is worth
the candle. Risk reduction necessarily implies redistribution of resources, to the
detriment of certain socio-economic sectors: a sacrifice that may be deeply
resented during times of economic slowdown. The decision-maker will thus be
forced to choose between reducing risks that have been only weakly demonstrated or meeting more immediate needs. This cruel dilemma has arisen in a
particularly acute form in the case of the continued operation of several nuclear
power plants in Ukraine and Bulgaria, where government leaders confront a
choice between supplying their populations with electricity while exposing them
to considerable danger of radiation or avoiding any possible risk of a nuclear
accident by closing down these obsolete installations.

At this level, in contrast to the usual application of the precautionary principle,
where the decision-maker balances the cost of a policy measure against the cost of
inaction, a third parameter comes into play and complicates decision-making.
The causal link between a hazardous activity and resultant ecological damage is
suspected at this stage but cannot yet be demonstrated. Ignorance thus replaces
full understanding of the risk involved, disturbing the decision-making process.

The decision-maker will undoubtedly be inclined to weigh the ecological cost
of inaction against the socio-economic cost of the measure intended to avert the
anticipated risk.[280] Yet such 'cost–benefit' analysis is no longer valid, since
the comparison between various parameters is unbalanced by the uncertainty
surrounding the risk. Even if the decision-maker is convinced that the seriousness
of possible ecological damage outweighs the economic advantage of not taking
action, he will hesitate to intervene simply because he has reason to believe that
the risk will not materialize. The cost of pollution avoidance measures will
then be augmented by the cost of uncertainty, which will substitute for the
internalization of externalities.[281] In this way, doubt leads to underestimating

---

[280] C. Gollier, B. Jullien, and N. Treich, 'Scientific Progress and Irreversibility: An Economic
Interpretation of the Precautionary Principle' (2000) 75 Journal of Public Economics 229–53;
C. Gollier, 'Should we Beware of the Precautionary Principle' (2001) 33 Economic Policy 303–21.

[281] G. Brüggermeier, 'The Control of Corporate Conduct and Reduction of Uncertainty by Tort
Law' in R. Baldwin (ed.), n. 247 above, 65.

the cost of ecological damage in comparison to the cost of redistributing economic resources implicit in the adoption of a preventive measure. What price can we assign to damage that has not yet arisen? Once a risk is better understood, however, the decision-maker can more easily weigh the probable benefit of intervention against the cost of inaction.

3.2.3.2. Possible solutions

Several authors propose using the principle of proportionality to mitigate any excesses that might arise from an insufficiently nuanced application of the precautionary principle.[282] According to the European Commission's Communication on the precautionary principle, 'Measures based on the precautionary principle must not be disproportionate to the desired level of protection and must not aim at zero risk, something which rarely exists'.[283]

If the risks must be weighed, the same should be true of precaution. In the German debate about *Vorsorge* a central issue is the proportionality of administrative action (*Verhältnismässigkeit*). In its decision of 8 August 1978 on the operation of the Kalkar fast breeder reactor. Germany's Federal Constitutional Court recalled that 'it is appropriate to proceed to a reasonable evaluation of the risks'.[284] Proportionality should in any case lead the decision-maker to evaluate the need for and usefulness of proposed measures by considering how they will affect the interests of the various parties influenced by a decision. A precautionary measure will be deemed disproportionate and should be abandoned if it brings into question in an inappropriate manner interests that are worthy of legal protection.[285] More recently the EFTA Court stated that precautionary measures taken by a Contracting Party must be proportionate. Under this principle the need to safeguard public health must be balanced against the principle of the free movement of goods. The mere finding by a national authority of the absence of a nutritional need will not justify an import ban, a most restrictive measure, on a product which is freely traded in other EEA States. [286]

According to some definitions the proportionality of a precautionary measure should be assessed by means of a cost–benefit analysis based on economic criteria. The explanatory memorandum of the French legal provision enunciating the principle proposes that the cost of a precautionary measure should be 'correlated

---

[282] In favour of applying the proportionality principle, see E. Rehbinder, 'The Precautionary Principle...', n. 249 above, 103; A. Kiss and D. Shelton, *International Environmental Law* (London: Graham & Trotman, 1991) 43.

[283] Para. 6.3.1, Communication from the Commission on the Precautionary Principle. For food safety issues, Article 7(2) of EC Regulation No. 178/2002, laying down the general principles and requirements of food law, provides that the precautionary measures 'shall be proportionate'.

[284] Cf. the comment on this decision in Subsection 2.3.1. above.

[285] While precautionary measures to reduce emission loads need to be proportionate to the risks they are intended to address, a programme that seeks to reduce emission loads across the board and is tailored to provide for uniform and regular implementation has been upheld as complying with this requirement of 'global' or overall proportionality (BVerwGE 69, 37: Heidelberger Heizkraftwerk). See also S. Rose-Ackerman, n. 210 above, 77; G. Roller, 'Environmental Law Principles', n. 151 above, 165–7.

[286] *EFTA Surveillance Authority v. Norway*, paras. 17–19.

with the seriousness of the risk and the economic capacity of the operators'.[287] According to the 1998 Swedish Environmental Code, precautionary rules cannot be deemed unreasonable. In this respect, 'Particular importance shall be attached ... to the benefits of protective measures and other precautions in relation to their cost. The cost–benefit relationship shall also be taken into account in assessments relating to total defence activities or where a total defence measure is necessary.'[288] By requiring that the 'cost' of the measure be 'economically acceptable', the legal definition of the principle confirms this interpretation. A similar position was adopted in 1990 by the British Government, when it undertook to develop a precautionary policy: 'to limit the use of potentially hazardous substances or to avoid the dissemination of potentially hazardous substances, even when the state of scientific knowledge does not make possible a definitive judgement, as long as the balance of costs and benefits of this action justify it'.[289]

This concern is also expressed in international law, notably in the 2001 POPs Convention,[290] the 2001 London IMO Convention on the Control of Harmful Anti-Fouling Systems on Ships,[291] and in the 1992 UNFCCC, which states that the precautionary principle should lead to the adoption of measures that are 'cost-effective so as to ensure global benefits at the lowest possible cost'. Several provisions of EC law set out a similar requirement.[292] Thus, Article 174(3) of the EC Treaty provides that 'in preparing its action relating to the environment, the Community shall take account of ... the potential benefits and costs of action or of lack of action'. Such requirements are also found in US environmental law.[293]

Just as it is necessary to undertake some form of scientific assessment to trigger application of the precautionary principle, it might also be necessary to undertake an economic assessment.[294] The question then arises whether the public authorities should carry out a classic cost–benefit analysis (CBA) before taking any precautionary action. However, the requirement to carry out a CBA might be inappropriate for the following reasons.

---

[287] G. Cesar, *J.O.*, déb. Sénat, meeting of 12 October 1994, 4174, and P. Herisson, *J.O.*, déb. Sénat, meeting of 9 November 1995, 2413.

[288] Chapter 2, Section 7 of the 1998 Swedish Environmental Code.

[289] Dept. of the Environment, *This Common Inheritance: Britain's Environmental Strategy*, UK White Paper on Environmental Policy (London: HMSO, 1990) 7.

[290] Annex C.

[291] Article 6(4)(a)(iii).

[292] See especially Directive 91/339/EEC concerning the placing on the market of PCB-PCT, amending Directive 76/769/EEC on the approximation of the laws, regulations, and administrative provisions of the Member States relating to restrictions on the marketing and use of certain dangerous substances and preparations. The European Commission's Communication on the Precautionary Principle calls for the 'least restrictive alternative. This means that controls and bans are only a means of last resort.'

[293] Under FIFRA, pesticides can be regulated only if both the benefits and the burdens of the proposed regulation are considered. Fg R.L. Revesz, *Foundations of Environmental Law and Policy* (Oxford, New York: OUP, 1997) 78.

[294] K. von Molkte, 'The Relationship between Policy, Science, Technology, Economics and Law in the Implementation of the Precautionary Principle' in D. Freestone and E. Hey (eds.), *The Precautionary Principle*, n. 181 above, 106.

First, a CBA does not address the issue of defining what 'costs' are 'economically acceptable', and for whom. In addition, it will never be accurate as long as economic analysis remains incapable of correctly internalizing all externalities in a context of uncertainty. From an economic point of view there are clearly no simple or comprehensive rules for integrating risk and uncertainty into decision-making.[295] Indeed, the uncertainty inherent in precaution increases the possibility that ecological interests could be systematically compromised compared to competing interests since, as recalled above, the gravity of suspected damage can only be known in an approximate manner.[296] The fact that causation may not be entirely clear (and continuing theoretical conflict as to how this question should be handled) also serves to complicate the decision-maker's task. In any event, such a calculation can never be as precise as might be the case for a measure adopted in a hypothetical stable universe where risks could be completely mastered.

In addition to the irreversible, we must acknowledge the problem of the irreparable. Increasingly, victims are no longer satisfied with receiving compensation, no matter how high. The precautionary principle contradicts the postulates of an insurance-based society, which presupposes that one can assign a price to everything.[297] For these reasons balancing the disadvantages of a precautionary measure against the advantages it is meant to secure cannot be limited to carrying out a classical cost–benefit analysis. Everything cannot always be considered from an economic perspective. Environmental goods such as endangered species or landscapes are not commodities; their value can only be appreciated collectively.[298] Our duties to future generations or to the global commons must be understood as incommensurable with classical economic valuation in the sense that such values cannot be ranked in a scale of relative worth; in other words, they cannot be represented by cost–benefit techniques.[299] Therefore precaution must reintroduce common sense into decision-making: where risks are deemed unacceptable, they must be prevented absolutely and not subject to a cost–benefit analysis.

Decisions must thus also take into account other non-quantifiable values at the economic level. Examining costs and benefits entails comparing the overall cost to the community of action and lack of action, in both the short and long term.[300]

---

[295] D. Pearce, 'The Precautionary Principle and Economic Analysis' in T. O'Riordan and J. Cameron (eds.), *Interpreting the Precautionary Principle* (London: Cameron & May, 1994) 194.

[296] See the discussion in Subsection 3.2.2.2. above.

[297] Fr. Ewald, n. 266 above, 62.

[298] M. Jacobs, *The Green Economy* (London: Pluto, 1991) 212.

[299] D. Pearce and R.K. Turner, *Economics of Natural Resources and the Environment* (London: Harvester Wheatsheaf, 1990) 149–53; J.T. Winpenny, *Value for the Environment: A Guide to Economic Appraisal* (London: HMSO, 1991) 59–61; T. Hayward, *Ecological Thought* (Cambridge: Polity Press, 1995) 104; J. Connelly and Gr. Smith, *Politics and the Environment* (London: Routledge, 1999) 139. According to other authors, if suitably constrained CBA is consistent with a broad array of appealing normative commitments. Eg M.D. Adler and E. Posner, 'Rethinking CBA' (1999) 2 Yale LJ 165–245.

[300] According to the Communication from the Commission on the Precautionary Principle, this is not simply an economic CBA: its scope is much broader, and includes non-economic considerations, such as the efficacy of possible options and their acceptability to the public.

Potential long-term effects must especially be taken into account in evaluating the proportionality of measures in the form of rapid action to limit or eliminate a risk whose effects will surface in several decades or will affect future generations.[301]

We should note, moreover, that most of the definitions of the principle found in international law do not contain restrictions referring to 'economically acceptable' costs.[302] Some national laws go so far as to proscribe weighing ecological against economic interests, on the ground that fundamental values should be protected at any price. For example, in the USA, even though the ESA does not recognize the precautionary principle as such, it gives absolute priority to the existence of species. Under this Act endangered species have an 'incalculable value'. In addition, the Federal Appeals Court of the District of Columbia has held that the US CAA should be applied independent of economic considerations,[303] and the Delaney Clause concerning food additives requires no balancing between potential harm to persons and the costs of regulating a substance.[304] In the *Alpharma* case, the President of the EC Court of First Instance held that 'the mere existence of the risk so identified is enough in itself to justify taking into account, in the balancing of interests, the protection of human health'.[305] Finally, it is reasonable to wonder to what extent the criterion of economic balance should continue to be allowed in cases where precautionary measures refer back to a constitutional right to environmental protection.

In assessing the proportionality of a precautionary measure, one should also consider non-targeted risks that might arise: to refuse to run a risk is often to accept other, opposite risks.[306] Even if the decision-maker is convinced of the need to intervene in order to eliminate a risk, he may have to abandon the planned measure if it is likely to give rise to a different hazard.[307] He may find

---

[301] According to the Communication from the Commission on the Precautionary Principle, risk reduction measures should not be limited to immediate risks where the proportionality of the action is easy to assess. It is in situations in which adverse effects do not emerge until long after exposure that cause—effect relationships are more difficult to prove scientifically and that the precautionary principle must consequently often be invoked. In this case the potential long-term effects must be taken into account in evaluating the proportionality of measures in the form of rapid action to limit or eliminate a risk whose effects will not surface until 10 or 20 years later or will affect future generations. This applies in particular to ecosystem effects (para. 6.3.1).

[302] For instance, the 2000 Cartagena Protocol on Biosafety, the latest piece of international legislation to recognize the precautionary principle, does not have a threshold requirement of 'cost-effective measures' as laid down in Principle 15 of the 1992 Rio Declaration.

[303] *Natural Resources Defense Council v. US EPA*, 824 F.2d (D.C. Cir. 1987), p. 1163.

[304] 21 U.S.C. §348(c)(3)(a).

[305] Case T-79/99P, *Alpharma* [1999] ECR II-2027. See the discussion in Subsection 2.2.4.1. above.

[306] On risk trade-off analysis, eg J. Graham and J. Wiener, *Risk v. Risk* (Cambridge, Mass.: Harvard U.P., 1995); J.B. Wiener, 'Managing the Iatrogenic Risks of Risk Management' (1998) 9 Risk: Environment Health & Safety 39–84; idem., 'Precaution in a Multi-Risk World' in D. Paustenbach (ed.), *The Risk Assessment of Environmental and Human Health Hazards* (2nd edn., London: John Wiley, 2001).

[307] Some US authors go so far as to defend the thesis that policies based on a precautionary approach act to generate risks whose scope exceeds those of the risks that have been avoided. Eg F. Cross, 'Paradoxical Perils of the Precautionary Principle' (1996) 53 Wash & Lee L Rev 851. This argument does not appear to be supported by recent case studies carried out by the European Environment Agency. In cases involving BSE, asbestos, and fisheries (collapse of Canadian cod stocks)

himself confronting competing scenarios which, as the following examples illustrate, are difficult to prioritize.

In order successfully to eliminate the risk arising from nuclear catastrophe it would be necessary to close all nuclear plants. But could this not lead to the risk of accelerating global warming through the increase in fossil fuel use that would inevitably result from such a step? Is it appropriate to combat famine worldwide by opening the way for the growth of biotechnology or, on the contrary, must we brake its development in the name of still uncertain risks? Should the construction of dams be encouraged on the ground that they could produce clean energy, even at the cost of the irreplaceable ecosystems that will be submerged in the process? Or should we endeavour to conserve natural resources at any price? What about the construction of high-speed trains? Should this be encouraged because these trains compete with more polluting modes of transport without consideration for the natural areas that will be disturbed by the infrastructure they require?

The question of trade-offs became particularly relevant in Europe at the end of 2000, when some States, including France (followed by the European Commission) prohibited the use of animal-based feeds. While discontinuance of these feeds reduced the risk associated with eating beef, it also put an end to an important recycling activity for animal fats that would otherwise have to be eliminated through more polluting methods such as incineration and increased the import of genetically modified maize from the USA, of which European consumers are wary.

However, there are limits to the trade-offs that can be considered in risk analysis. It would be excessive to oblige regulatory agencies to consider the environmental consequences resulting from the financial impact of risk-reduction decisions. Thus, for example, the District of Columbia Court of Appeals rejected the argument that the EPA 'erred in refusing to consider the health consequences of unemployment in determining the primary National Air Quality Standards for particulate matter' and held that 'it is only health effects relating to pollutants in the air that EPA may consider'.[308]

The concept of the general interest is inherent in the approach to ecological risk. In practice, however, that general interest will be defined in a variety of ways by different societal groups. Therefore it will again fall ultimately to the political establishment to arbitrate between the conservation of biodiversity and the production of less polluting energy, between modernizing agricultural production and genetic upheaval, etc., on the basis of the values it upholds. Yet the ramifications of these alternatives should, at the very least, be clarified in the light of the precautionary principle, with the aim of ensuring that final decisions conform to the general interest.

---

regulatory inaction to prevent uncertain risks led to far greater costs than if precautionary measures had been taken. Better targeted research at an earlier stage would have helped to minimize future costs. Eg European Environmental Agency, n. 243 above, 17–27, 52–61, 157–67, and 181.

[308] *NRDC*, 902 F.2d at 972–3; *American Trucking Associations Inc. v. EPA*, 175 F.3d at 94.

3.2.4. Critical assessment

The precautionary principle has been put forward as the best as well as the worst of principles. Applied strictly according to the letter it would condemn us to inaction. The principle would become inapplicable if taken to the extreme: it would lose its way, a substitute for good intentions. On the other hand, to place absolute faith in the competence of techno-science is sooner or later to court irreversible damage which could be averted by timely action. We no longer have a right to err. But at what price action? That is the question. While a certain number of markers must be fixed to prevent the precautionary principle resulting in absurd decisions, it is nevertheless essential that these be set out intelligently in order to use precaution wisely.

Conscious of these problems, both legislators and courts are attempting to define the scope of the precautionary principle within the limits of what is reasonable, by gradually giving shape to *stricto sensu* risk, anticipated damage, and the scope of policy measures. Even the most progressive formulations of the principle are circumscribed in scope, allowing for regulatory actions under a host of conditions.[309] However, careful consideration of several definitions makes it clear that the limits being set for the principle at times contradict its stated objective. Is it reasonable to require that a decision be based upon the existence of relevant scientific and technical data in the case of hypothetical damage which would be both significant and irreversible and where the decision will not even seriously affect socio-economic interests? Under multiple conditions of this sort, it appears that recourse to the precautionary principle is subject to excessive precaution.

Throughout this section we have sought an equitable path that would preserve the useful effect of the precautionary principle without paralysing innovation. We have drawn several conclusions from this exercise. Even if the principle does not require that the probability of damage be fully demonstrated, it should nevertheless not take purely hypothetical risks into account. Entirely speculative considerations are thus excluded. Common sense also suggests that the principle should not apply in the case of an extremely low probability of very slight damage. Thus the injury to be averted should be reasonably specific, even if the much cited criteria of seriousness and irreversibility are not always satisfactorily met. Finally, proportionality should not be limited to measuring the cost of the socio-economic sacrifices that will be caused by a precautionary measure. Rather, it should be broadened to take into account long-term non-economic advantages for society as a whole.

To conclude, we should ask ourselves if it is reasonable to expect such conditions to be reflected in normative texts. The nature of a legal principle is precisely *not* to be the subject of a complete and exhaustive definition in positive law; what is sought is a flexible norm able to adapt to the heterogeneous situations in

---

[309] A. Stirling, *Science and Precaution: The Management of Technological Risk* (Sevilla: IPTS, 1999) 14.

which it will be used. Any attempt to define a legal principle by overly precise wording would definitively restrict its meaning, thereby rendering it useless. Moreover, although a legal principle may remain vague, its scope will gradually be clarified as it is applied in various situations. Legal analysis will carry out this beneficial work.

4. SCIENCE VERSUS PRECAUTION: A FALSE DICHOTOMY

The principle of precaution runs up against the need for certainty that permeates the legal system as a whole. In order to derogate from the principle of the free movement of goods national measures must demonstrate the existence of risk; to obtain compensation for damage a victim must establish a clear causal link between that damage and an event; authorization to place a product on the market or to employ a new technology cannot be refused unless a suspected risk is firmly established. Positive law is thus partnered by scientific certainty. This presupposes continuous recourse to scientific expertise, with experts being able to provide flawless advice to both courts and decision-makers. Yet growing uncertainty has eroded this faith in science at the service of power. In addition, the perception of what constitutes risk is strongly influenced by psychological elements that cannot be quantified.

It is not surprising that critics of the principle often set precaution and scientific knowledge against one another. The implication of this opposition is that the adoption of the principle might somehow be seen *a priori* as being antithetical to the principles of scientific rigour in the regulation of risk (systematic methodology, scepticism, transparency, emphasis on learning, etc.).[310] Within such a perspective, implementation of the precautionary principle essentially becomes a politically determined compromise which has nothing to do with 'sound science'.

The purpose of this fourth section is precisely to demonstrate that the precautionary principle and the principles of scientific rigour are not antithetical, but rather mutually reinforcing. We base our analysis upon the following antimony:

—a *thesis* according to which precaution frees the decision-maker from the constraints of scientific expertise (Subsection 4.1 below), and
—an *antithesis* according to which precaution reinforces the position of experts to the detriment of decision-makers (Subsection 4.2), in order to derive
—a *synthesis* which shows, by focusing on the practical implications of the subtle relationship between science and precaution in risk analysis and risk management, that the precautionary principle could serve to reconcile the roles of scientists and decision-makers (Subsection 4.3).

---

[310] A. Stirling, n. 309 above, 4.

Even though this section is firmly based on the empirical elements of Section 2 above (primarily case-law relating to risk assessment in the US and at the WTO level and EC legislation on GMOs and chemicals) we have tried to adopt a multidisciplinary approach by referring to recent research in the field of social sciences (political sciences, philosophy, sociology).

4.1. Thesis: Returning decision-making to the political sphere

Environmental law has its source in a paradox that has not yet played itself out: the fact that the vulnerability of terrestrial ecosystems became apparent in the mid-1960s, at the very time when technology had most firmly established its mastery over nature. Since then the innovative powers of technology have consistently exceeded the capacity of science to anticipate potential adverse effects. Environment policy and science therefore stand in a paradoxical relationship to one another: while science (and its technological offspring) stand accused of being largely responsible for environmental damage, we rely upon science to identify the very ills to which it gives rise and to prescribe their necessary remedies.

Several factors explain why science is much more in evidence in environment law than in other branches of law. First, the sciences detect, identify, and set out the ecological problems to which the law must respond. Secondly, environmental crises are increasingly perceived through scientific descriptions of our physical world. Only scientists are capable of discerning the threats posed by nuclear power, biotechnology, synthetic chemistry, and other technologies. No one actually observed the hole in the ozone layer, and the lay gaze will never manage to scrutinize the stratosphere, animal tissues, or the oceans' shoals. Science may thus claim to be both the problem and its solution.[311] And science still plays a dominant role in setting standards of environmental protection. Risk assessments performed by scientists provide the cornerstone for much environmental legislation. Thus, environmental regulations remain heavily dependent upon science in the form of technical regulations, acoustic thresholds, chemical concentrations, fishing quotas, etc. Last but not least, science is often called upon to play a decisive role in judicial procedures.

It is hardly surprising, then, that environmental law should be deeply marked by a heavy reliance on science. In fact, no area of public policy is comparably dependent on science.[312]

Scientists thus play a decisive role in the conception and implementation of this legal discipline; all the regulations adopted in this field, without exception,

---

[311] J. Theys and B. Kalaora, 'Quand la science réinvente l'environnement' (1992) 1 Sciences et société 21.

[312] K. von Moltke, 'The Relationship between Policy, Science, Technology, Economics and Law in the Implementation of the Precautionary Principle' in D. Freestone and E. Hey (eds.), *The Precautionary Principle*, n. 181 above, 98.

are based on their calculations, their computations, or their affirmations.[313] Whether it is a question of setting a nuisance threshold, delimiting a protected area, or listing a species for legal protection, decisions are based on scientific considerations. By establishing their validity, science is linked to legal standards to such an extent that environment law would be crippled without its contribution.[314] Science has become both the basis and the justification for political decision-making: political decisions are legitimate because they are based on risk assessment performed by risk assessors who are legitimate because they apply sound science.[315]

Yet this marriage of reason is not entirely free of strife: to the extent that science postulates what exists while law lays down what should be, their respective logics are mutually inconsistent. Where the jurist conceives of resource protection in terms of the number of persons to be protected or hectares to be conserved, the ecologist thinks in terms of ecosystems. The latter conform to the long rhythm of natural cycles, the former to the staccato tempo of human expectations. Legal rules are meant to provide predictability, yet nature is unpredictable. While the jurist seeks certainty, the scientist points to the uncertainty inherent in ecological risk. Environment law attempts to resolve these contradictions. While it relies heavily on scientific data, it nevertheless remains a legal system: that is, a means of managing a fictitious social order, able to regulate conflicts with its own set of conceptual tools.

At the same time we are now seeing the appearance of post-industrial risks that could endanger the very conditions that sustain life on Earth.[316] From the erosion of genetic resources to depletion of the ozone layer, from global warming to the spread of persistent and bioaccumulable pollutants throughout the world's

---

[313] The reliance on science is reflected in regulatory instruments. This relationship is particularly obvious in the EC Treaty's provisions relating to environmental protection. According to Article 174(3), 'in preparing its action relating to the environment, the Community shall take account of available scientific and technical data'. In addition, Article 95(3) relating to the harmonization of the internal market requests that the EC legislator take 'as a base a high level of protection, taking account of any new development based on scientific facts'. At the international level, multilateral conventions specify that decision-making must 'take into account' scientific advice. UNCLOS, Article 61(2) on the EEZ provides that: 'The coastal state, taking into account the *best scientific evidence available* to it, shall ensure through proper conservation and management measures that its resources are not endangered by over-exploitation'. The Whaling Convention requires that regulations be based on '*scientific findings*'. According to the 1995 UN Agreement relating to the Conservation and Management of Straddling Fish Stocks and Highly Migratory Fish Stocks: 'In order to conserve and manage straddling fish stocks and highly migratory fish stocks, States . . . shall, in giving effect to their duty to cooperate in accordance with the Convention: . . . (b) ensure that such measures are based on the *best scientific evidence available* (Article 5(b)) (emphasis added). For a discussion of the role of scientific research in the regulatory process, see J. Wettestad and S. Andersen, 'Science and North Sea Policy-Making: Organization and Communication' (1990) 5 Int'l J Estuarine & Coastal L 111–22; P. Birnie, 'International Environmental Law: Its Adequacy for Present and Future Needs' in A. Hurrell and B. Kingsbury (eds.), *The International Politics of the Environment* (Oxford: Clarendon 1992) 75.

[314] E. Naim-Gesbert, *Les dimensions scientifiques du droit de l'environnement* (Brussels: VUB Press, Bruylant, 1999) 63–229.

[315] V. Heyvaert, *Coping With Uncertainty: The Regulation of Chemicals in the European Union*, Ph.D. (Florence, European University Institute, 1999) 186.

[316] See the discussion in Subsection 3.1.2. above.

waters, all global ecological problems present specific characteristics relating to scientific uncertainty. It is precisely the impossibility of measuring and anticipating all their effects on the environment and human health that set them apart from anything we have known before. Faced with the growing complexity and globality of ecological phenomena, science has ceased to be omnipotent. Strictly speaking, it is no longer possible to have so-called technical standards that express the facts in a definitive manner. Complete scientific certainty is the exception, rather than the norm. As pointed out in Hans Jonas' *The Imperative of Responsibility*, a paradigm of uncertainty has taken the place of certainty: 'Whereas Descartes recommended that we hold as false everything that can be questioned, faced with planetary risks it would on the contrary be advisable to treat doubt as a possible certainty and thus as a fundamentally positive element in any decision'.[317]

Classical science has tended to privilege 'hard' scientific fact. This made it easy to determine what decisions could be considered well grounded. Henceforth, post-Cartesian science will call for hard fact to be replaced by flexibility. Such science seeks to apprehend the greatest uncertainty—that is, ignorance[318]—and assess its dialectical interaction with knowledge. No longer omniscient, science will not have the power categorically to express a single truth. Scientific and technical progress will from now on be ruled by laws very different from those in place at the time of its most rapid advances. Furthermore, science is not neutral and above the political fray as previously believed; the choice of apparently neutral scientific assumptions often reflects political power relations. Values, which are meant to be safely sequestred during risk management, significantly influence the outcome of risk assessments. For instance, both scientific research and monitoring in the climate change assessment process are tinged by political values and ideological conflict.[319] In the field of chemical substances, what gets chosen for toxicity testing, by whom, and by what methods are crucial political questions.[320]

The reversal of certainty and doubt seriously disturbs the relations with the political authorities that scientific circles have patiently built up over time. The decision-maker always seeks reassurance through certainty; he therefore expects scientists to provide simple and categorical answers from which he can deduce political decisions. Henceforth, however, when scientists are consulted they will

---

[317] H. Jonas, *The Imperative of Responsibility* (Chicago: Univ. of Chicago Press, 1984).

[318] See the discussion on ignorance in Subsection 3.1.2. above.

[319] J. Jäger and T. O'Riordan, 'The History of Climate Change Science and Politics' in T. O'Riordan and J. Jäger (eds.), *Politics of Climate Change: A European Perspective* (London: Routledge, 1996) 5. See also for global change, M. Jacobs, 'Sustainable Development Assumptions, Contradictions, Progress' in J. Lovenduski and Stanyer (eds.), *Contemporary Political Studies: Proceedings of the Annual Conference of the Political Studies Association* (London: PSA, 1995) 1473; J. Connelly and Gr. Smith, *Politics and the Environment* (London: Routledge, 1999) 119.

[320] J.S. Applegate, 'The Perils of Unreasonable Risk: Information, Regulatory Policy and Toxic Substances Control' (1991) Colum LR, 279; W.D. Ruckelshaus, 'Risk in a Free Society' (1984) 14 Ent'l L Rep 10190; A. Kellow, *International Toxic Risk Management: Ideals, Interests and Implementation* (Cambridge: CUP, 1999) 32–3.

inform the decision-maker that their knowledge is incomplete and express doubts and differences, even ignorance. They will have to work to overcome the aversion of the political elite to everything that is imprecise, improbable, or uncertain. The disappearance of the alliance between knowledge and power will shatter the Weberian myth of the expert providing indisputable knowledge to a politician who takes decisions that reflect the values he defends.[321] This will in turn exacerbate the recurrent tensions between a public decision-making process dominated by pragmatism and a scientific approach which, to its credit, is characterized by doubt.

As we have seen, this context of uncertainty has given rise to the precautionary principle, which has its roots in an epistemology that posits the relativity of scientific knowledge. Precaution in fact gives evidence of a deeply disturbed relationship to science, which is consulted less for the knowledge that it offers than for the suspicions and doubts to which it gives rise. In the framework of prevention the search for security was oriented towards a steady growth of the scientific and technological arsenal; from the perspective of precaution security consists in strengthening the duty of care to the detriment of science and technology. This new principle would involve going beyond the classic scientific-technological model for combatting risk. We would no longer reason in terms of thresholds; rather, we would have to take the trouble to assess what cannot be assessed. The principle invites one to anticipate what one does not yet know, to take into account the most far-fetched forecasts and simple suspicions.[322]

No longer dependent on the current level of scientific knowledge, decisions could—indeed, should—be taken in the presence of doubt. It will not be possible to avoid recourse to extra-scientific judgements. This amounts to a powerful return to political decision-making, for the decision-maker will no longer be able to take refuge behind a screen of scientific pseudo-certainties provided by the expert. More than ever before, the decision-maker will find himself constrained to make choices: or more precisely, to choose among more or less acceptable hypotheses. In any case, he will have to explain his decisions and confront the consequences of his choices. The decision to act or to abstain from action will consequently be placed back in political hands. Only in this way can environmental law free itself from domination by science.

If the precautionary principle makes it difficult to delay adopting measures to prevent environmental degradation on the ground that scientific certainty has not been established, scientific certainty or 'sound science' can no longer, *a contrario*, be considered as the absolute reference criterion for decision-making.

We may wonder about the legal implications of such a transformation of scientific knowledge. Does disengagement from the requirement to provide rational and objective grounds for binding norms mask an abrupt return to the

---

[321] M. Weber, *Le savant et le politique* (Paris: Union générale des éditions, 1963).
[322] Fr. Ewald, n. 266 above, 66.

arbitrary? Should public authorities be allowed to discriminate among those they administer without being able to justify their actions on the basis of reliable proofs? Does this not amount to implicit acceptance that authorities may regulate without justifying their acts: in other words, to granting them unlimited discretionary power?

4.2. Antithesis: Reinforcing the role of experts

At first glance the precautionary principle appears to relativize the role played by scientists in the decision-making process. Should we then fear that they will be rendered superfluous? That would be an exaggeration. We develop in this Subsection the antithesis according to which the operational contents of the precautionary principle are entirely consistent with and even reinforce the use of expertise in the decision-making process.

First of all, arguing that 'sound science' is the sole arbiter of policy action undermines trust in the concept of scientific analysis.[323] The precautionary principle is there to respond to intractable problems in risk assessment, such as ignorance and incommensurability, and this is entirely consistent with sound scientific practice. Acknowledging uncertainty is thus part of science; it clarifies what is known and not known and stimulates further researches.[324]

Secondly, a minimal degree of scientific expertise is needed to set in motion a policy of precaution, which may take extremely varied forms according to the nature of the risk in question.[325] Rather than exclude science, precaution thus legitimizes it.

Thirdly, the requirement that scientific uncertainty not delay the adoption of a measure intended to enhance environmental protection does not prevent immediate action being supplemented by scientific follow-up in order to reduce the margin of uncertainty about the scope of the problem confronting the decision-maker. Indeed, one of the central features associated with the precautionary principle is the continuous re-evaluation of scientific evidence: all decisions taken in a context of uncertainty should regularly be revised in the light of new information. In the field of food safety follow-up measures are widely used: they allow the authorities to control the health impacts of food products from the farm to the fork.[326] The efforts of the international community to fight

---

[323] B. Haerlin and D. Parr, 'How to restore public trust in science' (1999) 400 Nature 499.

[324] A. Stirling, *Science and Precaution*, n. 309 above, 12; J. Tickner, *Precaution in Practice: A Framework for Implementing the Precautionary Principle* (University of Massachusetts Lowell, 2000) 106.

[325] For a discussion of the minimal degree of scientific expertise needed to set in motion a policy of precaution, see above the discussion in Subsection 3.2.1 above.

[326] According to Article 5(7) of the SPS Agreement, a State taking a precautionary measure must seek to obtain 'additional information necessary for a more objective assessment of risk'. According to Article 4 of the Directive 89/107/EEC concerning food additives authorized for use in foodstuffs intended for human consumption, all food additives must be kept under continuous observation and must be re-evaluated whenever necessary in the light of changing conditions and new scientific information. The Preamble (4th recital) of Directive 1999/93/EC on baby food states, for example,

atmospheric pollution perfectly illustrate such a scientific review procedure. In this case a necessary transition was effected from a classical international law approach (the timely adoption of conventions setting out rather vague legal obligations) to a continuous normative process characterized by the adoption at regular intervals of protocols setting out more precise obligations than those contained in their framework conventions. Scientific progress in identifying the causes and effects of regulated phenomena makes it essential that legal obligations be adapted through additional protocols. The science of climatic change is therefore increasingly being drawn into political structures, to the point where 'climate change science' is not always separable from the political process that shapes it.[327] Rather than constituting an obstacle to decision-making, scientific expertise makes possible the continuous adaptation of the decision-making process.

Science therefore needs to play a vital role in implementing the principle.[328] Nevertheless, in all likelihood scientists will have to play a fundamentally different role in this new arrangement from the one reserved for him in the framework of the preventive model. As scientists learn more about the effects of various hazards they may come to realize that greater knowledge does not necessarily translate into greater understanding about the complexity of environmental disturbances.[329] Rather than formulating solidly established truths, the scientist's task will in future be to transform the evaluation of scientific uncertainty into functional estimates of what data could be useful in implementing policies. Consequently, the scientist will provide the decision-maker with uncertain but evolving knowledge. This new discourse will also stimulate discussion about essential values. The precautionary principle will thus extend the autonomy of policy without constraining research; on the contrary, it will encourage it.

4.3. Synthesis: Reconciling science (risk assessment) and politics (risk management)

There is growing international debate about the relationship between the precautionary principle and risk assessment methodology, spurred by recent trade controversies concerning environmental issues (POPs) or food safety issues (beef

that 'whereas, taking into account the Community's international obligations, in cases where the relevant scientific evidence is insufficient, the precautionary principle allows the Community to provisionally adopt measures on the basis of available pertinent information, pending on additional assessment of risk and a review of the measure within a reasonable period of time'.

[327] T. O'Riordan and J. Jäger, 'Beyond Climate Change Science and Politics' in T. O'Riordan and J. Jäger (eds), *Politics of Climate Change*, n. 319 above, 346.

[328] K. Barrett and C. Raffensperger, 'Precautionary Science' in R.C. Raffensperger and J. Tickner (eds), *Protecting Public Health & the Environment*, n. 279 above, 107.

[329] S. Krimsky, *Hormonal Chaos: The Scientific and Social Origins of Environmental Endocrine Hypothesis* (Baltimore: Johns Hopkins U.P., 2000); J. Tickner, *Precaution in Practice*, n. 324 above, 100.

hormones and GMOs).[330] By narrowly defining the scientific basis for health or environmental decision-making in terms of quantitative assessment, the classical risk assessment methodology required by international organizations can limit the ability of national authorities to take precautionary measures. The question then arises how to reconcile the risk assessment analysis typically used by regulatory agencies and the tendency of political authorities to break free of these procedures in the name of the precautionary principle.

This discussion, which has significant implications for international trade, allows us to establish a synthesis between the thesis and antithesis described in the two preceding subsections. That synthesis is as follows: while the precautionary principle simultaneously reinforces the weight of expertise and political decision-making, it also requires these two areas to interact in order to master the challenges posed by the risks they must assess and manage.

After examining the advantages and shortcomings of a structured approach to risk analysis (Subsection 4.3.1. below) we explore how the precautionary principle could redefine both *risk assessment* (Subsection 4.3.2.) and *risk management* (Subsection 4.3.3.).

4.3.1. Advantages and shortcomings of a structured approach to risk analysis

Even though few standards for national risk regulation have emerged in a systematic and rationalist manner, international law as well as US and EC law have progressively emphasized a structured approach to risk analysis. The advantages and drawbacks of this approach are synthesized in this Subsection.

4.3.1.1. The attraction of a structured approach to risk analysis

The traditional structured risk analysis approach comprises a two-step process. First, the probability of the occurrence of harm is determined using a *risk assessment* procedure, in which experts examine both hazard and exposure, generally by mathematical modelling, in order to calculate an acceptable or tolerable level of contamination or exposure.[331] This systematic process involves a four-step approach: hazard identification (does a substance give rise to an adverse effect such as cancer, birth defects, etc.?), dose-response assessment (how potent a carcinogen is it?), exposure assessment (which groups of people are exposed to the substance, what is the environmental vehicle of exposure -air, water, soil-, for how long, and at what levels?), and risk characterization (what is the likelihood that any particular exposed person will get cancer?). Because risk assessment rules are strongly procedural in nature, they structure the decision-making process. Imbued with the 'magic of numbers', risk assessment offers the

---

[330] While the precautionary principle was initially applied to environmental issues, such as dumping of pollutants, that are characterized by sparse scientific data useful for setting policy, it has now been expanded to protect against environmental health risks for which extensive toxicological and epidemiological data are available. Eg K.R. Foster, P. Vecchia, M.H. Repacholi, 'Science and the Precautionary Principle' (12 May 2000) Science, 979.

[331] NRC (1983) 3 *Risk Assessment in the Federal Government: Managing the Process* 13.

decision-maker a structured information set: namely, an estimation of the probability of adverse effects occurring as the result of use of a particular substance or product. When the risk assessment procedure is completed, a *risk management* decision must be taken by politicians, taking into account both legislative requirements and economic, political, and normative dimensions of the problem.[332] Risk management, in contrast to risk assessment, is the public process of deciding how safe is safe. It necessarily requires 'the use of value judgements on such issues as the acceptability of the risk and the reasonableness of the costs of control'.[333]

Although controversial,[334] risk assessment is widely applied in international law in the field of 'food-borne' or 'pest-or-disease-related' risks,[335] technical barriers to trade,[336] and GMOs.[337] In EC law, risk assessment requirements are found in the areas of worker health and safety,[338] food safety,[339] drugs,[340]

---

[332] This clear-cut distinction is found, for instance, in Articles 15 and 16 of the Cartagena Protocol on Biosafety. See also the Communication from the Commission on the Precautionary Principle (COM(2000) 1)) and Regulation No. 178/2002 on food law (Article 6). However, in the *EC Hormones* case the Appellate Body rejected the distinction made by the panel between risk assessment and risk management, considering that such distinction had no textual support either in Article 5 or the rest of the Agreement (Appellate Body, *EC Hormones*, para. 181).

[333] NRC (1983) 18.

[334] NRC, *Understanding Risk: Informing Decisions in a Democratic Society* (National Academy Press, Washington, 1996).

[335] Article 5(1) of the SPS Agreement which imposes a specific obligation that SPS measures are 'based on an assessment, as appropriate to the circumstances, of the risks to human, animal or plant life or health, taking into account risk-assessment techniques developed by the relevant international organizations'. More detailed rules on the procedure of risk assessment are set forth in Article 5(2) to 5(8).

[336] TBT Agreement, Article 2(2). For pesticides, see the 1998 Rotterdam Convention.

[337] Articles 10(1) and 15 of the CPB require that a decision to prohibit or restrict the import of an LMO under the AIA procedure has to be based on a 'risk assessment carried out in a scientifically sound manner' and taking into account recognized risk assessment techniques. Annex III of the CPB further defines scope, general principles, and methodology of the risk assessment.

[338] Directive 80/1107/EEC on the protection of workers from the risks related to exposure to chemicals, physical, and biological agents; Directive 89/391/EEC on the introduction of measures to encourage the improvements in the safety and health of workers at work; Directive 90/394/EEC on the protection of workers from the risks related to exposure to carcinogens at work.

[339] Directive 89/107/EEC concerning food additives authorized for use in foodstuffs intended for human consumption according to which the food additive must be subjected to appropriate testing and evaluation. The White Paper on Food Safety (COM (1999) 719 final) and EC Regulation No. 178/2002 laying down the general principles and requirements of food law (Article 6(1)) stresses that risk analysis, including risk assessment, must form the foundation on which food safety is based.

[340] The preambular sections of Regulation (EEC) No. 2309/93 laying down EC procedures for the authorization and supervision of medicinal products for human and veterinary use and establishing a European Agency for the Evaluation of Medicinal Products states that 'in the interest of public health, it is necessary that decisions on the authorization of such medicinal products should be based on the objective scientific criteria of the quality, the safety and the efficacy of the medicinal product concerned to the exclusion of economic or other consideration...' In the event of a disagreement between Member States about the quality, safety, or efficacy of a medicinal product, the matter should be resolved by a binding Community decision following a scientific evaluation of the issues involved. A formal risk assessment is also required by Article 23a(2) of Council Directive 81/851/EEC on the approximation of the laws of the Member States relating to veterinary medicinal products and Article 9 of Regulation No. 2377/90 laying down a Community procedure for the establishment of maximum residue limits of veterinary medicinal products in foodstuffs of animal origin.

environmental protection,[341] and authorization schemes for dangerous substances,[342] GMOs,[343] pesticides,[344] and biocides.[345] Its attraction is reflected in political statements such as the Communication of the EC Commission on the precautionary principle, which emphasizes that any approach based on the precautionary principle should start with as complete a scientific evaluation as possible.[346] While there are few explicit requirements in US regulations for agencies to conduct quantitative risk assessments, regulatory agencies have adopted this requirement as the most methodical way to defend and isolate the decision-making process.[347]

Judicial circles are also keen to favour decisions based on sound science. Even though the precautionary principle has been aknowledged in several important cases, the ECJ has recently tended to tighten the duty of the European Commission to refer and even defer to scientific expertise to justify its decisions.[348] On the other side of the Atlantic, the US Supreme Court has progressively obliged regulatory agencies to base their decisions on scientific evidence.[349] Finally, the requirement to ensure that SPS measures are based on risk assessment has proved to be of central importance in the WTO Appellate Body case-law concerning the enforcement of the SPS Agreement.[350]

[341] According to Article 16(2) of Directive 2000/60/EC establishing a framework for Community action in the field of water policy, the hazardous substances included in the priority list have to be selected according to specific scientific methods.

[342] Risk assessment of new chemicals are dealt with in Commission Directive 93/67/EEC laying down the principles for assessment of risks to man and the environment of substances notified in accordance with Directive 67/548/EEC. Risk assessment of existing chemicals can be found in Council Regulation (EC) No. 793/93 and Commission Regulation (EC) No. 1488/94.

[343] Directive 2001/18/EC on the deliberate release of GMOs, Article 4(1) and (2); Annexes II and III. Under Article 8 of the Regulation (EC) No. 258/97, a novel food or food ingredient is deemed to be 'equivalent' to its conventional counterpart unless established risk assessment techniques can show this not to be the case.

[344] Directive 91/414/EEC concerning the placing of plant protection products on the market.

[345] Directive 98/8/EC concerning the placing of biocides on the market.

[346] According to the Commission, 'the reliance on the precautionary principle is no excuse for derogating from the general principles of risk management' (Section 6.3, para. 2 of the Communication on the Precautionary Principle).

[347] Unlike EIAs, which originated from a statutory requirement, risk assessments are not generically required by statutes. However, specific statutes requiring risk—benefit analysis and the obligation to justify proposed regulation according to administrative procedure had a strong impact on the development of risk assessment.

[348] The ECJ resort to scientific assessment in its supervision of secondary law is well illustrated by its *Angelopharm* judgment where the Court stated that 'the drafting and adaptation of Community rules governing cosmetic products are founded on scientific and technical assessments which must themselves be based on the results of the latest international research...' The necessity to refer to extra-legal bodies (Community's Scientific Committee for Food, Codex Alimentarius Committee, etc.) and their standards arises, according to the Court, almost from the 'nature of things'. Eg Case C-212/91, *Angelopharm* [1994] ECR I-171. See also case C-41/93, *France v. Commission* [1994] ECR I-1829.

[349] See the discussion in Subsection 2.3.6. above.

[350] D. Robertson and A. Kellow, *Globalisation and the Environment: Risk Assessment and the WTO* (London: Routledge, 2001).

4.3.1.2. The failure of the current system to address health and environmental concerns

Firmly based on facts and falsifiable test results, *risk assessment* has been considered a purely *scientific* evaluation involving hazard identification and characterization, exposure assessment, and risk characterization. As a technical, analytical, and objective exercise, risk assessment does not require any public involvment.[351] Moreover, subjective or ethical considerations must be excluded and relegated to the decision-making process. Inversely, *risk management* has been considered a *political* process involving risk evaluation, option assessment, option implementation, monitoring and review in order to achieve an appropriate level of protection.[352] This distinction between risk assessment and risk management is based on the assumption that experts are best suited to weigh uncertain scientific evidence and produce objective results that will lead to optimal political decisions. However, this clear-cut division between scientists, who discuss facts (objective approach), and politicians, who discuss values (subjective approach), has recently been thrown into question.[353] Paradoxically, while reliance on sound science is increasing at international and regional levels, sharp criticism of risk regulation is growing, particularly in the US; the limitations of the risk assessment procedure have never been so clear.

According to critics, when the risk assessment procedure is overburdened by analytical requirements it becomes a resource-intensive and time-consuming process, too stringent to suit regulatory goals.[354] It can be so slow that it may lead to a process of ossification or 'paralysis by analysis'.[355]

Secondly, the scope of assessment may be too narrow, excluding certain disciplines and failing to achieve a holistic understanding of complex ecosystems (eg analysis may focus only upon cancer, ignoring other potentially harmful effects). The impact of multiple exposure paths and possible cumulative or synergistic effects is rarely captured.

Thirdly, the experts cannot begin to assess something unless they have been instructed to do so. The current risk assessment process has a negligible input from those dealing with risk management as regards practical options for change or the validity and effectiveness of control measures. On the other hand, all the steps in risk analysis are becoming increasingly dependent on the assumptions of risk assessors (about exposures, human behaviour, etc.) which may be explicit or

---

351 V. Heyvaert, 'Reconceptualizing Risk Assessment' (1999) 8 RECIEL 140.

352 The latter phase takes place without expert consultation.

353 The basis for the distinction between risk assessment and risk management has been criticized in Europe in the fields of health and environmental regulation, on both practical and theoretical grounds. See C. Noiville and N. de Sadeleer, 'La gestion des risques écologiques et sanitaires à l'épreuve des chiffres: Le droit entre enjeux scientifiques et politiques' (2001) 2 RDUE 389–449.

354 The European Commission estimates that 11 years of testing the approximately 30,000 existing chemical substances would result in total costs of above 2.1 billion euros: a burden that should be shared by the private sector (Stategy for a Future Chemicals Policy, para. 3.4).

355 This ossification process has affected US risk regulation as well as the EC chemicals policy; see the discussion in Subsections 2.2.3.2. and 2.3.6. above.

implicit, with the attendant danger of bias caused by external factors (eg industrial or commercial interests).[356] The results of assessments carried out according to a single methodology may as a result differ significantly from one another.[357]

Fourthly, it is relatively difficult to meet the requirements of risk assessment at the international level in areas such as sanitary measures in the face of scientific uncertainty, despite the attempt by the WTO Appellate Body to allow some margin for scientific uncertainty.[358] The Appellate Body's case-law seems ambiguous on this point.[359]

More fundamentally, risk assessment focuses on quantifying threats rather than preventing them. It leads to a policy of pollution control (how much of a given contaminant are we able to assimilate? Is one death in a million an acceptable risk?) rather than a policy of prevention (what is the availability of less hazardous alternatives?).[360]

Budgetary constraints, uncertainties, and pressing deadlines call for faster, better, and more representative assessment techniques that are meaningful for regulatory decision-making and more suited to cope with the numerous uncertainties affecting the process. We do not share the viewpoint that risk assessment and risk management should be seen as opposites. In the light of the precautionary principle, the expert and the political sphere must be mutually supportive. What is at stake here is not just a blurring of the boundaries between risk assessment and risk management procedures, but rather creating an opening between these two areas.

The innovations we propose as regards both risk assessment and risk management should boost the level of environmental and health protection. Our analyses are largely based on our comparative analysis of WTO Appellate Body, ECJ, and US case-law regarding the validity of standards decided under conditions of scientific uncertainty.

---

[356] M. O'Brien, *Making Better Environmental Decisions* (Cambridge, Mass.: MIT Press, 2000) 27.

[357] A quantitative risk assessment exercise performed by 11 different teams in the EC came up with 11 different results that differed by a million fold. See S. Contini, A. Amendola, and I. Ziomas, *Benchmark Exercise on Major Hazard Analysis* (Ispra : European Commission Joint Research Center, 1991).

[358] See the discussion in Subsection 2.1.2.3. above.

[359] On one hand, a 'minimum magnitude of risk' is not required; a 'divergent opinion coming from qualified and respected sources' can be sufficient scientific evidence (Appellate Body *Australia Salmon*, paras. 120–30). On the other hand, the Appellate Body has set high conditions as regards the 'specificity' of such a risk assessment, and rejected studies that lend 'more weight to unknown and uncertain elements' (Appellate Body, *EC Hormones*, para. 186 and *Japan Varietals*, para. 77). It also held that under Articles 2(2) and 5(1) of the SPS Agreement the risk must be 'ascertainable' as opposed to 'theoretical uncertainty' (Appellate Body, *Australia Salmon*, para. 125).

[360] C.F. Cranor, *Regulating Toxic Substances: A Philosophy of Science and Law* (Oxford, New York: OUP, 1993) 14; idem., 'Risk Assessment, Susceptible Subpopulations, and Environmental Justice' in M.B. Gerrard (ed.), *The Law of Environmental Justice: Theories and Procedures to Address Disproportionate Risks* (Chicago: American Bar Association, 1999) 327.

4.3.2. Reviewing risk assessment in the light of the precautionary principle

Risk assessment, unlike the precautionary principle, assumes that it is possible to quantify and compare risks. In contrast, the precautionary principle is not neutral towards uncertainty; it is biased in favour of safety. Due to this *prima facie* opposition, a number of public authorities assume that the principle will be contrary to a sound scientific basis for risk assessment. Therefore they consider the precautionary principle merely a risk management tool that has nothing to do with risk assessment.[361]

However, we do not share the viewpoint that risk assessment and risk management should be seen as opposites. Indeed, we hope to demonstrate that the precautionary principle may influence both assessment methodology (4.3.2.1. below) and the proper role of scientific expertise (4.3.2.2.).

4.3.2.1. Reviewing risk assessment methods

- Broadening the scope of risk assessment

Traditional risk assessment procedures focus only on a small sub-set of the totality of issues of concern in the wider debate. The selected issues are more readily quantifiable because they are more amenable to measurement under an individual favoured metric (such as human mortality or monetary value). A number of risks thus lie outside the conceptual framework of formal risk regulation.[362] Furthermore, synergistic or additive effects of different compounds are not assessed under current regulatory appraisal in the EC and in the US, each substance being taken in isolation on a case-by-case basis.[363] Finally, the potential benefits of a technological risk which might be offset against any adverse effects are excluded from the scope of present regulatory risk assessment.

However, the total risk for a person is an aggregate of many individual risks. Protective measures should therefore be based on risk assessment, taking into account all relevant risk factors.[364] This requires that the scope of risk assessment be broadened to evaluate all uncertainties. These include direct or indirect and immediate or delayed risks, as well as any of their additive, cumulative, and

---

[361] See for instance, the positions defended by the EC Commission in its Communication on the Precautionary Principle and by the Scientific Steering Committee's Working Group on Harmonization of Risk Assessment Procedures in the Scientific Committees advising the European Commision in the area of human and environmental health (First Report on the Harmonisation of risk assessment procedures, 2000).

[362] For instance, hormonal effects are still excluded from current animal toxicity test protocols within the EC. See eg F. Bro-Rasmussen *et al.*, 'The Non-assessed Chemicals in the EU' (Copenhagen: Danish Board of Technology, 1996).

[363] D. Santillo, R. Stringer, P. Johnston, and J. Tickner, 'The Precautionary Principle: Protecting Against Failures of Scientific Method and Risk Assessment' (1998) 36: 12 MPB 939–50; C.F. Cranor, 'Risk Assessment, Susceptible Subpopulations, . . .', n. 360 above, 329.

[364] European Commission's Green Paper on 'The General Principles of Food Law in the European Union'; Communication from the Commission on the Precautionary Principle, para. 6.3.1.

synergistic effects, not only foreseeable risks.[365] These limitations of the risk assessment approach have become even more obvious in the face of new environmental challenges such as endocrine disrupting substances and POPs. Scientific proof of cause—effect relationships between these classes of chemicals and adverse effects on human health and the environment may take several years or decades to establish and may never be fully demonstrated owing to limitations in experimental design and the complexity of natural ecosystems. Therefore the wider the scope adopted during appraisal, the more 'precautionary' and 'scientifically sound' the associated regulatory decisions.[366]

Secondly, greater emphasis should be given to comparative assessment with substances or products with less harmful effects.[367] At present risk assessment procedures are usually designed to provide quantitative estimates of the risk associated with a single proposed action rather than to compare alternatives.[368] Therefore regulatory authorities are often presented with a more or less finished product by risk assessors, in the form of a risk recommendation which leaves them very little margin in choosing an alternative.[369] Normative decisions are thus completely determined by the scope of the assessment.

Nevertheless, a broader consideration of problems might give rise to more beneficial solutions and foster innovation in other areas.[370] Thus, to give more leeway to the decision-maker, decisions should be taken only after comparing the risks and benefits associated with a range of alternative options rather than a single option considered in isolation.[371] Risk assessment must therefore be conceived in such a way that it serves to inform decision-makers and allow them to select the right regulatory action rather than leave decisions to assessors. Comparing information relating to different classes of chemicals, for example, makes it possible for regulatory authorities to prioritize according to the relative degree of assessed risks. In this way hazardous substances can be prohibited on the grounds that less hazardous alternatives have been identified.[372] In the same

---

[365] A. Stirling, *On Science and Precaution in the Management of Technological Risk*, Vol. 1, A Synthesis Report of Case Studies (Seville: European Commission, Joint Research Centre & Institute for Prospective Technical Studies, 1999) 20. See, for instance, Article 2(8) and Annex II of the Directive 2001/18/EC on the deliberate release of GMOs.

[366] A. Stirling, n. 365 above, 33.

[367] For instance, the 1989 Massachusetts Toxics Use Reduction Act requires that manufacturing firms using specific quantities of industrial chemicals identify every two years alternatives to reduce use of those chemicals.

[368] R.N. Andrews, 'Environmental Impact Assessment and Risk Assessment: Learning from Each Other' in P. Wathern (ed.), *Environmental Impact Assessment: Theory and Practice* (London: Routledge, 1994) 89.

[369] V. Heyvaert, *Coping with Uncertainty*, n. 315 above, 198.

[370] The regulation of specific substances such as CFCs and PCBs has not only reduced overall environmental costs but has also stimulated scientific innovation in the search for commercial substitutes. Eg European Environmental Agency, n. 243 above, 182.

[371] M. O'Brien, n. 356 above, 213; A. Stirling, n. 365 above, 20; J. Tickner, *Precaution in Practice*, 122; European Environmental Agency, n. 243 above, 177.

[372] Article 8 of Directive 98/8/EC on biocides.

way, the environmental impacts of the deliberate release into the environment of GMOs should be compared with the effects of agricultural production methods (ranging from intensive to organic) in order to allow public authorities carrying out risk management to favour products or substances whose effects are most likely to be reversible.[373]

• Refining the methodology of risk assessment

In the hazard evaluation phase, a problem must be assessed and assigned a ranking to determine the full risk assessment procedure. A risk assessment approach must then be chosen. However, experts will only assess what they are told to assess. Therefore review of the system will require new thinking about the normative assumptions proper to the assessment procedure, such as a high level of environmental or health protection. This would include experts more fully considering normative needs following from the management of risk. We identify below a number of key elements that should be taken into account.

(a) Conservative assumptions for quantitative assessment
Scientific uncertainty is inherent in most situations. In fact, at every stage of the assessment process risk assessors are confronted with incomplete information and knowledge gaps. When data is imperfect or clear indications about impacts are lacking, risk assessment leaves room for uncertainty and error.[374] The precautionary principle should attempt to bridge gaps in our knowledge by making conservative assumptions that tend to overestimate risk. Even though they might appear overcautious, public expectations of safer standards should also be taken into account by risk assessors. Experts should err on the safe side by incorporating a number of such conservative assumptions in their procedures. In this regard, worst-case analysis should also be conducted, especially when risks include the possibility of accidental contamination.[375]

This trend is not entirely new, although it needs to be developed further. For example, even in the absence of statutory authorization, US environmental law is precautionary, using conservative evidentiary presumptions that tend to overestimate risk, and US agencies administering environmental and public health laws are known to overestimate true risks.[376] In the EC context, conservative

---

[373] P. Kourilsky and G. Viney, *Le Principe de Précaution* (Paris: La Documentation Française O. Jacob, 2000).

[374] C.F. Cranor, *Regulating Toxic Substances*, n. 360 above, 12–48.

[375] J. Gray and J. Bewers, 'Towards a Scientific Definition of the Precautionary Principle' (1996) 32: 11 MPB 768–71. See also Annex IV, para. 56 of Directive 98/8/EC on biocides.

[376] The 1996 US Food Quality Protection Act institutes safety factors. When setting standards for Superfund Cleanups, EPA uses very conservative assumptions through far-fetched exposure scenarios to increase the apparent risk. For an overview of the agencies conservative assumptions in the field of risk assessement, eg D. Bodansky, 'The Precautionary Principle: The US Experience' in T. O'Riordan and J. Cameron (eds.), *Interpreting the Precautionary Principle* (London: Cameron and May, 1994) 215; F. Cross, 'Paradoxical Perils of the Precautionary Principle' (1996) 53 Wash and Lee L Rev 851, 10. The dose—response relationship for a chemical is based on a threshold such as 'No observable adverse effect level' (NOAEL) which is divided by a safety factor in view of protecting sensitive

assumptions and broad safety margins are to be applied in the treatment of carcinogens.[377]

(b) Generic v. substance-by-substance assessment

There is a temptation to demand more detailed scientific evaluation on a case-by-case basis of substances considered for regulation, in order to overcome the uncertainties inherent in the various steps of risk assessment. For instance, courts in the US[378] and the WTO Appellate Body[379] both require regulatory bodies to undertake a substance-by-substance approach.

Nevertheless, too much scientific analysis can produce regulatory paralysis, with little useful information gained as a result. Identification and assessment methods are all too slow to evaluate on a case-by-case basis the risks posed by the 100,000 chemical substances currently in commercial circulation and the 1,000 new ones that are added to that number each year.[380] One should therefore avoid the temptation to require more detailed information in the face of uncertainty.[381] The regulatory challenge in the light of the precautionary principle is precisely to favour alternative approaches which could be based on generic regulation of classes of activities or chemicals according to hazard.[382] Certain single characteristics of a chemical or activity could trigger regulatory action, which avoids the need to perform an entire risk

segments of human populations. Eg A. Rosenthal, G. Gray, and J. Graham, 'Legislating Acceptable Cancer Risk from Exposure to Toxic Chemicals' (1992) 19: 2 ELQ 269–362. Such a cautious approach has been accepted by the US Supreme Court in the *Benzene* case. The Court ruled that: 'So long as [assumptions] are supported by a body of reputable scientific thought, [agencies are] free to use conservative assumptions in interpreting the data with respect to carcinogens, risking error on the side of overprotection rather than underprotection' (*Industrial Union Dept., AFL-CIO*, 448 U.S. at 656). On the obligation to carry out worst-case analysis in EIAs, see the discussion in Subsection 5.1.3. below.

[377] Directive 93/67/EEC laying down the principles for assessment of risks to man and the environment of substances notified in accordance with Directive 67/548/EEC. For example, the maximum allowable concentration of pesticides in water intended for human consumption has been fixed, with a view to precaution, at 0.1 ug/l by Directive 98/83/EC relating to the quality of water intended for human consumption. That threshold is relatively close to zero; more traditional risk assessment methods would have led EC authorities to authorize a contamination level 20 times higher. Eg D.M. Pugh, 'Deciding on the regulatory limits which have ensured that exposures of people to chemicals were without unacceptable risks' in D.M. Pugh and J.V. Tarazona (eds.), *Regulation for Chemical Safety in Europe: Analysis, Comment and Criticism* (Dordrecht: Kluwer, 1998) 15–16.

[378] See, for instance, the requirement made by the 11th Circuit Court that the OSHA has to develop an elaborate record for each chemical: *AFL-CIO v. OSHA* 965 F.2d. 962 (11th Cir. 1992).

[379] Appellate Body, *EC Hormones*, para. 194.

[380] For a critical analysis of the pace of the regulatory assessment procedures for chemical substances in the EC see the discussion in Subsection 2.2.3.2. above.

[381] C.F. Cranor, *Regulating Toxic Substances*, n. 360 above, 103, 116–29; idem., 'Risk Assessment, Susceptible Subpopulations . . .', n. 360 above, 333; European Environmental Agency, n. 243 above, 181–2.

[382] In this case, the intrinsic properties of chemicals or groups of chemicals are taken into consideration in order to arrive at a description of any and all hazards presented by the chemical or the group. Eg D. Santillo *et al.*, 'Hazard Based Risk Assessment and Management' in G. Winter (ed.), *Risk Assessment and Risk Management of Toxic Chemicals in the EC* (Baden-Baden: Nomas, 2000) 98–112.

assessment on a case-by-case basis, which can be time and resource consuming.[383] This alternative will make possible a more rapid evaluation of potentially harmful substances for human health and the environment.

(c) Qualitative v. quantitative assessment

Although techniques may vary tremendously from one discipline to another, the most commonly used analytical tool of prediction is quantified risk assessment. Required to adhere to established laboratory procedures, risk assessors have until now excluded public perceptions, priorities, and needs from the assessment procedure. Established assessment methodologies leave hardly any scope for the integration of non-scientific factors.[384]

However, risk is multidimensional.[385] Nearly all studies of public risk perception show that ordinary people bring more to their definitions and evaluations of risk than is recognized in the reductionist framework used by experts. Public perceptions may be influenced by a number of non-scientific factors, such as the origin of the risk (natural or man-made), whether it is assumed voluntarily or not (people will accept far greater risk when driving a car than they will from breathing its emissions), whether it is general or particular (the risk can be distributed throughout the population or may affect a small identifiable group), its degree of familiarity (smoking v. indoor pollution) and its time element (immediate v. long term). As subjective perceptions are not fully captured by risk assessments, experts and the public have rather different ways of looking at risks.[386] This can be explained partly by the fact that risks will often be imposed on those who are not the recipients of the benefits of a risk-creating activity. It can also be explained by the inevitable gap between the controlled and artificial conditions assumed in the analytical process (given the inherent difficulties of extrapolating data obtained in controlled laboratory conditions to human beings living in complex ecosystems) and the real-world conditions in which risks are actually experienced;[387] the knowledge created through testing is

---

[383] C.F. Cranor, *Regulating Toxic Substances*, n. 360 above, 103.

[384] V. Heyvaert, 'Reconceptualizing Risk Assessment', n. 351 above, 140.

[385] Major sociological studies of the 1990s in Germany, France, and the UK have shown that the traditional distinction between scientific facts and values is constantly blurred. Eg U. Beck, *Risk Society: Towards a New Modernity* (London: Sage, 1992); B. Latour, *Nous n'avons jamais été modernes* (Paris: La Découverte, 1991); R. Smith and B. Wynne, *Expert Evidence: Interpreting Science and the Law* (London: Routledge, 1989); S. Lash, B. Szerszynski, and B. Wynne (eds.), *Risk, Environment and Modernity* (London: Sage, 1996). See also S. Jasanoff, 'The Songlines of Risk' (1999) 8 Environmental Values 135. Sociologists assert that climate change science is itself a social construction that cannot be disentangled from political biases. Eg S. Jasanoff, *The Fifth Branch: Science Advisers as Policymakers* (Cambridge, Mass.: Harvard U.P., 1990); B. Wynne, 'Scientific Knowledge and the Global Environment' in M. Redclift and T. Benton (eds.), *Social Theory and the Global Environment* (London: Routledge, 1994).

[386] Nuclear power, for example, is regarded as relatively non-risky by experts and relatively dangerous by lay persons. Contrariwise, X-rays are regarded as quite risky by experts and not very risky by lay persons. Eg P. Slovic, 'Risk Perception' (1987) Science 280–5.

[387] B. Wynne, 'May the Sheep Safely Graze? A Reflexive View of the Expert—Lay Knowledge Divide' in S. Lash, B. Szerszynski, and B. Wynne (eds.), n. 385 above, 58.

partial, and at best approximate. And the belief that increased risk communication will obviate the fears of the layman is naïve.

However, qualitative information seems to be needed in order to obtain a more comprehensive understanding of complex scientific situations. Because risks are co-determined by sets of social values which affect their public acceptability, it might be more productive to accept those values as an integral part of the procedure, by making them explicit and co-ordinating them with regulatory goals instead of excluding them. In addition, a responsive risk assessment should not neglect lay knowledge (eg industry workers, users of the technology) which might be more firmly grounded in real-world conditions (eg workplace awareness of emerging patterns of ill health) than are laboratory experiments.[388] In other words, rather than hiding behind the fortress of science, risk assessment should become better attuned to public perceptions and lay knowledge as well as to regulatory goals.

The case-law and legislation described in the second section of this Chapter indicate that qualitative assessment is beginning to be integrated in risk assessment procedures. For instance, in its 1983 Report on 'Risk Assessment in the Federal Government' the US National Research Council already stressed that as quantitative estimates are not always feasible they may be eschewed for policy reasons in favour of qualitative expressions of risk. The WTO Appellate Body acknowledged in the *EC Hormones* case that risk assessment should take into account qualitative elements as well as quantitative information.[389] 'Matters not susceptible of quantitative analysis by the empirical or experimental methods commonly associated with the physical sciences' should therefore also be considered.[390] Such an option can already be found in some EC chemicals legislation.[391]

In this perspective, risks arising from difficulties of control, inspection, or enforcement or from the possibility of accidental pollution are relevant for the public authorities because they are related to the real world. As reflected in the recent WTO *Asbestos* case, concrete technological applications and the difficulty of controlling risks should be taken into account when assessing

---

[388] Often, too, lay knowledge may be based on different assumptions about what is salient, or what degree of control is reasonable to expect. Eg A. Stirling, 'Risk at a Turning Point' (1998) 1: 2 Journal of Risk Research 97–109; European Environmental Agency, n. 243 above, 177–8.

[389] The WTO Appellate Body has decided that risk assessment can be conducted either quantitatively or qualitatively (*EC Hormones*, paras. 184–6; *Australia Salmon*, para. 124). The Appellate Body clearly overturned the view of the Panel that social value judgements made by politicians, as 'non-scientific elements', pertained to risk management rather than to risk assessment (US Panel Report, para. 8.94; Canada Panel Report, para. 8.97).

[390] Appellate Body, *EC Hormones*, para. 187.

[391] For instance, several EC acts on chemicals leave the Member States a choice between qualitative and quantitative approaches when they have to estimate the dose/response concentration to which a population is or may be exposed (Commission Regulation (EC) No. 1488/94 laying down the principles for the assessment of risks to man and the environment of existing substances in accordance with Council Regulation (EEC) No. 793/93, Annex I, section 3.1; Directive 98/8/EC on biocides, Annex VI).

the need for a ban. Canada, although not disputing that chrysolite fibres pose health risks, claimed that those risks ceased to exist once asbestos was encapsulated in chrysolite-cement materials. However, both the Panel and the Appellate Body considered that there was enough evidence to show that such products continued to pose a risk to health in this type of application.[392] In fact, since most safety regulations are poorly implemented—especially those relating to environmental protection, as became evident during the 1999 Belgian dioxin crisis—it is important that risk assessors take such situations into account.[393]

Clearly, confining scientific expertise to an ivory tower serves no purpose. On the contrary, the precautionary principle means that scientific expertise and the decision-making process should be brought closer to one another.

4.3.2.2. Strengthening expertise

• Transparent expertise

It is not unusual for scientists viewing the same evidence to draw different conclusions. Indeed, the history of science is full of contradictory theories and fierce competition between diametrically opposed views and ideas. Consequently the progress of scientific research is punctuated by ruptures, and those responsible for breakthroughs must often wander in the scientific wilderness before their theories are widely accepted. Many important discoveries were born as controversial ideas that were initially contested bitterly by the mainstream scientific establishment.

Changes to the methodology of risk assessment such as those described above would strongly influence the type of expertise needed to carry out such assessments. The fact that science would no longer constitute an absolute criterion does not mean that it is no longer necessary to heed the advice of scientists: indeed, they have never been so important. However, their contribution to political decision-making must be substantially modified. By requiring the active exercise of doubt, the precautionary principle invites decision-makers to open the debate to marginal and dissident opinions and to the conjectures and questions of a minority of the scientific community.[394] The appraisal of risks should therefore be conducted in an open fashion: 'only in this way are the framing

---

[392] The Panel noted that, owing to the diversity of applications for chrysolite fibres in industrial, commercial, and residential buildings, 'there are areas in which health controls are difficult to apply'. (*European Communities: Measures Affecting the Prohibition of Asbestos and Asbestos Products* (WT/DS 135), para. 8.200). See also Appellate Body, *EC: Measures Affecting the Prohibition of Asbestos and Asbestos Products* (WT/D135/AB/R), paras. 162, 174 (hereinafter Appellate Body, *Asbestos*).

[393] In the summer of 1999 Belgium was struck by an important economic and political crisis due to the contamination of animal food products by PCB. The origin of the scandal was the mismanagement of hazardous wastes.

[394] It is an awesome responsibility for decision-makers to choose between majority and minority opinion. On one hand, unorthodox new ideas put forward by scientific minorities may ultimately constitute sound science. On the other hand, dissenting opinions can turn out to be based on false hypotheses.

assumptions adopted in the risk assessment and the treatment of associated uncertainties and trade-offs tested and validated against the wider socio-political realities'.[395] As a result, it will no longer be possible systematically to ignore the alarms sounded by a small group of experts until such time as the entire scientific community supports a minority opinion.[396] Decision-making will no longer be the prerogative of majority discourse alone, or the preserve of a scientific class close to the political elite. Expertise should therefore be employed in an open, transparent, and pluralistic fashion.

As noted above, some case-law is already characterized by this new relation to science. Of particular interest in this regard is the case of the *Whyl* nuclear power plant, where the German Federal Administrative Tribunal ruled that the administrative authorities should not have relied on majority opinion alone but should have given equal consideration to minority views.[397] As was acknowledged by the WTO Appellate Body in the *EC Hormones* case, the fact that a risk assessment is based on a scientific minority viewpoint does not invalidate the procedure.[398] Indeed, responsible authorities can act in good faith on the basis of contradictory opinions from equally qualified or respected sources.[399]

Experts, for their part, should more explicitly acknowledge the fact that they cannot eliminate all scientific uncertainties. Substantial uncertainties must be addressed through normative choices (high level of protection, precaution, substitution, etc.); they should rely upon such choices and make those choices explicit.[400]

- Pluralistic expertise

By primarily taking into account quantifiable, direct, and linear factors (eg toxicity leading to cancer) risk assessors tend to address single hazards, single effects, and single media. Qualitative factors (eg poverty, consumer habits) as well as multiple pathways of exposure tend not to be analysed. However, compartmentalized science, no matter how erudite, is an insufficient basis for anticipating or mitigating the impacts of complex substances in ecosystems characterized by feedback loops and complex interactions. Reflecting the different perceptions of risk, multidisciplinary risk assessment could better strike a balance between facts and values and between science and society than does compartmentalized research. Wherever possible, the precautionary principle

---

[395] A. Stirling, n. 365 above, 7.

[396] Such a demand has seemed particularly important since the discussion on reducing CFC emissions into the stratosphere demonstrated that initial regulation had been delayed by certain scientific groups insisting on ever-greater certainty about the phenomenon of ozone layer destruction.

[397] See the discussion in Subsection 2.3.1. above.

[398] In the *Beef Hormones* dispute, the WTO Appellate Body did not believe that: 'a risk assessment has to come to a monolithic conclusion that coincides with the scientific conclusion or view implicit in the SPS measure. The risk assessment could set out both the prevailing view representing the "mainstream" of scientific opinion, as well as the opinions of scientists taking a divergent view.' (Appellate Body, *EC Hormones*, para. 194).

[399] Appellate Body, *EC Hormones*, para. 194.

[400] C.F. Cranor, *Regulating Toxic Substances*, n. 360 above, 131.

calls for an interdisciplinary approach, which pools wisdom garnered from the natural and social sciences.[401] The information assembled by multidisciplinary teams (ecologists, biologists, neurologists, economists, sociologists) must be used to complement the quantitative probability of harm determined through epidemiologic and toxicological studies, exposure assessments, and monitoring studies (for instance, one cancer for one million persons exposed to a hazard). Of course, a mixed quantitative/qualitative risk assessment will increase the level of complexity and sophistication of ranking different types of risks and setting priorities.[402] Nevertheless, that is the way forward, because science is complex. Its complexity must be accepted rather than dissipated through a simplistic and abstract image of reality.

• Independent expertise

In order to develop risk-regulatory strategies in a more systematic and coherent manner, some authors have recently supported the idea that the problems of risk regulation call for the creation of an administrative organization that is mission-oriented and enjoys broad authority, independence, and prestige, with the goal of bringing a degree of uniformity and rationality to decision-making.[403] If the precautionary principle is to be observed, such an organization would have to remain independent, with that independence being both fostered and monitored (open to independent peer review).[404] Realistically, however, such experts are always subject to political and industrial pressures that can lead to less than independent results. Given these circumstances it would perhaps be more satisfactory to acknowledge the dependence of experts by measures such as 'declarations of interests'.

• Participation by interest groups

Unlike environmental impact assessment, which is intended to increase the accountability of decision-making to interest groups,[405] risk assessment

---

[401] Eg European Environmental Agency, n. 243 above, 4; J. Tickner, 'A Map towards Precautionary Decision-Making' in R.C. Raffensperger and J. Tickner (eds.), *Protecting Public Health and the Environment*, n. 179 above, 169 and *Precaution in Practice*, n. 324 above, 80.

[402] V. Heyvaert, *Coping with Uncertainty*, n. 315 above, 191.

[403] S. Breyer and V. Heyvaert, 'Institutions for Regulating Risks' in R.L. Revesz, Ph. Sands, and R. Stewart (eds.), *Environmental Law, the Economy, and Sustainable Development* (Cambridge: Cambridge U.P., 2000) 302.

[404] This has been recognized at the European Commission level by the shifting of scientific advisory committees from the 'producer' directorates (eg agriculture) to the Health and Consumer Directorate. In this regard, recitals 20 and 21 of the Preamble of Directive 2001/18/EC on the deliberate release of GMOs state: 'It is necessary to establish a common methodology to carry out the environmental risk assessment based on *independent scientific advice*.... Member States and the Commission should ensure that systematic and *independent research* on the potential risks involved in the deliberate release or the placing on the market of GMOs is conducted' (emphases added). See also European Environmental Agency, n. 243 above, 178–80.

[405] Article 4(2) of the 1991 Espoo Convention on Environmental Impact Assessment in a Transboundary Context; Article 6(2) of Directive 85/337/EEC on EIA; Article 6(3) of Directive 92/43/EEC on the conservation of natural habitats and of wild fauna and flora.

frequently functions as a more arcane expert procedure, couched in technical terms such as 'risk probability' or 'dose-response curve' that have little meaning to most laymen.[406] At present values are hidden behind quantitative models that leave very little room for deliberation. Scientists adhere to the view that risk assessment is in essence a scientific undertaking, and interest groups are therefore afforded few possibilities to make recommendations. Thus, risk assessment is technocratic rather than democratic. However, as we noted earlier, risk regulation is beset by divergent perceptions, interests, and value judgements. Complex environmental risks cannot be adequately addressed through a purely expert-driven 'sound science' approach. Risk assessors should therefore become more aware of the 'social dimensions' of their expertise by creating greater room for deliberation. Risk assessment must not be considered as a purely scientific enterprise to which only experts have access; it should become more pluralistic in character. Public consultation is thus a necessary part of any 'sound scientific' approach to the regulatory appraisal of ecological risks.[407] For this reason public authorities should ensure that the viewpoints of various stakeholders (eg workers, consumers, environmentalists, industrialists) are openly discussed in the risk assessment process.[408] These stakeholders should also be allowed to contribute to determining the relevant factors that scientists should take into consideration when carrying out assessments and the form in which those findings should be expressed. [409]

4.3.3. Reviewing risk management in the light of the precautionary principle

Owing to the pluralistic character of democratic society and the multidimensional character of risk, risk management cannot be dealt with by a single approach, nor can it lead to a definitive or unique authoritative conclusion. Recognizing plural interests also leads automatically to the acceptance of a certain pluralism in the decision-making process.

---

[406] R.N. Andrews, 'Environmental Impact Assessment and Risk Assessment: Learning from Each Other' in P. Wathern (ed.), *Environmental Impact Assessment: Theory and Practice* (London: Routledge, 1994) 89 *et seq.*

[407] A. Stirling, *Science and Precaution*, n. 365 above, 34; J. Tickner, *Precaution in Practice*, n. 324 above, 129; European Environmental Agency, n. 243 above, 185–6.

[408] According to the Communication from the European Commission on the Precautionary Principle, it is essential that the decision-making process gathers the views of all interested parties at a very early stage: 'the decision-making procedure should be transparent and should involve as early as possible and to the extent reasonably possible all interested parties' (para. 5). On this issue, see the discussion in Chapter 5, Subsection 4.3.2. below.

[409] 'Adequate risk analysis depends on incorporating the perspectives and knowledge of the interested and affected parties from the earliest phase of the effort to understand the risks. . . . Deliberation is important at each step of the process that informs risk decisions. . . . Appropriately structured deliberation contributes to sound analysis by adding knowledge and perspectives that improve understanding and contributes to the acceptability of risk characterization' (NRC, *Understanding Risk* (1996) 4).

4.3.3.1. Aiming at a high level of health and environmental protection

The precautionary principle is not taking root in virgin soil; it has neighbours: other rules that occupy a high position in the hierarchy of norms.[410] Among these are the obligation to promote a high level of health and environmental protection. EC institutions must seek to achieve a high level of environmental protection (see, for instance, Articles 95(3) and 174(2) of the EC Treaty), public health (eg Articles 95(3) and 152(1)), and consumer protection (eg Articles 95(3) and 153(1)). According to their constitutional provisions concerning environmental and health protection, most national authorities in Europe must also seek to achieve a high level of protection.[411] Several US environmental statutes, such as the CAA, require protection with an 'adequate' or 'ample' margin of safety.[412] Last but not least, according to the WTO Appellate Body's case-law, WTO Members have the right to establish the level of protection that they deem appropriate: a level which might be higher than that implied in existing international standards, guidelines, and recommendations.[413] A Member's acceptable level of risk may even be set at 'zero risk'.[414]

Public authorities may thus determine the level of risk they are ready to accept in the light of their international and constitutional obligations. In doing so they should embrace the precautionary principle's devotion to erring on the side of caution. They must have the discretion to base their measures on social or policy choices, as long as these bear a relation to the scientific conclusions of a risk assessment procedure,[415] which may, as we have seen, include the assessment of non-quantifiable factors.[416] Finally, the objective of a high level of human health and environmental protection is not to be made subordinate to the objective of minimizing trade effects or encouraging free enterprise.

4.3.3.2. Science should be on tap, not on top

Decision-making must obviously be based on available scientific information. However, scientific analysis is unavoidably and inextricably intertwined with subjective assumptions: risk analysts often have no choice but to make simplifying, and scientifically questionable, assumptions which can either underestimate

---

[410] On the interaction between the precautionary principle and the obligation to seek a high level of environmental protection, see Chapter 5, Section 2, below.

[411] See the discussion in Chapter 5, Subsection 4.1. below.

[412] R.L. Revesz, *Foundations of Environmental Law and Policy* (Oxford University Press, 1997) 77; C.F. Cranor, 'Risk Assessment, Susceptible Subpopulations, . . .' in M.B. Gerrard (ed.), *The Law of Environmental Justice: Theories and Procedures to Address Disproportionate Risks* (Chicago, American Bar Association, 1999) 307–56.

[413] Appellate Body, *EC Hormones*, para. 124.

[414] Appellate Body, *Australia Salmon*, para. 125; *Asbestos*, paras. 168, 174. For instance, a zero-risk policy can be justified for carcinogenic substances such as asbestos, as there is no known threshold of safety. Eg D. Gee and M. Greenber, 'Asbestos: From magic to malevolent mineral' in European Environmental Agency, n. 243 above, 57.

[415] Appellate Body, *Japan Varietals*, para. 84.

[416] Appellate Body, *EC Hormones*, paras. 184–6; *Australia Salmon*, para. 124.

or overestimate risks.[417] Therefore, risk assessment must be understood to be nothing more than a tool; it has a role to play in decision-making, but only a partial role. It is not up to scientists to decide on the acceptable level of risk imposed on society as a whole. Decisions on how far and how fast to reduce assessed risks are essentially political or societal value judgements to be made by the responsible regulatory authorities.[418] The public authorities must therefore enjoy a degree of discretion in regard to risk assessment:[419] that is, they should bear a reasonable relationship to the relevant scientific findings.[420] Science is thus a necessary but not a sufficient basis of regulation.

4.3.3.3. Acting when information is at the frontiers of scientific knowledge

When information is at the frontier of scientific knowledge or a full risk assessment is not possible, regulatory bodies must be able to regulate risks even though a risk assessment procedure has not conclusively demonstrated adverse health or environmental effects. Regulatory measures ought to be based on the precautionary principle. The question of what society should do in the face of uncertainty regarding cause and effect relationships is necessarily a question of public policy, not science. In those circumstances, decision-making must depend to a greater extent upon policy judgements that do not wait upon absolute scientific proof. In other words, the decision to act or to abstain must be a political decision where there is an indication that action is justified, as we know that 'awaiting certainty will often allow for only reactive, not preventive regulation'.[421]

In practical terms this means that risk assessment should be simplified. Where experts are not able to fully perform the four steps of the assessment procedure because information is lacking, inaccurate, or inconclusive, a preliminary assessment of hazard should be sufficient.[422]

---

[417] A. Stirling, *Science and Precaution*, n. 365 above, 29.

[418] R.B. Stewart, 'The Role of the Courts in Risk Management' (1986) 16 Ent'l L Rep 10208. See also the Comments from the European Commission Services to the Codex Secretariat on its Communication on the Precautionary Principle.

[419] S. Breyer has been advocating that, in the US institutional context, more, not less, discretionary power must be granted to regulatory agencies to allow them to deal with problems of risk management. S. Breyer, *Breaking the Vicious Circle: Toward Effective Risk Regulation* (Cambridge, Mass.: Harvard U.P., 1993); S. Breyer and V. Heyvaert, n. 403 above, 283.

[420] In this respect, the WTO Appellate Body considers that in order for an SPS measure to be based on a risk assessment, the measure must be rationally related to a risk assessment (Appellate Body, *Japan Varietals*, para. 84).

[421] On this point see the case-law of the US Appeals Courts (Subsection 2.3.6 above). Eg *Ethyl Corp. v. US EPA*, 541 F.2d1, 24–25 (D.C. Cir, 1976); *Lead Indus. Ass'n Inc. v. US EPA*, 647 F.2d 1130 (D.C. Cir. 1979).

[422] The EC has moved to an intermediate approach between classical risk assessment and assessment based on hazard, in the form of a simplified risk assessment. This is set out in the new framework 2000/60EC Directive establishing a framework for Community action in the field of water policy (Article 16(1)(c)). This would allow substances to be prioritized for regulatory action on the basis of a procedure based largely on evidence of intrinsic hazard of the substance concerned. The 2001 European Commission White Paper on the Strategy for a Future Chemicals Policy (COM(2001)88 final) calls for 'accelerated risk assessments' and 'targeted risk assessments' to replace the comprehensive risk assessments of the past (para. 4.4.)

In addition, when public authorities fear significant or irreversible damage, action should precede risk assessment.[423] This is particularly the case when scientists conclude that they are unable to assess a risk clearly or when their conclusions are inconclusive or divergent. In this case the risk manager should be able to take provisional measures without having to wait until the reality and seriousness of the identified risk become fully apparent.[424]

Nonetheless, public authorities should seek to obtain the additional information needed for a more objective risk assessment. Efforts should be made to reduce the uncertainty that may have prompted the adoption of a precautionary measure. This viewpoint seems to be shared by international organizations. According to the Commission's Communication on the precautionary principle, 'the measures must be of a provisional nature pending the availability of more reliable scientific data' and 'scientific research shall be continued with a view to obtaining more complete data'. Analagously, the case-law of the WTO Appellate Body stresses that SPS Agreement Members must seek to obtain the 'additional information necessary for a more objective assessment of risk'.[425] A precautionary measure decided according to Article 5(7) of the SPS Agreement is only provisional.

However, it must be stressed that under most international and national legislation precautionary action is not always confined to 'provisional measures'. For example, under the 2000 Cartagena Biosafety Protocol there is no requirement that a precautionary measure be provisional or that a review be carried out within a reasonable period of time, as it is the case under the SPS Agreement.

Moreover, the question of how provisional such measures should be is difficult to answer. The above statements from the European Commission and SPS case-law presume that it is only a matter of time until certainty can be achieved.[426] It is thus assumed that science can always provide definitive answers. However, as uncertainty is rarely due to a simple need to do more research, one may ask what a national authority is to do when no additional information becomes available, or when such information is still insufficient. There are areas where it is likely that no amount of time will allow for full certainty and where the seriousness of possible harm justifies a precautionary approach even in the long run.[427] The

---

[423] Such a possibility is recognized by several international agreements. See eg Article 5(7) of the SPS Agreement. In EC law see eg the EC Green Paper on the General Principles of Food Law, and Article 16(1) of Directive 2001/18/EC on the deliberate release of GMOs.

[424] Comments from the European Commission Services to the Codex Secretariat on its Communication on the Precautionary Principle.

[425] In the view of the Appellate Body, what constitutes a 'reasonable period of time' has to be established on a case-by-case basis and depends on the specific circumstances of each case, including the difficulty of obtaining the additional information necessary for the review of the provisional SPS measure (Appellate Body, *Japan Varietals*, para. 92).

[426] However, according to the WTO Appellate Body, 'what constitutes a "reasonable period of time" has to be established on a case-by-case basis and depends on the specific circumstances of each case, including the difficulty of obtaining the additional information necessary for the review and the characteristics of the SPS measure' (Appellate Body, *Japan Varietals*, para. 93).

[427] E. Fisher, 'Drowning by Numbers: Standard Setting in Risk Regulation and the Pursuit of Accountable Public Administration' (2000) 20: 1 OJLS 115.

maintenance of a precautionary measure should therefore not be linked to a time limit, but rather to the development of scientific knowledge. Precautionary measures should be maintained as long as scientific data remains incomplete, imprecise, or inconclusive and as long as a risk is considered too high to be imposed on society.

4.3.3.4. Balancing advantages and disadvantages and not merely costs and benefits

For practical reasons, achieving a 'zero-risk' policy might be difficult to achieve, and the precautionary principle does not tell the authorities how much risk uncertainty should be allowed under a regulation. Risk management is primarily a question of decision-making. Authorities must determine a level of acceptable risk. Yet that decision is likely to come up against economic interests in cases where risk-producing activities are prohibited, and ecological interests where they are authorized. What is action to one is inaction to the other; what one gains, the other loses. As we demonstrated in the third section of this Chapter, settling these claims calls for a balancing of interests.[428]

In some legal systems (eg the USA) cost–benefit analysis (CBA) has become the method most often used by the law-maker to weigh the various interests at stake. Action is taken only if the cost of damages exceeds the cost of intervention. Economic effects are expressed in monetary units, health and safety effects are expressed in mortality and morbidity terms, and environmental effects are expressed in appropriate descriptive terms. Then the traditional CBA translates all consequences into their current monetary value.

However, this method raises problems in that current estimates of regulatory benefits are too low: possibly far too low.[429] In addition it tries to quantify the unquantifiable. It is already difficult to translate all adverse effects of a project into monetary units, as many dimensions of risk are irreducibly qualitative in nature. In other words, they are irreducible: they cannot readily or unambiguously be reduced to a single measure of performance (in this case, monetary value).[430] In addition, CBA fails to take into account the long-term benefits of regulation (which are more difficult to quantify) by overestimating the cost of regulatory intervention (which is usually easy to quantify). The monetarization of non-traded goods is misleading and should be avoided.

In order to ensure that the assessment of the proportionate or disproportionate character of a measure is as objective as possible, public authorities should have at their disposal all the elements needed to compare the costs and benefits of the

---

[428] See Subsection 3.2.3.2. above.

[429] Eg R.H. Frank and C.R. Sustein, 'Cost-Benefit Analysis and Relative Position' (2001) 68:2 Univ. Chicago LR 323–3.

[430] Eg R. Baldwin, n. 247 above, 5; N. Ashford, 'A Conceptual Framework for the Use of the Precautionary Principle in Law' in C. Raffensperger and J. Tickner (eds.), *Protecting Public Health & the Environment*, n. 179 above, 200; A. Stirling, *On Science and Precaution*, n. 365 above, 18. See also Subsection 3.2.3.2. above.

contested measure. Without being thoroughly informed, the decision-maker will not be able to form a precise idea of the justification for allowing one interest to encroach upon another. Categories of interests which cannot be translated into monetary units should therefore also have to be considered as legitimate subjects of public policy. Consequently the traditional CBA should be replaced by a more global comparison of the advantages and disadvantages of a regulatory measure. Considerations other than purely economic ones, usually relating to free trade, must also be taken into account.

This viewpoint seems to be shared by some regional organizations. According to the EC Communication on the precautionary principle, examining costs and benefits has a much broader scope than CBA and includes non-economic considerations such as the efficacy of possible options and their acceptance by the public.[431] Indeed, health and environmental protection levels are largely derived from societal choices which are more subjective than objective. For example, the banning of hormones in beef in the EC can be justified by social considerations ranging from animal welfare to consumer safety.

Article 26 of the 2000 Cartagena Biosafety Protocol allows Parties to take socio-economic considerations into account when reaching a decision on import insofar as those considerations arise from the impact of LMOs on the conservation and sustainable use of biodiversity, and especially on the value of biological diversity to indigenous and local authorities. The inclusion of such considerations is innovative in international law, in comparison with the SPS Agreement provisions, according to which risk management measures shall only be imposed to the extent necessary to prevent adverse effects detected in a risk assessment carried out in a scientifically sound manner.[432]

Moreover, the US Court of Appeals[433] and EC courts[434] both clearly favour non-economic elements such as human health in the process of reviewing regulatory standards, where those interests must be balanced against economic interests.

4.4. Critical assessment

At first glance the precautionary principle seems to occupy a paradoxical position at the interface between science and normative decision-making. On one

---

[431] According to the European Commission, 'Examining costs and benefits entails comparing the overall cost to the Community of action and lack of action, in both the short and long term. This is not simply an economic cost—benefit analysis: its scope is much broader, and includes non-economic considerations, such as the efficacy of possible options and their acceptability to the public.' Article 174(3) of the EC Treaty lists a number of criteria which must be taken into account in the field of environmental policy. Among them, the criteria 'the costs and benefits of the measure' are translated into French as '*les avantages et les charges*' of action or lack of action. Eg L. Krämer, *EC Environmental Law* (4th edn., London: Sweet & Maxwell, 2000) 21–2. It must also be noted that the SPS Agreement does not direct WTO panels to apply a cost—benefit analysis.

[432] SPS Agreement, Article 2(2).

[433] See eg *Lead Industr. Ass'n v. EPA*, 647 F.2d 1130, 1148–1149 (D.C. Cir. 1980); *American Petroleum Institute v. Costle*, 665 F.2d 1176, 1185 (D.C. Cir. 1981).

[434] Case T-199/96, *Bergaderm* [1998] ECR II-2805; Case T-79/99P, *Alpharma* [1999] ECR II-2027.

hand, it would reaffirm the primacy of political decision-making in determining the contents and timing of preventive measures, thereby limiting the role of scientists. On the other hand, although arising from a lack of scientific information, precaution calls for ever increasing scientific knowledge, thus serving to reinforce the power of experts and consequently the dependence of decision-makers on science. Scientific expertise, initially rejected as insufficient, would thereafter be sought to balance the scope of anticipatory measures.[435] However, as we have demonstrated in this section through consideration of the articulation between risk assessment and risk management, these two tendencies can operate in a complementary fashion. In other words, the problems of precaution come within the competence of engineers and toxicologists working to assess a particular type of risk as much as that of the decision-maker: it is a question of knowing how to arbitrate between these two fields when knowledge is uncertain and imperfect, so that no single party can make a decisive case to convince others, obtain their agreement, and put an end to the debate.

The precautionary principle is thus in no way anti-scientific. On the contrary, it is precisely at that level that it demonstrates its innovative character, by forcing scientists to admit the existence of uncertainty and decision-makers not to hide behind Fortress Science.

5. Applications of the principle

The appearance of new principles is generally signalled by both major and minor modifications of existing laws. These could be significant in the case of the precautionary principle, which is based on assumptions completely contrary to those underlying the principle of prevention, the latter having until now shaped environmental law. This renegade principle could ruffle the tranquil course of positive law by leading to a genuine change of perspective in the elaboration of norms. Both *ex ante* and *ex post* procedures for environmental decisions will change owing to the effect of the precautionary principle. For the sake of greater clarity, we have distinguished between the effects of the principle on the elaboration of standards (Subsection 5.1 below) and its effects on civil liability (Subsection 5.2 below).

5.1. The effects of the precautionary principle on the elaboration of standards

5.1.1. Introductory note
The precautionary principle has its greatest impact prior to decision-making, since its logic relates to the formulation of decisions rather than their

---

[435] O. Godard, 'Social Decision-Making under Conditions of Scientific Controversy, Expertise and the Precautionary Principle' in C. Joerges, K.-H. Ladeur, and E. Vos (eds.), *Integrating Expertise into Regulatory Decision-Making* (Baden-Baden: Nomos, 1997) 65–7.

implementation. Under the principle duty of care becomes essential. It is no longer a question merely of foreseeing or averting a known danger, but of preventing a risk that cannot be fully assessed: a new type of risk, an uncertain risk. Consideration of such risks as part of the decision-making process must above all aim to avoid irreversible situations; the absence of certainty should no longer delay the adoption by the public authorities of suitable measures to protect against risks, nor the cessation of certain dangerous activities.

The precautionary principle should at the very least lead to the generalization of procedures for assessing and reducing risks, including those which have a low probability of occurring. However, it is not sufficient to gather relevant information: authorities must also be prepared to take decisions before full information has become available. In addition to enhanced information requirements, public authorities should henceforth consider the reversibility of their decisions in order to reflect advances in scientific knowledge. By urging the decision-maker to choose a different course of action or to declare a moratorium, the principle may play a decisive role in the battle against risk. Finally, the statement of reasons for a given decision should reflect not only factual elements but also those uncertainties that can no longer be ignored. These aspects of the precautionary principle are considered below.

5.1.2. *Reversal of the burden of proof in regulating risks*

5.1.2.1. The need for a shift

Public authorities should demonstrate the need to ban or regulate a given activity.[436] That requirement derives from the need to justify any constraining regulatory measure on the basis of objective considerations; in the field of environment, this implies that decisions must be based on proven scientific fact. The decision to protect a species or to ban the production of a chemical substance may be censured for exceeding an authority's powers, lacking adequate substantiation, or violating the principle of non-discrimination if the scientific assumptions upon which it is based bear no relation to the objective towards which the legislator or his administration is working.

This logic, which has strongly marked the evolution of environment law up to the present day, should be reconsidered in the light of the precautionary principle.[437] If the absence of scientific certainty may no longer serve as a pretext

---

[436] See, for example, Article 2 of the SPS Agreement providing that 'Members shall ensure that any sanitary or phytosanitary measure is applied only to the extent necessary to protect human, animal or plant life or health, is based on scientific principles and is not maintained without sufficient scientific evidence, except as provided for in paragraph 7 of Article 5'.

[437] J. Cameron and W. Wade-Gery, 'Addressing Uncertainty: Law, Policy and the Development of the Precautionary Principle' in B. Dente (ed.), *Environmental Policy in Search of New Instruments* (Dordrecht: Kluwer Academic, 1995) 95; J. Cameron, W. Wade-Gery, and J. Abouchar, 'Precautionary Principle and Future Generations' in E. Agius and S. Busuttil (eds.) *Future Generations and International Law* (London: Earthscan, 1998) 93–113, 108; E. Rehbinder, 'The Precautionary Principle in an International Perspective' in *Miljørettens Grundsporgsmaal* (Copenhagen, 1994) 91;

for delaying the adoption of measures to protect the environment, those who formulate standards should no longer be required to justify their actions on the basis of absolute scientific certainty.

According to the adage *in dubio pro natura* deduced by some authors[438] from the constitutional right to environmental protection, harmlessness is a prior requirement for authorization of any technology liable adversely to affect the environment. More concretely, the precautionary principle posits a presumption in favour of protection of the environment and public health. Therefore the principle places the responsibility for demonstrating safety on those undertaking potentially harmful activities.[439]

Parties seeking to introduce new and risky substances into the environment should be required to provide conclusive evidence of their safety. In the absence of sufficient scientific data, the authority should refuse to authorize the substance or the practice at issue. Thus the principle could serve to delay the decision to commercialize a product or undertake an activity until such time as a reasonable proof of its adequate safety has been provided. From a regime where any activity must be permitted unless the regulator is able to prove that it is hazardous, we would thus move to a regime where any activity that has not been proved safe by its developer would be forbidden. It would no longer be for those who fear a hazard to prove that such a hazard exists; rather, sectors affected by regulation would have to demonstrate, on the basis of scientific evidence, that regulation of their activity would be inappropriate. This is quite simply a new paradigm: previously the polluter benefited from scientific doubt; henceforth doubt will work to the benefit of the environment.

5.1.2.2. The tendency to shift the burden of proof in international, EC, and US law

There is a clear need to alleviate the burden of proof when information is 'at the frontiers of scientific knowledge'.[440] If the burden of proof cannot be shifted to the operator, the law-maker should at least lessen the burden of proof required to trigger a public intervention to prevent or mitigate harm to the

A. Nollkaemper, 'What You Risk Reveals What You Value...' in D. Freestone and E. Hey (eds.), *The Precautionary Principle* (London: Kluwer Law Int'l, 1995) 73; A. Kiss and D. Shelton, *International Environmental Law* (London: Graham & Trotman, 1997) 43.

[438] F. Ost, *La Nature Hors la Loi* (Paris: La Découverte, 1995) 100.

[439] See the thesis of C.F. Cranor, J. Tickner, and P.L. de Fur in C. Raffensperger and J. Tickner (eds.), *Protecting Public Health and the Environment*, n. 179 above, 94, 163, 345–6.

[440] According to the EC Commission's Communication on the Precautionary Principle, 'action taken under the head of the precautionary principle must in certain cases include a clause reversing the burden of proof and placing it on the producer, manufacturer or importer, but such an obligation cannot be systematically entertained as a general principle. This possibility should be examined on a case-by-case basis when a measure is adopted under the precautionary principle, pending supplementary scientific data, so as to give professionals who have an economic interest in the production and/or marketing of the procedure or product in question the opportunity to finance the necessary research on a voluntary basis' (para. 6.4.).

environment.[441] Several instruments of international and EC law have used this reversal in an anticipatory manner.

The 1982 UNGA World Charter for Nature established this change by requiring that: 'Activities which are likely to pose a significant risk to nature shall be preceded by an exhaustive examination; their proponents shall demonstrate that expected benefits outweigh potential damage to nature...'.[442]

It is international instruments for protection of the marine environment, however, which have given concrete form to this advance. Created within the framework of the 1972 Convention for the Prevention of Marine Pollution by Dumping, the Oslo Commission in 1989 adopted a decision that clearly illustrates this change.[443] Whereas formerly industrial wastes could be dumped at sea freely, with the entry into force of this decision those seeking to dispose of such wastes found that disposal could only be authorized if they had proved, according to an *ad hoc* procedure, that there was no practical alternative on land and that disposal at sea would pose no harm to the marine environment. In the same way, the 1992 OSPAR Convention requires parties wishing to continue to dump low- and intermediate-level radioactive substances to report at two-yearly intervals on 'the results of scientific studies which show that any potential dumping operations would not result in hazards to human health, harm to living resources or marine ecosystems, damage to amenities or interference with other legitimate uses of the sea'.[444] This evolution is even more marked as regards the management of marine resources, particularly the use of drift-nets. According to UNGA Resolution 44/225, States choosing not to observe the international moratorium on drift-nets are required to 'anticipate all unacceptable impacts of such practices'.[445] According to Freestone, this Resolution shifts the burden of proof (ie the use of 'statistically sound analysis') in favour of conservation, even though it does not constitute a complete reversal of the burden of proof.[446] This trend is even more remarkable in the 1995 Fishery Agreement. For instance, while UNCLOS Articles 61(2) and 119(1)(a) require the use of 'best scientific evidence available', Article 6(3)(a) of the 1995 Agreement, which sets out how States should implement the precautionary principle, refers to 'adequate scientific information', a less stringent requirement. Last but not least, in the 2000 CPB the party proposing to export an LMO can be required by the potential importing country to undertake and finance risk assessment studies to prove that its product is safe.[447]

---

[441] N.A. Ashford, n. 430 above, 163.

[442] UN General Assembly Resolution 37/7 on a World Charter for Nature, 37 UN GAOR (Supp. No. 51) 17, para. 11(b).

[443] OSCOM Decision 89/1 of 14 June 1989 on the Reduction and Cessation of Dumping Industrial Wastes at Sea.

[444] Article 3(3)(c) of Annex II of the 1192 OSPAR Convention.

[445] Resolution 44/225 of the General Assembly of the United Nations on Drift-Nets and their Impact on the Conservation of Marine Resources, ILM, 29 (15 March 1990), 1555.

[446] D. Freestone, 'International Fisheries since Rio...', n. 19 above, 152.

[447] CPB, Article 10(2) and (3).

EC law is also demonstrating a tendency to shift the burden of proving the harmlessness of certain activities to their operators. In view of *a priori* potential risk, decisions on drugs, pesticides, food products, additives, feedstuffs, and GMOs require a pre-marketing approval based on scientific studies and experimental data that must be supplied by the applicant company. The burden of proof is thus shifted onto the latter. For example, firms wishing to place new dangerous substances or active substances for pesticides on the EC market may do so only if they can first establish that these are safe for human health and the environment.[448] Similarly, the Community's new hazardous waste regime rests on a presumption of toxicity with regard to 200 categories of listed wastes. That presumption is only rebuttable in 'exceptional cases' and 'on the basis of documentary proof furnished in an appropriate manner' by the holders of such wastes.[449] This mechanism is clearly advantageous for the public authorities in that it places the burden of proof for the harmlessness of wastes on the waste holder.[450]

In US law, in general, the proponent of the regulation (i.e. the regulator) must prove that an activity or product poses a risk and that environmental measures are warranted, as the Supreme Court emphasized in *Industrial Union Department, AFL-CIO v. American Petroleum Institute*.[451] However, several statutes shift the burden of proof.[452] For example, under the Federal Food and Drug Act manufacturers of food and colour additives are required to prove that the 'proposed use of the food additive, under the conditions of use to be specified, will be safe' before the additive may enter the market.[453] In this context safety has been defined to mean 'reasonable certainty of no harm'.[454] This requirement obliges manufacturers to meet what is considered a relative standard of safety. The Federal Insecticide, Fungicide and Rodenticide Act (FIFRA) establishes a similar burden of proof on the producers of pesticides, which must be registered before being marketed in the US. A reversed burden of proof is also applied to animal drugs[455] and toxic substances.[456] In the Toxic Substances Control Act

---

[448] Article 7 of Directive 67/548/EEC on the approximation of laws, regulations, and administrative provisions relating to the classification, packaging, and labelling of dangerous and consequent amendments; Article 5 of Directive 91/414/EEC concerning the placing of plant protection products on the market.

[449] Article 3 of Commission Decision 2000/532/EC of 3 May 2000 establishing a list of hazardous wastes as required under Article 1, para. 4 of Directive 91/689/EEC on hazardous wastes.

[450] Concerning the controversies raised by the assumption of hazard in regard to certain types of wastes, see N. de Sadeleer and J. Sambon, 'The Concept of Hazardous Waste in European Community Law' (1997) 1 EELR 9.

[451] See Subsection 2.3.6.1. above. APA, 5 U.S.C. § 556(d); *Industrial Union Department, AFL-CIO*, 448 US at 652–655. Eg J.S. Applegate, n. 209 above, 427–9.

[452] D. Bodansky, 'The Precautionary Principle in US Environmental Law' in T. O'Riordan and J. Cameron (eds.), *Interpreting the Precautionary Principle*, n. 376 above, 209.

[453] 21 U.S.C. 348(c)(3)(A).

[454] 21 U.S.C. §301.

[455] 21 U.S.C. Sec 360b, (a) (4) (B), whereby pre-marketing approval of animal drugs is refused if there is a reasonable probability that its use may present a risk to the public health.

[456] The US apply a strict reverse-listing approach under the US Toxic Substances Control Act, whereby EPA is allowed to prohibit or limit the manufacture, processing, distribution, use, or disposal

there is no clear shifting of the burden of proof onto the applicants; rather, the task to prove harm or the absence of harm shifts back and forth between the chemical producers and the EPA.[457]

In the field of biodiversity conservation, the Marine Mammal Protection Act requires applicants for permits to take marine mammals to show that the taking will not have adverse effects.[458] The 'no jeopardy' procedure of the ESA,[459] which requires agencies to ensure that their actions are not likely to jeopardize the continued existence of any endangered or threatened species, shifts the burden of proof by requiring agencies to give 'the benefit of the doubt to the species' and stating that they should not proceed in the face of inadequate knowledge.[460] Nevertheless, the Department of the Interior cannot list an endangered species until it has completed an exhaustive study of the 'best scientific and commercial data available'.

5.1.2.3. The probatio diabolica

In its Sanitary and Phytosanitary case-law, the WTO Appellate Body has already ruled that there is no requirement for a risk assessment to establish a certain magnitude or threshold level of degree of risk.[461] Members are permitted during risk assessment to choose their own 'acceptable level of risk' when adopting health-related measures; an SPS Member's acceptable level of risk could even be set at 'zero risk'.[462] As long as the level of protection is based on scientific findings, a State may require its producers or importers to prove that the products they plan to place on the market meet safety requirements.

Must the operator or importer then be able to prove a complete absence of risk to the environment? Would that not be to require a *probatio diabolica*?[463] Taken to an extreme, this requirement, which is in many respects impossible, would merely serve to recreate the current problem in other terms. On the ground that the impact of certain technologies is uncertain, operators would be asked to provide absolute proof of their safety. Yet the very elements that give rise to that uncertainty make it impossible to provide absolute proof. In the uncertain and controversial contexts in which the precautionary principle applies, science is no more capable of providing definitive proof of the absence of risk than of its presence.

---

of a new chemical if there is concern about safety and existing information is 'insufficient to permit a reasoned evaluation of the health and environmental effects' of the substance. See 15 U.S.C. §2604(e)(1)(A).

[457] J. Tickner, *Precaution in Practice*, n. 324 above, 58.

[458] 16 USC §1371.

[459] ESA §7(a)(2), 16 USC §1536.

[460] *Roosevelt Campobello Int'l Park v. EPA*, 684 F.2d 1041, 1049 (DC Cir. 1982).

[461] Appellate Body, *EC Hormones*, para. 186.

[462] Appellate Body, *Australia Salmon*, para. 125.

[463] In the French GMOs case, Advocate General J. Misho judged that the precautionary principle 'does not require that, whenever the complete absence of any risk may not be scientifically demonstrated, an activity be forbidden or subjected to Draconian restrictions, since everyone knows that it is not for nothing that negative proof has always been characterised by jurists as *probatio diabolica*' (Opinion of 25 November 1999 in Case C-6/99, *Greenpeace France*, para. 72).

The reversal of the terms to be substantiated merely reformulates the positivist belief that science could reduce uncertainty by simply carrying out further research.[464] Yet demonstrating 'zero risk' necessarily leads to perplexity, since all human activity is likely to have an impact of one sort or another on the environment. Nothing will entirely eliminate the unforeseeability inherent in certain dangerous activities. It would accordingly be useful to modify the requirement to prove the absence of significant risk so that it relates to the seriousness of suspected damage. This would lead us back to the proportionality test. In fact, the reversal of the burden of proof is only one step in the complex process of decision-making and does not necessarily exclude the possibility that competing interests will subsequently be balanced against one another.

We must nonetheless ask whether this discussion is not overly theoretical. In the previous Subsection we saw that most legal regimes apply a 'reversal of the burden of proof' in one way or another. The onus is on the applicant who requests authorization for placing a product on the market rather than on the public authority; nonetheless, there is no obligation to prove harmlessness, the *probatio diabolica*.

In fact, the applicant seeking to obtain authorization for a product is not responsible for proving the harmlessness of that product, but rather for bearing the burden of the research needed to reduce uncertainty to the greatest degree possible, and finally develop the necessary proof. Logically, the scope of that burden will vary as a function of the seriousness of the suspected damage, the usefulness of the installation or the product, etc.

Finally, burden shifting need not be an all-or-nothing proposition. It might be possible to lower the burden of proof (from beyond all reasonable doubt to a balance of probabilities). It might also be possible to share the burden of proof between the regulatory authority and the industry. For example, in proceedings to suspend or cancel existing substances, the regulatory agency could have the initial burden of producing evidence suggesting that a substance is unsafe, and the holder of the substance would subsequently have the chance to establish the safety of his substance on the basis of documentary proof furnished in an appropriate manner.[465]

5.1.3. Environmental impact assessment

Like risk assessment, impact assessment procedures (EIA) are intended to reduce the uncertainties associated with the potential impacts of a project. The jewel in the crown of the preventive principle, EIA procedures are nonetheless weakened by serious shortcomings. To the extent that the decision-maker retains complete freedom of choice as to whether to carry out a project—the

---

[464] B. Wynne, 'Uncertainty and Environmental Learning: Reconceiving Science and Policy in the Preventive Paradigm' (1992) 2: 2 Global Environmental Change 111.

[465] For instance, only after the EPA has produced evidence suggesting that a registered pesticide is unsafe does the burden shift to the manufacturer to establish that his pesticide does not pose an unreasonable risk to the environment (*EDF v. EPA*, 598 F.2d at 1004, 1012–1018).

obligation to integrate the results of an impact assessment into a decision being of a purely formal nature—its preventive effects remain dependent upon the authority's willingness to take evaluation results into account. Consequently, we should consider whether it might not be possible to take assessment a step further with the help of the precautionary principle, through procedural modifications that accord a greater role to uncertainty. First of all, EIAs should not be restricted merely to the known impacts of a project but should also consider those impacts that are less clearly determined and define ways to take precautions against these, or at least attempt to reduce them. Therefore EIA procedures should not only reduce uncertainty but also explicitly acknowledge sources of uncertainty that remain, instead of burying these in arbitrary assumptions.

United States law is particularly instructive in this regard.[466] Having required the authors of impact assessments to carry out 'worst case analysis' for several years, the National Environmental Policy Act (NEPA) has since 1986 settled for an assessment of 'reasonably foreseeable' adverse effects based on theoretical approaches and research methods taking into account 'credible scientific evidence'. This amendment of the NEPA will undoubtedly exclude the assessment of purely hypothetical risks, but the requirement to assess reasonably foreseeable risks—in other words, those we are terming uncertain—has been maintained.[467] On this point the US model is far more anticipatory than Directive 85/337/EEC on the assessment of the effects of certain public and private projects on the environment.

An even more important step would be for the EIA procedure to force decision-makers to consider a number of reversible courses of action in order to take advantage of new knowledge. Even if it means forgoing a project, the author of an EIA should recommend reversible options in preference to those which are irreversible. The search for variants should become his principle task. While this requirement is at present ignored in most regulations, it would eliminate the partisan character of assessment and would oblige planners to reason on the basis of other than purely financial criteria.

As long as risks evolve as a function of scientific and technological knowledge the final word will never have been said. It is difficult to imagine that the assessment of a dangerous activity might one day be definitively concluded; it will always be advisable to repeat the EIA at regular intervals so that public authorities can adapt their decisions to new results. The 1991 Espoo Convention

---

[466] D. Shelton, 'The Impact of Scientific Uncertainty on Environmental Law and Policy in the United States' in D. Freestone and E. Hey (eds.), *The Precautionary Principle*, n. 181 above, 216.

[467] When information is incomplete or unavoidable on 'reasonably foreseeable' risks, the agency is instructed to assess uncertainties and to include potential catastrophic impacts if there is credible scientific evidence to support them, even if their probability of occurrence is low. Even the simple fact that a geological study differed from the conclusions of preliminary studies of the risks of a dam bursting was able to create a scientific uncertainty that obliged the author of the study to carry out further investigations. See *Warm Springs Dam Task Force v. Gribble*, 621 F.2d 1017, 1025 (9th Cir. 1980).

on Environmental Impact Assessment in a Transboundary Context reflects that understanding in its Article 7, which foresees a 'post-project analysis' that has no equivalent in EC law. Even if the ICJ did not address in *Gabcíkovo-Nagymaros* case the need for a prior EIA for a hydro-electric project on the Danube, the Court stressed that new environmental norms have to be taken into account not only when states contemplate new activities but also when continuing activities begun in the past. States are required to monitor ongoing environmental risks throughout the life of the project they have been allowing.

5.1.4. Strengthening the statement of reasons for standards

The formal obligation to provide a statement of reasons for certain decisions, an obligation found in most Continental administrative legal systems and in several EC environmental Directives[468] as well as in international conventions,[469] would also be influenced by the precautionary principle. Public authorities are required to provide reasons for their choice of standards based on the principles intended to guide their actions. Of course the authorities have the option of not applying a principle such as that of precaution (for example, if an anticipatory measure proves to be disproportionate compared to the importance of the potential risks or damages); but if the authorities decide to forgo the principle they must nonetheless be able to state the reasons for that decision. Faced with the possibility that a statement of reasons may be considered unacceptable, authorities cannot indefinitely avoid action to avert uncertain risks. The impossibility of recourse to a precautionary approach would therefore have to be set out in the statement of reasons for the decision. The effect of this obligation on the decision-making process should not be underestimated. The requirement to justify a deviation from the precautionary principle forces the authority to consider the impact of its decision carefully.

The precautionary principle could also modify the requirements for the statement of reasons for administrative decisions, which is meant to depend on considerations of fact and law. Administrative case-law in Belgium, France, Germany, and the Netherlands requires that considerations of fact be certain and duly established and does not allow an administrative authority to base decisions on uncertain elements. The effect of this overly restrictive perspective is to exclude as a basis for administrative decisions those presumptions which are not fully supported by scientific evidence. The precautionary principle will lead to a wider concept of 'considerations of fact' by integrating uncertainty therein. By reference to this principle, administrations can validly take decisions which might not be based entirely on considerations of certain and duly established fact, for example, a decision ordering that a polluting installation be closed or

---

[468] Directive 85/337/EEC on EIA, Article 9; Directive 90/313/EEC on the freedom of access to information on the environment, Article 3(4).

[469] Article 6(9) of the 1998 Århus Convention on Access to Information, Public Participation in Decision-Making Process, and Access to Justice in Environmental Matters.

that a product be withdrawn from the market for reasons of health, even when the evidence of harm is not yet irrefutable.[470]

5.1.5. Monitoring of activities giving rise to risk

It is not sufficient that the precautionary principle guide a decision, because a risk may only become apparent subsequently and thus not have been identified, or may have appeared insignificant, when the evaluation was taking place. A number of international instruments already require Parties to reconsider their obligations continually in the light of improved scientific knowledge, and if necessary to undertake more stringent requirements.[471] Precaution therefore does not call for stasis: on the contrary, management of risk must be flexible and progressive, and measures must continuously be adapted and revised as a risk is more thoroughly understood.[472] In other words, acting prudently means to design resilient measures that allow flexible responses to unexpected developments. Precaution should thus lead public authorities to establish mechanisms to monitor products and activities, in order to make necessary adjustments to decisions by suspending an activity or withdrawing a product. In that perspective, monitoring products which present a potential risk, eg GM foods or beef that may be contaminated by BSE, is essential, since it creates an information feedback mechanism that will allow the public authorities to withdraw a product from the market quickly if a problem arises.[473]

EC secondary law contains different provisions relating to the monitoring of activities giving rise to risk. According to the ECJ, Article 11(6) of Directive 90/220/EEC on the deliberate release into the environment of genetically modified organisms reflects the precautionary principle, in that the notifier is obliged to inform the competent national authority immediately of new information concerning the risk posed by a product to human health or the environment, and the authorities must subsequently inform the Commission and other Member

---

[470] For example the decision *Pro-Nat* of 1999 of the French Conseil d'Etat set out in Subsection 2.3.2. above.

[471] This obligation is reflected, for instance, in 1982 UNCLOS, Article 200; 1979 LRATP Convention, Article 2; 1991 ECE Convention on EIA in a Transboundary Context, Article 9; 1992 UNFCCC, Article 7; 1992 CBD, Article 23.

[472] Thus the precautionary principle does not imply a definitive decision that would permanently penalize the economic operator who generates a risk. On the contrary, it entails waiting in order to avoid an irreversible situation later on, simply because we no longer have the right to make errors. Even though destruction leads to irreparability, the nature of a moratorium is never definitive. A precautionary measure should therefore be understood in the legal sense as a temporary arrangement affecting a situation that could prove injurious. The case-law referred to above underlines the dynamic, rather than static, character of the precautionary principle. This is undoubtedly the meaning of the decision by the Belgian Court of Arbitration concerning exploitation of the Meuse quarries, which tipped the scales in favour of reversibility of the legal norm and against a risk of irreversible damage to the aquatic environment due to continuing gravel quarrying. See Subsection 2.3.3. above.

[473] In the case of the French embargo on British beef, Advocate General J. Misho stated that 'traceability is one of the preferred techniques of preventive action' (Opinion of 20 September 2001 in Case C-1/00, para. 86).

States of that information.[474] This presupposes that a product will be traced throughout the chain of production and commercialization ('from the farm to the fork'). For listed installations, the monitoring of activities that pose a risk is widespread. Thus Article 13 of the Integrated Pollution Prevention and Control Directive requires that competent authorities 'periodically reconsider and, where necessary, update permit conditions' when it appears that substantial changes in best available techniques make it possible significantly to reduce emissions.

Pre-market testing on chemicals is considered insufficiently reliable to remove all uncertainties surrounding their effects on the environment. Reliable data becomes available only after the substances have been put on the market and released into the environment. To fill this gap and in order to enable competent national authorities to request further testing on chemicals, Article 7(2) of the 67/548/EEC Directive on the classification, packaging, and labelling of dangerous substances requires the notifier to alert the authorities when the quantity of the substance on the market reaches a specific threshold.

5.2. The effect of the precautionary principle on civil liability

5.2.1. Introductory note

We should first ask whether the premises of the precautionary principle are inherent in liability or if, by contrast, liability hinders the principle's progress. To the extent that civil liability is above all intended to guarantee the reparation of existing damage, one is tempted to respond that it bears no relation to measures meant to prevent the occurrence of future damage. Consequently the precautionary principle, which is meant to protect against uncertain risk, is not relevant to civil liability. In fact, however, the incompatibility between a legal institution oriented towards the past and a principle oriented towards the future is only apparent. The days of absolute certainty are over; in the future greater importance will necessarily be attached to doubt and consequently to the precautionary principle within the mechanisms of liability.

Such an evolution is particularly desirable given the obstacle course which confronts the victim of ecological damage, who must not only prove that damage has occurred but also show a causal link to the tortfeasor. The sometimes considerable time and space between the event and the damage, as well as the difficulty of determining the extent of reparation, constitute formidable barriers. Even if a plaintiff manages to produce such proof, the defendant can always seek refuge in unforeseeability. Thus the uncertainties inherent in the three conditions of liability—fault, damage, and the causal link between the two—make compensation uncertain.

If liability is to play an effective role in the reparation and prevention of ecological damage, it will probably be necessary to remove the multiple constraints resulting from the certainty requirement. If we are to take account of

---

[474] Case C-6/99, *Greenpeace France*, para. 44.

ecological damage we will in effect have to leave behind the overly rigid realm of civil liability. We will have to require a lesser degree of certainty: in other words to replace certainties with probabilities.

The precautionary principle should shed new light on the duty of care which dominates the field, and at the same time lessen the severity of having to prove causation.[475]

5.2.2. Fault

5.2.2.1. Shedding a new light on the duty of care

We must first verify whether the precautionary principle can be instrumental in interpreting fault, which forms an integral part of the civil liability regime in both common law and continental legal systems. Until now the notion of fault has been defined with regard to duty of care. In effect, most liability regimes consider that normal and reasonable care is required and that measures taken under normal circumstances are sufficient to avoid incurring responsibility in the case of damage to the environment. In other words, the fact of having acted as a *bonus paterfamilias* or respecting the standards of professional conduct or professional rules currently in force is sufficient to exonerate a person from liability. The duty of care is thus linked to well established practices (state of the art) where doubt and uncertainty have no place.[476] A person cannot be blamed for something he could not know and can only be held responsible to the extent that knowledge is possible.

Precaution, however, echoes doubt: uncertainty replaces knowledge, and anticipation takes the place of foreseeability. The duty of care must therefore be rethought in the light of this new principle. In this context, it is not merely the person who has failed to take all preventive measures against a well understood or foreseeable risk who should be considered at fault, but also the person who, in a situation of uncertainty or doubt, has failed to adopt a precautionary approach in order to avert a still uncertain risk. There would thus be fault where an operator failed to take the specific precautions implied by the management of his activity. A person who failed to explore all the potential risks posed by his activity would be liable. The fact of having acted according to the current level of scientific knowledge and established techniques would no longer be sufficient to exonerate an operator from liability. In practical terms, the precautionary principle translates into a duty to investigate.[477]

---

[475] This analysis was originally written on the basis of civil liability regimes in the French and Belgian Civil Codes. For an overview of those regimes see W. Van Gerven, *Tort Law* (Oxford: Hart, 1999).

[476] Fr. Ewald, 'The Return of the Crafty Genius: An Outline of a Philosophy of Precaution' (1999/2000) Conn Ins LJ 47.

[477] In the Netherlands, the *Hoge Raad* ruled in an asbestos case that when there are no specific statutory rules on the dangers of hazardous substances the employer is under a 'duty to investigate which dangers may be created for his employees by the substances he produces or processes'. The Court also insisted that 'depending on the circumstances, it may be relevant to the duty to investigate whether information concerning the danger was available outside the Netherlands, in particular when

The determination of fault would not be limited to the information in the defendant's possession at the time an act occurred but would also consider information that should have been known, including working hypotheses not yet fully proved at the time of the event. As a result, the principle would preclude the defence 'I did not know'.

In addition to its *ex ante* dimension, the precautionary principle thus sets in place *ex post* the conditions to ensure that those who cause ecological damage will more easily incur liability for their acts. By raising the requirement for care a notch, the principle could prompt more prudent anticipation of injurious consequences that might result from activities and compel economic actors to discover facts they would generally not seek to know. By imposing a requirement that risks be anticipated, uncertainty redefines the extent of liability.

Given the highly flexible character of the concept of fault, Article 1382 of the French and Belgian Civil Codes, for example, should pose no obstacle to this evolution.[478] English and US Courts already impose a duty of 'high care', 'highest care', or 'utmost care' on firms that deal in dangerous substances, proportional to the magnitude of the risk.[479]

The Dutch case-law on danger creation is also particularly relevant to the precautionary measures required in environmental litigation. Under Dutch tort law, anyone who creates a danger is under a duty to prevent damage arising as a result of that danger;[480] a person who fails to take measures to that effect or does so inadequately will be liable for the ensuing damage.[481] However, this is not a true strict liability regime, in that a person who is not aware, and is not legally obliged to be aware, of a possible danger cannot be deemed to have acted negligently.[482] The following list of possibly obligatory measures has been derived from this case-law: duty to warn (and/or consult), duty to monitor and to carry out maintenance, duty to investigate or undertake research, and duty to take residuary safety measures.[483]

---

the substance had been occupationally utilised or produced abroad prior to [use] in the Netherlands' (HR 6 April 1990). Eg G. Betlem, *Civil Liability for Transfrontier Pollution* (London, Dordrecht: Graham & Trotman/ Martinus Nijhoff, 1993) 480.

[478] French and Belgian doctrinal and judiciary approaches to the concept of fault emphasize protection against all kinds of harmful behaviour, regardless of who has suffered from it. Eg W. Van Gerven, *Tort Law*, n. 475 above, 36.

[479] K. Zweigert and H. Kötz observe that: 'The degree of "care" demanded of the defendant is often so extreme as to be barely distinguishable from liability without fault. In general, whenever it seems necessary in order to achieve a socially acceptable distribution of the accident risks peculiar to modern life, the courts tend to insist on precautions which it is virtually impossible to satisfy, and they can do this because, judging a case *ex post facto*, they can always discover some precaution or other which, had the defendant adopted it in time, would have prevented the occurrence of the harm': K. Zweigert and H. Kötz, *Introduction to Comparative Law* (2nd edn., Oxford: Clarendon, 1992) 690.

[480] An example is the duty of a wreck's owner to remove the wreck when it creates a danger for other users of a waterway: HR 14 October 1994, NJ 1995, 720.

[481] G. Betlem, n. 477 above, 411.

[482] HR, 23 June 1989.

[483] G. Betlem, n. 477 above, 417.

5.2.2.2. Foreseeability of damage as an obstacle to further advances

If used to justify exoneration from liability, unforeseeability could hinder recourse to liability as a means of compensating environmental damage arising
from activities which had not been proved harmless at the time that damage
occurred. The requirement of foreseeability of damage is in effect a necessary
condition of fault, even if the question remains controversial in French, Belgian,
and Dutch law.[484] Even under a no-fault liability regime, unforeseeability is
relevant.

For instance, the requirement for foreseeability in English law may serve to
limit the liability of the person causing pollution. This was the case for a tannery
whose liability for aquifer pollution was not upheld by the House of Lords on the
ground that its operators could not reasonably have foreseen that their solvents
would contaminate groundwater at the time the activities in question took
place.[485]

However, the requirement of foreseeability should be put into perspective by
distinguishing between foreseeability *in abstracto* and foreseeability *in concreto*.[486] The tortfeasor may be considered liable from the time he was unable
in law to exclude the possibility of risk or when he could foresee the emergence
of damage *in abstracto*. It is thus not a requirement that damage *in concreto*
be foreseeable. The person responsible for damage would consequently not be
permitted to take refuge behind the impossibility of foreseeing the precise results
of his action. It suffices that damage within a certain category can be foreseen. In
other words, only the complete unforeseeability of an occurrence of damage
could justify exoneration from liability. This restrictive interpretation leaves the
door wide open to precaution in the field of fault. The condition of foreseeability
of damage is thus less absolute than it at first appears and is in fact able to
integrate uncertainty.

5.2.2.3. Possible misuse of the precautionary principle

A number of criticisms could be raised in response to the preceding discussion on
the precautionary principle. Reformulating the notion of duty of care could give
rise to certain reservations from the perspective of equity. Care would no longer
be judged on the basis of what should have been known, for example, but rather
of what ought to have been suspected. Operators might consequently incur
liability in cases where they had neglected to explore possible risks before
undertaking action. But would it not be unjust to hold them liable in situations

---

[484] For France, see Ph. Letourneau, *Droit de la responsabilité* (Paris: Dalloz, 1996) 263 no. 911.
For Belgium, see L. Cornelis, *Les principes du droit belge de la responsabilité extra-contractuelle*
(Brussels: Bruylant, 1991) 46. For the Netherlands, G. Betlem, n. 477 above, 454.

[485] *Cambridge Water Co. v. Eastern Counties Leather Plc* (1994) 2 AC 264; (1994) I All ER, 53
(HL).

[486] For Dutch Law, see G. Betlem, n. 477 above, 415; for Belgian civil law, see L. Cornelis, n. 484
above, 46 nos. 25–6; R.O. Dalcq and G. Schamps, 'La responsabilité délictuelle et quasi délictuelle'
(1995) 3: 6 RCJB 537.

where they could neither foresee nor avoid damage? Is it acceptable that a court would penalize behaviour eventually proved to have been negligent on the basis of methods, arguments, and concepts not yet unanimously accepted within the scientific community at the time when the acts in question took place and which could only be formulated after the event? Is it not unfair to judge an act according to a state of knowledge different from that under which it was carried out?

This would amount to judging the operator according to rules that evolved to meet risks that he did not know about at the time of the acts in question and that he could not have known in advance. An individual needs to know what rule applies to him; he cannot respect a rule except under those terms. Moreover, he will only consider himself liable if he has failed to comply with the law.

In response to these criticisms, we would distinguish between the person who could in the strict sense not have known the consequences of his activities and the person who could have been aware of them had he taken the trouble to explore more carefully the risks his activities posed to the environment. It is the liability of the latter which must be judged according to precaution, not that of the person who could not possibly have detected a risk. The opposite would amount to excluding any notion of fault, which would be equivalent to establishing an absolute liability regime, as was done in Germany for genetically modified organisms.[487] In this respect, Article 7(e) of Directive 85/374/EEC concerning liability for defective products permits a 'development risk' defence[488] and allows producers to prove that the objective state of scientific and technical knowledge, including the most advanced level of such knowledge, was not such as to enable the defect to be discovered. In order for the relevant knowledge to be successfully pleaded as arguing against the producer, that knowledge must have been accessible at the time when the product in question was put into circulation.[489]

It will also be necessary to determine at what moment the operator must become aware of a risk in order to incur liability. Should he only have known of the risk at the time of the act that caused the damage? Must it be proved that he knew? Concern for precaution should in any case lead to a restrictive interpretation of exoneration for liability on the basis of development risks.

5.2.2.4. The Trojan horse of fault

The precautionary principle would allow a return in full force to the concept of fault, which has increasingly been disregarded in recent legal developments.[490]

---

[487] Article 32 of the Law of 1 July 1990 on Biotechnology (*Gentech*) which, on the basis of the precautionary principle, excludes a 'development risk' defence.

[488] Under this provision, 'the producer shall not be liable if he proves ... that the state of scientific and technical knowledge at the time when he puts the product into circulation was not such as to enable the existence of the defect to be discovered'.

[489] Case C-300/95, *Commission v. United Kingdom* [1997] ECR I-2649.

[490] See the discussion in Subsection 4.2.1.1. above.

Fault would return to centre stage, decked out in new finery. According to Martin,[491] if the obligation to assume a risk—the sign of a system that is sure of itself—gives way to an ethic of duty of care, where each person is expected to take multiple precautions in the face of the unknown, the concept of fault will be revived. Rediscovered, fault could unexpectedly legitimate a questioning of the axioms of liability for risk, despite its extensive presence in environmental law. We should therefore ask ourselves whether the precautionary principle threatens to put an end to the further development of strict liability regimes in this legal discipline. The advantages and disadvantages of these two competing regimes must be carefully weighed.

It is true that classic fault liability is capable of providing compensation to victims of industrial hazards, eg personal injury as a result of exposure to asbestos.[492] However, considered from the perspective of risk theory, the person who profits from a technology must engage its risks regardless of any fault on his own part. The advantage of a strict liability regime for the plaintiff is precisely that he need not produce proof of negligence, since this is assumed. It could even be an advantage for the defendant to know what risks he will be held responsible for.

From the perspective of the precautionary principle, civil liability can only be understood with reference to negligence. Nevertheless, an evolution may be observed in countries like Belgium and France.[493] The disadvantage for the plaintiff of being required to prove negligence by the author of the damage would be partially compensated by the extension of the concept of fault, which henceforth—in pursuance of the precautionary principle—must cover behaviour in situations that could not easily be foreseen. The relaxation of the burden of proof, dictated by the same principle, would also benefit the plaintiff.

Must we therefore conclude that fault and non-fault liability regimes are of equal merit? Such a conclusion disregards the fact that even when it is imbued with the precautionary principle, a fault-based liability regime will always be less favourable to the victim than a strict liability regime. Demonstrating negligence which has caused damage constitutes an obstacle that even the boldest interpretation of the precautionary principle cannot easily brush aside. Restructuring the notion of fault by integrating precaution should therefore not be allowed to bring into question the advances already made in strict liability regimes relating to environmental damage.

Should the precautionary principle really be seen as a Trojan horse that will open the way to blocking the development of strict liability? It might make sense to use precaution to influence classical fault-based regimes where they still dominate. But this is not the case in most Continental liability regimes, where activities that threaten the environment are not subject to strict liability.

---

[491] G. Martin, 'Précaution et évolution du droit' (1995) D. chr. 304.

[492] See, for example, Court of Appeals, 2 April 1996, *The Times*, 17 April 1996.

[493] N. de Sadeleer, *Les principes du pollueur-payeur, de prévention et de précaution* (Brussels: Bruylant/Agence Universitaire pour la Francophonie, 1999) 217.

As we have seen, whether or not strict liability regimes are developed depends on political will rather than case-law development. It is up to the legislator to opt either for a regime of strict liability, where precaution plays no role in informing norms of conduct, or for a fault-based regime where the behaviour of the tortfeasor would be judged in light of the precautionary principle. In the latter case, the precautionary principle should enlarge the field of foreseeability. It should encourage courts to interpret foreseeability by adopting a stricter approach to what the defendant should and could have known at the time when the act in question occurred. However, there is no reason why a plaintiff could not be given a choice between two complementary regimes.

5.2.3. Damage

5.2.3.1. The exclusion of uncertain harm

It is crucial to delimit ecological damage, since this will determine the type of liability proceedings that may be used, and consequently the extent of the reparations that the polluter may be obliged to assume. Oriented towards the past, civil liability is in principle limited to guaranteeing the reparation of damage that has already occurred. Nevertheless, the extension of existing damage which carries a continuing risk may render its agent liable when injury is deemed certain. Continuing risk therefore does not in and of itself represent an obstacle to admitting the principle of reparation. Otherwise courts would be obliged to hand down an infinite series of successive judgments every time further evidence of progressive damage becomes apparent.

It is true, however, that a higher coefficient of uncertainty will make the right to reparation problematic.[494] To envisage reparation for existing damage which is likely to develop further, one must be able to trace its outlines with at least a minimum of precision. Even if it only becomes apparent in the future, damage must be seen, according to the case-law of the French *Cour de cassation*, to be 'the certain and direct extension of an existing situation, admitting of immediate assessment'.[495] Application of the principle is not a problem as long as the future—but certain—damage is the inevitable extension of existing damage. However, demonstrating this could be difficult when a plaintiff is unable to anticipate all the possible consequences of damage which has just begun to appear. Future damages that are purely 'hypothetical' are thus overlooked by liability law,[496] which is quite stubborn on this point. The virtual may never give rise to compensation when a judgment is handed down. The victim must therefore wait until new damage actually occurs before bringing a new action.

To the extent that it rests more on a difference of degree than on one of nature, the distinction between damage that may be characterized as the 'direct

---

[494] G. Viney, *Traité de droit civil* (Paris: L.G.D.J., 1982) 339.

[495] Cass. fr., 1 June 1932. The French courts and tribunals have never departed from this principle.

[496] H.-L. Mazeaud and A. Tunc, *Traité théorique et pratique de la responsabilité civile délictuelle et contractuelle* (6th edn., Paris: Montchrestien, 1965) no. 216; P. Le Tourneau, *La responsabilité civile* (3rd edn., Paris: Dalloz) 240; Y. Chartier, *La réparation du préjudice* (Paris: Dalloz, 1989) 27.

extension of the current situation' and that which is virtual or 'potential' is not easy to draw.[497] As a result, the case-law of French courts and tribunals is divided between an overly generous and a too severe interpretation of the hazardous nature of damage.

In dealing with nuisance, some jurisdictions have recognized damage caused to crops by factory emissions as well as depreciation of a good resulting from the establishment of a polluting activity in its vicinity as certain, although future.[498] On the other hand, the French *Cour de Cassation* refused to compensate an owner for property depreciation due to risk of electrocution from the installation of an electric lead, since this was a purely contingent injury.[499] The French *Conseil d'Etat*, for its part, sometimes recognizes the certainty of damage on the basis of mere probability.[500]

Whatever its nature, future damage must proceed from the 'certain and direct prolongation of an existing situation' if it is to be compensated. Yet this limits the effectiveness of civil liability law as a remedy against environmental degradation.[501] To require that damage be certain is to demand that there be no lingering doubt whatsoever as to its existence or how it will develop in future, although in practice both its character and its scope will constantly be the subject of scientific uncertainty. Nothing is sure in this sense: pollution may be reabsorbed owing to the regenerative capacity of a natural ecosystem; but it may instead grow worse as the result of cumulative or synergistic effects. Natural scientists trained in methods of rigorous proof will in any case be reluctant to assess the precise scope of a particular case of damage, pleading the uncertain and progressive character of the phenomena concerned.

5.2.3.2. Contradictory logics: precaution and the reparation of damage

Does the precautionary principle offer a new opportunity to victims seeking to establish the liability of polluters for damage that is still uncertain in nature? The response to this question must be negative, for this venerable legal institution is unable to manage uncertainty and would have to alter its character completely to do so. Moreover, a liability regime that established damage on the basis of doubt would hardly be equitable for all the parties involved. We must therefore express serious reservations about how the precautionary principle would affect the reparation of uncertain future damage. Below we consider two examples of how the precautionary principle cannot influence damage assessment.

Some international texts appear to open up new perspectives. The 1993 Lugano Convention on Civil Liability for Damage Resulting from Activities Dangerous to the Environment, for example, includes 'the cost of measures of

---

[497] G. Viney, *Traité de droit civil*, n. 494 above, 339.
[498] See the case-law cited by Y. Chartier, n. 496 above, 28.
[499] Cass. fr., 19 March 1947 (1947) D. 2.313.
[500] C.E. fr., 28 July 1951 (1952) D. 22.
[501] H. Bocken, *Het aansprakelijkheidsrecht als sanctie tegen de verstoring van het leefmilieu* (Brussels: Bruylant, 1979) 81 and 112.

reinstatement that have been taken or that will be taken' among those losses liable to be compensated. Plaintiffs could consequently be awarded compensation although costs are not yet accurately known. In practice, however, this provision is less revolutionary than it might appear, since nothing prevents a judge from awarding the plaintiff an advance on damages.

Secondly, the precautionary principle is irrelevant in determining the amount of damage, even though a system of fixed compensation for certain types of injury (such as the loss of a leg) reduces uncertainty relating to the assessment of damage and, as a result, allows the plaintiff to avoid being caught up in a net of interminable and costly expert opinion.

While the precautionary principle can play a significant role with respect to the extent of fault and causality, it is not obvious how it could restructure the question of damage. This is because precaution is dependent on a different logic from that underpinning civil liability, which requires that damage has already been caused in order for it to be made good.

5.2.4. *Causation*

5.2.4.1. Proof of causation under scientific uncertainty

In addition to both fault and damage, causation must—like the other basic elements of liability—be certain. The point of departure is that the onus is on the plaintiff to establish this requirement. Required under both strict liability and fault-based regimes, proof of a causal connection between the tortious act and the ensuing damage is the main stumbling block for victims of pollution, in particular in air and water pollution cases. In its 1867 report on the pollution of rivers,[502] the Royal Commission on the Pollution of Rivers had already drawn attention to the fact that: 'The plaintiff may prove that he has suffered injury from the pollution of the river and that the defendant has polluted the river above him; but this is not enough. The plaintiff has also to prove that what he has suffered has been caused wholly or in part by the special act of the defendant, which is always difficult—often impossible.'

Moreover, the introduction of a polluting substance into the natural environment does not directly affect private property. In the first instance it affects either air or water, *res communes*, and the question of liability will only arise to the extent that these collective goods are connected to economic rights: for example, saltwater fish caught by fishermen. It is extremely difficult to establish causation in cases involving compensation for indirect damages, and proving causation has become even more difficult as environmental deterioration increasingly comes to be caused by new and less well understood types of pollution.

Damage caused by diffuse pollution, for example, from automotive emissions and individual heating systems, results from the accumulation of emissions which may be inoffensive taken individually. Added together, however, they rapidly exceed the absorptive and regenerative capacity of receiving media and

---

[502] Cited by Howarth, *Water Pollution Law* (1988) 119.

cause damage of an often unexpected character. In addition, when pollutants mix with various substances synergies may create yet other pollutants, the precise sources of which are particularly difficult to identify. In such situations a plaintiff is confronted with intermixed, multiple, and confused causations which further erode the concept of individual liability.

These new pollutions are no longer indicative of the proximity, acuteness, or instantaneousness which generally characterize localized pollution of the chronic or accidental variety. Considerable distance and extremely long time lags often separate their detrimental effects from their cause. It then becomes difficult for experts to express opinions on causation with even a minimum of certainty. Pollution shifts in space; causation weakens over time. Despite this, the law remains firm: the requirement of causation between the defendant's tortious act and the ensuing damage is carved in stone.

By introducing a new manner of conceptualizing time within the legal system and allowing wider scope for presumptive evidence, will the precautionary principle eventually increase the flexibility of the traditional elements of causation? To answer this question, we consider the progress of the principle in case-law as well as in legislation.

5.2.4.2. Reforms in comparative law

The context of uncertainty justifies replacing full, scientifically proven cause and effect with a more probabilistic approach. Scientific uncertainty cannot be an obstacle for victims seeking to demonstrate the link between an event and damage when there are indications that the substance or activity in question is capable of having caused that harm.

Even where no explicit claims are being made for its use, the precautionary principle is advancing in both national legal systems and international law. Thus §6 of the 1990 German Environmental Liability Act facilitates proof of causation through a presumption of liability which is integrated into the industrial process that gives rise to damage.[503] The plaintiff need only show, through expert opinion or statistics, that the defendant's facility is likely to have caused the damage. The presumption can be rebutted by the operator by showing that his facility was complying with the conditions of its licence or that other circumstances may have caused the damage.

Article 10 of the 1993 Lugano Convention on Civil Liability for Damage Resulting from Activities Dangerous to the Environment attempts to echo this

---

[503] This provision is worded as follows: 'When, in the case in question, an installation is likely to have caused the damage that has occurred, it is presumed that the damage was caused by this installation. The capacity to cause damage is calculated in relation to the development of the operations of use, the installations used, the nature and concentration of substances employed and their residues, meteorological conditions, the time and place the damage occurred, and the form of the damage, as well as all circumstances which in the instant case may have had some importance in causing the damage.' Even before the adoption of this statute, German case-law had made several breakthroughs in this direction. See the cases cited by P. von Wilmowski and G. Roller, *Civil Liability for Waste* (Frankfurt: Peter Lang, 1992) 56.

advance in a more modest fashion by inviting the judge who evaluates a proof of causation to adopt probabilistic reasoning in considering the risks inherent in the activity in question. This must 'take due account of the increased danger of causing such damage inherent in the dangerous activity'. While this technique eases the burden of proof, it does not eliminate it.

Finally, in the United States, the Comprehensive Environmental Response, Compensation, and Liability Act practically relieves the Federal Administration of the need to demonstrate causation. Liability is engaged from the moment the EPA succeeds in proving that polluted land was being used for the disposal of wastes, that these were placed in the area where the pollution appeared, and that the polluting substances correspond to those found in the wastes.

The precautionary principle should at least encourage the adoption of mechanisms which make the requirement to demonstrate causation more flexible and accord greater importance to doubt in the field of civil liability, thereby preventing litigation from turning into a battle of experts. This of course does not alter the fact that the plaintiff must always be able to demonstrate some link, no matter how tenuous, between the damage suffered and the source of pollution. Such demonstration may prove difficult when the emission source is geographically or temporally distant from where the damage occurred.

6. CONCLUDING OBSERVATIONS

In matters of the environment everything has become a matter of time: we must not lose any more time, we cannot make up for lost time, we cannot predict the future . . . But a change in thinking about time should translate into a change of tone. The precautionary principle symbolically marks just such a passage. It transforms duty of care into an essential element of any policy: in other words, 'a policy for action in the face of uncertainty'.

Conceived to prevent serious or irreversible harm, the principle urges the authorities to act, or to abstain from action, in cases of uncertainty. In all cases it should encourage the delay, and in some cases even the abandonment, of activities suspected of having serious consequences for environmental protection; this will be the case even in the absence of full scientific proof for such suspicions. Inversely, it should accelerate the adoption of decisions intended to ensure better environmental protection, even if their validity is not unanimously accepted by expert opinion.

Precaution is determined by the characteristics of sectoral policies: fishing, climate, marine pollution, technological risks, food security. The standard of precaution is therefore likely to vary as a function not only of the technical requirements related to the nature of a risk, but also of the political needs of the field in question. As a result, no single regulatory scheme is capable of implementing the principle. One can envisage as many types of precaution as there are situations in which the principle might be applied; thus there is no point in seeking to set a precautionary standard *in abstracto*. For the same reason a multitude of differing measures may follow from this one principle: precaution is to act, and abstention is merely one way of acting. According to the magnitude of harm which is suspected, different types of measures ranging from weak to strong precautions can thus be taken (bans, phase-out, BAT, notification procedures, etc.).

In any case, the principle must be seen as part of a dynamic process. Decisions taken under the aegis of precaution should be understood as open to review: it must be possible to forbid something that has already been authorized, just as it must be possible to relax protective controls in cases where fears are dissipated by more accurate information. Irreversible decisions are the antithesis of the precautionary principle. Restructuring the very nature of standards, the principle's implementation goes far beyond simply setting procedures for decision-making, even though that step does allow consideration of differing points of view and interests.

In some ways prevention and precaution appear intimately linked: two sides of the same coin. However, these two principles should not be confused: while certain risk calls for a preventive approach, uncertainty requires precaution. Therefore, while precaution may well be the natural extension of prevention, it is far more than a simple variant. A difference in both degree and nature separates the principles: a difference of degree in that precaution urges prevention forward in the hope of closing the gap that always exists between decision-making and the mastery of risk. Institutionalizing duty of care at a higher level than has yet been achieved, the principle is a landmark in the battle against environmental threats. A difference of nature, in that the precautionary principle transforms doubt into possible certainty and hence strengthens action by the public authorities in the face of uncertainty. In this way it restructures, sometimes substantially, the policy measures on which environment policy depends. This is particularly the case for risk assessment procedures, which are expected to integrate uncertainty more effectively than other approaches.

The implementation of the precautionary principle also presents other difficulties, which are no less serious for being identical in the various legal orders considered above. Since it does not determine the degree of care needed to protect against risk, the principle's application will in effect depend on the potential seriousness of damages and their probability. Will it impel the authorities to set constraints on behalf of hypothetical stakes and to require compensation for uncertain damage, thereby undermining confidence in the legal system?

Perception of the data underlying uncertain risks is largely subjective. A serious danger in certain circumstances is not necessarily serious in another case. Moreover, the definitive elimination of risk—'zero risk'—is an ideal, as risk is inherent in our activities. Interpreted in too radical a manner, the precautionary principle could sacrifice innovation to security. Guidelines must therefore be established; in particular, scientific hypotheses must be minimally verifiable. Yet one should be wary of pushing these requirements too far, for they would then deprive the principle of its substance.

We observed in Section 4 above that by marking the passage from a Cartesian science that obeys the laws of reason to a science of uncertainty, the precautionary principle contributes to the emergence of a plurality of truth which could fundamentally redefine the relation between science and law. In the long run, a classical conception of science, based on objective data and facts derived from experiment and verified—in short, clothed in the appearance of truth—will give way to a type of scientific expertise whose essential function would consist in the qualitative and comprehensive presentation of scientific data bearing the stamp of uncertainty.

The road that remains to be travelled before we see the precautionary principle begin to take root in positive law at first glance appears strewn with obstacles, given the heavy reliance of legal systems on certainty rather than uncertainty. We have had occasion to observe, however, throughout the developments related in Section 5 above, that most of the reforms advocated in the name of precaution may already be found, in bits and pieces, in normative texts. This movement will undoubtedly develop further as legal systems are forced to adapt in order to anticipate ecological risks. To the extent that the precautionary principle aims to govern decision-making in a situation of uncertainty, it will very quickly be exported beyond its original territory into areas such as public health and product safety.

Now that the era of certainty has passed precaution must take over from prevention. Yet, despite the high hopes attached to this new principle, we must not expect it to replace the principle of prevention entirely. The latter is more pertinent than ever given that most deleterious effects on the environment are not attributable to a lack of foresight.[504] If our knowledge of the state of the environment has indisputably grown over the past two decades and has made it possible to determine the cause of many environmental assaults, policy has unfortunately not always been able to deduce from this exactly what measures should be taken. It is disturbing to see public authorities follow policies which they know full well will cause harm to the environment. The advent of precaution should therefore not cause us to forget that the battle for prevention is far from won.

---

[504] The delay by public authorities in taking preventive measures when confronting the risk of damage has been analysed through various case studies (fisheries, asbestos, halocarbons, benzene, BSE, etc.) in European Environmental Agency, n. 243 above.

Part I Conclusions

Part I, given over to consideration of the origin, legal status, and applications of the polluter-pays, prevention, and precautionary principles, has led us to elaborate a first thesis. As a result of the strong growth of a generation of risks permeated by uncertainty, environmental law is today profoundly marked by a reflex towards security. Emphasis is being given to prevention and even anticipation of risks in a quest for a more sustainable form of development. Although linked to distinct models, the principles of precaution and prevention are thus the most striking symbols of this reaction, which seeks to frustrate the occurrence of ecological risk and thereby avoid irreparable damage.

Consequently we should consider these three principles in terms of interaction rather than opposition, particularly since they are operationally interdependent. The precautionary principle calls for the presence of prevention, which in turn implies support for the polluter-pays principle. A preventive policy that would no longer be financed by the polluter-pays principle would be destined to fail. With a few adjustments, preventive techniques such as thresholds and impact assessment could equally well serve anticipatory objectives. Similarly, the polluter-pays principle is capable of assuming both a preventive dimension (for example, through a sizeable tax) and an anticipatory dimension (for instance, a dissuasive tax that would apply to an activity even while its deleterious effects remained a matter of controversy). Moreover, it is not uncommon to see these different principles contained within a single regulation. Thus, even if they sometimes result in contradictory solutions, the three principles are in reality interdependent.

The polluter-pays, prevention, and precautionary principles are certainly well represented in positive law; they are helping to shape new legal instruments and adapt mechanisms, not necessarily specific to environmental law, intended to achieve protective ends. Brought into the realm of civil liability, the three principles have, each in its own way, succeeded in modifying this classical legal institution. Moreover, the diversity of their applications is striking: they have given rise to widely differing norms, in fields ranging from administrative law to civil law. The polluter-pays principle translates into dispositions relating to State aid, environmental fiscal instruments, the management of compensation funds, and civil liability. The precautionary principle is found in conventions regulating marine pollution, air pollution, and natural resource exploitation, as well as in biotechnology directives. The salient characteristic of a legal principle is precisely that it may be applied in a wide variety of cases.

These principles appear to be self-evident but tend to become increasingly elusive the more precisely one tries to define them. Whether it is a question of the polluter pays, which has passed from a partial to a full internalization of cost, or of precaution, which is being applied to increasingly uncertain risks, the progressive character of these principles is obvious. We can conclude from this that all three principles, despite their seeming simplicity, contain concepts that are nebulous, protean, and flexible and will therefore not be easy to implement. Part I of this work has sought to clarify these problems by examining the difficulties of interpretation and application the principles confront when called upon to integrate positive law.

We can see from that examination that it is crucial to introduce greater rigour into these principles. This is fully justified by a recognition of the right to environmental protection, which we consider in Part II below, which requires that public authorities do everything possible towards that end. Consequently the precautionary principle should not be encumbered by too many limitations, the polluter-pays principle should be viewed in a perspective of utmost prevention, and the principle of prevention should favour the adoption of those instruments that will best guarantee environmental protection.

Of course this theoretical presentation is merely a partial reflection of reality. The establishment of a legal principle only becomes effective if it is reflected in significant changes in positive law. Although the precautionary principle has given rise to a great deal of hope, we should remember that the principles of the polluter pays and of prevention have not yet succeeded in deeply penetrating legal systems, as shown by the growth in ecological problems. It would not be unreasonable to denounce the hypocrisy of international institutions and national Governments that solemnly proclaim principles which they then take great care not to apply. In the light of these realities it appears we have a long road to travel before we witness the emergence of environmental policies that are truly informed by these guiding principles.

PART II

THE LEGAL STATUS AND ROLE OF THE POLLUTER-PAYS, PREVENTIVE, AND PRECAUTIONARY PRINCIPLES:

A SHIFT FROM MODERN TO POST-MODERN LAW

Part II   Introduction

In Part I of this work we examined the role played by the principles of the polluter pays, prevention, and precaution in the gradual progression from a curative model of approaching ecological risks to a preventive model, which in turn gave way to an anticipatory model. That evolution demonstrates how the law, having grasped the concept of *certain* risk, has proceeded to tackle the problem of *uncertain* risk. This initial thesis was based on a systematic analysis of the genesis, definition, and legal scope of each of these three principles.

In Part II we demonstrate that the polluter-pays, preventive, and precautionary principles described in Part I mark an epistemological shift between modern law, which rests on the fixed standards of traditional legal rule-making, and post-modern law, which emphasizes the pragmatic, gradual, unstable, and reversible nature of rules. This calls for a change of perspective; we therefore consider these three principles horizontally, with a view to their legal status and functions, rather than separately, as was done in Part I. We also comment on other, related principles (rectification at source, integration, etc.) where these are relevant to our analysis.

We describe the paradigm shift from modern to post-modern law in the course of Chapters 4 to 6. As was emphasized in the General Introduction, environmental law has undergone a number of transformations during the past two decades, which have brought it far from the assumptions of modern law. It has experienced a more profound transformation than any other field of law. Since the concepts of modernity and post-modernity are both ambiguous, clarification of these terms must necessarily precede further analysis. Chapter 4 therefore begins by identifying the various elements that together define modern and post-modern law. We explain how legal principles function within each of these legal models, for both international and municipal law, with particular attention to the role they assume in the field of environment law. We particularly stress the distinction that must be made between General Principles of Law, which are characteristic of modernity, and directing principles, which are better suited to adapting to the shifting forms that characterize current public policies, including environment policy. At the same time, however, we shall see that directing principles do not represent a complete break with modernity, since they eventually result in the rediscovery of the same values upon which modernity is based. In other words, postmodernity is not merely a chaotic system composed of anti-modern elements; rather, it is a system whereby chaotic elements are ordered[1] differently from modern law (eg regulatory flexibility *v.* codification, chaos *v.* rationality). The result is a complex model that can only be understood by means of extensive comparison.

The analysis of general legal theory presented in this first Chapter forms an essential basis for the reasoning that follows in Chapters 5 to 7. There, we attempt to show that the polluter-pays, preventive and precautionary principles serve to re-establish rationality, which did not in fact disappear in the shift to post-modernity.

Symbolizing the increasing importance of environmental public policy, directing principles such as the polluter-pays, preventive and precautionary principles present undeniable advantages within a changing concept of the State wherein coercion gives way to negotiation as State sovereignty cedes ground to globalization and a third generation of human rights refashions the character of the polity. Indeed, the mechanical model of modern law, whereby solutions to an infinite number of cases may be deduced from a legal norm, is now being replaced by other types of reasoning, which seek to balance interests by applying directing principles set out in legislative instruments. In this context, directing principles are preferable to rigid rules, since their flexibility makes it possible for divergent values and interests or contradictory policies to coexist. Couched in extremely vague terms, directing principles are able to make an important contribution to the development of positive law by providing conceptual flexibility for legislators, administrators and courts in their practical work. Constituting a common resource for international, EC and national legal orders, such directing principles also encourage a *rapprochement* among various legal spheres. These principles allow us to construct bridges between the global and local levels and between international and EC law. Chapter 5 considers the various functions that the polluter-pays, preventive and precautionary principles may fulfil within a post-modern legal prospect, seeking to strike a balance among multiple and conflicting interests.

Recourse to directing principles such as the polluter-pays, preventive and precautionary principles described in Part I is often disparaged despite their usefulness, on the ground that they are not sufficiently definite to ensure legal certainty. These principles are generally described as having no prescriptive effect—until one fine day a court makes use of them, to the great surprise of the legislator. These principles may thereby serve to conceal a return to judicial activism. This possibility raises the question of the legal status of the principles in both international and EC law, as well as in national legal orders. Some authors consider that these directing principles should be devoid of any legal effect; others demand that their autonomous normative content be recognised. In Chapter 6, we shall explain that the fact that these directing principles are set out in texts of varying status does not deprive them of normative effect. On the contrary: by being recognised in provisions with normative effect, the principles

---

[1] I. Prigogine and I. Stengers, *Order out of Chaos* (London: Flamingo, 1992) 291–313.

of the polluter pays, prevention and precaution have specific normative effect rather than being mere regulatory ideals. Nonetheless, their legal status is quite unusual and typifies post-modern law, in that it is concerned with norms whose content is quite vague and which therefore lend themselves to a wide range of applications.

The potential importance of directing principles in weighing differing interests will be considered in greater detail in Chapter 7, which focuses on the conflict between environmental principles and free trade within the WTO and the EC. That conflict illustrates the role that these principles can play in reshaping a debate with major legal as well as societal implications. This Chapter highlights the odd twists and tangled hierarchies characteristic of post-modern law which may be encountered in disputes involving trade and the environment.

This four-stage approach will allow us to demonstrate how the polluter-pays, preventive and precautionary principles help shape an ideal of rationality in a chaotic legal universe. While that ideal differs significantly from the concept of rationality that characterized modern law, it remains an essential element if legal systems are to survive in the face of proliferating regulatory instruments, an accelerated legal process and a weakening of the command and control approach. Thus, the directing principles that have emerged within the framework of post-modern law do not represent a complete break with modernity, but rather a revitalization of some of its values with respect to the new challenges that legal systems will have to confront in future (weighing of interests instead of conflict of interests; codification instead of a fragmented regulatory approach; harmony among different legal orders instead of segregated legal regimes).

We should stress that the following analyses are based on recent theoretical research in France, Belgium and Switzerland, much of which has not yet been translated into English. For that reason, we have chosen to use the term 'directing principles' instead of the usual English term 'policy principles', which does not fully convey the meaning of the French *principes directeurs*. The term 'policy principles' is not, moreover, appropriate to our analysis, as its use in English implies that such principles are devoid of any prescriptive effect. We defend precisely the opposite thesis in Part II.

4

Theoretical Presentation of Modern and Post-Modern Principles

1. Introductory remarks

Environmental law and policy do not always co-exist harmoniously. Political scientists have forgotten that the most important aspect of environmental policy is the fact that it is set out in legal form (for instance, taxes are not merely economic instruments but also fiscal regulations), while lawyers for their part have not yet grasped that the law is changing shape.

In effect, a new legal model that reflects post-modern conditions is replacing the classical law of modern societies. Under pressure from a globalizing economy, the State has lost its monopolist role as a producer of norms for multilateral and supranational institutions. The nation-state and even the system of states may be either in crisis or heading toward crisis in the face of the increasing seriousness of many environmental problems.[1] In addition, law-makers have had to renounce general legal formulations and turn to more flexible modes of action, better adapted to dynamic social realities, in order to ensure the effectiveness of public policies. Similarly, they have had to abandon simplicity, systematization, and coherence so that legal norms might respond more rapidly to urgent and complex social needs.[2] Finally, they have had to relinquish constraint in favour of a flexible and decentralized system of rule-making, based on regulatory flexibility.

These conditions have taken our societies fully into the age of post-modernity, a new intellectual construct heavy with ambiguities. In fact the most precise and coherent problem evoked by post-modernity is a series of critical questions concerning the new forms taken by positive law in today's world: a law that has become pluralistic, soft, and negotiated.[3]

While general principles of law have come to occupy an important place in the modern legal framework, particularly in ensuring a coherent legal order,[4] new

---

[1] A. Hurrell and B. Kingsbury (eds.), *The International Politics of the Environment* (Oxford: Clarendon, 1992) 146; R. Falk, 'Environmental Protection in an Era of Globalization' (1995) 6 YbIEL 3–25; T. Evans, 'International Environmental Law and the Challenge of Globalization' in T. Jewell and J. Steele, *Law in Environmental Decision Making* (Oxford: Clarendon, 1998) 207–27.

[2] Ch.-A. Morand, *Le droit néo-moderne des politiques publiques* (Paris: L.G.D.J., 1999) 209.

[3] Fr. Moderne, 'Légitimité des principes généraux et théorie du droit' (1999) 15: 4 RFD Adm. 737.

[4] See the discussion in Subsection 2.3.1. below.

principles linked to specific public policy advances—which we refer to as 'directing principles'—have come into existence within the post-modern legal framework.

With the guidance of modern and post-modern legal models, legal theory will help us to assess the emblematic role of these 'directing principles' by comparing them to the general principles of law. The term 'directing' clearly indicates the function assumed by the principles of the polluter pays, prevention, and precaution, particularly in the field of environment law. To assure maximum clarity we examine the modern and post-modern models individually, consider how they are related, and then assess how they differ from one another (Sections 2 and 3 below). We must keep in mind, however, that the two models are not strictly sequential, since post-modern law in no way displaces modern law. There is no 'point' at which modern law can be said to end and post-modern law to begin. We shall also see that while rationality is inherent in both models, it differs considerably from one to the other. Finally in this Chapter we shall demonstrate how environmental law bears the mark of post-modernity (Section 4 below).

2. MODERN LAW

2.1. The elements of modern law

The term 'modern law' is today used to define the legal system which has been in place in our societies since the eighteenth century, based largely on the concept of formal and material rationality set out by Max Weber.[5] While pre-modern societies were bound by the laws of nature, modern society puts its faith in the virtues of reason. This empire of reason is accompanied by a set of beliefs: in the virtues of science, which will endow mankind with an ever-greater mastery of nature; in unstoppable progress; and in a Western model that is the very embodiment of reason and will therefore compel recognition throughout the world.[6] Modernity also places the individual at the centre of society and restrains State intervention, which could threaten public freedoms.

2.2. The characteristics of modern law

Strongly conditioned by rationality, modern law is seen as an autonomous system that is made up of general and abstract rules[7] and is complete and coherent to the extent that it is organized in a systematic fashion to form a hierarchical whole. As stressed by Koskenniemi, 'lawyers have a political responsibility to justify their decisions so that they appear coherent with the

---

[5] M. Weber, *Wirtschaft und Gesellschaft* (5th edn., Tübingen : J.C.B. Mohr, 1980).

[6] J. Chevallier, 'Vers un droit post-moderne? Les transformations de la régulation juridique' (1998) 3 RDP 674.

[7] It thus mirrors mathematics.

decision-making activity (by legislators as well as judges) within the legal system as a whole'.[8]

2.2.1. A legal system of general and abstract rules

In a liberal vision the function of modern law is to provide for the coexistence of individual freedoms: each person has the right to enjoy maximum freedom to pursue his own interests, as long as he does not impinge upon the freedom of others. In order to provide every person with the maximum degree of freedom, modern law concentrates political power in the hands of the State: 'an institution which is capable of standing above the contention of private wants'.[9] In that context the need for legal certainty and foreseeability has led relations between individuals to be bound by general rules that refer to abstract concepts grouped together in general categories. Both generality and abstraction guarantee impartiality by drawing a veil of indifference between a norm and specific situations.[10] With the advent of modern law the general has taken the place of the individual, and the abstract has replaced the concrete. This coherent system of general and abstract rules is able to provide a single, precise solution for every dispute. Judicial decisions are mechanistically deduced from general and abstract norms. Within this formally rational legal system the legal subject is an abstract and autonomous entity entitled to formal equality.[11]

2.2.2. A hierarchical legal system

Modern law presents itself as a pyramidal construction, with the most general rules at the apex. It thus appears to constitute a coherent whole—that is, a system of hierarchical rules linked to each other by logical and necessary relationships.[12] This systematization confers upon the law the attributes of clarity, simplicity and certainty. Moreover, the legal hierarchy is secured by the fact that the power of constraint is invested in the State, which therefore puts itself forward as the sole creator of rules.

2.2.3. An autonomous legal system

Formally rational, modern law is characterized by its axiological neutrality—that is, its refusal to take into consideration any elements external to the legal sphere, such as value judgements or ideological considerations. Modern law seeks clearly to distinguish itself from both morality and other pragmatic rules, whether these be scientific, social, or economic.[13] Fending off rules from outside its own boundaries, modern law defines itself as an autonomous system. Therefore, lawyers

---

[8] M. Koskenniemi, *From Apology to Utopia: The Structure of International Legal Argument* (Helsinki: Lakimiestliiton Kustannuys, 1989) 410.

[9] A. Barron, 'Legal Discourse and the Colonization of the Self in the Modern State' in A. Carty (ed.), *Post-Modern Law* (Edinburgh: Edinburgh U.P., 1990) 110.

[10] Ch.-A. Morand, n. 2 above, 30.

[11] A. Barron, n. 9 above, 113.

[12] H. Kelsen, *General Theory of Law and State* (Cambridge: Harvard U.P., 1946).

[13] Ch.-A. Morand, n. 2 above, 47.

believe that 'they can produce statements relating to the social world which are "objective" in some sense that political, ideological, religious, or other such statements are not'.[14]

2.3. General principles of law in a modern legal perspective

The concept of the 'General Principles of Law' is central to modern law, even if it is subject to wide-ranging doctrinal debate at the level of both municipal and international law. The controversy surrounding the exact definition of general principles of law can be explained by varying concepts of the origin and functions of those principles and by the fact that they may be found in different legal orders and in several fields of law.

In addition, the classification of these principles presents difficulties.[15] First, some principles can be seen as tools for describing positive law. Such descriptive statements are more or less factual reconstructions of the law by academic scholars rather than acts of law-making. In other words, they are a kind of a summary of positive law and nothing more portentous.[16] These are not examined here in any detail as we consider that general principles of law are normative principles. Secondly, some principles of law embody legal logic (eg *non bis in idem, ubi major minor cessat, lex specialis derogat legi generali*, and *lex posterior derogat legi priori)* for the use of courts.[17] Thus they are not so much a source of law as a method of interpretation. For that reason they are not analysed. Thirdly, at both municipal and international levels, general principles of law have been created by courts to provide greater coherence to the legal system on one hand, and to fill gaps or mitigate the obscurity of the legal system on the other hand.[18] Given their prescriptive application, we consider this third category of principles highly emblematic of modern law.

2.3.1. *General principles of law and the coherence of the legal system*

From a theoretical point of view, general principles of law are perceived as essential to modern law for the coherence of the legal system: 'they make the law a consistent system in the sense that they make it possible to ensure systematic unity of the law amid the disorder of positive rules'.[19] Such a system is above

---

[14] M. Koskenniemi, n. 8 above, 458.

[15] For a typology of the different categories of principles in legal theory see eg A. Peczenik, 'Principles of Law: The Search for Legal Theory' (1971) 2 Rechtstheory 17; J. Wrobelski, *Principes du droit* (Paris: PUF, 1979) 474. For a typology in public international law see eg H. Mosler, 'General Principles of Law' in *Encyclopedia of Public International Law*, vol. 7 (Amsterdam, New York, Oxford: North Holland) 90.

[16] A. Peczenik, n. 15 above, 29.

[17] Reference may be here made to Article 31 of the Vienna Convention on the Law of Treaties, discussed in Chapter 7 below.

[18] For a critical analysis of the 'principes généraux du droit' in continental legal regimes see eg N. de Sadeleer, *Les principes du pollueur-payeur, de prévention et de précaution* (Brussels: Bruylant/Agence Universitaire pour la Francaphonie, 1999) 231–71.

[19] M. van de Kerchove and Fr. Ost, *Legal System Between Order and Disorder* (Oxford: OUP, 1994) 82.

all one in which various elements are carefully set out and arranged with regard to a hierarchy of norms, according to which primary rules generate secondary rules.[20] In his work on *Legal Reasoning and Legal Theory*, MacCormick defended the functional legitimacy of recourse to legal principles in contemporaneous legal systems, based on a need for coherence that is inherent in the rationality of modern law. MacCormick wrote that: 'Working out the principles of a legal system to which one is committed involves an attempt to give it *coherence* in terms of a set of general norms which express justifying and explanatory values of the system.'[21]

One can only agree with this analysis. Taken in isolation, the rule of law often appears obscure; doubts rapidly arise as to its precise effect. When the meaning of a rule within a given context is uncertain, recourse to the principle from which it derives explains why that rule should be applied. Linking a rule to a principle allows the court to clarify with some degree of precision the fundamentals of which any given rule is but a fragmentary manifestation. Faced with the difficulties of interpreting a normative text, the court will be able, prior to choosing among several possible readings, to base its reasoning on the principles it considers relevant to resolving the dispute in conformity with the *ratio legis* of the legal system.

General principles of law will also provide courts with a firmer basis for navigating the intricacies of often conflicting texts. If a rule consists in implementing a principle, the court may go back to that principle to shed new light on the merits of a case; if a rule takes the form of derogation from a principle, the court should interpret it restrictively. Thus, for example, exceptions for public order, public health, and the protection of animals and plants set out in Article 30 of the EC Treaty, which derogate from the principle of the free circulation of goods following from Articles 28 and 29, are interpreted restrictively by the ECJ. The existence of general principles thus authorizes interpretations of a teleological nature; that is, solutions are sought in the values that inspired the lawmaker rather than solely on the basis of a legal formula. Instead of according absolute value to a legal text, principles allow the spirit rather than the letter of the law to prevail. They thereby invite the courts to evaluate the latter in the light of the objectives of the legal system in which it occurs.

In addition, it is widely recognized that the completeness of the legal system is an important element of the formal rationality of modern law, which is strongly supported by general principles of law. General principles of law are thus called upon to help fashion the legal system by filling possible lacunae. At the level of international, EC, and national legal orders courts regularly find themselves confronting gaps in written sources. To the extent that courts must rectify such

---

[20] For a critical examination of the pyramid proposed by Kelsen see eg P. Golding, 'Kelsen and the concept of legal system' in R.S. Summers (ed.), *More Essays in Legal Philosophy: General Assessments of Legal Philosophies* (Los Angeles: Berkeley, 1971) 69.

[21] N. MacCormick, *Legal Reasoning and Legal Theory* (Oxford: OUP, 1978) 177 (emphasis added).

deficiencies to rule on a case, they will do so by deducing a relevant principle from a mass of rules. Once enunciated, the principle will be applied as an autonomous norm to resolve the dispute. Subsequently, that same principle can be applied in other cases.[22]

2.3.2. The creation of general principles of law

Whether they are called general principles of law, *principes généraux du droit, principios general del derecho, Rechtsbeginselen,* or *Rechtsprinzipien,*[23] a large number of general principles of law have been created by national courts, in continental legal regimes, since the end of the Second World War, especially in constitutional,[24] administrative,[25] and judicial[26] case-law. Some of those general principles cover an extremely wide field of application (eg the principle of proportionality). Other principles are only applicable in a single field of law (eg the principles of criminal law, *nullum crimen and nulla poena sine lege*). The future for general principles of law appears bright, even if recourse to these principles is progressively tapering off in some court systems following a period during which they were widely recognized.[27] Their success in continental legal regimes is attributable to several factors. On one hand some national legal systems, such as French or Belgian civil law, require courts to rule even when the law is silent on an issue and consequently authorize the court to fill in gaps in the written law by recourse to general principles of law.[28] On the other hand the success of these principles in fields

---

[22] We shall not review legal theory discussions about whether it is the judge's function to create general principles of law. We would merely recall that positivists argue that when there is no clear rule to guide them, judges must create legal rules in exercising their discretion; Dworkin, on the other hand, argues that judges are generally bound by existing principles of law and thus are not intended to fulfil the creative role that positivism seems to assign them. See eg R. Dworkin, *Taking Rights Seriously* (Cambridge: Harvard U.P., 1977) 35. For a critique of the general legal theory of ideological postulates underlying the creation of general principles of law, see Ph. Gerard, *Droit, égalité et idéologie* (Brussels: Saint-Louis, 1980) 177.

[23] It is not unusual for the term 'general' to be omitted when discussing principles; eg A. Peczenik, n. 15 above, 17; J. Raz, 'Principles and the Limits of Law' (1972) Yale LJ 81

[24] It is not possible to suggest a complete bibliography, given the numerous texts devoted to general principles of law in national legal systems. For French law see in particular Duhamel and Y. Meny, *Dictionnaire de droit constitutionnel* (Paris: PUF, 1992) 827; B. Genevois, 'Une catégorie de principes de valeur constitutionnelle: Les principes fondamentaux reconnus par les lois de la République', and F. Moderne, 'Actualité des principes généraux du droit' (1998) 14: 3 RFD Adm. 477. For Belgian law see F. Leurquin-De Visscher, 'Principes généraux et principes fondamentaux dans la jurisprudence de la Cour d'Arbitrage' (1996) 3 Ann Dr Louvain 275.

[25] In France, B. Jeannau, *Les principes généraux du droit dans la jurisprudence administrative* (Paris: Sirey, 1954); R. Chapus, 'De la valeur juridique des principes généraux du droit et des autres règles jurisprudentielles du droit administratif' (1996) I D. 99; G. Morange, 'Une catégorie juridique ambiguë: Les principes généraux du droit' (1977) RDP 761.

[26] For Belgian law see W. Ganshof van der Meersch, 'Propos sur le texte de la loi et les principes généraux du droit' (1970) JT 557.

[27] E. Larsonnier, 'La consécration par le Conseil d'Etat d'un principe fondamental reconnu par les lois de la République: Prémice d'une reconnaissance de la catégorie?' (1997) 2 Rev b Dr const 123.

[28] For France, C.civ., Article 4; for Belgium, Article 6, Code judiciaire.

such as administrative and constitutional law may be explained by the need for courts to find coherent solutions in the face of the gaps that characterize these legal fields. In common law countries principles that are primarily elucidated by the court sometimes provide a basis for the constitutional system of law;[29] at other times they are used to complement statute law.[30]

The technique of inducing a principle relevant to solving a case from a mass of rules is also widely applied at the level of EC law, where the ECJ has been strongly influenced by national techniques for creating general principles of law.[31]

Since the international legal system is not sufficiently developed[32] fully to address the problems it confronts,[33] the technique of general principles of law also exists at this level. In this context general principles 'constitute both the backbone of the body of law governing international dealings and the potent cement that binds together the various and often disparate cogs and wheels of the normative framework of the international community'.[34] It was for that reason that the provision of 'the general principles of law recognised by civilised nations' was inserted into Article 38(I)(c) of the Permanent Court of International Justice, the forerunner of the International Court of Justice, as a source of law.[35] Since the introduction of that provision, the concept of general principles of law has been the subject of numerous analyses, the main lines of which

---

[29] J. Raz, 'The Rule of Law and its Virtue' (1977) LQR 195; T.R.S. Allan, *Law, Liberty and Justice: The Legal Foundation of British Constitutionalism* (Oxford: Clarendon, 1993).

[30] See for example A. Kemp Kareleton, *Law in the Making* (Oxford: Clarendon, 1964) 456: 'there is the dominant principle never absent in the mind of judges, that the Common Law is wider and more fundamental than Statute and that wherever possible legislative enactments should be construed in harmony with established Common Law principles rather than in antagonism with them'.

[31] P. Reuter, 'Le recours de la Cour de justice des Communautés européennes à des principes généraux de droit' in *Mélanges H. Rolin* (Paris: Pédone, 1964) 263; J. Boulouis, 'A propos de la fonction normative de la jurisprudence: Remarques sur l'oeuvre jurisprudentielle de la Cour de justice des Communautés européennes' in *Mélanges Waline* (Paris: L.G.D.J., 1974); M. Akehurst, 'The Application of General Principles of Law by the ECJ' (1981) 52 BYbIL 25; G. Goletti, 'The General Principles of Law in the European Community' (1985) II: 61 Foro Aministrativo 2623; B. Spitzer, 'Les principes généraux de droit communautaire dégagés par la Cour de justice des Communautés européennes' (1986) Gaz Pal 732; D. Simon, 'Y a-t-il des principes généraux du droit communautaire?' (1991) Droits 73; R. Papadopoulou, *Principes généraux du droit et principes du droit communautaire* (Brussels: Bruylant, 1996).

[32] Several doctrinal views on international law as a legal system exist. See for example G.J.H. Van Hoof, *Rethinking the Sources of International Law* (Deventer: Kluwer, 1983) 17–56; J. Combacau, 'Le droit international: Bric à brac ou système ?' (1986) 31 Arch Ph Dr 85–105 ; R. Higgins, *Problems and Process: International Law and How We Use It* (Oxford: Clarendon, 1994) 1–16; H.J. Steiner, 'International Law, Doctrine and Schools of Thought in the Twentieth Century' in R. Bernardt (ed.), *Encyclopedia of Public International Law*, vol. II (Amsterdam: Elsevier, 1995) 1216–27.

[33] M. Shaw, *International Law* (4th edn., Cambridge: CUP, 1997) 78.

[34] A. Cassese, *International Law* (Oxford: OUP, 2001) 151.

[35] I. Brownlie, *Principles of Public International Law* (5th edn., Oxford: Clarendon, 1998) 15; M. Shaw, n. 33 above, 81.

are considered below.[36] Three schools of thought may be distinguished in the debates concerning this highly controversial source of international law.

Positivist jurists refuse to consider general principles as a formal source of international law.[37] Other authors, by contrast, consider that general principles are simply principles that are generally found in national legal systems.[38] A third group of jurists recognizes that Article 38 (I)(c) includes two categories of 'general principles': in addition to general principles arising from national legal systems, other general principles can be induced from positive rules of international law (eg the principles of non-intervention, reciprocity, equality of States, etc.).[39] Finally, there is a group which considers purely academic the question of whether general principles of law constitute a third source of law, distinct from treaties and customary law.[40]

This doctrinal controversy as to whether general principles of law constitute a formal source of law should not obscure the fact that a distinction has gradually been established between the general principles that can be induced in accordance with Article 38(I)(c) of the ICJ Statute and the general principles of law that are applicable to inter-State relations without being drawn from *foro domestico*. We would briefly recall the essential characteristics of this distinction, for while the legal status of principles of international law remains controversial they

---

[36] For an overview see: G. Fitzmaurice, 'The General Principles of International Law Considered from the Standpoint of the Rule of Law' (1957) II: 92 RCADI 5; M. Akehurst, 'Equity and General Principles of Law' (1976) *ICLQ* 801; W. Friedmann, 'The Use of General Principles in the Development of International Law' (1963) AJIL 279; C. Parry, *The Sources and Evidences of International Law* (Manchester: Manchester U.P., 1965) 83–91; J.G. Lammers, 'General Principles of Law Recognized by Civilized Nations' in *Essays on the Development of the International Order* (Panhuys) (Alphen a/d Rijn: Sijthof and Noordhoff, 1980) 53–75; A. Vitanyi, 'Les positions doctrinales concernant les sens de la notion de "Principes généraux" de droit reconnus par les nations civilisées' (1982) 86 RGDIP 45–116; I. Brownlie, n. 35 above, 15–19; M. Shaw, n. 33 above, 81; G.J.H. Van Hoof, n. 32 above, 131–50.

[37] Eg H. Kelsen, *Principles of International Law* (2nd edn., New York: Holt, Rhinehart, and Winston, 1956) 539–40; R.Y. Jennings, 'The Identification of International Law' in Bin Cheng (ed.), *International Law: Teaching and Practice* (London: Stevens and Sons, 1982) 4; A. Cassese, *International Law in a Divided World* (Oxford: Clarendon, 1986) 173–4; A. Cassese and J.H. Weiler (eds.), *Change and Stability in International Law-Making* (Berlin: De Gruyter, 1988) 33–7.

[38] H. Lauterpacht, *Private Law Sources and Analogies of International Law* (Weesp: Archon, 1970) 69–71; H. Bokor-Szegö, 'General Principles of Law' in M. Bedjaoui (ed.), *International Law: Achievements and Prospects* (Paris, Dordrecht: Martinus Nijhof, 1991) 217; J. Combacau and S. Sur, *Droit international public* (2nd edn., Paris: Montchrestien, 1995) 46; Nguyen Quoc Dinh, *Droit international public* (6th edn., Paris: L.G.D.J., 1999) 347–8. International courts are therefore keen to develop general principles of law by borrowing elements that are either common to all or most national systems of law or stem from domestic legal systems and have been transplanted into international law (*in dubio pro reo*, denial of justice). Eg P. Malanczuk, *Akerhust's Modern Introduction to International Law* (London: Routledge, 1993) 49.

[39] I. Brownlie, n. 35 above, 19; M. Virally, 'Le rôle des principes dans le développement du droit international' in *Recueil d'études de droit international en hommage de Paul Guggenheim* (Genève, 1968) 533; H. Mosler, 'General Principles of Law' 7 EPIL 89; J.G. Lammers, 'General Principles of Law...', n. 36 above, 57–9, 66–9.

[40] K. Wolfke, *Custom in Present International Law* (2nd edn., Dordrecht: Martinus Nijhoff, 1993) 108.

ought nevertheless to help ensure the coherence of the international legal order within a perspective that we are terming 'modern'.

In inserting Article 38(I)(c) into the Statute of the Court, the intention was clearly 'to enable the Court to fill the gaps in the body of law deriving from Convention and custom',[41] in order to avoid the *non-liquet* effect.[42] This is what may be called the 'gap-filling function'.[43] This doctrine is, according to Koskenniemi, based on the idea of the law as a *complete and coherent system*.[44] That said, the category of 'General Principles of Law Recognised by Civilised Nations' is only applicable when a treaty or customary provision is lacking.[45]

The general principles recognized by civilized nations referred to in Article 38(I)(c) of the Statute should be comparable to the general principles in *foro domestico* in terms of how they are elaborated.[46] However, States have seldom based claims before the ICJ on general principles of law recognized by civilized nations, and no decision of the Court has yet been based explicitly upon such a principle.[47] The difficulty for the ICJ in recognizing such principles arises from the prerequisite that that they be common to various national legal regimes.[48] Even if serious research on comparative law were to be undertaken, it would probably be quite difficult to derive common principles from a multitude of national and highly heterogeneous legal systems. In addition, the ICJ as well as other international courts exercise great caution in applying general principles of law, because they 'depend for their jurisdiction, as well as for the acceptability of their decisions and opinions, upon the consent of states'.[49] Finally, it would seem that the main reason for the decline of these principles is that scores of treaty rules have been established in the past few decades and that, in addition, numerous customary rules have emerged, translating dormant or potential general principles of law into treaty or customary rules.[50]

---

[41] H. Thirlway, 'The Law and the Procedure of the ICJ (1960–1989)' (1990) XI BYbIL 305.

[42] M. Koskenniemi, n. 8 above, 26–7.

[43] J.G. Lammers, 'General Principles of Law . . . ', n. 36 above, 64; P. Birnie and A. Boyle, *International Law and the Environment* (2nd edn., Oxford University Press, 2002) 19–20.

[44] M. Koskenniemi, n. 8 above, 24, 36–7. See also J.G. Lammers, 'General Principles of Law . . . ', n. 36 above, 64. For a criticism of the idea of material completeness, see J. Stone, '*Non liquet and the International Judicial Function*' (1959) XXXV BYbIL 124–61.

[45] *Rights of Passage (Portugal v. India)*, ICJ *Rep* [1960] 43. In contrast to custom, general principles of law have a life of their own; their existence does not depend on their being actively applied in international relations or State practice.

[46] H. Bokor-Szegö, n. 38 above, 215.

[47] H. Thirlway, n. 41 above, 110–11; J.G. Lammers, 'General Principles of Law . . . ', n. 36 above, 71. In its 1996 advisory opinion on the Legality of the Threat or Use of Nuclear Weapons, the majority of the ICJ made no reference to general principles of law to fill the lacuna caused by the lack of any relevant treaty obligations in this field. *Legality of the Threat or Use of Nuclear Weapons*, Advisory Opinion, ICJ Rep [1996] 226.

[48] *Contra* A. Verdross, 'Les principes généraux de droit dans le système des sources de droit international public' in *Recueil P. Guggenheim*, n. 39 above, 525; Nguyen Quoc Dinh, n. 38 above, 347.

[49] W. Friedmann, *The Changing Structure of International Law* (London: Stevens and Sons, 1964) 189. See also G.J.H. Van Hoof, n. 32 above, 144–6; J. Combacau and S. Sur, n. 38 above, 46.

[50] A. Cassese, *International Law*, n. 34 above, 157.

On the other hand, to the extent that other principles are set forth by international courts, there exists an additional source of international law distinct from the sources provided by Article 38. While not common in *foro domestico*, this second category of principles is applicable to inter-State relations.[51] Thus, despite its reticence about formulating general principles in the meaning of Article 38(I)(c), ICJ case-law abounds in references to principles of all kinds, sometimes qualified as 'general'.[52] This terminology is not always consistent, however.[53]

This second category of principles is derived through a process of induction from positive rules of international law, similar to the method used by constitutional courts and administrative high courts in national legal orders.[54] Procedural rules can be deduced from substantive obligations through this process of induction.[55] As stressed by Nollkaemper, 'compliance with certain procedural rules can be a necessary condition for compliance with substantive rules'.[56] In many cases these principles have been so long and so generally accepted that they are no longer directly connected to state practice.[57]

The principles falling into this second category may fulfil various functions. They may serve to fill gaps in cases where treaty law and customary law do not foresee solutions, with the aim of ensuring the coherence of the legal system, which is characteristic of modern law. They may also fulfil an interpretative function,[58] serving to clarify uncertainties in conventional law.[59] In both cases they play an important role as an autonomous source of law since, in contrast to customary rules, they may be applied even in the absence of State practice. The

---

[51] W. Friedmann, n. 49 above, 188; G.J.H. Van Hoof, n. 32 above, 139–48; H. Thirlway, n. 41 above; idem., (1989) 60 BYIL 7–76; J.G. Lammers, *Pollution of International Watercourses* (Dordrecht: Martinus Nijhoff, 1984) 164; P.-M. Dupuy, *Droit International Public* (Paris: Dalloz, 1999) 261; A. Cassese, *International Law*, n. 34 above, 151; J. Salmon (ed.), *Dictionnaire de Droit International Public* (Brussels: Bruylant-AUF, 2001) 880–1.

[52] The ICJ has applied general principles of a broad kind not derived from analysis of municipal systems without making any reference to Article 38. See *Nuclear Tests* Case (*Australia v. France*), ICJ Rep [1974] 253. In this case, for instance, the ICJ declared that 'One of the basic principles governing the creation and performance of legal obligations, whatever their source, is the principle of good faith. Trust and confidence are inherent in international co-operation, in particular in an age when this co-operation in many fields is becoming increasingly essential. Just as the very rule of *pacta sunt servanda* in the law of treaties is based on good faith, so also is the binding character of an international obligation assumed by unilateral obligation'. See also *United States Diplomatic and Consular Staff in Tehran* case (*US v. Iran*), ICJ Rep [1980] para. 86.

[53] *Military and Paramilitary Activities in and Against Nicaragua* (*Nicaragua v. USA*), ICJ Rep [1986] 111, paras. 190 and 202.

[54] M. Akerhust, *A Modern Introduction to International Law* (3rd edn., London: George Allen and Unwin, 1977) 40–1; G. Schwarzenberger, *The Inductive Approach to International Law* (London: Stevens and Sons, 1965) 8–42, 109–92; G.J.H. Van Hoof, n. 32 above, 139–44.

[55] *Nicaragua Case*, ICJ Rep [1986] para. 202.

[56] A. Nollkaemper, *A Legal Regime of Transboundary Water Pollution: Between Discretion and Constraint* (London, The Hague, Boston: Martinus Nijhoff/Graham & Trotman, 1993) 222.

[57] I. Brownlie, n. 35 above, 19.

[58] J.G. Lammers, 'General Principles of Law . . .', n. 36 above, 65.

[59] Ibid., 64–5, 69, 75; A. Cassese, *International Law*, n. 34 above, 152.

behaviour and consent of States is thus not a prerequisite to recognition of these principles.[60]

As can be seen from this brief analysis, general principles of law—whether in international or national law—can be seen as a logical postulate for the coherence and completeness of the legal system, despite the controversies surrounding them.

2.4. General principles of international environmental law in a modern perspective

Despite an increasing number of instruments expressed in the form of 'Declarations of Principles', the international community has not yet adopted a binding international instrument of global application which sets out the general principles of environmental law.[61] Nevertheless, these principles could play an important role by creating coherence in an international environmental legal order made up of a large number of treaties, each of which addresses a different global or regional environmental issue in response to a specific threat. Not surprisingly, legal scholars have expended considerable effort in identifying, elaborating, and developing various general principles of international environment law; these can be deduced from a wide variety of sources, ranging from soft law (the Stockholm and Rio Declarations)[62] to arbitral decisions (eg the *Trail Smelter* Arbitration) and judicial decisions by the International Court of Justice.[63] Some of the principles, such as good neighbourliness and international co-operation, simply reflect the application of general international law principles to environmental issues.[64] Others, like the obligation not to cause environmental harm, are specific to international environmental law. In the informal taxonomy of international environmental principles developed by scholars,[65] some general principles of international law are widely accepted as reflecting customary law; others constitute emerging legal obligations.[66] Consequently, principles such as the obligation not to cause environmental damage or the

---

[60] Dissenting Opinion by Judge Tanaka, in *South West Africa Case*, ICJ Rep [1966] 298. According to M. Bos, 'With a general principle of law... there is no practice to be taken into account—at least not in the sense attributed to the term in the context of custom...' Eg 'The Identification of Custom in International Laws' (1982) 25 GYbIL 11.

[61] P. Birnie and A. Boyle, *International Law and the Environment*, n. 43 above, 21; D. Hunter, J. Salzman, and D. Zaelke, *International Environmental Law and Policy* (New York: Foundation, 1998) 320–1; P. Sands, *Principles of International Environmental Law* (Manchester: MUP, 1995) 185–6.

[62] The 1972 Stockholm Declaration must be seen as a first attempt to elaborate international environmental law principles. Though not binding law, the 1992 Rio Declaration also reflects an important consensus within the international community regarding the basic principles of environmental policies.

[63] D. Hunter, J. Salzman, and D. Zaelke, n. 61 above, 319. See the discussion in Chapter 4, Section 1 above.

[64] P. Sands, *Principles of International Environmental Law*, n. 61 above, 197.

[65] P. Sands, n. 61 above, 183–242; D. Hunter, J. Salzman, and D. Zaelke, n. 61 above, 318–85.

[66] P. Sands, n. 61 above, 183.

principle of co-operation can be invoked;[67] principles that are not supported by significant practice through repetitive use in an international legal context cannot give rise to a legal remedy (eg the right to a healthy environment, or the principles of common but differentiated responsibility and of subsidiarity).[68]

Despite the wide use of principles of legal logic and general jurisprudence, courts have been reluctant to create general principles of international environmental law, however. Birnie and Boyle concluded in 1992 that, in practice, the most frequent use of general principles by international courts 'derives from the drawing of analogies with domestic law concerning rules of procedure, evidence, and jurisdiction and these are only marginally useful in an environmental context'.[69]

This may change in future; the ICJ and arbitral tribunals have already invoked various equitable 'principles' and 'concepts' as a means of resolving certain kinds of environmental disputes, for example over shared natural resources such as watercourses.[70] In the *Gabcíkovo-Nagymaros* case, the ICJ invoked the 'concept'—not the 'principle'—of sustainable development and stated that it should be given proper weight in interpreting existing environmental obligations. This means that as new environmental norms and standards are developed, they must be taken into consideration 'not only when States contemplate new activities but also when continuing with activities begun in the past'.[71] Similarly, the ECJ used the integration principle in the *Titanium Dioxide* case as a means to support the choice of a legal basis intended to ensure the functioning of the internal market (former Article 100A, new Article 95 of the EC Treaty) instead of a legal basis relating to environmental protection policy (former Article 130S, new Article 175 of the EC Treaty).[72] Although this remains controversial, the possibility that an international court will proclaim the principles of the polluter pays, prevention or precaution as general principles of international environmental law therefore cannot be excluded.[73]

---

[67] A. Kiss and J.-M. Beurier, *Droit international de l'environnement* (Paris: Pédone, 2001) 105 *et seq.* See also P. Birnie and A. Boyle, n. 43 above, 88, 109–11, 127.

[68] P. Sands, n. 61 above, 183–4.

[69] P. Birnie and A. Boyle, *International Law and the Environment* (Oxford University Press, 1992) 24.

[70] G. Handl, 'The Principle of Equitable Use as Applied to Internationally Shared Natural Resources: Its Role in Resolving Potential International Disputes over Transfrontier Pollution' (1977–78) 14 Rev b Dr intl. 46.

[71] *Gabcíkovo-Nagymaros* Case (*Hungary v. Slovakia*), ICJ Rep [1997] para. 140.

[72] Case C-300/89, *Commission v. Council* [1991] ECR I-2867, para. 23. See eg N. de Sadeleer, 'Legal Basis of EC Environmental Legislation' (1993) 5: 2 JEL 291–300.

[73] P. Birnie, 'International Environmental Law: Its Adequacy for Present and Future Needs' in A. Hurrell and B. Kingsbury (eds.), *The International Politics*, n. 1 above, 61; P. Birnie and A. Boyle, n. 43 above, 19. There is no contradiction between the function these three principles can carry out in a post-modern law perspective (see the discussion in Subsection 3.3. below) and the fact that they could also be deduced by courts from a wide range of legal instruments in order to fill a gap in the international legal system. However, we shall see in the next Chapter that courts are still relatively reluctant to deduce the precautionary principle as such and to apply it as a binding principle (see the discussion in Chapter 6, Subsection 3.2.3., below).

3. POST-MODERN LAW

3.1. The elements of post-modernity

The issue of post-modernity goes far beyond the legal context.[74] Based on theories of the history of science developed by Thomas Kuhn,[75] this concept describes the conceptual frameworks of modern culture in its aesthetic, artistic, and political dimensions.[76] Yet while there has been an explosion of discourse about 'modernity' and 'post-modernity' during the past two decades, both terms are vague and ambiguous and have been used in conflicting and contradictory ways.[77] In Jean-François Lyotard's *The Post-Modern Condition*, which gave rise to a great deal of controversy when it first appeared, post-modernity is defined as 'incredulity toward meta-narratives. This incredulity is undoubtedly a product of progress in the sciences; but that progress in turn presupposes it.'[78] Post-modernity questions the very legitimacy of knowledge, the status of which is shifting as societies enter a post-industrial age and cultures a so-called post-modern period.[79]

The uncertainties attending the exact meaning of post-modernity are also to be found in discussions about the general theory of law. As a result post-modern law remains an incomplete intellectual construct within which a large number of concepts, divergent as well as convergent, jostle each other,[80] creating significant confusion. In addition, post-modern law is less a phenomenon whose beginnings can be pinpointed at a precise moment of modern history than a complex process built up incrementally as the result of the upheavals which have at regular intervals shaken the order of modern law. As the result of these upheavals, post-modern law is going through a process that is radically different from any of those that characterize modern law.

Several factors have contributed to modern law losing the attributes of generality, systematicity, and autonomy, thus hastening its passage to post-modernity. First, the sovereign State has given way to a plurality of institutions which are as

---

[74] The term 'post-modern' was popularized in French primarily by J.-F. Lyotard, *La condition post-moderne* (Paris: éd. de Minuit, 1979); A. Touraine, *Critique de la modernité* (Paris: Fayard, 1992); A.J. Arnaud, *Entre modernité et mondialisation* (Paris: L.G.D.J., 1998) 145. In English see also B. Smart, *Postmodernity* (London: Routledge, 1992).

[75] T. Kuhn, *The Structure of Scientific Revolution* (Chicago: University of Chicago, 1962).

[76] Fr. Jameson, *Postmodernism, or The Cultural Logic of Late Capitalism* (London: Verso, 1991).

[77] R.J. Bernstein, *The New Constellation: The Ethical-Political Horizons of Modernity/Postmodernity* (Cambridge: Polity, 1991) 200; Fr. Jameson, n. 76 above, 55–66.

[78] J.-F. Lyotard, *The Postmodern Condition: A Report on Knowledge* (Minneapolis: University of Minnesota, 1984) xxiii–iv.

[79] Ibid.

[80] R.M. Unger, *Law in Modern Society: Toward a Criticism of Social Theory* (New York: Free Press, Collier Macmillan Publ., 1977); A. Carty 'Introduction: Post-Modern Law' in A. Carty (ed.), n. 9 above, 1–39; B. de Sousa-Santos, 'The Post-Modern Transition: Law and Politics' in A. Sarat and T.R. Kearns (eds.), *The Fate of Law* (Ann Arbor: University of Michigan Press, 1991); *Towards a New Common Sense: Law, Science and Politics in the Paradigmatic Transition* (London: Routledge, 1991); C. Douzinas, R. Warington, and Sh. McVeigh, *Postmodern Jurisprudence* (London: Routledge, 1991); P. Goodrich and D. Gray, *Law and Postmodernity* (Ann Arbor: University of Michigan, 1998).

much infra-national as supranational. 'Upstream', inter-governmental institutions such as the WTO, the EC, and NAFTA, which aim to govern the actions of their members and directly influence the elaboration of rules at national level, are growing in number. 'Downstream', public policies concerning education, health, land-planning, and natural resources generally fall within the competence of the numerous national actors (regions, provinces, communities, etc.) most closely involved with the areas being regulated, thus increasing the number of relevant regulators even further. In addition, standard-setting bodies (ISO, CEN, etc.) have established their own functional norms and procedures, giving rise to a non-statal law that vies with State law.

Secondly, although the number of regulators has increased dramatically, the speed at which norms are produced has also accelerated drastically.[81] In the past two decades time seems to have become unhinged. Events are proceeding as though we had become detached from the straight line of historical development that binds the present to the past and the future. Time is no longer a measure of duration; radically accelerated, it reduces the long term to a short term and continuance to immediacy.[82] Our societies, living in a permanent state of emergency, now favour flexibility over long-term action and action over prediction. Reflecting this, the legal universe has become one of short-term programmes and constant change. By seeking to adhere closely to constantly shifting scientific data, environment law has become the expiatory victim of this acceleration in legal time.

Thirdly, in a world of permanent change action will be more efficient the more easily it can be modified to take account of evolving contexts. This is particularly true since action is expected to result immediately in tangible results. The legitimacy of the State is no longer acquired as of right but is rather a function of the relevance of State-generated programmes.[83] Therefore both States and the international community increasingly act on the basis of recommendations, resolutions, and statements of intent: that is, subdued forms of intervention. This type of law, agreeably termed 'soft law', is replacing the 'hard law' advocated by those who support control and command systems: as if law no longer dared speak its name. This new approach tends to downplay the role of legislation and to dilute the responsibility of public authorities in formulating and implementing public policies.

Fourthly, in order to act efficiently under these conditions, the national lawmaker no longer proceeds via a system of unilateral constraints imposing a definition of the common good upon social actors. The State has in effect altered its method of societal intervention by abandoning the classical legal imperative

---

[81] Fr. Ost, M. van de Kerchove, and Ph. Gérard (eds.), *L'accélération du temps juridique* (Brussels: Saint-Louis, 2000).

[82] Fr. Ost, *Le temps du droit* (Paris : Od. Jacob, 1999) 273.

[83] Ch.-A. Morand, n. 2 above, 69–89. A typical example is provided by Directive 2000/60/EC establishing a framework for Community action in the field of water policy. The central administrative tools to implement this Directive are the river management plans which Member States are required to produce for each river basin district.

(the 'thou shalt not' approach) in favour of a 'let's work together' approach that mingles aspirations, encouragement, and threats. Voluntary participation by those whom the State intends to regulate has in this way come to replace classical forms of State intervention, in the name of 'shared responsibility'. Self-regulatory mechanisms (eg voluntary labels, eco-audits, tradable pollution rights) under which those being administered are considered fully involved actors ('stakeholders') play a major role in most of these new public policies. Contract is thus transformed into a technique of governance, whereby everything is negotiable.[84]

Fifthly, the decline of State authority is often associated with an increased political role for civil society. New rights to information, participation, and remedy have been accorded to citizens in order both to integrate them into the process of defining and implementing public policies and to facilitate the subsequent acceptance of negotiated norms. In counterpart to this trend, law-makers at both the international and national levels have become increasingly open to the influence of human rights advocates, environmental NGOs, and other activist groups.[85]

Last but not least, the questioning of the primacy of Reason has brought in its wake a loss of confidence in science. The emergence of the precautionary principle faithfully reflects this scepticism about a mode of science which has too long been convinced of its supremacy over policy.[86]

To conclude, the evolution of various goal-oriented public policies and their legal instruments gives evidence of a continuous gradation—or degradation—among various normative options, ranging from command and control to contractual agreement. Rigidity (hard law) has given way to flexibility (eg ephemeral programmes, soft law instruments), vertical action (eg market licensing) to horizontal measures (eg the Global Environment Facility), and hierarchical practices to co-ordination (such as the EC's environmental action programmes). These changes undermine the core premises of modern law (eg hierarchy between legislative and executive norms, autonomy of the legal system, the identity of the legal subject). It would be easy to take international, EC, and national legislators to task for these developments, but we must accept that there are legitimate, factual reasons underlying them. Situations that were once simple have become extremely complex; foreseeable situations have become unpredictable. Belief in a single, indisputable scientific truth able to serve as a basis for rational policy decisions has given way to a 'plurality of truths' bearing the imprint of the risk society. These developments are obliging jurists to re-examine the theoretical foundations of law in gradualist terms rather than in terms of a binary opposition between law and non-law.

---

[84] Ph. Gérard, Fr. Ost, and M. van de Kerchove (eds.), *Droit négocié, droit imposé?* (Brussels: Saint-Louis, 1999).

[85] O. Schachter, 'The Decline of the Nation-State and its Implications for International Law' in *Essays in Honor of Prof. L. Henkin* (The Hague, London, Boston : Martinus Nijhoff, 1997) 18–20.

[86] See the discussion in Chapter 3 Subsection 4.1.1. above.

3.2. The characteristics of post-modern law

Modernity has entered a period of crisis, leading to the emergence of the concept of post-modernity. The linear and ordered structure of modern law has been succeeded—but not replaced—by complex, indeterminate, and disordered forms which recall the rhizome, the labyrinth, or the network: forms better able to account for a complex social organization that has left the path of order and simplicity.[87] In the world of post-modernity, law loses the attributes of autonomy, systematicity, generality, and stability that characterize modern law. Instead it becomes individualized, complex, and open to other disciplines.

3.2.1. *An individualized legal system*

One of the most significant characteristics of the post-modern legal paradigm is the individualization of rules in place of generality. Legal output is based less on deductive logic than on initiatives taken by multiple decision-makers enjoying an increasingly wide power of discretion. This has resulted in an anarchic proliferation of rules that has served to blur the outlines of the legal order, undermining the coherence of the system and disturbing its structure.

At both the international and national levels, legislation increasingly takes the form of framework laws formulated in line with major principles, leaving to administrations the task of defining how objectives are to be achieved.[88] Such a legal structure can only encourage the proliferation of fragmentary and unstable implementing measures. These in turn produce a haphazard collection of very precise rules setting out a wealth of detail in a desperate attempt to adhere to a shifting reality. The application of these rules is narrowly circumscribed in terms of both time and location, thus robbing the legal system of any pretence at the universality and long-term validity to which modern law laid claim.

3.2.2. *A legal system of mingling yet competing norms*

While modern law was conceived as being monolithic and hierarchical, post-modern law is characterized by circularity,[89] or at least a baroque approximation thereof.[90] International norms arising in different subject areas (trade law, human rights, economic and social rights, etc.) mingle and compete at the same time. As the globalization of economies progresses national legal orders are converging, at least at the regional level (eg the EC, NAFTA). EC law and the ECHR tend to merge into the legal orders of the Member States of the

---

[87] J. Chevallier, n. 6 above, 668; Fr. Ost and M. van de Kerchove, *De la Pyramide au Réseau? Pour une théorie dialectique du droit* (Brussels: Saint-Louis, 2002) 49–50.

[88] At the EC level there is a clear preference for framework directives instead of detailed legal acts. This is particularly the case of EC environmental law. Eg M. Pallemaerts, 'The Decline of Law as an Instrument of Community Environmental Policy' (1999) 3–4 L & EA 348–50.

[89] E. Luhmann, *Rechtssoziologie* (2nd edn., Opladen: Westdeutscher, 1999).

[90] On the concept of 'tangled hierarchies', see M. van de Kerchove and Fr. Ost, *Legal System Between Order and Disorder* (Oxford: OUP, 1994) 67–72; M. Delmas-Marty, *Pour un droit commun* (Paris: Le Seuil, 1994) 109.

European Community and the Council of Europe. New legal disciplines (such as consumer law or environmental law) challenge established boundaries between private and public law, international and national law, public and private interests.[91] Furthermore, the line between soft law and hard law is becoming indistinct as treaty mechanisms increasingly turn towards 'soft' obligations and non-binding instruments, in turn, incorporate mechanisms traditionally found in hard-law texts.[92] Even within national legal regimes the classical distinction between private and public law is growing blurred.

3.2.3. *An open legal system*

While modern law seeks to distinguish itself sharply from non-legal disciplines, rules of law in the post-modern perspective are no longer seen as being completely autonomous in relation to the extra-legal sphere. Rather, post-modern law is characterized by a much greater openness towards the economic, ethical, and policy spheres: in many cases legal and socio-economic realities are interdependent. Indeed, it is neither useful nor ultimately possible to work with international law in isolation, without reference to the social theory that describes inter-State relationships as well as normative views about the principles of justice which should govern international conduct.[93] In post-modern law highly abstract rules are open-ended in character, providing opposing values with the possibility of dialogue. That opening simultaneously serves to blur the boundaries of the legal system.

Courts will be tempted to draw inspiration from the social and political objectives of institutions that observe these principles to the extent that their wording provides a wide margin for interpretation. On the other hand, the more precise the formulation of these norms, the more restricted that margin will become.

3.3. The emergence of directing principles in post-modern law

Post-modernity is strongly marked by the emergence of a multitude of public policies intended to deal with welfare, unemployment, poverty, and violent crimes. Those post-modern policies are designed to achieve concrete ends in a way that general, impersonal rules are intended not to be. The programmes put in place are vast in scope and may include both legal and other types of measures.[94] The intentions that determine the definition and application

[91] W. Friedmann, *The Changing Structure of International Law*, n. 49 above, 190–5.

[92] D. Shelton, 'Law, Non-Law and the Problem of "Soft Law"' in D. Shelton (ed.), *Commitment and Compliance: The Role of Non-Binding Norms in the International Legal Systems* (Oxford: OUP, 2000) 10.

[93] M. Koskenniemi, n. 8 above, xiii.

[94] Thus, establishing the EC internal market was achieved following the entry into force of the Single European Act, on the basis of an enormous programme. In national legal systems, legally binding programmes (known as *lois-programmes* in France) are numerous, ranging from social security to the fight against pollution. For examples see Ch.-A. Morand, n. 2 above, 74–90.

of these programmes affect the workings of the legal order. Consequently, the interpretation of post-modern legislations requires 'a purposive, rather than a deductive mode of reasoning, and this in itself appears to erode the distinction between the process of making laws and that of applying them'.[95]

While modern law is devoid of precise objectives, these goal-oriented public policies are characterized by the proclamation of legal objectives and principles meant to set various social actors in motion. In the perspective of post-modern law, 'principles' no longer serve merely to rationalize law or to fill gaps in a given legal system, as did the general principles of law.[96] Rather, they are intended to spur public policies, to allow courts to weigh and reconcile highly divergent interests. These principles mark a policy path to be followed, outline the context within which the law-maker must act, and guide the course of his passage. For this reason we use the term 'directing principles'.[97] Breaking with the hierarchical model of modern law, which presents itself as a unified whole, directing principles rather serve to reconcile differing legal systems. As legal systems multiply and intersect, this new generation of principles plays an important role in maintaining the links among weakly structured networks, ensuring the practical effectiveness of the legal system as a whole.[98] While directing principles make it possible more effectively to integrate public laws with differing objectives (eg economic development and the environment; the Common Agricultural Policy and protection of the natural environment) they must also be capable of ensuring or guaranteeing effective conciliation between supra-national, national, and sub-national public policies.

In addition, post-modern law is characterized by a range of competing or conflicting social interests (eg full employment, clean environment). The task of defining and weighing them is delicate, putting a heavy burden on legislatures.[99] Executive authorities, under the control of courts, must carefully balance these various interests in order to reconcile them. Consequently, the technique of weighing interests is crucial in the resolution of conflicts (eg the principle of proportionality).[100]

Nevertheless, the emergence of a post-modern legal system and directing principles does not mean that its precedents have been set aside. There is no question of drawing a line under earlier forms of law-making and turning the page.[101] Codification is still fashionable in France, Germany, and the Netherlands, as well as in the Scandinavian countries. Despite the ascendancy of

---

[95] A. Barron, n. 9 above, 112.

[96] Fr. Moderne, n. 24 above, 740.

[97] This term is used by Ch.-A. Morand in his work on post-modern law and public policy, n. 2 above.

[98] Ch.-A. Morand, n. 2 above, 205; M. Delmas-Marty, n. 90 above, 117.

[99] A. Barron, n. 9 above, 113.

[100] That principle is considered at length in Chapter 5, Subsection 5.2. below.

[101] We therefore reject the deconstructionist theories put forward by many critics of post-modernism.

regulatory flexibility, the general principles of law are for the most part drawn up and applied by courts. In this context directing principles represent a continuation of modern law.[102] They are needed to introduce a degree of rationality in a world that has become Kafkaesque through the production of an excessive number of rules and a high degree of instability, which social actors find it extremely difficult to master. These principles serve to reassemble dispersed rules into a coherent whole, which in continental Europe has taken the form of attempts at codification. They provide order to this new view of the legal system. Used in this way, the principles assume a major role in carrying out codification.[103]

Thus, the crisis that is shaking legal systems is at the same time giving rise to a return to sources and a revival of rationality. The current phenomenon is therefore more one of coexistence between modern and post-modern law than replacement of the former. Just as it does not condemn rationality, post-modern law does not signal the end of principles. On the contrary: they will have to be rediscovered and adapted to an environment different from that in which they were conceived. In this new model the stress will not be on 'general principles of law', *principes généraux du droit*, *principios general del derecho*, or *Rechtsprinzipien* that ensure the coherence of the legal order, but rather on 'directing principles' intended to act as a spur to public policy.

4. ENVIRONMENTAL LAW BEARS THE MARKS OF POST-MODERNITY

The factors leading to post-modernity have been felt much more sharply in the field of environment than in other disciplines. Nuisances, originally specific as to location and time, have become diffuse and sustained. The ecological crisis that was once local has become planetary in nature. For this reason the number of institutional actors dealing with environmental risks has increased tremendously, in turn multiplying the number of regulations. In addition, the traditional relationship between science and policy has been disturbed. Harm to the environment, once considered reversible, is now understood often to be irreversible; scientific certainty has given place to uncertainty. Law must therefore constantly adapt to new policy requirements as the policy-maker tries to cope with the latest scientific developments. As a result, rather than being a strongly hierarchical system based on ideas of order, simplicity, and unity, environment law is flexible, its structure unsettled, and its outlines uncertain (Subsection 4.1 below). Nonetheless, this legal discipline continues to produce its own 'directing principles' (Subsection 4.2).

---

[102] See the discussion in Chapter 5, Section 2 below.

[103] In fact, codification remains a cherished ambition of governments. In France, for instance, a general programme of codification, aimed at creating 42 codes, was ordered on 4 December 1995. The Environment Code was published in 2000.

4.1. The characteristics of environmental law in a post-modern perspective

4.1.1. The opening of environmental law to non-legal disciplines

While modern law attempts to distinguish itself from non-legal disciplines, post-modern rules are characterized by much greater openness towards other sectors. This is particularly true for environment law: the borders separating this legal discipline from technology and science are becoming increasingly blurred.[104] On one hand legal norms are tending to lose their specificity in relation to other normative provisions as they come to rely more heavily on the latter (this is the case for precautionary measures that adhere too closely to the latest scientific discoveries). On the other hand rules of varying types are increasingly being muddled. Technical standards are being applied as though they were binding norms (for example, Codex Alimentarius standards are applied as international standards under the SPS Agreement) while classical legal rules are taking on a technical aspect meant to improve their efficiency, as the result of greater contact with science (eg EC regulations on hazardous substances or hazardous wastes).[105] In addition, the principles of environmental law are more strongly permeated by values than precise and complete rules, because of their high degree of abstraction and generality resulting from the use of vague concepts (precaution, prevention, reduction, integration) with their own dynamic. More-over, as discussed in Part I of this work, the principles of the polluter pays, prevention, and precaution are located precisely at the point where legal, economic, and scientific disciplines meet. Thus, as has long been evident, the polluter-pays principle has been considered more from an economic than from a legal perspective. Similarly, the precautionary principle, far from condemning the use of scientific expertise, demands an abundance of research. The same observation applies to the relationship between law and ethics: the polluter-pays principle translates an ideal of equity, while the precautionary principle brings ethics into play to defend the interests of future generations.[106]

4.1.2. The absence of a comprehensive and systematic legal order

The plurality of institutional actors in the field of environmental protection is impressive. 'Upstream', inter-governmental institutions such as the OECD, UNEP, UNECE, Council of Europe, OAU, and EC have been deeply involved

---

[104] E. Naim-Gesbert, *Les dimensions scientifiques du droit de l'environnement* (Brussels: Bruylant-VUB, 1999).

[105] P.H. Sand, 'Methods to Expedite Environment Protection: International Ecostandards' (1972) 66 AJIL 37–59; idem., *Transnational Environmental Law* (London, Boston, The Hague: Kluwer Law Int'l, 1999) 11–33.

[106] R. Attfield, 'The Precautionary Principle and Moral Values' in T. O'Riordan and J. Cameron (eds.), *Interpreting the Precautionary Principle* (London: Cameron & May, 1994) 157; A. Kiss, 'The Rights and Interests of Future Generations and the Precautionary Principle' in D. Freestone and E. Hey (eds.), *The Precautionary Principle and International Law* (London, Boston, The Hague: Kluwer Law Int'l, 1995) 19; W. Beckerman, 'The Precautionary Principle and our Obligations to Future Generations' in J. Morris (ed.), *Rethinking Risk and the Precautionary Principle* (London: IEA Publications, 2001).

in the elaboration of international standards. 'Downstream', public policies concerning the environment generally fall within the competence of numerous national actors (regions, provinces, communities, etc.) thus increasing the number of relevant regulators even further. Thus the global aspects of environmental law (harmonization of product norms, etc.) are being taken over by international institutions, while its local elements (nuisances, discharge authorizations, soil decontamination, land planning, nature conservation, etc.) are being assigned to domestic actors. In Europe the situation is further complicated by the addition of an extra legal level comprising EC law on one hand and the ECHR on the other. As the result of direct effect, these two legal orders are an integral part of national legal systems. Consequently, European legal output is the result of initiatives taken by multiple decision-makers enjoying an increasingly wide margin of discretion.[107] Directing principles of environment law, set out in both international law and in national legal regimes, are in turn characterized precisely by the fact that they are subject to widely varying definitions determined by any of the large number of institutions acting in this field.[108] In addition, those principles are indicative of the quasi-circularities referred to above.[109]

Whether in the context of international law, EC law, or national legal regimes, environment law is at present not monolithic in character. It in no way constitutes a coherent model. Law-making is decentralized, and the absence of adequate co-ordination between various initiatives taken at the global, regional, and sub-regional levels often results in measures that are duplicative, and sometimes even inconsistent.[110]

[107] D. Liefferink, P.D. Lowe, and P.J. Mol (eds.), *European Integration and Environmental Policy* (London, New York: Belhaven Press, 1993); D. Liefferink and M. Skou Andersen (eds.), *The Innovation of EU Environmental Policy* (Oslo, Copenhagen, Stockholm, Oxford, Boston: Scandinavian U.P., 1997); C. Demmke (ed.), *Managing European Environmental Policy: The Role of the Member States in the Policy Process* (Maastricht: European Institute of Public Administration, 1997).

[108] As we saw in Chapter 3 above, the number of actors involved in defining the precautionary principle, each in his own way, is so great that it is sometimes difficult to grasp the substance of the principle precisely; disagreements about the correct definition are thus frequent. See eg the discussion concerning the conflict between the SPS Agreement and the Cartagena Protocol on Biosafety, in Chapter 3, Subsection 2.1.1. above.

[109] With its origins in the German legal order, the precautionary principle was rapidly recognized in international conventions and subsequently integrated into the EC Treaty in 1993. Thereafter the relatively bold application of the precautionary principle within EC law (hormones, mad cow disease, ozone depletion) influenced both the national legal regimes of EC Member States and the international legal order (eg the adoption in 2000 of a definition of the precautionary principle within the *Codex Alimentarius*). This indicates to what extent a large number of legal regimes have influenced one another within less than a decade. Similarly, as we examine in greater detail in Chapter 7 below, recourse to the principle of reduction at source also demonstrates confused hierarchies, intermingling rules of law with clear content and the principles inspiring those rules. See the discussion in Chapter 7, Subsection 3.2. below.

[110] Ph. Sands, 'Environmental Protection in the Twenty-First Century: Sustainable Development and International Law' in R.L. Revesz, Ph. Sands, and R. Stewart (eds.), *Environmental Law, the Economy and Sustainable Development* (Cambridge University Press, 2000) 372.

Particularly problematic is the nature of international environment law, 'which has proceeded incrementally and in a piecemeal fashion'.[111] It has not so far been 'the product of any comprehensive or systematic scheme of law making, nor has it been based on any clearly defined pre-existing code of principles', despite the attempts made in 1992 at Rio.[112] Almost every issue has its own specific treaty and institutional structures and mechanisms (eg ozone pollution, whaling, oil pollution, etc.).

EC environment law, for its part, is particularly characteristic of this fragmentation. Under the pretext of integration, the legal bases for directives and regulations that contribute to protecting the environment are particularly numerous. Instead of being based solely on Article 175 of the EC Treaty—a provision that comes under Title XIX, 'Environment'—these acts may be based on Article 95 (internal market), Article 37 (Common Agricultural Policy), or Article 133 (common economic policy). Yet the objective of the internal market does not necessarily correspond to that of environment policy, which also has a conflictual relationship to the Common Agricultural Policy. And although ecological risks are generally interlinked they are not considered in a global manner; on the contrary, they are understood through sectoral EC regulations and directives with appreciably differing emphases.[113]

National laws, pulled in several directions by varying logics (civil, public, administrative, patrimonial, etc.) and based on reasoning that looks at once to ecosystems (water, air, soil), species (flora and fauna), activities (economic, social, recreational), and nuisances (pollution, hazardous substances, wastes, discharges, etc.) often consist of a set of disconnected provisions of diverse origins, constructed according to autonomous logics (rural, industrial, and land-use law) one part of which happens to have been recycled with the aim of protecting the environment.[114] The numerous rules that comprise environmental law—general and sectoral, recent and expired, progressive and conservative—espouse differing and at times conflicting objectives. Some of these provisions are intended to 'protect' or 'conserve' the environment, while others serve merely to 'manage' it, a neutral concept that seeks to reconcile varying socio-economic

---

[111] A. Boyle, 'Codification of International Environmental Law and the International Law Commission: Injurious Consequences Revisited' in A. Boyle and D. Freestone (eds.), *International Law and Sustainable Development*, (Oxford University Press, 1999) 64. International law relating to nature protection provides a classical illustration of this regulatory jumble: the 1971 Ramsar Convention on Wetlands of International Importance Especially as Waterfowl Habitats, the 1973 CITES Convention, the 1979 Bonn Convention on the Conservation of Migratory Species of Wild Animals, the 1979 Bern Convention on the Conservation of European Wildlife and Natural Habitats, and last but not least, the 1992 Rio Convention on Biological Diversity all deal with the conservation of biodiversity in one way or another, but it is not easy to map clear relationships between them.

[112] A. Boyle, n. 111 above, 64.

[113] C. Noiville and N. de Sadeleer, 'La Gestion des risques écologiques et sanitaires à l'épreuve des chiffres: Le droit entre eujeux scientifiques et politiques' (2001) 2 RDUE 389–449, 393–405.

[114] See, for instance, the case of German law, eg H. Pehle, 'Germany: Domestic Obstacles to an International Forerunner' in M. Skou Andersen and D. Liefferink (eds.), *European Environmental Policy: The Pioneers* (Manchester: Manchester U.P., 1997) 173–5.

interests.[115] Last but not least, environment law appeals to certain concepts that are themselves highly ambiguous: the laws that protect wild game at the same time set out the right to kill these animals; environmental taxes impose charges on the polluter while at the same time legitimizing his act of pollution.[116] We may therefore wonder whether the end result being sought is case-by-case regulation of ecological problems, devoid of any over-arching vision.

4.1.3. *The uncertain character of environmental norms*

Environmental law bears the marks of post-modernity particularly strongly, owing to the uncertain character of a number of its norms. Three factors explain why environmental norms have become uncertain:[117] the increasing influence of regulatory flexibility, evolving and controversial scientific and technical data, and the shattering of traditional legal boundaries. The interactions between these three factors have produced a legislative restlessness that is compromising the very concept of law.

In societies that are deeply divided about their core values and what projects should form the basis for societal action (economic growth or environmental protection, sustainable development or tenable growth) law-makers are no longer able to deal with problems in a clear-cut manner. Consequently, the rules of contemporary law seek not so much to order solutions according to a political programme as to manage complex systems through a series of adjustments aimed at achieving an (always provisional) balance. More than other branches of law, environment law has shown itself to be a field of unresolved compromise, where tensions between opposing interests are partly calmed but never completely eliminated (for example, authorization systems for placing dangerous substances on the market or operating listed installations).

Decisions generally follow a careful balancing of divergent interests through the use of over-refined procedures. When they do address the heart of a problem, compromise texts immediately peter out in a plethora of detail.[118] Or they make do with setting out the bases for minimal agreement, surrounded by a degree of woolliness that will allow each party provisionally to turn them to account: until the norm is once again renegotiated, having ceased entirely to satisfy the various actors concerned. Environment law at the international, EC, and national levels is completely submerged in this regulatory wave, at once master and slave of the policy it supports.

---

[115] N. de Sadeleer, 'La conservation de la nature au-delà des espèces et des espaces: L'émergence de concepts écologiques en droit international' in Ph. Gérard, Fr. Ost, and M. van de Kerchove (eds.), *Images et usages de la nature en droit* (Brussels: Saint-Louis, 1993) 186.

[116] See the discussion in Chapter 1, Subsection 3.1.2., above.

[117] X. Thunis, 'Le droit européen de l'environnement: Le discours et la règle' in E. Le Hardy de Beaulieu (ed.), *L'Europe et ses citoyens* (Brussels, Bern, Berlin, Frankfurt: Peter Lang, 2000) 153–6.

[118] This technique was strikingly evident in the regulatory approach put in place to prevent climate change. The very general 1992 UNFCCC gave birth to the 1997 Kyoto Protocol, which still needs clarification (2001 Marrakesh Agreement).

The regulatory flexibility phenomenon translates into a weighing of conflicting interests, either through preventive procedures (public inquiries, consultative committees) or deliberative procedures (negotiation among stakeholders). As a result the procedural aspect often overrides the substantive, with procedures serving to settle decisions among conflicting interests. Environmental norms are expressed on a case-by-case basis more often than in a general manner, which adds to their uncertainty. In the context of a profound questioning of the traditional functions of the State, contracts have become a favoured means of regulating the relationships between the public authorities and private actors.[119] When the law assumes a more substantive aspect—in other words, when it dares to prohibit—such systems are subject to multiple derogations that deprive basic texts of most of their meaning.[120]

A second element has increased the uncertainty of norms. In addition to being the result of successive political compromises, environmental law is constrained to adapt to a constantly changing dynamic even while, as part of the legal system, it must continue to anticipate long-term developments in order to ensure legal security. Indeed, the volume of legislation is merely keeping step with the development of the ecological crisis, like a belated and partial compensation for the results of growth. Law is thus being forced to run along behind evolving and controversial scientific and technical facts.[121] And scientific controversies rapidly turn into social—if not political—controversies about acceptable levels of risk (how safe is safe?). This constant questioning leads to the continual rewriting of the rules intended to protect the environment. The duration, content, stringency, and preciseness of norms cannot help but be affected by this process.

---

[119] Fr. Ost, 'A Game without Rules? The Ecological Self-Organization of Firms' in G. Teubner, L. Framer, and D. Murphy (eds.), *Environmental Law and Ecological Responsibility: The Concept and Practice of Ecological Self-Organization* (London: J. Wiley, 1994) 337; J. Golub (ed.), *New Instruments for Environmental Policy in the EU* (London, New York: Routledge, 1998); U. Collier (ed.), *Deregulation in the European Union* (London, New York: Routledge, 1998); P. Glasbergen (ed.), *Cooperative Environmental Governance* (Dordrecht, Boston, London: Kluwer, 1998); Elni, *Environmental Agreements: The Role and Effects of Environmental Agreements in Environmental Policies* (London: Cameron and May, 1998); R. Khalatschi and H. Ward, 'New Instruments for Sustainability: An Assessment of Environmental Agreements under EC Law' (1998) 10: 2 JEL 257–90; E. Rehbinder, 'Market-based Incentives for Environmental Protection' in R. Revesz, Ph. Sands, and R. Stewart (eds.), *Environmental Law*, n. 110 above, 245–79. At the EC level, see the European Commission Communication on Environmental Agreeements of 9 December 1996 (COM (96) 561 Final).

[120] For example, a wide-ranging reform aimed at natural habitats protection will necessarily require the adoption of a host of derogations on behalf of the interests affected by the new system (see Article 4 of Directive 79/409/EEC on wild birds). Another example is provided by Article 4(4) and (5) of Directive 2000/60/EC establishing a framework for Community action in the field of water policy, which allows a number of derogations regarding the objective of achieving a good ecological status.

[121] Directive 67/548/EEC on the classification, packaging, and labelling of dangerous substances has been modified 27 times. It is difficult and sometimes impossible in these circumstances to know the exact content of the provisions that have most often been modified and what exactly is in force. Eg A. Guggenbühl, 'Codification and Simplification of European Environmental Law' in C. Demmke (ed.), *Managing European Environmental Policy* (Maastricht: European Institute of Public Administration, 1997) 228. The need constantly to re-assess and amend existing environmental law in the light of new practices further burdens an already over-loaded agenda. Eg T. Evans, n. 1 above, 224.

Finally, norms have become uncertain as the traditional borders between legal regimes and branches of law are eroded by the constant to and fro between the specific and the general, the local and the global, the proximate and the biosphere. The distinctions between classical legal categories such as international and domestic law[122] or public and private law are becoming blurred:[123] victims of environmental damage do not distinguish between public law pollution and private law pollution: they experience pollution, full stop. Similarly, the jumbling of traditional categories is affecting the legal nature of regulatory acts. Both international and EC law give evidence of this confusion. A number of recent multilateral conventions contain a string of good intentions which place them in the category of soft rather than hard law. Some EC directives have become so precise and binding that they resemble regulations, while other directives are so vague in nature that they are essentially no more than statements of intent. As for EC regulations, although their provisions are obligatory and directly applicable in Member States (Article 242 of the EC Treaty) they are at present used as a framework for forms of voluntary participation by businesses (eco-audits, eco-labels).[124] In a rather unorthodox manner, their binding character has become dependent upon the agreement of the firms they are meant to regulate. This technique of contractualization gives rise to problems of legality in that directives are in principle meant to be transposed by regulatory acts.[125]

Environmental law is thus akin to Penelope's tapestry: what is accomplished in the light of day is unravelled under cover of darkness, as the performer-State attempts to avoid displeasing any member of its audience.[126] The result is an ephemeral body of law, subject to continuous revision as it seeks to grasp a shifting and uncertain body of scientific data and to satisfy conflicting interests. The effects of that meandering path are clear: normative value is inversely proportional to bureaucracy, while rules become weaker as their numbers grow. The greater the volume of a rule, the flimsier its content; the more prolific a legislator becomes, the less he is heeded; the more often he persists in turning to

[122] J. Ebbesson, *Compatibility of International and National Environmental Law* (London, The Hague, Boston: Kluwer Law Int'l, 1996), xxiii; 'The Notion of Public Participation in International Environmental Law' (1997) 8 YbIEL 55; Ph. Sands, 'Sustainable Development: Treaty, Custom, and the Cross-fertilization of International Law' in A. Boyle and D. Freestone (eds.), *International Law and Sustainable Development*, n. 111 above 42–3; F.L. Morrison, 'The Relationship of International, Regional, and National Environmental Law' in F.L. Morrison and R. Wolfrum (eds.), *International, Regional and National Environmental Law* (The Hague: Kluwer Law Int'l, 2000) 124–6.

[123] K.-H. Ladeur, 'Post-Modern Constitutional Theory: A Prospect for the Self-Organising Society' (1997) 60:5 MLR 620–2.

[124] Regulation (EC) No. 1980/2000 on a revised Community eco-label award scheme; Regulation (EC) No. 761/2001 allowing voluntary participation by organizations in a Community eco-management and audit scheme (EMAS).

[125] In this regard the recent Commission Communication on Environmental Agreements allows Member States to implement their obligations under environmental directives through negotiated agreements between Government authorities and the private sector. This of course constitutes an anomaly in the context of ECJ case-law, according to which only binding instruments can implement directives (Case C-361/88, *Commission v. Germany* [1991] ECR I-2567).

[126] Fr. Ost, *La nature hors la loi* (Paris: La Découverte, 1995) 115.

technology for solutions, the more firmly he becomes its slave. The result is law by experts, in full contradiction to the democratic ideal of participation and transparency put forward by those who want to protect the environment.[127]

This growing instability of rules gives rise to permanent insecurity among those governed by such systems. The core function of law—to stabilize social relations—is being called into question. Moreover, the proliferation and obsolescence of texts contributes to a failure to apply them. Finding themselves in a legal tangle, courts and administrators will finally adopt an opportunistic approach to law. Rules will only be applied to the extent that they suit a given situation.

4.2. The emergence of directing principles of environmental law in a post-modern perspective

We have noted at several junctures in this work how strongly environmental law has been marked by the presence of principles (precaution, prevention, the polluter-pays, sustainability, substitution, self-sufficency, proximity, integration, participation, reduction of pollution at source, co-operation, stand-still)[128] compared with other legal disciplines. Several factors have contributed to the success of principles in the field of environment law. First, they assume a symbolic function, in that law-makers readily set forth principles when they are instituting new regimes. It is no accident that the activating principles whose absence had long been proclaimed a major failing began to flourish in substantive texts just as a process of codification began. It took the amendment of the Treaty of Rome by the SEA in 1987 formally to recognize a number of principles in EC policy, although they had already been propagated through numerous recommendations and directives. By proclaiming the principles in a treaty or a framework law, States Parties and national legislators elevate an emerging field of law to the level of more established regimes which have over time already taken shape around their own principles. The affirmation of environmental principles thus also fulfils a programmatic, and even pedagogical, function. As instruments that involve public authorities in a process of change, they are reformatory rather than stabilizing. By setting out these principles, the legislator is in fact announcing the norms of tomorrow.

Secondly, in addition to their symbolic and programmatic dimensions, these directing principles also function as the keystone for the structuring and systematization intended to remedy the deficiencies of a law that developed in a piecemeal manner on the basis of scattered and fragmentary provisions. From a number of directions at once, law-makers brought forth principles intended to serve as guide-posts around which dispersed laws could be reassembled and

---

[127] See the discussion in Chapter 5, Section 3 below.

[128] For an overview of the different environmental principles in Europe eg N. de Sadeleer, *Les principes du pollueur-payeur, de prévention et de précaution*, n. 18 above, 25–215; P. Gilhuis and A.H.J. Van den Biesen (eds.), *Beginselen in Het Milieurecht* (Alphen a/d Rhine, Kluwer, 2001) 7–12. See the discussion in Subsection 3.3. above.

structured within an entirely new rule-making entity. The codification of environment law and the enunciation of the principles underpinning that new law constitute the culmination of this process of rationalization. Thus, directing principles are primarily intended to impel environment law towards the reforms necessary for adaptation of the new challenges that are constantly arising in the field of the environment.[129]

Thirdly, strategic needs also encourage recourse to these principles. Their generality makes it easier to overcome the protests that habitually greet rules that are too precisely formulated. They attract agreement from various interest groups more easily than their more precise counterparts, owing to their relative flexibility. They inevitably facilitate the adoption of reforms that do not dare proclaim their true nature. For instance, international environmental regulation cannot be achieved immediately by clear and precise legal rules applicable in all circumstances. Directing principles, however, make it possible to set parameters for new obligations and thereby encourage subsequent negotiations on more detailed commitments. Principles enshrined in environmental framework conventions are known to facilitate the adoption of more detailed implementation mechanisms through protocols.[130]

In particular, the polluter-pays, preventive, and precautionary principles are emblematic of the functions that directing principles must assume in the context of a public policy that stresses flexibility, adaptability, and pluralism. They constitute key means by which to attenuate contradictions and antagonisms and harmonize domestic and supra-national policies. Their presence in both soft and hard law is due precisely to the fact that environmental law is more strongly characterized by post-modern elements than any other. These principles may properly be referred to as 'directing principles'. As we shall see in the next Chapter, recourse to those directing principles is encouraged to the extent that, unlike precise rules, they make it possible for divergent values and interests to coexist, by providing the flexibility needed for adaptations able to balance all the interests that must be taken into consideration in a given case. Overly precise rules are far too decisive to support multiple public policies liable to contradict each other at every turn. The directing principles of the polluter pays, prevention, and precaution do not suffer from this burden of detail and thus allow courts to weigh and reconcile highly divergent interests with maximum flexibility.

Consequently, the highly creative function that the court assumes when elaborating general principles of law is no longer relevant when setting forth these principles. The judicial alchemy that makes it possible to build a general principle of law from a number of dispersed rules by use of inductive

---

[129] N. de Sadeleer, *Les principes du pollueur-payeur, de prévention et de précaution*, n. 18 above, 280; C.W. Backes, C.J. Bastmeijer, A.A. Freriks, R.A.J. van Gestel, J.M. Verschuuren, *Codificatie van milieurechtelijke beginselen in de Wet milieubeheer* (The Hague: Boom, 2002).

[130] For instance, Article 3, UNFCCC sets out 'Principles' intended to guide the Parties 'in their actions to achieve the objective of the Convention and to implement its provisions'. See the discussion in Chapter 5, Section 2.2. below.

reasoning[131] has no place here. These three principles, which have already been put forward by law-makers at both the international and national levels, are meant to be applied by public authorities. Nonetheless, the distinction in the field of environmental law between general principles of law on one hand and directing principles of statutory origin on the other is more subtle than might at first appear.

The statement that general principles of law are merely the result of judicial activism cannot be taken as absolute, for these principles are often specifically set forth in statute provisions. In addition, *a priori* nothing prevents courts from inferring these principles from sources of written law. The polluter-pays principle could thus be induced from fiscal laws based on the fact that these tend to insist that the polluter bear the cost of the pollution he has caused, while the principle of prevention could be derived from a wide range of legal instruments (planning, assessment, authorization, monitoring, auditing, etc.) that give evidence of an intention to prevent rather than repair environmental damage. Thus, no one may be considered to have a monopoly over the elaboration and use of environmental law principles: the judge as well as the legislator may systematically set forth such principles.

Consequently, the distinction to be made between general principles of law and the polluter-pays, preventive, and precautionary principles relates to the functions these latter principles fulfil within the legal order rather than to their origin. In Chapter 5 below we fully examine the varied functions that the polluter-pays, preventive, and precautionary principles play in an increasingly complex legal world.

5. Concluding observations

A new type of law is today emerging which clearly departs from the coherent and deductive methods that form the basis of modern law, considered as an autonomous system. The structure in which basic norms generate derived rules is today being challenged by the appearance of confused hierarchies where norms and derived rules may no longer be distinguished. At first glance this new type of law appears extremely disordered: the general is to give way to the particular and continuity to timeliness, and imprecision is to replace rigour.

How can law be taught in these circumstances? How can it be applied, except by keeping up with legal developments and taking great care to keep abreast of the latest legal texts and most recent case-law? Influenced by the acceleration of legal time, an emphasis on negotiation and a rapid growth in the number of law-makers, can such a system remain viable? Not if post-modernism continues to express itself in a form that appears to be chaotic.

---

[131] See the discussion in Subsections 2.2.1 and 2.4. above.

Now, it is not at all certain that post-modernism is ringing the knell of rationality. Indeed, there has never been such great need for rationality as there is today, where the legal system is in a state of extreme agitation. For that reason, to posit a rupture between modern law and post-modern law is to underestimate the heritage of modernity. In fact, today's States are based on the rule of law, which has not yet been seriously challenged by contending systems: codification is continuing apace and rules continue to be interpreted according to a principle of the hierarchy of norms. The structure of legal rules has thus resisted the challenge of post-modernity much more effectively than the champions of post-modernity would have us believe.

Following upon a series of doctrinal studies carried out in francophone Europe, this book has strongly supported the thesis that post-modernity cannot be understood in a deconstructionist perspective[132] as an anti-modernist system; rather, it must be seen as the rediscovery of the values that form the basis for modernity.[133] Hence rationality must be restored to its rightful place, serving as a corrective to the results of post-modernity, even if it differs conceptually from the rationality that permeated the elaboration of modern law. This rediscovery of rationality, expressed particularly through the mediation of directing principles, should lead us to reconsider the relationships among conflicting interests, different branches of law, and varying legal systems. Their purpose is to construct the bridges needed to provide rationality to a system characterized by multiplicity rather than unity.

In addition, we consider that post-modernism in no way threatens the legitimacy of general principles of law[134] but rather serves to establish them more firmly, by adding a new category of principles—directing principles—which play an essential role in defining and implementing public policies. They are more useful in identifying the aims that public authorities should pursue than as a postulate of coherence and completeness. Finally, nothing would prevent the directing principles that we have described in Part I from eventually evolving into general principles of law that could be used to fill the gaps arising in a legal discipline which has not yet attained full maturity.

---

[132] The deconstruction of secular rationalism is central to post-modernism. Eg A. Carty, (ed.), *Post-Modern Law*, n. 9 above, 4.

[133] J. Chevallier, n. 6 above, 682–7.

[134] Fr. Moderne, n. 3 above, 742.

5

The Evolving Function of Environmental Directing Principles in the Transition from Modern to Post-modern Law

1. INTRODUCTORY REMARKS

In the Introduction to Part II we emphasized the modifications that legal principles have undergone in the passage from modern to post-modern law. General principles of law formulated by the courts in order to fill legal gaps (eg the principle of good faith) would be supplemented by directing principles set forth by the legislator with the aim of providing a more precise orientation for public policies (eg the principles of social security). Nevertheless, the emergence of this new category of principles does not replace the general principles of law, just as the growing importance of post-modernity does not eliminate all the characteristics of modern law. Indeed, in Chapter 4 we put forward the thesis that postmodernity is less a complete rupture with modernity than the rediscovery of the values underlying modernity within an evolving context. In reality the passage from modern to post-modern law is an extremely subtle phenomenon of constant interaction between these two models. The tensions between them appear precisely at the level of legal principles.

In the field of environment law the principles of the polluter pays, prevention, and precaution discussed in Part I lie at the heart of the interaction between modernity and post-modernity: Janus-like, modernity looks to the past while post-modernity looks towards the future. We consider these two facets in the two first sections of this Chapter, through a theoretical analysis of the phenomena of procedural law and codification, among others (Sections 2 and 3).

Post-modern law is characterized by the emergence of a new generation of human rights, among them the human right to environmental protection. That right could reinforce the duty of the public authorities to err on the side of caution by granting greater protection to environmental interests. We therefore also address the subtle interaction between this right and the polluter-pays, preventive, and precautionary principles (Section 4).

Furthermore, in a post-modern context directing principles make it possible to resolve hard cases and bear heavily on the weighing of interests. Looking carefully at recent WTO, ECJ, and ECtHR case-law one can already observe the impact those principles could have on the constitutive elements of proportionality (Section 5).

2. DIRECTING PRINCIPLES MAINTAIN A LINK WITH MODERN LAW

The ideal of rationality upon which modernity is based does not disappear with the emergence of the three directing principles of the polluter pays, prevention, and precaution. To the contrary, as we shall see below, these may serve to enhance the importance of this slightly tarnished ideal. Rationality in this context takes the form of an antidote against the transformations undergone by the legal system as a whole under the influence of regulatory flexibility, the acceleration of legal time, and the multiplicity of normative authorities. Nonetheless, the establishment of directing principles such as the polluter-pays, preventive, and precautionary principles could provide greater coherence to this field of law; indeed, without directing principles there is a risk that the evolution of environment law will continue to be determined by political fashion. They should serve to clarify the object of environment law. Such precision is indispensable given the conflicts of interest that set this branch of law apart from other public policies and from basic rights and fundamental freedoms (Subsection 2.1). At the same time, these directing principles can also play a major role in the codification processes taking place in several continental States (Subsection 2.2).

2.1. Directing principles serve to refine the purposes of environmental law

Under modern law the State renounced the right to introduce specific public policy objectives into private law. Thus private law, particularly contract law, has always been considered a mere framework within which economic actors could freely engage in contractual relations, without State interference. Modern law thus leaves actors (for example contracting parties) free to follow their own ends.

By contrast, as we saw in Chapter 4 above, post-modern law is characterized by the increase in public policies, including that of environmental protection. Those policies are strongly marked by the objectives assigned them, expressed in the form of either goals or principles. In that context public authorities attempt to depart from the role of arbiter that modern law had assigned them, seeking instead to assist directly in realizing the major goals that will henceforth define public policies (eg environmental protection, full employment, right to housing, etc).[1] But these policies, particularly environment policy, are not devoid of rationality, which would constitute a complete rupture with modernity. To the

---

[1] R. Dworkin opposes principles to policies. He calls a policy 'that kind of standard that sets out a goal to be reached, generally an improvement in some economic, political or social feature of the community'. Thus the standard that the incidence of car accidents is to be reduced is a policy. See *Taking Rights Seriously* (Cambridge, Mass.: Harvard U.P., 1978) 22.

contrary, we shall see how the principles of the polluter pays, prevention, and precaution serve to re-establish the coherence of the legal system by specifying the purposes of environment law, in an extremely modern perspective.

First, the insertion of directing principles such as the polluter pays, preventive, and precautionary principles into framework laws can help to clarify the purpose of the multitude of laws relating to the environment. In displaying such principles, environment law should pursue a *sui generis* course. Decked out in its new finery, it could transform itself into a 'right to the environment' or a 'right for the environment'. This choice is not an innocent one. Understood in terms of 'protection' rather than 'management', the rules that comprise environment law could no longer be analysed and interpreted in a neutral manner: the affirmation of prevention, precaution, and the responsibility of the polluter for pollution implies a commitment to protect the environment in order to meet the needs of present and future generations.[2]

Some examples demonstrate how the use of directing principles can transform borrowings from relatively classical disciplines into instruments adapted to the pursuit of a new objective: protection of the environment. The enunciation of a principle of waste management without danger for health and the environment set out in Article 4 of Directive 75/442/EEC on waste, for example, provides an environmental objective for a whole series of provisions relating to the management of waste.[3] The precautionary principle appears to be shifting the orientation of impact assessment regimes, which until now have been based more on formal obligations (through means of an impact assessment) than on substantive requirements (consideration of the ecological admissibility of a project).[4] Environmental taxation strongly reflects the influence of the prevention and polluter-pays principles on environmental taxation. This is less a tax in the classic sense of the term than an innovative fiscal instrument intended to alter the behaviour of both producers and consumers.[5]

The reparation of ecological damage, a central theme of environmental law, assumes a highly specific character when moulded by the preventive principle, to the extent that it breaks completely with the classical understanding of liability law. Fault is called upon to give way to risk, the certainty of causation is thrown into question in the name of presumptive evidence, and damage is presumed to be collective in character rather than individual and personal.[6] Thus the directing principles help ensure the coherence of environmental law by enhancing the ideal of rationality.

---

[2] J. Cameron, W. Wade-Gery, and J. Abouchar, 'Precautionary Principle and Future Generations' in E. Agius and S. Busuttil (eds.), *Future Generations and International Law* (London: Earthscan, 1998) 110–13.

[3] Cases C-175/98 and C-177/98, *Paolo Lirussi* [1999] ECR I-6881, paras. 51 and 53.

[4] See the discussion in Subsection 5.1.3., Chapter 3, above.

[5] T. O'Riordan (ed.), *Ecotaxation* (London: Earthscan, 1997).

[6] G. Martin, *Le droit de l'environnement* (Paris: Publications périodiques spécialisées, 1979); *idem*, *Le dommage écologique* (Paris: PIREN, 1989).

2.2. Directing principles are indispensable to the codification of environmental law

Since the beginning of the 1970s, when the Stockholm Declaration on the human environment was proclaimed and the first environment laws adopted, considerable progress has been made in the field of environment law. The structures set in place at the international, European, national, and local levels have contributed largely to the multiplication of normative texts intended to protect the environment. University teaching and a profusion of books and articles dedicated to the subject attest to the growing interest of jurists in this field of law, as much for what is at stake as for the originality of the instruments deployed.

A success of this kind should indicate that environment law will henceforth display all the characteristics of a settled legal discipline. When we speak of a new branch of law this should necessarily imply that the legal rules comprising that branch be sufficiently structured around a common object. Environment law, however, has no defined object and concept that permit of a unitary systematization. It is of course oriented towards preservation of the natural basis of life, but this is a weak justification for recognizing a body of law as a separate discipline. In addition, some of the instruments intended to distinguish environmental law from other legal disciplines are not in any way original: the permits required to operate listed installations are essentially the same as other administrative authorizations; criminal offences relating to the environment are merely a special aspect of criminal law; procedural rights such as the right to participation, *locus standi*, or the right to information may also be found in other parts of the legal system such as administrative regulations; and strict liability is not specific to environment law.

The proliferation of norms intended to protect the environment calls to mind the birth of labour law. Despite pressing requests from legal scholars for greater homogeneity, regulations continue to be adopted in isolation rather than as part of a comprehensive vision.[7] Legal production snowballs as ecological problems increase. Yet while the volume of laws is increasing their quality is declining: hence the chain of new rules being tacked on to out-of-date and unsuitable legal frameworks, rapidly obsolescent in turn.[8] Owing to the diversity and fragility of its sources, international environment law is even less cohesive than national laws. And EC environment law, splintered amongst a multitude of legal bases, is hardly a model of coherence. As we noted above, such fragmentation is particularly characteristic of post-modernity.[9]

---

[7] A lack of legal clarity and transparency, as well constant amendment of provisions, are particularly characteristic of the environmental field, both within the EC Member States and at EC level. See, for example, C. Demmke and J. Hochgürtel, 'The Quality of EC Law: The Case of the Environment' in C. Demmke (ed.), *Managing European Environmental Policy: The Role of the Member States in the Policy Process* (Maastricht : European Institute of Public Administration, 1997) 192.

[8] N. de Sadeleer, 'L'universitaire confronté à la régulation: L'expérience du droit de l'environnement' in Fr. Ost and B. Jadot (eds.), *Elaborer la loi: Mission impossible?* (Brussels: Saint-Louis, 1999) 155–64.

[9] See the discussion in Chapter 4 above.

Yet without a minimal degree of coherence environment law will in the long run be composed of many laws but little law. A reordering of environment law, at all political levels, is thus a priority of the first order. Codification has been put forward as one possible response[10] and could become the favoured vehicle for the rationalization of law. It would allow environment law to regain coherence and would thus perpetuate a modern vision of the law.

Yet such a code should not limit itself to reflecting the present state of law; it must go beyond simply compiling various provisions relating to a specific subject in a single text.[11] By systematically and exhaustively assembling scattered rules into a common body, codification must not merely put an end to the dispersion of sources but must also order those sources along rational lines.[12]

Legal principles represent precisely those lines that would make it possible to put some order into the current legal chaos. In conformity with their etymology (from the Latin *principium*) principles should act as a first cause, a matrix from which more precise rules naturally follow. On that basis principles play an essential role in the construction of legal systems; reflecting values and guiding concepts, they transcend the rules of positive law and provide them with a rational structure.[13] They thus represent one facet of a systematic process of rationalization which translates specifically into a logical systematization of the rules that make up the subject.[14]

Directing principles of environmental law, such as the polluter-pays, prevention, and precaution principles, should propel codification by providing a system to underpin any new code.[15] In this way, rather than being compiled and

[10] E. Rehbinder, 'Points of Reference for a Codification of National Environmental Law' in H. Bocken and D. Ryckbost (eds.), *Codification of Environmental Law* (The Hague: Kluwer Law Int'l, 1996) 157; *idem*, 'Towards a Codification of European Chemicals Law' in G. Winter (ed.), *Risk Assessment and Risk Management of Toxic Chemicals in the EC* (Baden-Baden: Nomos, 2000) 197.

[11] Concerning the difficulty of distinguishing between 'consolidation', 'codification', and 'simplification' in EC environment law see eg A. Guggenbühl, 'Codification and Simplification of European Environmental Law' in C. Demmke (ed.), *Managing European Environmental Policy*, n. 7 above, 221–50. For France, see the criticisms of the environmental code made by P. Lascoumes and G. Martin, 'Des droits épars au Code de l'environnement' (1995) 30–1 Droit et Société 334.

[12] M. van de Kerchove and Fr. Ost, *Legal System: Between Order and Disorder* (Oxford University Press, 1994) 74–7.

[13] 'General principles of international law may, as a *material* source of law, have an important persuasive force and formative function, in that they may influence the content of new rules of international law to be formed through international agreement or custom'. Eg J.G. Lammers, 'General Principles of Law Recognized by Civilized Nations' in *Essays on the Development of the International Order* (Panhuys) (Alphen a/d Rijn: Sijthaf & Noordhoff, 1980) 53–75, 69.

[14] N. de Sadeleer, 'Het milieurecht, een rechtsgebied in wording' in R. Foqué and S. Gutwirth (eds.), *Vraagstukken van milieurechtelijke begripsvorming* (Rotterdam: Goda Quint, 2000) 147–65.

[15] It would be advisable to codify only those principles of real relevance, for example directing principles such as precaution, prevention, and the polluter-pays. In any case these must be flagged, for example by inclusion in general articles, in order to indicate what the law-maker considers fundamental values. This is what the authors of the SEA did in amending the Treaty of Rome, by placing principles immediately after the Treaty's purposes. That step was subsequently followed by the French, Belgian, and Swedish legislators. For France, see Article 100–1 of the French Environmental Code; for Belgium, see Article 1.2.1, para. 2 of the 1995 Decree of the Flemish Region containing general provisions for environment policy and Article 4 of the 1999 Belgian law aiming at protection

juxtaposed through the addition of purely formal modifications, rules could be set out in a hierarchy according to a logical system. By removing contradictions, eliminating redundancy, and completing unfinished portions of the subject, principles should serve to guide the codifier in fully reworking the relevant normative texts. A long-term effort is required to arrest the current proliferation of compromise texts, which are both provisional and fragmented. Directing principles clearly guarantee the coherence—the main characteristic of modern law—at present lacking in environment law. They provide systematic unity for heterogeneous rules, thereby resolving contradictions and filling in gaps.

In addition to serving as a basis for codification, environmental directing principles clearly distinguish environmental law from other bodies of law and help it to become a specific branch of law. Environmental law is particular precisely because it is largely governed by directing principles, which do not exist in other areas of law.[16] Moreover, environment policy is the only policy area for which the EC Treaty lays down a set of principles upon which to 'base' secondary legislation. No directing principle has been foreseen for other EC policies: social, education, professional training, youth, culture, public health, consumer protection, industry, etc.

The autonomy and coherence suitable for a new legal discipline thus go together with the affirmation of fitting directing principles. Imprinted with those principles, environment law may continue its rise and eventually achieve the same status as other branches of law. But that result can only be realized after serious reform. Given the current proliferation of rules intended to protect the environment, an in-depth renovation of the field's legal structure is more necessary than ever. The mere existence of principles is not sufficient to turn environment law into a branch of law. Failing substantial reform, it is to be feared that this area of law will be condemned to follow in the wake of the fashion of the day.

3. Directing principles restrain the excesses of post-modern law

Even though they serve to restore coherence to the legal system, the polluter-pays, preventive, and precautionary principles are highly characteristic of

---

of the marine environment in marine areas under Belgian jurisdiction; for Sweden, see the 1998 Environment Code (*Miljöbälk*). For the proposal to codify in German law the precautionary, polluter-pays, and co-operation principles see Kloepfer/Rehbinder/Schmidt-Assmann/Kunig, *Umweltgesetz-buch*, Allgemeiner Teil, Berichte [reports] 7/90 (Berlin, Umweltbundesamt [Federal Environmental Agency] 1990) 40 and 138. For Netherlands see the proposals for a codification of various environmental principles in the *Wet milieubeheer* made by C.W. Backes, C.J. Bastmeijer, A.A. Freriks, R.A.J. van Gestel, and J.M. Verschuuren, *Codificatie van milieurechtlijke beginselen in de Wet milieubeheer* (The Hague: Boom, 2002).

[16] E. Rehbinder, 'The Precautionary Principle in an International Perspective' in *Miljorettens grundsporgsmaal* (Copenhagen, 1994) 91.

post-modern law. First and foremost, by openly proclaiming new orientations these directing principles enrich the formulation and implementation of environment law by State authorities within a post-modern perspective. In other words, they can stimulate new public policies. We consider below how these three principles could guide law-makers and frame the discretionary power of administrations. Influencing legislative procedures, these directing principles promote legislative reform and inspire environmental law to adapt to new challenges (Subsection 3.1.) By more clearly defining the limits within which public administrations exercise their discretionary powers, they provide authorities with a more coherent orientation and consequently legitimize their actions (Subsection 3.2.). Finally, we show that these principles will not necessarily have an effect on legal certainty (Subsection 3.3.).

3.1. Directing principles guide the legislator

Principles are in the first instance meant to guide the legislator, who must breathe life into them by adopting specific implementing laws. At the national level the law-maker then implements the principles through sectoral legislation. For example, the general provisions of most fiscal legislation relating to environment are firmly grounded in the polluter-pays principle.[17] The precautionary principle, recognized in a number of German sectoral laws, has decisively influenced the development of German environment law despite its vagueness, notably by setting ambitious objectives that in turn give rise to implementing mechanisms.[18] Adopted by the Swedish authorities, the precautionary principle has played a similarly important role in chemical products policy in that country.[19] The same is true for international environment law, with implementing agreements (protocols) being guided by the basic principles set out in framework conventions.[20] In EC law, Directives concerning impact assessment, industrial risks, and listed installations transpose the preventive principle set out in Article 174(2) of the EC Treaty, while Directives related to biotechnology and biocides are beginning to bring the precautionary principle into play.[21]

It is true that such sectoral controls might have come into being in the absence of directing principles, but it is highly likely that the dynamic character of those principles has propelled legislative advances. Thus, far from merely providing a sensible basis for ordering norms already in force, those principles help promote the reforms required to confront new challenges.

---

[17] See the discussion in Chapter 1, Subsection 4.1. above.

[18] S. Bolhmer-Christiaensen, 'The Precautionary Principle in Germany: Enabling Government' in T. O'Riordan and J. Cameron (eds.), *Interpretating the Precautionary Principle* (London: Cameron and May, 1994) 55.

[19] A. Kronsell, 'Sweden: Setting a Good Example' in S. Andersen (ed.), *European Environmental Policy: The Pioneers* (Manchester, New York: Manchester U.P.,1997) 53.

[20] D. Hunter, J. Salzman, and D. Zaelke, *International Environmental Law and Policy* (New York: Foundation Press, 1998) 319.

[21] See the discussion in Chapter 3, Subsection 2.2.3.2. above.

Their dynamic is indispensable to such reforms, in that the environmental measures to which they give rise must correspond to realities that are undergoing constant modifications, disappearances, and reappearances. Some of the principles we have considered are also likely to evolve on their own as the result of feedback from the reforms they have themselves set in train. The importance of the polluter-pays principle, for example, originally limited to considering the suppression of State aids, has evolved within two decades into a much more comprehensive internalization of pollution costs.[22]

Yet, although set out in law, the directing principles nonetheless evidence a certain fragility. Even when they are recognized in framework conventions or legislations, they are never secure from the forces of circumstance, since nothing prevents the law-maker from renouncing their use. Similarly, they may at any time be contradicted by the protocols or the sectoral laws intended to put them into effect, because they occupy the same level in the hierarchy of norms. If they are to play a significant role in guiding law-makers, it would be preferable to set them out at the highest level of the legal order: in the case of Continental legal regimes, in the Constitution.

In the EC legal order that was certainly the intention of the authors of the European Single Act, who inserted these principles among the highest rules of that legal order rather than, as earlier, among the rules of secondary legislation. The results of their choice are far from negligible: EC institutions are constrained to 'base' the Directives, Regulations, and Recommendations adopted in the field of environment on, among others, the polluter-pays, preventive, and precautionary principles.[23]

We should not forget, however, that principles are never sufficient in and of themselves. The law-maker cannot merely set forth principles in the form of a wish-list without engaging in concrete legislative revisions. Rather, he must legislate—area by area, procedure by procedure—in order to breathe life into the principles set out in framework laws. Precaution, for example, must be translated into provisions that oblige administrations to call on expert opinion and allow them to reconsider decisions when a new risk emerges. Only a profound reform of administrative policies regarding environmental principles can provide a framework for public administrations and facilitate the task of courts, which will be more likely to review all procedural obligations in this context.

3.2. Directing principles delimit the discretionary power of administrations

When the law-maker proclaims the polluter-pays, preventive, and precautionary principles he is also addressing subordinate administrations: regulatory as well as individual decisions will henceforth be required to conform to the principles

---

[22] See the discussion in Chapter 1, Subsection 2.2.2. above.
[23] See the discussion in Chapter 6 below.

set out in the law. These directing principles will thus serve as guides and signals for the use of discretionary powers by administrative authorities. Taking this a step further, German doctrine considers that the precautionary principle derived from various sectoral laws constitutes a line of legal policy that constrains State agencies charged with enacting the law.[24]

This effect of principles on administrative practice is fully justified. Public authorities increasingly require guidance as they find themselves daily having to balance interests that demand the use of wide discretionary powers. Balancing interests in the field of environment policy is so complex that it demands that impact assessments be carried out to draw up a detailed analysis of biotic and abiotic conditions and the environmental, economic, and social consequences of projects.[25] These preliminary analyses constitute a powerful means of rationalizing the balancing of interests, which should subsequently be carried out in the light of principles meant to ensure that discretionary powers are not used arbitrarily.

For instance, the central provision governing the issuance of environmental licences in the Netherlands simply stipulates that 'a licence may only be refused in the interest of protecting the environment'.[26] Such a norm, which is open to varying interpretations, increases the discretionary power of the licensing authorities. Introducing directing principles into a framework environment law would add content to this norm and thus render the administrative decision-making process more precise.[27] The issuing and revision of licences and the formulation of general rules for individual industrial sectors might all have a sounder legal basis by reference to directing principles, which could clarify the grounds for administrative decisions for both citizens and the legal authorities. Other examples can be found in EC law. For instance, when authorizing a project with significant effects on a protected natural area, national authorities must balance the 'imperative reasons of overriding public interest' that justify the project against the obligation to prevent irreversible damage to biodiversity.[28] The implementation of the obligation to use the best available technologies under the IPPC Directive, related to the preventive principle, also leads to some balancing of environmental and economic interests.[29]

---

[24] B. Bender *et al.*, *Umweltrecht* (3rd edn., Heidelberg: C.F. Müller, 1995) 26.

[25] 1991 Espoo Convention on Environmental Impact Assessment in a Transboundary Context; Directive 85/337/EEC on EIA.

[26] Article 8(10), Netherlands Environmental Management Act.

[27] P. Gilhuis, 'Consequences of the Introduction of Environmental Law Principles in National Law' in M. Sheridan and L. Lavrysen (eds.), *Environmental Law Principles in Practice* (Brussels: Bruylant, 2002) 45.

[28] Article 6(4) of Directive 92/43/EEC on the conservation of natural habitats and of wild fauna and flora. On the weighing of conflicting interests in the case of projects affecting special bird protection areas, see eg A. Nollkaemper, 'Habitat Protection in EC Law: Evolving Conceptions of a Balance of Interests' (1997) 9 JEL 271; N. de Sadeleer, 'L'étendue de la marge de manœuvre dans la transposition des règles communautaires' (2000) 16: 3 RFD Adm. 611–35.

[29] IPPC Directive, Article 3(c). See the discussion in Chapter 2, Subsection 4.2. above.

Scholars recognize the guiding role played by certain principles of environmental law as regards subordinate powers in EC law.[30] Article 6 of the EC Treaty specifies the principle of integration, by which environmental protection requirements must be integrated into the definition and implementation of other EC policies, including the discretionary power of the European Commission to review competition law. Thus, for example, when the Commission must decide individual requests for exemption from the prohibition on anti-competitive practices under Article 81(3) of the EC Treaty, it should not exempt practices with harmful consequences for the environment; at the same time, it should adopt greater flexibility regarding projects that would be favourable to the environment. The same reasoning can be applied to State aids, which must be approved by the Commission under Article 87 of the Treaty. When considering the proportionality of the aids being proposed by a Member State the Commission should consider respect for the polluter-pays principle set out in Article 174(2) of the EC Treaty. If State aid is financed by revenue from charges paid by polluters, it should *a priori* be given favourable consideration.

At the level of international law, the reiteration of environmental principles in a soft-law instrument such as the 1992 Rio Declaration also means that UN organizations cannot ignore these principles in their decision-making processes.[31]

3.3. Directing principles and legal certainty

The introduction of the principles of the polluters pays, prevention, and precaution into international treaties or national framework laws has been objected to on the ground that they would jeopardize legal certainty. Thus the general use of these principles in a wide number of international and national laws has revived the fear that the law-maker has created a series of time-bombs that will make it easier for judges to revolutionize environment law.[32] As a result of these imprecise norms, courts rather than legislators will eventually be making law.[33]

---

[30] J. Jans, *European Environmental Law* (2nd edn., Groeningen: Europa Law Publishing, 2000) 31; N. de Sadeleer, *Le droit communautaire et les déchets* (Brussels: Bruylant-L.G.D.J., 1995) 176.

[31] Fr. Maes, 'Environmental Law Principles...' in M. Sheridan and L. Lavrysen (eds.), *Environmental Law Principles*, n. 27 above, 73. See for instance, F. Mucklow, 'An Overview of the Integration of Environmental Principles into the World Bank' (2000) 9: 1 RECIEL 100–11.

[32] Y. Jegouzo, 'Les principes généraux du droit de l'environnement' (1996) 12: 2 RFD Adm. 209.

[33] In two recent cases the German Federal Constitutional Court (*Bundesverwaltungsgericht*) referred to the co-operation principle, based upon the idea that environmental protection should not be the exclusive responsibility of the State but also of industry, to declare local taxation regimes on one-way packaging and on industrial hazardous wastes unconstitutional (BVerfG, 2 BvR 1991 u. 2004/95, 7 May 1998 (*Packaging Waste Tax*) repr. in (1998) UPR 261). According to the Federal Court those taxes came into conflict with the underlying co-operation principle of the Federal Waste Act and the Federal Emission Control Act. However, those statutes do not expressly prevent local authorities from using such taxes. This case-law serves as a reminder of the interpretative pitfalls that lie ahead when deliberating on abstract principles that have been artificially severed from the specific legislative context in which they were first adopted. Eg G. Roller, 'Environmental Law Principles in the Jurisprudence of German Administrative Courts' (1999) 2 ELNI Newsletter 34.

In addition, some legal analysis criticizes recourse to these directing principles in the name of legal certainty, above all when those principles allow courts to deviate from the straightforward course of established precedent. Commentators have thus reproached the ECJ for not having followed its own case-law relating to the free circulation of goods when, in its *Wallonia Waste* decision, the Court invoked the principle of correction of environmental harm at source to determine whether the Wallonian restrictions were discriminatory.[34] Indeed, this was the first time the Court used the rule of reason to uphold trade restrictions which appeared to be discriminatory.

A priori, these concerns are far from devoid of any basis, to the extent that uncertainty about the scope of the polluters-pays, preventive, and precautionary principles is inversely proportional to the lack of precision in their formulation. As the result of their multiplicity of meanings—and hence their plurality of virtual meanings—application of these principles is often unpredictable. When faced with other principles they give rise to solutions that are all different to one another, because each new situation is different from all past situations.

While directing principles provide general discretion for making decisions, precise and complete rules can more easily be applied in individual cases since they do not allow the judge any choice about whether or not to apply them. Unlike principles, rules are all-or-nothing in character. The application of one rule automatically excludes another; consequently two contradictory rules cannot coexist. Rules are static; they do not adapt themselves to specific situations as principles do.[35] They therefore produce homogeneity: the ability to deduce an infinite number of similar solutions from a single norm. As a result they generate foreseeability and legal certainty. Legal certainty in turn requires that judges be subservient to a text that is clear, precise, and complete and not to flexible norms such as the principles we have been considering.

Should the principles therefore be thrown open to criticism under the pretext of legal certainty? Such a reaction appears exaggerated, given that signs of legal pathology are currently multiplying everywhere under the influence of postmodern law. Lack of time and means, the complexity and changeability of the questions to be addressed, pressure from lobbies, lack of interest in legal questions: these difficulties are giving rise to a proliferation of specific laws edited in haste and littered with gaps and contradictions, whose duration dwindles in direct proportion to their mediocrity.[36] Such is the result of an endless process of legislative patching-up engaged in by the public authorities in their attempts to satisfy a number of conflicting interests.

---

[34] See the critical analyses of *Wallonia wastes* by D. Geradin, 'The Belgian Waste Case' (1993) 5 Eur LR 144; *Trade and the Environment* (Cambridge: Cambridge U.P., 1997) 19; L. Hanscher and H. Sevenster, comment on this decision (1993) CML Rev 351; L. Krämer, 'General Principles of Community Environmental Law and their Translation into Secondary Law' (1999) 3: 4 L & EA 355–62.

[35] About this distinction, see the discussion in Chapter 6 below.

[36] See the discussion in Chapter 4, Section 4 above.

In addition environmental law is experiencing a true flight forward: the ineffectiveness of its existing regulatory regimes is compelling legislators constantly to adopt new texts, which are superimposed on existing law without increasing its effectiveness. The need to adopt new legislation often rests on a permanent state of reluctance to apply existing legislation. Thus environmental regimes in most industrialized countries are teeming with laws whose effectiveness leaves a great deal to be desired, owing to their precarious and confused nature. Jurists will find it difficult to discover the dogma of legal certainty in this jumble.

The resultant legal uncertainty is of course not specific to environment law; all branches of law are affected by this problem. It is not surprising that the major international courts are developing brakes and counterweights to this tendency, notably in the form of general principles (eg the principles of legitimate confidence, non-retroactivity, and legal certainty).

The directing principles of environmental law could similarly temper this increase in legal precariousness. Malleable and adaptable by nature, those principles function within a long-term perspective absent from more precise rules which must be formally modified every time circumstances change. Yet while specific rules are continually being modified to conform to changing situations, directing principles remain imperturbable. To remain in existence legal systems must have in hand directing principles authorizing change while at the same time avoiding inopportune legislative revisions. Thanks to their permanence, principles allow the legal system to rest on more stable axes than do the shifting and chaotic regulations that characterize environment law, which needs rapidly to acquire a minimum of stability. By acting to reduce uncertainty, directing principles may thus have the opposite effect to that claimed by their detractors.

To this we must add that principles do not in fact give courts carte blanche to settle disputes as they wish. If it is true that principles such as 'the polluter-pays' to some extent increase the freedom of interpretation enjoyed by the courts, the latter nonetheless remain bound to find solutions in harmony with the spirit of the legal system and must adhere to the values promoted by that system. Moreover, courts only have recourse to directing principles when they see the need to make one interpretation prevail over another. In addition, principles are always used in tandem with more precise rules, which serves to reduce the threat of legal uncertainty even further. We must therefore conclude that judicial discretion does not amount to arbitrary judgement. Courts may never act arbitrarily. Even when discretion is not limited courts are still legally bound to act according to the values of their legal order.[37] Moreover, it is always possible to reduce the margin of interpretation inherent in directing principles, since doctrine and case-law will refine their scope over time.

Finally, we should note that in a post-modern vision of law principles are elements that stabilize rather than perturb the legal system. Thanks to principles,

---

[37] J. Raz, *The Authority of Law* (Oxford: Clarendon, 1979) 96.

very dissimilar laws securing conflicting interests manage to coexist: the principles build bridges between these laws and make it possible, following a weighing of interests, to come to a solution that troubles the various interests concerned as little as possible.

Thus the flexible nature of principles does not put legal certainty into question; indeed, certainty has been ill served by a profusion of overly specific laws, revised at regular intervals.

4. DIRECTING PRINCIPLES ARE LINKED TO A HUMAN RIGHT TO ENVIRONMENTAL PROTECTION

Modern law places the individual at the centre of society. Individualism is the affirmation of an important degree of autonomy and freedom. Yet post-modern law is characterized by the ebbing of the concept of the 'individual' and the rise of 'welfare rights' or 'socio-economic rights' (*droits-créance*) which are no longer accorded to the individual as such but rather to the individual as a member of a specific group or social category (for example, housing rights, social security rights, etc. which are of a collective character). In modern law public freedoms served to limit the State's prerogatives; in post-modern law, by contrast, welfare or socio-economic rights require intervention by the public authorities. As a logical corollary, post-modern law has resulted in the emergence of a new generation of human rights, including the human right to environmental protection. While not expressly recognized by binding international instruments, this right (to be distinguished from other environmental rights such as the right to life or the right to freedom from interference with one's home and property) is expressed in the Constitutions of most European States (Subsection 4.1 below). Environmental directing principles, such as the polluter-pays, prevention, and precaution, may strengthen constitutional provisions that recognize environmental protection by setting out markers for action by public authorities (Subsection 4.2). Conversely, the procedural principles guiding participation, information, and access to justice that follow from a constitutional right to environmental protection could usefully complement the polluter-pays, preventive, and precautionary principles (Subsection 4.3).

As noted above, this interaction—to the point of entanglement—between constitutional rights, directing principles, and procedural rights is particularly symptomatic of post-modernity, where a complex alchemy of extremely general norms of varying legal status and functions replaces a uniform hierarchy of first- and second-level rules.

4.1. Recognition of a right to environmental protection

The proclamation of environmental law principles in basic legislation is often accompanied by the recognition of a right to environmental protection.[38] However, under international law the right to live in a clean environment is generally expressed through non-binding declarations adopted by international conferences rather than in legally binding international human rights covenants.[39] The first principle of the 1972 Stockholm Declaration on the Human Environment proclaimed that 'Man has the fundamental right . . . to adequate conditions of life, in an environment of a quality that permits a life of dignity and well-being'. Other international texts, such as the 1981 African Charter on Human Rights and the 1982 World Charter for Nature, expressed similar views. By setting out in its first principle that 'Human beings are at the centre of concerns for sustainable development. They are entitled to a healthy and productive life in harmony with nature', the 1992 Rio Declaration on Environment and Development showed itself to be significantly weaker than the international texts that preceded it, as a result of the pre-eminence accorded the right to development.[40] Indeed, Principle 3 of the Declaration envisages that: 'The right to development must be fulfilled so as to equitably meet developmental and environmental needs of present and future generations.'

That said, as Judge Weeramantry wrote in his separate opinion for the International Court of Justice in the *Gabcíkovo-Nagymaros* case: 'the protection of the environment is . . . a vital part of contemporary human rights doctrine, for it is a *sine qua non* for numerous human rights such as the right to health and the right to life itself'.[41]

Nevertheless, the right to protection of the environment may be related to several first-generation human rights—namely, the right to health and to respect of private and family life.[42] In the *López-Ostra* case, the European Court of Human Rights (ECtHR) firmly set environmental protection among the human rights protected by the application. The Court ruled that under Article 8 of the European Convention on Human Rights (ECHR) the State had the duty to take

[38] I. Koppen and K.-M. Ladeur, 'Environmental Rights' in *Human Rights and the European Community: The Substantive Law* (Baden-Baden: Nomos, 1991) 1; idem, 'Environmental Constitutional Law' in *European Environmental Law: A Comparative Perspective* (Dartmouth, 1995) 15; S. Deimann and B. Dyssli (eds.), *Environmental Rights* (London: Cameron and May, 1995); A. Boyle and M. Anderson (eds.), *Human Rights Approach to Environmental Protection* (Oxford: Clarendon, 1996); J. Verschuuren, *Het grondrecht op bescherming van het leefmilieu* (Zwolle: Tjeenk Willinck, 1993).

[39] P. Pevato, 'A Right to Environment' in Ph. Sands (ed.), 'International Law: Current Status and Future Outlook' (1999) 3 RECIEL 313.

[40] M. Pallemaerts, 'International Environmental Law from Stockholm to Rio: Back to the Future' in Ph. Sands (ed.), *Greening the Treaty* (London: Earthscan, 1993) 5; D. Shelton, 'What happened in Rio to Human Rights' (1994) 4 YbIEL 5.

[41] Separate Opinion of Judge Weeramantry, at 4.

[42] R. Churchill, 'Environmental Rights in Existing Human Rights Treaties' in A. Boyle and M. Anderson (eds.), *Human Rights Approach to Environmental Protection* (Oxford: Clarendon, 1996) 90. On the ECHR, see R. Descagne, 'Integrating Environmental Values into the European Convention on Human Rights' (1995) 2 AJIL 263; M. Dejeant-Pons, 'The Right to Environment in Regional Human Rights System' in Mahoney and Mahoney (eds.), *Human Rights in the Twenty-first Century* (1993) 595.

the necessary measures to ensure effective protection of the right of the complainants to respect of private and family life. The Court found in *López-Ostra* that even if serious damage to the environment did not put a person's health in grave danger, it 'could affect the well-being of a person and deprive him of the use of his home in such a way as to harm his private and family life'.[43] More recently the ECtHR has ruled that the authorities should provide potential victims of risky activities (chemical factories, nuclear plants, etc.) with the information they need in order to assess the risk they run.[44] Therefore a substantive environmental protection right may be derived from Articles 2 and 8 of the ECHR.[45]

Unlike international law, where a right to environmental protection is generally expressed through non-legally binding resolutions and declarations, most Western European constitutions expressly recognize such a right in one form or another.[46] All these constitutional and legal provisions give rise to both rights and obligations: rights to the extent that most of these Articles recognize, either explicitly or implicitly, the right of citizens to be able to live in a healthy, balanced, or protected environment. As we shall see below, procedural rights follow from this fundamental constitutional right, particularly as regards information, participation, and access to justice.

Obligations are created where constitutional provisions include a statement of public policy: the State thereby commits itself to protecting its citizens against the dangers posed to them by environmental threats, just as it is obliged to guarantee them a safe environment. Article 37 of the December 2000 Charter of Fundamental Rights of the European Union, which may some day form the preamble to a European constitution, is typical of such statements of public policy: 'A high level of environmental protection and the improvement of the quality of the environment must be integrated into the policies of the Union and ensured with the principle [*sic*] of sustainable development.'

As we shall see later in our analysis, environmental law principles provide consistency to these two facets of the fundamental right to protection of the environment.

---

[43] *López-Ostra v. Spain*, 9 December 1994, A 303–C.

[44] *Guerra* case, 19 February 1998, Reports 1998–I, 210; *McGinley and Egan v. United Kingdom*, 9 June 1998, Reports 1998–III, 1334.

[45] M. DeMerrieux, 'Deriving Environmental Rights from the ECHR' (2001) 21:3 OJLS 521–61.

[46] Article 66 of the Portuguese Constitution, Article 45 of the Spanish Constitution, Article 24.1 of the Greek Constitution, Article 21 of the Dutch Constitution, Article 23 of the Belgian Constitution, Articles 2 and 73–80 of the Swiss Constitution, Article 20a of the German Constitution, Article 14A of the Finnish Constitution, Article 110B of the Norwegian Constitution. Even when that right is not expressly recognized in the Constitution it may sometimes be found in framework laws, for example Article L-110–2 of the French Environmental Code. Eg E. Brandl and H. Bungert, 'Constitutional Entrenchment of Environmental Protection: A Comparative Analysis of Experiences Abroad' (1992) 16 Harv Env L Rev. 1–99. For a list of constitutional provisions on environmental rights and duties see E. Brown-Weiss, *Fairness to Future Generations* (Tokyo, New York: UN University, Transnational Pub., 1989) 297–327.

4.2. The interaction between directing principles and the right to environmental protection obliges public authorities to act

Public authorities do not generally serve as dependable and unconditional defenders of the environment. In the past they have been more likely to contribute to environmental degradation than to its protection. In future they will have to take ecological interests into consideration, but those interests are in practice always weighed against competing, if not conflicting, interests, such as economic growth, competitiveness, and employment security.

However, when a constitutional provision situated at the apex of the hierarchy of norms anticipates that the State should intervene to defend the environment, it imposes on the law-maker and subordinate authorities an obligation that they may not evade. Equivocation is no longer an option; were the public authorities to fail to take all possible measures to prevent environmental destruction, they would be disregarding their constitutional obligation.

Yet while action by the public authorities comprises the very heart of environmental protection, it is still unclear how authorities will act to guarantee that right. Both constitutional and legal provisions are silent on that point.

As we observed in our above analysis of the polluter-pays, preventive, and precautionary principles, public authorities have a considerable range of measures at their disposal. In order to give concrete form to a constitutional right to environmental protection, intervention by the public authorities must be framed and guided, even led, by principles. The polluter-pays, prevention, and precautionary principles, generally set forth in laws that are hierarchically inferior to constitutional provisions, may usefully fill in this constitutionally recognized right to environmental protection or the right to environmental protection that can be deduced from Articles 2 and 8 of the ECHR.[47]

In this way the right to environmental protection and the main principles of environmental law mutually reinforce one another through a dialectical relationship rather than acting in isolation. In other words, recognition of a constitutional right to environment only has meaning if it is informed by principles whose function is precisely to guide the public authorities in taking action intended to protect the environment more effectively.

For instance, both the Federal Constitutional Court and the administrative courts have held that the German legislature is under a constitutional obligation to afford the citizens of the Federal Republic adequate procedural protection against the risks associated with the use of potentially very hazardous technologies such as nuclear energy or genetic engineering and biotechnology.[48]

---

[47] M. DeMerrieux, n. 45 above, 557. This author supports the cross-fertilization between Article 174(2) EC Treaty principles and the ECHR.

[48] The Federal Constitutional Court derived this obligation from a reading of Article 2 of the Basic Law that views this provision's guarantee of 'life and bodily integrity' not only as a negative freedom to protect against straightforward State intrusion but also as a positive duty to provide for at least minimal protection against the potentially devastating effects on the right to life and security of the

The presence of principles is so essential in this respect that German doctrine deduces the principles of precaution (*Risikovorsorgeprinzip*), prevention (*Gefahrenabwehr*), sustainable management of renewable resources (*Nachhaltigkeitsprinzip*), and careful management of non-renewable resources (*Sparsamkeitsprinzip*) from Article 20a of the Federal Constitution.[49] Belgian doctrine and case-law support the same analysis: Article 23 of the Constitution, which lays down the right to a clean environment, contains the precautionary principle.[50]

4.3. The interaction between directing principles and the procedural rights that follow from the right to environmental protection

The implementation of environment law is not the sole prerogative of the public authorities; since its beginnings, environment policy has been driven forward by pressure groups acting at the international, national, and local levels. In addition to imposing obligations upon State organs,[51] the right to environmental protection has given rise to calls from pressure groups for procedural rights, among them the right to information, participation, and legal action.[52]

Therefore, whether it be preventive or anticipatory in nature, environment policy must have as a corollary the dissemination of accurate information, a dynamic process of participation for interested parties, and a guarantee of effective recourse against public decisions. The effectiveness of environmental rules will be enhanced if various actors are accurately informed about the choices being considered as well as the reasons underpinning them and are allowed to participate in drawing up environmental regulations. Subjective rights may in this way cause statutory law to evolve in a direction that favours environmental protection.[53]

---

person flowing from the use of hazardous technologies in industrial production processes or other activities undertaken by private third parties. BVerfG, Beschl. v. 8.8.1978, 2 BvL 8/77, (*Nuclear Power Plant Kalkar*), vol. 49, 89; BVerfG, Beschl. v. 20.12.1979, 1 BvR 385/77, (*Nuclear Power Plant Mülheim-Kärlich*), vol. 53, 30. G. Roller, 'Environmental Law Principles in the Jurisprudence of American Administrative Courts' in M. Sheridan and L. Lavrysen (eds.), *Environmental Law Principles in Practice* (Brussels: Bruylant, 2002) 160–1.

[49] The mandate to protect the environment set out in Article 20 of the German Constitution reads as follows: 'The State, bearing responsibility also for future generations, protects the natural bases of life within the existing constitutional order through legislation and, pursuant to statute law and justice, through its executive power and the judiciary'. The precautionary principle and the prevention principle are regarded as coming within the purview of this provision: see D. Murswiek, 'Der Bund und die Länder Schutz der natürlichen Lebensgrundlagen' in M. Sachs (ed.), *Grundgesetz: Kommentar* (Munich: Beck'sche Verlagsbuchhandlung, 1996) 660–1; S. Werner, 'Das Vorsorgeprinzip: Grundlagen, Maßstäbe und Begrenzungen' (2001) 21 Umwelt-und Planungsrecht, 336.

[50] C.E.b., no. 82.130, 20 August 1999, Venter (2000) 1 Amén.-Env. comment by N. de Sadeleer; no. 85.936, March 2000, Daeten.

[51] I. Koppen and K.-M. Ladeur, 'Environmental Rights', n. 38 above, 13.

[52] In environmental matters those three procedural rights draw from established human rights concepts. See J. Ebbesson, 'The Notion of Public Participation in International Environmental Law' (1997) 8 YbIEL 70–5.

[53] The concept of 'subjective right' is well known to continental legal systems such as the German (*subjektive Recht*) or the French (*droit subjectif*). It is generally opposed in Germany to *objektives Recht* and in France to the *droit objectif*. Eg W. Van Gerven, *Tort Law* (Oxford: Hart, 1999) 38.

International legal instruments regularly call for recourse to procedural rights. For instance, Principle 10 of the 1992 Rio Declaration on Environment and Development provides that:

Environmental issues are best handled with the participation of all concerned citizens at the relevant level. At the national level, each individual shall have appropriate access to information concerning the environment that is held by public authorities... and the opportunity to participate in decision-making processes. Effective judicial and administrative proceedings, including redress and remedy, shall be provided.

Elements of Principle 10 are reflected in the 1991 Espoo Convention on Environmental Impact Assessment in a Transboundary Context, in the 1992 CBD, and in the 1993 Lugano Convention on Damage Resulting from Activities Dangerous to the Environment.[54] The 1998 Århus Convention on Access to Information, Public Participation in the Decision-making Process, and Access to Justice in Environmental Matters is the most far-reaching expression to date of Principle 10: in order to 'contribute to the protection of the right of every person of present and future generations to live in an environment adequate to his or her health and well-being', its Article 1 binds States to 'guarantee the right of access to information, public participation in decision-making and access to justice in environmental matters'.

The emergence of these three categories of procedural rights (information, participation, and access to justice) goes hand in hand with the implementation of several directing principles that apply to public authorities.

4.3.1. The procedural right to information

The solitary exercise of power linked to the administrative tradition of secrecy has long been reflected in the considerable inertia that arises when it comes to disclosing information about technical choices relating to environmental issues. Yet information constitutes the core of the struggle to protect the environment, since ignorance renders rights to participation and access to justice ineffective. The right to information is therefore central among procedural rights.[55]

That right is not limited to requiring public authorities to make information accessible when interested parties request it. For such a right to be fully realized, authorities must also make information public in a systematic manner, so that any citizen may obtain information about the state of the environment in which he lives without having to go through long and costly administrative procedures.

---

[54] A. Boyle, 'The Role of International Human Rights Law in the Protection of the Environment' in A. Boyle and M. Anderson (eds.), *Human Rights Approach*, n. 38 above, 61.

[55] S. Weber, 'Environmental Information and the European Convention on Human Rights' (1991) 12 HRLJ 177; H. Smets, 'The Right to Information on the Risks Created by Hazardous Installations at the National and International Levels' in F. Francioni and T. Scovazzi (eds.), *International Responsibility for Environmental Harm* (London, Dordrecht: Graham and Trotman, 1991) 449; R.E. Hallo (ed.), *Access to Environmental Information in Europe* (The Hague: Kluwer Law Int'l, 1996).

The active dissemination of information by the public authorities is particularly important because degradation of the quality of environmental components directly threatens public health.

For that reason, recent regulations require that public authorities act to inform populations when they have been exposed to major technological risks,[56] when specified thresholds for concentrations of atmospheric pollutants have been exceeded,[57] or when GMOs are released.[58] In the absence of such measures public authorities would be guilty of exposing populations to environmental risks of whose existence they were unaware.

The right to examine official documents held by administrations[59] or individuals[60] should thus be accompanied by active efforts on the part of public authorities to inform the populations concerned about the state of the environment.[61] This naturally implies that authorities must have the technical and scientific means to obtain such information. In conjunction with the requirement that public authorities disseminate information, this procedural right is thus no longer determined by purely subjective criteria.

As can be seen in the case-law of the ECtHR, access to environmental information plays an important role as a procedural aspect of substantive rights. In *Guerra*, the ECtHR ruled that the failure by the Italian State to obtain essential information for the potential victims of industrial pollution, which would have allowed them to evaluate the risks they ran in residing near a dangerous industrial

---

[56] According to Article 13 of Directive 96/82/EC on the control of major accident hazards involving dangerous substances: 'Member States shall ensure that information on safety measures and on the requisite behaviour in the event of an accident is supplied, without their having to request it, to persons liable to be affected by a major accident originating in an establishment covered by Article 9. The information shall be ... made permanently available to the public.'

[57] Article 5 of Directive 92/72/EEC on air pollution by ozone states that in the event of air quality values being exceeded 'the Member States shall take the necessary steps for the public to be informed (eg by means of radio, television and the press)'. One of the general aims of Directive 96/62/EC on ambient air quality assessment and management is 'to obtain adequate information on ambient air quality and ensure that it is made available to the public, *inter alia* by means of alert thresholds'. The alert threshold means the level beyond which there is a risk to human health from brief exposure and at which immediate steps shall be taken by the Member States.

[58] Articles 24 and 31(2) of Directive 2001/18/EC on the deliberate release of GMOs.

[59] Case C-321/96, *Mecklenburg v. Kreis Pinnenberg* [1998] ECR I-3797.

[60] See Article 16 of the 1993 Lugano Convention on Civil Liability for Damage Resulting from Activities Dangerous to the Environment, not yet in force, which recognizes the right of a person who has suffered damage at any time to request the court to order an operator to provide him with specific information, insofar as this is necessary to establish the existence of a claim for compensation under the Convention.

[61] According to Article 5 of the 1998 Århus Convention, each party should act in such a way that 'in the event of an imminent threat to health or the environment, whether imputable to human activities or due to natural causes, all information likely to allow the public to take measures to prevent or limit eventual damages which is in the possession of a public authority should be disseminated immediately and without delay to those people who risk being affected'. According to Article 7 of Directive 90/313/EEC on the freedom of access to information on the environment: 'Member States shall take the necessary steps to provide general information to the public on the state of the environment by such means as the periodic publication of descriptive reports'.

activity, constituted a violation of Article 8 of the ECHR.[62] The Court in this decision was defending a novel and bold concept of the role of information in the full enjoyment of the right to respect for privacy and family life granted by the Convention. First, it did not require an ecological catastrophe already to have occurred in order to press for a positive obligation for the public authorities to provide information. Residence in a high-risk zone was considered sufficient to generate such information requirements. In addition, the Court did not require that the information to be communicated to affected populations exist and be available. According to the decision, the duty to inform requires public authorities to collect and elaborate the information that would ensure the safety of those affected. In the decision in *McGinley and Egan v. United Kingdom* the ECtHR considered that there was a positive obligation according to Article 8 of the ECHR for national authorities to establish an effective and accessible procedure enabling persons taking part in hazardous activities, such as nuclear testing, to seek all relevant and appropriate information about the risks to which they are exposed.[63]

Indeed, several directing principles of environment law are linked to preoccupations concerning the right to information. Since it is not possible to foresee harm that is not known, any preventive policy must be based on the mastery of sufficient information to allow decision-makers to set out relevant choices in full knowledge of the facts. A rapid examination of preventive policies, moreover, makes clear the central role of information, given the constant need for inventories, assessment reports, inquiries, and supplementary studies whose object is to improve the state of current knowledge. As the culmination of the preventive principle, the EIA procedure focuses entirely on the information the operator must obtain and disseminate to all those involved in a project. That information, which will be used to assuage or corroborate concerns expressed by third parties concerning the project under evaluation, will allow the author of the environmental impact study to carry out timely modifications. This process is intended to overcome any hesitations expressed by concerned parties and to require the competent authority to take a decision with all the facts to hand. A command of information thus constitutes the corner-stone of this preventive instrument.

The precautionary principle should also substantially enrich the right to information. First of all, it should profoundly transform the obligation that private entrepreneurs inform public authorities about the contents and impacts of their projects, by requiring them to carry out supplementary research on project aspects that were formerly neglected or that reflected a minority view within the scientific community. As guarantors of the general interest, the authorities must be correctly informed about the risks covered by the precautionary principle.

---

[62] *Guerra* case, 19 February 1998, Reports 1998–I, reproduced in JEL (1999) 157 with a comment by C. Miller. According to the ECtHR, the authorities must also have the relevant information at their disposal.
[63] *McGinley and Egan v. United Kingdom* case, 9 June 1998, Reports 1998-III, p. 1334, para. 101.

Similarly, while a certain number of laws secure a right to information for citizens as regards established risks,[64] that right should be extended to other categories of risks, since it is henceforth the ensemble of knowledge which must be considered and not merely proven facts.

Furthermore, the public should benefit from a serious right to professional information. For instance, in Dutch case-law on danger creation, the duty of care requires not only that precautionary measures be taken if the possibility of damage exists, but also imposes a duty to investigate possible dangers whenever there is reason to question whether an activity is harmless.[65] The precautionary principle must therefore include a requirement that professionals extend and complete their information obligations: information should be provided to consumers on a regular basis. A requirement closely to observe the evolution of a risk would therefore be imposed on producers or distributors who place on the market products likely to pose a danger to health, safety, or the environment. Indeed, in the context of a precautionary approach, producers would normally be required to continue to supervise their products even after these have been placed on the market and to alert the public as soon as any risk becomes apparent.[66] As the Belgian crisis of June 1999, resulting from dioxin contamination of poultry, clearly demonstrated, labelling and product traceability are corollaries of transparency and constitute key elements of crisis resolution. This is particularly true of information concerning the placing of GMOs on the market.[67] The EC White Paper on food safety recognizes that a 'successful food policy demands the traceability of feed and food and their ingredients'.[68]

---

[64] Directive 90/313/EEC on freedom of access to information on the environment.

[65] G. Betlem, *Civil Liability for Transfrontier Pollution* (London: Graham & Trotman/Martinus Nijhoff, 1993) 454.

[66] Several examples of such an approach can be found in EC product and food safety law. According to Article 5(1) of Directive 2001/95/EC on general product safety: 'Within the limits of their respective activities, producers shall provide consumers with the relevant information to enable them to assess the risks inherent in a product throughout the normal or reasonably foreseeable period of its use, where such risks are not immediately obvious without adequate warnings, and to take precautions against those risks . . . , adopt measures commensurate with the characteristics of the products which they supply, enabling them to (a) be informed of risks which these products might pose, and (b) take appropriate action including, if necessary, withdrawing the product in question from the market, warning customers adequately and effectively, and recalling products from consumers.'

[67] Commission Regulation 50/2000/EC on the labelling of foodstuffs and food ingredients containing additives and flavourings that have been genetically modified or produced from genetically modified organisms; Article 20 of Directive 2001/18/EC on the deliberate release of GMOs. On the other hand, the 2000 CPB does not address the issue of the domestic food labelling requirement for consumer information.

[68] According to the EC White Paper on Food Safety (COM (1999) 719 final): 'Adequate procedures to facilitate such traceability must be introduced. These include the obligation for feed and food businesses to ensure that adequate procedures are in place to withdraw feed and food from the market where a risk to the health of the consumer is posed.' Article 9 of the EC Regulation No. 178/2002 laying down the general principles and requirements of food law states that 'the traceability of food, feed, food-producing animals, and any other substance . . . incorporated into a food or feed shall be established at all stages of production and distribution'. See also the European Commission Proposal for a Regulation concerning the traceability and labelling of genetically modified organisms and the traceability of food and feed products produced from GMOs. The proposed regulation makes it

However, there are limits to the usefulness of information, since even natural products are not free of all impurities or extraneous substances. Thus the ECJ ruled that notwithstanding the presence of traces or residues of lead, cadmium, and pesticides in strawberry jam, use of the term 'naturally pure' on jam labels is not liable to mislead consumers as to its characteristics.[69] Given the environment in which garden fruit is grown, it is inevitably exposed to ambient pollutants.[70]

Finally, the precautionary principle could have an impact on freedom of the press, since journalists contribute significantly to the dissemination of information, including by calling attention to risks for which full scientific proof is lacking. The ECtHR ruled in *Hertel* that the order by a Swiss tribunal forbidding a journalist to assert that foods prepared in microwave ovens are dangerous to health and that their consumption gives rise to blood modifications of a pathological character constituted a restriction of the freedom of expression and thereby violated Article 10 of the ECHR.[71] In *Bladet Tromso* the Court again took a position favourable to freedom of the press in connection with the highly controversial subject of seal hunting in Norway. It ruled that Article 10 of the ECHR does not apply only to information or ideas that are favourably received or are considered inoffensive or neutral but also to those that offend, shock, or disturb the State or some portion of the population.[72]

4.3.2. *The procedural right to participation*

Besides demanding to be better informed, the public today also insists on being more closely associated with discussions on known or potential risks. Ulrich Beck's work on the risk society has widely promoted the idea of publicly debating decisions of a technical nature by creating an ecological public sphere in which individuals and groups would be represented on an equal footing.[73]

The desire to participate may take two forms: contributing to the debate or participating in the decision-making process. Yet any such encounter must remain sterile if it is not institutionalized through the recognition of subjective rights of a procedural nature. That 'proceduralization' of rights proves to be all the more necessary as public authorities increasingly find themselves called upon to arbitrate among divergent interests.

The conditions for responsible participation were already present in Principle 19 of the 1972 Stockholm Declaration on the Human Environment. Recommendation 97 of the Plan of Action adopted at that Conference invited States to facilitate 'the participation of the public in the management and supervision of

---

possible to trace GMOs through the production and distribution chain. Traceability facilitates monitoring of any effects on human health and the environment for accurate labelling and for controlling labelling claims. It is also necessary to enable withdrawal from the market in case of unexpected adverse effects.

[69] Case C-465/98, *Adolf Darbo* [2000] ECR I-2321, para. 33.

[70] Ibid., para. 27.

[71] *Hertel v. Switzerland* case, 25 August 1998, Reports 1998–IV.

[72] *Bladet Tromsø and Stensaas v. Norway* case, 20 May 1999, Reports 1999-III.

[73] U. Beck, *Risk Society: Towards a New Modernity* (London: Sage, 1992) 183.

the environment' by specifying that, towards that end, 'it is necessary to envisage ways to encourage the active participation of citizens'.

Principle 23 of the 1982 UNGA World Charter for Nature, provided that: 'All persons shall have the right to participate . . . in the formulation of decisions of direct concern to their environment, and shall have access to means of redress when their environment has suffered damage or degradation'.

Henceforth, the principle of participation will take its place next to the polluter-pays, prevention, and precautionary principles. In that regard, Principle 10 of the 1992 Rio Declaration on Environment and Development states that: 'Environmental issues are best handled with the participation of all concerned citizens, at the relevant level. At the national level, each individual shall have . . . the opportunity to participate in decision-making processes.' In addition, most recent multilateral conventions contain references to or guarantees of public participation.[74]

In the framework of a preventive policy, in both international law and national legal regimes, public inquiries constitute the best means for realizing the right to participation.[75] These go beyond merely guaranteeing that project information gathered during consultations will be disseminated; they also invite interested parties to set out their points of view directly. Inversely, public participation constitutes a useful source of information for those charged with taking decisions. Ebbesson states that 'public participation is likely to improve the quality of environmental decisions by bringing knowledge, insights, and subjective perceptions into the procedure, which would otherwise risk being ignored'.[76] Under pressure from demands by interest groups, the classic decision-making procedure has had to cede ground to a wider co-operation, which is no longer limited to experts.[77]

---

[74] See the list given by D. Shelton, 'Environmental Rights' in Ph. Alston (ed.), *People Rights* (Oxford: OUP, 2001) 204–5.

[75] The Århus Convention insists on this point; under its Article 6(4): 'each Party [must] take steps to ensure that public participation begins at the start of the procedure—that is, when all options and solution are still possible—and that the public may exercise a real influence'. In addition, under its Article 8: 'each Party shall make efforts to promote effective public participation at an appropriate stage—and while options are still open—during the phase when public authorities are drawing up regulatory provisions and other binding legal rules of general application which could have a significant effect on the environment'. IPPC Directive, Article 15 states that: 'Member States shall take the necessary measures to ensure that applications for permits for new installations or for substantial changes are made available for an appropriate period of time to the public, to enable it to comment on them before the competent authority reaches its decision'. See also Article 24 of Directive 2001/18/EC on the deliberate release of GMOs; Directive 85/337/EEC on EIA, Article 2(3)(b).

[76] J. Ebbesson, *Compatibility of International and National Environmental Law* (London: Kluwer, 1996) 68, 95.

[77] International law has similarly shown itself more open to civil society, by providing for the participation of certain groups in the work of committees established by treaty. Thus Article 13(3) of the 1979 Bern Convention on the Conservation of European Wildlife and Natural Habitats provides for the participation at the meetings of its Standing Committee of bodies that are technically qualified in the conservation of wild flora and fauna, unless one-third of the Contracting Parties object. In addition, NGOs have played an important and varied role with respect to the CITES Convention,

The precautionary principle seems even better placed than the preventive principle to further the right to participation. The uncertainty inherent in the former makes it difficult to adopt decisions that do not give rise to at least some degree of spirited controversy. As long as the scientific premises justifying decisions have not been fully proved, controversy concerning their justification will continue to rage. Specifically intended to apply in situations of scientific uncertainty, the precautionary principle distances decision-making from the notion that risk assessment should almost automatically determine what decision will be adopted. Under conditions of uncertainty, decisions concerning risk management will increasingly be the result of arbitration and value judgements; they are thus vulnerable to challenge, making public justification and debate especially important.[78]

Reflecting this, the Communication from the EC Commission on the Precautionary Principle states that: 'All interested parties should be involved to the fullest extent possible in the study of various risk management options that may be envisaged once the results of the scientific evaluation and/or risk assessment are available and the procedure be as transparent as possible'.[79] Precaution thus provides greater transparency in determining risk management and closer involvement of the public in making technological choices. In the perspective of the precautionary principle, risk management results in a new social contract between those giving rise to and managing risks and those likely to be exposed to them: a contract that implies a new type of decision-making.[80]

The tensions that characterize decisions taken in a context of uncertainty could also to some extent be alleviated if experts representing interested parties could work together. For that to happen, it is essential that the public authorities widen debate by requiring co-operation: minority scientific hypotheses must be compared to mainstream theory, thereby making it possible to exclude one-sided expertise.

One must not forget, however, that participation has limits. These generally relate to the late stage at which it occurs, the manipulation it may produce, and

---

monitoring compliance and participating directly in the development of law through involvment in conferences of the Parties. UNFCCC, Article 4(1)(i) requires States to encourage the participation of non-governmental organizations in the process of education, training, and public awareness related to climate change. Finally, NGOs played an active role during the negotiation of the 1998 Århus Convention to an extent unprecedented in the elaboration of an international instrument. Eg J. Cameron and R. Mackenzie, 'Access to Environmental Justice and Procedural Rights in International Institutions' in A. Boyle and M. Anderson (eds.), *Human Rights*, n. 38 above, 5; J. Ebbesson, n. 76 above, 81–9; U.P. Thomas, 'Civil Society and its Role in the Negotiation of the Biosafety Protocol' (2000) 4 RSDIE 350–7; special issue on 'NGOs and International Environmental Protection' (2001) 10: 2 RECIEL 149–98.

[78] See the discussion in Chapter 3, Section 4 above.

[79] Communication from the Commission on the precautionary principle (COM(2000) 1)), para. 6.2.

[80] C. Noiville, 'Principe de précaution et gestion des risques en droit de l'environnement et en droit de la santé' (2000), 239 LPA 41. See also J. Steele, 'Participation and Deliberation in Environmental Law: Exploring a Problem-solving Approach' (2001) 21: 3 OJLS 415–42.

the significant human and technical resources needed for its implementation. A show of discussion also often hides the fact that a decision has already been taken in the corridors of political power, with citizen participation merely serving to confirm what has been decided.

4.3.3. *The right to access to justice*

Access to justice is the logical culmination of the right to information and participation.[81] The right to consultation would remain a dead letter if its beneficiaries were deprived of the right to challenge a final decision taken by an administration. More fundamentally, if every individual is granted the right to live in a protected environment, that person must be able to contest decisions that impair his exercise of that right through all the means provided by the legal system. The ECJ thus ruled, in connection with the provisions used to transpose an air quality Directive, that 'whenever the exceeding of the limit values could endanger human health, the persons concerned must be in a position to rely on mandatory rules in order to be able to assert their rights'.[82] As this decision held that the Directive must be implemented in such a way that plaintiffs can compel public authorities to comply with their obligations, the ECJ implicitly recognizes that the Directive creates an enforceable right to clean air.[83]

The recognition of a basic right to protection of the environment necessarily has implications for determination of access to justice in this area. When a fundamental right is at issue any owner of that right has an interest in ensuring it is not violated. Restrictions may be applied to standing in order to ensure that the legal system runs smoothly; for all that, they may not render such a right devoid of substance. Yet standing remains the most serious stumbling block for applicants hoping to act on behalf of environmental protection, and in some cases it may even serve to obscure the substance of the challenge.

For litigation involving regulatory issues, standing to contest regulatory or administrative rulings is seen primarily in terms of the fear of popular action and the floodgate effect that detractors warn is likely to ensue.[84] EC jurisdictions, for instance, apply conditions that are so strict that their practical effect is to block any possibility of standing in the field of environmental law. *Locus standi* before EC courts requires that applicants be 'directly concerned' by the act that

---

[81] On the right to access to justice see M. Führ and G. Roller (eds.), *Participation and Litigation Rights of Environmental Associations in Europe* (Frankfurt: Peter Lang, 1991); S. Deimann and B. Dyssli, *Environmental Rights, Law, Litigation and Access to Justice* (London: Cameron and May, 1995).

[82] Case C-361/88, *EC Commission v. Germany* [1991] ECR I-2567, para. 16.

[83] G. Betlem, *Civil Liability for Transfrontier Pollution*, n. 65 above, 132.

[84] S. Douglas-Scott, 'Environmental Rights in the EU: Participatory Democracy or Democratic Deficit' in A. Boyle and M. Anderson (eds.), *Human Rights Approaches*, n. 38 above, 125.

adversely affects them, but the ECJ and the CFI have determined that this is not the case for nuclear testing[85] or atmospheric pollution,[86] for example.

The result of this restrictive interpretation of access to justice is to ensure that the violation of preventive measures may not be challenged in any way by those intended to benefit from them. The existence of pockets of illegality within positive law is consequently tolerated, although in principle violations of substantive legal rules should not be allowed.

As regards subjective rights, the conditions required to obtain compensation are equally strictly interpreted: the victim must establish a private interest in the case: that is, he must prove direct injury to his financial assets or to a physical or psychological aspect of his person. Consequently a victim may not obtain compensation for damage caused to environmental goods, which cannot depend on personal interest since they belong to everyone. Only the authorities could, if necessary, obtain indemnification for costs they have had to assume in order to halt damage, but this solution does not make it possible to cover all ecological damage.

The polluter-pays principle should, rather, encourage the law-maker and the courts to widen standing, in order to guarantee full reparation of ecological damage. Opening up the right to obtain damages for loss of environmental goods to persons or groups of persons who have suffered particular damage, such as environmental protection associations, would also conform more closely to the spirit of a principle which seeks to ensure that the polluter pays for pollution.[87] At the same time, the precautionary principle combined with a basic constitutional right to environmental protection should encourage administrative courts to alleviate the burden on applicants to prove serious damage before a contentious administrative act can be suspended. In Germany, for instance, an individual can assert under the Nuclear Energy Act that the authorities have not taken all measures necessary to ensure optimum prevention and precaution.[88] As we saw above, the responsible authorities should consider not only hazards that have a certain probability of occurring but also those risks for which no cause and effect relationship has yet been empirically shown to exist or the uncertainty of which makes the formulation of reliable prognoses impossible.[89] Nevertheless, an

---

[85] Case T-219/95, *M.-T. Danielson, P. Largenteau and E. Haoa v. EC Commission and France* [1995] ECR II-305.

[86] Case T-585/93, *Greenpeace International v. EC Commission* [1995] ECR II-2209; Case C- 321/ 95, *Greenpeace v. EC Commission* [1998] ECR I-1651. Eg D. Torrens, '*Locus standi* for Environmental Associations under EC Law: *Greenpeace* a Missed Opportunity for the ECJ' (1999) 3 RECIEL 313.

[87] Article 18 of the 1993 Lugano Convention on Civil Liability for Damage Resulting from Activities Dangerous to the Environment, not yet in force, provides for a right of action to be conferred upon associations or foundations whose statutes aim at protection of the environment to bring legal proceedings in order to obtain a judgment requiring an operator responsible for ecological damage to take measures of reinstatement.

[88] Traditionally, however, the Federal Administrative Court has refused to grant standing to individual plaintiffs. Eg G. Roller, n. 48 above, 163–65, 167.

[89] BVerwG, Urt. v. 19.12.1985, 7 C 65.82, (*Nuclear Power Plant Wyhl*), vol. 72, 300. See Chapter 3, Subsection 2.3.1. above.

individual cannot challenge an administrative authorization on the ground that 'residual risks' (eg the hypothetical crash of a jet liner into a nuclear power station) have not been assessed by the administration.[90] In Belgium, the *Conseil d'Etat* has decided that while risks to health cannot be proved, neither can they be excluded. To the extent that they threaten basic constitutional rights to health and environmental protection, risks from electric cables or mobile telephone masts could be considered sufficiently serious to warrant suspending construction licences.[91]

To conclude, the conditions applying to standing should also be made more flexible in order to ensure that recognition of the right to protection of the environment and the guiding principles that follow from that right do not become a dead letter.

5. DIRECTING PRINCIPLES, HARD CASES, AND THE WEIGHING OF CONFLICTING INTERESTS IN POST-MODERN LAW

From the perspective of modern law, both national and international courts fulfil an important role by elaborating general principles of law to fill gaps in the legal system.[92] While that role does not disappear in post-modern law, courts are certainly not able to use this method to the same extent. In effect the principles they will have to apply will be those set out in legal texts such as framework conventions or framework laws (directing principles) rather than principles derived from case-law (general principles of law). The role of the court will thus shift from judge-made principles to the implementation of principles recognized by the legislator.[93] Nevertheless, the discretion of the court will not disappear; indeed, in a post-modern perspective it will be supported by the weighing of interests.

Long relegated to a background role, the directing principles of environmental law such as the polluter-pays, prevention, and precaution should receive far greater attention from the courts. Indeed, these principles play a determinant role in the transition from modern to post-modern law. Enriching the arsenal of interpretative methods, these principles could encourage courts to break free of their status as servants of the law. In a post-modern context they make it possible to resolve hard cases (Subsection 5.1. below) and bear heavily on the weighing of interests (Subsection 5.2.).

5.1. Resolving hard cases in the light of directing principles

When antagonistic principles enter into conflict (eg the free movement of goods *versus* protection of the environment) the court enjoys wide discretion

---

[90] BVerwG, Urt. v. 22.12.1980, 7 C 84/78 (*Nuclear Power Plant Stade*), vol. 61, 256.
[91] See the discussion in Chapter 3, Subsection 2.3.3. above.
[92] See the discussion in Chapter 4, Section 2 above.
[93] Fr. Moderne, 'Légitimité des principes généraux et théorie du droit' (1995) 15: 4 RFD Adm. 722–42, 742.

in determining the respective weight of such principles. In theory principles make it possible to tip the scale in either direction. In practice the use of directing principles as a means of interpretation may prove extremely useful to courts in settling 'hard cases', that is, borderline cases where, *a priori*, it is not possible to settle an argument except by validating certain values.[94] As we saw in the *Greenpeace* GM Bt Maize case, the principle of precaution implies that the EC Directives relating to GMOs be interpreted in a way that gives full weight to environmental protection requirements.[95]

EC courts use the environmental directing principles set out in Article 174(2) of the EC Treaty to resolve particularly difficult cases. Thus the ECJ appealed directly to the principle of integration in three cases in order to confirm the interpretation that Article 175 of the Treaty specific to environment policy does not alter Community competences under other provisions of the EC Treaty, even if the measures taken under the latter also pursue an environmental protection goal.[96] Article 174(2) principles clearly have an interpretative value that enables them to resolve hard cases in the field of determining the legal basis for EC regulations. The ECJ recently received a request for an Opinion lodged by the European Commission, relating to the choice of the most appropriate legal basis for a proposed decision concluding the CPB (Articles 133 and/or 174(4) and/or Article 175(1) of the EC Treaty). The ECJ gave its opinion that the conclusion of the Protocol on behalf of the EC must be founded on a single legal basis, specific to environmental policy. In reaching that conclusion the ECJ stressed that: 'as regards the Protocol's purpose, it is clear beyond doubt from Article 1 of the Protocol, which refers to Principle 15 of the Rio Declaration on Environment and Development, that the Protocol pursues an environmental objective, highlighted by mention of the precautionary principle, *a fundamental principle of environmental protection* referred to in Article 174(2) EC'.[97]

In its decision in the *Wallonia Waste* case, the ECJ referred to the principle that environmental damage should as a priority be rectified at source to decide whether an obstacle to the free circulation of waste was discriminatory. It concluded that protection of the environment in this case constituted a 'mandatory requirement' that justified the contested regulation.[98] Subsequently, the Court thrice referred to this principle in order to favour environmental protection over considerations linked to the internal market.[99] This clearly shows that

---

[94] M. Koskenniemi, *From Apology to Utopia: The Structure of International Legal Argument* (Helsinki: Lakimiesliiton Kustannuys, 1989) 27; J. Bengoetxea, *The Legal Reasoning of the European Court of Justice* (Oxford: Clarendon, 1993) 218–70.

[95] Case C-6/99, *Greenpeace v. France*. See the discussion in Chapter 3, Subsection 2.2.4.3. above.

[96] Case C-62/88, *Greece v. Council* [1990] ECR I-1527, para. 22; Case C-300/89, *EC Commission v. Council* [1991] ECR I-2867, para. 22; Case C-405/92, *Armand Mondiet* [1993] ECR I-6133, para. 27.

[97] Opinion, 6 December 2001, [2001] ECR I-9713, para. 29 (emphasis added).

[98] Case C-2/90, *EC Commission v. Belgium* [1992] ECR I-4431, paras. 34–6.

[99] Case C-155/91, *EC Commission v. Council* [1993] ECR I-971, para. 13; Case C-187/93, *Parliament v. Council* [1994] ECR I-2857, para. 22; Case C- 422/92, *EC Commission v. Germany* [1995] ECR I-1097, para. 34. For a comment on those decisions, see the discussion in Chapter 7 below.

environmental principles can influence or even determine the outcome of cases.[100]

A further example is the differentiation between waste and product, which has been the subject of much heated academic debate as well as litigation in EC law. According to the ECJ, the concept of waste must be interpreted in light of the aim of Directive 75/442/EEC, which is to protect human health and the environment against harmful effects caused by waste. Furthermore, the ECJ has pointed out that, pursuant to Article 174(2) of the EC Treaty, EC policy on the environment is to aim at a high level of protection and must be based, in particular, on the precautionary principle and the principle that preventive action should be taken.[101] It follows that the concept of waste cannot be interpreted restrictively. This case-law shows again how the principles embodied in Article 174(2) can play a determinant role in resolving hard cases.

5.2. Impact of directing principles on the constitutive elements of the proportionality principle

5.2.1. Background

Decisions taken by the public authorities to protect the environment may have favourable or unfavourable repercussions on interests unrelated to their actual objectives. In practice, environmental decisions may entail the use of coercive mechanisms that restrict economic freedoms, limit property rights, impose conditions on freedom of movement in protected areas, or threaten the right to work as the result of the closure of polluting installations. On the other hand, certain fundamental rights may profit from environmental protection measures. For instance, neighbours of listed installations or airports may demand measures to limit nuisances affecting their right to respect for private and family life according to Article 8 of the ECHR.[102] Environmental measures are thus at the centre of a broad range of conflicts of interest.

Many different categories of interests have to be considered legitimate subjects of public policy, whether they belong to economic operators or to citizens entitled to environmental protection. In the perspective of post-modern law, a fundamental right and an opposing public interest may well coexist if their main elements of contention can be smoothed over. When a dispute opposes norms that are very general in character, for example the free movement of goods against the precautionary principle, the court may apply these norms concomitantly. On the other hand, if a court is settling a dispute between two legal rules whose provisions are more precise, it excludes the rule that does not apply to the case before it.[103]

---

[100] This seems to be particularly clear in Case C-2/90 on Wallonia waste. For a comment on this decision, see Chapter 7, Subsection 3.2.1. below.

[101] Cases C-418/97 and C-419/97, *ARCO Chemie Nederland* [2000] ECR I-4512, para. 39.

[102] *López-Ostra v. Spain* case, 9 December 1994, Series A No. 303-C.

[103] See the discussion in Chapter 6, Subsection 2.1. below.

In order to guarantee the coexistence of conflicting general norms, courts try to balance the interests involved. In particular they are keen to determine, in the light of the proportionality principle, whether the advantages of a contested measure exceed the disadvantages it will cause to the interests or freedoms of third parties. Where this is disproportionate the measure must be nullified in order to protect the interest affected; where the opposite is the case the measure should be confirmed and the resultant limitations on rights and freedoms will have to be tolerated.

The proportionality principle thus allows conflicting interests to coexist by curbing their potentially extreme elements, should this prove necessary. If a measure appears disproportionate the law-maker may adopt a measure that achieves the same end through less restrictive means. The principle of proportionality is thus specifically intended to arbitrate and settle conflicts by weighing the pursuit of a public objective against the private interests that may be threatened in the process.

Even though the concept of proportionality is not specifically mentioned in the EC Treaty or the ECHR and its Protocols, it has become a general principle of law in those two legal orders. The principle of proportionality is applied widely by the ECtHR and ECJ to assess the validity of limitations imposed by national authorities on basic human rights (as under the ECHR) and fundamental economic freedoms (as under the EC Treaty).[104] Furthermore, in some countries (Germany, Belgium) the principle has acquired constitutional status, in that it is applied to control legislative measures; it also plays an important role in administrative law (eg *la théorie du bilan* in French administrative law). Finally, it is acquiring a similar status at the international level within the WTO.

While the function of the proportionality principle is easily understood, its modes of application are less clear. As the constitutive elements of the principle are not laid down in statutory provisions their application by various courts is flexible and varies over time. For instance, in the *Shrimp/Turtle* case the WTO Appellate Body stated that the 'equilibrium' between the commercial interests of the plaintiffs and the legitimate right of a Member to invoke an exception under Article XX 'is not fixed and unchanging; the line moves as the kind and the shape of the measure at stake vary and as the facts making up specific cases differ'.[105] The proportionality principle may therefore be applied differently in different contexts. Consequently its content is not easy to categorize for any court system.

It is nevertheless possible to identify three essential stages for its application in the case-law of both the ECtHR and the ECJ: suitability, necessity, and the absence of disproportionate character of the measure under review (proportion-

---

[104] N. Emiliou, *The Principle of Proportionality in European Law* (London: Kluwer Law Int'l, 1996).

[105] Appellate Body Report on *United States—Prohibition of shrimp and certain shrimp products*, WTO Doc. WT/DS58/AB/R, adopted 12 October 1998, para. 159 [hereinafter, Appellate Body, *Shrimp*].

ality *stricto sensu*).[106] A good illustration of this three-pronged approach is found in *Fedesa*, where the ECJ was asked to examine the validity of a Directive imposing an outright prohibition on the administration of certain hormone substances to animals owing to their potential risks for human health.[107] The Court stated in its judgment: 'The principle of proportionality...requires that the prohibitory measures are *appropriate* and *necessary* in order to attain the objectives legitimately pursued by the legislation in question; when there is a choice between several appropriate measures recourse must be had to the least onerous, and the disadvantages caused must not be *disproportionate* to the aims pursued'.[108]

Below, we consider how each of these tests could evolve under the impetus of the polluter-pays, prevention, and precautionary principles.

5.2.2. First test: suitability of the measure under review

A measure affecting a protected interest (personal freedom, economic freedom) must first demonstrate a causal link to the purpose being pursued, in that it is capable of achieving that object (suitability test). So for example the prohibition of hormones in beef in response to scientific uncertainty about their effects must be able to achieve the health protection goals of EC law. A policy measure that would in no way avert the risk it is intended to combat must be considered inadmissible.[109] Thus an export prohibition for a species which is not at risk would not satisfy this first test.[110]

The principles of environment law may clarify the choices made by the law-maker. Thus the suitability of prohibitive or restrictive measures applying to waste imports and exports must be reviewed against the principle that environmental damage should be rectified at source; according to the case-law of the ECJ, this implies that 'it is for each region, commune or other local entity to take appropriate measures to receive, process and dispose of its own wastes'.[111] In the light of that principle, a prohibition on the import of wastes intended for disposal seems suitable to achieve the desired object; this would not necessarily be the case for other goals.

5.2.3. Second test: necessity of the measure under review

In a second stage, the measure affecting a protected interest must prove to be indispensable in achieving the purpose being pursued (necessity test). If it

[106] W. Van Gerven, 'The Effect of Proportionality on the Actions of Member States of the European Community: National Viewpoint from Continental Europe' in E. Ellis (ed.), *The Principle of Proportionality in the Laws of Europe* (Oxford: Hart, 1999) 37.

[107] Case C-331/88, *Fedesa* [1990] ECR I-4023. As regards the consistency of a national measure with EC law, see also Case 302/86, *EC Commission v. Denmark* [1989] ECR I-4607, paras. 20–1, and the opinion of Advocate General Slynn at 4625–6.

[108] *Fedesa*, at para. 13 (emphases added).

[109] See the discussion in Chapter 7, Section 3 below.

[110] Case C-169/89, *Gourmetterie Van den Burg* [1990] ECR I-2143.

[111] Case C-2/90, *EC Commission v. Belgium* [1992] ECR I-1, para. 34.

appears that an alternative measure would make it possible to achieve the same goal in a less restrictive manner, the contested measure is not necessary and may thus be challenged. In that case the authority must refrain from action or replace the contested measure by an alternative measure.

At this stage the proportionality principle involves comparing measures likely to achieve a desired result and accepting the one that gives rise to the fewest disadvantages. This second stage is based on the idea that the least harmful measure should be preferred if it offers the same basic degree of protection. This equates to requiring a demonstration that the measure being challenged cannot be avoided or replaced. As is clear from the following examples, this test is of particular relevance in the GATT/WTO dispute settlement procedure.[112]

In the *Gasoline* case, the WTO Appellate Body found that an EPA rule to implement the Clean Air Act constituted 'unjustifiable discrimination' between national gasoline producers and countries exporting gasoline to the US and 'a disguised restriction on international trade', because the US had not adequately considered alternative, less trade-restrictive approaches that would have accomplished similar ends:[113]

There was more than one alternative course of action available to the US in promulgating regulations implementing the CAA. These included the imposition of statutory baselines without differentiation as between domestic and imported gasoline. This approach, if properly implemented, could have avoided any discrimination at all. Among other options open to the US was to make available individual baselines to foreign refiners as well as domestic refiners...

Therefore a national measure can only be considered 'necessary' within the meaning of Article XX(b) of GATT if there were no alternative measures reasonably available which could achieve the aim sought with less impact on international trade.[114]

In an environmental case involving Article XX(g) of GATT, the Appellate Body found that the US measure protecting sea turtles was valid under the exception set out in paragraph (g): this measure was not disproportionately wide in its scope and reach in relation to the policy objective of protection and conservation of sea turtle species.[115]

When considering the SPS Agreement in the *Japan Varietals* case, the Appellate Body ruled that the complainant must demonstrate that an alternative

---

[112] M. Montini, 'The Necessity Principle as an Instrument to Balance Trade and the Protection of the Environment' in F. Francioni (ed.), *Environment, Human Rights and International Trade* (Oxford: Hart, 2001) 136–55.

[113] Appellate Body Report on *United States: Standards for Reformulated and Conventional Gasoline*, adopted 20 May 1996, (WT/DS2) at p. 620, [hereinafter Appellate Body, *Gasoline*].

[114] The necessity test is applied to review the exception of Article XX(b) of GATT which refers to national measures '*necessary* to protect human, animal or plant life or health'. However, the exception of Article XX(g) relating to the 'conservation of exhaustible natural resources' does not mention a necessity requirement.

[115] Appellate Body, *Shrimp*, para. 141.

measure exists: a panel may not merely posit an alternative based on expert advice.[116]

In the *Asbestos* case, the Appellate Body considered that a French ban on chrysolite asbestos as a necessary high level of protection, as 'controlled use' of this substance, which consists in taking precautionary measures to avoid the release of fibres, was not a 'reasonably available alternative' since its efficacy had not yet been demonstrated.[117] In the earlier *Gasoline* case, 'necessary' basically meant 'the least trade restrictive measure', while in the more recent case-law of the Appellate Body the least restrictive test gives way to a sort of reasonableness test.[118]

At the EC level, the ECJ also favours measures that are least trade-restrictive. The Court has ruled, for instance, that protection of native crayfish in Germany is better achieved by administrative rules, forbidding the release of exotic crayfish into the aquatic environment, and the enactment of programmes to save native crayfish populations, than by an embargo on all imports of foreign crayfish.[119]

While the necessity test occupies a central role in determining proportionality, particularly in the ECJ's case-law, its use is questionable. In some cases the ECJ has considered as comparable measures that are not equally useful in protecting the environment. Thus, it considered comparable:

—the obligation to deliver waste oils to undertakings required to recycle them on national territory and the possibility of delivering them to foreign undertakings authorized to incinerate them, a much more polluting operation than the contested option chosen by the French authorities at the time;[120]
—an import prohibition on live freshwater crayfish, intended to protect native species, and instituting health checks of highly uncertain effectiveness;[121]
—the obligation to obtain administrative permission to market bottles, intended to limit the amount of packaging placed on the market, and a particularly vague requirement to reuse those same bottles.[122]

In each of these cases the ECJ concluded that the challenged national measure was disproportionate because alternative measures made it possible to reach the

---

[116] Appellate Body, *Japan Varietals*, paras. 126 and 130.

[117] Appellate Body, *Asbestos*, para. 174.

[118] M. Montini, n. 112 above, 154.

[119] Case C-131/93, *Commission v. Germany* [1994] ECR I-3303. Inversely, in a rather similar case (*Maine v. Taylor*) the US Supreme Court upheld a state regulation banning the importation of baitfish, which the State of Maine argued threatened native species (477 U.S. 131 (1986)). In this case Maine offered unrefuted evidence that no adequate scientific testing procedures existed to inspect live baitfish before they entered the state (ibid., 147). According to the US Supreme Court, Maine was not required to 'sit idly by and wait until potentially irreversible environmental damage had occurred or until the scientific community agrees on what disease organisms are or are not dangerous before it acts to avoid such consequences'.

[120] Case C-172/82, *Syndicat National des Fabricants Raffineurs d'Huiles de Graissage* [1983] ECR I-555, para. 14.

[121] Case C-131/93, *EC Commission v. Germany* [1994] ECR I-3303, para. 24. In particular, see the conclusions of Advocate General W. van Gerven, para. 14.

[122] Case C-302/86, *EC Commission v. Denmark* [1988] ECR I-46, para. 21.

same objective with less restriction of intra-Community trade, but it did not take into consideration the fact that national authorities had justified their choices by the greater efficiency of the contested measures. One is thus led to wonder whether the ECJ is really qualified to compare widely divergent methods with respect to a desired result when it does not necessarily possess the relevant technical information.

By focusing on the commercial damage arising from a contested measure, the ECJ effectively favours measures that present less of a hindrance to commercial activities. Weighing the disadvantages of the contested measure against all other possible measures is thus likely to ensure that the most moderate measure will always have an advantage over the most rigorous, to the detriment of the intended goal. This method runs counter to the principle of a high level of environmental protection set out in Article 174(2) of the EC Treaty, as well as in a number of national laws. Nonetheless, ECJ case-law appears to be evolving on this point. Thus, in the case of a Swedish ban on tricholorethylene, the ECJ did not carry out a comparative assessment of alternative mesures (ecolabels, use limitations, warnings, etc.). It was satisfied with the fact that the Swedish Chemical Inspectorate was pursuing a legitimate interest in phasing out a harmful substance.[123]

The use of the necessity test by courts should be limited to cases where measures exhibit a similar degree of effectiveness. This would make it possible to avoid subjective assessments.[124] Comparative tests between an environmental measure and a less restrictive measure should thus clearly be made subject to specific conditions, in order to prevent the court replacing the law-maker.[125]

5.2.4. *Third test: absence of disproportionate character of the measure under review*

The third stage in establishing proportionality is the requirement that the disadvantages to which a contested measure gives rise do not exceed its advantages *in globo*, despite the fact that a less restrictive measure does not exist. The contested measure is not compared to other measures in this test, but analysed in its own right. At this stage courts are carrying out a balancing test (known as the proportionality test *stricto sensu*) weighing a legitimate public freedom against a specific measure (internal market *versus* health or environmental protection; free speech *versus* national security; human rights *versus* free trade). This test, which

---

[123] Case C-473/98, *Kemikalieinspektionen and Toolex Alpha AB*, para. 45.

[124] N. de Sadeleer, 'Le principe de proportionnalité: Cheval de Troie du marché intérieur?' (1999) 3–4 L&EA 379.

[125] Interestingly, some international conventions already provide a set of specific conditions for correctly comparing various available measures. For instance, under Article 5(6) (footnote 3) of the SPS Agreement a measure must be considered more trade-restrictive than required if there is another SPS measure which (1) is reasonably available, taking into account technical and economic feasibility; (2) achieves the Member's appropriate level of protection; and (3) is significantly less restrictive to trade than the SPS measure contested. Thus a contested national measure can be nullified only if an alternative measure fulfils all these requirements.

is little used by the ECJ, is important in the case-law of the ECtHR, as well as in several national case-laws.[126] Examples are varied, in the context of basic rights as well as that of fundamental economic freedoms. The third test plays an important role in verifying the conformity of national measures under GATT provisions.

Although the US measure protecting sea turtles served a legitimate interest under Article XX(g) of GATT, the Appellate Body must still submit it to a proportionality test *stricto sensu*. According to the *chapeau* of Article XX, the environmental measure cannot be applied 'in a manner which would constitute a means of arbitrary or unjustifiable discrimination . . . or a disguised restriction on international trade'. In the Appellate Body's view, the task of applying the *chapeau* is essentially: 'a delicate one of locating and marking out a line of equilibrium between the right of a Member to invoke an exception under Article XX and the right of the other Members under varying substantive provisions of the GATT 1994, so that neither of the competing rights will cancel out the other and thereby distort and nullify or impair the balance of rights and obligations constructed by the Members themselves in that Agreement'.[127]

In other words, an 'equilibrium' must be found between conflicting interests. In the *Shrimp/Turtle* case, the Appellate Body concluded that the US measure was unjustifiable because an alternative course of action was reasonably open to it. The measure would have been more acceptable had it been agreed upon multilaterally, and not resulted from unilateral measures to ban shrimp imports (eg 'the heaviest weapon of a Member's armory of trade measures').[128] In other words, the measure is disproportionate even if unilateral trade measures represent the most effective practical means to protect a global resource (sea turtles) and to remove the incentive of access to a large market for those States that fail to protect that resource.[129]

The third test is applied in an even stricter manner in the field of human rights. For instance, the injunction that prevented a Swiss journalist from making statements about the dangers of microwave ovens—a highly controversial subject from a scientific point of view—was deemed unacceptable by the ECtHR because it affected the very essence of the freedom of speech.[130] In that case,

---

[126] While the tripartite test has received some support in the opinions of Advocate General Van Gerven, in practice the ECJ does not distinguish between the second and third tests. See T. Tridimas, 'Proportionality in Community Law: Searching for the Appropriate Standard of Scrutiny' in E. Ellis (ed.), *The Principle of Proportionality*, n. 106 above, 66; N. de Sadeleer, 'Le principe de proportion-nalité . . . ', n. 124 above, 379. On the other hand, the ECtHR directly tackles the third test. Eg J.G. Schokkenbroeck, *Toetsing aan de vrijheidsrechten van het Europees Verdrag tot bescherming van de rechten van de Mens* (Zwolle: Tjeenk Willink, 1996) 197; S. Van Drooghenbroeck, *La proportionnalité dans le droit de la Convention Européenne des Droits de l'Homme* (Brussels: Saint-Louis/Bruylant, 2001) 292–423.

[127] Appellate Body, *Shrimp*, para. 159.

[128] Ibid., para. 171. See however, the more muanced appreciation of the Appellate Body in its Report of 22 October 2001, WT/DS558/AB/RW, para. 134.

[129] J. Cameron, 'Dispute Settlement and Conflicting Trade and Environment Regimes' in *Trade and the Environment: Bridging the Gap* (London: Cameron and May, 1998) 22.

[130] *Hertel v. Switzerland* case, 25 August 1998, Reports 1998-IV.

contributing to the public debate about the possible hazards of a new technology weighed more heavily than the economic interests of the companies producing the technology, especially as there was no evidence that the sale of microwave ovens had been affected by the journalist's criticisms.

Similar balancing of interests may be found in challenges concerning economic freedoms, particularly as regards the application of Article 30 of the EC Treaty. For instance, Advocate General Van Gerven considered that the Dutch law prohibiting trade in Scottish grouse, which may legally be shot in the UK, was disproportionate given the measure's minimal contribution to achieving the objective of conserving a species of bird in no danger of extinction.[131] In that case, marketing of the species overrode the benefits of the Dutch trade prohibition. In the *Danish Bottles* case, Advocate General Gordon Slynn clearly endorsed the third test: 'There has to be a balancing of interests between the free movement of goods and environmental protection, even if in achieving the balance the high standard of the protection sought has to be reduced. The level of protection sought must be a reasonable level...'[132] In the *Fedesa* case, which considered whether a Council of Ministers measure to ban hormones because of their potential risk to human health was proportional *sensu stricto*, the plaintiffs argued that 'the prohibition in question entails excessive disadvantages, in particular considerable financial losses on the part of the traders concerned, in relation to the alleged benefits accruing to the general interest'.[133] However, the ECJ held that the Council had committed no manifest error of appraisal and that the prohibition of several hormones, even though it might have caused financial loss to certain traders, could not be regarded as manifestly inappropriate. The precautionary approach, taken to protect human health, in this case weighed more heavily than the economic interest.

Needless to say, this last test is the most controversial of the three. Assessment of the proportionate or disproportionate character of a measure may, at this final stage, take on a subjective character. Consequently, by clarifying the elements involved in conflicts of interest, the proportionality principle transforms the court into a true arbitrator, with a considerable margin of discretion to decide between the interest underlying the restraining measure and the rights and freedoms affected by that measure. In this way the proportionality principle could have an extremely serious impact on environmental policy.

In order to avoid too great a degree of subjectivity on the part of the court, the interests that are to be weighed against each other should be inventoried. In other words, the court should clearly identify the interests that are in conflict, determine whether these are legitimate, and establish a hierarchy among them according to the legislative options available and the public policy

---

[131] Case C-169/89, *Gourmetterie Van den Burg* [1990] ECR I-2143.
[132] AG Opinion of May 24 1988, Case C-302/88, *Commission v. Denmark* [1988] ECR I-46.
[133] Case C-331/88, *Fedesa* [1990] ECR I-4023.

principles at stake.[134] This is clearly the path followed by the Swiss Federal Tribunal.[135]

Once the court has identified the interests involved it can compare them and select the most relevant option. Under an economic analysis of law, 'every serious question of social order can be resolved by aggregating the overall net good promised by alternative options in terms of a simple commensurating factor, namely wealth measured in terms of the money which relevant social actors would be willing and able to pay to secure their preferred option'.[136] In this context, cost–benefit analysis serves as a scaling procedure for ranking different options by assigning each option a number equalling its net monetarized benefits or costs.[137] While it is possible to calculate the financial losses that economic operators will suffer as the result of an environmental protection measure, since these losses are expressed in monetary terms, it is much more difficult to evaluate the benefits resulting from such a measure. What economic value can be assigned to the conservation of natural resources, the health of the environment, or the quality of life? These are qualitative evaluations; they are inevitably subjective and cannot be quantified. As a result the balancing test cannot usually be reduced to a purely mathematical assessment.[138] As noted above, the interests at stake are incommensurable; the comparative worth of options must therefore be judged using parameters that go beyond monetary worth.[139]

The fact that a mathematical weighing cannot be carried out does not mean that the legal system may not indicate its preferences through directing principles set out in framework legislation however.[140] For instance, the directing principles of environmental law may express an abstract preference in favour of greater environmental protection. Thus Swiss law shows a marked abstract preference favouring forests against conflicting interests: for a road to be allowed to pass through a forest, a particularly strong interest must justify carrying out the project. [141]

Various arguments favour according greater importance to environmental protection or public health when weighing interests by bringing directing principles into play. First, in some cases directing principles may be considered to

---

[134] W. Van Gerven, 'The Effect of Proportionality', n. 106 above, 58.

[135] Ch.-A. Morand, 'Pesée des intérêts et décisions complexes' in Ch.-A. Morand (ed.), *La pesée globale des intérêts* (Geneva: Helbing and Lichtenhahn, 1996) 41.

[136] J. Finnis, 'Natural Law and Legal Reasoning' in R.P. George (ed.), *Natural Law Theory: Contemporary Essays* (Oxford: Clarendon, 1992) 150.

[137] M. Adler, 'Law and Incommensurability: Introduction' 146 (1998) Univ of Pennyslvania LR 1172.

[138] L. Krämer, *Focus on European Environmental Law* (2nd edn., London: Sweet & Maxwell, 1997) 203–4; N. de Sadeleer, *Le droit communautaire et les déchets* (Brussels: Bruylant, 1995) 93.

[139] C.R. Sunstein, 'Incommensurability and Valuation in Law' (1994) 92 Mich LR 810–12 and 841–3; F.M. Coffin, 'Judicial Balancing: The Protean Scales of Justice' (1988) 63 NYU LR 19.

[140] Ch-A. Morand, 'Pesée d'intérêts et décisions complexes' in Ch.- A. Morand (ed.), *La pesée globale des intérêts*, n. 135 above, 68–9.

[141] Article 5 of the Swiss Federal Forest Code.

represent an irreducible core of values that leads the court to exclude the weighing of interests. Such is the case when a measure intended to protect extremely rare ecosystems or endangered species comes into conflict with other interests. In the decision in *TVA v. Hill* the US Supreme Court judged that a principle of conservation provided no basis upon which to compare the worth of an endemic species of incalculable value with the economic loss that would result from halting the construction of a dam, since Congress had recognized the intrinsic value of endangered species.[142] Similarly, in the *Leybucht* case the ECJ ruled that only a prevailing public interest, such as the protection of persons against floods, can override the nature protection interest in a special protection area for water birds.[143]

Secondly, a further fundamental value is represented by the precautionary principle when public health is in question: an interest closely related to environmental protection. Thus the European Community's courts determined that upholding a ban on beef exports justified by the precautionary principle in view of the risk of infection by bovine spongiform encephalopy must inevitably take precedence over the economic interests of the UK, which was being pro-hibited from exporting its products.[144] US case-law takes a slightly more nuanced view of public health protection requirements. In the 1987 *Vinyl* case the Federal Court of Appeal for the District of Columbia judged that emission standards for hazardous air pollutants should reduce the risk of death or serious, irreversible illness to a minimum; any further reduction of risks, however, would be subject to risk—benefit analysis.[145]

Thirdly, the needs of future generations, represented by the precautionary principle, should carry as much weight as the immediate present when balancing interests. The Belgian Constitutional Court decision in a case involving the closure of gravel works underlines how a constitutional court may weigh specific legal measures against injurious activities even in the absence of irrefutable scientific proof concerning the effects of the activities in question on the aquatic environment. It is always possible to reconsider a closure if it eventually becomes clear that such a measure is excessive, while maintaining high-risk activities could lead to irreversible damage in the long term.[146]

Fourthly, mere reference to the economic benefits of the measure should not be sufficient to overweigh fundamental rights such as the right to respect for private and family lives. For instance, in the recent case of *Hatton and Others v. the United Kingdom* the ECtHR judged that 'despite the margin of appreciation' left

---

[142] *TVA v. Hill*, 437 U.S. 153 (1978). See Chapter 3, Subsection 2.3.6. above.

[143] Case C-56/90, *Leybucht* [1996] ECR I-883, para. 22, reproduced in *JEL* 4 (1992) 139 with a comment by D. Baldock and in (1992) 3 RJE 351 with a comment by N. de Sadeleer.

[144] Case C-180/96, *United Kingdom v. Commission* [1996] ECR I-3903, para. 90; Case T-76/96P, *N.F.U.* [1996] ECR II-815, paras. 103 and 104. See the discussion in Chapter 3 above.

[145] *NRDC v. US EPA*, 824 F.2d (D.C. Cir. 1987), p. 1163. See the discussion in Chapter 3, Subsection 2.3.6.1 above.

[146] C.A., no. 35/95 of 25 April 1995.

to the British authorities, the State had failed to strike a fair balance between the United Kingdom's economic well-being (night flights at Heathrow Airport) and the applicants' effective enjoyment of their right to respect for their homes and their private and family lives. The Court underlined that 'in striking the required balance, States must have regard to the whole range of material considerations. Further, in the particularly sensitive field of environmental protection, mere reference to the economic well-being of the country is not sufficient to outweigh the rights of others.'

Last but not least, environmental interests should weigh more heavily than they usually do to the extent that they respond to the EC's public interest, as in the case of French nuclear testing.[147] At the international level one might say that environmental concerns relate to a core of public policy values pursued by the international community as a whole, and encompassing not only fundamental human rights[148] but also the protection of global environmental resources that constitute a common concern of humankind.[149]

5.2.5. Critical assessment

In conclusion, directing principles of environmental law such as the polluter-pays, prevention, and precaution principles, should draw attention to the suitability, necessity, and proportionality *stricto sensu* of an environmental protection measure whose validity is contested.

First, the relevance of the measure should be assessed in the light of its underlying principles rather than merely in relation to the disadvantages that third parties will suffer. Secondly, the weight of the interest—or proportionality *stricto sensu*—demands rigour and method: all relevant conflicting interests should be set out, balanced, and weighed. Failing a method that makes it possible correctly to assess and weigh the relevant interests, courts should turn to abstract preferences drawn from principles. Furthermore, the environmental protection goal or health standard chosen by a party should not itself come under scrutiny.

By shedding new light on an environmental measure when it comes into conflict with intersecting interests, the environmental principles that we have analysed may serve to tilt the scales more strongly in the direction of environmental protection.

---

[147] See also the opinion of Advocate General Cosmas in Case C-321/95 P, *Greenpeace v. Commission* [1998] ECR I-1669, para. 18.

[148] See in particular the recent case-law of the ECtHR: *López-Ostra v. Spain* case, 9 December 1994, A 303–C; *Guerra* case, 19 February 1998, Reports 1998-I; *Hatton and Others v. the United Kingdom* case, 2 October 2001, not yet reported.

[149] A. Kiss, 'The Common Concern of Mankind' (1997) Envt P & L 244; R. Pavoni, 'Biosafety and Intellectual Property Rigths: Balancing Trade and Environmental Security' in F. Francioni (ed.), *Environment, Human Rights and International Trade*, n. 112 above, 101.

6. Concluding observations

We may ask ourselves whether there is any point in establishing principles in normative texts, since environment law already suffers from chronic non-compliance. By legislating through principles rather than binding norms, is the law-maker not merely admitting that he is incapable of tackling ecological challenges? Would it not be better to consider reinforcing the effectiveness of existing laws rather than proclaiming principles that we then take care not to apply?

In response to these questions we have emphasized the multiple functions that principles can assume within environmental law. We demonstrated in Part I that three principles—those of the polluter pays, prevention, and precaution—have given rise to significant transformations in whole areas of environmental law; furthermore, we have explained in this Chapter that their role is not confined to triggering timely reforms on very precise points of law. Beyond their influence on certain institutions (liability, taxation, etc.) or mechanisms (risk assessment, environmental impact assessment, administrative regimes, etc.) directing principles of environmental law are able to affect the functioning of environmental law as a whole.

In Section 2 of this Chapter we saw how those principles play an essential role in fashioning the internal structure and organization of environment law when applied to institutional actors. They gather fragmented rules into a coherent whole, renew institutions, and refine legal techniques. They thereby provide solidity to a legal discipline that is still seeking an identity. The momentum they provide will add the dimension needed to develop a fully fledged branch of law. This aspiration to greater coherence is very much a modern law concern.

In Section 3 of this Chapter we identified the functions that most strongly characterize post-modern law. First, in regulating the functioning of environment law, these principles have a reforming rather than a stabilizing effect. Their influence over the various powers of the State is immediate: they guide the conceptual work of the law-maker and the enforcement function of subordinate authorities in a dynamic fashion. Their inclusion in normative texts may lead, by the interposition of flexible concepts, to a more supple application of a law that is often criticized as too rigid. By legislating through such indeterminate norms, the law-maker grants the executive and the administration wide powers to evaluate the respective weights of conflicting interests. As they are not adaptable, in the words of Dworkin, to an 'all or nothing' form of application, these guiding principles provide direction in determining dominant values. They are sufficiently flexible to adapt to changing circumstances and to render overly rigid rules more tractable. Principles allow the legislator to achieve economies of means, thus replacing a pointillist regulatory technique that finds expression through a multitude of detailed rules. Such flexibility has the added advantage of making it easier to adapt rules to changing circumstances, ensuring for the principles the type of sustained use that more precise and complete rules no longer enjoy; being malleable, principles do not need to be formally modified when circumstances change.

In Section 4 of this Chapter we saw that if these principles are to stimulate public policies, they should be co-ordinated with another norm whose substance is not yet clearly defined: that is, the constitutional right to protection of the environment, which also requires public authorities to act to protect the environment. It is not merely the obligations of the public authorities under such law that are clarified by the directing principles of the polluter pays, prevention, and precaution; these also serve as a source of inspiration for the procedural rights granted in the areas of information, participation, and access to justice.

In Section 5 we saw that the polluter-pays, preventive, and precautionary principles may play a determining role in balancing interests—an activity which plays an important part in post-modern law—by helping courts to understand the specific value of environmental protection measures in the context of proportionality testing; this will increase the importance of such measures when conflicting interests are being balanced.

As shown by the perspectives considered above, the transformations brought about by these three directing principles of environmental law are not timely and local but also continuous and global. These principles are not abstract and isolated; they serve to integrate a series of normative processes that are in their present form necessary but insufficient. By promoting reforms, calling for change, and freeing courts from the constraint of an overly literal interpretation of texts they set environment law in motion. In this way they symbolize the subtle transition from modern to post-modern law.

6

The Legal Status of the Directing Principles of Environmental Law: From Political Slogans to Normative Principles

1. INTRODUCTORY REMARKS

Like most legal disciplines, environmental law produces principles in order to affirm its specificity. Indeed, there is such an abundance of principles in this discipline that one is forced to wonder whether, given the relative lack of rigour of the approach, the law-maker and doctrine will end up misusing them.

Despite the success of the principles of the polluter pays, prevention, and precaution in international and EC law as well as national environment laws, neither doctrine nor case-law has succeeded in clearing up the mystery of their legal status. How should we class these three principles? Do they display the characteristics that typify normative principles? Are we dealing with complete rules? Are they sufficiently precise to allow legal effects to be deduced? Do they call for the adoption of more precise rules?

These questions do not admit of clear-cut answers. Whether it is a matter of their origin, their formulation, their basis, or their place in the hierarchy of norms, the directing principles of environmental law such as the principles of the polluter pays, prevention, and precaution constitute a theoretical challenge to any effort at classification. On one hand their normative character is likely to vary as a function of the legal system in which they are being applied. On the other hand the heterogenieity of the functions these principles are supposed to fulfil—described in the preceding Chapter—only add to the confusion: inspiring the law-maker and guiding positive law, filling gaps, resolving conflicts for some, and serving as a norm for others.

Our attempt to elucidate the legal nature of the directing principles of environmental law consists first in recalling, at the level of legal theory, what distinguishes a principle from other rules (Section 2 below). We must then verify, this time at the level of the international, EC, and national legal orders, under what conditions the polluters-pays, preventive action, and precautionary principles are apt to assume an autonomous normative value (Section 3) in order to analyse their potential in administrative, civil, and criminal proceedings (Section 4).

Notwithstanding the theoretical character of this approach, inevitable given the diversity of legal systems considered in this work, we put forward the practical effects of each choice of classification proposed.

2. Principles and rules of indeterminate content

Despite its long-standing popularity with jurists, the term 'principle' remains controversial as a result of its multiple meanings. By turn used to indicate the essential characteristics of legal institutions (descriptive principles), to designate fundamental legal norms (basic principles), or to fill gaps in positive law by assigning a constitutional or legal value to rules which are not yet formally set forth in written sources of law although they are considered essential (general principles of law), the notion of principle is closely linked to legal classifications. Several factors obscure their nature and legal effect, however. First, the term 'principle' serves as a rubric for both high-level rules that set out the foundations or main objectives of the rule of law (eg the principles of equality and of legal certainty) and rules of legal technique (eg the principle of proportionality). An additional problem is that principles have extremely diverse origins. They are sometimes expressly stated in fundamental legal texts (constitutions and basic laws). Failing formulation in this type of provision, principles may be the product of a purely judicial construction (as is the case for the principles set forth by the ECJ, constitutional courts, and administrative high courts). The latter situation gives rise to some confusion about the role of judges, who do not have the power in Continental legal systems to create legal norms. Their main function is confined to settling disputes by applying the constitutional, legislative, and regulatory norms at their disposal, not to produce legal rules.

By recourse to the teachings of the general theory of law, we attempt to clarify the status of environmental law principles. We first set out what distinguishes these principles from legal rules (Subsection 2.1 below) in order to put forward a new concept: that of rules of indeterminate content (Subsection 2.2). These are abstract models, which will become more nuanced through practical application (Subsection 2.3).

2.1. The theoretical distinction between principles and legal rules

The distinction between principles and rules has given rise to an important discussion within the general theory of law, whose main lines may constitute early signposts for resolving the problem of the legal status of environmental law principles.[1] We first recall the analyses carried out by Dworkin,[2] who used

---

[1] For a standard definition of what should be properly called 'legal rule', see L.A. Hart, *The Concept of Law* (Oxford: Clarendon, 1961) 8–12, 27–32, 38–4, 97 *et seq.*

[2] R. Dworkin, *Taking Rights Seriously* (Cambridge: Harvard U.P., 1977) 35.

principles to counter certain positivist theories, in particular those developed by Hart.[3]

According to Dworkin, a rule sets forth a precise solution for specific facts. Once its conditions of application have been fulfilled it leads directly to a legal solution. By contrast, a principle is a legal proposal which does not necessarily exist in written form and which provides the general orientation and direction to which positive law must conform. It is not applicable in an all-or-nothing fashion, but is limited to providing the court with a reason that argues in favour of a particular solution, but without constituting a binding norm.[4] Thus, exaggerating somewhat, we may qualify the rules as 'little dictators' while principles are merely 'counsellors' since they do not produce immediate legal consequences.[5]

As a result, principles allow a great deal more discretion to their interpreters than do rules, which are naturally less subject to interpretation. Principles are therefore 'flexible instruments of action', which can be adapted and manipulated to suit the specific situations to which they are being applied, while rules are a great deal more rigid. This first distinction, according to Dworkin, implies a second. Principles have a dimension absent in rules of positive law: they have variable weight, which rules do not have.[6] They can therefore withstand contradictions, whereas rules offer no possibility of compromise. When several principles are in conflict the judge allows himself to be guided by the one he believes to have the greatest weight. Such a balancing is not possible among rules, which either apply or do not apply in a specific case.

This thesis has been the subject of many critiques, among them by Raz, who observed that competing legal rules are likely to apply to a single situation and that conflicts may consequently break out among rules of positive law.[7] Raz believes, moreover, that while principles may be characterized by weight, the same may be said of rules, since some of these (for example those relating to public policy) are likely to carry more weight than others. Raz concludes from this that principles could more clearly be identified by recourse to the degree of abstraction of a norm. In that regard, he notes that principles give rise to indeterminate actions while rules determine specific actions. The distinction would thus be one of degree rather than nature. Moreover, according to Raz, principles are able to incorporate a number of values into the legal system that rules of law may not recognize as such. The sharp distinction between principles and rules that looms so large in the work of Dworkin should thus be strongly nuanced.

---

[3] L.A. Hart, n. 1 above, 89–96.

[4] R. Dworkin, n. 2 above, 24.

[5] N. de Sadeleer, 'Réflexions sur le principe de précaution' in E. Zaccaï and J.M. Missa (eds.), *Le principe de précaution* (Brussels: ULB U.P., 2000) 118.

[6] R. Dworkin, n. 2 above, 26.

[7] J. Raz, 'Legal Principles and the Limits of the Law' (1972) Yale LJ 823.

2.2. Nuancing the distinction between principles and legal rules: The emergence of rules of indeterminate content

Based on the conclusions of this controversy, we may ask whether it is in fact reasonable to want to distinguish directing principles of environmental law from other rules at all costs. The difference between principles and rules developed by Dworkin in any case does not take into account one of the main characteristics of post-modern law: the declaration of legal principles in public policy. As policies become more targeted, an intermediate category has arisen: that of rules of an indeterminate nature, which may be set against rules of complete and precise content.[8] The polluter-pays, prevention, and precautionary principles of environment law illustrate the emergence of such rules, which weaken the dichotomy put forward by Dworkin.

Rules of determinate content are endowed with unequivocal meaning owing to their degree of precision. The cases they regulate are precisely determined, thanks to the rigour of legal terms, which makes it possible to narrow the multiple meanings of ordinary language.[9] Their degree of precision allows them to regulate, prohibit, or authorize types of behaviour by reducing the risk of interpretation, and thence of contention, as regards their application. By giving rise to predictability—that is, the ability to deduce an infinite number of similar solutions from a single norm—they guarantee legal certainty. Environmental law is essentially composed of rules formulated with a high degree of precision. Norms for products, the operation of facilities or waste all strictly establish the thresholds that producers, contractors, or operators must respect, under pain of punishment; none of these norms allows those to whom they are addressed any choice other than full compliance.

Rules of determinate content constrain because they permit no latitude concerning their application; those of indeterminate content are more flexible. Their degree of abstraction is so great that it is not possible to deduce obligations from them with the same degree of certainty that can be assumed when considering rules of determinate content. Consequently, they cannot constrain those to whom they are addressed to adopt or avoid one or another type of behaviour in the same way as rules of determinate content. They always retain a wide margin of interpretation to ensure their implementation. International law, for instance, is loaded with expressions which are of indeterminate content.[10]

Conceived to regulate situations that are both complex and heterogeneous, most directing principles of environmental law are far more general than other rules. Thus, for example, one might refer to the 'principle' of preventing trans-

---

[8] We note, however, that this distinction is rather abstract, for a legal rule is in fact never intended to be completely final; each of its applications makes it more precise, polishes it, provides shades of meaning, and indeed transforms it.

[9] A. Jeammaud, 'La règle de droit comme modèle' (1990) 28 D. 207.

[10] M. Koskenniemi, *From Apology to Utopia: The Structure of International Legal Argument* (Helsinki: Lakimiestliiton Kustannuys, 1989) 22–3.

boundary harm but the 'rule' that requires carrying out an environmental impact assessment for a project with significant transboundary impacts. The analysis in Part I of this book highlighted that particularity. It soon becomes obvious that the polluter-pays principle is able to encompass legal regimes as different as those for State aids for enterprises, taxation intended to reduce nuisances, and strict liability for damages caused by pollution. Similarly, the preventive principle does not determine the degree of constraint of a policy measure or the time at which it should enter into force and it does not identify those to whom it is addressed. All such questions are left to the discretion of the public authorities. Indeed, it is the nature of these principles to leave a wide margin of manoeuvre to the bodies that must implement them. The directing principles could not in any case be confined within a complete and final definition: this would have the effect of setting limits to their meaning and preventing them from evolving to meet new contingencies.

In environmental law the distinction between directing principles of environmental law and rules of determinate content may be illustrated by the following example. When a measure requires importers of waste to deliver these to duly authorized installations for treatment, it is laying down a categorical instruction. For each import the administration will be obliged to verify whether the wastes have in fact been delivered to an authorized enterprise; it will not enjoy any discretion. The situation is quite different when a measure provides that imports and exports of waste should be governed by the principles of self-sufficiency and proximity. These two principles are only weakly specific; they do not lay down the distance that must separate the site where waste was produced from the treatment installation or set a capacity threshold for the installation receiving waste shipments. The lack of precision of the terms 'self-sufficiency' and 'proximity' allows the administration considerable discretion in determining what transfers may be authorized, thereby allowing it to apply the two principles in different ways depending on the details of a given situation. Nonetheless, administrations must respect these principles and may not fail to verify whether waste transfers are covering too great a distance and thus threatening to overwhelm available treatment capacity.

In the same way, authorities are not required to forbid an activity in the name of precaution if such a response would prove disproportionate. In a given case they may decide not to follow a principle by clearly setting out the reasons for that choice. In contrast, more precise provisions on the pollution of soil or water provide the automatic cessation of polluting activities once quality standards have been exceeded. The authorities do not have the choice of not applying such provisions.

2.3. Nuancing the distinction between rules of indeterminate content and those of determinate content

An overly clear distinction between the polluter-pays, prevention, and precautionary principles and the other rules that make up environment law risks disturbing the often subtle relation that unites the two. The connection between them should be understood less in terms of opposition than of gradation, in that each of these principles presents varying degrees of precision and thereby more closely resembles or further differs from the model of a rule of determinate content.

In this way a constitutional rule formulated in a very general manner (the right to a healthy environment) may take on a more concrete form through a gradual series of modifications, each more precise than the last. Its first application may be as a principle set out in framework legislation (the preventive principle), then as a subsidiary principle laid down in sectoral legislation (the principle requiring the use of best available technologies), finally to reappear in an individual decision, the form taken by a legal rule that is complete and precise (the requirement to use a specified technology in a given situation). These successive uses gradually make a principle more normative: the more precisely and completely a legal norm is drafted, the more easily it can be applied to a particular case. That being said, the generality of principles implies that subsidiary principles, and following from that even more precise norms, make their use more concrete.

3. The autonomous normative value of environmental law principles

3.1. The centrality of autonomy

For some authors the principles of environmental law are nothing more than political principles intended to guide legislative and regulatory action.[11] Thus, in the absence of a specific legal or regulatory application to provide a supporting dynamic, principles would lack immediate and autonomous applicability. If the law-maker decided to ignore them, applicants could not depend on them.

The question then arises whether, in the context of international, EC, and national legal systems, environmental law principles such as the principles of the polluter pays, prevention, and precaution may achieve the status of direct applicability in the absence of specific regulations, or whether they merely constitute interpretive rules for such regulations. In other words, do those principles have direct application or do they need additional action by the legislator to make them operative through more specific rules?

Everything hinges on this question. If directing principles of environmental law are true and autonomous normative principles, they may be directly raised

---

[11] L. Krämer, 'General Principles of Community Environmental Law and their Translation into Secondary Law' (1999) 3:4 L & EA 361, according to whom 'General principles constitute rather leitmotives, guiding principles, than legal provisions'. Other critics have argued that principles such as the precautionary principle are too elusive to be binding. Eg L. Gündling, 'The Status in International Law of the Precautionary Principle' (1990) 23 Int'l J Estuarine & Coastal L 25.

by States before national courts or by individuals before EC and national courts. In addition, the autonomy of environmental law directing principles would justify significant derogations being applied to other principles that have long been explicitly recognized: in particular, freedom of competition, free trade and industry, and even the free circulation of goods. On the other hand, if these principles are devoid of autonomous normative value they could not be relied upon by litigants or used to hold intersecting principles in check.

At present neither legal texts, doctrine, nor court practice is able to supply a definitive response to the questions raised above. It is nevertheless possible to fix a certain number of markers to guide our interpretation of the role of these principles. There can be no legal norm, and hence no normative principle, when language is purely descriptive or narrative. An optimal degree of precision is indispensable if a legal provision is to fulfil its function.[12] Whether it proscribes, prohibits, enjoins, permits, or provides, a legal provision exists in order to dictate particular behaviour in a sufficiently precise and unequivocal manner.

Environment law is particularly vulnerable as concerns this 'optimal degree of precision'. The field is constantly veering between a complete absence of rules and excessive stringency: at times rules are set out in exaggerated detail and are thus always under threat of being outpaced by changes in the context of their application as set out in regulations; at other times rules are so vague that it is difficult to know where they could be applicable.

The prevention, precautionary, and polluter-pays principles are *directing principles*: principles that guide the actions of public authorities. They attempt to cope with this twofold risk by giving rise to a quantity of more precise and binding rules.[13] In order to assume an autonomous character and to bind those to whom they are addressed, these principles must fulfil two conditions: first, they must appear in a normative text (formal approach); and secondly, they must be formulated in a sufficiently prescriptive manner (substantive approach). Using this twofold approach, we attempt to verify the autonomous character of these three principles in three distinct legal spheres.

3.2. International law

Specific features of international environmental law make this discipline a particularly fertile ground for the development of principles. However, the precise legal status of specific principles is also the object of considerable uncertainty and disagreement.[14]

There are three aspects to the question of the legal value of the directing principles of environmental law we have analysed. First, we must consider

---

[12] N. de Sadeleer, *Les principes du pollueur-payeur, de prévention et de précaution* (Brussels: Bruylant/Agence Universitaire pour la Francophonie, 1999) 235.

[13] See the discussion in Chapter 4 above.

[14] L. Paradell-Trius, 'Principles of International Environmental Law: An Overview' (2000) 9: 2 RECIEL 93.

their status when they are set out in soft-law texts (Subsection 3.2.1 below). Secondly, we must verify that they can be regarded as part of so-called hard law, which imposes mandatory obligations on States, when they are affirmed by international conventions (Subsection 3.2.2). Finally, we must ask whether the precautionary principle may not be accorded the status of customary law, based on its constant reiteration in normative texts (Subsection 3.2.3).

3.2.1. Soft-law instruments

Abounding in declarations, resolutions, and guidelines, international environment law is a favoured discipline for the use of soft-law instruments.[15] The 1972 Stockholm Declaration on the Human Environment identified twenty-six principles; the 1982 World Charter for Nature proclaimed five general principles; more recently, the 1992 Rio de Janeiro Declaration on Environment and Development proclaimed twenty-seven principles. Agenda 21, intended to clarify the scope of the UN Declaration, contains an impressive string of principles in its own right. As we saw in Part I above, the principles of the polluter pays, prevention, and precaution are set out in most of these instruments. The various principles proclaimed in those three instruments have a universal significance. As core principles of international law, they cannot be dismissed as the work of one segment of international society.[16]

Soft-law instruments such as recommendations, guidelines, and declarations by heads of states or ministers at international conferences do not fit neatly into any of the traditional categories of international legal sources.[17] Moreover, the provisions entitled 'principles' set out in these texts are devoid of binding effect.

First, principles declared in soft-law instruments may not be put in the same category as normative principles, since soft law is not legally binding *per se*. Secondly, owing to their imprecise formulation, they cannot be likened to normative principles on the substantive level. For example, the fact that Principle 21 of the Rio Declaration on Environment and Development encourages mobilization of the 'creativity, ideals and courage of the youth of the world . . . to forge a global partnership in order to achieve sustainable development and ensure a better future for all' is obviously of no legal consequence for either the youth of the world or the international community.

---

[15] See the various studies on non-binding norms in environmental law published in D. Shelton (ed.), *Commitment and Compliance* (Oxford University Press, 2000) 121–242.

[16] A. Boyle and D. Freestone (eds.), *International Law and Sustainable Development* (Oxford University Press, 1999) 4.

[17] P. Weil, 'Towards Relative Normativity in International Law' (1983) 77 AJIL 413; T. Gruchalla-Wesierki, 'A Framework for Understanding "Soft law" ' (1984) 30 McGill LJ 37–88; C.M. Chinkin, 'The Challenge of Soft Law: Development and Change in International Law' (1989) 38 ICLQ 85–6; P.-M. Dupuy, 'Soft Law and the International Law on the Environment' (1991) 12 Mich. J Int'l L 420; P. Birnie and A. Boyle, *International Law and the Environment* (2nd edn., Oxford University Press, 2002) 165; A. Boyle, 'Some Reflections on the Relationship of Treaties and Soft Law' (1999) 48 ICLQ 901; O. Elias and C. Lim, ' "General Principles of Law", "Soft Law" and the Identification of International Law' (1997) 28: 3 NYIL 45; C.M. Chinkin, 'Normative Development in the International Legal System' in D. Shelton (ed.), *Commitment and Compliance, See* n. 15 above, 21–42.

Thus, despite their laudable intentions, soft-law 'principles' do not take on the features that lead to recognition of a normative principle. Nevertheless, the commitments made by States should be understood in the light of the principles set out in this type of instrument, among other things; taken up in soft-law provisions, they assume a purely interpretative value. In addition, directing principles of environmental law can be used as a precursor to hard law; they may thus serve as forerunners of treaty law.[18] They can also play a catalytic role in the customary international law-making process: they may act as magnetic poles attracting and channeling State practice. The hardening of soft law is therefore important for the development of hard law and can be a good indication of a principle of law in *status nascendi*. Indeed, the recalling, repetition, and reiteration of the same principles in various non-binding instruments can gradually contribute to the development and establishment of true normative principles. Consequently, reference to soft law can be used as evidence of State practice that might support the existence of a rule of customary law.[19]

3.2.2. Hard-law instruments

In order to be accorded the status of normative principles, the polluters-pays, preventive, and precautionary principles must first be set out in the operative provisions of a convention (formal approach) and their wording must render them binding upon Parties (substantive approach).

3.2.2.1. Formal approach

At a formal level, when one of those directing principles is set out in a treaty or international convention, it should have the normative value that attaches to that instrument. In national legal regimes where international treaties and conventions have a value superior to that of national law, recognition of the directing principle should then be imperative for the national legislator.

Neither the form nor the type of instrument, however, determines the legal status of the directing principle which is enunciated.[20] Thus, the fact that a directing principle is taken up in an international convention does not necessarily indicate that it is a normative principle.[21] In fact, the three principles examined in Part I of this work do not always occupy the same position in conventions:

---

[18] D. Shelton, 'Law Non-Law and the Problem of "Soft Law"' and A. Kiss 'Commentary and Conclusions' in D. Shelton (ed.), *Commitment and Compliance*, see n. 15 above, 10 and 229. See also C.M. Chinkin, 'Normative Development in the International Legal System' in D. Shelton (ed.), *Commitment and Compliance*, n. 15 above, 31–4. See also P. Birnie and A. Boyle, *International Law and the Environment* (2nd edn.), n. 17 above, 119–20.

[19] A. Boyle, 'Codification of International Environmental Law...', in A. Boyle and D. Freestone, *International Law and Sustainable Development* (Oxford University Press, 1999) 64; Fr. Maes, 'Environmental Law Principles and the Legislator: The Law of the Sea' in M. Sheridan and L. Lavrysen (eds.), *Environmental Law Principles* (Brussels: Bruylant, 2002) 17–18.

[20] C.M. Chinkin, 'Normative Development...', n. 18 above, 37.

[21] P. Martin-Bidou, 'Le principe de précaution en droit international de l'environnement' (1999) 3 RGDIP 660.

some of them occur in preambles,[22] while others are found in the operative provisions of conventions, either in the form of general obligations[23] or specific provisions.[24] Obviously, a distinction should be drawn between the principles found in the preambular sections of treaties and those elaborated in the operational parts. A principle can be normative only to the extent that it is affirmed by an operative provision of a convention. When it is merely mentioned in the preamble its role is simply to inform the more precise legal norms contained in the convention's operative paragraphs.

3.2.2.2. Substantive approach

The issue of the legal status of the principles set out in international conventions becomes more complicated when we turn our attention to their wording. The way in which the polluters-pays, preventive action, and precautionary principles are expressed in international treaties appreciably weakens their effect, for they are not always presented as normative principles that are directly binding on States and which courts must take into account in their decisions. When a convention expressly provides for the adoption of implementing norms, these principles are devoid of autonomous character. This argument finds support in the structure of international law as well as in a literal interpretation of certain legal provisions setting out the principles.

First, we note that the polluters-pays, preventive, and precautionary principles generally figure in framework conventions.[25] Although this technique, widely used in international environmental law, makes it possible to gather the support of a large number of States, it is merely a first step in the elaboration of normative principles.[26] For that to occur these directing principles have to be made operational through protocols adopted to implement the framework conventions.

Secondly, in a number of international conventions the polluters-pays, preventive action, and precautionary principles are worded in such a way that they are deprived of all immediate and autonomous applicability. Use of terms such as 'form a basis for', 'inspire', 'endeavour', etc. imply that these three principles are merely intended to prepare States to implement their international obligations.

---

[22] This is the case for the precautionary principle in the 1992 CBD and in the 1994 Oslo Protocol to the LRATP. This is also the case for the polluter-pays principle found in the preambular sections of the 1996 Protocol for the Protection of the Mediterranean Sea Against Pollution from Land-Based Sources (not yet in force), the 1990 OPRC, the 1992 Helsinki Convention on the Transboundary Effects of Industrial Accidents, and the 2000 London Protocol on Preparedness, Response and Co-operation to Pollution Incidents by Hazardous and Noxious Substances (not in force).

[23] For the precautionary principle see UNFCCC, Article 3(3).

[24] For the precautionary principle see Article 4 of the 1991 Bamako Convention on the Import into Africa and the Control of Transboundary Movement and Management of Hazardous Wastes Within Africa (not in force).

[25] See the final annex below listing the international conventions that set out the polluter-pays, preventive, and precautionary principles.

[26] G. Palmer, 'New Ways to Make International Environmental Law' (1992) 86: 2 AJIL 259; T. Gehring, 'International Environmental Regimes: Dynamic Sectoral Legal Systems' (1990) 1 YbIEL 35.

For example, according to the 1991 Bamako Convention on the Import into Africa and the Control of Transboundary Movement and Management of Hazardous Wastes Within Africa, 'Each Party shall strive to adopt and implement the preventive, precautionary approach to pollution problems...'; the 1992 Helsinki Convention on the Protection and Use of Transboundary Watercourses and International Lakes states that Parties 'shall be guided' by the precautionary and polluter-pays principles; the 1994 Sofia Convention on Co-operation for the Protection and Use of the Danube provides that the polluter-pays and precautionary principles constitute 'the basis' for all measures intended to protect the Danube and the waters of its catchment basin; the 1999 Bern Convention on the Protection of the Rhine states that 'the contracting Parties take their inspiration from the principles...'; and the 1992 UNFCCC states that 'The Parties should take precautionary measures...'.

At the same time, however, international environment law also contains provisions in which these directing principles are recognized as being directly binding on States Parties. For instance, the 1992 OSPAR Convention requires that Parties 'shall apply' the precautionary principle.

Nevertheless, these directing principles are rarely set out in a precise manner and most international conventions do not bother to define them or to spell out their implications. One must therefore consider on a case-by-case basis whether the terms used to describe the polluters-pays or the precautionary principle are sufficiently prescriptive, in order to determine if these principles could be considered to directly apply to States without in turn being laid down in implementing norms such as protocols.

By merely referring to a 'precautionary principle' without providing a minimal amount of content through more substantive provisions, States will not be bound to any great extent. Mere reference to this principle is not sufficient to allow it to emerge as a normative principle of international law. It is therefore time to develop the precautionary principle beyond the stage of mere intentions. Treaties should be more explicit about the binding precautionary obligations that could be deduced from the principle.[27]

3.2.3. *Customary value*

The difficulty of determining the legal status of some directing principles of environmental law, particularly that of the precautionary principle, becomes even more acute when we consider whether they have acquired functional autonomy by becoming general principles of customary international law.

---

[27] To avoid a mere statement of intentions, some authors propose that the principle should be submitted to several criteria: (1) a reasonably precise statement of the desired environmental goal and the environmental condition that justifies invoking the precautionary principle; (2) identification of the jurisdictional scope of the agreed precautionary obligations under the principle; (3) specification of those human activities for which precautionary measures are required; and (4) a clear statement of the precautionary measures that must be undertaken before engaging in a covered activity. Eg J.E. Hickley and V.R. Walker, 'Refining the precautionary principle in international environmental law' (1995) 14: 3 Va Envtl LJ 453–4.

While the principle of ensuring that activities within a State's jurisdiction or control do not cause damage to the environment of other States or of areas beyond national jurisdiction[28] and the principle of prevention[29] have already obtained that status, the procedure appears to be a great deal more delicate in the case of the precautionary principle. Only the repeated use of State practice is likely to transform precaution into a customary norm. A number of authors believe that sufficient State practice currently exists to support the view that the precautionary principle should be considered a principle of customary international law.[30] Others, however, argue that the principle has not yet achieved the status of a principle of international law, or at least consider such status doubtful, amongst other reasons because the principle is still subject to a wide range of interpretations.[31]

This question is important. While treaties create law between parties, the recognition of the precautionary principle as an international custom will make it applicable to all States.[32]

Thus far the argument that the precautionary principle has customary value has come up against the refusal by various international courts to rule in favour of this interpretation. The precautionary principle has been put forward twice

---

[28] *Legality of the Threat or Use of Nuclear Weapons*, Advisory Opinion, ICJ Rep [1996] 226, at 241–2. See the discussion in Chapter 2, Section 2 above.

[29] In its advisory opinion in the *Nuclear Weapons* case [1996] the ICJ held that the general obligation to take all measures to ensure that activities under their jurisdiction or control are so conducted as not to cause damage by pollution to other States and their environment has become part of the corpus of international law relating to the environment (para. 29). Nevertheless, balanced against principles of international law, the ICJ was of the opinion that this general obligation was not intended to be an obligation of total restraint during a military conflict. See also *Gabcíkovo-Nagymaros (Hungary v. Slovakia)*, ICJ Rep [1997] paras. 53, 87, and 140.

[30] See, for example, P. Sands, *Principles of International Environmental Law*, (Manchester: MUP, 1995) 212; J. Cameron, 'The Status of the Precautionary Principle in International Law' in T. O'Riordan and J. Cameron (eds.), *Interpreting the Precautionary Principle* (London: Cameron & May, 1994) 283; J. Cameron and J. Abouchar, 'The Status of the Precautionary Principle in International Law' in D. Freestone and E. Hey (eds.), *The Precautionary Principle in International Law* (London: Kluwer, 1995) 52; Z. Plater, 'From the Beginning, a Fundamental Shift in Paradigms: A Theory and Short History of Environmental Law' (1994) Loy LAL Rev 1000; H. Hohmann, *Precautionary Legal Duties and Principles of Modern International Environmental Law* (London: Graham and Trotman, 1994) 184; O. McIntyre and T. Mosedale, 'The Precautionary Principle as a Norm of Customary International Law' (1997) 9: 2 JEL 221; A. Trouwbost, *Evolution and Status of the Precautionary Principle in International Law* (London: Kluwer Law International, 2002). Furthermore, Australian courts have held the principle was relevant even when it is not included in a legislative framework because it is a 'customary norm of international law'. See the discussion in Chapter 3, Subsection 2.3.7. above.

[31] See eg L. Gündling, n. 11 above, 30; P. Birnie and A. Boyle, *International Law and the Environment*, n. 17 above, 119–20. It should be noted, however, that those authors who do not consider the precautionary principle as a principle of customary law were writing before 1992; thereafter, the principle made important advances in international law. P. Birnie and A. Boyle, in their 2nd edition of *International Law and the Environment*, find that there are good reasons for 'judicial hesitation' concerning the legal status of the precautionary principle. 'These uncertainties in the meaning, application, and implications of the precautionary principle or approach suggest that the propositions that it is, or it is not, customary international law are too simplistic'. They recognize, however, that the principle can be considered as a principle of international law on which decision-makers and courts may rely.

[32] *Contra* A. Cassese, who considers that 'custom ultimately rested on a consensual basis.' Eg *International Law in a Divided World* (Oxford: Clarendon, 1986) 169.

before the ICJ, which refused to take a decision on those grounds. In the 1992 *French nuclear testing* case the ICJ used a procedural argument to avoid a decision on the complaint put forward by New Zealand based on the precautionary principle.[33] In the *Gabcíkovo-Nagyramos* case the Court again managed to avoid a direct ruling on the application of the precautionary principle, which had been advanced by Hungary to justify its failure to meet its commitments.[34]

In the WTO *Beef Hormones* case the United States did not consider that the precautionary principle represented customary international law, but suggested it was an 'approach' rather than a 'principle'.[35] Canada, too, took the view that the precautionary principle has not yet been incorporated into the corpus of public international law; however, it conceded that the 'precautionary approach' or 'concept' was 'an emerging principle of law' which may in future crystallize into one of the 'general principles of law recognised by civilized nations' within the meaning of Article 38(1)(c) of the Statute of the International Court of Justice.[36] The opinion of the Appellate Body on the normative value of the precautionary principle in international law was diffident, at best:[37]

The status of the precautionary principle in international law continues to be the subject of debate among academics, law practitioners, regulators and judges. The precautionary principle is regarded by some as having crystallized into a general principle of customary international environmental law. Whether it has been widely accepted by members as a principle of general or customary international law appears less than clear. We consider, however, that it is unnecessary, and probably imprudent, for the appellate body in this appeal to take a position on this important, but abstract, question. We note that the panel itself did not make any definitive finding with regard to the status of the precautionary principle in international law and that the precautionary principle, at least outside the field of international environmental law, still awaits authoritative formulation.

On the basis of this statement the Appellate Body concluded that the disputes caused by the desire of some WTO contracting parties to oppose the import of products coming from other States on health grounds would have to be settled by strictly applying WTO Agreements. The implicit reference to the precautionary principle in Articles 3(3) and 5(7) of the SPS Agreement could not lead to the conclusion that the principle would prevail over the obligation imposed by Articles 2 and 5(1) of the SPS, which require that risk be scientifically proved. In the other two SPS disputes the Appellate Body did not rule on the customary value of the principle.[38]

While these decisions are characterized by a relatively nuanced assessment, they nonetheless demonstrate that international courts are not favourable to

---

[33] ICJ Rep [1992] 288.

[34] *Gabcíkovo-Nagymaros (Hungary v. Slovakia)* ICJ Rep [1997] para. 56.

[35] United States appellee's submission, para. 92.

[36] Canada appellee's submission, para. 34.

[37] Appellate Body, *Hormones*, para 123. See the discussion in Chapter 3, Subsection 2.1.2.3. above.

[38] Appellate Body, *Japan Varietals*.

the direct and autonomous application of the precautionary principle. Moreover, a general principle of integration, such as that set out in Article 6 of the EC Treaty, is missing from major international conventions,[39] even though the need to integrate environmental protection and economic development was regarded by the ICJ as one of the decisive elements of the *Gabcíkovo-Nagymaros* case.[40]

Proving the existence of a customary international law principle requires sufficient support in both State practice (*usus*) and *opinio iuris*.[41] State practice must be uniform, extensive, and representative in character. Policy statements, comments by governments on draft treaties, legislation, decisions of national courts and executive authorities, pleadings before international tribunals, statements in international organizations, and the resolutions those bodies adopt are all examples of State practice that should be taken into account when considering the precautionary principle as a principle of customary international law.[42]

Does the recent origin of the precautionary principle not prevent it from becoming such a principle, however? Although normally a certain amount of time elapses before there is sufficient practice to satisfy the criteria referred to above, no specific time requirement exists.[43] In fact, some customary principles have sprung up quite quickly (for example, the *régime* of the continental shelf) because there was a substantive and representative quantity of State practice. In addition, one must recall that while State practice must be both extensive and representative, it does not need to be universal. Much will depend on the degree of representativeness of the practice.[44]

In our view, the prevalence of the principle in recent State practice and in international law[45] suggests that, contrary to the opinion of the WTO Appel-

---

[39] With the exceptions of Article 2(1) of the 1985 ASEAN Agreement on the Conservation of Nature and Natural Resources; Articles 6(b) and 10(a) of the 1992 CBD; Article 4(2) of the 1994 Paris Convention to Combat Desertification; and Articles 1 and 32(1) of the 2000 ACP-EC Cotonou Agreement.

[40] A. Boyle and D. Freestone (eds.), *International Law and Sustainable Development*, n. 16 above, 10.

[41] Both case-law and doctrinal analyses support this view. *North Sea Continental Shelf* case [1969] ICJ Rep 44; para. 77, see also 42, para. 71; *Continental Shelf (Libya v. Malta)*, ICJ Rep [1985] 29–30, para. 27; *Military and Paramilitary Activities in and Against Nicaragua* case (Nicaragua v. USA), ICJ Rep [1986] ICJ Rep 97, paras. 183–4, 108–9, 207. See further I. Brownlie, *Principles of Public International Law* (Oxford University Press, 5th edn., 1998) 4–11; A. D'Amato, *The Concept of Custom in International Law* (Ithaca, London: Cornell, 1971) 74–87; H. Thirlway, *International Customary Law and Codification* (Leiden: Sijhoff, 1972) 145–6; G.J.H. van Hoof, *Rethinking the Sources of International Law* (Deventer: Kluwer, 1983) 87; Hoggenmacher, 'La doctrine des deux éléments du droit coutumier dans la pratique de la Cour Internationale' (1986) 90: 5 RGDIP 114; M. Bos, 'The identification of Custom in International Law' (1982) 25 GYbIL 22.

[42] I. Brownlie, n. 41 above, 5.

[43] *North Sea Continental Shelf* case [1969] ICJ Rep 43, para. 74.

[44] In the words of the ICJ in the *North Sea Continental Shelf* case, the practice must 'include that of States whose interests are specially affected'.

[45] Multilateral treaties can provide the inspiration for the adoption of new customary rules. Eg *North Sea Continental Shelf* case (*Germany v. Denmark; Germany v. Netherlands*) [1969] ICJ Rep 41, para. 71. In other words, the numerous multilateral treaties recognizing the principle of precaution can constitute the source of a new customary rule. Nevertheless, the normal conditions for the formation of a customary rule must be fulfilled.

late Body, it may indeed have attained this status.[46] Our own analysis of the evolution of the precautionary principle in international and EC law and a number of national legal orders provides firm evidence to substantiate that conclusion.[47]

3.3. European Community law

For EC law, as for public international law, one must distinguish between the directing principles set out in soft-law texts (Subsection 3.3.1. below) and those put forward in texts with normative effect, that is, in the EC Treaty and secondary EC law (Subsection 3.3.2.)

3.3.1. Soft-law instruments

Almost all the directing principles laid down in Article 174(2) of the EC Treaty—with the exception of the precautionary principle—were already present in Title II of the 1973 First Environmental Action Programme, which did not contain any legally binding requirements.[48] In fact, hardly any policy programmes, political statements, strategy documents, or White or Green Papers do not refer to one or more principles. For instance, the EC's Environmental Action Programmes have always referred to different environmental principles, which are meant subsequently to be defined more clearly through measures adopted by normal legislative procedures.

Nonetheless, such soft-law principles do not constrain the EC institutions to act in a strictly determined manner, even if statements of principles set out in earlier Action Programmes were regularly transformed into binding requirements.[49] According to ECJ case-law, resolutions are 'basically' or 'primarily' expressions of political will.[50] Referring to the Fifth Action Programme, the ECJ judged that the Programme was 'designed to provide a framework for defining and implementing Community environment policy, but does not lay down rules of a mandatory nature'.[51]

---

[46] According to Freestone, its explicit endorsement 'by a wide range of international and national bodies, by a large and growing number of international and natural resource treaties, national constitutions and legislation, as well as by courts and tribunals' suggests a pattern of State practice in the area of national and international law which strongly supports the argument that it has emerged as a principle of customary international law'. Eg D. Freestone, 'International Fisheries Law since Rio...' in A. Boyle and D. Freestone (eds.), *International Law and Sustainable Development*, n. 16, above.

[47] See the discussion in Section 2, Chapter 3 above.

[48] L. Krämer, 'General Principles of Community Environmental Law...', n. 11 above, 355.

[49] L. Lavrysen, 'Good Intentions and Less Good Results: The Five Environmental Action Programmes and their Translation into Secondary Legislation' (1999) 3: 4 L & EA 322.

[50] Case C-142/94P, *Rovigo* [1996] ECR I-6669, para. 32.

[51] Case C-9/73, *Schlüter* [1973] ECR I-1135, para. 40; Case C-59/75 *Manghera* [1976] ECR I-91, para. 21.

If soft-law principles cannot be binding, they can nevertheless be interpretive in nature when taken up in recommendations.[52] National courts are thus obliged to take them into account when resolving conflicts, particularly when such recommendations clarify the interpretation of national provisions intended to transpose these principles or when their objective is to complete EC provisions of a binding nature.[53]

3.3.2. Hard law instruments

3.3.2.1. Formal approach

Directing principles of environmental law such as the polluter-pays principle appeared in secondary EC legislation throughout the 1970s,[54] but they have only been expressed in EC primary law since 1987, with the adoption of the Single European Act. Subsequently, four environmental law principles received full recognition in the Maastricht Treaty, thanks to the insertion of Article 130r(2) (new Article 174(2)), which states that: 'Community policy on the environment...shall be based on the precautionary principle and on the principles that preventive action should be taken, that environmental damage should as a priority be rectified at source and that the polluter should pay'.

Other directing principles are explicitly laid down in the EC Treaty. The integration principle, set out in Article 6 of the Treaty,[55] provides that: 'Environmental protection requirements must be integrated into the definition and implementation of the Community policies and activities referred to in Article 3, in particular with a view to promoting sustainable development'.

The principle of a high level of environmental protection follows from several provisions of the EC Treaty: Article 2, which specifies 'a high level of protection and improvement of the quality of the environment'; Article 174(2), which provides that 'Community policy on the environment shall aim at a high level of protection taking into account the diversity of situations in the various regions of the Community...'; and Article 95(3), which stipulates in

---

[52] The polluters-pays and precautionary principles have been made clear in recommendations. This is the case for the polluter-pays principle, for instance, as set out in Recommendation 75/436/ Euratom, ECSC, EEC of 3 March 1975 regarding cost allocation and action by public authorities on environmental matters. Thus, State obligations must be understood in the light of the principles set out therein. In this perspective, soft law can be regarded as a useful tool in interpreting EC hard-law obligations. Eg G. Betlem, *Civil Liability for Transfrontier Pollution* (London: Graham and Trotman/ Martinus Nijhoff, 1993) 256. However, the Commission's Communication on the precautionary principle, which is not a recommendation, does not fall under this heading.

[53] Case C-322/88, *Grimaldi* [1989] ECR I-6669, para. 32.

[54] See Chapter 1 above.

[55] Applied by the ECJ in Case C-300/89, *Commission v. Council* [1991] ECR I-2867, paras. 22–4; Case C-379/98, *PreussenElektra AG* [2001] ECR I-2159, para. 76. In the *PreussenElektra AG* case, Advocate General Jacobs stressed that Article 6 was not merely programmatic but imposed legal obligations. Special accounts of environmental concerns must be taken in interpreting the Treaty provisions on free movement of goods (Opinion, para. 224). See the discussion in Chapter 7, Subsection 3.2.1. below.

regard to internal market policy that: 'The Commission, in its proposals...
concerning health, safety, environmental protection and consumer protection,
will take as a base a high level of protection, taking account in particular of
any new development based on scientific facts. Within their respective powers,
the European Parliament and the Council will also seek to achieve this
objective.'.

It is striking that for no other field does the EC Treaty set out so many directing
principles to serve as the basis for public policy. The EC institutions—the
Commission, the Council, the European Parliament, the Economic and Social
Committee, and the Committee of the Regions—are obliged to take these
directing principles into consideration in the course of the normative process;
in this way, all acts of secondary legislation will be subordinated to those
principles.[56] In addition, as was demonstrated by the *Safety Hi-Tech* and *Standley* cases, the ECJ must ensure respect for the principles laid down in Article
174(2) in the cases it is called upon to settle.[57]

3.3.2.2. Substantive approach

(a) Mandatory language

The EC Treaty provisions setting out the directing principles of environment law
are drafted in such a way that the institutions are obliged to apply them when
carrying out action in the environment field. The use of the indicative rather than
the conditional confirms that such provisions are obligations: 'Environmental
protection requirements must be integrated' (Article 6); 'Community policy on
the environment shall aim at a high level of protection' (Article 95 (3)); 'Community policy on the environment...shall be based on the precautionary
principle and on the principles that preventive action should be taken, that
environmental damage should as a priority be rectified at source and that the
polluter should pay' (Article 174(2)).[58]

This binding formulation is striking when one compares the three first paragraphs of Article 174, which define successively the objectives, principles, and
factors of the Community's environment policy. Thus, the *principles* embodied
in paragraph 2 of Article 174 involve language ('Community policy...shall be
based') whose effect is more mandatory than that used to describe the *objectives*
contained in paragraph 1 ('Community policy...shall contribute to pursuit of
the following objectives...'), whilst the *factors* in paragraph 3 need merely to be
taken into consideration ('in preparing its policy..., the European Community
shall take account of...').

---

[56] L. Krämer, 'The Polluter Pays Principle in Community Law: The Interpretation of Article 130r of
the EEC Treaty' in *Focus on European Law* (2nd edn., London: Graham and Trotman, 1997) 244.

[57] Case C-284/95, *Safety Hi-Tech* [1998] ECR I-4301; Case C-341/95, *Bettati* [1998] ECR I-4358;
Case C-293/97, *Standley* [1999] ECR I-2603, paras. 51–2.

[58] The conditional is sometimes appropriate for certain principles. While most official versions of
the EC Treaty state that the polluter shall pay, the English version states that the polluter should pay.

(b) A degree of discretion

The requirements that action by the EC relating to the environment shall aim at a high level of environmental protection, 'based on the precautionary principle and on the principles that preventive action should be taken, that environmental damage should as a priority be rectified at source and that the polluter should pay', and that other policies must integrate environmental protection requirements do not, however, prevent the EC institutions from exercising a wide degree of discretion in shaping the EC's environmental policy.[59] For example, according to Article 6, the obligation to aim at a high level of environmental protection must take into account 'the diversity of situations in the various regions of the Community'. This is reinforced by the need for the EC institutions to weigh the Article 174(2) principles against each other and against other policy objectives. In his conclusions on the status of these principles, Advocate General Léger indicated that the phrase 'Community policy in the EC Treaty' necessarily implied the assessment of complex and generally conflicting situations. This results in a process which 'consists in weighing the respective merits and drawbacks of any given action'.[60]

Thus, in contrast to rules of determinate content, the principles set out in the Article 174(2) always admit the possibility of accommodation. In other words, the EC institutions may depart from the principles set out in the Treaty under particular circumstances. This interpretation is corroborated by case-law such as the *Peralta* case, where the ECJ ruled that former Article 130r 'confines itself to defining the general objectives of the Community in environmental matters'[61] and that the Council was responsible for deciding what action was to be taken in this respect.

Ludwig Krämer deduces from this that: ' . . . since, by nature, any principle allows for exemptions or derogations, it is not possible to consider them as of legally binding nature. In other terms, one cannot measure a specific directive or regulation or even a specific provision of such a directive or regulation against the requirement of an environmental principle.'[62]

However, we do not agree with Krämer's argument that principles set out in Article 174(2) are not 'legally binding'. First, there is nothing astonishing in legal provisions which allow for exemptions or derogations implicitly rather than explicitly. EC law has long contained norms of indeterminate content which are implicitly subject to derogation. One need only think of the principles of equality—a basic provision of any democratic legal order—which allow a certain flexibility, as demonstrated by the case-law of constitutional courts.

Secondly, the case-law of the EC Courts has already demonstrated that there is a possibility to review secondary legislation according to Article 174(2)

---

[59] J.H. Jans, *European Environmental Law* (London: Kluwer Law Int'l, 1997) 29.
[60] Opinion in Cases C-284/95 and C-341/95, *Safety Hi-Tech* [1998] ECR I-4301, para. 73.
[61] Case C-379/92, *Peralta* [1994] ECR I-3453, para. 58.
[62] L. Krämer, 'General Principles . . .', n. 11 above, 357; *EC Environmental Law* (4th edn., London: Sweet and Maxwell, 2000) 10.

principles. A distinction must be drawn, however, between review of the omission to act and review of the content of EC secondary legislation.

(c) Review of the omission to act according to the Article 174(2) principles
Due to their indeterminacy, Article 174(2) principles do not require the EC to legislate on a particular subject in a specific and detailed manner. Thus, for example, it would be difficult to conceive of an Article 232 action (review due to an omission to act on behalf of the EC institutions) being successful on the basis of the polluters-pays, preventive action, and precautionary principles.[63]

(d) Review of the substance of EC secondary legislation
It is not in the context of a failure to act but in that of reviewing the content of EC secondary legislation and the procedures leading to its adoption that the polluter-pays, preventive action, and precautionary principles can become normative principles.[64] Indeed, the ECJ has in several cases reviewed EC secondary legislation to determine whether it is in breach of Article 174(2) principles.

For example, the new Articles 95 and 174(2) of the EC Treaty provide, for both internal market and environment policy, that secondary legislation must achieve a 'high level of environmental protection'. This particular obligation is particularly vague, since determining any degree of protection depends on numerous elements more likely to arise from subjective assessment than from objective analysis. What is considered a high level in some quarters will not necessarily be seen in the same light by others. Some authors have stated that it seems hardly conceivable that such an obligation would be open to review by the courts.[65]

The indeterminacy of this obligation does not, however, imply that EC institutions have total discretion as to how the obligation to achieve a 'high level of environmental protection' is to be applied. While the level of protection need not necessarily be the highest level possible,[66] a level of protection that is non-existent, weak, or even intermediate in nature must be considered contrary to the obligation and therefore to be reviewed by the court dealing with a relevant dispute. An EC institution, a Member State that cast a minority vote in the Council of Ministers, even an individual, in the framework of a preliminary ruling, may always contest an EC legal act whose level of protection is clearly below what might be expected in a given case before an EC court.[67] If the court, after weighing various parameters, determines that the level of protection is too

---

[63] M. Doherty, 'The Status of the Principles of EC Environmental Law' (1999) 2 JEL 379. On the actions against failure to act where such a failure is contrary to EC law, see P.J.G. Kapteyn and P. Verloren van Themaat, *Introduction to the Law of the European Community* (3rd edn., London: Kluwer Law Int'l, 1998) 466–71.

[64] M. Doherty, n. 63 above, 380.

[65] J.H. Jans, *European Environmental Law*, n. 59 above, 19.

[66] Case C-341/95, *Safety Hi-Tech* [1998] ECR I-4328, para. 47.

[67] Article 6 of the EC Treaty, which embodies the integration principle might also be subject to a control of legality. According to M. Wasmeier, 'any EC legislation that does not integrate environmental protection properly, in particular if a resulting harmful effect on the environment cannot be justified by clear and overriding reasons, is therefore subject to annulment by the ECJ in accordance with Articles 230 *et seq*.' Eg 'The Integration of Environmental Protection as a General Rule for Interpreting Community Law' (2001) 38 : 1 CMLR 164.

weak and that no valid justification has been put forward for not having satisfied the obligation in question, it may annul the disputed act.

In its decisions in the *Safety Hi-Tech* and *Bettati* cases[68] the European Court of Justice considered whether an ozone regulation was adopted in breach of principles embodied in Article 174(2) (former article 130r), among them the obligation of a 'high level of environmental protection'. This judgment clearly rejected the Council's submission that review of this obligation was beyond the reach of the Court. In both cases the Court found that a high level of protection was ensured, particularly because the EC regulation was more stringent than the EC's international obligations in this area.[69] This case-law clearly raises the possibility that failing to comply with international standards could be seen as a violation of the requirements associated with the goal of a high level of protection.

However, the Court held that the review was necessarily limited 'to the question whether the Council, by adopting the Regulation, committed a manifest error of appraisal regarding the conditions for the application of Article 130r of the Treaty' and this 'in view of the need to strike a balance between certain of the objectives and principles mentioned in Article 130r and the complexity of the implementation of those criteria'.[70] As a result of the rather limited scope of the review, Article 174(2) grants a wide discretion as to the measures that can be taken by the EC institutions.

The approach laid down by the Court in the *Safety Hi-Tech* and *Bettati* cases is that for each legal action the EC institutions must correctly assess the meaning of Article 174(2) principles and the conditions for their application in the specific context being considered;[71] however, only if EC measures are manifestly inappropriate having regard to the aim pursued would their legality be in issue. This is a complex task, and the Court will only find an action invalid if the error of appraisal is manifest. But a review by the Court is far from impossible; it is particularly conceivable in other policy areas where environmental considerations have to be taken into consideration. In those areas the EC institutions must weigh directing principles of environmental law against conflicting policy objectives. Consequently, an error of appraisal of the implications of Article 174(2) principles is more likely than in traditional environmental policy areas.[72]

---

[68] Cases C-284/95, *Safety Hi-Tech* [1998] ECR I-4301 and C-341/95, *Bettati* [1998] ECR I-4358. On the high level of protection of consumers: Case C-127/97, *Burstein* [1998] ECR I-6005.

[69] *Safety Hi-Tech*, n. 68 above, para. 46.

[70] Case C-284/95, para. 37 and Case C-341/95, para. 35.

[71] M. Doherty, n. 63 above, 383.

[72] Nonetheless, applicants are likely to come up against the significant difficulty of being allowed to institute legal proceedings before the Community courts, which have ruled that local residency, occupations such as fishing and agriculture, or the status of being affected by the results of environmental degradation do not constitute circumstances that permit applicants to demonstrate individual concern and thereby allow them standing under Article 230 of the EC Treaty. Case 219/95, *M.-T. Danielson, P. Largenteau and E. Haoa v. EC Commission* [1995] II-3051; Case C-321/95, *Greenpeace v. EC Commission* [1998] ECR I-1651.

Furthermore, a strict application of the principle of legality may combine with the obligation 'to aim at a high level of environmental protection'. For instance, the Council of Ministers had adopted a Directive aimed at implementing some technical aspects of the Directive concerning the placing on the market of plant protection products. That implementing Directive excluded groundwater from its field of application, although the framework Directive required impact assessment for both drinking water and groundwater. This partial execution of the obligations in the framework Directive had the effect of lowering the level of environmental protection, since the required assessment of the environmental impacts of plant protection products would only apply to groundwaters intended for the production of drinking water. Based on a teleological reading of the recitals of the framework Directive, the ECJ annulled the implementing Directive on the ground that its overly restrictive field of application modified an essential obligation, that of protecting groundwaters not intended for use as drinking water. The ECJ supported its reasoning by recalling that the basic Directive's recitals stated that the Directive aimed to ensure a 'high level of environmental protection' in order to avoid pesticides having any unacceptable influence on the environment and health.[73]

The ECJ has already considered cases where it reviewed whether secondary legislation was in breach of Article 174(2) principles. In the *Standley* case the ECJ examined whether Directive 91/676/EEC concerning the protection of waters against pollution caused by nitrates from agricultural sources infringed the polluter-pays principle. The Court ruled that the Nitrates Directive did not mean that farmers had to take on burdens for the elimination of pollution 'to which they have not contributed'.[74] In *Safety Hi-Tech* the ECJ accepted that the principles of Article 174(2) could be used as a means of marginally testing the validity of EC measures.[75]

To sum up, the above cases make clear that the ECJ reviews the validity of EC measures in a marginal manner. Only in cases where the institutions have made a manifest error of appraisal, misused their powers, or exceeded the limits of their discretion will the Court be prepared to declare a measure invalid.[76]

(e) The review of the content of EC Commission decisions
Other possibilities exist for reviewing EC law to determine whether there has been a violation of the environmental law principles set out in Article 174(2) of

---

[73] Case C-303/94, *European Parliament v. Council* [1996] ECR I-2943, para. 31. Also, see P. Cardonnel, 'The Annulment of the EU Uniform Principles for Evaluation and Authorisation of Pesticide Products by the ECJ' (1996) RECIEL 271.
[74] Case C-293/97, *Standley* [1999] ECR I-2603, para. 51.
[75] Case C-341/95, See nn. 68 and 70 above.
[76] W. Th. Douma, 'The European Union and the Precautionary Principle' (2000) 2 RECIEL 132.

the EC Treaty. The obligation to implement directing principles in secondary legislation is reinforced by Article 230 of the EC Treaty, under which any natural or legal person may ask the ECJ to review the legality of acts of the institutions. If, for example, the Commission were to authorize a national authority to grant State aids to a proven polluter for clean-up costs and those State aids provided the polluter with a competitive advantage over competitors from other Member States, a judicial review of the Commission's decision could take place, based on Article 87 of the Treaty and interpreted in the light of the requirements of the polluter-pays principle.[77]

3.3.3. *The normativity of Article 174(2) principles for Member State authorities*

3.3.3.1. Article 174(2) principles are addressed to EC institutions

Member State actions may not, in principle, be reviewed on the basis of the Article 174(2) principles. In the *Peralta* case the ECJ held that former Article 130R 'confines itself to defining the general objectives of the Community in environmental matters. The responsibility for deciding upon the action to be taken is entrusted to the Council by Article 130S (new Article 175).'[78] That case makes clear that the directing principles of the EC Treaty do not apply directly to national authorities; they are addressed to EC institutions.

This interpretation is insufficiently nuanced, however. First, from a political point of view, the 1975 EEC Commission's Recommendation on the Polluter-Pays Principle and the December 2000 Council Resolution on the Precautionary Principle state that these principles also apply to the Member States. Second, from a legal point of view, a distinction must be made between areas covered by secondary law and those which are not. A distinction should also be made between principles that are explicit in EC secondary legislation and those that are implicit.

In areas that have not been harmonized Article 174(2) principles cannot constrain national authorities and are devoid of direct effect (see Subsection 3.3.4. below). Nevertheless, in areas that have been harmonized the Treaty's environmental principles as set out in Article 174(2) may apply both directly and indirectly to Member States through secondary legislation (see below, Subsections 3.3.3.2. and 3.3.3.3.).

3.3.3.2. Article 174(2) principles apply to Member State authorities when explicitly set out in secondary legislation

The principles may apply in an autonomous manner to national authorities if the latter are obliged to apply EC regulations which recognize one or several of

---

[77] L. Krämer, 'The Polluter Pays Principle in Community law...', n. 56 above, 252.

[78] That case concerned a preliminary question relating to criminal offences. No EC secondary legislation concerning the environment was being directly considered, since the Italian legislation transposed an international convention to which the EC was not party. In this case the ECJ ruled that Article 130R did not contravene the Italian legislation being considered (Case C-379/92, *Peralta* [1994] ECR I-3453, para. 58).

the principles contained in Article 174(2) as such.[79] For example, specific reference to such principles is not exceptional in EC waste law.[80] According to Article 15 of the Waste Framework Directive 75/442/EEC, Member States must implement the polluter-pays principle.

In the 2001/18/EC Directive on the deliberate release of GMOs, the precautionary principle is explicitly mentioned in two Articles.[81] In this instance the principle embodied in secondary legislation constrains the national authorities to conduct risk assessment of GMO release notifications in the light of the precautionary principle.

Other general provisions of EC secondary legislation also function as directing principles. Article 4 of the Waste Framework Directive aims to put the principles of precaution and preventive action found in Article 174(2) of the Treaty into practice as regards waste management.[82] That provision requires the EC and Member States to prevent, reduce, and as far as possible to eliminate the sources of pollution or nuisances by adopting measures to eradicate known risks. The general nature of this provision marks the boundaries within which State activities for waste treatment should occur, even if it does not actually require the adoption of concrete measures.[83] Despite the provision's general character and consequent absence of direct effect, the Commission may sue a Member State for non-compliance with such an obligation before the ECJ against a State that has not ensured the correct management of wastes within its territory.[84] Furthermore, in applying the criteria of the degree of seriousness of the infringements to EC waste legislation, to ensure that penalty payments have coercive force and EC waste law is applied in Greece, the ECJ has ruled that 'failure to comply with the obligation resulting from Article 4 of Directive 75/442 could, by the very nature of that obligation, endanger human health directly and harm the environment and must, in the light of the other obligations, be regarded as particularly serious'. Therefore a high penalty payment is the means best suited to the circumstances.[85]

Similarly, Article 3(1) of Directive 75/439/EEC of 16 June 1975 on the disposal of waste oils, according to which 'Where technical, economic and organisational constraints so allow, Member States shall take the measures necessary to give priority to the processing of waste oils by regeneration,' is sufficiently general as to provide no concrete indication of what steps must be taken to meet that objective. Nevertheless, although it is not for the ECJ to

---

[79] N. Dhondt, 'Environmental Law Principles and the Case Law of the Court of Justice' in M. Sheridan and L. Lavrysen (eds.), *Environmental Law Principles*, n. 19 above, 141–55.

[80] By contrast, most EC Directives on water, air pollution, and nature protection, as well as those relating to horizontal measures, rarely refer directly to the principles laid down in the EC Treaty. Eg L. Krämer, 'General Principles of Community Environmental Law . . .', n. 11 above, 358.

[81] See the discussion in Chapter 3 Subsection 2.2.3.1. above.

[82] Cases C-175/98 and C-177/98, *Paolo Lirussi and Francesca Bizzaro* [1999] ECR I-6881, para. 51.

[83] Case C-236/92, *Comitato di coordinamento per la difesa della cava* [1994] ECR I-483, para. 14. Eg M. Reddish, 'Direct Effect of Environmental Directives' EELR (1994) 308.

[84] Case C-365/97, *Commission v. Italy* [1999] ECR I–7773, paras. 60–1.

[85] Case C-387/97, *Commission v. Greece* [2000] ECR I-5092, para. 94.

determine the measures a Member State should take to implement the obligation contained in that Article, it has the responsibility, when determining constraints within the meaning of Article 3, to consider whether it is possible to adopt measures aimed at prioritizing the processing of waste oils by regeneration and satisfying the criteria of technical, economic, and organizational feasibility.[86]

3.3.3.3. Article 174(2) principles apply to Member State authorities even when not explicitly set out in secondary legislation

Many directives follow a preventive or a precautionary approach without specifically mentioning Article 174(2) principles. In such cases, even when they are not explicitly set out in secondary legislation, those principles may directly apply to Member States.

Article 10 of the EC Treaty obliges the Member States to 'take all appropriate measures ... to ensure fulfilment of the obligations arising out of this Treaty or resulting from action taken by the institutions of the Community' and 'facilitate the achievement of the Community's tasks' as well as to 'abstain from any measure which could jeopardise the attainment of the objectives' of the Treaty. Read in the light of the polluter-pays, prevention, and precautionary principles of Article 174, Article 10 imposes on national authorities wide-ranging obligations of environmental protection, preservation, conservation, prevention, and precaution.[87]

In other words, even if a directive or a regulation does not expressly proclaim one of the principles of Article 174(2), those principles do constrain the Member State within the scope of EC environment legislation, since national administrations are obliged to interpret national legal texts in conformity with EC rules and the principles that follow therefrom.[88] Consequently, it no longer appears possible for Member States to carry out a policy of environmental protection that ignores the environmental principle set out in Article 174(2).

3.3.4. The normativity of Article 174(2) principles for individuals

It is unlikely that the polluters-pays or the precautionary principle as set out in Article 174(2) would ever be attributed direct effect, in the sense that an individual could plead before a national court that Member State action or legislation conflicted with a Treaty article and should therefore be put aside or declared inapplicable.[89] Therefore, it seems extremely doubtful that individuals could rely upon the Article 174(2) principles before a national court to challenge Member State legislation for failure to respect them. This seems to be the

---

[86] Case C-102/97, *Commission v. Germany* [1999] ECR I-5051, para. 48.

[87] A. Doyle and T. Carney, 'Precaution and Prevention: Giving Effect to Article 130r Without Direct Effect' (1999) 8 EELR 44.

[88] Case C-14/83, *von Colson and Kamann* [1984] ECR I-1891, para. 26; Case C-106/89, *Marleasing* [1990] ECR I-4135, para. 8.

[89] L. Hancher, 'EC Environmental Policy: a Pre-cautionary Tale?' in D. Freestone and E. Hey (eds.), *The Precautionary Principle*, n. 30 above, 202.

position taken by national courts, for example, in the UK's Queen's Bench Division decision of 3 October 1994.[90] In France, in the *Superphoenix* case involving the closure of a nuclear power plant, the *Conseil d'Etat* refused to consider the precautionary principle embodied in the EC Treaty as a self-executing norm.[91]

3.3.5. *The autonomous normative value of the precautionary principle in EC law*

In contrast to the ICJ and WTO dispute settlement bodies, EC courts have made the precautionary principle a true normative principle. Both the ECJ and the CFI have used it to confirm the validity of food safety measures[92] and the protection of marine resources.[93] At times the precautionary principle is implicit in these decisions;[94] at other times, it is expressly set out in the operative words of a judgment.[95] The importance of these decisions is twofold: first, the EC courts have explicitly put forward the precautionary principle to justify measures that frustrate the principle of the free circulation of goods within the EC internal market[96] or the principle of freedom of trade and industry;[97] and secondly, they do not limit the principle to environment policy but also use it to validate health protection measures, although health is an independent policy area whose links to environment policy remain ambiguous.[98]

3.4. National laws

When considering national laws a distinction must also been drawn between principles embodied in soft-law and hard-law instruments. While the former are not binding, the latter can play an important role in litigation.

3.4.1. *Soft law instruments*

Several national authorities—for example, in the UK—have limited themselves to proclaiming the polluters-pays, preventive action, and precautionary principles in policy documents. Such principles are generally devoid of legal effect: they are not formally adopted by the legislator, and the administration continues

---

[90] *Duddridge* case; see Subsection 2.3.5. of Chapter 3 above.

[91] C.E. fr., 28 Febr. 1997, WWF Geneva and others.

[92] Case C-331/88, *Fedesa* [1990] ECR I-4023, para. 9; Case C-180/96P, *United Kingdom v. Commission* [1996] ECR I-3903, para. 93; Case T-76/96P, *NFU* [1996] ECR II-815, para. 88.

[93] Case C-405/92, *Armand Mondiet* [1993] ECR I-6176, paras. 31–6.

[94] Case C-355/90, *Commission v. Spain* [1993] ECR I-6159, para. 28; Case C-435/93, *Association pour la protection des animaux sauvages et préfet de Maine-et-Loire et Préfet de la Loire-Atlantique* [1994] ECR I-67, para. 21.

[95] Case T-79/99P, *Alpharma*, [1999] ECR II-2027.

[96] Case C-331/88, *Fedesa* [1990] ECR I-4023, para. 9; Case C-180/96P, *United Kingdom v. Commission* [1996] ECR I-3903, para. 93.

[97] Case C-405/92, *Armand Mondiet* [1993] ECR I-6176, paras. 31–6; Case T-76/96P, *NFU* [1996] ECR II-815, para. 88.

[98] Case C-331/88, *Fedesa* [1990] ECR I-4023, para. 9.

to enjoy a wide degree of discretion as to what principles it lays down for itself. In order to assess each individual case precisely, the administration must always have the choice of ignoring the lines it has set for itself, but in that case it must put forward good reasons for its action. Thus, as it considers each individual case, an administration must ask whether the principle set out in policy documents it is attempting to follow is relevant; if not, it must find reasonable grounds for setting it aside. In this way, even though these principles are set out in soft-law instruments, they may strongly influence administrations by providing coherence to their actions.

3.4.2. Hard law instruments

3.4.2.1. Formal approach

As we have seen, several national legislators have followed the example of the international institutions, and particularly of the EC, by setting forth the polluters-pays, preventive action, and precautionary principles in their framework laws.[99] In Germany important legislation such as the Federal Emmissions Control Act (*Bundesimmissionsschutzgesetz*), the Atomic Energy Act (*Atomgesetz*), and the Biotechnology Act (*Gentechnikgesetz*) specify that various activities subject to authorization are to be constructed and operated in such a manner that precaution is exercised against damaging environmental effects. In addition, processes of codification of environment law have presented an occasion to insert basic principles into framework laws. The French Environmental Code and in Belgium the 1995 Flemish Decree and the 1999 Federal Act aimed at protection of the marine environment in Belgium have taken up and adapted the principles set out in Article 174(2) of the EU Treaty. In addition, many national laws also contain recitals whose purpose is to set out guidelines for implementing rules or measures. Although not termed 'principles', these provisions share the attributes of legal principles, such as a high degree of generality or authority, as the result of their wording and their high ranking in the hierarchy of norms.[100]

Contrary to international or EC legal orders, which are only addressed to international institutions and States parties, environmental principles recognized in national legal systems are generally addressed to all users of the environment, both public and private. For instance, according to the Danish Environmental Protection Act 358 of 6 June 1991: 'Any party proposing to commence activities likely to cause pollution shall choose such a site for the activities that the risk of pollution is minimized [and] shall take measures to prevent and combat pollution'; the Dutch Law of 1 March 1993 on environmental management (*Wet milieubeheer*) requires that 'All persons accord sufficient consideration to the environment'; the French Environmental Code affirms that it is 'is incumbent upon all persons to take care to safeguard and contribute to protecting the

---

[99] See Chapter 3 above.

[100] P. Gilhuis, 'The Consequences of Introducing Environmental Law Principles' in M. Sheridan and L. Lavrysen (eds.), *Environmental Law Principles*, n. 19 above, 49.

environment'; the 1999 Belgian Federal Act on the protection of the marine environment stipulates that 'users of the marine environment and the government shall take into consideration...the precautionary principle...when carrying out activities in the marine environment'.

From the perspective of the precautionary principle this extension *ratione personae* is justified, for it implies that the State does not intend to exclude professionals from precautionary obligations.[101] Indeed, the precautionary principle should apply to all those engaged in activities that carry a risk; this would serve to extend the general duty of care and due diligence, which requires avoiding exposing others to risks and subsequently managing such risks, to potential as well as actual risks. We must ask, however, whether the imprecision of the principle, and indeed its unpredictability, represent a serious obstacle to its application in particular cases. We might respond to this doubt by noting that the European Court of Human Rights, when reviewing the legality of national regulations restricting individual freedoms, has shown great flexiblity when reviewing relatively imprecise rules applied to professionals in a given field.[102]

3.4.2.2. Substantive approach

While at the formal level the normative character of the polluter-pays, preventive, and precautionary principles does not really give rise to discussion when those directing principles are set out in framework laws, various substantive arguments have been put forward in an attempt to deny them any binding legal character.

First, directing principles of environmental law are often presented as 'guiding' principles meant solely to inspire the law-maker or executive. As an example, the 2000 French Environmental Code provides that principles exist to 'inspire' environment legislation 'within the framework of the laws that define their effect'. Yet this wording has not prevented the French *Conseil d'Etat* from directly invoking the precautionary principle in several cases related to the protection of public health.

Similarly, there is a refusal to liken directing principles to normative principles, on the ground that no penalty attaches to their violation.[103] This is to confuse sanction with criminal punishment. While a rule always entails a sanction, it is not necessarily provided with penalizing measures—far from it. The fact that violations of most rules of indeterminate nature,[104] including the three directing principles of environmental law, are not censured under criminal law does not mean there are no other sanctions. For instance, under administrative

---

[101] P. Kourilsky and G. Viney, *Le Principe de Précaution* (Paris, La Documentation Française-O. Jacob, 2000) 143–4.

[102] *Groppera Radio AG v. Switzerland*, 28 March 1990, A 173, para. 68.

[103] O. Godard, 'L'ambivalence de la précaution et la transformation des rapports entre science et décision' in O. Godard (ed.), *Le principe de précaution dans la conduite des affaires humaines* (Paris: Maison des Sciences de l'Homme, 1997) 287.

[104] See above, Section 2.

law an authority can always refuse or withdraw a licence on the ground of breach of an environmental principle. It is also worth noting that a breach of the duty of care can in any case also entail civil liability.[105]

Finally, there is opposition to the fact that the directing principles set out in framework laws could have normative effect, owing to the extremely vague nature of the concepts they convey. What is in fact being prescribed by notions as intangible as those of the polluter pays, precaution, or prevention? In Part I of this book we saw how difficult it was to determine the effect of those principles. In fact, directing principles of environmental law such as the polluters-pays, preventive action, and precautionary principles sketch out very general orientations, from which it is difficult to deduce precise provisions; their lesser degree of precision, or inversely their greater degree of abstraction, attenuates their obligatory character. As we demonstrated in the first section of this Chapter, however, a rule need not necessarily have an uniquivocal content to be normative. Even if it remains closed at the strictly normative level, a legal system is characterized by its openness to other systems, whether these be moral, economic, or scientific. If legal norms must be able to integrate external legal elements, their meaning should then be able to evolve as a function of that level of integration. Consequently, by referring to elements outside the legal system, the definition of principles is more dynamic than static.

Even if the number of court decisions invoking the polluters-pays, preventive, and precautionary principles has been small to date, evolution has led to some of those principles being given an autonomous normative value that makes them directly applicable in German, French, Belgian, and Dutch law.

For instance, in Belgium the *Conseil d'Etat* judged that a noise regulation which constituted a relaxation of the level of protection for man and the environment against the harmful effects of racing circuits was incompatible with the constitutional right to a clean environment and the standstill principle, which had been laid down in regional legislation:

whereas Article 23 of the Constitution enshrines for each person the right to the safeguarding of a healthy environment; whereas this basic right appears to imply, among other things, that a relaxation of the existing environmental regulations can only be deemed compatible with the Constitution if there are compelling reasons for doing so; whereas the 'standstill principle' that flows from this provision has been laid down for the Flemish Region in the decree of 5 April 1995 laying down general provisions of environmental policy; . . . whereas the Flemish government should be mindful of these principles when . . . it decrees general environmental conditions or conditions that apply per category of establishment. . . . Whereas it appears from the foregoing that the challenged provision gives rise to an attenuation of the protection of man and the environment against the harmful effects of the operation of racecourses for motor vehicles; whereas, as has already been said, if such an arrangement is to be compatible with Article 23 of the Constitution, compelling reasons must be given for doing so; whereas no such reasons can be inferred

---

[105] A. Cliquet, 'Recente ontwikkelingen inzake natuurbehoudswetgeving in het mariene en kust-zonemilieu van België' (1999) 5 TMR 346.

from either the administrative records or the defence put forward by the defendant; whereas the argument is serious.[106]

The Belgian Court of Arbitration has several times referred to the polluter-pays principle in order to verify whether taxes on discharges of wastewater and the management of wastes were adequate and proportionate.[107]

Favoured by a strong trend towards tighter risk control which national courts cannot ignore, the future of the precautionary principle seems to be assured. Since the 1980s German administrative courts have accorded it the role of a fundamental principle of environmental law which compels consideration by the decision-making authorities.[108] More recently French administrative courts have also begun to use it, not only in the field of environment but also in that of public health.[109] As is the case for EC courts, the *Conseil d'Etat de France* has extended the scope of the precautionary principle to the field of public health despite the absence of legal backing equivalent to that provided by the framework law on the protection of the environment.[110] In the Netherlands the President of the Leeuwarden Court applied the precautionary principle in a decision of 28 April 1997 deduced from the EC Habitats Directive, which implements Article 174 of the EC Treaty, to suspend an authorization to drill new gas wells in the North Sea on the ground that an impact study had not been able to exclude with certainty the risk that special protection zones designated to protect wild birds might be damaged as a result.[111]

In light of these case-law developments, the principles of environmental law, particularly that of precaution, should constitute a true legal rule independent of the regulations they influence.

4. The effects of directing principles of environmental law on litigation

As autonomous norms, the directing principles of environmental law may produce concrete results at the criminal, civil, and administrative levels.

---

[106] C.E.b., 29 April 1999, no. 80.018, Jacobs, (1999) 4 TMR 301. Eg I. Larmuseau, 'The Precautionary Principle...' in M. Sheridan and L. Lavrysen (eds.), *Environmental Law Principles*, n. 19 above, 187–90.

[107] C.A., no. 16/92, 12 March 1992, B3.3.; no. 41/93, 3 June 1993, B 3.4; no. 42/97, 14 July 1997, B. 52.4.

[108] BVerwGE, 17 February 1984, Bd. 69 (1985), p. 43.

[109] O. Sachs, 'Principe de précaution et contrôle de légalité' (December 1999) CJEG 420; C. Cans, 'Le principe de précaution, nouvel élément de légalité' (July–August 1999) 15 : 4 RFD Adm. 750–763; A. Rouyere, 'L'exigence de précaution saisie par le juge' (March–April 2000) 16 : 2 RFD Adm. 266–283.

[110] C.E.fr., 21 April 1997, Barbier, no. 180.274; 24 February 1999, Pro-Nat, no. 192.465; 30 June 1999, Germain. Even if all these decisions do not explicitly rely on the precautionary principle, they apply it without basing themselves on a specific text.

[111] Pres. Rechtbank Leeuwarden, 28 April 1997 (1997) 10 M & R 214, comment by Backes. Eg Ch. Backes, P. Gilhuis, and J. Verschuuren (eds.), *Het voorzorgbeginsel in het natuurbeschermings-recht* (Deventer: Tjeenk Willink, 1997).

4.1. Principles and the control of legality

In the framework of litigation over legality, both EC and national administrative courts (notably in France, Belgium, and Germany) exercise control over the substance of a decision (internal legality) and on its respect for procedure (external legality). While control of respect for procedure is relatively extensive, control of the substance of a decision is limited in that EC and national legislations allow a wide margin of discretion to administrations. We discuss below how the precautionary principle may at times reinforce and at other times weaken controls of the internal and external legality of administrative decisions.

4.1.1. The control of manifest error of appraisal (internal legality)

It may happen that petitioners, in litigation over legality, claim that an administration has committed a manifest error of appraisal by having taken an unreasonable decision relating to public health protection although it was not fully justified by the current state of scientific understanding. Courts have a tendency to reject such complaints in a context of controversy, invoking the precautionary principle to justify adopting the contentious measure.

Thus, in the case of bovine spongiform encephalopathy the ECJ referred to the precautionary principle set out in Article 174 (2) of the EC Treaty to support the Commission's decision to ban British beef, on the ground that the Commission could take measures to protect public health without having to wait until the reality and seriousness of the risk of developing Creutzfeld-Jakob's Disease had been fully proved.[112] Similarly, the French *Conseil d'Etat* has on several occasions had recourse to the precautionary principle, both to validate health protection norms[113] and to suspend a decision authorizing the commercialization of genetically modified maize.[114]

By proceeding in this way EC and national courts allow administrations a wide margin of discretion when they adopt measures of administrative policy in a context of scientific uncertainty. Unlike the reviewing of procedural obligations (*contrôle de légalité externe*) recourse to the precautionary principle sets aside the possibility of reviewing the measure on the ground that it violates internal legality (for example, for reasons having to do with the absence of proportionality or manifest error of appraisal).

The use thus made of the precautionary principle is connected to the aversion of courts to scientific debate; they are not ready to involve themselves in highly technical points of scientific controversy. In German case-law, for example, while legal control of the precautionary principle has been increased, the role of the courts in verifying respect for the current state of science and technology nonetheless remains marginal.[115] German courts believe that judicial control

---

[112] Case C-180/96, *United Kingdom v. Commission* [1998] ECR I-2269, paras. 99 and 100.
[113] C.E.fr., 24 February 1999, Société Pro-Nat.
[114] C.E.fr., 19 February 1998, Association Greenpeace France.
[115] Judgment of 8 August 1978 of the Federal Constitutional Court (*Bundesverfassungsgericht*).

should be limited to ensuring that a contentious assessment is based on sufficient information and non-arbitrary assumptions.[116] UK courts have also shown judicial restraint in reviewing risk regulations. Such decisions are in the realm of administrative authorities.[117]

This reserve on the part of courts in carrying out controls of internal legality does not appear to have been questioned thus far. Indeed, the fact that legal doctrine sets out the need to allow administrations a wide margin of manoeuvre favours a restrained control of internal legality. In any case, a court is no substitute for an administration. Such discretion in assessing the facts of a case is all the more useful when the scientific proofs assembled by an administration do not dictate a clear solution to a problem. Moreover, when risk is involved public decisions must often be taken very quickly. National courts are aware of the difficulties involved in ruling in emergency conditions and thus are rarely strict as regards possible errors made by public authorities in their haste to protect the public interest.

The precautionary principle also supports judicial prudence when a public authority takes refuge behind the need to act under conditions of scientific uncertainty. Environmental principles thus do no more than reaffirm the wide discretion that administrations already enjoy in carrying out their prerogatives.[118]

4.1.2. *Control of procedural regularity (contrôle de légalité externe)*

By contrast, control of the external legality of administrative decisions should be reinforced by contact with the precautionary principle. For example, the decision by the French *Conseil d'Etat* in a case concerning genetically modified maize indicates the willingness of the high administrative court to review the risk assessment procedure in the light of the precautionary principle.[119]

The only irregularity in this case was that the dossier was incomplete, as a result of which an opinion required by the relevant legislation had been delivered by a scientific committee. Although this procedural irregularity might have been of no importance in another case, in this particular case it was deemed sufficiently serious for the *Conseil d'Etat* to order that the decision by the Ministry of Agriculture authorizing the commercialization of a variety of genetically modified maize be suspended. Although quite minor, this type of irregularity seems to be sufficient to constitute a serious ground for annulment.

This judicial trend closely corresponds to the spirit of the precautionary principle, which calls for procedural arrangements that allow the most complete examination possible of risk, so as to minimize uncertainty. When risk assessment

---

[116] OVG Hamburg, 27 January 1995, (1995) 2 Umweltrecht 93.

[117] E. Fisher, 'Is the Precautionary Principle Justiciable?' (2001) 13: 3 JEL 315–34, 323.

[118] N. de Sadeleer, 'Les avatars du principe de précaution en droit public' (2001) 3 RFD Adm. 555–7; *idem*, 'L'émergence du principe de précaution' (2001) 6010 JT 393–401.

[119] C.E. fr., 19 February 1998, Association Greenpeace France. See Chapter 3 above, Subsection 2.3.2.

procedures are envisaged in order to prevent risks arising, it is normal that courts should verify respect for these procedures in an extremely rigorous, even punctilious, manner and that they would accordingly not hesitate to nullify decisions that disregard any of their requirements. The precautionary principle thereby serves to reinforce the formal control of respect for procedure in cases involving scientific controversy.

4.2. Principles and civil liability

The preventive and precautionary principles may be implemented entirely by the presence of procedural regimes and administrative structures, to the extent that these never altogether preclude harm. On the other hand, they may gain in consistency through civil liability: the threat that the operator may be liable should give rise to preventive behaviour beyond that envisaged by strict respect for norms and procedures. Seen from this angle, civil liability appears an indispensable complement to the administrative policies on which the preventive and precautionary principles are traditionally based.[120]

Although civil liability still performs an essentially reparative or curative function, it should fulfil its potential by evolving in those areas where the preventive and precautionary principles are most used—the environment, health, and safety—with a view to preventing or even anticipating damages. This development proves particularly necessary where there is a question of serious and irreversible damage. In such cases it is important that action be taken to avert the irreparable; prevention and anticipation must override reparation.

As discussed in Part I of this work, the polluter-pays, preventive, and precautionary principles may enter the civil liability litigation process in various forms, with the reparative function of liability giving way to that of preventing damage.[121] In other words, these three principles may be invoked in turn to support legal arguments favouring victims or the environment. Fault, for example, should be interpreted more widely, and the burden of proof for those exposed to risk should be reduced, particularly by easing the requirement to show causation.

In Chapter 3 above we indicated that the precautionary principle did not necessarily conflict with risk theory; on the contrary, risk theory and the precautionary principle both have the same objective: that of protecting people against risks.[122] The prevalence of strict liability regimes in environmental law is fully justified by the polluter-pays, preventive, and precautionary principles.

---

[120] International soft law clearly demonstrates that there is a need to give access to the victims to civil law remedies. According to Article 13 of the 1992 Rio Declaration on the Environment and Development, 'States shall develop national law regarding liability and compensation for the victims of pollution and other environmental damage'. See also Council of Europe Model Act on the Protection of the Environment (Strasbourg, 1994) which includes both regulatory approach and civil liability.

[121] See the discussion on civil liability regimes in Chapters 1–3 above.

[122] See the discussion in Chapter 3, Subsection 5.2.2.4 above.

The precautionary principle should prevent operators from taking advantage of scientific uncertainty to justify damage brought about by their activities; the very fact of operating an activity that poses risks to others must be considered to give rise to an obligation to repair damage resulting from the normal activity of an installation.

The influence of the precautionary principle should by the same token be felt in the context of civil liability in assessing the 'information requirement' that applies to professionals. In effect, that principle requires that information provided by operators is not limited to scientifically established risks but also includes those that are likely or which give rise to suspected effects that have not yet been fully proved. In assessing professional liability the courts should take a stricter stand on the information communicated to consumers and should penalize those who have been content to disseminate information that downplays the risks generated by their products.

Furthermore, the duty to interpret national law in conformity with EC law can influence the content of tort liability. It can be said that, via the doctrine of indirect effect, the civil liability of the tortfeasor might increase in the light of the requirements of environmental law principles found in EC directives and regulations. For example, under the EC interpretative obligations of the polluter-pays principle the defendant could be held more strictly liable than under the liability regime of national legislation taken in isolation.[123]

However, some people are concerned that the precautionary principle might eventually turn into a legal time-bomb which, years after the fact, could engage liability for operators who took decisions without full knowledge of the consequences. They would then find themselves dragged before the courts and held liable for risks accepted at an earlier time on the basis of hoped-for benefits. We consider these fears excessive. While it is true that courts could more easily penalize a lack of duty of care by invoking the precautionary principle, they are unlikely to wish to abuse the correct application of the principle in this way.

4.3. Principles and criminal liability

There are several reasons why decision-makers at present feel far more exposed to prosecution than was formerly the case. First, the legislative excitement that today characterizes the fields of environment, health, and consumer protection is being accompanied by the multiplication of offences, with each new provision giving rise to a penalty. In addition, owing to the rather painless character of civil judgments as the result of general insurance and the growth of guarantees or compensation funds, those who have suffered serious injuries to health or safety to themselves or their families are increasingly turning from civil to criminal

---

[123] G. Betlem, n. 52 above, 222. However, one has to differentiate between the impact of indirect effect doctrine on civil and on criminal liability. See Subsection 4.3. below.

proceedings.[124] Finally, decision-makers are worried by the willingness of judges to be more severe towards those defendants who wielded the greatest power when a violation was committed.

Among the possible consequences of applying the precautionary principle, a multiplication of criminal proceedings is obviously that most feared by public or private decision-makers whose negligence might have given rise to risks with injurious consequences. This tendency towards penalization will feed their fear of criminal proceedings. In order to avoid the risk of liability they will tend to make excessive use of the precautionary principle, to the detriment of innovation.

Nevertheless, in order to give substance to criminal liability, violation of the precautionary principle should be specifically set out by the penal Code or by a special criminal law. This need results from the fundamental principle of legality [*nullum crimen, nulla poena sine lege*] under which any criminal conviction must be based on a legal offence that has been provided for in a sufficiently clear provision and defined before the facts subject to prosecution took place. In effect, respect for individual liberties demands that it be the law that strictly defines the elements comprising an offence and the penalties incurred by the defendant.

In almost all legal systems, absence of precaution is not an offence with general effect. Similarly, no penal sanction specifically set out in special laws censures the violation of this principle, even if numerous offences are related to a lack of precaution (for example, in the area of hazardous waste management).[125] Failing a penal provision expressly applying to a non-precautionary attitude, the defendant will not experience any greater penalty. For this reason an extensive interpretation of penal legislation in the light of the precautionary principle will run counter to the principle of legality. Moreover, the fact that the principle is enunciated in a Directive cannot determine or aggravate the liability in criminal law of persons who act in contravention of the provisions of that Directive.[126]

That said, the precautionary principle could eventually insinuate itself into a certain number of offences that are defined in very general terms.[127] Until a little while ago the elements comprising endangerment were largely based, for a specific technical field, on the common norms, obligations, and prohibitions characteristic of a trade or profession. For several years now, however, many national laws have recognized offences based on the 'endangerment of

---

[124] In France several ministries have been prosecuted and found guilty by the *Cour de Justice* of the Republic for infractions committed in the exercise of their powers in connection with AIDS-contaminated blood.

[125] A. Marchal, 'Le délit de mise en péril et son objet' (1968–1969) Revue de droit pénal et de criminologie 299.

[126] Case C-322/88, *Pretore di Salo v. X* [1987] ECR I-2545; Case C-80/86, *Kolpinghuis Nijmegen* (1987) ECR I-3989.

[127] P. Kourilsky and G. Viney, n. 101 above, 124.

others'.[128] In such cases the offence is complete even when no concrete injury has occurred. The realization of damage is not required: it is the offender's clear lack of concern that is condemned, in that it demonstrates his indifference to the possible consequences of his act.

Such offences allow an extremely wide power of discretion to judicial authorities, which must assess on a case-by-case basis the degree of danger created by an offender. The precautionary principle could in this case lead a judge to be more severe with defendants who did not bother to explore all the possible consequences of their acts and might thereby have exposed society to clear risks. In any case it is dangerous to convict someone for purely hypothetical endangerment. Finally, the type of reasoning inherent in civil law, where the precautionary principle faces a promising future, cannot necessarily be transposed to criminal law owing to the principle of the legality of penalties and the unusual character of the conviction.

5. CONCLUDING OBSERVATIONS

In seeking to throw light on the legal nature of the polluters-pays, preventive action, and precautionary principles, we must take care not to rely on appearances. All the provisions in this legal discipline that are designated as 'principles' do necessarily constitute true normative principles; inversely, certain provisions that are not termed 'principles' nonetheless share the characteristics of normative principles.

The identification of the legal status of these provisions should be determined by conceptual rather than nominalistic steps. Similarly, it requires a nuanced assessment rather than an overly categorical judgement, since the latter would merely destroy their flexibility.

In order to qualify as normative principles, provisions must be taken up in legally binding text (formal approach) and be addressed to specific categories of people—in this case State bodies—as well as in national administrative systems (substantive approach). The wide discretion given to public authorities in formulating environmental legislation under principles such as precaution or preventive action has been identified as a significant barrier to granting the status of normative principles to those obligations. However, the fact that some provisions may be highly abstract, that their binding character may be less marked than that of precise substantive norms, and that they do not impose direct penalties does not deprive them of all normative effect, as long as they are taken up in binding legal sources and set out in sufficiently prescriptive terms.

---

[128] See Article 223–1 of the French Penal Code, under which 'the fact of directly exposing another to an immediate risk of death or wounding...by an obviously deliberate violation of a specific requirement of safety or duty of care set out by law or regulation is punishable by one year's imprisonment...' see also Article 9 of the Swedish Penal Code, and Article 211–2 of the US Model Penal Code.

When they are laid down in text with normative effect in international law (eg a multilateral convention), in EC law (eg the EC Treaty, a Directive, or a Regulation), or in national legal systems (eg framework legislation) the majority of directing principles thereby assume the characteristics of rules of indeterminate content.

Of course, their high degree of generality entails a twofold corollary: on one hand they are somewhat less binding than more prescriptive rules, and on the other hand their legal predictability remains uncertain. We have seen, however, that the most emblematic environmental law principles described in Part I are not necessarily synonymous with legal uncertainty.

7

Environmental Directing Principles versus Free Trade

1. Introductory Remarks

The end of the twentieth century will be remembered for two parallel developments without precedent in the history of mankind: on one hand the emergence of ecological crises of global scope (climate change, loss of biodiversity, ozone depletion, etc.) and on the other hand a progressive liberalization of world trade, embodied at the international level by the conclusion of the Uruguay Round in 1994 and at the European level by the adoption of the SEA in 1987. Underlying these parallel developments is a clash of legal rules on several fronts that goes well beyond the disputes of the past. The doctrine of free trade, based on the postulate that products should be able to circulate freely without hindrance from technical obstacles erected by States, is traditionally opposed to national or regional regulation in the areas of public health or environmental protection. Indeed, the need to open up markets directly conflicts with the need to promote legitimate environmental objectives; until now efforts to reconcile these two goals have been unsuccessful.

In an attempt to attenuate these conflicts international organizations have sought to harmonize national rules (positive harmonization) by setting common denominators able to facilitate commercial exchanges.[1] Nevertheless, positive harmonization is difficult to achieve at international level,[2] and even at EC level.[3] When no common ground can be found between States that do not share the same goals, free trade is encouraged by a principle of mutual recognition that allows goods lawfully produced and marketed in one State to be commercialized in another State (negative harmonization) and by requiring

---

[1] In this regard it should be noted that the TBT and SPS Agreements promote the harmonization of standards (Articles 2(4), 2(6), and 9 of the TBT Agreement; Article 3(4) of the SPS Agreement). Article III:2 of the WTO Agreement also mentions that 'the WTO shall provide the forum of negotiations among its Members concerning their multilateral trade relations in matters dealt with under the agreements in the Annexes to this Agreement'. Positive harmonization is transposed into EC law through the adoption of directives and regulations based on Article 95 of the EC Treaty intended to guarantee the working of the Internal Market.

[2] One must fear that the international negotiation process will lead to the lowest common denominator, as few States in the world have very high protection levels.

[3] The establishment of the internal market after the SEA entered into force has been seen by some Member States as a downward harmonization.

States that impose stricter standards than those applied in the producer country to prove that those standards are necessary to protect the citizens of the State imposing them, and to prove that they are not discriminatory to the producer State.

Ideally, free trade presupposes that States share concepts of product safety on one hand and of human health and the environment on the other. In fact, goals for the protection of human health, the environment, and consumers vary appreciably from one State to another. Hormones in meat, for example, which are banned in the EC because of consumer concerns about their effects, are freely available across the Atlantic.

A wave of recent food production scandals has put public health in the spotlight and undermined the confidence of European consumers, and as a result also that of their public representatives in food production techniques such as hormones and genetically modified organisms. Consumers in the developed countries have also become concerned about the collective risks (emissions of greenhouse gases, non-sustainable industrial operations, etc.) to which they contribute through their consumption patterns. By adopting a higher level of safety as their norm to respond to such concerns, the more advanced States are acting in ways likely to restrict commercial trade with States that do not share these goals; their compet-tititors will view such measures as disguised protectionism. There is thus every reason to believe that the WTO's criticism of Europe's measures against hormones and of the United States' actions in cases relating to the exploitation of marine resources (the *Tuna-Dolphin* and *Shrimp-Turtle* cases) are only the first in a wider series of trade crises.[4]

Some principles of environmental law, particularly the precautionary principle, have taken these conflicts to a higher stage by widening the gap between the conditions underlying international trade liberalization and the urgent need, recognized particularly by the EC, to adopt a high level of protection for the environment, consumers, and public health.[5] Does the EC, which is more likely than its trading partners to invoke that principle in international forums, have the right to apply it beyond the scope envisaged in the various WTO agreements? In other words, does repeated State use of the precautionary principle render it a general principle of international customary law? That question, which has been the subject of important debates in international legal circles, has yet to be definitively addressed by international courts.

The purpose of this final Chapter is to demonstrate how some of the environmental directing principles described in Part 1 of this book can shed new light on the conflict between free trade and environment protection. Since the relationship between trade and environment has been examined in numerous legal

---

[4] Report on US—Restrictions on Imports of Tuna, 3 September 1991, not adopted, BISD 39S/155 (hereinafter *Tuna I*); Report on US—Restrictions on Imports of Tuna, 10 June 1994, not adopted, DS 29 R (hereinafter *Tuna II*); US—Import Prohibition of Certain Shrimp and Shrimp Products, adopted 6 November 1998.

[5] Articles 95(3), 152(1), 153(1), 174(2) of the EC Treaty.

analyses over the past several years,[6] we confine our consideration here to how such principles have influenced the resolution of conflicts.

2. WTO LAW

2.1. Background

Before 1991 the environment—trade debate was primarily an arcane speciality that attracted little attention within the legal community. In endeavouring to encourage 'the full use of the resources of the world',[7] the GATT 1947 system paid very little attention indeed to environmental concerns; consequently trade policy and environmental policy evolved along separate paths for several decades.

Despite the change of tone in 1994 in the wording of the WTO's aims—'an optimal use of the world's resources in accordance with the objective of sustainable development'[8]—the fundamental principles of GATT remain unaltered;[9] environmental concerns are still considered the black sheep of the trading community. Indeed, Principle 12 of the Rio Declaration on Environment and Development, which states that 'Trade policy measures for environmental purposes should not constitute a means of arbitrary or unjustifiable discrimination or a disguised restriction on international trade' in its own way also recognizes

---

[6] For WTO law, J. Cameron and J. Robinson, 'The Use of Trade Provisions in International Environmental Agreements and their Compatibility with GATT' (1992) 2 YbIEL 3–30; S.L. Walker, *Environmental Protection Versus Trade Liberalization: Finding the Balance. An Examination of the Legality of Environmental Regulation Under International Trade Law Regimes* (Brussels: Saint-Louis, 1993); J. Cameron, P. Demaret, and P. Geradin (eds.), *Trade and the Environment: The Search for Balance*, vol. I (London: Cameron & May, 1994); E.-H. Petersmann, *International and European Trade and Environmental Law after the Uruguay Round* (London: Kluwer Law Int'l, 1995); A. Fijalkowski and J. Cameron (eds.), *Trade and the Environment* (London: Cameron and May-Asser Instituut, 1997); G. Van Calster, *International and EU Trade: The Environmental Challenge* (London: Cameron and May, 2000); P. Birnie and A. Boyle, *International Law and the Environment* (2nd edn., Oxford University Press, 2002) 697–750.

[7] Preamble to the GATT 1947.

[8] Preamble to the 1994 WTO Agreement. As noted by the WTO Appellate Body, this change in orientation must 'add colour, texture and shading to the interpretation of the agreements annexed to the WTO Agreement' (*Shrimp*, para. 153). The Doha WTO Ministerial Declaration of 14 November 2001 strongly reaffirms the commitment to the objective of sustainable development, as stated in the Preamble to the Marrakesh Agreement: 'We are convinced that the aims of upholding and safeguarding an open and non-discriminatory multilateral trading system, and acting for the protection of the environment and the promotion of sustainable development can and must be mutually supportive. . . . We recognize that under WTO rules no country should be prevented from taking measures for the protection of human, animal or plant life or health, or of the environment at the levels it considers appropriate, subject to the requirement that they are not applied in a manner which would constitute a means of arbitrary or unjustifiable discrimination between countries where the same conditions prevail, or a disguised restriction on international trade, and are otherwise in accordance with the provisions of the WTO Agreements.'

[9] L. Guruswamy, 'Environment and Trade: Competing Paradigms in International Law' in A. Anghie and G. Sturgess (eds.), *Legal Visions of the 21st Century: Essays in Honour of Judge Ch. Weeramantry* (London, The Hague, Boston: Kluwer Law Int'l, 1998) 550–2.

the primacy of free trade over environmental interests. Furthermore, Principle 12 clearly discourages unilateral action to deal with environmental challenges outside the jurisdictions of importing countries; transboundary or global issues should be based as far as possible on international consensus.

As a result trade restrictions to achieve environmental goals have given rise to an increasing number of international commercial disputes during the past decade; the relationship 'trade—environment' has thus become one of the hottest topics in a number of political circles.

2.2. Environmental directing principles v GATT/WTO obligations

As we have seen in the WTO EC *Hormones* case,[10] environmental principles such as those of prevention or precaution are important factors in the trade—environment debate, since they can be used under Multilateral Environmental Agreements (MEAs) to justify the adoption of trade measures which potentially conflict with WTO obligations. First, it must be stressed that several trade-related environmental measures (TREMs) have been justified in the light of environmental directing principles (Subsection 2.2.1 below). Secondly, those principles could be invoked before WTO Dispute Settlement Bodies (DSBs) to justify these trade measures. At this point we should recall that TREMs are not always the result of international co-operation but can also be the expression of unilateral State policy. We will therefore distinguish between multilaterally agreed (Subsection 2.2.2.) and unilaterally enacted TREMs (Subsection 2.2.3.), even though the distinction is at times an uneasy one.[11]

2.2.1. *Justification of trade-related environmental measures (TREMs) in the light of environmental directing principles*

Among the hundreds of environmental treaties a small number of multilateral environmental agreements (MEAs) allow TREMs in order to increase their effectiveness. In particular, restrictions on trade with non-Parties may be put in place to prevent free riders from enjoying benefits without adhering to a multilateral agreement, as well as to encourage non-Parties to become signatories to a convention.[12]

For instance, TREMs occur in the context of waste management in instruments such as the 1989 Basel Convention on the Transboundary Movement of Hazardous Wastes. The Basel Convention aims to reduce hazardous waste movements through the treatment and disposal of hazardous wastes in an environmentally sound manner (principle of prevention) as close as possible to the place where they were generated (proximity principle) and to minimize the production of wastes (principle of rectification of environmental harm at

---

[10] See the discussion in Chapter 3, Subsection 2.1.2.3. above.

[11] P. Demaret, 'TREMs, Multilateralism, Unilateralism and the GATT' in J. Cameron, P. Demaret, and P. Geradin (eds.), *Trade and the Environment*, n. 6 above, 59.

[12] R.G. Tarasofsky, 'Ensuring Compatibility between MEAs and GATT/WTO' (1996) 7 YbIEL 54.

source).[13] Article 4(2)(e) of that Convention requires that States of export ban shipments of hazardous wastes if there is reason to believe these will not be managed in an environmentally sound manner in the country of import. In addition, Article 4(5) bans exports and imports of hazardous and other wastes by Parties to the Convention to and from States non-Party. Furthermore, the controversial Decision III/1, adopted at the third meeting of the Conference of the Parties, restricts exports of hazardous wastes from OECD countries to non-OECD countries for disposal or recycling, even for States that are not Parties to the Basel Convention.[14] These trade mechanisms have been partially justified in the light of the self-sufficiency principle.

Among MEAs relating to wildlife protection, 1973 CITES, which has progressively been based on a precautionary approach,[15] is the only multilateral treaty which seeks to protect endangered species through the regulation of international trade. Recommendations made by the CITES Standing Committee can require Parties to prohibit all trade with a Party that is not complying with the Treaty's obligations. Furthermore, CITES authorizes Contracting Parties to take stricter measures than those set out in the Treaty.

Trade restrictions on non-Parties are also to be found in the 1987 Montreal Protocol on Substances that Deplete the Ozone Layer, which is influenced by a precautionary approach.[16] Parties to the Protocol are required to ban trade in ozone-depleting substances such as CFCs with non-Parties.

While the 1997 Kyoto Protocol on climate change does not contain trade sanctions, it contains a number of provisions whose implementation could conflict with WTO law. According to Article 2(1)(a)(i) of the Protocol, Parties are encouraged to implement policies and measures aimed at 'enhancement of energy efficiency in relevant sectors of the economy', which might prompt Parties to apply technical regulations to save energy. The Technical Barriers to Trade (TBT) Agreement of the WTO, however, requires among other things that WTO members ensure that in applying technical regulations imported products are treated no less favourably than products of national origin and that technical regulations are not more trade-restrictive than necessary to achieve the 'legitimate objectives' allowed under the TBT Agreement, which include 'protection of human health or safety, animal or plant life or health, [and] the environment'.[17] Both the EC and Japan voiced concern in the year 2000 about the other's energy efficiency requirements, each arguing that the other discriminates unfairly against imported vehicles.[18] While no dispute has been brought to the WTO,

[13] K. Kummer, *International Management of Hazardous Wastes: The Basel Convention and Related Legal Rules* (Oxford: OUP, 1999).

[14] J. Krueger, *International Trade and the Basel Convention* (London: Earthscan, 1999) 106.

[15] CITES Resolution of the Ninth Conference of the Parties, known as Conf. 9.24.

[16] See the discussion in Chapter 3 Subsection 2.1.1. above.

[17] Article 2(2).

[18] L. Campbell, 'WTO and Climate Change: Trade, Investment and the Kyoto Protocol', 23: 17 Int'l Env Rep, 654; G. Loibl, 'Trade and Environment. A Difficult Relationship: The Kyoto Protocol and Beyond' in *Liber Amicorum Prof. I Seidl-Hohenveldern* (The Hague: Kluwer Law Int'l, 1998) 430–42.

this case illustrates the increased scrutiny of national or regional environmental product standards for consistency with WTO rules, including those implemented to comply with the Kyoto Protocol.

The 2000 Cartagena Protocol on Biosafety (CPB) addresses the 'transboundary movement, transit, handling and use of all LMOs [living modified organisms] that may have adverse effects on the conservation and sustainable use of biological diversity'.[19] Its key element is a prior notification and consent procedure for the import and export of LMOs. The Protocol explicitly endorses the precautionary principle for the regulation of imports or exports, allowing import restrictions in the face of scientific uncertainty due to insufficient scientific information.[20] According to several authors, an unlimited import ban on LMOs[21] would undoubtedly conflict with the SPS Agreement, which only allows provisional precautionary measures, while a more objective risk assessment must be obtained within a reasonable period of time.[22] As the relationship between the Protocol and WTO obligations has been one of the core areas of disagreement during negotiations, the Preamble to the CPB reflects a delicate compromise between the trade and environmental interests at stake. The Preamble emphasizes that it 'shall not be interpreted as implying a change in the rights and obligations of a Party under any existing international agreements'; in other words, the Protocol shall not affect WTO obligations. Nevertheless, the CPB proclaims that this recital is not intended to subordinate it to other international agreements. To reconcile those conflicting views, the Preamble recognizes that 'trade and environment agreements should be mutually supportive with a view to achieving sustainable development'. The wording of these two recitals implies that although the CPB and WTO agreements are on equal footing, they are not impervious to one another.[23]

The use of TREMs in the major MEAs described above clearly indicates their potential for achieving specific environmental goals, in conformity with directing principles.[24] Since the 1989 Basel Convention entered into force the worst forms of waste dumping in developing countries have ceased, while the 1987 Montreal Protocol has served to reduce drastically the production of substances known to destroy the ozone layer.

2.2.2. *Multilaterally agreed TREMs versus GATT/WTO obligations*

Although no WTO contracting party has ever complained of alleged conflicts between GATT/WTO rules and MEAs containing environmental trade meas-

---

[19] Article 1.

[20] CPB, Article 11(8). See Chapter 3, Subsection 2.1.1. above.

[21] S. Zarrilli, 'International Trade in Genetically Modified Organisms and Multilateral Negotiations: A New Dilemma for Developing Countries' in F. Francioni (ed.), *Environment, Human Rights and International Trade* (Oxford: Hart, 2001) 39–86.

[22] SPS Agreement, Article 5(7). Eg T.J. Schoenbaum, 'International Trade in Living Modified Organisms' in F. Francioni (ed.), *Environment, Human Rights and International Trade*, n. 21 above, 33. See Chapter 3, Subsection 2.1.2.3. above.

[23] St. Charnovitz, 'The Supervision of Health and Biosafety Regulation by World Trade Rules' (2000) 13 Tulane Envt LJ 271.

[24] D. Brock, 'The Shrimp-Turtle case: Implications for the MEA-WTO Debate' (1998) 9 YbIEL 14.

ures,[25] such environmental agreements have given rise to questions about their consistency with the legal order regulating world trade. The core of the conflict is that the TREMs found in environmental agreements discriminate between countries on the basis of their membership in an MEA or of their environmental performance, whereas the GATT/WTO system is specifically designed to eliminate discriminatory trade practices for reasons of economic efficiency. In other words, TREMs are intentionally discriminatory, with the purpose of compelling States to change their policies or to phase out hazardous production. TREMs could thus constitute a most favoured nation (MFN) violation under Article I, contravene the non-discrimination clause in Article III, or violate the prohibition on quantitative restrictions for imports or exports according to Article XI of the GATT 1994.

A few well aimed changes to GATT could enable the concerns of MEAs to find a counterweight in international trade regimes.[26] As there is no general consensus on this issue for the moment it remains to be seen which obligation should prevail. The conflict between a convention provision that restricts trade and a WTO obligation prohibiting restrictions on trade will have to be resolved in the light of the rules in force. That solution will differ according to the membership of the Parties: in some cases all disputants might be members of both the WTO and the MEA; in other cases only one of the disputants might be a Party to the MEA. Therefore one should distinguish between conflicts where MEA membership is identical to that of the WTO and the situation where not all WTO Parties are members of the MEA. Article 30 of the 1969 Vienna Convention on the Interpretation of Treaties provides for resolution of such conflicts.

—Membership is identical

It must be recalled that the membership of the WTO Agreements is quite similar to the membership of CITES and the Basel and Vienna Conventions. For instance, only twenty-six WTO members are not Party to the Basel Convention and only eleven are not Party to CITES.[27] Therefore in most cases litigants would be Parties to both the conflicting regimes, for example WTO Member States that are also Parties to the Basel Convention. Being a valid international agreement, the MEA *a priori* enjoys equal status with WTO obligations.

When the consistency of an MEA with GATT/WTO obligations is challenged, TREMs must be considered a limited derogation by mutual agreement,[28] and in

---

[25] Since the WTO—MEA debate began eight years ago not a single dispute over an MEA-related trade measure has occurred.

[26] G. Van Calster, *International and EU Trade Law*, n. 6 above, 183.

[27] R. Schwartz, 'Trade Measures Pursuant to Multilateral Environmental Agreements: Developments from Singapore to Seattle' (2000) 9 RECIEL 69. *Contra* G. Marceau, 'A Call for Coherence in International Law' (1999) 33: 5 JWT 124. The latter author considers that as the WTO membership grows, fewer MEAs will match its membership.

[28] T. Schoenbaum, 'Free International Trade and Protection of the Environment: Irreconcilable Conflict?' (1992) 86 AJIL 719; D. Wirth, 'Trade Implications of the Basel Convention Amendment Banning North-South Trade in Hazardous Wastes' (1998) 3 RECIEL 242; P. Demaret, n. 11 above, 55.

particular as a consensual departure from mutual State obligations relating to import and export.[29] Therefore trade restrictions with an environmental purpose in MEAs should be rebuttably presumed to be 'necessary' and not 'unjustifiably discriminatory' in terms of Article XX of GATT.[30] In practical terms there can be no nullification or impairment of GATT/WTO obligations between Parties to the MEA, at least to the extent that national measures employed to implement an Agreement are consistent with that instrument.[31]

This reasoning is supported by Principle 4 of the 1992 Rio Declaration, which provides that 'in order to achieve sustainable development environmental protection shall constitute an integral part of the development process and cannot be considered in isolation from it'. In addition, it must be recalled that the WTO Appellate Body, in the *Shrimp-Turtle* dispute, expressed a strong preference for multilateral action over unilateral action.[32] Therefore a strong case may be made that TREMs are permissible if they are agreed and applied multilaterally in a way that does not distinguish arbitrarily between countries. Trade restrictions of this type would be free of the unilateral taint of the US *Shrimp-Turtle* restraints.[33]

—*Membership is not identical*

If both litigants are parties to, for example, the SPS and TBT Agreements, it is possible that the State challenging an environmental measure may not be a Party to the MEA under dispute, for example the CPB. In such a situation the CPB Party could oppose the import of LMOs from the other party by taking precautionary measures according to the Protocol, without being bound by the requirements set out by the WTO Appellate Body in its SPS case-law: for instance, that the precautionary measure must be provisional and should be reviewed within a reasonable period of time. However, in this case the LMO approval procedure under the CPB is likely to be considered an SPS measure; additional require-

[29] Some authors suggest that MEAs should be viewed as a *lex specialis* compatible with the trade regime, even if it preceded the Uruguay Round/WTO agreements in time. Nevertheless, it is difficult to decide the issue of priority of MEAs over WTO obligations on the basis of the *lex posterior derogat* rule (Article 30(3) of the Vienna Convention on the Interpretation of Treaties). Prior to the Marrakesh Agreements, all the MEAs entered into force after the GATT 1947. After the entry into force of the GATT 1994, the MEAs must be considered as prior agreements in the *lex posterior* rule. In addition, the rule *generalia specialibus non derogant*, which suggests that more specific treaties enjoy priority over more general treaties whatever their date, is also difficult to apply in the MEA-WTO debate. Eg G. Van Calster, *International and EU Trade Law*, n. 6 above, 137.

[30] As an exception to the substantive GATT obligations, Article XX allows 'the adoption or enforcement by any contracting party of measures ... (b) necessary to protect human, animal or plant life or health, ... (g) relating to the conservation of exhaustible natural resources if such measures are made effective in conjunction with restrictions on domestic production or consumption'. Of particular importance to the balance between the need to open markets and the need to regulate them in order to promote other legitimate objectives, this provision has been the focal point for most environment-related disputes. Eg E.-H. Petersmann, *International and European Trade and Environmental Law*, n. 6 above, 42.

[31] D. Wirth, n. 28 above, 243.

[32] Appellate Body, *Shrimp*, paras. 43 and 55. See also the Appellate Body Report of 22 October 2001, WT/DS58/AB/RW, para. 134.

[33] T. Schoenbaum, 'The Decision in the Shrimp-Turtle case' (1998) 9 YbIEL 39.

ments, such as labelling,[34] could be considered technical measures falling under the TBT Agreement.

In such a conflict, SPS and TBT obligations should apply because the mutual rights and obligations of the litigants are determined by the treaties to which both are Party—the SPS and TBT Agreements—and not by the treaty to which only one is Party—the CPB.[35] The underlying logic is that WTO obligations can be altered by another treaty obligation only with the consent of the other Party (*pacta sunt servanda*).[36]

Nevertheless, the use of Article 31(3)(c) of the 1969 Vienna Convention on the Interpretation of Treaties can assist in the interpretation of a WTO Agreement even where membership in an MEA is not identical. Marceau has advocated that the obligation under this Article of the Vienna Convention to take into account, 'together with the context: . . . (c) any relevant rules of international law applicable in the relations between the parties' may provide some guidance in interpretating WTO obligations.[37]

If we follow the argument of Marceau, the precautionary principle embodied in the CPB could be taken into account by WTO DSBs even in cases where not all WTO litigants are also CPB Parties and could be considered 'relevant' within the meaning of Article 31(3)(c) in interpreting, to take but one example, Article 5(7) of the SPS Agreement.[38] Furthermore, it must be stressed that this conciliatory interpretation of the SPS obligation in the light of the precautionary principle finds support in the preambular recital of the CPB according to which 'trade and environment agreements should be mutually supportive'.

Justification for multilaterally agreed TREMs in the light of environmental directing principles has been put forward by several authors. It has been argued that the directing principles of environmental law, prescribed in Article 174(2) of the EC Treaty, should also be taken into account in interpreting WTO obligations, since those principles have been universally adopted in the Resolution of the 1992 UN Conference on Environment and Development.[39] The decisions of the ECJ could also provide important support for some TREMs. For instance, according to one author:

---

[34] Article 18(2)(a) of the CPB states that each party shall take measures to require that documentation accompanying LMOs that are intended for direct use as food or feed or for processing clearly identifies that they 'may contain' LMOs.

[35] P.T. Stoll, 'Controlling the Risks of GMOs: The Carthagena Protocol on Biosafety and the SPS Agreement' (1999) 10 YbIEL 82–119, 117.

[36] Ph. Sands, *Principles of International Environmental Law* (Manchester: MUP, 1995) 686.

[37] G. Marceau, n. 27 above, 123–6.

[38] This seems to have been acknowledged by the Appellate Body in the *Shrimp* case, where it used a number of MEAs, to which all the disputants were not members, in order to interpret the term 'exhaustible natural resources' found in Article XX(g) (Appellate Body, *Shrimp*, footnote 111). In the *Gasoline* case, by virtue of Article 3(2) of the Dispute Settlement Understanding, the Appellate Body linked the WTO legal system to the rest of the international order and imposed on Panels the duty to interpret WTO Agreements in accordance with the customary law of interpretation.

[39] H. Peterson, 'Trade and Environmental Protection: The Practice of GATT and the EC compared' in J. Cameron, P. Demaret, and P. Gerardin (eds.), *Trade and the Environment*, n. 6 above, 151.

the ban on imports of waste from non-Parties imposed by the 1989 Basel Convention could be considered as necessary to protect the importing Party's own environment under the polluter-pays principle and the proximity principle. The claim can be made that, with respect to waste, a new international rule is emerging according to which each State is in principle responsible for dealing with its own waste and is, as a result, entitled to exclude waste from abroad in order to protect its environment.[40]

In the case of GMOs, it would be difficult to maintain that a modified organism is indeed the same ('like product') as a non-modified organism, whatever their outward appearance. This distinction finds support in the precautionary principle.

2.2.3. *Unilaterally enacted TREMs versus GATT/WTO obligations*
—*The pros and cons of unilaterally enacted TREMs*
The absence of international co-operation in a number of environmental fields has led States with high standards of environmental or health protection increasingly to regulate imports of hazardous products, not only in order to safeguard their own domestic resources but also to protect public health and the environment at a global level. In such instances trade measures are either adopted in the absence of agreed international standards or rules, or go beyond existing international standards.[41] This trend is likely to take on greater importance with the adoption of measures intended to protect the environment beyond a national jurisdiction, for example the US ban on killing dolphins or endangered sea turtles when harvesting tuna or shrimp, or EC Regulation No. 3254/91 on leghold traps which bans the import into the EC of fur products originating from animals trapped by methods that do not meet 'internationally agreed humane trapping standards'.[42] Beyond ethical or conservationist grounds, importing States concerned by a situation where competitive advantage is obtained through lower standards which cannot be eliminated by environmental duties will be willing to restrict the import of products based on those standards.

On one hand, unilateral trade measures may be needed under certain conditions to avoid the degradation of global commons which lie outside any national jurisdiction. For instance, unilateral measures to protect the global commons should be accepted when irreversible damage might occur before a relevant international agreement could be concluded, particularly if the adoption of such measures could hasten international consensus on the need to protect the global commons.[43] On the other hand, such trade restrictions raise important

---

[40] P. Demaret, n. 11 above, 58.

[41] Ph. Sands, *Principles of International Environmental Law*, n. 36 above, 687; L. Boisson de Chazournes, 'Unilateralism and Environmental Protection: Issues of Perception and Reality of Issues' (2000) 11: 2 EJIL 315–38. For the theoretical justifications of unilateral measures see Birnie and Boyle, n. 6 above, 713–4.

[42] A. Nollkaemper, 'The Legality of Moral Crusades Disguised in Trade Laws: An Analysis of the EC Ban on Furs from Animals Taken by Leghold Traps' (1996) JEL 237–57.

[43] E. Brown-Weiss, 'Environment and Trade as Partners in Sustainable Development' (1992) 86 AJIL 733; P. Demaret, n. 11 above, 64.

concerns under international trade law, since they act to close markets to countries that cannot afford strict environmental controls. In sum, the willingness to influence the domestic standards of another State through import bans raises concerns about eco-imperialism.[44]

—The importance of scientific justification for unilaterally enacted TREMs
Some Uruguay Round instruments, notably those on TBT and SPS, establish a legal presumption that national standards are compatible with the system if they conform to international standards. For instance, according to Article 3(2) of the SPS Agreement: 'SPS measures which conform to international standards, guidelines or recommendations shall be deemed to be necessary to protect human, animal or plant life or health, and presumed to be consistent with the relevant provisions of this Agreement and of GATT 1994'. Similarly, according to Article 2(2) of the TBT Agreement, technical standards based on relevant international standards 'shall be rebuttably presumed not to create an unnecessary obstacle to international trade'.

However, international standards can be deemed ineffective or inappropriate owing to varying geographical or climatic conditions or production systems. Therefore Article 2(4) of the TBT Agreement states that Member States are not obliged to use international standards as a basis for their technical considerations: 'for instance because of fundamental climatic or geographic factors or technological problems'. In this case, if a Party implements a stricter standard than the international one, the complainant bears the burden of proving *prima facie* that the higher standard is inconsistent; thereafter the onus shifts to the defendant, which will have to prove that its measure needs to be stricter than international standards, guidelines, or recommendations in order to achieve specific goals and that it is not discriminatory. Furthermore, a higher level of protection than that afforded by international standards, guidelines, or recommendations can be justified only if there is scientific justification according to the SPS Agreement.[45] According to the TBT Agreement, in assessing the health or environmental risks that a technical regulation is intended to avoid the national regulator is obliged to consider, among other things, 'the available scientific information'.[46]

Where disputes arise scientific analysis is called upon as an essential means of conflict resolution. A State that is unable to provide scientific justification for its measures may not maintain them. The appropriateness of a measure is reviewed on the basis of scientific assessment alone, since the SPS and TBT Agreements do not permit economic and social factors to determine such choices. Difficulties arise, however, when the level of protection adopted is based on scientific

---

[44] E. Brown-Weiss, n. 43 above, 732.
[45] Article 3(3) SPS Agreement. According to Article 3(3) SPS Agreement, however, the application of measures which result in a lower standard of protection than the level afforded internationally is not deemed to be inconsistent with the SPS Agreement.
[46] Article 2(2) TBT Agreement.

grounds that are disputed owing to the absence of definitive proof. We have seen earlier in this work how WTO DSBs have until now subjected uncertainty to strict constraints, making it difficult for States to pursue a higher level of protection than that set by international standards or guidelines (eg Codex Alimentarius, CEN, ISO) within a context of scientific uncertainty.[47] Thus scientific justification lies at the heart of conflicts between the free circulation of goods and national or regional policies of health and environmental protection.

In this context assessing risk becomes a task of paramount importance. Recognition of scientific uncertainty by virtue of the precautionary principle would make it easier for States to seek a higher level of protection; requiring scientific certainty to justify stricter national measures would, on the contrary, re-establish the primacy of free trade.

—The role of environmental directing principles

Principles of general or customary international law[48] – among them, in our view, the precautionary principle—must under certain conditions be taken into account by Dispute Panels and the Appellate Body in their interpretation of Article XX or other related provisions, even if they are not specifically embodied in an MEA.[49] Recent Appellate Body decisions, including *Gasoline*[50] and *Shrimp*[51] have acknowledged that even in the case of unilateral trade measures the WTO system remains part of a broader body of international law. According to this new jurisprudential trend, which represents a departure from earlier GATT panel jurisprudence, the WTO system is not a hermetically sealed regime that may refuse to take basic principles of environmental law into account.

Article 31(3)(c) of the 1969 Vienna Convention on the Interpretation of Treaties is once again of particular relevance for customary environmental principles. This Article provides that 'there shall be taken into account, together with the context ... (c) any relevant rules of international law applicable in the relation between the parties'. Article 31(3)(c) could be developed into an operationally useful tool to oblige the WTO DSBs to interpret classical obligations in the light of new principles of customary international law, such as the precautionary principle and the obligation to prevent transboundary environmental

---

[47] See the discussion on SPS case-law in Chapter 3, Subsection 2.1.2.3. above.

[48] See the discussion in Chapter 4, Subsection 2.3.2. above.

[49] G. Marceau, n. 27 above, 87.

[50] In that case the WTO Appellate Body stated that 'customary rules of interpretation' would include Article 31 of the 1969 Vienna Convention which 'has attained the status of a rule of customary or general international law' (Appellate Body, *Gasoline*, p. 17).

[51] For instance, the concept of 'natural exhaustible resources' embodied in the words of Article XX(g) must be interpreted, according to the Appellate Body, 'in the light of contemporary concerns of the community of nations about the protection and conservation of the environment' (Appellate Body, *Shrimp*, para. 129). The Appellate Body also considered the 1992 Rio Declaration on Environment and Development to illustrate international support for a multilateral approach to the adoption of environmental measures (ibid., para. 168).

harm.[52] If such an approach were taken in future it would enhance the value and authority of the directing principles of environmental law identified in Part I.[53]

Although WTO DSBs have in the past referred to various MEAs, and in that connection to Article 31(3)(a) and (b), when reviewing unilateral trade measures they have thus far resisted any reference to Article 31(3)(c) of the 1969 Vienna Convention. However, this situation might be set to change. In the *EC Hormones* case the WTO Appellate Body reviewed the status of the precautionary principle; while it did not rule on its status in international law,[54] it supported its application by acknowledging the right of a Party to establish its own level of protection and softening the requirements for risk assessment in such a way as to allow a wider margin for consideration of the principle. The Appellate Body also made extensive use of the general principle of *in dubio mitius* in this case, enlarging the scope of the EC's discretion to determine its own health standards.[55] However, by stressing that all national precautionary measures must be based on 'sufficient scientific evidence' gathered as the result of a risk assessment, as required under SPS Article 5,[56] the Appellate Body seems to have overestimated the role which scientific evidence may legitimately play in resolving trade disputes.[57]

Two examples illustrate how more systematic recourse to the principles could prove particularly useful in supporting some unilateral measures. First, according to one author, an absolute ban on imports of hazardous wastes from abroad could be considered consistent with Article XX if it could be justified in the light of the polluter-pays and proximity principles;[58] the latter aims to restrict transboundary movements of wastes and hazardous substances to the greatest possible extent.[59] In this respect interesting comparisons could be made with the case-law of the ECJ, which has ruled that such a unilateral prohibition is permissible under the EC Treaty.[60]

---

[52] P. Sands, 'Environmental Protection in the Twenty-First Century: Sustainable Development and International Law' in R.L. Revesz, Ph. Sands, and R. Stewart (eds.), *Environmental Law, the Economy, and Sustainable Development* (Cambridge: CUP, 2000) 403; 'Sustainable Development: Treaty, Custom, and the Cross-fertilization of International Law' in A. Boyle and D. Freestone (eds.), *International Law and Sustainable Development* (Oxford University Press, 1999) 48–60.

[53] The Appellate Body concluded that the precautionary principle, at least outside the field of international environmental law, still awaits authoritative formulation and does not override the provisions of the SPS Agreement (Appellate Body, *EC Hormones*, para. 403).

[54] Appellate Body, *EC Hormones*, para. 123.

[55] J. Cameron, 'Dispute Settlement and Conflicting Trade and Environment Regimes' in A. Fijalkowski and J. Cameron (eds.), *Trade and the Environment*, n. 6 above, 20.

[56] Appellate Body, *EC Hormones*, para. 177.

[57] R. Pavoni, 'Biosafety and Intellectual Property Rights: Balancing Trade and Environmental Security— The Jurisprudence of the European Patent Office as a Paradigm of an International Public Policy Issue' in F. Francioni (ed.), *Environment, Human Rights and International Trade*, n. 21 above, 95.

[58] P. Demaret, n. 11 above, 60–1.

[59] The proximity principle is embodied in the 1998 POPs Protocol to the LRATP Convention. Article 3(1) of the Protocol stipulates that, whenever feasible, disposal should be carried out domestically.

[60] N. de Sadeleer, *Le droit communautaire et les déchets* (Brussels: Bruylant, L.G.D.J., 1995) 115—21, 481–92. See Subsection 3.2. below.

Secondly, the principle of rectification of environmental harm at source may shed new light on the ability of Parties to ban imports of goods produced using environmentally unsustainable practices. From the viewpoint of sustainable development the production process is as important as the characteristics of the good itself.[61]

Nevertheless, Article 31(3)(c) of the 1969 Vienna Convention only requires States 'to take into account . . . the relevant rule'; therefore although the customary principle of rectification at source can influence the contested conventional norm it cannot replace it. Furthermore, there is no guarantee whatsoever that international environmental law principles, supposing they were to be included in the reasoning of WTO DSBs, would be correctly implemented by those bodies.[62]

3. EUROPEAN COMMUNITY LAW

3.1. Introductory remarks

Unlike the GATT/WTO system, the EC Internal Market—which ensures the free movement of goods, among other things—is not a closed system that can afford to ignore health or environmental concerns. Indeed the task of the EC actually requires 'a harmonious, balanced and sustainable development of economic activities . . . with a high level of protection and improvement of the quality of the environment'.[63] In contrast to the GATT/WTO system, the EC legal order provides explicitly or implicitly for comprehensive public policies in the field of health, consumer, and environmental protection. In addition it should be noted that the internal market is not an end in itself, but one of the means by which EC objectives are to be achieved. Nevertheless, the relationship between the internal market and the environment can also be very strained within the EC legal order.[64]

National or regional environmental protection measures appear in many ways to be vestiges of a neo-protectionist policy which threatens the development of the internal market, and particularly one of its most basic elements: the free circulation of goods. This has provoked criticism of some national environmental protection measures.

[61] From an environmental point of view the possibility of discriminating between products according to the sustainability of their production process is important because environmental policy intends to discrimate against environmental unfriendly products in favour of less damaging substitutes. Eg Brown-Weiss, n. 43 above, 730. However, WTO DSBs have not recognized that process and production methods could serve to distinguish products. In a recent report the WTO Appellate Body recognized that the 'effects of a product, such as carcinogenicity or toxicity' constitute a defining aspect of the physical properties of the product which have to be taken into account in assessing the likeness of two products (Appellate Body, *Asbestos*, paras. 113–14).

[62] J.L. Dunoff, 'Border Patrol at the WTO' (1998) 9 YbIEL 27.

[63] Article 2 EC Treaty.

[64] N. de Sadeleer, *Le droit communautaire et les déchets*, n. 60 above; A.R. Ziegler, *Trade and Environmental Law in the European Community* (Oxford: Clarendon, 1996); D. Geradin, *Trade and the Environment: A Comparative Study of EC and US Law* (Cambridge: CUP, 1997); J. Jans, *European Environmental Law* (2nd edn., Groeningen: Europa Law Publishing, 2000).

Some consider import restrictions on polluting products as a particularly sound excuse for strengthening domestic competitiveness; the requirement to return used bottles favours national firms over their foreign competitors, and the use of a national logo or label on environmentally friendly products can serve to advertise the advantages of domestically produced goods. Two institutional mechanisms have been promoted in order to ensure that the unity of the internal market is not damaged by wide divergences in national policies. The first consists in preventing Member States from adopting regulations that affect intra-Community trade by requiring strict compliance with Articles 28 and 29 of the EC Treaty, which recognize the free circulation of goods (negative harmonization). A national measure that is inconsistent with free trade will be challenged before the ECJ or in national courts and invalidated if found to be discriminatory or disproportionate. The second mechanism, known as positive harmonization, complements the first: common rules (directives, regulations) are adopted that apply to all Member States, with the purpose of avoiding market fragmentation through the application of diverging national rules. In this second mechanism the tensions that arise between free trade and environmental protection measures are generally resolved through positive harmonization, especially product regulation and directives based on Article 95 (former Article 100A) of the EC Treaty. However, this harmonization does not prevent Member States from adopting rules stricter than the EC measure under some circumstances, thus giving rise to the prospect of further trade conflicts.[65] Indeed, the majority of environmental regulations not relating to product standards are based on Article 174 of the EC Treaty and allow Member States to adopt stricter measures. Neither positive nor negative harmonization can thus completely prevent national environment policies from entering into conflict with the principle of the free movement of goods; harmonization can merely reduce the likelihood of conflict.

Whatever the option chosen, the principles of prevention, rectification at source, and precaution are likely to shed new light on the conflicts between national environment measures and the principle of the free movement of goods. This thesis is demonstrated in the following sections. First, we examine how the self-sufficiency and proximity principles can validate measures that conflict with the principle of the free movement of wastes (Subsection 3.2. below). Secondly, we consider how the precautionary principle can shed new light on the principle of pre-emption (Subsection 3.3.).

3.2. Negative harmonization

In contrast to the reports of the WTO DSBs, the case-law of the ECJ reveals that directing principles of environmental law may be used in assessing national

---

[65] On the issue of the choice of the legal basis of EC legislation concerning environmental protection: N. de Sadeleer, *Le droit communautaire et les déchets*, n. 60 above, 34–67; D. Geradin, *Trade and the Environment*, n. 64 above, 75–90.

measures that affect the principle of the free circulation of goods. We consider below ECJ decisions relating to three groups of principles: the self-sufficiency and proximity principles, the precautionary principle, and the substitution principle. As we have already stressed, there is nothing to prevent the reasoning underlying ECJ case-law from being used by analogy to resolve WTO conflicts.

3.2.1. Derogations to the free movement of waste in the light of the self-sufficiency and proximity principles

The *Wallonia Waste* case is the clearest illustration of the role that environmental principles can play in fine-tuning the balance between the principle of the free movement of goods and environmental needs.

Throughout the 1980s important quantities of industrial wastes were illegally exported from Germany and The Netherlands into Belgium, particularly into the Wallonia region, which at that time did not possess the administrative and technical structures needed efficiently to control their disposal. Some of these wastes had been illegally dumped and had subsequently given rise to serious pollution, to which the local population reacted strongly. The Wallonia region tried to remedy the situation by banning the import of any waste into Wallonia.

In response to a complaint, the European Commission challenged the validity of the Walloon measure, in terms of the provisions of EC waste Directives and of the principle of the free circulation of goods recognized in the Treaty. In a 9 July 1992 judgment that has since become famous, the ECJ ruled against the Belgian decree insofar as it related to the provisions of EC secondary legislation.[66]

The Court accepted the argument that mandatory requirements relating to environmental protection justified the adoption of measures contested by the Commission. But mandatory requirements could only be relied upon if the measure, in this case the prohibition of waste imports, applied indiscriminately to both national and foreign wastes. In that respect the Commission held that the Wallonian restrictions were discriminatory because they applied only to foreign wastes. Advocate General Jacobs thus had no difficulty in holding that 'the measure in question, which favours waste produced in one region of a Member State, is plainly not indistinctly applicable to domestic and imported products'.

Unexpectedly, the ECJ assessed the discriminatory nature of the measure in quite an original manner, taking into account the specific nature of wastes: 'so far

---

[66] Case C-2/90, *Commission v. Belgium* [1992] ECR I-1. Eg N. de Sadeleer, 'Les limites posées à la libre circulation des déchets par les exigences de protection de l'environnement' (1993) 5–6 Cah Dr Eur. 672–96; H. Somsen, 'Case C-2/90, Commission v. Belgium/Free Movement of Goods, Transfrontier Movement of Waste' (1992), EELR 107; M. Wheeler, 'The Legality of Restrictions on the Movement of Wastes under Community Law' (1993) 5: 1 JEL 140; L. Hancher and H. Sevenster, (1993) CMLR 351; P. von Wilmowsky, 'Abfall und freier Warenverkehr: Bestandaufnahme nach dem EUGH-Urteil Wallonisches Einfuhrverbot' (1992) EuR, 416 and 'Waste Disposal in the Internal Market: The State of Play After the ECJ's Ruling on the Walloon Ban' (1993) CMLR 541; H.J. Jans, 'Waste Policy and European Community Law: Does the EEC Treaty Provide a Suitable Framework for Regulating Waste?' (1993) ELQ 165.

as the environment is concerned ... waste has a special characteristic. The accumulation of waste, even before it becomes a hazard, constitutes a threat to the environment because of the limited capacity of each region or locality for receiving it.'[67]

Subsequently, in order to assess discrimination, the Court referred to the principle of the rectification of environmental harm at source set out in former Article 130r(2) (new Article 174(2)) of the EC Treaty, which applied to the present case implies that it is incumbent on each region and other local government to take appropriate measures to treat and eliminate its own waste.[68] The ECJ justified these restrictions on the grounds that 'waste should be disposed of as close as possible to the place where it is produced' (proximity) and 'it is for each region, commune or other local entity to take appropriate measures to receive, process and dispose of its own waste' (self-sufficiency).[69] Finally the Court affirmed that its reasoning was in accordance with the principles of self-sufficiency and proximity embodied in the 1989 Basel Convention on the Control of Transboundary Movements of Hazardous Waste and their Disposal, a Convention to which the EC was a signatory.[70] The ECJ ruled that the Wallonia waste import ban could not be regarded as discriminatory in view of the differences between wastes produced abroad and wastes produced in Wallonia and their connection with the place where they were produced.

The use of the principle of rectification of environmental harm at source, combined with the principles of self-sufficiency and proximity, served in this case to blur the traditional differentiation between distinctly (Article 30) and indistinctly (rule of reason) applicable criteria and led the ECJ to endorse a limitation on the free movement of goods on environmental grounds. Environmental protection should justify distinctly applicable national measures (eg a waste ban) in the light of the environmental principle set forth in (new) Article 174(2) of the EC Treaty and the principles of the 1989 Basel Convention. By reading the Treaty in context, the ECJ found that the principle of free movement of goods had to be interpreted in a way that was compatible with environmental requirements. Therefore wastes could not be treated as just another type of goods.[71]

Following that decision, however, several analysts considered that the *Wallonia Waste* judgment was of limited scope, since the Wallonia Region's import prohibition was justified primarily as the result of the serious pollution that had been created at the time by massive and illegal imports of foreign industrial wastes.[72] These analyses concluded that this bold decision would not be

---

[67] Para. 30.   [68] Para. 34.   [69] Para. 34.   [70] Para. 35.

[71] M. Wasmeier, 'The Integration of Environmental Protection as a General Rule for Interpreting Community Law' (2001) CMLR 159–77.

[72] See among others P. von Wilmowsky, 'Waste Disposal in the Internal Market: the State of Play after the ECJ's Ruling on the Walloon Import Ban' (1993) CMLR 552. Other authors recognize the fundamental role played by these principles in case-law evolution. Eg D. Geradin, *Trade and the Environment*, n. 64 above, 19.

applicable to less striking situations than those pertaining in the Walloon region at the time the waste import ban was adopted. Consequently, reference to the proximity and self-sufficiency principles was seen as purely circumstantial and not as an authoritative decision.

We must thus ask whether *Wallonia* is in fact an authoritative judgment, or rather a judgment given in response to exceptional circumstances. At the time it quickly became evident that the judgment was going to have important consequences for systems of waste movements within the EC, to the extent that the ECJ subsequently used the same principles to validate measures relating to the management of wastes.

In a second judgment *(Commission v. Council)* concerning the Waste Framework Directive 75/442/EEC, which sets out the principles of proximity and self-sufficiency, the ECJ confirmed its earlier interpretation of the principle of rectification of environmental damage at source as a priority, as in *Wallonia Waste*.[73] It agreed that the contested Directive had to be based on the principle that environmental damage should as a matter of priority be rectified at source. This principle, embodied in Article 5 of the Directive, requires taking into account: 'the place where the waste is to be disposed of in relation to the place where it is produced in order to ensure, insofar as possible, that each Member State is responsible for the disposal of its own waste'.[74]

In a third judgment, *Parliament v. Council*, the ECJ once again referred to *Wallonia Waste* to confirm the environmental nature of Regulation 259/93/EC on the supervision and control of waste within, into, and out of the European Community, thereby justifying the choice of Article 130S of the Treaty (new Article 175) as its legal basis. The Court reasoned that: 'Those conditions and procedures have all been adopted with a view to ensuring the protection of the environment, taking account of objectives falling within the scope of environmental policy such as the principles of proximity, priority for recovery and self-sufficiency at Community and national levels'.[75]

In a fourth judgment, *Commission v. Germany*, the ECJ dismissed any doubts as to the role of environmental principles in assessing measures that restrict the transboundary movements of wastes within the EC. In this case the Commission was challenging the validity of a German law that gave priority to the elimination of wastes within national territory. The Court held that: 'the rule requiring disposal on national territory laid down in the German Law...cannot be regarded as a general and absolute prohibition on the export of dangerous waste...'[76] The ECJ stressed that the German rule reflected: 'the pursuit of an objective which is in conformity with the principle...that environmental damage should, as a priority, be rectified at source'.

---

[73] Case C-155/91, *Commission v. Council* [1993] ECR I-939.
[74] Ibid., para. 14.
[75] Case C-187/93, *Parliament v. Council* [1994] ECR I-2857, para. 22.
[76] Case C-422/92, *Commission v. Germany* [1995] ECR I-1097, para. 34.

In the *Düsseldorf* case the ECJ stated that the principle that environmental damage should as a priority be rectified at source must be limited to shipments of waste intended for disposal.[77] This argument was confirmed in the *Københavns Kommune* case, concerning the consistency of a prohibition on exporting construction wastes out of Denmark:

As regards the justification based on the protection of the environment, and in particular the principle referred to in Article 130r(2) (new Article 174(2)) of the Treaty that environmental damage should as a priority be rectified at source, it must be pointed out that the protection of the environment cannot serve to justify any restriction on exports, particularly in the case of waste destined for recovery (...). That is so *a fortiori* where, as in the case before the national court, environmentally non-hazardous building waste is involved.[78]

More recently, the ECJ judged that 'a national measure prohibiting exports of waste for disposal could be justified by the principles of proximity, priority for recovery and self-sufficiency, in accordance with Article 4(3)(a)(i) of the Waste Shipment Regulation'. It was not necessary for that national measure to be subjected to a further and separate review of its compatibility with Article 30 of the EC Treaty.[79]

The developments reflected in this case-law sharply emphasize how the principle of correction of environmental harm at source recognized in Article 174(2) of the EC Treaty, combined with the self-sufficiency and proximity principles, serves to clarify the interpretation of secondary EC legislation, with important consequences for a part of the waste market.

Environmental principles have in this way allowed the EC to develop a *ius singulare* based on the principle that free movement should be the exception rather than the rule in cases where wastes will be disposed of.[80] This dialectic between primary law principles and secondary legislation breaks down into three phases. First, in a conflict between the Commission and Belgium, environmental principles made it possible to modify the rigour of ECJ case-law in a way that favoured limiting the transboundary movements of wastes. In a second phase, the Community's legislator took the conclusions of this controversial judgment as a basis for setting out the principles of proximity and self-sufficiency in secondary law and consequently limiting certain categories of transboundary movements of wastes.[81] Finally, in a third phase, when asked to determine the appropriate legal basis of the Community's waste instruments, the ECJ based its judgment on the principles set out in *Wallonia Waste*.

---

[77] Case C-203/96, *Chemische Afvalstoffen Dusseldorp B.V.* [1998] ECR I-4077, para. 49.
[78] Case C-209/98, *Entreprenørforeningens Affalds v. Miljøsektion and Københavns Kommune* [2000] ECR I-3777, para. 48.
[79] Case C-324/99, *DaimlerChrysler AG*, [2001] ECR I-9918, para. 46.
[80] D. Geradin, n. 64 above, 201.
[81] Article 7 of Council Directive 75/442/EEC on waste; Article 3(a)(i) of Council Regulation (EEC) No. 259/93 of 1 February 1993 on the supervision and control of shipments of waste within, into, and out of the European Community.

In conclusion, the *Wallonia Waste* case-law provides a fine example of the integration of environmental principles into the field of trade law.[82] Whether the ECJ's approach is the result of an environmentally friendly interpretation, or a formal recognition of the duty to integrate, it constitutes implementation of the integration principle.[83] Finally, we should recall that this is a particularly clear illustration of an essential element of post-modern law: entangled hierarchies that intermingle legal rules of determinate content with the principles that inspire them.[84] Thus a paradigm of complexity replaces one of linearity, and brings with it a strong link to environmental legal principles.

3.2.2. *Derogations to the principle of the free movement of goods in the light of the precautionary principle*

Failing a requirement to apply the precautionary principle outside of the Community's legal framework, nothing prevents Member States from invoking it to justify derogations relating to health and the life of humans set out in Article 30 of the EC Treaty (former Article 36) and linked to mandatory requirements of

---

[82] It remains to be seen whether other types of distinctly applicable measures can be accepted under the rule of reason in the light of Article 174(2) principles. The case-law of the ECJ is not clear. For instance in *Asher-Waggon GmbH v. Germany*, concerning the discriminatory effects of a German regulation to control noise emissions from aircrafts, the Court ruled that even though there was a difference in treatment between aircraft previously registered in Germany and those that were not, 'such a barrier may, however, be justified by considerations of public health and environmental protection' (Case C-203/96, *Asher Waggon* (1998) ECR I-4473). However, the ECJ failed to address the question of the real nature of the national measure, distinctly or non-distinctly applicable. Nevertheless, the non-discriminatory nature of the measure was not unambiguous as it appears that aircraft are treated differently according to the country of registration. But it seems that the ECJ was raising the issue more in regard to whether the German regulations were proportionate than whether or not they were discriminatory in effect. Eg Duncan French, 'The Changing Nature of Environmental Protection: Recent Developments regarding Trade and the Environment in the EU and the WTO' (2000) NILR 21–2; H. Temmink, 'From Danish Bottles to Danish Bees: The Dynamics of Free Movement of Goods and Environmental Protection—A Case Law Analysis' (2000) I YbEEL 291. See also the Opinion of Advocate General Jacob delivered on 26 October 2000 in Case C-379/98, *PreussenElektra AG* [2001] ECR I-2159, para. 233: 'National measures for the protection of the environment are inherently liable to differentiate on the basis of the nature and origin of the cause of harm, and are therefore liable to be found discriminatory, precisely because they are based on such accepted principles as that "environmental damage should as a priority be rectified at source" (Article 130r(2) of the EC Treaty). Where such measures necessarily have a discriminatory impact of that kind, the possibility that they may be justified should not be excluded.'

[83] G. Van Calster, n. 6 above, 348; M. Wasmeier, n. 71 above, 175. See in particular the Opinion of Advocate General Jacob in Case C-379/98, *PreussenElektra AG*, para. 232: 'Special account must therefore be taken of environmental concerns in interpreting the Treaty provisions on the free movement of goods. Moreover harm to the environment, even where it does not immediately threaten—as it often does—the health and life of humans, animals and plants protected by Article 36 of the Treaty, may pose a more substantial, if longer-term, threat to the ecosystem as a whole. It would be hard to justify, in these circumstances, giving a lesser degree of protection to the environment than to the interests recognised in trade treaties concluded many decades ago and taken over into the text of Article 36 of the EC Treaty, itself unchanged since it was adopted in 1957.' The ECJ confirmed in that case that 'environmental protection requirements must be integrated into the definition and implementation of other Community policies. The Treaty of Amsterdam transferred that provision, in a slightly modified form, to Article 6 of the Treaty, which appears in Part One, headed "Principles"' (para. 76).

[84] See the discussion in Chapter 1, Subsection 3.2. above.

general concern related to environmental protection. This argument was put forward by France when it decided at the end of 1999 to prohibit the importation of British beef.[85] In other words, while EC institutions are required to take the precautionary principle into account when managing risks, Member States may take precautionary measures in areas that fall within their jurisdiction.[86] At the same time, however, a moratorium, a decision to withdraw a product from the market, or any other such measure adopted in the name of precaution constitutes a technical barrier to the principle of the free circulation of goods, which can only be justified under Article 30 of the EC Treaty or under the *Cassis de Dijon* case-law.

Although the precautionary principle has only recently been formally recognized in the EC Treaty and national legal orders, the Court of Justice has long drawn inspiration from the idea of precaution. Since the mid-1980s the ECJ has on several occasions been called upon to rule on trade-restrictive food safety measures while the risks being countered were still the subject of scientific controversy. In those cases the Court applied the precautionary principle on the basis of its consideration of the risk concerns put forward by Member States.[87] Only the existence of a risk to public health may permit a Member State to restrict the free movement of goods. To evaluate whether such a health hazard exists the ECJ refers to the results of international scientific research (FAO, WHO, Codex Alimentarius). In cases of insufficient evidence or lack of scientific consensus the ECJ has nonetheless ruled that Member States may uphold trade barriers for purposes of health protection.[88] For instance, in several cases concerning additives the ECJ accepted that despite an absence of scientific consensus on the potential effects of critical doses of additives in foodstuffs, Member States could have recourse to Article 30 of the EC Treaty to decide what level of protection was required for health and the life of humans in the light of national eating patterns.[89] In other words, protective measures restricting the free movement of goods could be accepted in cases where scientific research was being undertaken but 'appeared not to be sufficiently advanced to be able to determine with certainty the critical quantities and the precise effects' of additives consumed in large quantities.[90] The ECJ judged that particularly sensitive consumers (eg children and pregnant women) must be taken into account when evaluating health hazards.[91] On the other hand, a reference to risks that might potentially

---

[85] See the discussion in Chapter 3 Subsection 2.2.4.1. above.

[86] L. Gonzalez Vaque, L. Ehring, and C. Jacquet, 'Le principe de précaution dans la législation communautaire et nationale relative à la protection de la santé' (1999) 1 RMME 106.

[87] Eg S. Schlacke, 'Foodstuffs Law and the Precautionary Principle' in C. Joerges, K.-H. Ladent, and E. Vos (eds.), *Integrating Expertise into Regulatory Decision-Making* (Baden-Baden: Nomos, 1997) 172–82.

[88] Case 53/80, *Eyssen* [1981] ECR 409.

[89] Case 174/82, *Sandoz* [1983] ECR 2445; Case C-227/82, *Van Bennekom* [1983] ECR 3883, paras. 36 and 37; Case C-247/84, *Motte* [1985] ECR 3887; Case C-304/84, *Muller* [1986] ECR 1511, para. 21.

[90] Case 227/82, *Van Bennekom* [1983] ECR 3883.

[91] Case 97/83, *Melkunie* [1984] ECR 2367.

result from the ingestion of additives does not meet the requirements of the proportionality principle if such additives are authorized in the manufacture of other food products.[92]

Thus in cases of scientific controversy the ECJ does not support measures that disproportionately restrict the free movement of goods.[93] ECJ case-law indicates that a Member State must in every case be able to demonstrate that prohibiting a food additive is necessary in order effectively to protect human health, in the light of national consumption patterns and the results of international scientific research. Member States must also demonstrate that the additive being prohibited does not fulfil an important technical function.[94]

The precautionary principle, recognized in the EC Treaty, should support this case-law by clarifying the grounds for intervention by public authorities when a causal link has not yet been firmly established between a product or activity suspected of giving rise to risk and eventual damage. Precautionary measures adopted by Member States would thus constitute a legitimate restriction of the free movement of goods in cases characterized by an uncertain level of evidence according to the present state of scientific research, provided that the measure was proportional. The ECJ has ruled that in the absence of secondary legislation, in cases of uncertainty, Member State-specific eating habits and climate conditions must be seen as supporting intensive health protection.[95]

3.2.3. *Derogations to the principle of the free movement of goods in the light of the substitution principle*

Finally, a less well known principle that has links with precaution may also eventually affect the validity of national measures that derogate from the principle of the free circulation of goods. The ECJ recently ruled that a system of individual and conditional derogations to a general prohibition on the use of a chemical product was adequate and proportional in that it made it possible to improve worker protection while taking into account the continuing operation of firms. Such a derogation is granted subject to the conditions that no less dangerous substitute exists and that the applicant seek a replacement less dangerous to public health and the environment in the future.[96]

3.3. Positive harmonization

Harmonization of national legislation has been the centrepiece of the EC internal market. Article 95, the cornerstone of this policy, nevertheless allows Member States to maintain or adopt consumer, health, and environmental protection measures that are more stringent than EC measures, thereby creating derogations

---

[92] Case 178/84, *Commission v. Germany* [1987] ECR 1227.
[93] Case 74/82, *Commission v. Ireland* [1984] ECR 317.
[94] Case 178/84, *Commission v. Germany* [1987] ECR 1227.
[95] S. Schlacke, n. 87 above, 180.
[96] Case C-473/98, *Kemikalieinspektionen and Toolex Ab* [2000] ECR I-5702, paras. 46 and 47.

to the principle of full harmonization. However, the ability of Member States to take unilateral action is far from unlimited.

National measures set in place before an EC harmonization measure enters into force may, according to Article 95(4), be maintained if they are justified by the major needs referred to in Article 30 EC Treaty or protection of the environment or the working environment and pass the non-discrimination test.

In addition, Article 95(5) allows Member States to introduce provisions relating to protection of the environment or the working environment after adoption of an EC-wide harmonization if these are based on 'new scientific evidence'. In particular, a Member State wishing to take unilateral action must demonstrate that the problem justifying the measure is specific to its territory and has arisen after the adoption of the harmonization measure. In any case, these two types of measures must not constitute arbitrary discrimination or a disguised restriction on trade and must not constitute an obstacle to the functioning of the internal market.[97]

The inclusion of the precautionary principle in Article 174(2) of the EC Treaty should influence how Article 95(5) is to be interpreted. In the light of this principle, the condition that protection measures adopted after EC harmonization measures enter into force must be based on 'new scientific evidence' needs to be interpreted to allow Member States to introduce national protection measures even if the new evidence does not yet provide full scientific certainty.[98] This means that conclusive proof, as opposed to 'evidence', is not required and that it should be sufficient for the Member State to demonstrate on the basis of current scientific knowledge that an environmental problem could arise.[99]

Confirmation of this thesis can already be found in the practice of the European Commission.[100] In four decisions on creosote, a wood preservative classified as carcinogenic and which is highly toxic to aquatic organisms, the Commission acknowledged that the EC level of protection provided by a harmonization directive was insufficient. The Commission for the first time referred directly to the precautionary principle and confirmed the right of Member States to act in accordance with it. In addition to setting aside the requirement that a national measure must address a problem specific to the requesting Member

---

[97] H. Sevenster, 'The Environmental Guarantee after Amsterdam: Does the Emperor Have New Clothes?' (2000) I YbEEL 291; N. de Sadeleer, 'Les clauses de sauvegarde prévues à l'article 95 du traité CE: L'efficacité du marché intérieur en porte-à-faux avec les intérêts nationaux dignes de protection' (2002) 1 RTDE 53–73.

[98] B. Poostchi, 'The 1997 Treaty of Amsterdam: Implications for EU Environmental Law and Policy-Making' (1998) 1 RECIEL 76–84, at 80; W.T. Douma, 'The European Union and the Precautionary Principle' (2000) 1 RECIEL 133. See, however, Commission Decision of 13 July 2001 concerning the national provisions notified by Germany on limitations of the marketing and use of organostannic compounds, 2001/570/EC, [2001] OJ L202/37, para. 78; Commission Decision of 25 July 2001 concerning the national provisions notified by Belgium on limitations of the marketing and use of organostannic compounds, 2000/509/EC, [2001] OJ L205/37, para. 54.

[99] H. Sevenster, n. 97 above, 304.

[100] R. Verheyen, 'The Environmental Guarantee in European Law and the New Article 95 EC Treaty in Practice: A Critique' (2000) 1 RECIEL 180–7.

State, the Commission recognized that national measures 'aiming at reducing the probability of dermal exposure . . . with creosote . . . are justified in the light of the precautionary principle'.[101] In other words, if the EC level of protection is insufficient the precautionary principle can justify derogations.

Nevertheless, the weight of the precautionary principle seems to be less important in cases where EC harmonization legislation is less controversial. On the ground that a threat to public health justifies precautionary action, the Danish authorities have supported limiting as far as possible the use of nitrates, nitrites, and sulphite additives in foodstuffs. However, the European Commission rejected a Danish request to derogate from Directive 95/2/EC, which limits the use of those substances in foodstuffs, arguing that no particular threat to the Danish population from the intake of nitrates/nitrites or sulphites could be identified.[102] A Swedish request to apply stricter rules for food colours was rejected on similar grounds. The Commission decided that stricter measures could not be justified even if these were likely to reduce the risk of allergic reactions.[103]

It must also be stressed that it should not be necessary that an environmental problem be exclusive to the Member State invoking the derogation. Rather, it should be sufficient for a Member State to demonstrate that a national derogation is necessary to resolve a specific environmental problem. A stricter interpretation would be incompatible with the principle of a high level of environmental protection which the Commission must take into account when assessing national derogations under Article 95(5) of the Treaty.[104]

4. Concluding observations

Strongly characterized by pluralism, post-modern law is shot through by contradictory—if not conflicting—logics. Within both the WTO and the EC environmental and free trade regimes are clashing increasingly often. At the

---

[101] Commission Decision of 26 October 1999 concerning the national provisions notified by the Kingdom of Denmark concerning the limitations of the marketing and use of creosote, 1999/835/EC, [1999] OJ L329/82, para. 110; Commission Decision of 26 October 1999 concerning the national provisions notified by the Federal Republic of Germany concerning the limitations of the marketing and use of creosote, 1999/833/EC, [1999] OJ L329/43, para. 99; Commission Decision of 26 October 1999 concerning the national provisions notified by the Kingdom of Sweden concerning the limitations of the marketing and use of creosote, 1999/834/EC, [1999] OJ L329/63, para. 108; Commission Decision of 26 October 1999 concerning the national provisions notified by the Kingdom of the Netherlands concerning the limitations of the marketing and use of creosote, 1999/832/EC, [1999] OJ L329/25, para. 104.

[102] Commission Decision of 26 October 1999 concerning the national provisions notified by the Kingdom of Denmark concerning the use of sulphites, nitrites and nitrates in foodstuffs, 1999/830/EC, [1999] OJ L329/1, para. 42. The Danish Government has already decided to challenge the Commission's decision regarding the Danish rules on food additives and has submitted its case to the ECJ.

[103] Commission Decision of 21 December 1998 on the national provisions notified by the Kingdom of Sweden concerning the use of certain colours and sweeteners in foodstuffs, 1999/5/EC, [1999] OJ L 3/13, para. 18.

[104] H. Sevenster, n. 97 above, 302–3.

global level unilaterally enacted or multilaterally agreed TREMs enter into conflict with the WTO Agreements. At the EC level the use by Member States of trade restrictions for environmental purposes conflicts with the principle of the free movement of trade. This last Chapter has sought to demonstrate the role that certain directing principles of environmental law could play in such disputes (the principles of rectification of environmental harm at source, self-sufficiency, and proximity, the precautionary principle, the principle of a high level of environmental protection) by tipping the balance in favour of interests relating to the environmental or public health.[105] In doing so we have sought to stress one of the main elements of post-modernity: the presence of directing principles in the weighing of interests.[106]

We have also seen that the principles of prevention and precaution can build bridges between normative areas that pay scant attention to or conflict with one another (internal market *versus* environmental protection at the EC and Member State levels). They are thus able to serve as new interpretative tools for resolving disputes between various fields of international law (for instance, the conflict between MEA and WTO obligations).

While directing principles of environment law may have important consequences for dispute resolution by tipping the balance towards protection of the environment and human health (eg as regards trading in wastes) it is clear that they can merely smooth extreme points of conflict, not resolve them definitively. For that reason it is essential that legal requirements in this area be clarified, in the direction of greater integration of environmental concerns in legal trade regimes such as the WTO and the EC internal market.

---

[105] Of course, there is no single solution to the trade—environment conflict. There is not even a single conflict, but rather several different conflicts which may vary tremendously in intensity according to the legal order concerned. D. Geradin, *Trade and the Environment*, n. 64 above, 198.

[106] See Chapter 4, Subsection 3.3. above.

Part II   Conclusions

Both the international legal order and national legal regimes have recently undergone important changes. The systematization, generality, and coherence that characterized modern law seem to have given way to more regulative techniques that better reflect a complex and constantly changing world. The production of rules also seems suddenly to be racing ahead: legislators are competing against one another in a normative game whose rules are known only to a few, soft-law and hard-law instruments are proliferating rapidly and the State is abandoning its traditional means of command and control in favour of negotiation. Thus law has become an integral part of a complex and multiform model bearing the name post-modernity, which will cause the last vestiges of modernity—the basis of today's legal systems—to disappear.

Must we simply give in to this transformation and resign ourselves to applying a negotiated, flexible, adaptable, pluralist, networked form of law, without further discussion? That way lies increased confusion, for a number of important legal struggles are concealed within the post-modern phenomenon, which will determine how legislative systems confront a rapid increase in complexity. For this reason detached consideration is essential in the face of such rapid, radical, undefined, and complex changes.

In Part II we strongly defended the argument that the advent of post-modernity has not done away with all forms of rationality. To the contrary, based on recent works in the field of general legal theory published in French, we have tried to show that new legal principles, which we have called 'directing principles' in an effort to emphasize their dynamic nature, can contribute to a revival of rationality. Environment law is particularly suitable in this respect, for in addition to exhibiting many of the characteristics of post-modernity (growth in regulatory instruments, multiplication of levels of power, regulatory flexibility, etc.) it gives rise to more principles than any other branch of law.

Part II showed how these directing principles, Janus-like, present a double face: on one hand they recall the rationality inherent in modernity (function of coherence, codification) while on the other hand they are strongly shot through with post-modern characteristics (stimulation of public policy, weighing of interests). Facing towards the past and the future at once, these principles present striking particularities in comparison with the general principles of law that have been created by national and international courts in order to fill legal gaps and thereby ensure the coherence of the legal system.

We considered these issues above in four stages. First, in chapter 4 we attempted to define exactly, at the theoretical level, what is meant by modernity and post-modernity. It is impossible to pinpoint where modernity ends and post-modernity begins, for these two models interact more strongly than they conflict. Instead we therefore set out the main characteristics of both models and showed how directing principles differ from general principles of law. This theoretical approach allowed us to make preliminary observations concerning the status and functions of the polluter-pays, preventive, and precautionary principles described in Part I.

As demonstrated in Chapter 5, the functions of those three directing principles of environmental law emphasize a gradual shift from modernity to post-modernity. These principles increase the coherence of the legal system by gathering scattered rules into a coherent whole, rejuvenate institutions, and refine legal techniques (codification, etc.) thereby reintroducing an ideal of rationality—an essential element of modernity—into the legal system. At the same time they are able to mitigate the excesses of post-modernity. By promoting legal reform, they spur public policies; by clarifying objectives and freeing judges from having to interpret texts too literally, they set environment law in motion. They also help ensure the coexistence of public policies with often contradictory purposes and norms emanating from various legal regimes. They build bridges between the global and local levels, and between national, European, and international law. Rather than comprising a logic of exclusion, they form part of a series of normative processes (recognition of the right to a healthy environment at constitutional level, etc.) that are both necessary and insufficient.

These principles lie at the core of post-modernity when it comes to the weighing of interests. The mechanistic model of modern law has been replaced by new types of reasoning, which imply that the directing principles contained in legislation must be applied when weighing interests.

In Chapter 6 we identified a number of guideposts to help us understand the legal status of the polluter-pays, preventive, and precautionary principles within several legal systems that are not easily compared. Despite their indeterminate character, these directing principles have sufficient legal force to be considered normative—that is, giving rise to legal effects. For that to be the case they must fulfil two conditions: first they must be part of a binding text, and secondly they must be formulated in sufficiently prescriptive terms. Nonetheless, their normative character differs at several levels from that of the numerous more complete norms found in environment law. In addition, their legal force varies as a function of the legal system in which they occur: national, European Community, or international. These traits are all characteristic of a post-modern perspective.

The observations contained in Chapter 5 regarding the role of the principles in the weighing of interests were expanded in Chapter 7, which considered more precisely how the polluter-pays, preventive, and precautionary principles could help resolve the conflict between trade and environment. Needless to say, this function will become increasingly important in the near future.

Final Conclusions

We have chosen to base our analysis of the genesis and legal effect of the principles of environmental law on three principles found in international, European Community, and national law: the polluter-pays, preventive, and precautionary principles. That analysis rested on two theses: (1) vertical analysis of the origin, status, and application of these three principles in international, EC, and national legal systems indicates that a subtle shift in the battle against ecological risk is taking place; and (2) horizontal analysis of the status and functions of these three principles shows that they represent the interface between modern and post-modern law. Although we considered these two theses individually, the extent to which they complement one another became increasingly apparent. We next briefly summarize the main conclusions we have drawn from our study.

Despite the increased value of their status (they are rules rather than mere political slogans) and functions (those rules influence the course of law) these three principles will continue to clash with other rules that occupy a higher position in the hierarchy of norms. Weighing of interests is at the core of these conflicts. Nonetheless, as set out in the Epilogue below, a number of arguments support tilting the balance in favour of environmental concerns.

1. First thesis: directing principles point to a subtle shift in the battle against risks

In Part I of this book we explained that the three principles have a common denominator: the battle against environmental risks. For that reason they are complementary and cannot function in isolation. We put forward the proposition that these three principles of the polluter pays, prevention, and precaution could be described using three distinct models representing three paradigms of protection: a curative model (which would rely on civil liability and compensatory mechanisms financed by charges), a preventive model (relying largely on the enforcement power of public authorities), and an anticipatory model (informed by the precautionary principle).

The curative model rests on the hypothesis that nature has an infinite regenerative capacity. This model sees nature as invulnerable. In cases where damage occurs the polluter will pay for reparation, under the polluter-pays principle, either through the mechanisms of civil liability or by use of compensation funds financed by charges.

The preventive model is based on the understanding that some types of pollution are irreparable and must therefore be prevented. These must be addressed by special administrative measures relating to various environmental media such as water, soil, air, biodiversity, and natural habitats. The preventive model assumes the possibility of a scientific understanding of what level of damage will not compromise the restoration of ecosystems and their species: a level that can be technically repaired and economically compensated.

The culmination of this evolution is the precautionary model, born of the wish to break free of an assimilative approach and replace it with an anticipatory approach. While in some ways an extension of the preventive model, the precautionary model takes into consideration the fact that science cannot determine the degree of damage that nature can tolerate. This position does not indicate any particular mistrust of science; it merely acknowledges that scientists do not have the answers to some important questions. Consideration of the uncertainty that results from this stance compromises the relevance of the preventive model and at the same time makes untenable the idea that nature will always be able to regenerate.

Each of these models is thus based on an individual principle: a very general norm whose regulatory ramifications affect a number of fields of law, including international, public, liability, and fiscal law. We have attempted to show that there is an undeniable normative dimension to these three principles and that they will henceforth influence the course of positive law.

Whatever their formulations, however, these principles remain flexible, for several reasons. First, a principle is by nature difficult to define. Its application determines its substance. In addition, the principles of the polluter pays, prevention, and precaution set the conditions for action without actually describing that action, thus leaving a wide margin to those who must implement them. Finally, these principles are applied in extremely diverse ways, ranging from management of marine resources to health protection.

While there is certainly an element of slogan—of political manifesto—at work here, it is nevertheless impossible to reduce the use of principles such as those of the polluter pays, prevention, and precaution to a tool of political combat: since they are set out in substantive legal texts and are binding on categories of persons they constitute true legal norms, even if their effect is long-term rather than immediate. Nor is it possible to criticize them on the ground that they will give rise to too many or not enough legal effects, for their primary purpose is to guide and reform rather than to revolutionize.

2. SECOND THESIS: DIRECTING PRINCIPLES REPRESENT THE INTERFACE BETWEEN MODERN AND POST-MODERN LAW

The proposition that there has been a subtle shift in the battle against ecological risk must necessarily lead to a second thesis, even more basic than the first in the context of legal theory. This led us to demonstrate that the polluter-pays, preventive, and precautionary principles described in Part I mark an epistemological shift between modern law, which rests on the fixed standards of traditional legal rule-making, and post-modern law, which emphasizes the pragmatic, gradual, unstable, and reversible nature of rules. In order to clarify this epistemological shift we contrasted three environmental principles, characterized as 'directing principles' of environmental law, with 'general principles of law', more typical of modernity.

This contrast was of necessity nuanced; as we have stressed throughout this work, the shift from modernity to post-modernity has not been a radical one, nor has rationality been abandoned in that transition. The two models will continue to coexist, and the principles are the point where the conflicts of rationality that distinguish them from one another play themselves out.

This second thesis finds an echo in many other fields of positive law. Indeed, from the perspective of the general theory of law the emergence of a litany of directing principles in environmental law is part of a more general evolution affecting the entire legal system. If, in a modern perspective, there has long been a clear distinction between law, morality, and policy, this is no longer the case today. Law in a post-modern perspective is more likely to be organized around a group of very general norms that will provide the basis for conciliating conflicting interests. At both international and national levels a delicate interaction between law and other values has taken the place of a formal hierarchy of norms. Owing to their flexibility, the directing principles of environment law foreshadow the advent of a post-modern law dominated by the balancing of interests.

3. EPILOGUE: THE BALANCING OF INTERESTS AT THE HEART OF POST-MODERNITY

On the basis of our analyses should we conclude that the polluter-pays, preventive, and precautionary principles are harbingers of a radiant future for environmental law? We know they are currently in style; are they truly original as well? Or must we view the wide use of principles in the field of environmental law as a false start likely to have little subsequent effect; or even worse an excuse for an exercise in deregulation that will threaten the advances made as the result of prolonged battles? Does the renewed emphasis on principles merely betray the inability of States to move beyond a simple recognition of threats? In concluding we must try to answer some difficult questions about what role this new type of norm might play.

While the polluter-pays, preventive, and precautionary principles may help clarify the objectives of environmental law, they nonetheless risk having to take a back seat when various interests are weighed and other values and objectives of public policy take centre stage. It is thus always possible that public authorities and courts will set them aside, provided they have carried out a proportionality test and given an explicit statement of reasons for their decisions. The power of directing principles of environmental law is thus likely to find itself weakened at the first sign of a conflict of interests.

Should we therefore countenance a balancing of interests that would render those three environmental principles devoid of any useful effect? Can we accept that their effectiveness may be compromised simply by implementing the procedural principles of proportionality and statement of reasons? To pose these questions is to wonder about a possible 'hard centre' for the principles we have considered. Aside from clarifying the exact position of the protection guaranteed by these principles, determination of such a centre would reduce the legal insecurity linked to the rise of a 'government of judges'. It would also ensure more precise limits for principles of environmental law, thus protecting them from unreasonably wide application which would be likely to paralyse action. Several important considerations plead in favour of such a hard centre; however, important obstacles remain.

At the EC level, Article 174(2) of the EC Treaty, seat of the principles of the polluter pays, reduction at source, precaution, and prevention, provides the beginning of an answer to our questions, specifying that: 'Community policy on the environment shall aim at a *high level of protection*'. As the European Court of Justice ruled in the *Safety Hi-Tech* case, that level of protection need not be the highest possible level. In fact, the presence of that obligation has not prevented a progressive weakening of the degree of protection accorded the environment by Community law, with directives that contain extremely vague objectives increasingly replacing directives that set out precise obligations.

The 'right to the protection of a healthy environment' and the right to health which are the subject of constitutional recognition, in the way that the right to privacy and family life is protected by the European Convention on Human Rights, may also be invoked to prevent compromising ecological interests when there is a risk to human health. But this leads us back to the heart of the question, for protection of the environment is taken into consideration as a corollary to the 'right to lead a life in conformity with human dignity'. Should we conclude from this that ecosystem preservation remains subordinate to the protection of human interests, for example health or respect for privacy and family life, as the rulings by the European Court of Human Rights in the *López Ostra*, *Guerra* and *Hatton* cases appear to confirm? This is a formidable question: does the environment represent an autonomous and original facet of the public interest, or merely a corollary derived from more basic values (first-generation human rights) to which it will always be sacrificed if the need arises?

Consideration of the time factor undoubtedly strengthens the argument for a 'hard centre'. Beyond a certain threshold environmental degradation reaches a stage of no return. When damage proves to be *irreversible*, it becomes unacceptable and must therefore be averted no matter what the circumstances. Since we cannot make ancient forests grow back from their ashes nor reproduce extinct species by the use of biotechnology the hard centre of environmental principles must provide nature the opportunity and time needed for regeneration. We must not, however, lose sight of the fact that irreversibility is difficult to predict. It is therefore not easy for experts, courts, or legislators to fix irreversibility thresholds. Moreover, laws often combine irreversibility with a threshold of seriousness that is equally difficult to determine. Finally, seen in the context of human generations, legal 'time' is short: after several decades sanctions lose their force and responsibilities grow dim. We must ask ourselves if the remote future on whose behalf the precautionary principle pleads will always be as important in the balance of interests as the immediate present.

Time is also inherent in the concept of sustainable development, which leads to a long-term vision while taking care that present use does not jeopardize possible future use of natural resources. This reflects the human understanding of the limits set by the rhythms of nature. Retaining the potential for usefulness for both present and future generations thus becomes the hard centre. Nevertheless, caught between an economic logic seeking to maximize production for profitability and an ecological logic, sustainable development is situated at the junction of interests that are *a priori* at loggerheads. In keeping with an anthropocentric approach, the concept of sustainability remains imprecise in that it may apply to methods of exploitation as well as to natural resources.

While concentric circles are taking shape around environmental interests, each of those interests still gives evidence of a certain fragility. Yet they must be progressively strengthened, for that hard centre is essential if environmental directing principles are to succeed in increasing the coherence, cohesion, and rigour of this law, so painfully come to maturity. Only in this way will the environment have some hope of escaping the assaults committed in the name of progress.

Appendix I
Table of Materials

Main provisions embodying environmental principles, as discussed in this book (emphases on the principles have been added by the author).

1. INTERNATIONAL LAW

Soft law

United Nations

1972 Stockholm Declaration on Human Environment

Principle 7: 'States shall take all possible steps to prevent pollution of the seas by substances that are liable to create hazards to human health, to harm living resources and marine life, to damage amenities or to interfere with other legitimate use of the sea.'

Principle 21: 'States have, in accordance with the Charter of the United Nations and the principles of international law, the sovereign right to exploit their own resources pursuant to their own environmental policies, and the responsibility to ensure that activities within their jurisdiction or control do not cause damage to the environment of other States or of areas beyond the limits of national jurisdictions.'

1982 World Charter for Nature

Paragraph 11: 'Activities which might have an impact on nature shall be controlled, and the best available technologies that minimize significant risks to nature or other adverse effects shall be used; in particular:

(a) activities which are likely to cause irreversible damage to nature shall be avoided;

(b) activities which are likely to pose a significant risk to nature shall be preceded by an exhaustive examination; their proponents shall demonstrate that expected benefits outweigh potential damage to nature, and where potential adverse effects are not fully understood, the activities should not proceed;

(c) activities which may disturb nature shall be preceded by assessment of their consequences, and environmental impact studies of development projects shall be conducted sufficiently in advance, and if they are to be undertaken, such activities shall be planned and carried out so as to minimize potential adverse effects...'

1989 UNEP's Governing Council Decision 15/27 on the Precautionary Approach to Marine Pollution

'Recognizing that waiting for scientific proof regarding the impact of pollutants discharged into the marine environment may result in irreversible damage to the marine environment and in human suffering...Recommends that all governments adopt the *principle of precautionary action* as the basis of their policy with regard to the prevention and elimination of marine pollution.'

1990 Bergen Ministerial Declaration on Sustainability in the ECE Region

Section 7: 'In order to achieve sustainable development, policies must be based on the *precautionary principle*. Environmental measures must anticipate, prevent and attack the causes of environmental degradation. Where there are threats of serious or irreversible damage, lack of full scientific certainty should not be used as a reason for postponing measures to prevent environmental degradation.'

1990 Bangkok Declaration on Environmental Sound and Sustainable Development in Asia and the Pacific

'Community policy on the environment...shall be based on the *precautionary principle*...'

1992 Rio de Janeiro Declaration on Environment and Development

Principle 2: 'States have....the responsibility to ensure that activities within their juris-diction or control do not cause damage to the environment of other States or of areas beyond the limits of national jurisdiction.'

Principle 15: 'In order to protect the environment, the *precautionary approach* shall be widely applied by States according to their capabilities. Where there are threats of serious or irreversible damage, lack of full scientific certainty shall not be used as a reason for postponing cost-effective measures to prevent environmental degradation.'

Principle 16: 'National authorities should endeavour to promote the *internalisation of environmental costs* and the use of economic instruments, taking into account the approach that the polluter should, in principle, bear the cost of pollution, with due regard to the public interests and without distorting international trade and investment.'

1992 Agenda 21, Chapter 17

'*A precautionary and an anticipatory rather than a reactive approach* is necessary to prevent the degradation of the marine environment. This requires, *inter alia*, the adoption of precautionary measures, environmental impact assessments, clean production tech-niques, recycling, waste audits and minimization, construction and/or improve-ment of sewage treatment facilities, quality management criteria for handling hazardous substances, and a comprehensive approach to damaging impact from air, land and water.'

Organization for Economic Cooperation and Development

1972 OECD Council Recommendation on Guiding Principles concerning International Economic Aspects of Environmental Policies (C(72)128(Final))

A(4) 'The principle to be used for allocating costs of pollution prevention and control measures to encourage rational use of scarce environmental resources and to avoid distortions in international trade and investment is the so-called "*Polluter-Pays Principle*". This principle means that the polluter should bear the expenses of carrying out the above-mentioned measures decided by public authorities to ensure that the environment is in an acceptable state. In other words, the cost of these measures should be reflected in the cost of goods and services which cause pollution in production and/or consumption. Such measures should not be accompanied by subsidies that would create significant distortions in international trade and investment.'

1974 OECD *Council Recommendation on the Implementation of the Polluter-Pays Principle (C(74)223 (Final))*
'The Council . . . I. Reaffirms that:

- the *Polluter-Pays Principle* constitutes for Member countries a fundamental principle for allocating costs of pollution prevention and control measures introduced by the public authorities in Member countries;
- the *Polluter-Pays Principle*, as defined by the Guiding Principles Concerning International Economic Aspects of Environmental Policies, which take account of particular problems possibly arising for developing countries, means that the polluter should bear the expenses of carrying out the measures, as specified in the previous paragraph, to ensure that the environment is in an acceptable state. In other words, the cost of these measures should be reflected in the cost of goods and services which cause pollution in production and/or consumption;
- uniform application of this principle, through the adoption of a common basis for Member countries' environmental policies, would encourage the rational use and the better allocation of scarce environmental resources and prevent the appearance of distortions in international trade and investment.'

1989 OECD *Council Recommendation on the Application of the Polluter-pays Principle to Accidental Pollution (C89) 99 Final, July 7, 1989*
4. 'In matters of accidental pollution risks, the *Polluter-Pays Principle* implies that the operator of the hazardous installation should bear the cost of reasonable measures to prevent and control accidental pollution from that installation which are introduced by public authorities in Member Countries in conformity with domestic law prior to the occurrence of an accident in order to protect human health and the environment.'

1991 OECD *Council Recommendation on the Use of Economic Instruments in Environmental Policy (C(90)177 (Final))*
'The Council, . . . Considering that a sustainable and economically efficient management of environmental resources requires, *inter alia*, the internalisation of pollution prevention, control and damage costs;
Considering that such internalisation can be enhanced by a consistent use of market mechanisms, in particular those economic instruments defined in the Annex to this Recommendation;

1. Recommends that Member countries: . . . ii) work towards improving the allocation and efficient use of natural and environmental resources by means of economic instruments so as to better reflect the social cost of using these resources.'
. . . .
23. In implementing economic instruments, it is necessary to comply with . . . principles of environmental policy both at national and the international level. One of the most important of these is the *Polluter-Pays Principle*.'

North Sea International Conferences

1984 Bremen Ministerial Declaration of the International Conference on the Protection of the North Sea
A.7. 'Conscious that damage to the marine environment can be irreversible or remediable only at considerable expense and over long periods and that, therefore, coastal states and the EEC must not wait for proof of harmful effects before taking action;'

1987 London Ministerial Declaration of the Second International Conference on the Protection of the North Sea
'VII. 'Accepting that, in order to protect the North Sea from possibly damaging effects of the most dangerous substances, a *precautionary approach* is necessary which may require action to control imputs of such substances even before a causal link has been established by absolutely clear scientific evidence.'
XVI. 1. '(The Participants) accept the *principle of safeguarding the marine ecosystem* of the North Sea by reducing polluting emissions of substances that are persistent, toxic and liable to bioaccumulate at source by the use of the best available technology and other appropriate measures. This applies especially when there is reason to assume that certain damage or harmful effects on the living resources of the sea are likely to be caused by such substances, even where there is no scientific evidence to prove a causal link between emissions and effects ("the *principle of precautionary action*").'

1990 The Hague Ministerial Declaration of the Third International Conference on the Protection of the North Sea
'(The Participants) will continue to apply the *precautionary principle*, that is to take action to avoid potentially damaging impacts of substances that are persistent, toxic and liable to bioaccumulate even where there is no scientific evidence to prove a causal link between emissions and effects.'

1995 Esbjerg Ministerial Declaration of the Fourth International Conference on the Protection of the North Sea
'The Ministers agree that the objective is to ensure a sustainable, sound and healthy North Sea ecosystem. The guiding principle for achieving this objective is the *precautionary principle*. This implies the prevention of the pollution of the North Sea by continuously reducing discharges, emissions and losses of hazardous substances thereby moving towards the target of their cessation within one generation (25 years) with the ultimate aim on concentrations in the environment near background values for naturally occurring substances and close to zero concentrations for man-made synthetic substances.'

Multilateral treaties

Air pollution
1985 Vienna Convention for the Protection of the Ozone Layer
Preamble: 'Mindful . . . of the *precautionary measures* for the protection of the ozone layer which have already been taken at the national and international levels . . . '

1987 Montreal Protocol on Substances that Deplete the Ozone Layer

Preamble: 'The Parties to this Protocol (are) determined to protect the ozone layer by taking *precautionary measures* to control equitably total global emissions of substances that deplete it, with the ultimate objective of their elimination on the basis of developments in scientific knowledge, taking into account technical and economic considerations and bearing in mind the developmental needs of developing countries.'

1992 UNFCCC

Article 3(3): 'In their actions to achieve the objective of the Convention and to implement its provisions, the parties shall be guided, *inter alia*, by the following:

1. The Parties should protect the climate system for the benefit of present and future generations...
2. The parties should take the precautionary measures to anticipate, prevent or minimise the causes of climate change and mitigate its adverse effects. Where there are threats of serious or irreversible damage, lack of full scientific certainty should not be used as a reason for postponing such measures, taking into account that policies and measures to deal with climate change should be cost-effective so as to ensure global benefits at the lowest possible cost.
3. The parties have a right to, and should, promote sustainable development...'

1994 Oslo Protocol on Further Reduction of Sulphur Emissions to LRTAP Convention

Preamble: 'Convinced that where there are threats of serious or irreversible damage, lack of full scientific certainty should not be used as a reason for postponing such measures, taking into account that such *precautionary measures* to deal with emissions of air pollutants should be cost-effective.'

1998 Århus Protocol on Persistent Organic Pollutants to LRTAP Convention

Preamble: 'Resolved to take measures to anticipate, prevent or minimize emissions of persistent organic pollutants, taking into account the application of the *precautionary approach*, as set forth in principle 15 of the Rio Declaration on Environment and Development.'

1998 Århus Protocol on Heavy Metals to the LRTAP Convention

Preamble: 'Resolved to take measures to anticipate, prevent or minimize emissions of heavy metals and their related compounds, taking into account the application of the *precautionary approach*, as set forth in principle 15 of the Rio Declaration on Environment and Development.'

Marine pollution

1976 Barcelona Convention for the Protection of the Mediterranean Sea against Pollution (as amended in 1995)

Article 4(3)(a): 'In order to protect the environment and contribute to the sustainable development of the Mediterranean Sea, the Contracting Parties shall:

a) apply, in accordance with their capabilities, the *precautionary principle*, by virtue of which where there are threats of serious or irreversible damage, lack of full scientific certainty shall not be used as a reason for postponing cost-effective measures to prevent environmental degradation;

b) apply the *polluter pays principle*, by virtue of which the costs of pollution prevention, control and reduction measures are to be borne by the polluter with due regard to the pulic interest;'

1980 Athens Protocol for the Protection of the Mediterranean Sea against Pollution from Land-Based Sources and Activities (as amended in Syracuse on 7 March 1996)

Preamble: 'Applying the *precautionary principle* and the *polluter-pays principle*, undertaking environmental impact assessment and utilizing the best available techniques and the best environmental practice, including clean production technologies . . . '

1989 PARCOM Recommendation 89/1

'The contracting parties . . . accept the *principle of safeguarding the marine ecosystem* of the Paris Convention area by reducing at source polluting emissions of substances that are persistent, toxic and liable to bioaccumulate by the use of best available technology and other appropriate measures. This applies especially when there is reason to assume that certain damage or harmful effects on the living resources of the sea are likely to be caused by such substances, even when there is no scientific evidence to prove a causal link between the emissions and effects (*"the principle of precautionary action"*) . . . '

1990 London International Convention on Oil Pollution Preparedness, Response and Cooperation

Preamble: 'Taking account of the *polluter pays principle* as a general principle of international environmental law,'

1992 OSPAR Convention

Article 2(2): 'The Contracting Parties shall apply:

1. the *precautionary principle*, by virtue of which preventive measures are to be taken when there are reasonable grounds for concern that substances or energy introduced, directly or indirectly, into the marine environment may bring about hazards to human health, harm living resources and marine ecosystems, damage amenities or interfere with other legitimate uses of the sea, even when there is no conclusive evidence of a causal relationship between the inputs and the effects;
2. the *polluter pays principle*, by virtue of which the costs of pollution prevention, control and reduction measures are to be borne by the polluter.'

1992 Helsinki Convention on the Protection of the Marine Environment of the Baltic Sea Area

Article 3(2): 'The Contracting Parties shall apply the *precautionary principle*, i.e. to take preventive measures when there is reason to assume that substances or energy introduced, directly or indirectly, into the marine environment may create hazards to human health, harm living resources and marine ecosystems, damage amenities or interfere with other legitimate uses of the sea even when there is no conclusive evidence of a causal relationship between imputs and their alleged effects.'

1996 London Protocol to the Convention on the Prevention of Marine Pollution by Dumping of Wastes and Other Matter

Article 3(1): 'In implementing this Protocol, Contracting Parties shall apply a *precautionary approach* to environmental protection from dumping of wastes or other matter whereby appropriate preventative measures are taken when there is reason to believe that wastes or other matter introduced into the marine environment are likely to cause harm even when there is no conclusive evidence to prove a causal relation between inputs and their effects.'

(2) 'Taking into account the approach that *the polluter should, in principle, bear the cost of pollution*, each Contracting Party shall endeavour to promote practices whereby those it has authorized to engage in dumping or incineration at sea bear the cost of meeting the pollution prevention and control requirements for the authorized activities, having due regard to the public interest.'

2000 London Protocol on Preparedness, Response and Co-Operation to Pollution Incidents by Hazardous and Noxious Substances

Preamble: 'Taking into account of the *"polluter pays" principle* as a general principle of international environmental law...
Being mindful of the development of a strategy for incorporating the *precautionary approach* in the policies of the International Maritime Organization.'

2001 London Convention on the Control of Harmful Anti-Fouling Systems on Ships

Preamble: 'Mindful of the *precautionary approach* as set forth in Principle 15 of the Rio Declaration on Environment and Development...'
'Recognizing further the need to continue to develop anti-fouling systems which are effective and environmentally safe and to promote the *substitution* of harmful systems by less harmful systems or preferably harmless systems.'

Article 6 (Process for Proposing Amendments to Controls on Anti-Fouling Systems):

(1) 'Any Party may propose an amendment to Annex 1 in accordance with this Article...

(3) 'The Committee shall decide whether the anti-fouling system in question warrants a more in-depth review based on the intial proposal. If the Committee decides that further review is warranted, it shall require the proposing Party to submit to the Committee a comprehensive proposal containing the information required in Annex 3, except where the initial proposal also includes all the information required in Annex 3. Where the Committee is of the view that there is a threat of serious or irreversible damage, *lack of full scientific certainty shall not be used as a reason to prevent a decision to proceed with the evaluation of the proposal*. The Committee shall establish a technical group in accordance with Article 7.

(4) 'The technical group shall review the comprehensive proposal along with any additional data submitted by any interested entity and shall evaluate and report to the Committee whether the proposal has demonstrated a potential for unreasonable risk of adverse effects on non-target organisms or human health such that the amendment of Annex 1 is warranted. In this regard:

   (a) The technical group's review shall include: ...
     (v) consideration of the availability of suitable alternatives, including a consideration of the potential risks of alternatives.

(5) ... The Committee shall decide whether to approve any proposal to amend Annex 1, and any modifications thereto, if appropriate, taking into account the technical group's report. If the report finds a threat of serious or irreversible damage, *lack of full scientific certainty shall not, itself, be used as a reason to prevent a decision* from being taken to list an anti-fouling system in Annex 1 ... '

High seas fisheries

1995 UN Agreement for the Implementation of the Provisions of The Convention on the Law of the Sea of 10 December 1982 relating to the Conservation and Management of Straddling Fish Stocks and Highly Migratory Fish Stocks

Article 5. General principles:

'In order to conserve and manage straddling fish stocks and highly migratory fish stocks, coastal States and States fishing on the high seas shall, in giving effect to their duty to cooperate in accordance with the Convention: ...

   (c) apply the *precautionary approach* in accordance with Article 6;

Article 6. Application of the precautionary approach:

1. States shall apply the *precautionary approach* widely to conservation, management and exploitation of straddling fish stocks and highly migratory fish stocks in order to protect the living marine resources and preserve the marine environment.

2. States shall be more cautious when information is uncertain, unreliable or inadequate. The absence of adequate scientific information shall not be used as a reason for postponing or failing to take conservation and management measures.

3. In implementing the *precautionary approach*, States shall:
   (a) improve decision-making for fishery resource conservation and management by obtaining and sharing the best scientific information available and implementing improved techniques for dealing with risk and uncertainty;
   (b) apply the guidelines set out in Annex II and determine, on the basis of the best scientific information available, stock-specific reference points and the action to be taken if they are exceeded;
   (c) take into account, *inter alia*, uncertainties relating to the size and productivity of the stocks, reference points, stock condition in relation to such reference points, levels and distribution of fishing mortality and the impact of fishing activities on non-target and associated or dependent species, as well as existing and predicted oceanic, environmental and socio-economic conditions; and
   (d) develop data collection and research programmes to assess the impact of fishing on non-target and associated or dependent species and their environment, and adopt plans which are necessary to ensure the conservation of such species and to protect habitats of special concern.

4. States shall take measures to ensure that, when reference points are approached, they will not be exceeded. In the event that they are exceeded, States shall, without delay, take the action determined under paragraph 3(b) to restore the stocks.

5. Where the status of target stocks or non-target or associated or dependent species is of concern, States shall subject such stocks and species to enhanced monitoring in order to review their status and the efficacy of conservation and management measures. They shall revise those measures regularly in the light of new information.

6. For new or exploratory fisheries, States shall adopt as soon as possible *cautious conservation and management measures*, including, *inter alia*, catch limits and effort limits. Such measures shall remain in force until there are sufficient data to allow assessment of the impact of the fisheries on the long-term sustainability of the stocks, whereupon conservation and management measures based on that assessment shall be implemented. The latter measures shall, if appropriate, allow for the gradual development of the fisheries.

7. If a natural phenomenon has a significant adverse impact on the status of straddling fish stocks or highly migratory fish stocks, States shall adopt conservation and management measures on an emergency basis to ensure that fishing activity does not exacerbate such adverse impact. States shall also adopt such measures on an emergency basis where fishing activity presents a serious threat to the sustainability of such stocks. Measures taken on an emergency basis shall be temporary and shall be based on the best scientific evidence available.'

International watercourses

1992 ECE Helsinki Convention on the Protection and Use of Transboundary Watercourses and International Lakes

Article 2(5): 'In taking the measures referred to paragraphs 1 and 2 of the article, the Parties shall be guided by the following principles: ...

- the *precautionary principle*, by virtue of which action to avoid the potential transboundary impact of the release of hazardous substances shall not be postponed on the ground that scientific research has not fully proved a causal link between those substances, on the one hand, and the potential transboundary impact, on the other hand ...
- the *polluter-pays principle*, by virtue of which costs of pollution prevention, control and reduction measures shall be borne by the polluter.'

1994 Convention on Cooperation for the Protection and Sustainable Use of the Danube River

Article 4(4): 'The *Polluter pays principle* and the *Precautionary principle* constitute a basis for all measures aiming at the protection of the Danube River and of the waters within its catchment area.'

1999 Bern Convention on the Protection of the Rhine

Article 4: 'The Contracting Parties are guided by the following principles:
— principle of prevention
— principle of precaution
— principle of mainly fighting environmental deteriorations at the source
— polluter-pays principle
— principle of not increasing adverse effects
— principle of compensation for considerable technical interventions
— principle of sustainable development

—application and further development of the Best Available Technique and of the Best Environmental Practice
—principle of not transferring environmental pollution into other environmental media.'

Biodiversity

1991 Salzburg Convention on the Protection of the Alps
Preamble: 'The Contracting Parties, respecting the *principles of prevention, cooperation, and the polluter-pays*, shall maintain a comprehensive policy of protection and preservation of the Alps.'

1992 UN Convention on Biological Diversity
Preamble: 'Noting that it is vital to *anticipate, prevent* and attack the causes of significant reduction or loss of biological diversity at source.
Noting that where there is a threat of significant reduction or loss of biological diversity, lack of full scientific certainty should not be used as a reason for postponing measures to avoid or minimize such a threat.'

1994 CITES Resolution of the Conference of the Parties: Criteria for Amendment of Appendices I and II, agreed at the Ninth Meeting of the Conference of the Parties, Fort Lauderdale (US), 7–18 November 1994
'RECOGNISING that by virtue of the *precautionary principle*, in cases of uncertainty, the Parties shall act in the best interest of the conservation of the species when considering proposals for amendment of appendices I and II;
RESOLVES that when considering any proposal to amend appendix I or II the Parties shall apply the *precautionary principle* so that scientific uncertainty should not be used as a reason for failing to act in the best interest of the conservation of the species.'

1995 The Hague Agreement on the Conservation of African-Eurasian Migratory Waterbirds
Article 2(2): 'In implementing the measures prescribed in paragraph 1 above, Parties should take into account the *precautionary principle*.'

1996 Monaco Agreement on the Conservation of Cetaceans of the Black Sea, Mediterranean Sea and Contiguous Atlantic Area (ACCOBAMS)
Article 2(4): 'In implementing the measures prescribed above, the Parties shall apply the *precautionary principle*.'

2000 Cartagena Protocol on Biosafety
Article 1: 'In accordance with the *precautionary approach* contained in Principle 15 of the Rio Declaration on Environment and Development, the objective of this Protocol is to contribute to ensuring an adequate level of protection in the field of the safe transfer, handling and use of living modified organisms resulting from modern biotechnology that may have adverse effects on the conservation and sustainable use of biological diversity, taking also into account risks to human health, and specifically focusing on transboundary movements.'
Articles 10(6) and 11(8): 'Lack of scientific certainty due to insufficient relevant scientific information and knowledge regarding the extent of the potential adverse effects of a living modified organism on the conservation and sustainable use of biological diversity in the

Party of import, taking also into account risks to human health, shall not prevent that Party from taking a decision . . . in order to avoid or minimize such potential adverse effects.'

2001 Canberra Agreement on the Conservation of Albatrosses and Petrels

Article 2(3): 'In implementing such measures the Parties shall widely apply the *precautionary approach*. In particular, where there are threats of serious or irreversible adverse impacts or damage, lack of full scientific certainty shall not be used as a reason for postponing measures to enhance the conservation status of albatrosses and petrels.'

Waste management

1991 Bamako Convention on the Ban of Import into Africa and the Control of Transboundary Movement and Management of Hazardous Wastes within Africa

Article 4(3)(f): 'Each Party shall strive to adopt and implement *the preventive, precautionary approach* to pollution problems which entails, *inter alia*, preventing the release into the environment of substances which may cause harm to humans or the environment without waiting for scientific proof regarding such harm. The parties shall co-operate with each other in taking the appropriate mesasures to implement the *precautionary principle* to pollution through the application of clean production methods rather than the pursuit of a permissible emissions approach based on the assimilative capacity assumptions.'

Chemicals

2001 Stockholm Convention on Persistent Organic Pollutants

Preamble: 'Acknowledging that *precaution* underlies the concerns of all the Parties and is embedded within this Convention

Article 1: Mindful of the *precautionary approach* as set forth in Principle 15 of the Rio Declaration on Environment and Development, the objective of this Convention is to protect human health and the environment from persistent organic pollutants.'

Environmental impact assessment

1992 Helsinki UNECE Convention on the Transboundary Effects of Industrial Accidents

Preamble: 'Taking into account of the *polluter-pays principle* as a general principle of international environmental law.'

2. EUROPEAN COMMUNITY LAW

Soft law

Recommendation 75/436/Euratom, ECSC, EEC 1975 Regarding Cost Allocation and Action by Public Authorities on Environmental Matters

'Natural or legal persons governed by public or private law who are responsible for pollution must pay the costs of such measures as are necessary to eliminate that pollution or to reduce it so as to comply with the standards or equivalent measures which enable quality objectives to be met or, where there are no such objectives, so as to comply with the standards or equivalent measures laid down by the public authorities.'

1992 EC Commission Vth Programme for Sustainable Development and Environmental Policies:

Preamble: 'ACKNOWLEDGE that the programme presented by the Commission has been designed to reflect the objectives and *principles of sustainable development, preventive and precautionary action and shared responsibility* set out in the declaration of the Heads of State and the Government of the Community meeting in Council on 26 June 1990 and in the Treaty on European Union signed at Maastricht on 7 February 1992... In accordance with the European Council's Declaration 'The Environmental Imperative' the guiding principles for policy decision under this Programme derive from the *precautionary approach* and the concept of shared responsibility, including effective implementation of the *Polluter Pays Principle*.'

1997 EC Commission Green Paper on the General Principles of Food Law in the European Community

'The Treaty requires the Community to contribute to the maintenance of a high level of protection of public health, the environment and consumers. In order to ensure a high level of protection and coherence, protective measures should be based on risk assessment, taking into account all relevant risk factors, including technological aspects, the best available scientific evidence and the availability of inspection sampling and testing methods. Where a full risk assessment is not possible, measures should be based on *the precautionary principle*.'

2000 EC Commission White Paper on Food Safety

'Where appropriate, the *precautionary principle* will be applied in risk management decisions.'

2000 Communication from the EC Commission on the Precautionary Principle

'The Community has consistently endeavoured to achieve a high level of protection, among others in environment and human, animal or plant health. In most cases, measures making it possible to achieve this high level of protection can be determined on a satisfactory scientific basis. However, when there are reasonable grounds for concern that potential hazards may affect the environment or human, animal or plant health, and when at the same time the available data preclude a detailed risk evaluation, the *precautionary principle* has been politically accepted as a risk management strategy in several fields.'

'Although the *precautionary principle* is not explicitly mentioned in the Treaty except in the environmental field, its scope is far wider and covers those specific circumstances where scientific evidence is insufficient, inconclusive or uncertain and there are indications through preliminary objective scientific evaluation that there are reasonable grounds for concern that the potentially dangerous effects on the environment, human, animal or plant health may be inconsistent with the chosen level of protection.'

2000 Council Resolution on the Precautionary Principle

'...

2. considers that the precautionary principle applies to the policies and action of the Community and its Member States and concerns action by public authorities both at

the level of the Community institutions and at that of Member States; that such authorities should endeavour to have that principle fully recognised by the relevant international fora;

3. notes that the precautionary principle is gradually asserting itself as a principle of international law in the fields of environmental and health protection;

4. considers that WTO rules do basically allow account to be taken of the precautionary principle;

5. believes that under international law the Community and the Member States are entitled to establish the level of protection they consider appropriate in risk management, that they may to that end take appropriate measures under the precautionary principle and that it is not always possible to determine in advance the level of protection appropriate to all situations;

6. sees a need to establish guidelines for use of the precautionary principle, in order to clarify arrangements for its application;

7. considers that use should be made of the precautionary principle where the possibility of harmful effects on health or the environment has been identified and preliminary scientific evaluation, based on the available data, proves inconclusive for assessing the level of risk;

8. considers that the scientific assessment of the risk must proceed logically in an effort to achieve hazard identification, hazard characterisation, appraisal of exposure and risk characterisation, with reference to procedures recognised at Community level and internationally, and that, owing to insufficient data and the nature or urgency of the risk, it may not always be possible to complete every stage systematically;

9. considers that, in order to carry out the risk assessment, public authorities must have suitable research facilities and rely in particular on scientific committees and on relevant national and international scientific work; that the public authorities are responsible for organising the risk assessment, which must be carried out in a multidisciplinary, independent and transparent manner and ensure that all views are heard;

10. considers that an assessment of risk must also report any minority opinions. It must be possible to express such opinions and bring them to the knowledge of the parties involved, in particular if they draw attention to scientific uncertainty;

11. affirms that those responsible for scientific assessment of risk must be functionally separate from those responsible for risk management, albeit with ongoing exchange between them;

12. considers that risk management measures must be taken by the public authorities responsible on the basis of a political appraisal of the desired level of protection;

13. believes that, in selecting the risk management measures to be taken, consideration should be given to the whole range of measures enabling the desired level of protection to be achieved;

14. considers that all stages must be conducted in a transparent manner, in particular the risk assessment and management stages, including the monitoring of measures decided upon;

15. considers that civil society must be involved and special attention must be paid to consulting all interested parties as early as possible;

16. considers that appropriate means must be used for communicating information on scientific opinion and risk management measures;

17. considers that measures must observe the principle of proportionality, taking account of short-term and long-term risks and aiming to achieve the desired high level of protection;

18. considers that measures must not be applied in a way resulting in arbitrary or unwarranted discrimination; where there are a number of possible means of attaining the same level of health or environmental protection, the least trade-restrictive measures should be opted for;

19. considers that measures should be consistent with measures already adopted in similar circumstances or following similar approaches, having due regard to the latest scientific developments and developments in the level of protection sought;

20. stresses that the measures adopted presuppose examination of the benefits and costs of action and inaction. This examination must take account of social and environmental costs and of the public acceptability of the different options possible, and include, where feasible, an economic analysis, it being understood that requirements linked to the protection of public health, including the effects of the environment on public health, must be given priority;

21. considers that decisions taken in accordance with the precautionary principle should be reviewed in the light of developments in scientific knowledge. To that end the impact of such decisions should be monitored and additional research conducted in order to reduce the level of uncertainty;

22. considers that, when determining measures taken in accordance with the precautionary principle and in monitoring them, the competent authorities should be able to decide case by case, on the basis of clear rules established at the appropriate level, who is responsible for providing the scientific data required for a fuller risk assessment; Such an obligation may vary according to the circumstances and the aim must be to strike a satisfactory balance between the public authorities, scientific bodies and economic operators, taking into account in particular the responsibility held by economic operators by virtue of their activities.'

Hard law

European Community Treaty

Article 2 EC Treaty
'The Community shall have as its task, by establishing a common market and an economic and monetary union and by implementing common policies or activities referred to in Articles 3 and 4, to promote throughout the Community... a *high level of protection and improvement of the quality of the environment* ...'

Article 6 EC Treaty
'Environmental protection requirements must be *integrated* into the definition and implementation of the Community policies referred to in Article 3, in particular with a view to promoting sustainable development.'

Article 95(3) EC Treaty
'The Commission, in its proposal envisaged in paragraph 1 concerning health, safety, environmental protection and consumer protection, will take as a base a *high level of*

protection, taking account in particular of any new development based on scientific facts. Within their respective powers, the European Parliament and the Council will also seek to achieve this objective.'

Article 152(1) EC Treaty
'A *high level of human health protection* shall be ensured in the definition and implementation of all Community policies and activities...'

Article 153(1) EC Treaty
'In order to promote the interests of consumers and to ensure a *high level of consumer protection*, the Community shall contribute to protecting the health, safety and economic interests of consumers, as well as to promoting their right to information, education and to organise themselves in order to safeguard their interests...'

Article 174 EC Treaty
1. 'Community policy on the environment shall contribute to pursuit of the following objectives:
   – preserving, protecting and improving the quality of the environment;
   – protecting human health;
   – prudent and rational utilisation of natural resources;
   – promoting measures at international level to deal with regional or worldwide environmental problems.'
2. 'Community policy on the environment shall aim at a *high level of protection* taking into account the diversity of situations in the various regions of the Community. It shall be based on *the precautionary principle* and on *the principles that preventive action should be taken*, that *environmental damage should as a priority be rectified at source* and that *the polluter should pay*'
   ...
3. 'In preparing its policy on the environment, the Community shall take account of:
   —available scientific and technical data;
   —environmental conditions in the various regions of the Community;
   —the potential benefits and costs of action or lack of action;
   —the economic and social development of the Community as a whole and the balanced development of its regions...'

Porto Agreement of 2 May 1992 on the European Economic Area
Article 73(2): 'Actions by the Contracting Parties relating to environment shall be based on *the principles that preventive action should be taken*, that *environmental damage should as a priority be rectified at source* and that the *polluter should pay*. Environmental protection requirements shall be a component of the Contracting Parties' other policies.'

Secondary law

Decision 80/372/EEC concerning Chlorofluorocarbons in the Environment
Preamble: 'Whereas, in accordance with the common position of the Member States of 6 December 1978 and in accordance with recommendation III of the Munich Conference, a significant reduction should, as a precautionary measure, be achieved in the next few years in the use of chlorofluorocarbons giving rise to emissions...'

Directive 93/67/EEC Laying Down the Principles for Assessment of Risks to Man and the Environment of Substances Notified in Accordance with Directive 67/548/EEC

'Whereas the assessment of risks should be based on a comparison of the potential effects of a substance with the reasonably foreseeable exposure of man and the environment to that substance.'

Directive 96/61/EC concerning Integrated Pollution Prevention and Control

Article 3: 'Member States shall take the necessary measures to provide that the competent authorities ensure that installations are operated in such a way that:

> (a) all the appropriate *preventive measures* are taken against pollution, in particular through application of the best available techniques;
> (b) no significant pollution is caused;
> . . .
> (e) the necessary measures are taken to *prevent* accidents and limit their consequences;

For the purposes of compliance with this Article, it shall be sufficient if Member States ensure that the competent authorities take account of the general principles set out in this Article when they determine the conditions of the permit.'

ANNEX IV: Considerations to be taken into account generally or in specific cases when determining best available techniques, as defined in Article 2(11), bearing in mind the likely costs and benefits of a measure and the *principles of precaution and prevention*: . . .

10. the need to *prevent* or reduce to a minimum the overall impact of the emissions on the environment and the risks to it;

11. the need to *prevent* accidents and to minimize the consequences for the environment; . . .'

Directive 96/82/EC on the Control of Major-Accident Hazards Involving Dangerous Substances

Article 1: 'This Directive is aimed at the *prevention of major accidents* which involve dangerous substances, and the limitation of their consequences for man and the environment, with a view to ensuring high levels of protection throughout the Community in a consistent and effective manner.'

Article 5(1): 'Member States shall ensure that the operator is obliged to take all measures necessary to prevent major accidents and to limit their consequences for man and the environment.'

Directive 97/57/EC establishing Annex VI to Directive 91/414/EEC concerning the Placing of Plant Protection Products on the Market (Annex B, point 4)

'In interpretating the results of evaluations, Member States shall take into consideration possible elements of uncertainty in the information obtained during the evaluation, in order to ensure that the chances of failing to detect adverse effects or of under-estimating their importance are reduced to a minimum'.

Directive 98/81/EC modifying Directive 90/219/EEC on the Contained Use of Genetically Modified Micro-Organisms
Preamble:
(1) 'Whereas, within the meaning of the Treaty, action by the Community relating to the environment should be based on *the principle that preventive action is to be taken* and shall have as its objective to preserve, protect and improve the environment and to protect human health;
(2) Whereas contained uses of genetically modified micro-organisms (GMMs) should be classified in relation to the risks they present for human health and the environment; whereas such classification should be in line with international practice and based on an assessment of the risk;
(3) Whereas in order to ensure a high level of protection the containment and other protective measures applied to a contained use must correspond to the classification of the contained use; whereas in case of uncertainty the appropriate containment and other protective measures for the higher classification should be applied until less stringent measures are justified by appropriate data;

Article 5:
1. Member States shall ensure that all appropriate measures are taken to avoid adverse effects on human health and the environment which might arise from the contained use of GMMs.
2. To this end the user shall carry out an assessment of the contained uses as regards the risks to human health and the environment that these contained uses may incur, using as a minimum the elements of assessment and the procedure set out in Annex III, sections A and B.
3. The assessment referred to in paragraph 2 shall result in the final classification of the contained uses in four classes applying the procedure set out in Annex III, which will result in the assignment of containment levels in accordance with Article 6.
4. *Where there is doubt* as to which class is appropriate for the proposed contained use, *the more stringent protective measures shall be applied* unless sufficient evidence, in agreement with the competent authority, justifies the application of less stringent measures.'

Directive 99/39/EC amending Directive 96/5/EC on Processed Cereal-Based Foods and Baby Foods
Preamble: 'Whereas, taking into account the Community's international obligations, in cases where the relevant scientific evidence is insufficient, the *precautionary principle* allows the Community to provisionally adopt measures on the basis of available pertinent information, pending on additional assessment of risk and a review of the measure within a reasonable period of time.'

Directive 2001/18/EC on the Deliberate Release into the Environment of Genetically Modified Organisms and Repealing Council Directive 90/220/EEC
Article 1: 'In accordance with the *precautionary principle*, the objective of this Directive is ... to protect human health and the environment when carrying out the deliberate release of genetically modified organisms for any other purposes than placing on the market within the Community; placing on the market genetically modified organisms as or in products within the Community.'

Article 4: 'Member States, in accordance with the *precautionary principle*, shall ensure that all appropriate measures are taken to avoid adverse effects on human health and the environment which might arise from the deliberate release or the placing on the market of GMOs. GMOs may only be deliberately release or placed on the market . . .'

Regulation (EC) No 178/2002 of the European Parliament and of the Council Laying Down the General Principles and Requirements of Food Law, Establishing the European Food Safety Authority and Laying Down Procedures in Matters of Food Safety

Preamble:

(19) 'It is recognised that scientific risk assessment alone cannot, in some cases, provide all the information on which a risk management decision should be based, and that other factors relevant to the matter under consideration should legitimately be taken into account including societal, economic, traditional, ethical and environmental factors and the feasibility of controls.

(20) The *precautionary principle* has been invoked to ensure health protection in the Community, thereby giving rise to barriers to the free movement of food or feed. Therefore it is necessary to adopt a uniform basis throughout the Community for the use of this principle.

(21) In those specific circumstances where a risk to life or health exists but scientific uncertainty persists, the precautionary principle provides a mechanism for determining risk management measures or other actions in order to ensure the high level of health protection chosen in the Community.'

Article 7. Precautionary principle

1. 'In specific circumstances where, following an assessment of available information, the possibility of harmful effects on health is identified but scientific uncertainty persists, provisional risk management measures necessary to ensure the high level of health protection chosen in the Community may be adopted, pending further scientific information for a more comprehensive risk assessment.

2. Measures adopted on the basis of paragraph 1 shall be proportionate and no more restrictive of trade than is required to achieve the high level of health protection chosen in the Community, regard being had to technical and economic feasibility and other factors regarded as legitimate in the matter under consideration. The measures shall be reviewed within a reasonable period of time, depending on the nature of the risk to life or health identified and the type of scientific information needed to clarify the scientific uncertainty and to conduct a more comprehensive risk assessment.'

3. NATIONAL LAWS

Australia

1991 New South Wales Protection of the Environment Administration Act
'If there are threats of serious or irreversible environmental damage, lack of full scientific certainty should not be used as a reason for postponing measures to prevent environmental degradation.'

1992 Intergovernmental Agreement on the Environment

Section 3(5)(1): 'Where there are threats of serious or irreversible environmental damage, lack of full scientific certainty should not be used as a reason for postponing measures to prevent environmental degradation. In the application of the *precautionary principle*, public and private decisions should be guided by: (i) careful evaluation to avoid, wherever practicable, serious or irreversible damage to the environment; and (ii) an assessment of risk-weighted consequences of various options.'

1994 New South Wales Fisheries Management Act

Section 30: 'The TAC Committee is also to have regard to: ... (c) the *precautionary principle*, namely, that if there are threats of serious or irreversible damage to fish stocks, lack of full scientific certainty should not be used as a reason for postponing measures to prevent that damage.'

1999 Commonwealth Environment Protection and Biodiversity Conservation Act

Section 391: 'The Minister must take account of the *precautionary principle* in making a decision listed in the table in subsection (3), to the extent that he or she can do so consistently with the other provisions of this Act.'

'The *precautionary principle* is that lack of full scientific certainty should not be used as a reason for postponing a measure to prevent degradation of the environment where there are threats of serious irreversible environmental damage.'

Belgium

1995 Act of the Flemish Region concerning Environmental Policy

'Environmental policy shall seek to achieve a high level of protection...It shall be based on the *precautionary principle*, on the *principles that preventive action should be taken, that environmental damage should as a priority be rectified at source*, the *stand-still principle* and the *polluter pays principle*.'

1999 Federal Act Aimed at Protection of the Marine Environment in the Maritime Areas under Belgian Jurisdiction

Article 4(1): 'The users of the maritime areas and the public authorities shall take into consideration the *principle of preventive action*, the *precautionary principle*, the *principle of long-term management*, the *polluter pays principle* and the *restoration principle* when carrying out their activities in these areas.

(2) The *principle of preventive action* implies that action must be taken to prevent environmental damage rather than having to repair the damage afterwards.

(3) The *precautionary principle* means that preventive measures must be taken if there are reasonable grounds for concern about pollution of the maritime areas, even in cases

where there is no conclusive evidence of a causal connection between the introduction of substances, energy and materials into the maritime areas and the harmful effects.

(4) The *principle of long-term management* in the maritime areas implies that the natural resources are kept available in sufficient quantities for future generations and that the effects of human activity do not exceed the capacity of the environment in the maritime areas. To this end, the ecosystems and the ecological processes necessary for the proper functioning of the marine environment shall be protected, its biological diversity preserved and nature conservation stimulated.

(5) The *polluter pays principle* means that the costs of measures to prevent, limit and control pollution and to repair any damage are to be borne by the polluter.

(6) The *restoration principle* implies that, in case of damage or environmental disruption in the maritime areas, the marine environment is restored to its original condition as much as possible.

Article 5. Any person carrying out an activity in the maritime areas is obliged to take the necessary precautions to prevent damage and environmental disruption. More particularly, shipowners are obliged to take all the necessary precautions to prevent and limit pollution.'

Denmark

1998 Environmental Protection Act No. 698

Article 1(1): 'The purpose of this Act is to contribute to safeguarding nature and environment, thus enabling a sustainable social development in respect for human conditions of life and for the conservation of flora and fauna.

(2) The objectives of this Act are in particular:

(1) to prevent and combat pollution of air, water, soil and subsoil, and nuisances caused by vibration and noise,

(2) to provide for regulations based on hygienic considerations which are significant to Man and the environment,

(3) to reduce the use and wastage of raw materials and other resources,

(4) to promote the use of cleaner technology, and—to promote recycling and reduce problems in connection with waste disposal.

...

Article 3(1): In the administration of this Act weight shall be given to the results achievable by using the least polluting technology, including least polluting raw materials, processes and plants and the best practicable pollution control measures. In this evaluation special consideration shall be given to *preventive measures* in the form of cleaner technology.

(2) When determining the extent and nature of measures to *prevent pollution* consideration shall be given to:

(1) the nature of the physical surroundings and the likely impact of pollution thereon, and

(2) the whole cycle of substances and materials, with a view to minimizing wastage of resources.

Article 4(1): Any party proposing to commence activities likely to cause pollution shall choose such site for the activities that the *risk of pollution is minimized*.

(2) When choosing such site consideration shall be given to the nature of the area, including present and planned future uses, and to the possibilities for appropriate disposal of wastewater and waste.

(3) Any party commencing or carrying out activities likely to cause pollution shall take measures *to prevent and combat pollution* and design and operate the activities so as to cause the least degree of pollution, cf. section 3 above. In the design and operation of the plant, including choice of production processes, raw materials and auxiliary substances, measures shall be taken to minimize the use of resources, pollution and generation of waste. (4) Any person giving rise to or causing risks of pollution of air, water, soil or subsoil, shall take the measures required to *effectively prevent or combat the impact of pollution*. In addition, he shall seek to restore the original state of the environment.'

Finland

2000 Environmental Protection Act No. 86/2000

Article 1: 'The objective of this Act is:

...

3. to prevent the pollution of the environment and to repair and reduce damage caused by pollution;
4. to safeguard a healthy, pleasant ecologically diverse and sustainable environment;
5. to prevent the generation and the harmful effects of waste.'

Article 4: 'The following principles apply to activities that pose a risk of pollution:

(1) harmful environmental impact shall be prevented or, when it cannot be prevented completely, reduced to a minimum (*principle of preventing and minimizing harmful impact*);
(2) the proper care and caution shall be taken to prevent pollution as entailed by the nature of the activity, and the probability of pollution, risk of accident and opportunities to prevent accidents and limit their effects shall be taken into account (*principle of caution and care*);
(3) the best available technique shall be used (*principle of best available technique*) ... combinations of various methods, such as work methods, shall be used and such raw materials and fuels shall be selected as provide appropriate and cost-efficient means to prevent pollution (*principle of best environmental practice*).'

France

2000 French Environmental Code

Article L101-1: 'I. Natural areas, resources and environments, special sites and landscapes, animal and plant species, biodiversity and the biological systems to which they belong are part of the national patrimony.

II. Their protection, development, restoration, reparation and management are part of the public interest and ... draw inspiration, within the framework of the laws defining their effect, from the following principles:

1 The *precautionary principle*, according to which the absence of certainty, taking account of the current state of scientific and technical knowledge, ought not to delay the adoption of effective and proportionate measures intended to prevent the risk of serious and irreversible damage to the environment, at an economically acceptable cost;
2 The *principle of preventive action and rectification of damage to the environment as a priority at source*, using best available techniques not entailing excessive cost;

3 the *polluter-pays principle*, according to which the costs resulting from measures to prevent, reduce and fight pollution should be borne by the polluter;

4 the *principle of participation*, according to which each citizen should have access to information relating to the environment, including information relating to dangerous substances and activities.'

Article L101-2: 'Laws and rules provide the right of all people to a healthy environment ... It is the duty of each individual to help safeguard and contribute to the protection of the environment. Public and private persons should conform to these requirements in all their activities.'

Germany

1959 Atomic Energy Act (Atomgesetz)

§ 7: 'The authorisation may only be granted if the *precautions* demanded by the current level of scientific and technical knowledge are taken against possible damage caused by the establishment or operation of the installation.'

1973 Act for Protection against Harmful Environmental Effects on Air Pollution, Noise, Vibrations and Similar Processes (BImSchG)

§ 5: 'Installations subject to authorisation are to be constructed and operated in such a manner that:

1. No detrimental environmental effects or other hazards, noticeable adverse effects and nuisance to the public and the neighbourhood are caused.

2. *Precaution* is taken against damaging environmental effects, in particular by means of measures for the control of emissions in accordance with the state of technology.'

1993 Biotechnology Act (Gentechnikgesetz)

§ 6 (2): 'In conformity with the current level of science and technology, the operator must take all measures to protect the rights set out in § 1, no. 1 and *to anticipate the creation of dangers* ...'

§ 13: 'Authorisation for the operation and establishment of a biotechnology installation ... may not be granted until: ...

(4) It is guaranteed that the measures required have been taken at all necessary levels of protection, in conformity with the current level of science and technology, and this without it being necessary to wait for damaging effects by emissions on the rights protected under § 1, no. 1.'

Sweden

1998 Swedish Environmental Code (Chapter 2)

Section 2: 'Persons who pursue an activity or take a measure, or intend to do so, must possess the knowledge that is necessary in view of the nature and scope of the activity or measure to protect human health and the environment against damage or detriment.'

Section 3(1): 'Persons who pursue an activity or take a measure, or intend to do so, shall implement protective measures, comply with restrictions and take any other precautions that are necessary in order to prevent or hinder damage or detriment to human health or the environment as a result of the activity or measure. For the same reason, the best available technology shall be used in connection with professional activities.

(2) Such *precautions* shall be taken as soon as there is cause to assume that an activity or measure may cause damage or detriment to human health or the environment.'

Section 6: 'Persons who pursue an activity or take a measure, or intend to do so, shall avoid using or selling chemical products or biotechnical organisms that may involve risks to human health or the environment if products or organisms that are less dangerous can be used instead. The same requirement shall apply to goods that contain or are treated with a chemical product or a biotechnical organism.'

Section 7(1) 'The rules of consideration laid down in sections 2 to 6 shall be applicable where compliance cannot be deemed unreasonable. Particular importance shall be attached in this connection to the benefits of protective measures and other precautions in relation to their cost. The cost-benefit relationship shall also be taken into account in assessments relating to total defence activities or where a total defence measure is necessary.

(2) A decision reached in accordance with subsection (1) must not entail infringement of an environmental quality standard referred to in chapter 5.'

1999 Guidelines on Chemicals Policy

3. 'Man-made organic substances that are persistent and bioaccumulative occur in production processes only if the producer can show that health and the environment will not be harmed. Permits and terms of the Environmental Code are devised in such a way as to guarantee this guideline.'

United Kingdom

1990 White Paper This Common Inheritance: Britain's Environmental Strategy

'We must act on facts, and on the most accurate interpretation of them, using the best scientific and economic information . . . That does not mean we must sit back until we have 100% evidence about everything. Where the state of our planet is at stake, the risks can be so high and the costs of corrective action so great, that prevention is better and cheaper than cure. We must analyse the possible benefits and costs both of action and of inaction. Where there are significant risks of damage to the environment, the government will be prepared to take precautionary action to limit the use of potentially dangerous materials or the spread of potentially dangerous pollutants, even where scientific knowledge is not conclusive, if the balance of likely costs and benefits justifies it. The *precautionary principle* applies particularly where there are good grounds for judging either that action taken promptly at comparatively low cost may avoid more costly damage later, or that irreversible effects may follow if action is delayed.'

Bibliography

This bibliography regroups references according to the legal order to which they belong or to their discipline. Three specific sections regroup the references concerning the preventive action, the polluter-pays, and the precautionary principles.

1. LEGAL THEORY

Baldwin R. (ed.), *Law and Uncertainty: Risks and Legal Processes* (London: Kluwer Law Int'l, 1997)

Carty A., *Post-Modern Law* (Edinburgh: Edinburgh U.P., 1990)

Chevallier J., 'Vers un droit post-moderne? Les transformations de la régulation juridique' (1998) 3 RDP 674

Delmas-Marty M., *Pour un droit commun* (Paris: Seuil, 1994)

de Sadeleer N., 'Het milieurecht, een rechtsgebied in wording' in R. Foqué and S. Gutwirth (eds.), *Vraagstukken van milieurechtelijke begripsvorming* (Rotterdam: Goda Quint, 2000) 147–65

——, 'Gli effetti del tempo, la posta in gioco e il dirrito ambientale' (2001) Riv Giur Amb XVI:5 589–607

de Sousa-Santos B., *The Post-Modern Transition: Law and Politics*, in A. Sarat and T.R. Kearns (eds.), *The Fate of Law* (Ann Arbor: University of Michigan Press, 1991)

——, *Towards a New Common Sense: Law, Science and Politics in the Paradigmatic Transition* (London: Routledge, 1991)

Douzinas C., Warington R., and Sh. McVeigh, *Postmodern Jurisprudence* (London: Routledge, 1991)

Dworkin R., *Taking Rights Seriously* (Cambridge, Mass.: Harvard U.P., 1978)

Ewald Fr., *L'Etat providence* (Paris: Grasset, 1980)

Finnis J., 'Natural Law and Legal Reasoning' in R.P. George (ed.), *Natural Law Theory. Contemporary Essays* (Oxford: Clarendon, 1992) 150

Gerard Ph., *Droit, égalité et idéologie* (Brussels: Saint-Louis, 1981)

Gérard Ph., Ost Fr., and van de Kerchove M. (eds.), *Droit négocié, droit imposé?* (Brussels: Saint-Louis, 1996)

Golding P., 'Kelsen and the concept of legal system' in R.S. Summers (ed.), *More Essays in Legal Philosophy: General Assessments of Legal Philosophies* (Los Angeles: Berkeley, 1971) 69

Goodrich P. and Gray D., *Law and Postmodernity* (Ann Arbor: University of Michigan, 1998)

Hart H.L.A., *The Concept of Law* (Oxford: Clarendon, 1961)

Kelsen H., *General Theory of Law and State* (Cambridge, Mass.: Harvard, 1946)

Koskenniemi M., *From Apology to Utopia: The Structure of International Legal Argument* (Helsinki: Lakimiestliiton Kustannuys, 1989)

Ladeur K.-H., 'Post-Modern Constitutional Theory: A Prospect for the Self-Organising Society' (1997) 60: 5 MLR 617–29

Luhmann E., *Rechtssoziologie* (2nd edn., Opladen: Westdeutscher, 1999)

MacCormick N., *Legal Reasoning and Legal Theory* (Oxford: Oxford U.P., 1978)

Moderne F., 'Actualité des principes généraux du droit' (1998) 14: 3 RFD Adm. 477

——, 'Légitimité des principes généraux et théorie du droit' (1999) 15: 4 RFD Adm. 722–42

Morand Ch.-A., *Le droit néo-moderne des politiques publiques* (Paris: L.G.D.J., 1999)

Ost Fr., 'A Game Without Rules? The Ecological Self-Organization of Firms' in G. Teubner, L. Framer, and D. Murphy (eds.), *Environmental Law and Ecological Responsibility: The Concept and Practice of Ecological Self-Organization* (London: J. Wiley, 1994) 337–61

——, *La nature hors la loi* (Paris: La découverte, 1995)

——, *Le temps du droit* (Paris: O. Jacob, 1999)

Ost Fr., van de Kerchove M., and Gérard Ph., *L'accélération du temps juridique* (Brussels: Saint-Louis, 2000)

Ost Fr. and van de Kerchove M., *De la pyramide au réseau? Pour une théorie dialectique du droit* (Brussels: Saint-Louis, 2002)

Peczenik A., 'Principles of Law: The Search for Legal Theory' (1971) 2 Rechtstheory 17

Raz J., 'Legal Principles and the Limits of the Law' (1972) 81 Yale LJ 823

——, 'The Rule of Law and its Virtue' (1977) LQR 195

——, *The Authority of Law* (Oxford: Clarendon, 1979)

Unger R.M., *Law in Modern Society: Toward a Criticism of Social Theory* (New York: Free Press, Collier Macmillan, 1977)

van de Kerchove M. and Ost Fr., *Legal System Between Order and Disorder* (Oxford: Oxford U.P., 1994)

Wrobelski J., *Principes du droit* (Paris: PUF, 1979)

2. Philosophy, economy, and social theory

Andersen M.S., *Governance by Green Taxes: Making Pollution Prevention Pay* (Manchester: Manchester U.P., 1994)

Andersen S. and Liefferink D., *European Environmental Policy: The Pioneers* (Manchester: Manchester U.P., 1997)

Andrews R.N., 'Environmental Impact Assessment and Risk Assessment: Learning from Each Other' in P. Wathern (ed.), *Environmental Impact Assessment: Theory and Practice* (London: Routledge, 1994) 89 *et seq.*

Arnaud A.-J., *Entre modernité et mondialisation* (Paris: L.G.D.J., 1998)

Beck U., *Risk Society: Towards a New Modernity* (London: Sage, 1992)

Bel R., and Halffman W., (eds.), *The Politics of Chemical Risk: Scenarios for a Regulatory Future* (Dordrecht, Boston, London: Kluwer, 1998)

Bernstein R.J., *The New Constellation: The Ethical-Political Horizons of Modernity/ Postmodernity* (Cambridge: Polity, 1991)

Breyer S., *Breaking the Vicious Circle: Toward Effective Risk Regulation* (Cambridge: Harvard U.P., 1993)

Bro-Rasmussen F. *et al.*, *The Non-assessed Chemicals in the EU, report and recommendations from an interdisciplinary group of Danish experts* (Copenhagen: Danish Board of Technology, 1996)

Bro-Rasmussen F., 'The Precautionary Principle and Science-based Limits in Regulatory Toxicology' in D.M. Pugh and J.V. Tarazona (eds.), *Regulation for chemical Safety in Europe: Analysis, Comment and Criticism* (Dordrecht, Boston, London: Kluwer, 1998) 97–110

Coase R., 'The Problem of Social Cost' (1960) III JL & Econ 1–44

——, *The Firm, the Market and the Law* (Chicago: Univ. of Chicago Press, 1988)

Collier U. (ed.), *Deregulation in the European Union* (London, New York: Routledge, 1998)

Connelly J. and Smith Gr., *Politics and the Environment* (London: Routledge, 1999)

Contini S., Amendola A., and Ziomas I., *Benchmark Exercise on Major Hazard Analysis* (Ispra: European Commission Joint Research Center, 1991)

Cranor C.F., *Regulating Toxic Substances: A Philosophy of Science and Law* (New York, Oxford: Oxford U.P., 1993)

——, 'Risk Assessment, Susceptible Subpopulations, and Environmental Justice' in M.B. Gerrard (ed.), *The Law of Environmental Justice: Theories and Procedures to Address Disproportinate Risks* (Chicago: American Bar Association, 1999) 307–56

Demmke C. (ed.), *Managing European Environmental Policy: The Role of the Member States in the Policy Process* (Maastricht: European Institute of Public Administration, 1997)

Downing T., Olsthoorn A., and Tol R.S., *Climate, Change and Risk* (London, New York: Routledge, 1999)

European Environmental Agency, *Late Lessons from Early Warnings: The Precautionary Principle 1896–2000* (Copenhagen: Environmental Issue Report, no. 22, 2001)

Fisher E., 'Drowning by Numbers: Standard Setting in Risk Regulation and the Pursuit of Accountable Public Administration' (2000) 20:1 OJLS 115

Foster K.R., Vecchia P., and Repacholi M.H., 'Science and the Precautionary Principle' (2000) *Science* 979

Frank R.H. and Sustein C.R., 'Cost—Benefit Analysis and Relative Position' (2001) 68:2 Univ Chicago LR 323–3

Giddens A., *Modernity and Self-Identity: Self and Society in the Late Modern Age* (London: Polity, 1990)

Glasbergen P. (ed.), *Co-operative Environmental Governance* (Dordrecht, Boston, London: Kluwer, 1998)

Graham J. and Wiener J., *Risk v. Risk: Tradeoffs in Protecting Health and the Environment* (Cambridge: Harvard U.P., 1995)

Gray J. and Bewers J., 'Towards a Scientific Definition of the Precautionary Principle' (1996) 32: 11 MPB 768–71

Haerlin B. and Parr D., 'How to Restore Public Trust in Science' (1999) 400 Nature 499

Hayward T., *Ecological Thought* (Cambridge: Polity, 1995)

Heyvaert V., 'Reconceptualizing Risk Assessment' (1999) 8 RECIEL 135–43

——, 'The Changing Role of Science in Environmental Regulatory Decision-Making in the European Union' (1999) 3–4 L&EA 426–44

——, *Coping with Uncertainty: The Regulation of Chemicals in the European Union*, Phd. (Florence: European University Institute, 1999)

Jacobs M., *The Green Economy* (London: Pluto, 1991)

——, 'Sustainable Development Assumptions, Contradictions, Progress' in J. Lovenduski and Stanyer (eds.), *Contemporary Political Studies: Proceedings of the Annual Conference of the Political Studies Association* (London: PSA, 1995) 1473 et *seq.*

Jameson Fr., *Postmodernism, or The Cultural Logic of Late Capitalism* (London: Verso, 1991)

Jasanoff S., *The Fifth Branch: Science Advisers as Policymakers* (Cambridge, Mass.: Harvard U.P., 1990)

——, 'The Songlines of Risk' (1999) 2: 8 Environmental Values 135–52

Joerges C., Ladeur K.-H., and Vos E. (eds.), *Integrating Expertise into Regulatory Decision-Making* (Baden-Baden: Nomos, 1997)

Jonas H., *The Imperative of Responsibility* (Chicago: Univ. of Chicago Press, 1984)

Kellow A., *International Toxic Risk Management. Ideals, Interests and Implementation* (Cambridge: Cambridge U.P., 1999)

Klinke A. and Renn O., 'Precautionary Principle and Discursive Strategies: Classifying and Managing Risks' (2001) 4: 2 Journal of Risk Research 159–73

Krimsky S., *Hormonal Chaos: The Scientific and Social Origins of Environmental Endocrine Hypothesis* (Baltimore: Johns Hopkins U.P., 2000)

Kuhn T., *The Structure of Scientific Revolution* (Chicago: University of Chicago, 1962)

Lash S., Szerszynski B., and Wynne B. (eds), *Risk, Environment and Modernity* (London: Sage, 1996)

Latour B., *Nous n'avons jamais été modernes* (Paris: La Découverte, 1991)

Liefferink J.D., Lowe P.D., and Mol P.J. (eds.), *European Integration and Environmental Policy* (London, New York: Belhaven Press, 1993)

Liefferink D. and Skou Andersen M., *The Innovation of EU Environmental Policy* (Oslo, Copenhagen, Stockholm, Oxford, Boston: Scandinavian U.P., 1997)

Litfin K., 'Framing Science: Precautionary Discourse and the Ozone Treaties' (1995) 24: 2 Millenium: Journal of International Studies 251–77

Luhmann N., *Risk: A Sociological Theory* (Berlin: de Gruyter, 1991)

Lyotard J.-F., *La condition post-moderne* (Paris: éd. de Minuit, 1979)

——, *The Postmodern Condition: A Report on Knowledge* (Minneapolis: University of Minnesota, 1984)

National Research Council, *Risk Assessment in Federal Government: Managing the Process* (Washington: National Academy Press, 1983)

——, *Understanding Risk: Informing Decisions in a Democratic Society* (Washington: National Academy Press, 1996)

O'Brien M., *Making Better Environmental Decisions* (Cambridge: MIT Press, 2000)

O'Riordan T. (ed.), *Ecotaxation* (London: Earthscan, 1997)

O'Riordan T. and J. Jäger (eds.), *Politics of Climate Change: A European Perspective* (London, New York: Routledge, 1996)

Paulus A., *The Feasibility of Ecological Taxation* (Antwerp, Apeldoorn: Maklu, 1997)

Pearce D. and Turner R.K., *Economics of Natural Resources and the Environment* (London: Harvester Wheatsheaf, 1990)

Pigou A.C., *The Economics of Welfare* (2nd edn., London: Macmillan, 1924).

——, *A Study in Public Finance* (London: Macmillan, 1947)

Pravdic V., 'Environmental Capacity: Is a New Scientific Concept Acceptable as a Strategy to Combat Marine Pollution?' (1985) 16 MPB 295 *et seq.*

Prigogine I. and Stengers I., *Order out of Chaos* (London: Flamingo, 1984)

Pugh D.M. and Tarazona J.V. (eds.), *Regulation for Chemical Safety in Europe: Analysis, Comment and Criticism* (Dordrecht, Boston, London: Kluwer, 1998)

Revesz R.L., Sands Ph., and Stewart R. (eds.), *Environmental Law, the Economy, and Sustainable Development* (Cambridge: Cambridge U.P., 2000) 283

Robertson D. and Kellow A., *Globalisation and the Environment. Risk Assessment and the WTO* (London: Routledge, 2001)

Rosenthal A., Gray G., and Graham J., 'Legislating Acceptable Cancer Risk from Exposure to Toxic Chemicals' (1992) 19: 2 ELQ 269–362

Santillo D., Stringer R., Johnston P., and Tickner J., 'The Precautionary Principle: Protecting against failures of scientific method and risk assessment' (1998) 36: 12 MPB 939–50

Slovic P., 'Risk Perception' (1987) Science 280–5

Smart B., *Postmodernity* (London: Routledge, 1992)

Smith R. and Wynne B., *Expert Evidence: Interpreting Science and the Law* (London: Routledge, 1989)

Stanners D. and Bourdeau Ph. (eds.), *Europe's Environment: The Dobris Assessment* (Copenhagen: European Environmental Agency, 1995)

Stirling A., 'Risk at a Turning Point' (1998) 1: 2 Journal of Risk Research 97–109

——, *On Science and Precaution in the Management of Technological Risk*, volume I: A Synthesis Report of Case Studies (Sevilla: European Commission, Joint Research Centre & Institute for Prospective Technological Studies, 1999)

Theys J. and Kalaora B., 'Quand la science réinvente l'environnement' in *La Terre outragée: Les experts sont formels* (1992) 1 Sciences et société 21 *et seq.*

Touraine A., *Critique de la modernité* (Paris: Fayard, 1992)

Weber M., *Le savant et le politique* (Paris: Union générale des éditions, 1963)

——, *Wirtschaft und Gesellschaft* (5th edn., Tübingen: J.C.B. Mohr, 1980)

Wettestad J. and Andersen S., 'Science and North Sea Policy-Making: Organization and Communication' (1990) 5 Int'l J Estuarine & Coastal L 111–22

Wynne B., 'Uncertainty and Environmental Learning: Reconceiving Science and Policy in the Preventive Paradigm' (1992) 2 Global Environmental Change 111 *et seq.*

——, 'Scientific Knowledge and the Global Environment, in M. Redclift and T. Benton (eds.), *Social Theory and the Global Environment* (London: Routledge, 1994)

——, 'May the Sheep Safely Graze? A Reflexive View of the Expert-Lay Knowledge Divide' in Lash S., Szerszynski B., and Wynne B. (eds.), *Risk, Environment & Modernity* (London: Sage, 1996) 58 *et seq.*

WGBU, *World in Transition: Strategies for Managing Global Environmental Risks* (Berlin, Heidelberg, New York: Springer Verlag, 1999)

Winpenny J.T., *Value for the Environment: A Guide to Economic Appraisal* (London: HMSO, 1991)

3. International law

3.1 General works

Akehurst M., 'Equity and General Principles of Law' (1976) ICLQ 801

——, *A Modern Introduction to International Law* (3rd edn., London: George Allen and Unwin, 1977)

Bokor-Szegö H., 'General Principles of Law' in M. Bedjaoui (ed.), *International Law: Achievements and Prospects* (Paris, Dordrecht: Martinus Nijhof, 1991) 215

Bos M., 'The identification of Custom in International Law' (1982) 25 GYbIL 11–22

Boyle A., 'State Responsibility and International Liability for Injurious Consequences of Acts not Prohibited by International Law: A Necessary Distinction?' (1990) ICLQ 15 *et seq.*

——, 'The Role of International Human Rights Law in the Protection of the Environment' in A. Boyle and M. Anderson (eds.), *Human Rights Approach to Environmental Protection* (Oxford: Clarendon, 1996) 61

——, 'Some Reflections on the Relationship of Treaties and Soft Law' (1999) 48 ICLQ 901

Brownlie I., *Principles of Public International Law* (4th edn., Oxford: Clarendon, 1990)

Cassese A., *International Law in a Divided World* (Oxford: Clarendon, 1990)

——, *International Law* (Oxford: Oxford U.P., 2001)

Cassese A. and Weiler J.H. (eds.), *Change and Stability in International Law-Making* (Berlin: De Gruyter, 1988) 33–7

Chinkin C.M., 'The Challenge of Soft Law: Development and Change in International Law' (1989) 38 ICLQ 85–6

——, 'Normative Development in the International Legal System' in D. Shelton (ed.), *Commitment and Compliance: The Role of Non-Binding Norms in the International Legal Systems* (Oxford: Oxford U.P., 2000) 31–43

Combacau J., 'Le droit international: Bric à brac ou système?' (1986) 31 Arch Ph Dr 85–105

Combacau J. and Sur S., *Droit international public* (2nd edn., Paris: Montchrestien, 1995)

D'Amato A., *The Concept of Custom in International Law* (Ithaca, London: Cornwell U.P., 1971)

Dupuy P.-M., *Droit International Public* (Paris: Dalloz, 1999)

Elias O. and Lim C., ' "General Principles of Law", "Soft Law" and the Identification of International Law' (1997) 28: 3 NYIL 45

Fitzmaurice G., 'The General Principles of International Law Considered from the Standpoint of the Rule of Law' (1957) 92: II RCADI 5

Friedmann W., 'The Use of General Principles in the Development of International Law' (1963) AJIL 279

——, *The Changing Structure of International Law* (London: Stevens & Sons, 1964)

Gruchalla-Wesierki T., 'A Framework for Understanding "Soft Law" ' (1984) 30 McGill LJ 37–88

Higgins R., *Problems and Process: International Law and How We Use It* (Oxford: Clarendon, 1994) 1–16

Hoggenmacher, 'La doctrine des deux éléments du droit coutumier dans la pratique de la Cour internationale' (1986) 90: 5 RGDIP 114

Jennings R.Y., 'The Identification of International Law' in Bin Cheng (ed.), *International Law: Teaching and Practice* (London: Stevens & Sons, 1982) 4 *et seq.*

Kelsen H., *Principles of International Law* (2nd edn., New York: Holt, Rhinehart and Winston, 1956)

Lammers J.G., 'General Principles of Law Recognized by Civilized Nations' in *Essays on the Development of the International Order* (Panhuys) (Alphen a/d Rijn: Sijthof & Noordhoff, 1980) 53–75

Lauterpacht H., *Private Law Sources and Analogies of International Law* (Weesp: Archon Books, 1970)

Malanczuk P., *Akerhust's Modern Introduction to International Law* (London: Routledge, 1993)

Mosler H., 'General Principles of Law' in *Encyclopedia of Public International Law*, no. 7, (North Holland, Amsterdam, New York, Oxford, 1992)

Nguyen Quoc Dinh, *Droit international public* (6th edn., Paris: L.G.D.J., 1999)

Parry C., *The Sources and Evidences of International Law* (Manchester: Manchester U.P., 1965)

Salmon J. (ed.), *Dictionnaire de Droit International Public* (Brussels: Bruylant-AUF, 2001)

Schachter O., 'The Decline of the Nation-State and its Implications for International Law' in *Essays in Honor of Prof. L. Henkin* (The Hague, London, Boston: Martinus Nijhoff, 1997) 13–28

Schokkenbroeck J.G., *Toetsing aan de vrijheidsrechten van het Europees Verdrag tot bescherming van de rechten van de Mens* (Zwolle: Tjeenk Willink, 1996)

Shaw M., *International Law* (4th edn., Cambridge: Cambridge U.P., 1997)

Shelton D. (ed.), *Commitment and Compliance: The Role of Non-Binding Norms in the International Legal Systems* (Oxford: Oxford U.P., 2000)

Steiner H.J., 'International Law, Doctrine and Schools of Thought in the Twentieth Century' in R. Bernardt (ed.), *Encyclopedia of Public International Law*, vol. II (Amsterdam: Elsevier, 1995) 1216–27

Stone J., 'Non liquet and the International Judicial Function' in Ch. Perelman (ed.), *Le problème des lacunes en droit* (Brussels: Bruylant, 1968) 305

Thirlway H., *International Customary Law and Codification* (Leiden: Sijhoff, 1972), 145–6

——, 'The Law and the Procedure of the I.C.J. (1960–1989)' (1990) LXI BYBIL 10

Van Hoof G.H.J., *Rethinking the Sources of International Law* (Deventer: Kluwer, 1983)

Vitanyi B., 'Les positions doctrinales concernant les sens de la notion de "Principes généraux" de droit reconnus par les nations civilisées' (1982) 86 RGDIP 45–116

Weil P., 'Towards Relative Normativity in International Law' (1983) 77 AJIL 413

Wolfke K., *Custom in Present International Law* (2nd edn., Dordrecht: Martinus Nijhoff, 1993)

3.2 International environmental law

Betlem G., *Civil Liability for Transfrontier Pollution* (London: Graham & Trotman/ Martinus Nijhoff, 1993)

Birnie P. and Boyle A., *International Law and the Environment* (Oxford: Clarendon, 1992)

Birnie P. and Boyle A., *International Law and the Environment* (2nd edn., Oxford: OUP, 2002)

Birnie P., 'International Environmental Law: Its Adequacy for Present and Future Needs' in A. Hurrell and B. Kingsbury (eds.), *The International Politics of the Environment* (Oxford: Clarendon, 1992) 61 *et seq.*

——, 'The Status of Environmental "Soft Law": Trends and Examples with Special Focus on IMO Norms, in Competing Norms' in *The Law of Marine Environmental Protection* (London: Kluwer Law Int'l, 1997) 51 *et seq.*

Boisson de Chazournes L., 'Unilateralism and Environmental Protection: Issues of Perception and Reality of Issues' (2000) 11: 2 EJIL 315–38

Boyle A., 'State Responsibility and International Liability for Injurious Consequences of Acts not Prohibited by International Law: A Necessary Distinction?' (1990) ICLQ 15 *et seq.*

——, 'Some Reflections on the Relationship of Treaties and Soft Law' (1999) 48 ICLQ 901

Boyle A. and Anderson M. (eds.), *Human Rights Approach to Environmental Protection* (Oxford: Clarendon, 1996)

Boyle A. and Freestone D. (eds.), *International Law and Sustainable Development* (Oxford: Oxford U.P., 1999)

Brock D., 'The Shrimp-Turtle Case: Implications for the MEA-WTO Debate' (1998) 9 YbIEL 14

Brown-Weiss E., *Fairness to Future Generations* (UN University, Tokyo: Transnational Pub., New York, 1989)

——, 'Environment and Trade as Partners in Sustainable Development' (1992) 86 AJIL 733

Bugge H.C., 'General Principles of International Law and Environmental Protection' in M. Basse (ed.), *Environmental Law: From International to National Law* (Aarhus: Gadjura, 1997) 53–72

Cameron J., 'Dispute Settlement and Conflicting Trade and Environment Regimes' in *Trade and the Environment: Bridging the Gap* (London: Cameron & May, 1998) 16–34

Cameron J. and Mackenzie R., 'Access to Environmental Justice and Procedural Rights in International Institutions' in A. Boyle and M. Anderson (eds.), *Human Rights Approach to Environmental Protection* (Oxford: Clarendon, 1996) 5 *et seq.*

Cameron J. and Robinson J., 'The Use of Trade Provisions in International Environmental Agreements and their Compatibility with GATT' (1992) 2 YbIEL 3–30

Cameron J., Demaret P., and Geradin P. (eds.), *Trade and the Environment: The Search for Balance* (Cameron & May, London: 1994)

Cameron Hutchison, 'International Environmental Law Attempts to be "Mutually supportive" with International Trade Law: A Compatibility Analysis of the CPB with the SPS Agreement' (2001) 4: 1 J Int'l Wildlife L & Pol'y 1–34

Campbell L., 'WTO and Climate Change: Trade, Investment and the Kyoto Protocol', (2000) 23: 17 Int'l Env Rep 654

Charnovitz St., 'The Supervision of Health and Biosafety Regulation by World Trade Rules' (2000) 13 Tulane Envt LJ 271

Deimann S., 'WTO Panel on EC Measures concerning Meat and Meat Products (Hormones)' (1997) 2 Elni Newsl 1

Deimann S. and Dyssli B. (eds.), *Environmental Rights* (London: Cameron & May, 1995)

Dejeant-Pons M., 'The Right to Environment in Regional Human Rights System' in Mahoney and Mahoney (eds.), *Human Rights in the Twenty-First Century* (1993) 595

DeMerrieux M., 'Deriving Environmental Rights from the ECHR' (2001) 21:3 OJLS 521–61

de Sadeleer N., 'La conservation de la nature au-delà des espèces et des espaces: L'émergence de concepts écologiques en droit international' in *Images et usages de la nature en droit* (Brussels: Saint-Louis, 1993) 186

——, 'Gli effetti del tempo, la posta in gioco e il dirrito ambientale' (2001) Riv Gui dell Amb 589–607

Dunoff J.L., 'Border Patrol at the WTO' (1998) 9 YbIEL 20–7

Dupuy P.-M., 'Due Diligence in the International Law of Liability' in *Legal Aspects of Transfrontier Pollution* (OECD, Paris, 1977)

——, 'Soft Law and the International Law on the Environment' (1991) 12 Mich J Int'l L 420 *et seq.*

——, 'Où en est le droit international de l'environnement à la fin du siècle?' (1997) RGDIP 873

Ebbesson J., *Compatibility of International and National Environmental Law* (London, The Hague, Boston: Kluwer Law Int'l, 1996)

——, 'The Notion of Public Participation in International Environmental Law' (1997) 8 YbIEL 51–97

Eggers B. and Mackenzie R., 'The Cartagena Protocol on Biosafety' (2000) 3 JIEL 525–43

Evans T., 'International Environmental Law and the Challenge of Globalization' in T. Jewell and J. Steele, *Law in Environmental Decision Making* (Oxford: Clarendon, 1998) 207–27

Falk R., 'Environmental Protection in an Era of Globalization' (1995) 6 YbIEL 3–25

Fijalkowski A. and Cameron, J. *Trade and the Environment* (London: Cameron & May-Asser Instituut, 1997)

Francioni F. (ed.), *Environment, Human Rights and International Trade* (Oxford: Hart, 2001)

Francioni F. and Scovazzi T. (eds.), *International Responsibility for Environmental Harm* (London, Dordrecht: Graham and Trotman, 1991)

Gehring, 'International Environmental Regimes: Dynamic Sectoral Legal Systems' (1990) 1 YbIEL 35

Gruchalla-Wesierki T., 'A Framework for Understanding "Soft Law" ' (1984) 30 McGill LJ 37–88

Guruswamy L., 'Environment and Trade: Competing Paradigms in International Law' in A. Anghie and G. Sturgess (eds.), *Legal Visions of the 21st Century: Essays in Honour of Judge Chr. Weeramantry* (London: Kluwer Law Int'l, 1998) 550–2

Handl G., 'State Liability for Accidental Transnational Environmental Damage by Private Persons' (1980) AJIL 540 *et seq.*

——, 'Environmental Security and Global Change: The Challenge to International Law' (1990) YbIEL 1

Horvarth K. and Visser P., *National Experiences on Codifying Rio Principles in National Legislations*, Publikatie reeks Milieubeheer, D.-G. Milieubeheer – Ministerie van Volks-rijksvesting, Ruimtelijke ordening en Milieubeheer 2 (1996) 1–20

Hunter D., Salzman J., and Zaelke D., *International Environmental Law and Policy* (New York: Foundation Press, 1998)

IUCN Environmental Law Centre, Draft International Covenant on Environment and Development, *Environmental Policy and Law Paper*, no. 31

Kamto M., 'Les nouveaux principes du droit international de l'environnement' (1993) 1 RJE 11

Kaye S., *International Fisheries Management* (London: Kluwer Law Int'l, 2001)

Khavari A. and Rothwell D., 'The ICJ and the Danube Dam Case: A Missed opportunity for International Environmental Law?' (1999) 507 MULR 15 *et seq.*

Kiss A. and Shelton D., *International Environmental Law* (London: Graham & Trotman, 1991)

Kiss A. and Beurier J.-P., *Droit international de l'environnement* (2nd edn., Paris: Pédone, 2001)

Koppen I. and Ladeur K.-M., 'Environmental Rights' in *Human Rights and the European Community: The Substantive Law* (Baden-Baden: Nomos, 1991) 1 *et seq.*

——, 'Environmental Constitutional Law' in *European Environmental Law: A Comparative Perspective* (London: Dartmouth, 1995) 15

Krueger J., *International Trade and the Basel Convention* (London: Earthscan, 1999)

Kummer K., *International Management of Hazardous Wastes: The Basel Convention and Related Legal Rules* (Oxford: Oxford U.P., 1999)

Lammers J.G., *Pollution of International Watercourses* (London, Boston, The Hague: Martinus Nijhof, 1984)

—— (ed.), *Environmental Protection and Sustainable Development: Legal Principles and Recommandations* (Dordrecht, Boston, London: Graham & Trotman/Martinus Nijhof, 1987)

——, 'International and European Community Law: Aspects of Pollution of International Watercourses' in W. Lang, H. Neuhold, and K. Zemanek (eds.), *Environmental Protection and International Law* (London: Graham & Trotman/Martinus Nijhoff, 1991) 117 *et seq.*

Lang W. (ed.), *Sustainable Development in International Law* (London: Graham & Trotman, 1995)

Lefevere R., *Transboundary Environmental Interference and the Origin of State Liability* (The Hague: Kluwer, 1996)

Leggett K., 'The Southern Bluefin Tuna Cases: ITLOS Order on Provisional Measures' (2000) 9 RECIEL 75

Loibl G., 'Trade and Environment. A Difficult Relationship. New Approaches and Trends: The Kyoto Protocol and Beyond' in *Liber Amicorum Prof. I. Seidl-Hohenveldern* (London, The Hague, Boston: Kluwer Law Int'l, 1998) 430–42

Marceau G., 'A Call for Coherence in International Law' (1999) 33: 5 JWT 123–6

McNelis N., 'The Role of the Judge in the EU and WTO: Lessons from the BSE and Hormones Cases' (2001) J Intl Econ L 189–208

Morrison F.L. and Wolfrum R. (eds.), *International, Regional and National Environmental Law* (The Hague, London, Boston: Kluwer Law Int'l, 2000)

Mucklow F., 'An Overview of the Integration of Environmental Principles into the World Bank' (2000) 9: 1 RECIEL 100–11

Noiville C., *Ressources génétiques et droit* (Paris: Pédone, 1997)

Nollkaemper A., *The Legal Regime of Transboundary Water Pollution: Between Discretion and Constraint* (London, The Hague, Boston: Martinus Nijhof/Graham & Trotman, 1993)

Orrego Vicuna F., *The Changing International Law of High Seas Fisheries* (Cambridge: Cambridge U.P., 1999)

Pallemaerts M., 'International Environmental Law from Stockholm to Rio: Back to the Future' in Ph. Sands (ed.), *Greening the Treaty* (London: Earthscan, 1993) 5

Palmer G., 'New Ways to Make International Environmental Law' (1992) 86: 2 AJIL 259 *et seq.*

Paradell-Trius L., 'Principles of International Environmental Law: An Overview' (2000) 9: 2 RECIEL 93–9

Petersmann H., *International and European Trade and Environmental Law after the Uruguay Round* (London, Boston, The Hague: Kluwer Law Int'l, 1995)

Sacharien K., 'The Definition of Thresholds of Tolerance for Transboundary Environmental Injury under International Law: Development and Present Status' (1990) XXXVII NILR 193 *et seq.*

Sand P.H., *Transnational Environmental Law* (London, Boston, The Hague: Kluwer Law Int'l, 1999)

Sands Ph., 'The Greening of International Law: Emerging Principles and Rules' (1994) Indian Journal Global of Legal Study 293 *et seq.*

——, *Principles of International Environmental Law* (Manchester: Manchester U.P., 1995)

Schiffman H.S., 'The Southern Bluefin Tuna Case: ITLOS Hears Its First Fishery Dispute' (1999) 3 J Int'l Wildlife L & Pol'y 318

Schoenbaum T., 'Free International Trade and Protection of the Environment: Irreconcilable Conflict?' (1992) 86 AJIL 719

——, 'The Decision in the Shrimp-Turtle Case' (1998) 9 YbIEL 39

Schwartz R., 'Trade Measures Pursuant to Multilateral Environmental Agreements: Developments from Singapore to Seattle' (2000) 9 RECIEL 69

Shelton D. and Kiss C., *Manual of European Environmental Law* (2nd edn., Cambridge: Cambridge U.P., 1997)

Singh N., 'Sustainable Development as a Principle of International Law' in P. De Waart, P. Peters, and E. Denters (eds.), *International Law and Development* (Dordrecht, Boston, London: Martinus Nijhof, 1988) 1

Stoll P.-T., 'Controlling the Risks of GMOs: The Cartagena Protocol on Biosafety and the SPS Agreement' (1999) 10 YbIEL 82–119

Tarasofsky R.G., 'Ensuring Compatibility between MEA ans GATT/WTO' (1996) 7 YbIEL 54

Taylor P., *An Ecological Approach to International Law* (London: Routledge, 1998)

Van Calster G., *International & EU Trade Law: The Environmental Challenge* (London: Cameron & May, 2000)

Van Drooghenbroeck S., *La proportionnalité dans le droit de la Convention européenne des droits de l'homme* (Brussels: Saint-Louis/Bruylant, 2001)

Van Dunne J. (ed.), *Non-Point Source River Pollution: The Case of the River Meuse* (London, The Hague, Boston: Kluwer Law Int'l, 1996)

Walker S.L., *Environmental Protection Versus Trade Liberalization: Finding the Balance. An Examination of the Legality of Environmental Regulation Under International Trade Law Regimes* (Brussels: Saint-Louis, 1993)

Walker V.R., 'Keeping the WTO from Becoming the "World Trans-science Organisation": Scientific Uncertainty, Science Policy, and Factfindings in the Growth Hormones Dispute' (1998) Cornell ILJ 251

Weber S., 'Environmental Information and the European Convention on Human Rights' (1991) 12 HRLJ 177

Wirth D., 'Trade Implications of the Basel Convention Amendment Banning North-South Trade in Hazardous Wastes (1998) 3 RECIEL 242

World Commission on Environment and Development, *Environmental Protection and Sustainable Development: Legal Principles and Recommendations* (London, The Hague, Boston: Graham & Trotman/Martinus Nijhoff, 1987)

Zemanek K., 'State Responsibility and Liability' in *Environmental Protection and International Law* (London, The Hague, Boston: Graham & Trotman/Martinus Nijhoff, 1991) 192

4. EC LAW

4.1 General works

Akehurst M., 'The Application of General Principles of Law by the CJEC' (1981) 52 BYbIL 25

Bengoetxea J., *The Legal Reasoning of the European Court of Justice* (Oxford: Clarendon, 1993)

Boulouis J., 'A propos de la fonction normative de la jurisprudence: Remarques sur l'oeuvre jurisprudentielle de la Cour de justice des Communautés européennes' in *Mélanges Waline* (Paris: L.G.D.J., 1974)

Emiliou N., *The Principle of Proportionality in European Law* (London, The Hague, Boston: Kluwer Law Int'l, 1996)

Goletti G., 'The General Principles of Law in the European Community' (1985) 61: II Foro Amministrativo 2623

Kapteyn P.J.G. and Verloren van Themaat P., *Introduction to the Law of the European Community* (3rd edn., London: Kluwer Law Int'l, 1998)

Papadopoulou R., *Principes généraux du droit et principes du droit communautaire* (Brussels: Bruylant, 1996)

Reuter P., 'Le recours de la Cour de justice des Communautés européennes à des principes généraux de droit' in *Mélanges H. Rolin* (Paris: Pédone, 1964) 263 *et seq.*

Simon D., 'Y-a-t-il des principes généraux du droit communautaire?' (1991) Droits 73

Spitzer B., 'Les principes généraux de droit communautaire dégagés par la Cour de justice des Communautés européennes' (1986) Gaz Pal 732

Van Gerven W., 'The Effect of Proportionality on the Actions of Member States of the European Community: National Viewpoint from Continental Europe' in E. Ellis (ed.), *The Principle of Proportionality in the Laws of Europe* (Oxford: Hart, 1999) 37–63

4.2 EC environmental law

Cardonnel P., 'The Annulment of the EU Uniform Principles for Evaluation and Authorisation of Pesticide Products by the ECJ' (1996) RECIEL 271

Deimann S. and Dyssli B., *Environmental Rights, Law, Litigation and Access to Justice* (London: Cameron & May, 1995)

de Sadeleer N., 'Les limites posées à la libre circulation des déchets par les exigences de protection de l'environment' (1993) 5: 6 Cah Dr Eur 672–96

——, *Le droit communautaire et les déchets* (Brussels: Bruylant/L.G.D.J., 1995)

——, 'Le principe de proportionnalité: Cheval de Troie du marché intérieur?' (1999) 3: 4 L&EA 379–88

——, 'L'étendue de la marge de manoeuvre dans la transposition des règles communautaires: De nouveaux défis pour le droit public (à propos de la conservation des espaces naturels)' (2000) 16: 3 RFD Adm 611–35

——, 'Les clauses de sauvegarde prévues à l'article 95 du traité CE: L'efficacité du marché intérieur en porte-à-faux avec les intérêts nationaux dignes de protection' (2002) 1 RTDE 53–73

de Sadeleer N. and Noiville C., 'La directive communautaire 2001/18/CE sur la dissémination volontaire d'organismes génétiquement modifiés dans l'environnement: Un examen critique' 58 (2002) 58 JTDE 81 *et seq.*

de Sadeleer N. and Sambon J., 'The Concept of Hazardous Waste in EC Law' (1997) EELR 9–14

Doherty M., 'The Status of the Principles of EC Environmental Law' (1999) 2 JEL 378–86

Douma W.Th., 'The European Union and the Precautionary Principle' (2000) 1 RECIEL 132–44

Douma W.T. and Matthee M., 'Towards New EC rules on the Release of Genetically Modified Organisms' (1999) 8 RECIEL 152–9

Duncan French, 'The Changing Nature of Environmental Protection: Recent Developments regarding Trade and the Environment in the EU and the WTO' (2000) NILR 21–2

Elni, *Environmental Agreements, The Role and Effects of Environmental Agreements in Environmental policies* (London: Cameron & May, 1998)

Epiney A., 'Die umweltpolitische Handlungsprinzipien in Art. 130r EGV: politische Leitlinien oder rechtsverbindliche Vorgaben? Zu den Urteilen des EuGH in den Rs. C-284/95, C-341/95 (Safety Hi-Tech) vom 14.7.1998' (1999) 21: 14 Natur und Recht 181–5

Freestone D., 'The Road from Rio: International Environmental Law after the Earth's Summit (1994) 6 JEL 210–13

Führ M. and Roller G. (eds.), *Participation and Litigation Rights of Environmental Associations in Europe* (Frankfurt: Peter Lang, 1991)

Geradin D., 'The Belgian Waste Case' (1993) Eur L R 144

——, *Trade and the Environment: A Comparative Study of EC and US Law* (Cambridge: Cambridge U.P., 1997)

Grabitz E. and Zacker Ch., 'Scope for Action by the EC Member States for the Improvement of Environmental Protection under EEC Law: The Example of Environmental Taxes and Subsidies' (1989) CMLR 423 *et seq*

Hallo R.E. (ed.), *Access to Environmental Information in Europe* (London, The Hague, Boston: Kluwer Law Int'l, 1996)

Jans J.H., 'Waste Policy and European Community Law: Does the EEC Treaty Provide a Suitable Framework for Regulating Waste?' (1993) ELQ 165

——, *European Environmental Law* (London: Kluwer Law Int'l, 1995)

——, 'Objectives and Principles of EEC European Environmental Law' in G. Winter (ed.) *European Environmental Law* (Dartmouth: Aldershot, 1996) 277

——, *European Environmental Law* (2nd edn., Groeningen: Europa Law Publishing, 2000)

Khalatschi R. and Ward H., 'New Instruments for Sustainability: An Assessment of Environmental Agreements under EC Law' (1998) 10: 2 JEL 257–90

Krämer L., *EC Treaty and Environmental Protection* (London: Sweet & Maxwell, 1990)

——, 'Community Environmental Law under the Maastricht Treaty on European Union and the Fifth Environmental Programme' in *Recent Economic and Legal Developments in European Environmental Policy* (Leuven: Leuven U.P., 1995) 83

——, *Focus on European Environmental Law* (2nd edn., London: Sweet & Maxwell, 1997)

——, 'General Principles of Community Environmental Law and their Translation into Secondary Law' (1999) 3: 4 L&EA 355–62

Lavrysen L., 'Good intentions and less good results: The five environmental action programmes and their translation into secondary legislation' (1999) 3: 4 L&EA 298–326

Noiville C. and de Sadeleer N., 'La gestion des risques écologiques et sanitaires à l'épreuve des chiffres: Le droit entre enjeux scientifiques et politiques' (2001) 2 RDUE 389–449

Nollkaemper A., 'The Legality of Moral Crusades Disguised in Trade Laws: An Analysis of the EC Ban on Furs from Animals Taken by Leghold Traps' (1996) JEL 237–57

——, 'Habitat Protection in European Community Law: Evolving Conceptions of a Balance of Interests' (1997) 9 JEL 271 *et seq.*

Pallemaerts M., 'The decline of law as an instrument of Community environmental policy' (1999) 3:4 L&EA 338–62

Poostchi B., 'The 1997 Treaty of Amsterdam: Implications for EU Environmental Law and Policy-Making' (1998) 1 RECIEL 76–84

Reddish M., 'Direct Effect of Environmental Directives' (1994) EELR 308

Rowland S., 'EU Policy for Ozone Layer Protection' in Golub (ed.), *Global Competition and EU Environmental Law* (London: Routledge, 1998) 39 *et seq.*

Sevenster H.G., *Milieubeleid en Gemeenschapsrecht* (Deventer: Kluwer, 1992)

——, 'Milieubeginselen uit EG-Verdrag toetssteen voor CFK-verordening' (1998) 4 NTER 226–8

——, 'The Environmental Guarantee after Amsterdam: Does the Emperor Have New Clothes?' (2000) YbEEL 291

Sheridan B., *EU Biotechnology Law and Practice* (Benbridge: Palladion Law Press, 2001)

Somsen H., 'Case C-2/90, Commission v. Belgium/Free Movement of Goods, Transfrontier Movement of Waste' (1992) EELR 107

Temmink H., 'From Danish Bottles to Danish Bees: The Dynamics of Free Movement of Goods and Environmental Protection, A Case Law Analysis' (2000) I YbEEL 291

Thunis X., 'Le droit européen de l'environnement: Le discours et la règle' in *L'Europe et ses citoyens* (Frankfurt: Peter Lang, 2000) 151–65

Torrens D., '*Locus standi* for Environmental Associations under EC Law: *Greenpeace* a Missed Opportunity for the ECJ' (1999) 3 RECIEL 313

Verheyen R., 'The Environmental Guarantee in European Law and the New Article 95 EC Treaty in Practice: a Critique' (2000) 1 RECIEL 180–7

Vogelzang-Stoute E., 'European Community Legislation on the Marketing and Use of Pesticides' (1999) 8 RECIEL 144–51

von Wilmowsky P., 'Abfall und freier Warenverkehr: Bestandaufnahme nach dem EUGH-Urteil Wallonisches Einfuhrverbot' (1992) EuR 416

——, 'Waste Disposal in the Internal Market: The State of Play After the ECJ's Ruling on the Walloon Ban' (1993) CMLR 541

von Wilmowsky P. and Roller G., *Civil Liability for Waste* (Frankfurt: Peter Lang, 1992)

Wasmeier M., 'The Integration of Environmental Protection as A General Rule for Interpreting Community Law' (2001) 38 CMLR 159–77

Wheeler M., 'The Legality of Restrictions on the Movement of Wastes under Community Law' (1993) 5: 1 JEL 140 *et seq.*

Winter G. (ed.), *Risk Assessment and Risk Management of Toxic Chemicals in the EC* (Baden-Baden: Nomos, 2000)

Ziegler A.R., *Trade and Environmental Law in the European Community* (Oxford: Clarendon, 1996)

5. NATIONAL LAW

5.1 General works

Aberkane H., 'Du dommage causé par une personne indéterminée dans un groupe déterminé de personnes' (1958) RTD Civ 516 *et seq.*

Allan T.R.S., *Law, Liberty and Justice, the Legal Foundation of British Constitutionalism* (Oxford: Clarendon, 1993)

Brüggermeier G., 'The Control of Corporate Conduct and Reduction of Uncertainty by Tort Law' in R. Baldwin (ed.), *Law and Uncertainty: Risks and Legal Processes* (London: Kluwer, 1997) 57–74

Chapus R., 'De la valeur juridique des principes généraux du droit et des autres règles jurisprudentielles du droit administratif' (1966) I D 99

Chartier Y., *La réparation du préjudice* (Paris: Dalloz, 1989)

Cornelis L., *Les principes du droit belge de la responsabilité extra-contractuelle* (Brussels: CED Samson, Bruylant, Maklu, 1991)

Dalcq R.O. and Schamps G., 'Examen de jurisprudence (1987–1993): La responsabilité délictuelle et quasi délictuelle' (1995) 3: 6 RCJB 537 *et seq.*

Duhamel et Y. Meny, *Dictionnaire de droit constitutionnel* (Paris: P.U.F., 1992)

Ganshof van der Meersch W., 'Propos sur le texte de la loi et les principes généraux du droit' (1970) JT 557

Jeannau B., *Les principes généraux du droit dans la jurisprudence administrative* (Paris: Sirey, 1954)

Kemp Kareleton A., *Law in the Making* (Oxford: Clarendon, 1964)

Letourneau Ph., *Droit de la responsabilité* (Paris: Dalloz, 1996)

Leurquin-De Visscher F., 'Principes généraux et principes fondamentaux dans la jurisprudence de la Cour d'Arbitrage' (1996) 3 Ann Dr Louvain 275

Marchal A., 'Le délit de mise en péril et son objet' (1968–1969) Rev. droit pénal et de criminologie 299

Mazeaud H.-L. and Tunc A., *Traité théorique et pratique de la responsabilité civile délictuelle et contractuelle* (6th edn., Paris: Montchrestien, 1965)

Morand Ch.-A., 'Pesée des intérêts et décisions complexes' in Ch.-A. Morand (ed.), *La pesée globale des intérêts* (Geneva: Helbing & Lichtenhahn, 1996) 41–105

Morange G., 'Une catégorie juridique ambiguë: Les principes généraux du droit' (1977) RDP 761

Sachs M., *Grundgesetz: Kommentar* (München: C.H. Beck Verlag, 1996)

Shapiro M., 'The Frontiers of Science Doctrine: American Experiences with the Judicial Control of Science-Based Decision-Making' in C. Joerges, K.-H. Ladeur, and E. Vos (eds.), *Integrating Expertise into Regulatory Decision-Making* (Baden-Baden: Nomos, 1997) 325 *et seq.*

Van Gerven W., *Tort Law* (Oxford: Hart, 1999)

Viney G., *Traité de droit civil* (Paris: L.G.D.J., 1982)

von Bar, *The Common European Law of Torts* (Oxford: Clarendon, 1998)

Zweigert K. and Kötz H., *Introduction to Comparative Law* (2nd edn., Oxford: Clarendon, 1992)

5.2 National environmental law

Applegate J.S., 'The Perils of Unreasonable Risk: Information, Regulatory Policy, and Toxic Substances Control' (1991) Colum LR 279

Applegate J.S., Laitos J, and Campbell C., *The Regulation of Toxic Substances and Hazardous Wastes* (New York: Foundation Press, 2000)

Backes C.W., Bastmeijer C.J., Freriks A.A., van Gestel R.A.J., and Verschuuren J.M., *Codificatie van milieurechtelijke beginselen in de Wet milieubeheer* (The Hague: Boom, 2002)

Barton C., 'The Status of the Precautionary Principle in Australia: Its Emergence in Legislation and as a Common Law Doctrine' (1998) 22: 2 Harv Env L Rev 509 *et seq.*

Baun E., 'Alternative causaliteit en milieuschade: Enkele opmerkingen naar aanleiding van het arrest Moerman-Baak' (1998) 2 TMA 30 *et seq.*

Belsky M., 'Environmental Policy Law in the 1970s: Shifting Back the Burden of Proof' (1988) 12: 1 ELQ 5

Bender B., Sparwasser R., and Engel R., *Umweltrecht: Grundzüge des öffentlichen Umwelschutsrechts* (3rd edn., Heidelberg: R. Müller, 1995) 24–7

Bocken H., *Het aansprakelijkheidsrecht als sanctie tegen de verstoring van het leefmilieu* (Brussels: Bruylant, 1979)

Bothe M. and Scharp H., 'La juridiction administrative allemande empêche-t-elle le développement de l'utilisation pacifique de l'énergie nucléaire?' (1986) 4 RJE 420 *et seq.*

Brandl E. and Bungert H., 'Constitutional Entrenchment of Environmental Protection: A Comparative Analysis of Experiences Abroad' (1992) 16: 1 Harv Env L Rev 1–99

Brussaard W., Drupsteen T., Gilhuis P., and Koeman N., *Milieurecht* (Zwolle: Tjeenk-Willink, 1996)

Caballero F., *Essai sur la notion juridique de nuisance* (Paris: L.G.D.J., 1981)

Carette A., *Herstel van en vergoeding voor aantasting aan niet-toegeëigende milieubestanddelen* (Antwerpen, Groeningen: Intersentia, 1997)

Cliquet A., 'Recente ontwikkelingen inzake natuurbehoudswetgeving in het mariene en kustzonemilieu van België' (1999) 5 TMR 346

Deketekaere K., 'Flemish Environmental Policy Principles' (1996) EELR 275–86

de Sadeleer N., *Les principes du pollueur-payeur, de prévention et de précaution* (Brussels: Bruylant/Agence Universitaire pour la Francophonie, 1999)

Gilhuis P. and Van den Biesen A.H.J. (eds.), *Beginselen in het milieurecht* (Alphen a/d Rijn: Kluwer, 2001)

Hilson C., *Regulating Pollution: A UK and EC Perspective* (Oxford: Hart, 2000)

Holder J., 'Safe science? The Precautionary Principle in UK Environmental Law' in Holder, J. (ed.), *The Impact of EC Environmental Law in the UK* (Chichester: John Wiley, 1997) 123

Kloepfer M., 'Die Principien im einzelnen' in *Umweltrecht* (München: C.H. Beck Verlag, 1989) 74–83

——, *Umweltrecht* (2nd edn., 1998)

Kronsell A., 'Sweden: Setting a Good Example' in S. Andersen (ed.), *European Environmental Policy: The Pioneers* (Manchester, New-York: Manchester U.P., 1997) 53

Kruisinga A. and Lefevere J., 'De 30 september arresten: De historische vervuiler opnieuw buiten schot?' (1995) 2 TMR 99

Lascoumes P. and Martin G., 'Des droits épars au Code de l'environnement' (1995) 30: 31 Droit et Société 323–43

Lundmark T., 'Principles and Instruments of German Environmental Law' (1997) 4: 4 Journal of Environmental Law and Practice 43

——, 'Systemizing Environmental Law on a German Model' (1998) Dickinson Journal of Environmental Law and Policy 1 *et seq.*

Messer E.A., *Risico-aansprakelijkheid voor milieu-verontreiniging in het BW* (Arnhem: Goude Quint, 1994)

Murswiek D., 'Der Bund und die Länder Schutz der natürlichen Lebensgrundlagen' in M. Sachs (ed.), *Grundgesetz: Kommentar* (Munich: C.H. Beck Verlag, 1996) 653 *et seq.*

Naim-Gesbert E., *Les dimensions scientifiques du droit de l'environnement* (Brussels: Bruylant-VUB, 1999)

O'Leary R., 'The Impact of Federal Court Decisions on the Policies and Administrations of the U.S. Environmental Protection Agency' (1989) 41 Administrative Law Review 549

Parnell M., 'Southern Bluefin Tuna Feedlotting ESD, the Precautionary Principle and Burden of Proof' (1999) 2 J Int'l Wildlife L & Pol'y 334–7

Percival R.V. and Alevizatos D.C., *Law and the Environment: A Multidisciplinary Reader* (Philadelphia: Temple U.P., 1997)

Rehbinder E., 'Points of Reference for a Codification of National Environmental Law' in H. Bocken and D. Ryckbost (eds.), *Codification of Environmental Law* (London, The Hague, Boston: Kluwer Law Int'l, 1996) 157

Revesz R.L., *Foundations of Environmental Law and Policy* (Oxford, New York: Oxford U.P., 1997)

Roller G., *Genehmigungsaufebung und Entschädigung im Atomrecht* (Baden-Baden: Nomos (1994)

——, 'Environmental Law Principles in the Jurisprudence of German Administrative Courts' (1999) 2 ELNI Newsl. 29–34

Rose-Ackerman S., *Controlling Environmental Policy* (New Haven: Yale U.P., 1994)

Ruckelshaus W.D., 'Risk in a Free Society' (1984) 14 Ent'l LR 10190

Sheridan M. and Lavrysen L. (eds.), *Environmental Law Principles in Practice* (Brussels: Bruylant, 2002)

Sioutis G., 'La notion de développement durable dans la jurisprudence du Conseil d'Etat hellénique' (1998) 1 REDE 56

Steele J., 'Participation and Deliberation in Environmental Law: Exploring a Problem-solving Approach' (2001) 21: 3 OJLS 415–42

Stewart R.B., 'The Role of the Courts in Risk Management' (1986) 16 Ent'l LR 10208

Sunkin M., Ong D., and Wight R., *Sourcebook on Environmental Law* (London, Sydney: Cavendish, 1998)

Teubner G., 'The Invisible Cupola: from Causal to Collective Attribution in Ecological Liability' in Teubner, Farmer, and Murphy (eds.), *Environmental Law and Ecological Responsibility* (London: Kluwer, 1994) 17 *et seq.*

Verschuuren J., *Het grondrecht op bescherming van het leefmilieu* (Zwolle: Tjeenk Willink, 1993)
——, 'Naar een codificatie van beginselen van het milieurecht' (1995) 21: 4 Recht en Kritiek 421–5

6. LITERATURE CITED ON THE POLLUTER-PAYS PRINCIPLE

Bergkamp L., 'De vervuiler betaalt dubbel: Over de verhouding tussen privaat en publiek milieurecht' (1998) 6 TMR 400–7
——, *De vervuiler betaalt dubbel* (Antwerpen-Groeningen: Intersentia, 1999)
Boyle A.E., 'Making the Polluter Pay? Alternatives to State Responsibility in the Allocation of Transboundary Environmental Cost' in Fr. Franzioni and T. Scovazzi (eds.), *International Responsibility for Environmental Harm* (London: Graham & Trotman/Martinus Nijhoff, 1991) 363
Bugge H.C., 'The Principle of Polluter-Pays in Economics and Law' in E. Eide and R. Van den Bergh (eds.), *Law and Economics of the Environment* (Oslo: Juridisk forlag, 1996)
Gaines S., 'The Polluter-Pays Principle: From Economic Equity to Environmental Ethos' (1991) 26 Tex Intl LJ 470
Jans J.-H., 'State Aids and Articles 92 and 93 of the EC Treaty: Does the Polluter Pay?' (1995) EELR 108
Ketelwell U., 'The Answer to Global Pollution? A Critical Examination of the Problems and Potential of the Polluter-Pays Principle' (1992) 3 Colo J Int'l Envtl L & Pol'y 431
Kim H.J., 'Subsidy, Polluter-pays Principle and Financial Assistance Among Countries' (2000) 34: 6 JWT 1145 *et seq.*
Krämer L., 'The Polluter-pays Principle in Community Law: The Interpretation of Article 130R of the EEC Treaty' in *Focus on European Environmental Law* (London: Sweet & Maxwell, 1992) 244–63
Pezzey J., 'Market Mechanisms of Pollution Control: "Polluter Pays", Economic and Practical Aspects' in R. Kerri Turner (ed.), *Sustainable Environmental Management: Principles and Practice* (Boulder, 1988) 190
Smets H., 'The Polluter Pays Principle in the early 1990's' in L. Campiglio *et al.* (eds.), *The Environment after Rio: International Law and Economics* (London: Graham & Trotman, 1994) 131

7. LITERATURE CITED ON THE PRINCIPLE OF PREVENTION

de Sadeleer N., 'Le principe de prévention: Analyse coût—bénéfice de la mesure préventive' in S. Maljean-Dubois (ed.), *L'outil économique en droit international de l'environnement* (Paris: La Documentation Française, 2001) 7–15
Okowa P., 'Procedural Obligations in International Environmental Agreements' (1996) LXVII BybIL 275–336
Soljan L., 'The General Obligation to Prevent Transboundary Harm and its Relation to Four Key Environmental Principles' (1998) 3 ARIEL 209–32
Vessey J., 'The Principle of Prevention in International Law' (1998) 3 ARIEL 181–207

8. LITERATURE CITED ON THE PRECAUTIONARY PRINCIPLE

Applegate J.S., 'The Precautionary Preference: an American Perspective on the Precautionary Principle' (2000) 6: 3 Hum Ecol Risk Ass 413

Backes C. and Verschuuren J., 'The Precautionary principle in European and Dutch Wildlife Law' (1998) 43 Colo J Int'l Envtl L & Pol'y

Backes Ch., Gilhuis P., and Verschuuren J. (eds.), *Het voorzorgbeginsel in het natuurbeschermingsrecht* (Deventer: Tjeenk Willink, 1997)

Barcena I. and Schütte P., 'El Principio de precaucion medioambiental en la Union Europea: Aspectos juridico-politicos' (1997) 19 Rev Dr Amb 13–42

Barton C., 'The Status of the Precautionary Principle in Australia: Its Emergence in Legislation and as a Common Law Doctrine' (1998) 22: 2 Harv Env L Rev. 509–58

Bodansky D., 'Scientific Uncertainty and the Precautionary Principle' (1991) 4 Environment 33

Cameron J. and Abouchar J., 'The Precautionary Principle: a Fundamental Principle of Law and Policy for the Protection of the Global Environment' (1991) Boston CILR 1–27

Cameron J., Wade-Gery W., and Abouchar J., 'Precautionary Principle and Future Generations' in E. Agius and S. Busuttil (eds.), *Future Generations and International Law* (London: Earthscan, 1998) 93–113

Cooke J. and Earle M., 'Towards a Precautionary Approach to Fisheries Management' (1993) 3 RECIEL 252–9

Cross F., 'Pardoxical Perils of the Precautionary Principle' (1996) 53 Wash & Lee L Rev 851

de Sadeleer N., 'Het voorzorgsbeginsel: Een stille revolutie' (1999) 2 TMR 82–99

——, 'Réflexions sur le principe de précaution' in E. Zaccaï et J.M. Missa (eds.), *Le principe de précaution: Significations et conséquences* (Brussels: ULB U.P., 2000) 117–37

——, 'The Enforcement of the Precautionary Principle by German, French and Belgian Courts' (2000) 9: 2 RECIEL 144–51

——, 'Reflexiones sobre el estatuto juridico del principio de precaucion' (2000) 25 Rev Dr Amb 9–38

——, 'Le statut de principe de précaution en droit communautaire' (2001) 1 Cah Dr Eur 91–132

——, 'Les avatars du principe de précaution en droit public' (2001) 3 RFD Adm. 547–62

——, 'L'émergence du principe de précaution' (2001) 6010 JT 393–401

——, 'The Effect of Uncertainty on the Threshold Levels to which the Precautionary Principle Appears to be Subject' in M. Sheridan and L. Lavrysen (eds.), *Environmental Law Principles in Practice* (Brussels: Bruylant, 2002) 17–43

Dickson B., 'The Precautionary Principle in CITES: A Critical Assessment' (1999) 39: 2 NRJ 211–29

Douma W. Th., 'Status des Vorsorgeprinzips im internationalen Recht anhand des Urteils des IGH zu den französischen Atomtests des Jahres 1995' (1996) 4 Humanitäres Völkerrecht 187–92

——, 'Beginselen van international milieurecht: Een case study naar het gebruik van het voorzorgsbeginsel in het Nederlandse milieurecht' in *International milieurecht in Nederland: Consequenties van het international milieurecht voor de nationale rechtspraktijk* (Deventer: Tjeenk Willink, 1998) 117–33

——, 'The European Union and the Precautionary Principle' (2000) 1 RECIEL 132–43

Doyle A. and Carney T., 'Precaution and Prevention: Giving Effect to Article 130r Without Direct Effect' (1999) EELR 44–7

Ewald Fr., 'The Return of the Crafty Genius: An Outline of a Philosophy of Precaution' (1999/2000) Conn Ins LJ 47

Ewald Fr., Gollier Ch., and de Sadeleer N., *Le principe de précaution* (Paris: PUF, 2001)

Fabra A., 'The LOSC and the Implementation of the Precautionary Principle' (1999) 10 YbIEL 15–24

Fisher E., 'Is the Precautionary Principle Justiciable?' (2001) 13:3 JEL 315–34

Freestone D., 'The Precautionary Principle' in *International law and Global Climate Change* (London: Graham & Trotman, 1991) 24

——, 'Caution or Precaution: A Rose By Any Other Name . . . ?' (1999) 10 YbIEL 25–32

Freestone D. and Hey E. (eds.), *The Precautionary Principle and International Law* (London, Boston, The Hague: Kluwer Law Int'l, 1995)

Freytag E., Jackl T., Loibl G., and Wittman M. (eds.), *The Role of Precaution in Chemicals Policy* (Vienna: Diplomatishe Akademie Wien, 2002)

Fullem G., 'The Precautionary Principle: Environmental Protection in the Face of Scientific Uncertainty' (1995) Willamette Law Review 3

Garcia S.M., 'The Precautionary Principle: Its Implications in Capture Fisheries Management' (1994) Ocean and Coastal Management 99–125

Gollier C., 'Should we Beware of the Precautionary Principle?' (2001) 33 Economic Policy 303–21

Gollier C., Jullien B., and Treich N., 'Scientific Progress and Irreversibility: An Economic Interpretation of the Precautionary Principle' (2000) 75 Journal of Public Economics 229–53

Gonzalez Vaqué L., 'El principio de precaucion en la jurisprudencia del TJCE: La sentecia "Greenpeace France"' (2001) 2 Comunidad Europea Aranzadi 33–43

Gonzalez Vaqué L., Ehring L., and Jacquet C., 'Le principe de précaution dans la législation communautaire et nationale relative à la protection de la santé' (1999) 1 RMUE 79–128

Gullett W., 'Environmental Protection and the Precautionary Principle: A Response to Scientific Uncertainty in Environmental Management' (1997) 14: 1 Env't and Planning LJ 52

Gündling L., 'The Status in International Law of the Principle of Precautionary Action' (1990) 23 Int'l J Estuarine and Coastal L 10 *et seq.*

——, 'The Status in International Law of the Principle of Precautionary Action' in Freestone D. and Ijlstra T. (eds.), *The North Sea: Perspectives on Regional co-operation* (London: Graham & Trotman, 1990) 23–30

Harding R. and Fisher E., *Perspectives on the Precautionary Principle* (Sydney: Federation Press, 1990)

Hewison G.J., 'The Precautionary Approach to Fisheries Management: An Environmental Perspective' (1996) 3 Int'l J Marine & Coastal L 301–32

Hey E., 'The Precautionary Concept in Environmental Policy and Law: Institutionalizing Caution' (1992) 4 G Int'l Env't L Rev 303

Hickley J.E.. and Walker V.R., 'Refining the Precautionary Principle in International Environmental Law' (1995) 14: 3 Va Envtl LJ 423–54

Hohmann H., *The Precautionary Principle* (London: Kluwer/Graham & Trotman, 1994)

——, 'Precautionary Legal Duties and Principles of Modern International Environmental Law' (1996) 1 Colum J Env't L 183–203

Jernelöv A., 'The Precautionary Principle' in *On the General Principles of Environment Protection* (Stockholm: Swedish Government Official Reports, 1994) 45–51

Jordan A.J. and O'Riordan T., 'The Precautionary Principle in UK Environmental Law and Policy' in Gray T. (ed.), *UK Environmental Policy in the 1990s* (London: Macmillan, 1995)

Kourilsky P. and Viney G., *Le principe de précaution* (Paris: La Documentation Française-O. Jacob, 2000)

Ladeur K.-H., 'Zur Prozeduralisierung des Vorsorgebegriffs durch Risikovergleich und Prioritätensetzung' in *Jahrbuch des Umwelt* (Heidelberg: TechnikelB, 1994, 297–331

Lavrysen L., 'The Precautionary Principle in Belgian Jurisprudence: Unknown, Unloved?' (1998) EELR 75

Lübbe-Wolff G., 'IVU-Richtlinie und europäisches Vorsorgeprinzip' (1998) 1 Neue Zeitschrift für Umweltrecht 1

Maat B., 'Grensoverschrijdende verontreiniging van internationale waterlopen: Het belang van het voorzorgsbeginsel voor het nationale privaatrecht' (1997) 3 TMA 68–75

Martin G., 'Précaution et évolution du droit' (1995) D. 299–306

Martin-Bidou P., 'Le principe de précaution en droit international de l'environnement' (1999) 3 RGDIP 660

Mcintyre O. and Mosedale T., 'The Precautionary Principle as a Norm of Customary International Law' (1997) 9: 2 JEL 221

Morris J. (ed.), *Rethinking Risk and the Precautionary Principle* (London: IEA Publications, 2001)

Noiville C., 'Principe de Précaution et Organisation Mondiale du Commerce: Le cas du commerce alimentaire' (2000) 2 JD Int'l 263–97

——, 'Principe de précaution et gestion des risques en droit de l'environnement et en droit de la santé' (2000) 239 LPA 39–50

Nollkaemper A., 'What you risk reveals what you value and other dilemmas encountered in the Legal Assaults on Risk' in Freestone and Hey (eds.), *The Precautionary Principle and International Law* (London: Kluwer, 1995) 73–94

O'Riordan T. and Cameron J. (eds.), *Interpreting the Precautionary Principle* (London: Cameron & May, 1994)

O'Riordan T., Cameron J., and Jordan A. (eds.), *Interpreting the Precautionary Principle* (2nd edn., London: Cameron & May, 2001)

Philippopoulos-Mihalopoulos A., 'The Silence of the Sirens: Environmental Risk and the Precautionary Principle' (1999) Law & Critique 175–97

Raffensperger C. and Tickner J., *Protecting Public Health & the Environment: Implementing the Precautionary Principle* (Washington: Island Press, 1999)

Rehbinder E., 'Vorzorge Prinziepe und Präventive Umweltpolitiek' in UE Simonis (ed.), *Präventive Umweltpolitiek* (1988) 129–41

——, 'Prinzipien des Umweltrechts in der Rechtsprechung des Bundesverwaltungsgerichts: Das Vorsorgeprinzip als Beispiel' in *Bürger-Richter-Staat: Festschrift für Horst Sendler* (Münich: Hg. Franssen/Redeker/Schlichter/Wilke, 1991) 269–83

——, 'Precaution and Sustainability: Two Sides of the Same Coin?' in A. Kiss and F. Burhenne-Guilmin (eds.), *A Law for the Environment: Essays in Honour of Wolfgang E. Burhenne* (Gland: IUCN – The World Conservation Union, 1994) 93–101

——, 'The Precautionary Principle in an International Perspective' in *Miljorettens grund-sporgsmaal* (Copenhagen, 1994) 91

Reich A., *Gefahr-Risiko-Restrisiko, Umweltrechtliche Studien*, no. 5 (Düsseldorf: Werner-Verlag, 1989)

Sand P., 'The Precautionary Principle: A European Perspective' in *Transnational Environmental Law: Lessons in Global Change* (London, The Hague, Boston: Kluwer Law Int'l, 1999) 129–39

——, 'The Precautionary Principle: A European Perspective' (2000) 6 Hum Ecol Risk Ass 445

Shaw S. and Schwartz R., 'The Cartagena Protocol and the WTO: Reflections on the Precautionary Principle' (2000) 10:4 RSDIE 536–42

Stairs K.C. and Johnston P.A., 'The Precautionary Action Approach to Environmental Protection' (1991) 1 Environmental Pollution ICEP, 473–79

Streinz R., 'The Precautionary Principle in Food Law' (1998) 8:4 EFLR 413–32

Tickner J., *Precaution in Practice: A Framework for Implementing the Precautionary Principle. Dissertation completed for the Department of Work Environment* (University of Massachusetts Lowell, 2000)

Trouwbost, A., *Evolution and Status of the Precautionary Principle in International Law* (London: Kluwer Law International, 2002)

von Moltke K., 'The Vorsorgeprinzip in West German environmental policy' in *Royal Commission on Environmental Pollution, 12th Report: Best Practicable Environment Option*, Cmnd 310 (London: HMSO, 1988)

Wagner W.E., 'The Precautionary Principle and Chemical Regulation in the U.S.' (2000) 6: 3 Hum Ecol Risk Ass 459–77

Weintraub B.A., 'Science, International Environmental Regulation and the Precautionary Principle: Setting Standards and Defining Terms' (1992) NYI Env't L J 173

Wiener J.B., 'Precaution in a Multi-Risk World' in D. Paustenbach (ed.), *The Risk Assessment of Environmental and Human Health Hazards* (2nd edn., London: John Wiley, 2001)

Index